A Man of Principle

Contributors

Robert G. Anderson
Robert James Bidinotto
Peter J. Boettke
Juan C. Cachanosky
Clarence B. Carson
Camille P. Castorina
Edwin G. Dolan
Richard M. Ebeling
Ridgway K. Foley, Jr.
Bettina Bien Greaves
Robert L. Guarnieri
Mark W. Hendrickson
Sanford Ikeda
Bruce W. Ketler
Matthew B. Kibbe
Israel M. Kirzner
Robert D. Love
Charles S. MacKenzie
Luisa Zorraquin de Marcos
Robert H. Miller
Gary North
Judd W. Patton
William H. Peterson
Sylvester Petro
Lawrence W. Reed
George Reisman
John W. Robbins
Rousas John Rushdoony
Gary G. Short
Mark Skousen
Mark Spangler
John A. Sparks
Terree P. Wasley
Walter J. Wessels
Lawrence H. White
Richard A. White

HANS F. SENNHOLZ

A Man of Principle

Essays in Honor of Hans F. Sennholz

Presented on the Occasion
of his Seventieth Birthday
February 3, 1992

Volume Editors
John W. Robbins
Mark Spangler

Grove City College Press
Grove City, Pennsylvania 16127

ISBN 0-9631818-0-7

MANUFACTURED IN THE UNITED STATES OF AMERICA

DEDICATION

The middle of the twentieth century was an era marked by the further entrenchment of authoritarianism. One of the most ruthless of Soviet rulers controlled that country. In China, Mao Tse-Tung had defeated the Nationalists and installed his communist regime. Communist governments were situated in Eastern Europe and were to be solidified by the Warsaw Pact, and just over the horizon was the construction of the Berlin Wall. Indeed, Marxism and socialism controlled the lives of millions.

The political climate in the United States still afforded individuals the greatest freedoms on earth, yet the country was drifting ever closer to full statism as ideals of government intervention eroded the founding principles of the nation. A country built on limited government, individual initiative, free markets, and property rights gave way to the welfarism of the "New Deal." Social Security insurance and minimum wage laws were well established in society along with a host of other government welfare services to combat poverty, unemployment, sickness, old age, and inadequate housing. Marginal income tax rates had reached their highest level, and well over two thousand agencies, bureaus, and departments comprised the federal government. And yet this scope of government would come to seem narrow as "The Great Society" brought the next wave of welfarism in the decades that were to follow.

In the 1950s popular economic thought was sanctioning a transformation to a welfare state. The mainstay of the academic community was Keynesianism, which endorsed governmental management of demand and spending. And Galbraithian ideas supported political intervention for the "public good." Economists of the day no longer employed the methodology of deductive logic used by the "classical school" but shrouded their theories in mathematics and empiricism and became willing participants in government's administering of national "macroeconomic phenomena."

About this same time there came to the United States a young German immigrant whose destiny was to challenge the economic orthodoxy of his day. This was a man who had just earned a doctorate in political science in his native country, yet, wasting no time, he sought to improve his knowledge of the business world in the United States by enrolling in evening classes at New York University. He sought out a man whose name was familiar to him from his student days in Germany—the eminent Professor Ludwig von Mises, an Austrian School economist whose genius brought new depths of understanding to the field of economics, and whose class this young immigrant began attending. Inspired by the profound work of his professor, he became one of a handful of students to earn a full doctorate under the tutelage of Professor Mises. And so began the brilliant career of Hans F. Sennholz, a man who carried on the tradition of his teacher for the next four decades.

The Austrian school was by no means popular in academia. Austrian economists employed deductive reasoning and historical interpretation to express universal laws of economics not subject to the whims of dictators and politicians. Their analyses, based upon "methodological individualism," pointed to the only rational economic order—a private property order where the actions of free individuals generate the price information that coordinates the economy. Under socialism, economic calculation is impossible. A mixed economy of government intervention is illogical and generates results contrary to the vision of its planners; thus, the Austrian school occupied a position of little prominence in a world dominated by socialist thought and welfare state economics. However, Dr. Sennholz was not to be influenced by such appeals to popularity or "political" advantage in his search for truth and eternal principles. He became a consistent and reliable spokesman for individual freedom and free enterprise, and valiant in his defense of a free society.

Soon after his graduation from New York University, Hans Sennholz was discovered by J. Howard Pew, the Board Chairman of Grove City College. Nestled in the hills of Western Pennsylvania and demanding high academic standards, this small private school cherished and guarded its independence from government interference. Grove City College was to become the perfect arena for Dr. Sennholz to express his understanding of political economy and to impart his knowledge to those who sought it. Since his first day in 1956, he has chaired its Economics Department.

Rejecting the dialectical materialism of Marxist thought, Dr. Sennholz emphasized the power of ideas in shaping the world: all human endeavors and social change begin in the hearts and minds of acting individuals. One could feel his sense of obligation to explore the ideals of freedom with the youth of the country. Powerful logic and style illuminated his lectures as he described the rationale for free markets and limited government, whether he spoke from his chair to a small seminar or from a podium to the entire student body. His unwillingness to compromise sound principles for the sake of popularity or political gain has provided a wellspring of inspiration for countless students.

While Grove City College remained the nucleus of Professor Sennholz's endeavors, his influence reached far beyond the boundaries of the campus. With his gift of eloquent speech, a prolific pen, and an uncommon ability to communicate ideas to a popular audience, he distinguished himself as a public speaker and essayist. Over the course of almost forty years, he has made thousands of public addresses and published hundreds of articles, attracting a wide following. For the more ambitious students, his numerous books and monographs have proven to be invaluable sources of knowledge.

Professor Sennholz's influence has been acknowledged in this country and others as schools, professional associations, educational foundations, private organizations, and publications afforded him opportunities to present the precepts of a free society and to caution against encroaching government. As his career progressed, he argued not only for the efficiencies of the market, but exposed the immorality of plundering others through the political process, and espoused the moral case for individual responsibility, private property rights, and a restricted government. He won the admiration of students and colleagues alike as a tireless champion of personal and economic freedom.

As he reached outward from Grove City College, he made the school a special forum which attracted other renowned leaders of the freedom philosophy. Dr. Sennholz and his wife, Mary Homan Sennholz, often hosted distinguished associates and friends who, as visiting lecturers, found a receptive and eager audience on the campus.

A cross section of proponents of freedom reveals an abundance of students who have been touched directly by Dr. Sennholz.

Dozens have achieved responsible positions as full-time educators in colleges and advisors in private organizations, and anyone moving in libertarian and conservative circles today invariably encounters a "Sennholz student." Dr. Sennholz has been preeminent in developing successive generations of pupils committed to the ethical and economic principles of a free society.

In the mid-1970s, there was one particular personal project which Dr. Sennholz described with enthusiasm to his students, who perceived the excitement and satisfaction their professor anticipated from this undertaking—the foresting of his farm in central Pennsylvania with black walnut trees. He regularly taught that capital accumulation is the only means to raise standards of living. A mature black walnut is highly valued for its lumber and fruit, and the creation of a whole forest could become future capital wealth to satisfy needs of society. So with the aid of students, he planted literally thousands of seedlings. Of course decades would pass before the trees matured fully. Dr. Sennholz knew that he himself would never harvest the profits of this venture and loved to convey that thought to his students by proclaiming, "In a hundred years, I'll be a multi-millionaire." Plainly, his focus was on his future generations.

Thus, Dr. Sennholz has "forested" the field of economics—planting seedlings that will mature for future generations. He can take great pride in his accomplishments, being confident that as one educator, he has done much to lay the foundation for the regeneration of a truly free society.

As we observe communism collapsing throughout the world, we see the tragic toll among real individuals who have lived out the empirical experiments of Marxism. While the demolished Berlin Wall is a powerful symbol, the Communist world seems headed not toward truly free markets and freedom, but toward varieties of mixed economies with political control, while interventionism in the Western world is reaching new heights. Much work remains to be done in the battlefields of ideas to restore a private property order. In the sentiment of Dr. Sennholz, "Let us, therefore, make the best use of the present, with courage and dedication, and fulfill our parts. Even in evil we can discern the rays of light and hope, for man may gradually come to see, through suffering and misery, the error of his ways. ...we are ever hopeful that, in the end, right and virtue will prevail over error and evil."

To commemorate his salutary achievements in advancing an understanding of free societies, we—students, colleagues, and friends—offer these essays to honor one who has been a *Teacher* in the purest sense of the word. If future generations are to re-embrace freedom and the fruits of capitalism and reject the bondage and barren follies of statism, the trail surely will have passed through a maturing and flourishing grove grown from the seeds of knowledge sown by Professor Hans F. Sennholz throughout his academic career.

Table of Contents

Acknowledgments xvii

Introduction 1

Part One: *Grato Animo Beneficiique Memores*

Integrity and Economics
Robert D. Love 5

The Beacon Factor
Gary North 11

Part Two: *Veritas Praevalebit*

The Disintegration of Economic Ownership
Robert G. Anderson 33

What is Freedom For?
Robert James Bidinotto 47

Economic Education and Social Change
Peter J. Boettke 63

The Theory of Value and the Austrian School
Juan C. Cachanosky 75

Marx's Quantity Theory of Labor:
A Critique
Clarence B. Carson 91

On Some Forgotten Passages in the History of Liberty
Camille P. Castorina 105

Our Common Road to the Market
Edwin G. Dolan 119

Variations on the Demand for Money Theme:
Ludwig von Mises and Some Twentieth
Century Views
Richard M. Ebeling 127

The Anonymous Life
Ridgway K. Foley, Jr. 139

Mises's New York University Seminar and the
Austrian School of Economics in the United States
Bettina Bien Greaves 155

Capitalism and Women:
Some Principles of Political Economy of
Special Interest to Women
Robert L. Guarnieri 169

The Key Question
Mark W. Hendrickson 185

The Dynamics of Government Intervention:
Theory and Implications
Sanford Ikeda 201

The Legal Status of Money
Bruce W. Ketler 213

Tax, Borrow, and Spend:
The Dilemma of Federal Budget Reform
Matthew B. Kibbe 223

Human Action, Freedom, and Economic Science
Israel M. Kirzner 241

Equality and the Bible
Charles S. MacKenzie 251

Free Market Environmentalism
Luisa Zorraquin de Marcos 269

Supply-Side Economics:
A Critique
Robert H. Miller 289

The Inseparable Link Between Morality and Economics
Judd W. Patton 309

America's Second Democracy
William H. Peterson 327

Capitalism, Democracy, and Elections
Sylvester Petro 339

The Perils of Forecasting
Lawrence W. Reed 363

Freedom of Opportunity, Not Equality of Opportunity
George Reisman 373

The *Sine Qua Non* of Enduring Freedom
John W. Robbins 391

Christianity and Freedom
Rousas John Rushdoony 409

Deposit Insurance, the Use of Information, and the Current Crisis in the Financial Industry
Gary G. Short 417

Crowding Out
Mark Skousen 429

Behind the Bottom Line
Mark Spangler 453

Private Property, Non-Ownership, and the Third World
John A. Sparks 469

Health Care in the Twentieth Century:
A History of Government Interference and Protection
Terree P. Wasley 483

Are Unions All that Good?
Walter J. Wessels 507

Mises on Free Banking and Fractional Reserves
Lawrence H. White 517

The Ethical Setting of the Market:
The Perspective of Röpke
Richard A. White 535

Index 547

Acknowledgments

We would like to acknowledge, with our sincere appreciation, the contributions contained herein by the many students, friends, and colleagues of Dr. Sennholz. Their cooperation and enthusiasm in the preparation of this *Festschrift* have brought together an outstanding collection of essays.

We are especially indebted to Robert and Lyn Sennholz for their role in planning and directing editorial production. Toward that end, we wish to express our gratitude to Gay Taylor for serving as copy editor for the project. Her competent review of manuscripts and footnotes for factual and grammatical accuracy was invaluable to the successful completion of this work.

The ultimate completion of this volume was made possible by generous gifts from the following individuals, private foundations, and organizations:

The Foundation for Economic Education, Inc.
Grove City College
Mr. and Mrs. John S. Howell
Mr. and Mrs. J. P. Humphreys
The Charles G. Koch Charitable Foundation
Mr. and Mrs. Harry F. Langenberg
Mr. and Mrs. Robert D. Love
Philip M. McKenna Foundation, Inc.
Mr. and Mrs. Stanley O. Miller
Other Friends of Dr. Sennholz

Finally, we wish to acknowledge our gratitude to Grove City College as publisher of these essays and institutional employer of Dr. Sennholz as Chairman of the Economics Department these past 36 years.

INTRODUCTION

For more than a century, Grove City College has kept faith with its founders, who believed in liberty—civil, religious, political, and economic. For the past thirty-five years, the College has been immeasurably aided in fulfilling its mission by an internationally renowned advocate of free enterprise.

Hans Friedrich Sennholz, one of the great teacher-scholars of our time, has taught a generation of Americans about freedom.

Born February 3, 1922, in Brombauer, Westphalia, one of three sons of Friedrich and Karoline Sennholz, Dr. Hans Sennholz has lived a most remarkable life.

He received his pilot's license at age 13 and was drafted by the Third Reich at age 17. Flight Sergeant Sennholz flew for the *Luftwaffe* (an ME-109) in France, the Soviet Union, and North Africa; he was shot down and captured in North Africa in the spring of 1942 and spent several years as a prisoner of war in the United States. He returned to Germany in 1946, where he completed his education at the University of Marburg (M.A., 1948) and the University of Köln (Dr. rer. pol., 1949) in law and political science.

After practicing law for a year, Dr. Sennholz, still less than thirty years old and the only known surviving member of his immediate family, was sponsored by an aunt in America and came to the United States.

Dr. Sennholz went to New York City and worked while attending classes at New York University. There he studied under the Austrian economist, Ludwig von Mises, receiving the first economics Ph.D. from Mises in America in 1955. While in New York, he became a citizen of the United States, an associate (and later trustee and chairman) of the Foundation for Economic Education, and took Mary Homan as his wife.

Dr. Sennholz began his teaching career at Iona College, a small college just north of New York City. He was there for one year only, 1954–1955, as Assistant Professor of Economics, but he received the Professor of the Year Award from his students. In 1956, on the recommendation of Mises, J. Howard Pew, Chairman of the Board of Grove City College for forty years, persuaded Dr.

Sennholz to become Professor of Economics and Chairman of the Department of Economics at Grove City College, the post he has held for thirty-five years.

In the course of his academic career, Dr. Sennholz has published many books and booklets, and more than five hundred essays and articles. Among the titles are: *Moneda y Libertad,* 1961; *Gold is Money,* 1975; *Death and Taxes,* 1976, 1981; *Age of Inflation,* 1979; *Money and Freedom,* 1985; *The Politics of Unemployment,* 1987; and *Debts and Deficits,* 1987.

More recently, he has received two honorary degrees, the Doctor en Ciencias Sociales from the Universidad Francisco Marroquin in Guatemala, and the Doctor of Laws from Culver-Stockton College in Missouri.

The publication of this *Festschrift* by Grove City College is a natural outgrowth of the high esteem in which the College holds Dr. Sennholz. The essays have been divided into two parts: *Grato Animo Beneficiique Memores* contains two essays paying special tribute to Hans F. Sennholz. *Veritas Praevalebit* contains topical essays. The essays in each section are arranged alphabetically by author.

For my first convocation after coming to Grove City College as dean, I had the honor, in September 1988, to process next to Dr. Sennholz. As I told him, I considered it an honor to march shoulder to shoulder with him. I hold it as one of my highest privileges as new president of the college he loves to publish this tribute, evincing our respect and love for him.

Jerry H. Combee
President, Grove City College

PART ONE

Grato Animo Beneficiique Memores

1

INTEGRITY AND ECONOMICS

Robert D. Love*

It has always seemed to me that ideas are cheap; it is implementation that counts. This is not, of course, to denigrate the importance of ideas, for ideas do have consequences. That can certainly be demonstrated the world over by what has happened throughout history. America was based on an idea—the idea of religious freedom and all that it entails: freedom of association, freedom of speech, freedom of the press, etc. The implementation of that idea was difficult—sometimes fatal—for the Pilgrims and other Founding Fathers.

I first met Dr. Hans Sennholz more than thirty-five years ago and was at once impressed by his stalwart German bearing and, at the same time, the kindness and gentleness of a man with a twinkle in his eye. He demanded of those he was teaching no less than learning what he had to say. His audiences outside of the classroom were always treated to a barrage of reasoned arguments that came from years of study of Austrian economics.

I was attracted to Dr. Sennholz by his insistence that what he had to say in theory must be implemented in practice. His greatest gift to me was teaching me what money is. Money, of course, can have many forms, but it must be scarce, difficult to reproduce, durable, divisible, and portable. Above all, to be sound money, it must be out of the control of politicians.

Many people think money is a crass subject, yet it is fundamental to the way we live. We exchange our labor for something of value, and because we desire other things of value, we must have some means to store value for future exchanges. We certainly cannot trade labor for housing without a medium of exchange that is honest, true, reliable, and durable. Unfortunately,

* Mr. Love is president of the Love Box Company, Wichita, Kansas.

the control of money has been in the hands of politicians for too long.

Many years ago Leonard Read, Founder of the Foundation for Economic Education, wrote an essay entitled "The Macro Malady" about Napoleon and how he was "grossly ignorant of the limits of his own wisdom." No one can successfully run the life of another person, Read argued. He cannot tell another person how to be happiest or most productive by regulating his every move.

Leonard suggested an experiment to those who doubt their inability to command another successfully: put the man you want to control into a room by himself, blindfold him, and give him a fly swatter; turn a fly loose in the room, and standing on the outside, give the man instructions for every move to make to kill the fly. The fly will die of old age and the man with the swatter will be totally frustrated.

Government's response to this lesson is never to take the blindfold off and let the man solve the problem himself, but rather to send in more bureaucrats to tell him what to do. At that point, the obvious result is complete confusion, frustration, and the inability to do anything constructive. The collapse of central economic planning in Europe in the past few years is an example of the futility of trying to micro-manage other men's lives.

Some years ago we held a seminar in Wichita led by Dr. Sennholz and Dr. Schmolders of Germany on the question: what would a "wheelbarrow" inflation look like in the United States?

Dr. Sennholz reached into his profound knowledge of money and oppressive government and painted a bleak picture of what the economy would look like with runaway inflation. But he also contrasted the darkness with the light, in the manner of Rembrandt, by describing what might happen in this country were we to adopt measures similar to those Ludwig Erhard used in Germany in 1948. As I look back on that seminar, Dr. Sennholz predicted exactly what would happen. He argued that we would not have a "wheelbarrow" inflation such as the Germans experienced in the 1920s, but rather a gradual destruction of the value of money by the U.S. Treasury.

I also remember the many times Dr. Sennholz and I talked about business and his advice to me as a young businessman. First of all, he said, "As you build factories, buy plenty of land and build buildings that are first-class, because over a period of thirty or forty years, you will be able to finance and refinance those buildings for many more dollars than what you put into them in the first place, because of inflation and the increase in the money supply—which is the proper definition of inflation."

Not only did our company build good factories with plenty of land; we also bought first-class equipment and did everything we could to keep it modern. Thus, we tried not to overstate our profits through low depreciation expense or lack of repairs. Back in 1947 and 1948, industrialist J. Howard Pew was very interested in and vocal about depreciation. Because it was too low, the U.S. economy was not replacing capital lost due to inflation and high taxes on illusory profits. By consuming our capital, we were ensuring the collapse of our economy. In the past few decades our nation has substituted borrowed money for real earnings, and this has led to a greater demand for more inflation to postpone the day of reckoning a few years more.

Of course, Dr. Sennholz understood money and inflation, and as the first Ph.D. in economics in the United States under Ludwig von Mises, he certainly was qualified to understand the market place, money, and all of those things that properly fall under the rubric, economics. In addition to being well schooled in economics and the cold hard facts, Dr. Sennholz was also a gentle and kind spirit who had a simple moral principle: "If I advocate something, I will live by it." It is very difficult in this world today to speak the truth and live by it at the same time. But Dr. Sennholz did and does that.

Leonard Read laid down three axioms that I believe make a good cornerstone: first of all, know what you are talking about; second, live by what you say you believe; and third, if you do the first two, you will be so unusual that someone will ask why you believe what you do. At this point, you become a teacher, which is a high calling. To be a teacher is a very responsible position in God's eyes, and He will judge those who are teachers more severely than those who are not. Dr. Sennholz has lived by those axioms and earned for himself an estimable following.

Of course, because of Dr. Sennholz's attachment to honesty in all things, he was never accorded the political recognition he deserved. His consistency, and his advocacy of the idea that a dollar taken through taxation from somebody who earned it and given to someone else is immoral, earned him the enmity of most politicians and collectivists in government. The politicians were not sure why they avoided Dr. Sennholz; they knew only that they could not refute his penetrating analysis of situations that they wanted to make muddy and unintelligible.

But the lack of political recognition was more than compensated for by recognition of another sort. We have had seminars in Wichita for almost forty years, sponsored by the Foundation for Economic Education, and Dr. Sennholz has been a participant in over ninety percent of them. He is always sought after by the people here in our community and has been revered by them for almost four decades. I surmise the same is true in other cities across the United States.

Let me conclude by saying that I was asked to write an essay on some original subject, but I found that there aren't too many original subjects that have not already been discussed. My intention is to give glory to those who deserve it, and certainly Hans, and his right hand, Mary Sennholz, deserve every accolade that can possibly be given them by those of us who have benefited from his learning, his keen mind, and his consistent ethical position of not saying one thing and doing another.

Mine is certainly not a scholarly paper, but it tells my story as a businessman, friend, and admirer of Dr. Sennholz and what he has meant to me in the success of my own company and my life's work. Without his sound teaching on money, which touches all aspects of economic life, I would probably have been pulled and hauled back and forth across the collectivist threshold many times. But because of that sound teaching, it was not necessary to deviate from my course. It is difficult today to be in business and be completely consistent, but it can be done, and with success. However, there must be a will to do it, and Dr. Sennholz, as my teacher and mentor, has set an example for me that was hard to follow but easy to see in its truthfulness and integrity.

My wish for Hans and Mary Sennholz as his retirement from Grove City College approaches is that they will continue to be productive and enjoy the fruits of their labor which they so rightly deserve. They are blessed with a fine family: son, daughter-in-law, and grandson. If none of us had any more than that, we would be totally successful in God's sight. But God has given Hans Sennholz much more than that. His stout heart, his devotion to principle, and his willingness to stand by that principle through all adversity demands from us our admiration and respect.

May God bless the Sennholz family in their endeavors. May He also preserve the teaching of Dr. Hans Sennholz in all its ethical and moral dimensions.

2

THE BEACON FACTOR

Gary North*

Ye are the light of the world. A city that is set on an hill cannot be hid. Neither do men light a candle, and put it under a bushel, but on a candlestick; and it giveth light unto all that are in the house.

Matthew 5:14-15

When he was in college after World War II, Hans Sennholz suffered from the effects of the price and wage controls that Hitler had imposed in the 1930s and which were kept intact by the Allied occupation government, 1945-48.[1] Every night, the local electric power company blacked out most of the city of Marburg, leaving only one section with power. The power was allocated night by night, section by section, on a rotating basis. Sennholz and his fellow students had to organize into study groups, with each member living in a different section of the city. Each little band of students would move from one student's room to the other's, night by night, following the lights like moths, in order to study. He learned to appreciate the benefits of predictable lighting in one location. That was a luxury available only to the few.

In a very real sense, Sennholz dedicated his academic career to this allocation principle: *predictable light in one location.* In a mobile society, this principle is no longer honored except in the breach. Corporations require their executives to move from city to city as they move up the corporate ladder. To move up, executives are expected to move out. The American military no longer assigns a young officer to one unit and then keeps him with that

*Dr. North is president of the Institute for Christian Economics and a prolific author.

unit to build an esprit de corps. Instead, officers are treated like corporate managers, whom they resemble in many ways.[2] They are moved from command to command. The idea that a person should remain in one place for an entire career, shedding the accumulated light of experience and wisdom on those under his authority, is no longer taken seriously. Only in places like Grove City, Pennsylvania, do people occupy the same position decade after decade. Perhaps the greatest irony is that Grove City College does not offer tenure to its faculty. By not "locking in" its faculty, and thereby locking out others, it has created considerable academic stability. (The bureaucratic academic world is predictably unimpressed.)

Grove City College was a perfect place for Hans Sennholz. It was a college operated in terms of a vision. There are not many of these colleges still remaining. The positive influence of J. Howard Pew, the college's richest alumnus, has extended down through the years, both in terms of his original financial capital and his original visionary capital. Pew, a dedicated Presbyterian layman and dedicated defender of free market economics, used his money wisely when he provided the funds to build up a debt-free Presbyterian college. And he displayed both an entrepreneurial and an ecumenical vision when he persuaded Sennholz the Lutheran to come to the college and serve as a beacon in the department of economics.

To serve as a beacon, a man needs a permanent foundation, and this foundation is two-fold: ideological and geographical. He has to stay in one place for the long haul. He also needs sufficient ideological oil to keep his light burning. Sennholz had the oil, and he has stayed at his post until he decided it was time to relinquish his command.

Hans Sennholz is a good economist in an era dominated by degree-holding non-economists. But I think we would miss the point of his career if we evaluated him only in terms of his performance as an economist. We should not forget that Hans Sennholz is a good soldier. He was a "soldier" who once flew for the *Luftwaffe,* but beyond that, he was an ideological soldier who stayed at his assigned post for over thirty-five years. He accepted his ideological assignment from Ludwig von Mises, and he accepted his institutional assignment from J. Howard Pew. Soon, like a soldier at the end of an honorable career, he will step down to make room for a younger "officer" to serve. He will leave behind both a legacy and an example. It is appropriate at this point to summarize both the legacy and the example.

The Intellectual Assignment from Mises

Ludwig von Mises taught Hans Sennholz economics. Sennholz had read Mises's *Theory of Money and Credit* while in college in Germany. He decided that this was the kind of economics he wanted to devote his career to developing and proclaiming. He came to New York University to study with the master in the early 1950s. Sennholz learned Misesian economics well. Others learned, too. Four students of Mises were granted the Ph.D. at New York University in this period: Sennholz, Israel Kirzner, George Riesman, and Louis Spadaro.

It is one of those seeming peculiarities of history that no strict Misesians occupy the classroom today. There are followers of Mises, to be sure, but they all are "Mises plus something else, something different." There are Rothbardian anarchists, Lachmannite irrationalists, Kirznerian perceptionists, Christian Reconstructionists, and a host of academic spin-offs. But there are no more academic defenders of Mises without additions, or at least none who still teach.[3] Even Sennholz is no longer a Misesian, if he ever really was, for Sennholz was always a Lutheran, and he never divorced his Lutheran world view from his economics. His recent collection of essays, *Three Economic Commandments* (1990), begins with an essay on "The Judeo-Christian Foundation of the Private-Property Order." It ends with "Our Sins Shall Find Us Out."[4] This is not the kind of epistemological approach to economic science that we would have expected from Mises, who was a nineteenth-century Kantian rationalist and utilitarian.

The Master and His Disciples

The disciples of the master have not retained the whole of the master's world view. This is the fate of every man-made intellectual movement. The founder may expect his disciples to defend the faith as originally delivered, but this cannot happen for very long if the movement is to survive. Times change. People change.

Problems change. For any movement to survive over time, it must depart from some elements of the original creed; otherwise, it dies out, leaving behind at best only a memory of a few of its chief tenets. No human creed is perfect. Perfection is not possible in this world. Thus, the creeds of any faith must be revised and updated from time to time if they are to remain viable in men's lives as statements of faith. The alteration of the tenets of the faith is part of the historical process. The heirs of the legacy will have to modify it in order to keep it alive.[5]

The founder cannot determine in advance which elements of his original legacy will be preserved. He knows only that the best he can hope for is that the outline of his legacy will be familiar to those living a generation or a hundred generations later. What did not survive intact in Mises's system was its Kantianism. Rothbard went back to Aristotle's principles of natural rights; Lachmann and Kirzner have placed the Kantian noumenal (imperceivable)[6] at the heart of their entrepreneurial reconstruction of Mises; and the Christian Reconstructionists have substituted the Bible for Kant's *Critique*. Only Hayek defends the older Kantian faith;[7] but he has either abandoned or ignored much of Mises's original legacy in monetary theory, welfare policy, and taxation.

What does Sennholz still defend? He defends Mises's critique of socialist economic planning, his monetary theory, his theory of the trade cycle, his defense of free trade, his theory of profits and entrepreneurship, and his hostility to the use of state power to redistribute wealth. But here we find the key difference between the master and the pupil. Sennholz insists that the fundamental evil of coercive wealth redistribution is in fact its fundamental *evil.* It is immoral. Coercive wealth redistribution leads to economic inefficiencies, Sennholz has shown, but this is because such acts are inherently immoral. Morally evil acts have bad economic consequences.

The Question of Morality

Sometime in the early 1960s, I had a conversation with F. A. Harper.[8] Harper was an anarchist, and he defended his position in terms of the immorality of every action of the state. He told me that he once had asked Mises whether Mises would accept the legitimacy of socialism if socialism turned out to be more efficient than the free market. "But it isn't," Mises said. Harper pressed him, and again Mises answered, "But it isn't." Harper concluded that Mises was determined not to introduce any question of morality into his analysis of an economic system. The only thing that mattered to him was economic efficiency, an economic system's ability to allow acting men the unrestricted use of their assets.

Mises was a philosophical utilitarian. In the introductory chapter on epistemology[9] in *Human Action*, Mises wrote: "The idea that the incentive of human activity is always some uneasiness and its aim always to remove such uneasiness as far as possible, that is, to make the acting man feel happier, is the essence of the teachings of Eudaemonism and Hedonism. . . . The theological, mystical, and other schools of a heteronomous ethic did not raise any other objection than its neglect of the 'higher' and 'nobler' pleasures. It is true that the writings of many earlier champions of Eudaemonism, Hedonism, and Utilitarianism are in some points open to misinterpretation. But the language of modern philosophers and still more that of the modern economists is so precise and straightforward that no misinterpretations can possibly occur."[10] He had no use for either theology or mysticism.

Mises made it clear what he thought should be primary in economics: autonomous human reason. "We may leave aside the genuine dogmas such as Creation, Incarnation, the Trinity, as they have no direct bearing on the problems of interhuman relations. But many issues remain with regard to which most, if not all, Christian churches and denominations are not prepared to yield to secular reasoning and an evaluation from the point of view of social utility. Thus the recognition of natural law on the part of Christian theology was only conditional. It referred to a definite type of natural law, not opposed to the teachings of Christ as each of these churches and denominations interpreted them. It did not acknowledge the supremacy of reason. It was incompatible with the principles of utilitarian philosophy."[11]

It was this hedonistic, utilitarian aspect of Mises's epistemology that was abandoned by Sennholz:

> In God's world, causes and consequences are connected logically. To violate a natural law, to offend against an economic principle, or to disobey an ethical commandment is to suffer the inexorable consequences of our action. God may not reach out of heaven to punish

the offenders; His eternal laws and principles invariably exact a price for all offenses.

Many Jews and Christians pray piously to God for employment and prosperity, and at the same time blatantly violate His commandments. While they build synagogues and churches to the glory of God, they supplicate in the temples of politics, especially in Washington. When rabbis, priests, and ministers give moral legitimacy and intellectual validity to resentment and envy, their followers are likely to resort to political action.

Gross violations of the commandments call for prompt and severe consequences. The appeals for political coercion immediately generate social conflict and strife, which, in time, give rise to political power and authority. An envious society is a conflict society that needs many administrators, regulators, judges, and policemen; its prisons are forever overcrowded. A violent society is a poor society in which people linger in dire straits and many suffer from hunger and want.[12]

The Example Set by Mises

In his dedication to the approach to economics that Mises set forth in many of his works, but especially in *Human Action*, *Socialism*, and *The Theory of Money and Credit*, Sennholz always displayed a devotion to principle that has served as a beacon to younger scholars, including me. This was not merely a devotion to intellectual principle, as Mises himself displayed; it was also devotion to moral principle. I believe that it was his willingness to serve as a beacon in the midst of seemingly impenetrable darkness that constitutes the most important legacy from Mises that Sennholz preserved and passed on intact to the next generation of students and scholars. He learned more than economics from Mises; he learned to take his stand in the face of implacable intellectual opposition from his professional peers.

Mises had displayed this same trait. He met every intellectual challenge, answered every critic, and did not waver in his commitment to the free market. The spiritual heirs of the academic socialists (institutionalists) who had battled Carl Menger and Eugen Böhm-Bawerk in the late nineteenth century later challenged Mises. Then it was the Marxian socialists of the entire era. It was the democratic socialists (Social Democrats) of the 1920s. It was the national socialists of the 1930s. Finally, it was the Keynesian socialists of the 1940s through the 1970s. Mises did not give an inch. This is not a common human trait. Mrs. Mises recounts this incident in her biography of Mises. It is representative of a lifetime of opposition. New York University, where Mises taught for over twenty years, retiring in the late 1960s when he was well into his eighties, never paid him a dime in salary. His paycheck was picked up by Lawrence Fertig and other supporters. The school kept him listed as a visiting professor, never a full member of the faculty. A graduate student wanted to take Mises's seminar. Here is Mrs. Mises's account:

> His faculty advisor told him that he could take the seminar course on his own, but *not* as a part of his official program. "Mises's theory," said the professor, "is a religion, not economics."
>
> Eight years later that same professor, reminiscing over the great social experiments of the last generation, was greatly disturbed at the fact that the experiments were a dismal and known failure. "I had always tended to be liberal over the years and I favored all these new programs," he said. "But one by one I have seen them all fail and have to be discarded. You know, *perhaps Mises was right after all.*"[13]

Today, there is no "perhaps" about it. Mises had been right from the beginning. Now even his former opponents are beginning to admit this in print. In the final months of 1989, the ideology of communism died an unexpected death, unexpected in the West. It had been expected for a long time behind the Iron Curtain, recognized by all as a terminally ill patient in an insane asylum.[14] A kind of Alzheimer's disease had afflicted communism. The ideology of socialism, like a close relative suffering from the same incurable disease, shuffled along behind the casket at the funeral. Keynesianism, a second cousin, was also in attendance, sitting glumly through the brief and poorly attended service, pretending afterwards to be related only by marriage. But the same lapses of coherence and memory have afflicted Communism's Keynesian cousin. The main difference is that textbook royalties still support the aging second cousin in upper-middle-class comfort.

A Stunning Admission in 1990

In 1920, Mises wrote a classic essay on the impossibility of rational socialist economic calculation. He argued that without the private ownership of the means of production, there can be no free market system. But without a free market for services and goods, especially capital goods, there is no way for a socialist planning board to establish rational prices. So, he concluded, socialist planning is inherently irrational.[15] Mises wrote in 1922: "The problem of economic calculation is the fundamental problem of Socialism. That for decades people could write and talk about Socialism without touching this problem only shows how devastating were the effects of the Marxian prohibition on scientific scrutiny of the nature and working of a socialist economy."[16]

Mises's critics rejected both his economic theory and his analysis of socialism, and the economics profession for half a century consigned Mises's work, at most, to a brief footnote telling the reader that Oskar Lange's supposed refutation of Mises in 1936 had been definitive.[17] But in 1990, the socialist economist and best-selling author Robert Heilbroner admitted: "It turns out, of course, that Mises was right."[18] Mises's critics on this point had all been wrong.

Mises's essay and his 1922 book, *Socialism*, had persuaded a younger group of socialist economists in the early 1920s, including F. A. Hayek, Wilhelm Röpke, and Lionel Robbins. But not many others followed, and a majority of the few who did were epistemologically overwhelmed by the Great Depression. Several became followers of John Maynard Keynes in the late 1930s or early 1940s, including Gottfried Haberler, Fritz Machlup, and Robbins. Almost all references to Mises disappeared from professional economic literature after 1935, except for brief statements that he had been totally refuted by Lange. Yet Mises was still writing as late as 1966, specifically, an essay predicting that the proposed reforms of the Soviet economy would not work.[19] He was right once again; they didn't.

Heilbroner's own career is indicative of just how long and how thoroughly Mises's work had been suppressed by professional economists. Heilbroner's book, *The Worldly Philosophers*, first published in 1953, has sold over three million copies. It is the book on the history of economic thought that most economics majors in the United States have read, and many history majors, too. In it, there is not a word on Mises. But there is a whole chapter on Marx. Heilbroner wrote of Marx: "He called the trends the 'laws of motion' of a capitalist system, the path which capitalism would tread over future time. And the astonishing fact is that almost all these predictions have come true!"[20] Heilbroner's rhetoric on the breakdown of capitalism showed few restraints:

> In Russia and Eastern Europe capitalism has disappeared; in Scandinavia and Britain it has been partially abandoned; in Germany and Italy it drifted into fascism and emerged from its bath of fire in less than perfect health. Indeed, almost everywhere except in the United States capitalism is on the defensive; and while wars, brute political power, exigencies of fate, and the determined efforts of revolutionaries have all contributed their share, the grim truth is that its demise has largely been for the very reason Marx foresaw: it broke down.[21]

The collapse of Communist economies in 1989 changed Heilbroner's thinking overnight. He gave up hope in the future of socialism. "In a word, socialism as a desirable order that lies beyond the reach of advanced capitalism appears to me to be an unlikely prospect within the imaginable future. It seems unlikely in part because one residual effect of the collapse of Communism is apt to be an inhibition of the social imagination. In larger part, however, my skepticism stems from an absence of plausible social blueprints whose realization seems worth the risk of venturing beyond the known terrain of capitalism."[22] It was not the power of Mises's arguments, nor the power of his followers' arguments, that had persuaded Heilbroner to give up his socialist faith. It was the fact of Communism's failure.

Ironically, it was only with Gorbachev's admission in 1989 of the complete economic failure of Soviet Communism, coupled with the pull-back of the official, visible Communist control apparatus in Central Europe, that Western intellectual opinion reversed itself regarding the productivity of Communism. This shift came overnight, indicating that their previous commitment had not been based on strictly technical or academic factors, but had something to do with their humanistic religious presuppositions. The best example of the pre-1989 views of Western intellectuals is found in the most widely read textbook in economics in the West, Paul Samuelson's *Economics*. It has sold over three million copies, making the author a multi-millionaire. Samuelson was the first American to win the Nobel Prize in economics (1970). In the 1989 edition of the textbook, presumably written in 1988, he wrote this: "The Soviet economy is proof that, contrary to what many skeptics had earlier believed, a socialist command economy can function and even thrive."[23]

When the leaders of the Soviet Union and several satellite nations admitted in 1989 that the Soviet economy was economically bankrupt, they launched a revolution, in every sense. Almost overnight, socialism as an ideology perished. Like an overstressed dam, the economic reality of socialism could no longer be covered up by the leaders of Communist nations. With this public admission, people's confidence in socialism—not just Communism—collapsed, except perhaps in Communist China and North Korea. Within months, there were very few socialists still visible except in the West's universities. All the arguments that free market economists had brought against socialism had been ignored by socialists for over a century. Then, overnight, the intellectual battle seemed to be over. But is it?

What we need to understand is that the defenders of free market capitalism did not win this debate by the power of logic. They won only by default. Communist economies went bankrupt, taking socialist ideology with them. But the arguments of the defenders of capitalism have not triumphed. This is the problem. Those living in formerly Communist nations still have little understanding about the alternative: a social order based on free market voluntarism. This is why the ideological battle is not over. It is another reason why we need to understand Mises's legacy and Sennholz's continuation of it.

The Institutional Assignment from J. Howard Pew

Hans Sennholz received his doctorate in political science at the University of Köln. He served briefly as a lawyer, but he decided that this was not to be his life's work. He returned to the United States, this time to attend graduate school in economics under Mises, which was at least a more stimulating environment than his years as a German P.O.W. in Arkansas.[24] New York City in the 1950s was not New York City in the 1990s, an environment which no longer compares so favorably with Arkansas (although it is arguably superior, marginally, to a P.O.W. camp).[25]

In his early academic years, he taught political science at Iona College in New York. Dr. Ernst Winter, an Austrian immigrant who, like Mises, had fled from the Nazis in 1938 (his father had been the anti-Nazi Vice Mayor of Vienna), and who was married to one of the famous Von Trapp daughters, was the chairman of the Department. Four decades later, he reminisced: "We were the only political science department in the country that still taught traditional political science—a more organic view of the state. We were regarded as most peculiar." It did not matter what field Sennholz entered; he was always unconventional. This never seemed to disturb him. It has greatly disturbed his opponents and critics from time to time. Sennholz always seemed so stubborn, so arrogant in the face of the "known facts" of economic life, such as the economic benefits of wage controls. When Sennholz criticized Nixon's price and wage controls at a conference attended by conservatives in the early 1970s, a conservative political scientist who taught at a major midwestern state university rose from his seat, shouted "Bircher, Bircher!", and stomped out of the meeting. (So much for rational academic discourse.)

When he received his Ph.D. in economics in 1955, the academic world was fast becoming Keynesian. The few hold-outs were older professors who were left over from the early 1930s. Their days were clearly numbered. In this intellectual environment, he was asked by J. Howard Pew to come to Western Pennsylvania to teach at a four-year Presbyterian college whose very name suggests a two-year community college.[26] He accepted, and he created an undergraduate economics department that was notable for its commitment to the free market without the Chicago School's commitment to abstract equations. His department was the one economics department where the student learned about human action rather than lifeless equations, whether Keynesian or Chicagoan. Sennholz made sure that in his department the foundations of economic analysis rested on the decisions of acting men. In this, he isolated the department. It was so far out of the mainstream that few professional economists knew anything about it. When Milton Friedman announced that, "We are all Keynesians now,"[27] he was ignoring the economics department at Grove City College. Most professional economists have agreed with Friedman, and most of them also have continued to ignore Grove City College's economics department.

And so, the beacon now had an institutional academic base. Not large. Not prestigious. Not world-renowned. But a base. There was no other in degree-granting academia, 1956–80. Israel Kirzner was in this early period a lonely voice for a narrowly circumscribed academic Misesianism,[28] teaching at New York University.[29] George Riesman, was (and remains) a Randian, taught at St. Johns College (Roman Catholic) in New York City and then at the Church of Christ college, Pepperdine University, seemingly odd places of employment for a follower of Ayn Rand.[30] Louis Spadaro was Dean of the Graduate School of Business Administration at Fordham University, and, briefly upon retirement, served as President of The Institute for Humane Studies. There was only one institutional academic base: the economics department at Grove City College. Had Sennholz refused Pew's offer, there would have been none.

The Example Set by Sennholz

I first heard of Sennholz sometime in the late 1950s or in 1960. When I was in high school, I was given a copy of *The Freeman*, and in it I came across Sennholz's name. From time to time, I would read an article by him or see him quoted in some conservative college publication, and there were very few of them in 1960. In the summer of 1962, I attended a two-week summer school program sponsored by the Intercollegiate Society of Individualists (now the Intercollegiate Studies Institute). Sennholz was one of four main speakers at that seminar.[31] Every day for a week, he would give two hours of lectures. I can remember that he told about his young son who was buying up silver dollars. Sennholz warned that they would go out of circulation soon. They did. A year later, so did other U.S. silver coins, as Gresham's law once again made its presence felt.

From the first time I heard him, I was impressed by the real-world focus of his economics. Economics in his view is not simply an academic exercise; it is an intellectual tool for solving real-world problems and formulating economic policy. A year later, when I was employed by the William Volker Fund as a summer intern, I came across a typed report in the files that was highly critical of Sennholz. It had been written by a young Misesian anarchist who was still in graduate school. He reported on a conference he had attended at which Sennholz insisted that economic science should be used to make investment decisions. The author sneered at Sennholz's claim that this was how he made his own investment decisions. It was this commitment to making profits as an entrepreneur that outraged this strictly academic anarchist. (The critic subsequently produced very few published academic contributions, and none that I can think of in economics. He received academic tenure in a state university where he has taught, almost immune from market forces, for a quarter century.)

Sennholz has always taught his obligatory four courses per semester. Every instructor in the department must do the same. He has always lectured off-campus whenever possible. He has bought real estate. And he has written. How he has written! He has written several books, but the bulk of his output has been articles. Hundreds and hundreds of articles, not always for pay. He knew, as any author of essays knows, that no single essay is likely to have great impact. It will not re-shape the thinking of thousands of individuals. At best, it might be read by a few hundred, remembered by thirty, and taken to heart by a dozen. So, the only way to make essay writing into a force for positive intellectual and social change is to write lots and lots of them. This means that the author must continually be alert, Kirzner style, to possibilities for the application of permanent general principles to specific cases in history. This alertness was basic to Sennholz's career. He never ceased writing, even though he could not get his essays published in the prestigious economics journals. He was not interested in writing his way into a prestigious university; he was interested only in keeping the beacon shining. Wherever he thought he could get some editor to run one of his essays, he submitted it. There was no way to know who might be illuminated if it appeared in print.

The Remnant

He understood and believed the message in Albert J. Nock's famous essay, "Isaiah's Job."[32] It is the job of the prophet to keep telling the truth whenever and wherever someone is willing to listen. There is no way for men to ram the truth down people's throats and make them believe it; there is only the public testimony to the truth. The Remnant, Nock said, is always out there, invisible, waiting to see some light. It will not be pushed, but it will be led. It is drawn to men of principle who are not afraid to stand up for the truth.

In the 1950s and 1960s, there were not many members of the Remnant. It was a time of great spiritual and intellectual darkness. The liberal-interventionist world view was dominant on campus in the social sciences and the humanities. Milton Friedman was barely known then, and his insights were regarded by most of his peers as quaint, silly, or dangerous. Had they known of Mises, let alone Sennholz, they would have chortled. "What nonsense! How antiquated! When will you people enter the twentieth century?"

The imagery of swimming upstream does not do justice to the magnitude of the task, unless the stream flows into Niagara Falls. Any light shed from Western Pennsylvania or from various unscholarly journals of free market opinion was easily ignored by the academic guild. It would have caused no ripples for Sennholz to have gone the conventional route for an academic economist: writing mathematical essays to be read by no one, but which alone serve as the ladder into professional success in academia. It would also have created no sense of loss in the academic guild for Sennholz to have devoted more time to real estate and less to his essays. No one would have missed him at Harvard, Yale, or the University of Chicago, since no one knew who he was.

But I surely would have missed him, and so would other members of the Remnant of the early 1960s.

What did Sennholz do that was so important? He did what Mises did for Hayek, Röpke, Robbins, Haberler, Machlup, and others in the 1920s and early 1930s, and what he did for Kirzner, Sennholz, Rothbard, and others in the 1950s; what Hayek did in the 1930s through the mid-1970s; and what Röpke did in the late 1930s through the mid-1960s: *He kept the beacon lit in an era of great darkness.* He offered safe (though turbulent) intellectual passage through the rocky shoals during the Keynesian ideological storm. But Sennholz did this for undergraduates; the others didn't. No one else cared about undergraduates with the intensity that Sennholz did. No other follower of Mises wrote with equal dedication to housewives and businessmen, bankers and politicians. Not many of them listened; not many of them cared; but not many ever do.

The clouds began to lift in the mid-1970s. The Keynesian myth had begun to crack under the strain of worldwide stagflation. Hayek was a co-winner of the Nobel Prize in economics in 1974, the year after Mises's death (conveniently for the Nobel committee). He shared the prize with socialist Gunnar Myrdal. (The rumor at the time was that one of them never expected to win it, while the other never expected to share it.) Friedman and the Chicago School had penetrated the tenured walls of academia. Ronald Reagan made an unsuccessful bid for the Republican nomination for President in 1976. The tide had begun to turn.

What did Sennholz do? He wrote more articles, spoke at more conferences, and bought more real estate. And he taught more undergraduates. No one else wanted to teach undergraduates. He took advantage of a "natural monopoly": the unwillingness of senior professors to teach undergraduates. He remained where he had begun: in Western Pennsylvania. This was symbolically appropriate, for it was in Western Pennsylvania in the 1850s that crude oil was discovered. J. Howard Pew made his fortune by seeking better ways to refine and market that oil. So he did again late in his life when he persuaded Hans Sennholz to make the move to Western Pennsylvania, a century after oil was discovered there. The "oil" in Sennholz's lamp never ran low, and it was being refined constantly. All that was missing was the marketing.

In an age of marketing, the advertising experts "sell the sizzle, not the steak." Sennholz always had at least some sizzle—his accent, if nothing else—but he always sold steak. Worse, Sennholz was selling steak *sandwiches*—undergraduate education. This was the steak that killed the sale in the economics guild of the 1950s and 1960s. The guild was in the sizzle business: the dazzling promises and equations of the Keynesians, replaced in part only by the dazzling claims and equations of the Friedmanians. (By the late 1970s, both were being challenged by the ultra-dazzling equations but drastically reduced claims of the "rational expectationists.")

In teaching undergraduates exclusively, Sennholz placed himself in the outer darkness of academia. There was only one justification for a senior professor to do this: he wanted to get to the students before the cares of the world, or the cares of graduate school, got to them. He wanted to instill in as many as possible a way of reasoning, economic reasoning. Some learned how to do it; not many, but some. Few ever do. But if there is not a dedicated beacon like Sennholz to guide undergraduates through the shoals, most of them will wind up on the rocks. This was especially true in the era of Keynesian dominance.

Conclusion

Sennholz for years has warned against the immorality of the envy-driven American voter. He has warned that when the promises of the welfare state turn at last to gravel in men's mouths, as they surely will, there will be a social crisis. He has done what he could to warn people, not merely telling them ways of escaping the fury of the political reaction, but also warning them not to participate in the political plunder of the age. He has taken seriously the words of Solomon: "Bread of deceit is sweet to a man; but afterwards his mouth shall be filled with gravel" (Proverbs 20:17).

Not many have listened to his warning. But it was not his responsibility to make them listen. That is never a prophet's job. It was his responsibility to warn those who were willing to listen, and to make that warning as cogent as possible. That responsibility in the classroom he never forsook until he reached threescore and ten, which Moses tells us is as much as any man should be expected to do, lest weakness overtake him (Psalm 90:10).

So how do we encapsulate his career? Economist, teacher, promoter, author, entrepreneur (or, as he would call it, "spekoolator"), moral philosopher, watchman on the wall, beacon of light. They all apply. But I think they are all wrapped up into two words: *good soldier*. The good soldier Sennholz. We need an army full of men like him. Sadly, we do not have yet even an officer corps. But at least we have some non-coms: the best and brightest of the thousands of students who passed through his non-commissioned officer's candidate school. No more can be asked of a good soldier.

Notes and References

1. See Sennholz, Hans, "The Second German Inflation and the Destruction of the Mark (1933-1948)," *Journal of Christian Reconstruction*, VII (Summer 1980), pp. 53-71.
2. Grace Hopper, who remained on active duty in the U.S. Navy until she was well into her seventies, used to tell young officers: "The trouble is, officers need to lead, not manage."
3. Bettina Bien Greaves still keeps the Misesian torch filled with pure Misesian oil, but she has never taught in a classroom.
4. Sennholz, Hans, *Three Economic Commandments* (Spring Mills, PA: Libertarian Press, 1990).
5. Of course, the faith must retain some continuity in order to remain "the faith." The task of the faithful of every era must be to preserve the fundamentals of the faith without allowing the faith to become irrelevant.
6. Kroner, Richard, *Kant's Weltanschauung* (Chicago, IL: University of Chicago Press, [1914] 1956). The "kalaidic" economics of Ludwig Lachmann and G. L. S. Shackle, and the perceptional economics of Kirzner both rely on the non-rational element of Kant and Mises to make their systems coherent. The dualism in Mises's thought, following Kant, has become natural rights rationalism in Rothbard's system and irrationalism in Lachmann's, with Kirzner doing his best to skate down the middle of the melting epistemological ice.
7. In a 1985 interview with Mark Skousen and me, Hayek admitted that until he read John Gray's book on Hayek's system, he had not recognized that he was a Kantian. He told us that he thought Gray was correct.
8. A remarkable number of economists have the initials F. A.: Walker, Fetter, Hayek, Harper, and Lutz.
9. Epistemology: "What can man know, and how does he know it?"
10. Mises, Ludwig von, *Human Action: A Treatise on Economics* (New Haven, CT: Yale University Press, 1949), p. 15.
11. Mises, *Theory and History: An Interpretation of Social and Economic Evolution* (Auburn, AL: Ludwig von Mises Institute, 1985), pp. 46-47. Published originally by Yale University Press, 1957.
12 Sennholz, *Three Economic Commandments*, p. 42.
13. Mises, Margit von, *My Years with Ludwig von Mises* (Spring Mills, PA: Libertarian Press, 1984), p. 141.
14. See Leopold Tyrmand, *The Rosa Luxemburg Contraceptives Cooperative: A Primer on Soviet Civilization* (New York, NY: Macmillan, 1972).

15. Mises, Ludwig von, "Economic Calculation in a Socialist Commonwealth" (1920), in F. A. Hayek (ed.), *Collectivist Economic Planning* (London: Routledge & Kegan Paul, 1935), ch. 3. Reprinted by Augustus Kelly, New York.
16. Mises, Ludwig von, *Socialism: An Economic and Sociological Analysis* (New Haven, CT: Yale University Press, [1922] 1951), p. 135. Reprinted by Liberty Press, Indianapolis.
17. Lange, Oskar, and Taylor, Fred M. *On the Economic Theory of Socialism* (New York, NY: McGraw-Hill, [1938] 1965). Lange's essays were published in 1936 and 1937 in *Review of Economic Studies.*
18. Heilbroner, Robert, "After Communism," *New Yorker* (Sept. 10, 1990), p. 92.
19. Mises, Ludwig von, "Observations on the Russian Reform Movement," *The Freeman* (May 1966).
20. Heilbroner, Robert, *The Worldly Philosophers: The Lives, Times, and Ideas of the Great Economic Thinkers* (New York, NY: Simon & Schuster, [1953] 1961), p. 138. In the 1953 edition, this statement appeared on page 155.
21. *Ibid.*, p. 139. In the 1953 edition, this statement appeared on page 157.
22. Heilbroner, "After Communism," p. 99.
23. Samuelson, Paul, and Nordhaus, William D., *Economics* (13th edition; New York, NY: McGraw-Hill, 1989), p. 837.
24. On the day that Germany surrendered, Flight Sergeant Sennholz went to the American officer in charge of the P.O.W. camp and volunteered to join the U.S. Army Air Corps to fight the Japanese. He explained that he was no longer bound by his oath to the former German government. It would have created a sensation had his request been granted. It wasn't.
25. Few Americans are aware that there were 45,000 German prisoners of war and 5,000 Italians in P.O.W. camps inside the United States during World War II.
26. Perhaps it should be re-named: the College of Grove City.
27. He was speaking of methodology, not policy conclusions.
28. Kirzner's published concerns have been primarily related to capital theory. To some extent, this makes him more an academic heir of Böhm-Bawerk than of Mises. While he has pursued Mises's insights on methodological individualism, capital theory, and entrepreneurship, there was far more to Mises's legacy than this. Kirzner's intermediate level textbook, *Market Theory and the Price System* (Van Nostrand, 1963), shows that his concerns were much wider in his early years, but it was not reprinted, and his later books do not reveal a comparable interest in the broader themes of economics.

29. Originally assigned to the Graduate School of Business Administration, not the Department of Economics.
30. Actually, Christian colleges are rarely concerned very much about the relationship between their expressed theology and the academic subject matter taught in the classroom. They want their faculty members certified by secular and state universities.
31. The others were R. J. Rushdoony, then a Presbyterian minister, Leo Paul de Alvarez, a Straussian political philosopher, and Francis G. Wilson, a Catholic political scientist.
32. Reprinted by the Foundation for Economic Education, Irvington-on-Hudson, New York 10533.

PART TWO

Veritas Praevalebit

3

THE DISINTEGRATION OF ECONOMIC OWNERSHIP

Robert G. Anderson*

The great economic achievement of the twentieth century has been the development of a world market order. The coordinating power of the market process has created a global social division of labor unprecedented in human history. It has achieved an international social cooperation that was, and is, unattainable through political alliances. Consequently, the millions of people participating in this worldwide market economy have shared in an immense improvement in material living standards.

This historical accomplishment has resulted from a rule of law that eventually secured both private claims to property and the freedom to contract. Without the institution of private property in the ownership of productive economic resources and a legal framework securing contractual agreements in the transfer of economic resources, an advanced world market economy would never have developed.

The economic efficiency of the market process in directing scarce economic resources toward their most valued use, as determined by consumers, has been tested and proven. The functioning of prices provides both consumers and producers with the information required to assure that property owners gain maximum use of their economic resources. An unhampered price system enables consumers to exercise their sovereignty in the market. The prices at which consumers buy or abstain from

*Mr. Anderson, a 1957 graduate of Grove City College, was one of the first of many Sennholz students over the years. He is the vice president of the Foundation for Economic Education in New York, and a contributing editor to its monthly journal, *The Freeman.*

buying the goods and services offered in the market direct economic resources toward fulfilling their most urgent demands by imparting profits or losses to the owners of property used in production.

Legal and Economic Ownership

The ownership of economic resources by individual market participants is a fundamental requirement for the formulation of an advanced market order. And the concept of private ownership implicitly assumes full economic control as well. Discussions of legal ownership without addressing economic ownership are meaningless.

While the world market order has been an extraordinary achievement, a counteracting force operating in the world has been a blight on the market's progress. This is the force of statist policies which prevent individuals from exercising the freedom of choice needed for the market economy to bring its full benefits to all mankind and to direct the world's limited resources to their most productive uses. Statist interventionist policies causing massive wealth destruction have been inflicted upon the people of the twentieth century, resulting in the loss of productive activity, diminished prosperity, and a disintegration of economic ownership. Edicts and mandates which undermine private property ownership have been impeding economic growth and the quality of life within the social order.

Where the disintegration of economic ownership is most radical (where control over productive economic resources has been totally removed from private ownership), totalitarian societies quickly emerge to ravage the lives and freedom of the people. The inevitable collapse of such command systems (state socialism) is now occurring worldwide.

The failure of state socialism is not surprising, since the roots of its decline are inherent in its structure. The very essence of socialism was to deny the institution of private property ownership and the individual's freedom to contract. Instead, state socialism placed control over the means of production in a centrally planned and bureaucratically administered order without the essential information provided by market pricing. The socialist structure, thereby, was unable to coordinate economic activity rationally.

Without the benefit of a market price system to direct production and consumption, socialism became a system of failed promises and brought misery and loss of economic freedom to the millions of individuals under its control. Socialism lacked any objective means to evaluate the economic merits of an exchange between buyers and sellers at the point of trade—that is, economic calculation.

The New Statism

While the ordering of economic resources under a socialist structure is failing throughout the world today, a more insidious successor to state socialism has developed. A form of statism has evolved whose adherents are less concerned with outcome and more concerned with controlling the processes of society. These new statists are interested in a social order which can be manipulated politically to interfere with private property ownership without completely repudiating the market order framework. While state socialism seized all claims of private ownership to property, this new form of statism captures only the economic ownership of private property, achieving its political objectives by imposing mandates and injunctions upon the legal owners of the property. It has become a system of social organization which can best be described as a pragmatic, neo-fascist state.

This neo-fascism outwardly appears to be a market order where consumers and producers engage in the voluntary exchange of goods and services. But the state interventionists, having seized some or all of the economic powers of private property owners, use their political control over the property to supersede the price signals and production patterns of the market if full economic ownership had remained with the private legal owners. This system is particularly deceiving in that it permits the statists to fault the market economy for any declines in prosperity while attributing all gains under such a system to their interventionist policies.

Both consumers and producers have felt the heavy hand of interventionism through regulations and edicts that have caused a disintegration of economic control of their property. The consequential destruction of both economic resources and human creativity has been devastating. The separation of property from private ownership, in a total sense under state socialism and in an economic sense under pragmatic neo-fascism, has exacted an enormous toll in the material standard of living of the people of this century.

The nature of property ownership determines the economic development of a social order because property resources are the means through which wants are fulfilled. Because means of production are limited, those who own and control property are stewards with a responsibility to direct property efficiently to its most valued use. It also must be secured and maintained to avoid loss or abuse. Private ownership is essential to ensure such stewardship. Private property owners have incentives to conserve and to employ their resources in the most socially beneficial uses to gain profits and thereby improve their own well-being from economic decisions made. The absence of private ownership places existing resources at risk and jeopardizes the incentives for the creation of new resources.

The fundamental point of this essay is in understanding that the accumulation and productive employment of property is directly related to the nature of property ownership. Without incentives available for private property owners in the form of a profit potential from employing their resources productively, there is little reason that owners would, or should, subject their property to any kind of risk-taking activity. Without exception, the separation of ownership incentives from productive economic resources diminishes the probability that the property will be used prudently.

The growth and economic influence of the state in this era of neo-fascism has resulted in vast accumulations of private and public wealth falling under the control of individuals who possess no ownership claims of any kind to the property. The consequence has been an incredible wasting and misuse of these resources, both seen and unseen, and it has led to a steady decline in the standard of living for millions. Even more tragically, it has prevented many more millions from participating in the greater abundance that an unhampered world market surely would have yielded.

Government Ownership

In the realm of government property, where economic resources are under the total control of state bureaucratic managers, there are no such things as private ownership incentives. The lack of such incentives tends to create an indifference toward, and general lack of responsibility for, government property. Exceptional is the public servant who displays a sense of accountability for the use of government property. Incentives to conserve government resources are undermined, since the government bureaucrat is unable to realize any direct benefit from such conservation.

Instances of mismanagement and wasting of government resources are legion in our political history. Unfortunately, the response to public outcries for ending such waste is either to pursue a more tightly controlled regulation of the government bureaucrats or to replace them with their political adversaries. Few see, and even fewer admit, that the problem is the absence of economic ownership incentives for the bureaucratic managers who control the resources.

The problem is simply a characteristic of the given framework and cannot be otherwise. Consider the bureaucrat who controls certain government property. His first priorities are maintaining his job position and controlling ever greater quantities of government property in order to solidify his position and gain further political influence. A bureaucrat's use of government property is incited by these priorities rather than by any compelling sense of stewardship.

Indeed, the absence of economic ownership over property in the public sector has not only undermined incentives to conserve its resources but has encouraged the destruction or excessive consumption of them. Excessive consumption is commonly caused by the tendency to treat public property as a free good rather than a scarce economic resource. This occurs in many areas, but the classic case is the public highway system.

Drivers treat highways as a free good, provided by governments with no direct cost to their users. The resulting unlimited demand is abusive and accelerates the deterioration of this public-sector resource. The higher maintenance costs and earlier replacement of highways is but one example of what must inevitably occur when an economic good is treated as a free good. Without economic ownership as an integral part of private property, excessive consumption leads toward destruction of non-owned property.

Then there is the wholesale destruction of property practiced by the state through acts of war. This may be a tragic necessity of the political world in which we live, but it is, nonetheless, a graphic display of the vast destructive power of government. We have seen in this century unprecedented accumulation and destruction of military hardware, either by war or technological obsolescence. It is difficult to calculate how many ships, aircraft, tanks, trucks, and the like have been blown or thrown into oblivion in this age of statist conflicts. But that this destruction has exacted an awesome toll in the material standard of living no one can deny. To be sure, the lack of economic resources ownership in the public sector has been a major factor in the destruction of this property.

Modern Corporate Ownership

The lack of economic ownership in the public sector has been a major cause of wealth destruction; but interventionism has been inflicting its heavy toll within the private sector as well. Institutional structures, created either in response to interventionist regulations or by direct interventionist edicts, have generated powerful forces of economic destruction.

A primary example in the private sector has been the development of the corporate structure under the regulatory edicts and interventionist laws of this century. The modern corporation, comprised of a multitude of diverse owners and controlled by managers detached from that ownership, has evolved into a major hidden force of wealth destruction. The disintegration of economic ownership within the modern corporation, however, differs from that in the public sector in two essential ways. Because corporations remain privately owned by stockholders in a legal sense, they are profit-seeking. Second, even though corporate managers share with government bureaucrats the problem of not owning the resources under management, they are forced to remain mindful that the corporation must respond to market forces.

The disintegration of economic ownership within the corporation is not necessarily an inevitable consequence of the corporate concept of shared ownership. While the corporate entity is open to easy manipulation in a politically hampered market economy, it is not necessarily a flawed structure. The loss of ownership control within the modern corporation has little to do with the nature of the market economy. The causes are more likely to be found in the interventionist manipulations of the legal and political environment of the pragmatic, neo-fascist state. For example, confiscatory burdens of income and estate taxation, as well as distortions in tax rates between corporations and individuals, have had a much greater influence on the structure of the modern corporation than have the economic forces of market competition.[1]

Under neo-fascism, a manipulated corporate structure has evolved which today is virtually under the control and management of non-owners. Stockholder ownership of corporations has become so dispersed that in many instances no one individual, nor even an entire board of directors, owns a measurable interest in the firm. Edicts and mandates imposed by an interventionist state have caused such a complete disintegration of economic ownership in today's corporations that one can say, as is the case in the public sector, "since everyone owns it, no one owns it!" Such corporations, as public-sector counterparts, fall victim to economic waste and wealth destruction in the hands of their non-owner managers.

The modern corporate world, having evolved within a neo-fascist order, behaves in a manner radically different from how it would in an unhampered market economy. This claim can be demonstrated both by example and with general financial data. Probably the most striking financial evidence of a general failure of "public" corporations to pursue the best interests of their stockholders is in the dismal record of stock prices in recent decades. Calculated in constant dollars, share prices would have to increase by an additional 1000 points from today's levels to reach again the all-time historic high of the New York stock market (June, 1966). Corporate profitability and, ultimately, share market prices have borne the bulk of the waste of non-owner management of corporate property.

Examples of the squandering of corporate property by non-owner managers can be found throughout today's corporate world. From the construction of pretentious headquarters, to the private corporate jets which whisk corporate bureaucrats to their exotic resort conferences, the non-owner manager of corporate property creates a luxurious life-style for himself. The costs for executive limousines, personal aides, and fancy offices contribute little to productive output or bottom-line equity but have everything to do with a vanity-enhancing corporate life-style for the non-owner executives. The lowering of rates of return on corporate assets as a result of such expenditures are a real cost to the legal owners (the stockholders) but are little more than a minor embarrassment to the non-owner managers who control the property.

The economic structure of many of today's corporations, standing as monuments to corporate waste, evolved over a lengthy period of time. But not until such abuse of economic resources created chronic losses instead of profits did the market forces of competition begin to undermine these wasteful corporate entities. Because the corporate structure tends to possess the potential for immense productivity, non-owner managers have been able to forestall for long periods of time the impact from the disintegration of economic ownership and its associated waste. Obviously, the greater the entrepreneurial foresight and the greater the accumulation of corporate wealth, the longer will be the concealment of the economic waste generated by succeeding non-owner managements.

What must be understood is that these non-owner-managed corporations did not originate out of an unhampered market order but are, instead, a phenomenon of a regulated market economy operating in a pragmatic, neo-fascist state. Without exception, they all began as small entrepreneurial endeavors under the watchful eyes of a few owner managers. Controlling costs and enhancing production efficiency in an effort to better serve consumers were essential ingredients to success and the great hallmarks of the founding entrepreneurs of today's corporations. Unable to transfer their corporate wealth to the next generation of private property owners due to prohibitive tax burdens and antitrust laws, the founding generation of owners, under the pressure of statist mandates, surrendered their corporations to a broad-based spectrum of diverse stockholders. With legal ownership fragmented, the non-owner managers of these firms were the ones to gain economic control and build the Taj Mahal-like headquarters for themselves and their wasteful entourages.

Ultimately, of course, the market responds to such assaults on the private property order. In recent years, smaller and more efficient entrepreneurs have eroded the market shares of many of these corporations controlled by non-owner managers, and the global competition of the world market as well has been taking a toll on these firms. To the extent that an orderly price system and freedom of entry continue to prevail in a market mired by statist-constructed obstacles, the economic destruction inflicted by the disintegration of private ownership in public corporations will be limited. The danger, of course, is that regulatory measures and tax laws which created the political and economic setting for such disintegration to occur in the first place will be expanded. Clearly, the replacement of private ownership with government administration and publicly managed corporations has wasted economic resources and curbed the economic growth rate throughout this century.

Quasi-Public Ownership

Between the government and the private corporation lies a third form of economic ownership, a statist creation which epitomizes both the disintegration of private economic control of resources and a fundamental anti-market mentality. The creation of quasi-public entities, brought into existence by enabling statutory laws to pursue some partisan political agenda, has been an integral characteristic of pragmatic neo-fascism. Regardless of the motives or explanations for their creation, they are in actuality nothing more than a fascist license granted to the favored few who have successfully captured political power within government.

No more tragic a story can be told of what quasi-public organizations can beget than the financial disaster of the "Savings and Loan" industry (S&Ls). In an industry created by enabling statutes of government and regulated directly by political authorities, these monsters of economic waste and mismanagement have inflicted a toll on taxpayers into the billions.[2] Not only did government mandates forbid private economic ownership of these structures, but managers of these fascist charters became *de facto* bureaucratic clerks under the direct control of their statist regulators. Neither the competitive market economy nor economic ownership incentives guided the operations of the S&Ls.

The inevitable consequence was for the management of these fascist charters to seek out alternative means to profit personally from what little power they still retained over the resources. And seek out they did! The abuse from inflated appraisals and excessive loans to themselves and their associates became legion and, in the numbing disclosures of the S&L bailout, is now well-known. The criminal behavior which occurred under the structure of these fascist charters all too often was attributed exclusively to "human weakness." Only the rare analyst saw the disintegration of economic ownership within the savings and loan industry as a leading motivation for the criminality and the cause for lost deposits which this banking disaster inflicted upon its victims.

Hidden from public scrutiny are the thousands of similarly structured "fascist charters," just waiting their turn to collapse from the disintegration of private economic ownership in their management. The savings and loan industry is merely today's first and most visible example. Suffering from the same design afflictions of all bureaucratically regulated, quasi-public operations are such vulnerable activities as the mutual life and health care insurance industry, federal credit unions, electric utility and agricultural cooperatives, transportation authorities, and the like.

The common denominator of all these fascist charters is that economic ownership and the managerial control over their resources is vested in political authority rather than market forces emanating from private economic ownership. When managers are legally accountable to political regulators, decisions inevitably shift resources toward bureaucratic interests and away from the interests of consumers. Managements simply have no incentive to conserve the resources of these non-owned entities and to use them for long-term objectives of owners who don't even exist!

The final devastation that these political creatures of the pragmatic, neo-fascist state can inflict on our economy is yet to be felt. Meanwhile, the statist underwriting of the wasteful activities of these quasi-public creations, all too frequently concealed as off-budget expenditures by governments, continues to increase the burden of the state upon society, as private and public wealth is mercilessly ravaged.

Charitable Institutions and Ownership

There is, finally, a fourth area afflicted by the disintegration of private economic ownership which is rarely thought of as an institution for massive wealth consumption and waste. It is in the eleemosynary industry. Unlike governments or public corporations, where adversarial politics or competitive market forces provide some limit to the magnitude of wealth which these structures can destroy, the only force at work to conserve the resources of public charities is a sense of altruism and dedication to each charitable mission by those in control.

This fourth area of wealth destruction carries within itself the germs of disintegration of economic ownership. Operating charities can be particularly destructive of wealth because these organizations are not owned in an economic sense, and often are unaccountable to anyone for their activities. As a consequence, charities are frequently captured from an uninformed, uninvolved board of trustees, and used by their managements for personal ends. The actions of operating charities elude accountability to market forces, political adversaries, directorates, or anyone else. Consequently, the management of eleemosynary property remains insulated from private ownership incentives.

The momentum of charitable giving is a powerful force. Responding with sympathy and other emotions (and to tax incentives), productive individuals transfer billions of dollars annually to operating charities. While the power to control and use these resources is almost absolute for the managers of operating charities, there is a single limitation on their authority. Management can never receive full-ownership benefits from the charitable resources under their control. This may indeed be harmful, since any particular manager is faced with the temptation to pursue short-run personal goals with the entity's resources rather than long-term charitable goals.

Recent disclosures of such episodes do not reflect even the tip of the iceberg in wealth destruction by operating managements under this kind of legal structure. Eleemosynary organizations, routinely captured from detached and disinterested trustees, become incredible sources of wealth for personal use. Acting with impunity, secrecy, and little likelihood of any review, managers of charities create private empires of plunder for themselves. Untold billions in economic waste results from the junkets, pretentious consumption, and vanity-posturing which they are capable of inflicting on these non-owned and non-accountable charities. The absence of economic ownership in the legal structure of the charity, as presently exists under interventionist tax laws, results in billions of dollars being diverted from the charitable mission to the personal perquisites of the operating managers.

Conclusion

At roots of almost every case of continuing abuse and waste of productive resources can be found the absence of private economic ownership. As the twentieth century draws to a close, the economic well-being of millions of individuals is being dissipated by virtue of the separation of economic ownership from its private, legal owners. The bureaucratic institutionalization of vast amounts of wealth in the hands of governments, corporations, fascist charters, and charities, which statist regulations have either mandated or encouraged, has destroyed incredible magnitudes of wealth.

The self-interest of every individual to improve the quality of life for himself encourages both the conservation and the securing of the private property which he owns. If economic ownership does not exist in the hands of the people who control property, or if it is impossible for the people who control property to possess it, then there will be few incentives to use the resources prudently for the future but, rather, more incentives to squander the property.

The disintegration of economic ownership in the pragmatic, neo-fascist or hampered market economy of today has been a primary force in the destruction of wealth. Its continuance means the ethical corruption of participants in the interventionist order and the inevitable lowering of material living standards—a price too costly to pay. In a world where limited resources must be allocated toward serving unlimited human wants, it is imperative that the structure of the market economy be unimpeded.

Toward this end, it is essential that all property fall under the economic control of those individuals who legally own it. As economist and professor, Hans Sennholz has observed: "In the private property order and voluntary exchange system, private ownership means full control over the uses and services of property, not merely a legal title while government is holding the power of control."[3] Nothing less than this will ever assure the needed personal stewardship over the limited resources of this planet or the efficient employment of property for the benefit of all.

Notes and References

1. See Sennholz, Hans F., *Death and Taxes* (Grove City, PA: Center for Futures Education, 1982) for a further discussion of this issue.
2. See Sennholz, Hans F., *The Savings and Loan Bailout: Valiant Rescue or Hysterical Reaction?* (Spring Mills, PA: Libertarian Press, Inc., 1989) for a complete analysis.
3. Sennholz, *Death and Taxes*, p. 3.

4

WHAT IS FREEDOM FOR?

Robert James Bidinotto*

Some of us seem to have gotten so caught up in the abstract world of theory that we sometimes act as though freedom alone were the ultimate value, independent of and above all others. We have forgotten what our cherished abstract ideals, such as "freedom," ultimately are *for.* We have confused means with ends. Liberty cannot stand alone, as an end in itself. A free society itself depends upon, and is justified by, more primary values.

This essay reassesses first principles and reconsiders what position liberty may properly hold in our hierarchy of values.

Liberty As An End

Many sincere advocates of *laissez faire* treat "liberty" as our most basic premise or ultimate end—rather than as a necessary means to some more basic end. This impels them to formulate a philosophical starting point that is purely socio-political, rather than individual. The most popular example of this, in free-market circles, is what is usually called the "Nonaggression Axiom."[1]

An axiom is a basic, irreducible first principle upon which the rest of one's theory rests. The Nonaggression Axiom says, according to one prominent proponent, that "no man or group of men has the right to aggress against the person or property of anyone else." Some have gone so far as to argue that strict adherence to this axiom alone is sufficient to guarantee a free society.

*Mr. Bidinotto is a staff writer for *Reader's Digest,* specializing in cultural and political issues. His many articles and reviews have appeared in *The Boston Herald, The American Spectator, Reason,* and others.

But as an axiom, "nonaggression" leaves much unclear. What is "aggression?" Why is aggression always wrong? What is this notion of "rights" which the axiom refers to? What is meant by the term "property?" And why is holding exclusive rights to property morally proper? There is nothing in the wording of the axiom itself which offers even a clue to any answers.

In an attempt to address such thorny yet basic questions, others have expanded upon the bare axiom. According to one writer, for example, "Libertarianism is first and foremost the doctrine championing individual freedom, private property, unfettered capitalism, and free trade."[2]

But this elaboration only provokes more questions. What kind of trade is "free trade?" Do business deals between a private company in a free country and a dictatorial foreign government constitute "free trade?" Or is the selling of United States military secrets to a foreign, hostile government "free trade?" Or is sex-for-hire between an adult and a child prostitute? Or paying a blackmailer not to reveal personal information? Or "competing" with the government by paying one's bills with one's own private currency?

If so, is banning any of these things, therefore, an act of "aggression" by the state? According to many advocates of liberty, the answer is "yes" in each case; according to others, the answer is a resounding "no."

Another well-known libertarian once argued that "any child above some very low age (say, nine years old) who is willing to arrange for his own support should be free from the authority of his parents."[3] In a similar vein, the national Libertarian Party adopted a 1985 platform plank to give children the right to drink liquor.[4] Is parental discipline, then, an act of aggression, punishable in a truly "free" society? Or are other proponents of a "free" society correct to regard the drugging of a child by an adult to be abusive and criminal?

Some proponents of personal liberty regard *all* use of force to be immoral. One influential free-market pacifist, for example, argued that any use of force—even purely retaliatory or defensive—constituted aggression.[5] Others somewhat similarly believe that even a purely defensive war is "mass murder [of innocent citizens of the aggressor nation] and therefore totally illegitimate."[6] Still others argue that to arrest and subpoena suspected criminals *before* they have been convicted of a crime constitutes an act of aggression by the state, since these people should be considered innocent until proved guilty.

In fact, a sizable number of advocates of freedom believe that government itself is inherently aggressive, and hence immoral and unjustified. As two representatives of this view wrote, "Government is a coercive monopoly which has assumed power over and certain responsibilities for every human being within the geographical area which it claims as its own... [I]t must initiate force in order to prohibit any citizens from going into business in competition with it..."[7] Such advocates of philosophical anarchism instead would let all defensive activity—police, laws, courts, prisons, whatever—be handled by the competitive free market system.[8]

But others argue that a properly limited government is not inherently aggressive, and that anarchism itself would promote aggression by competing gangs, who would necessarily rely upon incompatible standards and arbitrary force.

Given the divergent interpretations of their philosophical starting point—"nonaggression"—it is not surprising that advocates of liberty profess logically incompatible conclusions about what a "free" society would look like.

For instance, the national Libertarian Party has declared itself to be based on the Nonaggression Axiom. Yet a 1983 survey of 672 Libertarian Party members[9] found no consensus interpretation of the axiom on any single issue. Sixty-five percent would have neither banned nor subsidized abortions—but the rest would have. Seventy-three percent would have decriminalized all drugs—but nineteen percent would have regulated and taxed them. Eighty-two percent opposed conscription—but 13 percent would have drafted in wartime, and five percent even in peacetime. Thirty-eight percent would have abolished the FBI and CIA, seventy-four percent favored either mutual or unilateral U. S. disarmament, and forty-one percent believed use of nuclear weapons always to be intrinsically immoral; of course, the remaining percentages in each category completely disagreed.

Nor was this survey an aberration. A 1986 survey of over 100 members of the libertarian group, Society for Individual Liberty, found similar divisions on each issue,[10] as did a more recent survey of Libertarian Party members and subscribers to the free-market magazine, *Liberty*.[11]

So what would happen to the dissenting minority in a libertarian "free" society? Would they retain the right not to be bound by the majority's interpretations of "nonaggression?" On the abortion question alone, it would seem that, in the absence of a final legal arbiter (a government), passionate disagreement would lead to civil war among all these morally uncompromising "nonaggressors."

Each camp, I hasten to emphasize, proclaims its allegiance to the Nonaggression Axiom quite sincerely. But there is nothing in that premise alone which gives a clue as to which *interpretation* of "nonaggression" is the correct one.

Upon reflection, the Nonaggression Axiom is not a very helpful starting place. It merely asserts that the initiation of aggression is bad without telling us why. It does not offer even a hint to help us decide which acts are aggressive, and which defensive. With all basic terms left undefined, we remain in the dark as to what the terms "liberty" and "freedom" really mean. And obviously, if you cannot specify what "liberty" is, you cannot describe what shape a free society will assume.

The Nonaggression Axiom and its related problems arise from the assumption that "liberty" is an end in itself, and can be interpreted or defended in a void. But liberty remains impossible to grasp, define or justify if it has no ultimate purpose. Freedom to do exactly *what*—and *why?*

To resolve some of these conflicting interpretations, a more fundamental end must be defined—one that can infuse liberty with a rationale and a purpose. What that end might be is an issue to which I shall return momentarily.

Failure to Communicate

It should come as no surprise that, in the absence of any clear-cut rationale and purpose, the freedom philosophy has been difficult to "sell" to a mass audience.

It is convenient for anyone in an intellectual minority to believe that the majority of people are basically evil, or, at best, hostile to their ideas. But in light of recent world events, this can no longer be seriously argued—at least, not in regard to the freedom philosophy. Even after generations of enslavement, whole nations have thrown off their shackles, demonstrating that the thirst for liberty is unquenchable. I believe that whatever remaining problems we have in persuading people lie in our dismal failure to address our abstract, theoretical arguments to the concrete, *value* concerns of ordinary people.

The typical American is not abstract and theoretical; he is practical and empirical. He has no time, interest or capacity to involve himself in abstract debates and philosophical inquiries. He has a job to go to, a family to support, bills to pay, and personal goals and commitments to fulfill. He is not interested in principles for their own sake, no matter how noble or true they may sound. He wants to know what some idea or principle will do for him personally—what its "pay value" is. (I do not say this as a criticism, by the way. All of us would suffer horribly if many people quit their productive jobs to join ideological undertakings.)

I firmly believe *laissez faire* could be "sold" to millions if it could be shown, concretely, to better the lives of ordinary people. But the proponent of liberty who thinks of freedom abstractly—as an end in itself, and not in terms of its impact on human lives, happiness and well-being—typically tries to "sell" his philosophy in purely theoretical terms, as an issue of principle. That approach is guaranteed to glaze the eyes and try the patience of most listeners.

All too often, we do not talk most people's language. We talk concepts, principles, ideals, *virtues*—while they are concerned about concretes, practicalities, realities, *values.* Of course, "virtue versus value" is a false dichotomy. But our failure to recognize that many people think in such terms is thwarting our efforts to communicate. And our blindness to their *value* concerns stems largely from our own habit of living, thinking and talking almost exclusively in a platonic realm of principle, about which only a few others like ourselves are concerned.

Viewing freedom as an end in itself hurts our persuasive efforts in a related way. It gives many the impression that we care more for abstract ideals and principles, than for the lives and well-being of real people. That, in too many cases, may not be a false impression. Let me give some examples.

- Simon Geller is an elderly eccentric who operated a one-man radio station in Massachusetts. Because he played only uninterrupted classical music, Geller ran afoul of Federal Communications Commission (FCC) regulations which require all broadcasters to air a certain amount of "public service" programming. The FCC voted to take his license and award it to a competing applicant who pledged to follow government content guidelines.

Here was a symbolic synthesis of civil liberties and property rights issues, and of an individual fighting against the state. A spontaneous, grassroots movement arose in his own community to support him. An embarrassed FCC eventually backed down.

The Geller case was a "natural" for proponents of liberty. Free marketers could have led the fight on his behalf, pointing out the vital link between free markets and free speech. Yet there was *no* organized effort on Geller's behalf by "our side"—and no participation by free marketers in the citizen's campaign in his defense.

- Several years ago a Soviet boy, Walter Polovchak, received worldwide media attention for abandoning his family and defecting to the United States. Though the Soviet Union—aided by the American Civil Liberties Union (!)—tried every legal path to get him back to the USSR, young Walter finally won a long, desperate fight to gain his American citizenship.

Here was another great morality play of the individual versus the state, in the form of the priceless life of one small boy. But except for the tireless work of his attorneys (including free marketers Erika and Henry Mark Holzer), there was *no* organized activity on the boy's personal behalf generated by other advocates of individual liberty.

- At a convention of libertarian activists, I asked, "How many of you know who Carl Pescosolido, Jr., is?" Not a hand went up. For the record, Pescosolido is a private California citrus grower and self-educated free marketer, who, virtually single-handedly, has been fighting for years against the government-mandated citrus quota system known as "agricultural marketing orders." Much has been written about this statist cartel system in free market literature, and some pro-market groups have even taken up the legal battle. But few free-enterprise journals have bothered to chronicle Pescosolido's own pivotal role in the struggle. As a result, few advocates of liberty even know his name—let alone care enough about one man's principled stand to offer him help.

These three examples illustrate the disturbing results of treating abstract theory as an end in itself. As I told the libertarian gathering, "I suspect that too often, men of principle lose sight of those whom their principles are supposed to serve. We concern ourselves with 'liberty'...but we don't even remember the name of the slave."

Those remarks summarized my growing impatience with a widespread malady in pro-freedom circles, of which these three cases are disturbing examples. Put bluntly, many of us pay lip service to "individualism" in which real *individuals* do not seem to matter.

There is an irony here that I find bitter. The advocates of *collectivism* manage to put a face on their every abstract cause. They, who advocate the sacrifice of the individual to social abstractions, nonetheless miss no opportunity to transform their abstractions into specific campaigns on behalf of specific *individuals*.

They know their heroes and martyrs intimately. In the Forties and Fifties, middle-aged Marxists chanted and demonstrated for Alger Hiss and Julius and Ethel Rosenberg. In the Sixties, their sons and daughters plastered dormitory walls with posters of Fidel Castro, Che Guevara, Mao Tse Tung and Ho Chi Minh, and turned Robert Kennedy and Martin Luther King, Jr. into mythic martyrs. In the Seventies, a new generation of budding collectivists canonized Robert Woodward and Carl Bernstein, Daniel Ellsberg, and John Lennon, while during the next decade they invoked reverently the names of Karen Silkwood, Daniel Ortega and Nelson Mandela.

But do we "individualists" even know the names of the three young men who fell to the tanks in Moscow, and in doing so, helped to vanquish the greatest statist threat of our time? Who among us has their photos on a poster?

Committed collectivists constantly *personalize* their causes. This helps to explain their ability to captivate and motivate the public—to bring home to a wide audience the living, dramatic reality of their ideals.

Yet with a world of collectivism's victims to champion, and a pantheon of heroes to honor, free marketers rarely give their cause a *human* face. Then we bridle when our collectivist opponents accuse us of not caring about people. And we wonder why a portion of the public continues to find the collectivists more morally compelling and inspiring.

The Pyramid of Values

This brings us directly to the answer to our question: What is freedom for?

Imagine that all our ideas, concerns, interests, emotions, passions, beliefs and values are building blocks, and that if stacked in the shape of a pyramid they would represent our hierarchy of values. Those blocks near the top would represent our more important ends and values; those below would be of lesser importance, and would support the higher values. At the very apex would be our highest value—that which gave meaning and justification to the whole structure.

In any moral decision, our choices and actions ultimately would be determined by whatever is at the top of the pyramid. And those things beneath it in the hierarchy would be, if necessary, expendable to whatever was at the top. They would be means to the ultimate end.

Now, consider what happens when we place different things at the top of the pyramid: Individualists place *individual human well-being* at the top of their hierarchy. The individual is an "end in himself." Everything else is regarded as a means to this, the highest end. By contrast, collectivists would place some group's well-being at the top. This would necessitate moving individual human well-being somewhere down the hierarchy. The group would be an end in itself; the individual would be reduced in status, as a mere tool of the group, a means to its ends. Thus, in any case where the group's well-being might be threatened, the lives and well-being of individuals would be expendable.

Suppose you put the state, or society, or the dictator, or future generations, or the environment at the apex of the pyramid, as the ultimate moral end. In every case, the lives and well-being of individuals would be diminished to the servile status of means to these higher ends in themselves.

Now what if one were to place some *abstraction*—however inspiring or noble-sounding—at the apex? Suppose it were some virtue, like "honesty" or "justice." What would be wrong with that?

Normally, virtues (moral principles) are considered to be the abstract means that we use in the pursuit of values, or ends. However, placing virtue at the top inverts this relationship of ends and means. Suddenly, principles are no longer regarded as tools by which to advance the end of human life; human life is now treated as the sacrificial means of promoting abstract principles, which are now *ends in themselves*. This inversion of virtue and value is the route to fanaticism.

What does this have to do with liberty? Consider a telling historical contrast. The American Revolution placed individual "life, liberty and the pursuit of happiness" at the apex of the nation's value pyramid. The Founders aimed at securing the rights of individuals to achieve their personal well-being. By contrast, the French Revolution, whose ultimate end was a utopian society of "liberty, equality, and fraternity," wound up sacrificing the life, liberty and happiness of individuals. The American Revolution brought moral principle into the social lives of men; the French Revolution brought men to the guillotine...in the name of "moral principle."

We need liberty in order to live happy, productive, fulfilled lives in society. In fact, *it is only the quest for individual well-being that morally justifies the need for a free society.*

But today, many modern champions of an abstract "liberty" have forgotten what our Founders knew. Under many confused conceptions of liberty, "freedom" or "rights" or "nonaggression" have become nebulous, platonic ends in themselves. By logical necessity, those holding such misconceptions then sacrifice themselves, and the well-being of others, to advance these platonic abstractions.

Do I exaggerate? Recall some of the examples cited earlier. There was the libertarian pacifist, whose highest value was the abstract principle of "nonviolence." He argued that one should not use force even in self-defense, but rather allow one's life and well-being to be sacrificed, in order that the principle of nonviolence survive.

Or recall those who would refuse to subpoena or arrest dangerous criminals until *after* their trials (allowing them to escape, of course). Here again, principles are torn from their ultimate purpose: the protection of human life and well-being. Instead, a formal premise of courtroom procedure (the legal presumption of innocence) is treated as an end in itself, to which the safety of real people must be sacrificed.

In the same fashion, sundry proponents of "liberty" would liberate children from their parents, and permit their psychological manipulation and physical exploitation by adults. Or they might free one's neighbor to build and store bombs in his apartment; or permit "competition" with the Federal Reserve (read: counterfeiting); or allow another nation to bomb ours into oblivion, while we unilaterally, "morally" refuse to retaliate against the noncombatant population of the invading nation; or allow American companies to sell military secrets to the enemy during our annihilation in the name of "free trade."

A similar form of the same error involves those free-marketers who insist on revolutionary, overnight abolition of all existing government interventions, regardless of any disruptive consequences to millions of people. To the abolitionist, the welfare state is immoral—period. That is his first concern, and his last. It's the *principle* of the thing, you see. The gradual abolition of any evil, he says, is itself evil. The evil must stop now—regardless of context or consequences. All welfare payments must be cut off—today. The Federal Reserve System must be shut down—overnight. "Stop payments" must be put on all Social Security checks, and the post offices which deliver them must be closed—right now. All public housing must be razed and all public schools locked—this afternoon.

And if millions of welfare state dependents starve, or if they are given no time to adjust and the economy collapses into chaos—so what? "Who cares about all those parasites anyway?" the abolitionist reasons; "at least, I abolished evil—even if, in the process, I also unfortunately abolished a lot of people."

Any resemblance of this attitude to that of the Marxists or Nazis, who wiped out millions in pursuit of their own utopian vision, is not coincidental: it stems from the same platonic roots.

The key to understanding all of these bizarre interpretations of "liberty" and "nonaggression" is to grasp that, in every case, a pure *abstraction* has replaced the well-being of real individuals at the apex of the value pyramid. As a result, the individual is to be sacrificed to an idea. As in Gilbert and Sullivan's "Pirates of Penzance," men become "slaves of duty," rigidly, absurdly, adhering to principles regardless of context or consequence.

Freedom ... As if Individuals Matter

To reject the notion that principles are ends in themselves is not to reject principles *per se.* One must simply keep ends and means firmly in mind, realizing that principles and ideals, properly understood, are the individual's servants, not his masters.

A truly principled approach to the task of ending governmental evils would take into account that principles have a higher purpose: the furtherance of the lives of *real* people. Thus, any valid approach to reform cannot ignore the fact that Rome was not built in a day, and cannot be dismantled in a day...at least not if the lives of individuals are to matter.

Individualists never lose sight of their ideals; but they aim to reform an imperfect society, not to "purify" it overnight by putting it self-righteously to the torch. Liberty is a constructive, not destructive, process; freedom demands the sober spirit of a Thomas Jefferson, not the fanatical fury of a John Brown.

To the fanatic, however, all this smacks of moral compromise, of a failure to uphold principles "absolutely." To fail to uphold principles, no matter what the context, is to be "unprincipled." Even under the threat of a gun, one must do the moral thing, he believes. We cannot allow mere consequences to deter our commitment to principles like rights.

By contrast, I argue that moral principles—including the principle of rights—are only *contextually* absolute. They apply absolutely within the appropriate context, but not in any context which renders them incoherent, impossible or meaningless. For example, does the virtue of "honesty" apply absolutely, regardless of circumstances? Would you feel "dishonest" if you lied rather than honestly revealed the whereabouts of a loved one to an armed intruder?

Likewise, the principle of rights can only arise and apply in a *non-coercive social context.* There is no "right or wrong" in coercive contexts, where one's options are limited to a choice among forms of destruction. If human well-being is the end, and principles are the means to further that end, then coercion limits one to an impossible alternative: your principles or your life.

There is no "principled" option in such a context. Deprived, by the threat of physical force, of principled ways to pursue one's well-being, one may be forced to pursue values any way one can, until one can get out of the coercive context. Deprived, under brutish circumstances, of the option of maximizing gain, one's only remaining moral obligation is to minimize loss—and try to escape.

Confusion about moral ends and means underlies a host of political positions taken by many proponents of liberty—for instance, debates about the "justice" of putting non-combatants in harm's way during war or hostage situations, or whether it is ever "moral" to accept government money. Those who would argue, *a priori*, that in each case the alleged principle must take precedence even over one's survival, have swallowed whole the bait and hook of platonism. They have accepted a false dichotomy between morality and life, and have rejected the end for the means.

Communicating the Ideas of Liberty

Many of us wonder why our message of *laissez faire* seems to fall on deaf ears. But perhaps the real deafness is our own. The public is, as I have said, not interested in ideas for their own sake. They are interested in their own individual lives, happiness and well-being.

But is this not the essence of an individualist outlook? If our philosophy of individualism is not convincing them, whose fault is it? We fail to communicate, I believe, because lost in the realm of theoretical argument, we remain deaf to their very legitimate, individual concerns.

Let me begin with a confession: I have been as guilty of many of these bad habits, confusions and thinking aberrations as anyone. For many years, my effectiveness in convincing others was minimal. But writing, as I now do, for the world's most widely read magazine, has taught me much about communicating ideas to an audience of millions.

My ideas remain the same today as they have been for many years. But I reach far more people now. What changed, basically, was my view of what is at the top of my value pyramid. Where I used to see virtues near the top, I now see values. And where I used to see philosophical abstractions like "the individual" at the very apex, I now see the faces of real individuals. They—not the abstractions—are the only real ends in themselves.

Because of this new perspective, I find it much easier to communicate. I address most people on the level of personal, shared values: their concerns about their homes, their jobs, their families, their futures, their personal health and safety. I choose my political issues accordingly. That is why, for a mass market, I write far more about crime than I do about the Federal Reserve Board. This does not mean I have abandoned "serious" writing. I merely save my abstract discussions for the appropriate forums, like this one, and for the rare individuals who show an interest in them.

There is nothing cynical or condescending in this approach, either. I respect the general public, and take "popular" writing every bit as seriously as "serious" writing. It is not necessary that one be on a college faculty, or writing treatises to tiny groups of intellectuals, in order to spread a radical philosophy. Once a theory is originated by some innovator, there is no subsequent mode of communication that is "more important" than any other. It is simply impossible to tell where a decisive cultural breakthrough may occur, or which person may prove pivotal.

Ideas move down through a culture over thousands of rungs; they are spread across a nation over thousands of links. To argue that the "intellectual professions" are more important than any other, is like arguing that the top rung of a ladder is more important than any below, or that the first link in a chain is more important than any other.

Simply because most people are not professional intellectuals does not make them stupid. In fact, most people are far more sensible about philosophical ideas than are many self-styled intellectuals. That is, they are not the least bit interested in ideas, except insofar as ideas pertain directly to their own lives and well-being. But most people are basically reasonable, and do have a fundamental sense of decency and justice. They can be aroused to action by a dramatic depiction of evils and injustices—as I have learned from personal experience.

The way to reach millions is to personalize abstract themes—to give principles and ideas a human face—to dramatize issues and events by relating them to the actual lives of real people. Not only is this the most effective way to do the public education job; it is also the method most consonant with our highest value: the supreme value of the individual.

But reaching others is not our first order of business. Before we can reform the culture, we must reform ourselves. We must commit ourselves, not to principles as ends in themselves, but to the principled pursuit of individual values. If others do not understand us, let us show them what true individualism means as embodied in our persons. If they think our way impossible, let us show them what is possible as an individual. If they would victimize the innocent, let us be the individual victim's personal champion.

The theoretical base of *laissez faire* capitalism has never been so sophisticated and complete; its empirical case is resounding around the world. The ideological battlefield is barren of competing theories and theorists. Yet the distance between the world of our dreams, and the world that is, remains considerable.

If we are not convincing the world, it is not for lack of theories, evidence or champions. It is because we are failing to win the moral battle for men's souls, failing to inspire them with a noble vision of human potential. If the world is still under the inertial influence of an anti-individualistic ideal, it is because we have lacked the imagination to posit another vision...or, perhaps, the courage to embody it ourselves.

"Certain moral standards," Dr. Hans Sennholz has written, "are basic to the social order: [the] sanctity of human life and dignity of the individual..."[12]

But we are not believed, because the world sees no clear image of those moral standards. Too often, they see uninspiring theoreticians, or demoralized misanthropes, or fanatical activists...but no human ideal, nothing around which to rally. We do not let them experience the living reality of our values and concerns, by helping them to walk in the shoes of a Geller, or a Polovchak, or a Pescosolido, or by filling such shoes ourselves.

For those of us in the business of persuasion our challenge is to accept George Washington's challenge and raise a moral standard to which the wise and honest may repair. But each of us bears a private responsibility: to create in himself a living testament to the standard of individual self-realization. For it is not simply that an individual's life matters. In the final analysis, an individual's life, well-lived, is the *only* thing that matters.

Notes and References

1. Rothbard, Murray N., *For a New Liberty* (New York, NY: MacMillan, 1973, first edition), p. 8.
2. Childs, Roy, "The Literature of Liberty," *Laissez Faire Books Catalog,* May 1987), p. 16.
3. Friedman, David, *The Machinery of Freedom* (New York, NY: Harper Colophon edition, 1973), p. 126.
4. Garvin, Glenn, "Whiskey for 4-year-olds? It's a Libertarian plank," *The Washington Times,* Aug. 16, 1985.
5. LeFevre, Robert, "To Catch a Thief," *Lefevre's Journal,* Summer 1975. Mr. LeFevre argued that to repossess by force any property stolen by a thief "would be a new act of theft," since "the thief now *owns* the property."
6. Rothbard, p. 9. See also Hummel, Jeffrey Rogers "The Great Libertarian Defense Debate," *Nomos,* May/June 1985 and August 1985.
7. Tannehill, Morris, and Tannehill, Linda, *The Market for Liberty* (Lansing, MI: privately published edition, 1970), Ch. 4.
8. For the most recent presentation of this argument, see Benson, Bruce L., *The Enterprise of Law: Justice without the State* (San Francisco, CA: Pacific Research Institute, 1990).
9. Published in *Frontlines,* a now-defunct newsletter of the Reason Foundation, May 1983.
10. Walter, David, "Commentary on Liberty," *Individual Liberty,* July 1986.
11. "The Liberty Poll," *Liberty*, July 1988.
12. Sennholz, Hans F., "Eternal Hope," in *Ideas on Liberty: Essays in Honor of Paul L. Poirot* (Irvington, NY: Foundation for Economic Education, 1987), p. 99.

5

ECONOMIC EDUCATION AND SOCIAL CHANGE

Peter J. Boettke

Significant reforms, in the final analysis, are moral reforms, changes in the perception of right conduct. Certain moral standards are basic to social order: sanctity of human life and dignity of the individual. They may not change much from one generation to the next. Other standards may undergo visible changes in the span of one generation or two, such as individual independence and self-reliance; the ethos of labor; thrift, honesty, and integrity; and respect for private property. Changes in these standards lead to changes in the system of economic and social organization. In this century, they sowed the seeds of economic and social conflict, and paved the way for political intervention in our lives. They gave birth to a transfer and entitlement system that is eroding the private property order. A reform that would restore it and remove the transfer predilection would have to restore the harmony of interests and repair the moral standards.

Hans F. Sennholz, *Debts and Deficits* (pp. 163-164)

We live in revolutionary times. Only ten years ago, for example, did personal computers begin establishing a market, and compact disk players were virtually unknown. New technologies which are the result of years of scientific research and development are introduced every day.

Our political climate has also experienced rapid change. Ten years ago, for example, the Soviet Union was characterized as the "evil empire." Today that view is no longer relevant, as the Soviet

*Dr. Boettke is Assistant Professor of Economics and a faculty member of the Austrian Economics Program at New York University. He contributes frequently to journals, and has authored two books.

Union has ceased to exist. Again, this is the culmination of decades of dissident movement and thought.

With the world changing around us, it may be useful to reflect on how knowledge in general is conveyed within society. Do ideas follow events or do events follow ideas? What role does interest-group pressure play in the flow of information? How complicated is the process by which abstract ideas are translated into concrete change?

This essay focuses on a particular aspect of the question of information transmission within society, exploring the role of economic education in social change.[1] After examining the function of the different stages of production within the intellectual structure of society, it will provide some observations on the relationship between *ideas* and *interests* in social change. The recent changes in Eastern and Central Europe, and the problems of the transformation, will be used to highlight the conflict between ideas and interests.

An Intellectual Structure of Production

Ideas can be viewed fruitfully as the social capital stock in a society, and as such can be analyzed from the perspective of capital theory. It takes time for ideas to be produced and disseminated. The production of abstract ideas is a roundabout process. F. A. Hayek has addressed aspects of the distilling of ideas in society in his analysis of the intellectuals and socialism.[2] Hayek focuses his analysis on what could be termed the intellectual pyramid of society, with academic specialists and scholars occupying the top, other traders of ideas occupying the lower levels, and the general public representing the base. This formulation of the production and distribution of ideas can be represented easily within a capital structure framework. Figure 1 represents the intellectual pyramid in modern society.

Figure 1

Scholars and Academic Specialists
Think Tanks Teachers
Politicians Journalists Students Business
The general public in society

The production of higher-order ideas, or ideas remote from final consumption, takes place mainly within research universities and is supported by charitable foundations or government agencies that invest in this research. For the sake of exposition let us examine how these ideas travel down the intellectual structure of production to the public policy community. Academic ideas are filtered down through academic journals, seminars, books, and lectures to the "think tanks," which take the latest developments and formulate possible public policy statements from them. Public policy think tanks, such as the Brookings Institute, American Enterprise Institute, The Heritage Foundation, and the Cato Institute, do not originate ideas but transform abstractions into public policy research in a manner similar to the factory that turns iron ore into steel.

The results from these public policy studies then pass down to broadcast and print media, and through media coverage these ideas will exert influence directly on politicians and the public, who rely almost exclusively on the media for information concerning public policy. The political dissemination of ideas is also aided by public-interest lobbyists or citizens' groups. These two groups, the media and citizen's groups, are like a car salesman who is trying to sell a car produced by an auto maker who depended on steel produced from iron ore. Without the iron ore, though, the salesman would not have much of a car to sell.

A similar story could be told concerning how abstract ideas travel through the intellectual structure to the educational community. Of course these communities—political and educational—are interconnected. Colleges and universities, in fact, have acquired a dominant role in shaping the intellectual landscape of society. *Money* magazine, for example, pointed out that *60 percent of our children go on to college.*[3] The preponderance of business, media, educational, and political leaders all come through the higher education system. This general point about the leveraged position of professors in the intellectual structure of idea production is not missed by those on the political left. Richard Wolf, for example, (a leading academic of the left) has argued:

> Today well over half of all eighteen to nineteen-year old Americans enter postsecondary schools. They comprise a public to whom professors speak in lectures, seminars, and informal discussions, and through arti-

cles, books and textbooks. This public audience is certainly far larger—by any measure—than that ever reached through the books and magazine articles of Jacoby's "public intellectuals." Moreover, the intensity and timing of their direct contacts with students suggests that the professors' influence is probably deeper and more lasting than that achieved through magazine articles and books. It is at least a very plausible supposition that leftists in American universities today have more, not less, of a public audience than ever before in the country's history.[4]

The fact that most politicians, journalists, business leaders, educators, etc., all come to their positions via their earlier university training has profound consequences for a strategy of liberty. The college professor, in fact, has obtained a unique position within the intellectual structure of society. Ideas are disseminated mainly through academicians. In classroom lectures, the books, articles and ideas of scholars are shared with students—who are actually the future politicians, directors of think tanks, journalists, business leaders, etc. In modern society ideas are primarily conveyed to the public through a vast interlocking network of intellectuals from scholars to political activists. But does that mean that ideas are the sole source of public policy?

Ideas and Interests

John Maynard Keynes concludes his *General Theory of Employment, Interest and Money* with the famous statement:

> The ideas of economists and political philosophers, both when they are right and when they are wrong, are more powerful than is commonly understood. Indeed, the world is ruled by little else. Practical men, who believe themselves to be quite exempt from any intellectual influences, are usually the slaves of some defunct economist. Madmen in authority, who hear voices in the air, are distilling their frenzy from some academic scribbler of a few years back. *I am sure that the power of vested interests is vastly exaggerated compared with the gradual encroachment of ideas* [emphasis added].[5]

But, can we be so sure? If political decisions are largely the outcome of interest-group pressure, then what role is left for ideas in changing the polity? Do ideas make any difference at all?

The so-called Thatcher and Reagan popular free-market "revolutions" provide some evidence about the relative strength of ideas and interests. Despite their popular mandates, neither transformed the basic institutions of the polity or instituted constitutional changes in the rules. As a result, irrespective of short-term gains in releasing the power of free markets that might have been achieved—a very doubtful proposition even at that level—the long-term prospect for both the United Kingdom and the United States is simply more of the same welfare/warfare policies that preceded Thatcher and Reagan. It was (and remains) "policy within politics" as usual.

The evidence from these "revolutions" suggests the analytical power and empirical relevance of public-choice economics. This argument stated in the extreme proclaims the victory of interests over ideas. Indeed, the world is ruled by little else. Politicians are vote seekers and most voters are rationally ignorant of the vast majority of issues—concentrating instead on those that are of special interest to them. The interaction between rationally ignorant voters and vote-seeking politicians produces a bias in government decision making toward policies that yield short-term and easily identifiable benefits at the expense of long-term and hidden costs. If we characterize the logic of the market as buying low and selling high, then the logic of the political process is to concentrate benefits on well-informed and well-organized interest groups, and to disperse costs among the ill-informed and unorganized mass of voters.

This public choice argument is a powerful one, but one that is generally misunderstood. Special interests do not preclude the influence of ideas; but within any *existing* polity, interests have certain advantages over rational arguments when it comes to satisfying the demands of political activists. But ideas can and do make a difference.

Political activists must make decisions concerning their political future within a *climate of opinion*. If the climate of opinion were one that challenged the transfer society, then politicians who were exposed as advocates of transfer programs would be challenged easily by their opponents. On the other hand, if the climate of opinion were such that the transfer system was the accepted norm, then a politician favoring individual freedom and free markets would be considered reactionary and suffer at the voting booth. Ideas matter in changing the constraints in which political activists seek to maximize their personal gain in terms of votes, campaign contributions, and personal prestige.

Educators and educational organizations, therefore, are not assigned a negligible role in society. Instead, they assume a role of fundamental importance by influencing the climate of opinion in society. But in addition to determining the climate of opinion, ideas also play an extremely important role within the political economy. Decision making occurs at both a pre- and post-constitutional level. The pre-constitutional level deals with ideas concerning good and appropriate rules by which to organize society. Post-constitutional analysis, on the other hand, seeks to understand and explain the various strategies politicians will employ within an already existing set of institutions or rules. The weaving together of pre- and post-constitutional analyses in order to tackle the problems at hand constitutes the method of the constitutional political economist.

The extreme variant of the public choice argument presented above is a correct representation of the role of interests in the political processes that occur in the post-constitutional arena. Ideas concerning what is moral, good, fair, or simply the most effective way to organize society, affect the rules of social interaction. Intellectual advances and the promotion of ideas represent remote stages in a time structure of production that eventually produces public policies.

In the end, therefore, Keynes's statement contains great truth. On the surface the paradox between interests and ideas presents a serious problem to liberalism—pointing out its inherent fragility in the face of interest-group pressure. This fragility exists because of the conflict between sound economics and good politics. The logic of concentrated benefits and dispersed costs biases the political process in a manner which tends to undermine the liberal society—leading instead to a transfer society governed by special interests. But this theoretical and empirical problem, while serious, is not as deadly as one may suspect. An understanding of the role of interests is fundamental to developing ideas which can protect economic liberties from dominance by special interests. At the constitutional level, as the American Founding Fathers sought to do, rules can be established which reduce the role of interests. Once we fully recognize that the original attempt, however noble, at constitutional democracy failed to protect our liberties, then liberal social theorists must attempt to build additional safeguards at the constitutional level to protect against erosion of the rules in the face of interest-group pressure. To do that requires a victory in the battle of ideas, both in the academic community where social philosophy emerges, and among the general populace where the climate of opinion is formed.

Free Market Activism

Since the mid-1970s free market ideas have gained in influence. The failure of Keynesian "demand management" policies, as represented in the stagflation of the 1970s, led to a flourishing of free market intellectual activity. Variant schools of free market thought such as monetarism, new classical, and supply-side all grew in popularity as a response to the failure of Keynesian economics. The Keynesian stranglehold on economic reasoning was broken. Even the most ardent defenders of the free market system, the Austrian school of economics, has grown in popularity in the past two decades. No longer limited to Grove City College and Hillsdale College, Austrian economics is now taught to undergraduates in such places as Auburn University, New York University, George Mason University, St. Lawrence College, Loyola University (New Orleans, LA), State University of California (Hayward), State University of New York (Oswego), State University of New York (Purchase), Holy Cross College, Dickinson College, and University of Nevada (Las Vegas). In addition, graduate programs have been established at Auburn, George Mason and New York Universities which train the next generation of scholars and teachers in the Austrian tradition.

Developments in the Austrian tradition in the areas of industrial organization, free banking, and comparative economic systems have had significant influence on the economics profession. This in turn has traveled down the intellectual structure of production to the arena of public opinion. *Forbes*, for example, devoted an article to the development of free banking theory as an alternative to the crisis in the current central banking system.[6] And the *New Yorker* has published Robert Heilbroner's reflections on the collapse of communism and his admission that "Mises was right."[7]

In the past two decades there have been some tremendous changes in the intellectual community. The political world has also changed, demonstrated most noticeably by the complete collapse of communism in Eastern Europe. Political leaders of the post-communist world, such as Vaclav Klaus (finance minister of Czechoslovakia), in fact draw inspiration from free market thinkers like Ludwig von Mises, F. A. Hayek and Milton Friedman. Even Western politicians like Ronald Reagan and Margaret Thatcher have been known to quote Mises and Hayek favorably. Nevertheless, little has changed in the basic structural organization of society. As a result, despite all the change in the intellectual landscape, the political economy in reality has not changed all that much. Truly free markets are far from existing anywhere. For example, a New York *Times* headline reads, "7 Rich Nations to Help Soviets Plan Economy."[8] Unfortunately, Western institutions and governments do not support real free market reforms, but rather the same policies that have failed repeatedly in other less-developed countries in Africa and Latin America will now be offered to the Soviet republics and will produce the same undesirable consequences.

The current reality seems to force us to reconsider the answer to the conflict between ideas and interests. In many ways, free market ideas are now an acceptable part of intellectual conversation. Theoretical developments in property rights economics, public choice economics, and Austrian economics have convincingly challenged a wide variety of traditional interventionist views of public policy on issues of market failure. The empirical evidence, moreover, on the power of free market processes to promote economic development and well-being is well documented. Consider the post-World War II development of the three Chinas: Hong Kong, Taiwan, and mainland China. These are three regions with a homogeneous population and a common cultural heritage, yet the economic well-being of their inhabitants varies greatly. In 1950, Taiwan and mainland China had about the same per capita income, Hong Kong slightly more; but today Taiwan's per capita income is thirty times that of the mainland and Hong Kong's is thirty-five times more.

These facts illustrate that economic prosperity depends far more upon economic institutions than cultural traits or natural resources. The institutional rules that govern economic processes either promote or discourage productive activity. The economic benefits of a free market require the underlying institutions that sustain the system: free entry and private property protected by a rule of law. The power of market forces once unleashed (even in controlled environments) to develop a region is also demonstrated in the experience with the Special Economic Zones in South China.

A recent *Economist* article points out that South China has experienced a twelve-year boom since Deng Xiaoping "created" fourteen "coastal open cities" and "special economic zones."[9] The open-door policy welcomed foreign firms and established freer trade rules. These rules brought with them the market discipline of world prices, resulting in real growth rates (using the Chinese version of GDP) of 12.5 percent a year. Even if such aggregate growth rates are a poor measure of economic development (regardless of whether they are the Chinese, Soviet or United States version), they do suggest a tremendous expansion of industrial development in a region that in 1980 subsisted mainly on fishing and farming.

Despite the overwhelming evidence of the flexibility and adaptability of the market to all kinds of situations, and the ability of unhampered markets to generate economic prosperity and opportunity for members of a society, the free market economy is not the policy of choice to politicians. Economic reform towards a liberal market order is nowhere in sight. Most of the talk in Eastern Europe, for example, is not of an unhampered free market, but rather a market circumscribed by a democratic welfare state which will protect the least-advantaged and the environment. Why, in the face of such overwhelming evidence about the power of unhampered markets to promote economic welfare, does the message not get through?

The problem, as Mancur Olson argued in his *Rise and Decline of Nations*, is that as political stability occurs, entrenched interests form which, eventually, through their rent-seeking activity, retard the further economic development of a country.[10] Reform in a situation with such entrenched interests is nearly impossible. The logic of reform runs directly contrary to the logic of politics. If the logic of politics is to concentrate benefits on the well-organized and well-informed and disperse costs across ill-informed and unorganized masses, then the logic of reform is actually to concentrate costs and disperse benefits. As long as the entrenched interests are not displaced, reform measures within a system will continually stall. Empirical illustrations of this simple point can be found in the failure of both Reagan and Thatcher, the Tiananmen massacre, and the troublesome reform efforts in the Soviet Union from 1986–1991.

Another side of Olson's argument, however, points to the window of opportunity that exists when an exogenous shock displaces the dominant interest groups. At such moments, intellectual entrepreneurs can act in a manner which changes the basic structural rules governing a society.

This also relates to our discussion of the intellectual structure of production. In a market economy, production is always for an uncertain future demand. Automobile manufacturers, for example, engage in research and development for cars that will be produced and marketed ten years hence even though the demand that will exist for cars then is uncertain. The system of profit and loss in an unfettered market helps to assure that production plans and consumption demands are somehow systematically coordinated through time. Similarly, the "R & D" of ideas is for an uncertain future demand. Mises's ideas, for example, have a much greater opportunity for impact on the intellectual climate of opinion today than at any time in his own life. But, the possibility of acting on that opportunity is only available because Mises labored in almost complete isolation for decades when his ideas ran contrary to the received wisdom of his day. In moments of revolutionary change, when dominant interest groups are dispersed, ideas can influence the basic institutions and attitudes of a society. Only in redefining the basic relationship between the citizen and the polity can reform in the direction of economic freedom be guaranteed.

The events of 1989 in Eastern and Central Europe and the failed coup attempt in August, 1991, in the Soviet Union have provided the exogenous shock necessary to displace the former beneficiaries of the communist system. This is not to say that reform will be easy—far from it. The heady days of 1989 have given way to the sober reality of the 1990s. But, at least, the previous system has been thoroughly de-legitimized. Market reform, which previously amounted simply to much talk, now is a distinct possibility. The task for the reformers is to construct a workable constitution of economic policy that establishes a rule of law which protects private property rights and allows market experimentation through freedom of entry in competition. In developing this constitution, the reformers can draw freely from the wealth of free market ideas which have become commonplace in the West over the past two decades. Perhaps if the reformers of Eastern Europe are successful, then the United States will also be able to pursue a *perestroika* of its own.

Conclusion

"The main objective of praxeology and economics," Ludwig von Mises wrote, "is to substitute consistent correct ideologies for the contradictory tenets of popular eclecticism"[11] But such a substitution does not occur just by winning the battle of ideas. Ideas are intertwined with interests, and for the substitution of correct ideologies for false beliefs, ideas must not only be developed but must be utilized to reconstruct the basic rules of social interaction when opportunities arise.

Karl Marx understood this in his appeals for *radical* change as opposed to simply reformist measures. The direction of the change he advocated is what was wrong. Free market activists must take their cue, however, from Marx. Reformism within the system does not lead to the kind of fundamental changes that economic freedom requires. Only structural change in the basic constitution of social interaction will "restore the harmony of interests and repair moral standards."[12]

Notes and References

1. I have tried to address some of these issues previously; cf., Boettke, P., "The Reagan Regulatory Reform: Rhetoric and Reality," In A. Sahu and R. Tracy, ed., *The Economic Legacy of the Reagan Years,* (New York, NY: Praeger, 1991) and in a book review of A. Gamble, ed., *Ideas and Interests* in *The Freeman,* (February, 1991).
2. Hayek, F. A., "The Intellectuals and Socialism," in *Studies in Philosophy, Politics and Economics,* (Chicago, IL: University of Chicago Press, 1967).
3. *Money,* (October, 1991), p. 90.
4. Wolf, R., Book review of Russell Jacoby, *The Last Intellectuals in Re-Thinking Marxism,* (Spring, 1989), p. 137.
5. Keynes, John M., *The General Theory,* (New York, NY: Harcourt Brace, 1936), p. 383.
6. *Forbes,* (May, 1988).
7. Heilbroner, Robert, "Reflections (After Communism)," *The New Yorker,* (September, 1990), pp. 91-100.
8. *The New York Times,* (October 14, 1991).
9. "The South China Miracle," *The Economist,* (October 5, 1991), pp. 19-22.
10. Olson, M., *Rise and Decline of Nations,* (New Haven, CT: Yale University Press, 1982).
11. Mises, Ludwig von, *Human Action,* (Chicago, IL: Henry Regnery, 1966), p. 185
12. Sennholz, Hans F., *Debts and Deficits.*

6

THE THEORY OF VALUE AND THE AUSTRIAN SCHOOL

Juan C. Cachanosky*

The Ancient Philosophers

Economic science began in Ancient Greece as a moral or ethical subject, and one of the main topics treated by the philosophers was the "just price." This essay will follow the path that the theory of value followed from those years to our century (concentrating in this brief space only on the most revolutionary contributions in this field). Aristotle was the first to address the question of value systematically. He was the first to distinguish, in spite of not using the terms, between "value in use" and "value in exchange":

> Every article or property has a double use; both uses are uses of the thing itself, but they are not similar uses; for one is the proper use of the article in question, the other is not. For example a shoe may be used either to put on your foot or to offer in exchange. Both are uses of the shoe; for even he that gives a shoe to someone who requires a shoe, and receives in exchange cash or food, is making use of the shoe as a shoe, but not the use proper to it, for a shoe is not expressly made for exchange purpose.[1]

Since Aristotle's time, the word "value" has had this double meaning, which unfortunately led to substantial confusion. Some thinkers used the word "value" in the sense of "value in use," and others used it in the sense of "value in exchange." Aristotle himself in his book *The Nicomachean Ethics*, (V, 5) when dealing with the problem of just price, used the word "value" in an am-

*Dr. Cachanosky is a research fellow and teacher in Argentina at ESEADE, an educational institute emphasizing Austrian economics. He is also a professor with the Faculty of Law, University of Buenos Aires.

biguous way. The Greek philosopher argued that for an exchange to be just the *values* of the things interchanged must be equal:

> It is required that the builder shall receive from the shoemaker some part of what the latter produces, giving him at the same time some part of what he produces himself. Now if they achieve, first, proportionate equality, secondly fair give and take, they will find the problem we have stated above. But if they fail to achieve this, there will not be equality, nor will there be fairness in their dealing and it cannot continue. For nothing prevents the product of one of the parties from being better valued than that of the other, and this requires a process of reducing them to equality. It is the same with all other arts and crafts. They would never have survived unless the active element—the producer—produced and received the same quantity and quality of products as the passive element—the recipient—gets.[2]

A few lines later he adds:

> In this way we arrive at the formula: As a builder is to a shoemaker, so are *x* shoes to a house. Unless it be carried out in accordance with this formula, there can be no true exchange or association, and such reciprocity will be found impossible, if the things exchanged are not somehow reduced to equal value.[3]

The question that arises is: What, to follow Aristotle's example, makes *x* shoes to be equal to one house? We may think of two answers: (1) the *utility* (or use value) of "x" shoes equals the *utility* of one house; or (2) the "labour and cost" of producing "x" shoes equals those of one house. Aristotle did not answer this problem, but we may speculate that if he was thinking of utility, then his theory is wrong because persons exchange goods only when each of them values the good he receives more than the good he gives. In other words, exchange takes place when there is *inequality* and not equality of "utilities."

This idea of Aristotle had an overwhelming influence during almost two centuries. As Hans Sennholz has pointed out:

> For almost two thousand years economic investigation was handicapped by the common notion that economic exchange is fair only as long as each party gets exactly as much as he gives the other. This notion of equality in exchange even permeated the writings of the classical economists.[4]

Carl Menger had already called attention to Aristotle's mistakes: "The error of regarding the quantities of goods as equivalents was made as early as Aristotle."[5] We may also contrast Aristotle's conclusion to that of Eugen von Böhm-Bawerk, "An exchange is economically possible only between persons whose valuations of the goods and of the medium of exchange differ and, indeed, differ in opposite directions."[6]

St. Thomas Aquinas, the main follower and interpreter of Aristotle in the Middle Ages, said that there is justice in an exchange when *the labor and costs* of production of the good are equal:

> Although a house has a higher price than shoes, many shoes equal, nevertheless, the price of a house, or the food of a man during a long period of time. It is necessary, to be justice in exchange, that x quantity of shoes should be given for a house or food, for the builder or farmer exceeds the shoemaker in *labor and costs*. If this principle were not attained there would be no exchange of things nor men would trade with each other.[7]

True, following this quotation, St. Thomas says that "human need" is the measure to compare the values of the goods. But to repeat, equality of value or need precludes an exchange. The fact that St. Thomas was thinking of value as something "objective" is quite clear in his *Summa Theologica* when he asks if a thing can lawfully be sold for a higher price than it is worth.[8] On the contrary a subjective theory of value implies that a thing may have a worth different for each and every person. The following quotation of Menger shows his differences with Aristotle and St. Aquinas:

> The *measure* of value is entirely subjective in nature, and for this reason a good can have great value to one economizing individual, little value to another, and no value at all to a third, depending upon the differences in the requirements and available amounts. What one person disdains or values lightly is appreciated by another, and what one person abandons is often picked up by another. While one economizing individual esteems equally a given amount of one good and a greater amount of another good, we may frequently observe just the opposite evaluations with another economizing individual.[9]

Some scholars think that Aristotle and St. Thomas had a subjective theory of value and that the classical economists had an objective one. Emile Kauder, for example, asserts, "...the father of our economic science wrote that water has a great utility and a small value. With these few words Adam Smith had made waste and rubbish out of the thinking of 2,000 years."[10] However the assertion of Ludwig von Mises is more correct:

> An inveterate fallacy asserted that things and services exchanged are of equal value. Value was considered as objective, as an intrinsic quality

inherent in things and not merely as the expression of various people's eagerness to acquire them. People, it was assumed, first established the magnitude of value proper to goods and services by an act of measurement and then proceeded to barter them against quantities of goods and services of the same amount of value. This fallacy frustrated Aristotle's approach to economic problems and, for almost two thousand years, the reasoning of all those for whom Aristotle's opinions were authoritative. It seriously vitiated the marvelous achievement of the classical economists and rendered the writings of their epigones, especially those of Marx and the Marxian school, entirely futile.[11]

Mises was quite right since almost all scholastic thinkers followed Aristotle and St. Thomas in their writings. In recent years, however, some scholars have argued that scholastic thinkers, especially those of the School of Salamanca, advanced a subjective theory of value.[12] The fact is that these scholastic doctors never truly departed from elements of "objective" value or holistic reasoning. They thought that value was determined by three elements: (1) *virtuositas*, which is the intrinsic qualities of the goods; (2) *raritas*, which is scarcity; and (3) *complacibilitas*, which is common estimation. Only *raritas* may be said to be a correct element, although its definition is lacking in accuracy.

Virtuositas is incompatible with a subjective theory of value. What are, for example, the "intrinsic" qualities of a chair? One can sit on it. But a chair can also be used as an ornament, to break a window, to knock somebody's head, to start a fire, to do exercises, to practice shooting, to kill a cockroach, etc., etc. In fact, a thing's uses depend only on human imagination. What the scholastic doctors seemed to have in mind when talking of *virtuositas* is the most "common" use of a thing. But it is an incorrect reasoning to associate the most "common" use of a thing with an intrinsic value. C. Menger would say many years later, "Value is ...nothing inherent in goods, no property of them, but merely the importance that we first attribute to the satisfaction of our needs."[13]

Complacibilitas, or common estimation, is a holistic concept. Only individuals act and value.[14] There cannot be a "common" estimation. There are as many estimations as persons, and the Austrian economists showed that utility is not measurable; there is no way to calculate an average or mean.

With these erroneous concepts, the scholastic thinkers could not have been forerunners of the Austrian economists. It also should be remembered, as Marjorie Grice-Hutchinson herself had to admit, that almost all scholastic doctors were in favor of price controls,[15] which are inconsistent with a subjective theory of value.

The Classical Economists

The classical economists also distinguished between "value in use" and "value in exchange," but in a more precise and explicit way than the scholastic doctors. Some scholars mistakenly assert[16] that the classical economists could not solve the "value paradox" because of their labor theory of value. Adam Smith had already solved this paradox in his *Lectures on Jurisprudence*:

> ...a thing of no use, as [a] lump of clay, brought into the market will give no price, as no one demands it. If it be useful the price will be regulated according to the demand, as this use is general or not, and the plenty there is to supply it. A thing which is hardly of any use, yet if the quantity be not sufficient to supply the demand, will give a high price; hence the great price of diamonds. Precious metals, which are certainly not so useful as gold, bear a far greater price, partly on this account. Abundance on the other hand does more than supply all possible demands, renders water of no price at all and other things of a price that is next thing to nothing.[17]

The classical economists also distinguished between natural price and market price. The first was determined by the costs of production, and the second by supply and demand. When the market price is above the natural price (costs), the entrepreneurs will expand the production encouraged by the higher profits. This additional supply of goods will lower the market price again towards its natural price. If, on the other hand, the market price is below the natural price, the entrepreneurs will reduce the production, discouraged by the losses or lower profits. The decline in the supply of goods will raise the market price until reaching the natural price. In this way the market price will tend to fluctuate around the natural price, or cost of production.

The classical economists concluded, then, that costs determine the prices, or value in exchange, of the goods. Later we will see that this is an erroneous conclusion. But this theory led them to another problem. Costs are also prices, and when these economists tried to explain the formation of costs, they based their reasoning on the prices of final goods. Wages, for instance, are costs of production for wheat, but the price of wheat is, for the classical economists, a part of the wages. The following quotation of David Ricardo shows the problem clearly:

> The natural price of labour is that price which is necessary to enable the labourers, one with another, to subsist and to perpetuate their race, without either increase or diminution ...
>
> ...The natural price of labour therefore, depends on the price of the food, necessaries, and conveniences required for the support of the labourer and his family.[18]

This fallacious reasoning (*circulus vitiosus* as Böhm-Bawerk called it) prevented the classical economists from providing a sound foundation for their remarkable explanation of the market process. In spite of this error John S. Mill wrote, "Happily, there is nothing in the laws of value which remains for the present or any future writer to clear up; the theory of the subject is complete...."[19] The classical theory of prices, or value in exchange, needed another theoretical justification. The marginal utility theory accomplished this goal.

The Revolution of Marginal Utility

In the 1870s three thinkers discovered independently and approximately at the same time the marginal utility theory. They were William S. Jevons in England, Leon Walras in Switzerland, and Carl Menger in Austria. Their followers helped to develop and spread the new theory: Alfred Marshall in England; Vilfredo Pareto in Switzerland; Eugen von Böhm-Bawerk and Friedrich von Wieser in Austria.

The Austrian economists followed a line of reasoning that allowed them to formulate a more consistent and accurate general economic theory than their fellows of England and Switzerland. As Böhm-Bawerk has said, "...the direction in which I believe the Austrians have outstripped their rivals, is the use they have made of the fundamental idea in the subsequent construction of economic theory."[20] We have seen that the classical economists concluded that in the long run the prices were determined by the costs of production. The theory of marginal utility as used by the English and Swiss economists did not completely unveil this error. These economists concluded that prices are determined by marginal utility and costs. On the other hand, the Austrian economists showed that costs have no influence whatever on prices. On the contrary, for this school the costs of production were determined by the prices, or more exactly by expected prices.

W. S. Jevons, one of the discoverers of the marginal utility theory[21], asserted:

> Repeated reflection and inquiry have led me to the somewhat novel opinion, the *value depends entirely upon utility*. Prevailing opinion makes labour rather than utility the origin of value; and there are even those who distinctly assert that labour is the cause of value.[22]

Here Jevons seems to discard completely the costs of production as a determinant of prices. But he contradicts himself in a later chapter:

> But though labour is never the cause of value, it is in a large proportion of cases the determining circumstance, and in the following way: *Value depends solely on the final degree of utility. How can we vary this degree of utility? By having more or less of the commodity to consume. And how shall we get more or less of it? By spending more or less labour in obtaining supply.* According to this view, then, there are two steps between labour and value. Labour affects supply, and supply affects the degree of utility, which governs value, or the ratio of exchange. In order that there may be no possible mistake about this all-important series of relations, I will re-state it in a tabular form, as follows:
>
> *Cost of production determines supply;*
> *Supply determines final degree of utility;*
> *Final degree of utility determines value.*[23]

The conclusion of the Austrian economists is the opposite: valuation, or the final degree of utility, is the source of prices (value-in-exchange) and costs.

In England it was Alfred Marshall who popularized the marginal utility theory. But Marshall stepped backwards to classical economists' conclusion that long-run costs determine prices:

> ...we may conclude that, as *a general rule*, the shorter the period which we are considering, the greater must be the share of our attention which is given to the influence of demand of value; and the longer the period, the more important will be the influence of cost of production on value.[24]

We have seen that the classical economists distinguished between market prices (which were determined by supply and demand) and natural prices (which were determined by costs of production). In the later quotation Marshall is following the same reasoning and reaching the same conclusion. This conclusion is reinforced in Appendix I of his book when he defends Ricardo's theory of value against the attack of Jevons:

> There are few writers of modern times who have approached as near to the brilliant originality of Ricardo as Jevons has done. But he appears to have judged both Ricardo and Mill harshly, and to have attributed to them doctrines narrower and less scientific than those which they really held.[25]

Later he asserts that Ricardo's doctrine "though unsystematic and open to many objections, seems to be more philosophic in principle and closer to the actual facts of life."[26] But then Marshall failed to use the marginal utility theory to escape from the *circulus vitiosus* of the classical economists.

Walras's analysis is looser. The use of a model based on a system of linear equations prevented him from formulating a teleological causality. He concluded that in the long run prices are equal to costs of production, but he did not specify if costs determine prices or prices determine costs:

> Given several services by means of which various products can be manufactured and assuming that these services are exchanged for their products through the medium of a *numeraire*, for the market to be in equilibrium, or for the prices of all the services and all the products in terms of the *numeraire* to be stationary, it is necessary and sufficient (1) that the effective demand for each service and each product be equal to its effective supply at these prices; and (2) that the selling prices of the products be equal to the cost of the services employed in making them. If this twofold equality does not exist, in order to achieve the first it is necessary to raise the prices of those services or products the effective demand for which is greater than the effective supply and to lower the price of those services or products the effective supply of which is greater than the effective demand; and, in order to achieve the second, it is necessary to increase the output of those products the selling price of which is greater than the cost of production and to decrease the output of those products of which the cost of production is greater than the selling price.
>
> This is the *law of the establishment of equilibrium prices* in production.[27]

Pareto arrived at a similar conclusion:

> What is the *value* of diamonds? You can resolve this question neither by considering the desires which they awaken in men and women, nor by considering the obstacles which their production encounters, nor the evaluation into which these desires and these obstacles are translated, nor the "limitations of quantity," nor the cost of production, nor the cost of

reproduction, etc. All these circumstances have an influence on the price of diamonds, but singly or even as a group they are not enough to determine it.[28]

Marshall, Walras, Pareto, and their followers have all concluded that value in exchange, or price, is neither determined by utility alone nor by costs of production alone, but by both utility *and* costs of production. Students of economics all over the world are taught that prices are determined by demand and supply. And they are taught to deduce the demand curve from *marginal utility*, and to deduce the supply curve from *marginal costs*. This is what any book of microeconomic theory, or general equilibrium theory, teaches about price determination.

The use of mathematics has led these economists to this erroneous conclusion. If prices are determined by utility and costs, then the *circulus vitiosus* has not been broken. The Austrian economist Eugen von Böhm-Bawerk was acquainted with this problem:

> It is well known that Jevons and Walras arrived at a similar [to the Austrian economists] law of price. Their statement, however, has considerable deficiencies, which were first supplied by the Austrians. It was the latter who first found the right way of escape from the *circulus vitiosus* in which the older theory of price as dependent upon supply and demand was involved.[29]

Mathematical economists started from the assumptions of a "perfect market," including that of perfect knowledge. Every consumer and producer knows perfectly all the conditions and alternatives to buy and sell in the market.

Under conditions of perfect knowledge there is no market process but market equilibrium. There is no difference between short-run and long-run prices; we are always in a long-run position. And in the long-run, prices and costs tend to be equal. Any change in the conditions, such as tastes or technology, produces an instantaneous adjustment in the markets. From one long-run price we pass to another long-run price; there is no "process" of adjustment. Many assumptions of the mathematical economists were, in fact, chosen only for the purpose of justifying the use of the mathematical tools and not for the purpose of theoretical fertility.

The Austrian economists have followed a different approach. They have not assumed a market of perfect competition. They have accented the market process and not the market equilibrium.

By not assuming perfect knowledge, they could distinguish clearly between *prices* and *expected prices*, and this distinction allowed them to break the *circulus vitiosus*. The decision of the entrepreneurs to produce or not to produce is not strictly based on prices but on *expected* prices. Production increases when *expected* profits grow, and decreases when losses are *expected*. The demand for production goods today depends on the *expected* prices of the final product. Carl Menger pointed it out clearly:

> ...it is evident that the value of goods of higher order is always and without exception determined by the prospective value of the goods of lower order in whose production they serve. The existence of our *requirements* for goods of higher order is dependent upon the goods they serve to produce having expected economic character and hence expected *value*...We therefore have the principle that the value of goods of higher order is dependent upon the expected value of the goods of lower order they serve to produce. Hence goods of higher order can attain value, or retain it once they have it, only if, or as long as, they serve to produce goods that we expect to have value for us. If this fact is established, it is clear also that the value of goods of higher order cannot be the *determining* factor in the prospective value of the corresponding goods of lower order...On the contrary, the value of goods of higher order is, in all cases, regulated by the prospective value of the goods of lower order to whose production they have been or will be assigned by economizing men.[30]

And finally he concludes:

> Hence the principle that the value of goods of higher order is governed, not by the value of corresponding goods of lower order at the present, but rather by the prospective value of the product, is the universal valid principle of the determination of the value of goods of higher order.[31]

Clearly, Menger broke the *circulus vitiosus* of the classical and of the mathematical economists. Böhm-Bawerk has also pointed out the mistakes of the classical economists and the imperfect solution of the English and Swiss marginalists, but he was less accurate than Menger in distinguishing between prices and expected prices. He comments the classical theory in the following way:

> ...without doubt we place a high estimate upon materials of production only when and because they are capable of furnishing valuable products. The relation of cause and effect is, therefore, exactly the reverse of what the older theory stated. The older theory explained the value of the product as the effect, and the cost—that is, the value of the materials of production—as the cause, and thought no further explanation necessary.

The Austrian economists found: (1) that the value of the materials of production needs, first of all, to be explained; and (2) that after this explanation is made, and after the net of complicated relations is untangled, the value of the materials of production is seen in the end to be the effect, and the value of the product the cause.[32]

Böhm-Bawerk could have been more accurate if he had said "expected value" and not simply "value." Let us remember that first comes production and then the sale of the product. Costs are prior to prices. Prices, as we will see, are determined only by the marginal utility of the good, once production is accomplished and costs disbursed. In his book *Capital and Interest*, Böhm-Bawerk reached the same conclusion:

> The value of every means of production is also determined directly by the value of the product of the next lower order which is derived from it.[33]

Years later, Ludwig von Mises enhanced and refined the theory of Menger. Mises emphasized the role that the entrepreneur plays as forecaster of changes and disequilibriums in the market:

> In drafting their plans the entrepreneurs look first at the prices of the immediate past which are mistakenly called *present* prices. Of course, the entrepreneurs never make these prices enter into their calculations without paying regard to anticipated changes. The prices of the immediate past are for them only the starting point of deliberations leading to forecasts of future prices. The prices of the past do not influence the determination of future prices. It is, on the contrary, the anticipation of future prices of the products that determines the state of prices of the complementary factors of production. The allocation of the nonconvertible factors of production and the amount of capital goods available for future production are historical magnitudes; in this regard the past is instrumental in shaping the course of future production and in affecting the prices of the future. But directly the prices of the factors of production are determined exclusively by the anticipation of future prices of the products.[34]

In this way the Austrian economists made a more complete and accurate use of the marginal utility theory. Breaking the *circulus vitiosus* of the classical economists, they gave us a complete and coherent theory of value and prices (unlike the mathematical economists of Cambridge and Lausanne).

We have seen that costs of production depend on "expected prices." Once production is finished, costs belong to the past; they are "sunk," and the entrepreneur is now the owner of the goods produced. How are the prices of these goods determined? By demand and supply, both determined by the subjective valuations (or the marginal utility) of buyers and sellers. Buyers do not pay prices which sacrifice marginal utility greater than the good they buy. The seller does not sell to receive lower marginal utility. Both Menger and Böhm-Bawerk have clearly explained the determination of prices from marginal utility as reflected in supply and demand. In this way costs were completely eliminated from price formation as explained by Mises:

> The ultimate source of the determination of prices is the value judgements of the consumers. Prices are the outcome of the valuation preferring *a* to *b*. They are social phenomena as they are brought about by the interplay of the valuations of all individuals participating in the operation of the market.[35]

A Foundation for Further Advancement

The Austrian economists not only used the marginal utility theory to break the *circulus vitiosus* of the classical economists, but they have also made other illuminating applications of the theory. It was Ludwig von Mises who made a wider use of the new theory of value in the following topics:

Money. Mises was the first economist to use the marginal utility theory to explain the determination of the value and of purchasing power of money;[36]

Epistemology. The marginal theory of value widened the field of economic science. The market, or *catallactics*, is only one aspect of a more general theory of human action: *praxeology*. The epistemological problems of praxeology are different from those of the natural sciences; and,

Economic calculation. The way in which the Austrian economists used the new theory of value allowed them to see more clearly the fundamental role that prices play in allocating the factors of production in the most efficient way. It was the Austrian school that demonstrated irrefutably that a rational allocation of resources is only possible in a free market economy, *i.e.* where ownership is private and individuals are free.

Notes and References

1. Aristotle, *Politics* (London: Penguin Books, 1970), p. 41.
2. Aristotle, *The Nicomachean Ethics* (London: Penguin Books, 1971), p. 152.
3. *Ibid.*, p. 152.
4. Sennholz, Hans F., "The Formation and Function of Prices," *The Freeman*, February, 1985, p. 3.
5. Menger, Carl, *Principles of Political Economy* (New York, NY: New York University Press, 1981), p. 305.
6. Böhm-Bawerk, Eugen von, *Capital and Interest* (Spring Mills, PA: Libertarian Press, 1959), p. 216.
7. Aquinas, St. Thomas, *Comentario de la Etica a Nicomaco,* (Buenos Aires: CIAFIC, 1983), p. 285. Raymond de Roover asserts that "... there is no contradiction, since the market price would then tend to coincide with cost or to oscillate around this point like the swing of a pendulum," in "The Concept of Just Price: Theory and Economic Policy," *Journal of Economic History* (December, 1958), p. 420. This seems to be forced interpretation; St. Thomas was only thinking of "justice" and not of market processes. However Marjorie Grice-Hutchinson, who has asserted that the schoolmen had a subjective theory of value, admitted that Albertus Magnus, the teacher of St. Thomas, "...bases justice in exchange on equality of labour and 'expenses,' and, at the same time, maintains that the primary object of exchange is the satisfaction of human wants," (*The School of Salamanca,* Oxford: Clarendon Press, 1952, p. 26.) Grice-Hutchinson arrives at the same conclusion with St. Thomas in her book *El Pensamiento Economico en España (1177–1740)* (Barcelona: Editorial Critica, 1982), p. 113.
8. Aquinas, St. Thomas, *Summa Theologica* (Buenos Aires: Club de Lectores, 1988), 2-2, q. 77, a. 1.
9. Menger, Carl, *op. cit.*, p. 146.
10. Kauder, E., "The Genesis of the Marginal Utility Theory," *The Economic Journal*, September, 1953, p. 650.
11. Mises, Ludwig von, *Human Action* (Chicago, IL: Henry Regnery Company, 1966), p. 203-204.
12. Among these scholars we may find Joseph A. Schumpeter, *History of Economic Analysis* (Oxford University Press, 1978), pp. 94-107; Marjorie Grice-Hutchinson, *The School of Salamanca*; Emile Kauder, *A History of Marginal Utility Theory* (Princeton, NJ: Princeton University Press, 1965); Murray N. Rothbard, "New Light on the Prehistory of the Austrian School," in Edwin G. Dolan (ed.) *The Foundations of Modern Austrian Economics* (Kansas City, MO: Sheed & Ward, Inc., 1976);

Alejandro A. Chafuen, *Christians for Freedom, Late-Scholastic Economics* (San Francisco, CA: Ignatius Press, 1986).
13. Menger, *op. cit.*, p. 116.
14. See Mises, Ludwig von, *The Ultimate Foundation of Economic Science* (Kansas City, MO: Sheed Andrews and McMeel, Inc., 1978), pp. 78-83; also *Human Action*, pp. 41-43.
15. Grice-Hutchinson, Marjorie, *El Pensamiento Economico en España (1177–1740)*, p. 116.
16. Among them George J. Stigler in "The Development of Marginal Utility," *Essays in the History of Economics* (Chicago, IL: The University of Chicago Press, 1989), p. 68.
17. Smith, Adam, *Lectures on Jurisprudence* (Indianapolis, IN: Liberty Classics, 1982), p. 358.
18. Ricardo, David, *Principles of Political Economy and Taxation* (London: Penguin Books, 1971), p. 115.
19. Mill, John S., *Principles of Political Economy* (New York, NY: Kelley Publishers, 1987), p. 436.
20. Böhm-Bawerk, Eugen von, "The Austrian Economists," *Shorter Classics of Böhm-Bawerk* (Spring Mills, PA: Libertarian Press, 1962), p. 8.
21. By "value" Jevons meant prices or value-in-exchange. And he did not use the term "marginal utility" but "final degree of utility."
22. Jevons, W. S., *The Theory of Political Economy* (New York, NY: Kelley Publishers, 1965), p. 1.
23. *Ibid.*, p. 165.
24. Marshall, A., *Principles of Economics* (London: Macmillan & Co., Ltd., 1946), p. 349.
25. *Ibid.*, p. 817.
26. *Ibid.*, p. 819.
27. Walras, L., *Elements of Pure Economics* (New York, NY: Kelley Publishers, 1977), pp. 253-54.
28. Pareto, V., *Manual of Political Economy* (New York, NY: Kelley Publishers, 1971), p. 179.
29. Böhm-Bawerk, Eugen von, *op. cit.*, p. 10.
30. Menger, *op. cit.*, p. 150.
31. *Ibid.*, p. 151.
32. Böhm-Bawerk, Eugen von, *op. cit.*, p. 12.
33. Böhm-Bawerk, *Capital and Interest*, Vol. II, p. 171.
34. Mises, *Human Action*, pp. 336-337.
35. *Ibid.*, p. 331.

36. See his *The Theory of Money and Credit* (New York, NY: The Foundation for Economic Education, 1971), Part II, Chapters 1 and 2. Also *Human Action*, Chapter XXVII.

7

MARX'S QUANTITY THEORY OF LABOR:
A Critique

Clarence B. Carson*

The apparent disintegration of Communism in the Soviet Union, Eastern Europe, and in other places in the world might be taken to mean that Marx's intellectual legacy has been spent. Indeed, there was much evidence that the hold of Marxian theory on the minds of even Communist leaders was loosening long before the Soviet Empire began to fold. For example, Hedrick Smith reported this conversation in a book published in 1976:

> "You have to go to these political meetings but nobody listens," said a plump Leningrad schoolteacher in her late thirties.... When the director of our school gives the lecture, he tries to make it interesting. He's a nice man—a Party member but a nice man. But everyone is bored and nobody believes it."
>
> "What about the person giving the lecture?" Ann asked her.
>
> "Even he doesn't believe what he's saying. The older generation really believed in Lenin and they felt this was the way to build a new society. But my generation doesn't even believe in it at all. We know it's false."[1]

There were those who doubted even a decade and a half ago that the members of the Politburo any longer believed in Communist theory.

Since that time, and especially since Gorbachev has introduced such reforms as he has, it has become increasingly clear that what remains of Communism is the attachment of the *Nomenklatura,* party bureaucracy, to their privileged positions within the Communist system. However, as their privileges are withdrawn, it now seems probable that the last vestiges of attachment to Marxist

* Dr. Carson is an historian, a prolific author, and a former colleague of Hans Sennholz at Grove City College.

ideology, *per se,* will disappear in the Soviet sphere. Of course, Communism is still very much alive in China and here and there in provinces under Chinese or other influences. But perhaps its passing there depends only on the passing of the old men who rule, which cannot be far distant.

In any case, the hold of Marxian theory by way of Communism is disintegrating and presumably disappearing in the former Soviet sphere and apparently is in decline around the world. Even so, Marx's ideas should retain an interest among academicians as long as the memory of them remains because of their tremendous influence on events and peoples over the past century. That is not, however, the only reason for continuing to examine and analyze them. Karl Marx's influence still remains strong by way of ideas that have entered into the stream of Western and world thought. The most obvious example might well be in how the class struggle idea still fortifies unionist theory and practice. More broadly, the near universal hold of various socialist premises today owes much of its currency to Marxist ideas.

This paper deals with something much narrower in scope than that, but it does have to do with an idea which is in considerable part a legacy from Marxian theory. Much of the continuing impact of Marxism, now that Communism is disintegrating, lies in the way its residue in our minds skews ideas that have become accepted in the West generally. That is certainly the case with his quantity theory of labor. It is now deeply ensconced both in our practice and our outlook in the payment for labor on the basis of time spent at the job. Perhaps all this will become clearer from an examination of what I am calling here Marx's quantity theory of labor.

To do so, it is necessary to separate and distinguish it from his labor theory of value. The labor theory of value has not only overshadowed the quantity theory but was also more directly crucial to the Marxian ideology. In essence, the labor theory holds that human labor provides the whole of the value which goods have for us. In the Marxian formulations, it should follow then that in a just society, those who perform the labor should receive the whole of the price paid for goods. In fact, however, Marx's thought was both more devious and complex than that. He did belabor the alleged injustices involved in such things as money being paid to rent and interest. He did base his class struggle thesis on the maldistribution of wealth in a capitalistic system. But he did not call for the distribution of wealth directly to those whose labor produced it, which would be the logical course, we may suppose. Instead, Marx was a collectivist, and the distribution he proposed was only tangentially, if at all, tied to his labor theory of value.

No matter, it was always a central piece in his ideology. Moreover, as I pointed out earlier, it has overshadowed the quantity theory of labor, which, in the Marxian formulation was very much a part of it. Not much has been made of the quantity theory of labor. Perhaps it is because, as one economist, David McCord Wright, observed: "Economists get so lost in blowing it [Marx's labor theory of value] up that they miss more important parts of his thought."[2] It is more probable, however, that they simply did not conceive of the quantity conception as distinct from the labor theory of value. Certainly, Marx made no such distinction, so completely were the two conceptions linked in his mind. At any rate, Marx stated his basic quantity theory of labor this way: "The *relative values of commodities are...determined by the respective quantities or amounts of labour, worked up, realized, in them.*[3] In turn, he reduced quantity of labor to "labor time," or "laboring power time." To wit: "The determination of price by the labour time necessary for the manufacture of a commodity, for the cost of production consists of 1) raw materials and depreciation of instruments, that is, of industrial products the cost of which has cost a certain amount of labour time, and 2) of direct labour, the measure of which is, precisely, time."[4]

Marx did qualify his quantity theory to get around some of the more obvious objections to it. Eugen von Böhm-Bawerk described the more elaborate theory this way: "Since labor constitutes the substance of value, the magnitude of the value of all goods is...measured by the quantity of labor they contain, or more specifically, by the labor time. But that does not mean the individual length of time that this or that person who may have fashioned the commodity happened to need for it. It means the 'socially necessary labor time.' Marx explains this as meaning 'the time required to produce any use value when operating under the conditions of production normally prevailing in a given society, and when utilizing the degree of skill and application normally available there.'"[5]

Here is a further elaboration in Marx's words: "It is only the quantity of socially necessary labor, or the labor time socially necessary for the production of a use value, which determines the magnitude of its value. Any single given commodity is considered the average of its kind. Commodities or goods which contain equal quantities of labor, or which can be produced in the same labor time, have the same amount of value. The value of one commodity bears the same relation to the value of every other commodity, as the labor time necessary for the production of the other. As values, all commodities are only definite measures of crystallized labor time."[6]

Goods are, then, "crystallized labor time." That is, "perhaps," the essence of Marx's quantity theory of labor. Friedrich Engels made it clear that for Marx goods are "crystallized labor time" whether the laborer is paid directly for his labor time or indirectly for it by way of the number of the pieces he produces.[7] It should be explained that Marx was a philosophical monist and hence a reductionist, that is, he tended to reduce all of reality to one level. His dialectical materialism was such a reduction writ large. He reduced all of reality to its material level. In the above case, he was trying to reduce all the diverse elements that go into production to a single level, *i.e.*, the labor time, or, as Marx would have it, the labor power time of the worker. In fact, he was saying the products themselves reduce to the labor time that went into producing them.

That is reductionism with a vengeance, it could be said with considerable justice. Marx had gone well beyond reducing something to its essence, a mental operation commonly done in reasoning in order to place it in a class with all other beings of its kind. Thus, man might be classified as a rational animal, thus reducing him to one of his essential features for purposes of classification. It would not do at all, however, to claim that man is essentially crystallized H_2O, though water is the main component of his body. That would be to alter the nature of his being by reduction. That is what Marx does with products with his crystallized labor time, even though he qualifies his classification by saying he is talking about products only as values. That is not true either. Crystallized labor time, if there were such a thing, would remain crystallized labor time. It is not the essence of any product or its value. That can and will be demonstrated below, but it is important to understand at the outset that Marx did not have his philosophical feet fully planted, so to speak.

But whatever the philosophical standing of Marx's quantity theory of labor, it fitted firmly into his ideology. It was a subordinate and integral part of the labor theory of value. The labor theory of value held that all value was imparted to commodities by labor. The quantity theory supposedly explained how this occurred, *i.e.*, by the application of labor time to the production of goods. It might be supposed, then, that if the labor theory of value were refuted and discredited, a like fate would befall the quantity theory. The labor theory of value has been refuted, and nowadays does not even much energize labor unions. Such Communists as remain do not appear to be of the opinion that all the proceeds of production should go to "labor." By contrast, the practice of compensating labor on the basis of the quantity of time worked has spread, become well established, and appears to be on its way to becoming universal.

This practice, if it is based on any theory at all, is of necessity based on a quantity theory of labor. Undoubtedly, the practice of basing wages on time worked antedated Marx. But Marx's theory gave great impetus to its spread, as labor unions became advocates of it, and governments began to prescribe minimums in terms of hours worked. As time has elapsed, the practice seems to have become almost completely separated from the ideological framework in which Marx enunciated it.

How this separation could have occurred takes us a little deeper into the Marxian theory. Marx had welded at least three distinct propositions from economics on to his ideology. One proposition, not mentioned thus far, is that value tends to equal price in a competitive market. He actually stated the notion both more emphatically and less absolutely. For example, he said, in the first volume of *Das Capital:*

> We have in fact assumed that prices equal values. We shall, however, see in Volume III, that even in the case of average prices the assumption cannot be made in this very simple manner.[8]

Still, the basic statement that value tends to equal price covers what Marx was maintaining. The second proposition was that labor contributes the whole value of commodities or goods. The third proposition was that the measure of labor's contribution is the (socially necessary, normal or average) labor time required to produce a good. These three propositions are neither causally, logically, nor temporally bound to or dependent upon one another. None follows from the others. For example, if it could be conclusively demonstrated that value tends to equal price in the market, this would not add one whit to the proof of the notion that labor adds the whole value to a product. Nor if either or both of the above propositions be accepted would it follow that the measure of that value is the quantity of labor time that went into it. Indeed, some economists, Adam Smith, for example, have held that the value of goods derived from labor without having declared or believed that it could be measured in labor time. These three propositions are held together only because Marx used them that way.

At any rate, there are three distinct propositions in Marx's formulation held together only by ideological glue. Dissolve the glue, so to speak, and each of the propositions is separate, must stand on its own merits or credibility, and can follow its own course. Substantially, that is what has happened, for whether the ideological glue has been entirely melted, the propositions now have different and separate standings. The value-price relationship has been taken in a quite different direction by the Austrian School, for example. Marx's labor theory of value has been refuted, abandoned, or generally ignored by economists. He inherited it from the classical economists, notably Adam Smith, who had arrived at his conclusion from the angle of natural law theory. Unfortunately, many economists have long since thrown the natural law baby out with the labor theory of value bath water, substituting utilitarian theory for natural law. In any case, the labor theory of value has to stand on its own without support from the other propositions.

The quantity theory of labor has also gone its own way. But in contrast with the decline in the standing of at least one of the propositions, labor time is one of the major determinants, if not the only one, in fixing the total amount of wages and salaries. That is not to say that labor time determines the hourly wage or monthly or annual salary received by particular employees. It is rather to say that labor time provides the terms in which these are calculated and paid. Wages and hours legislation in the United States prescribes minimum wages per hours worked, and time and-a-half pay for overtime work. Union wages are cast in this framework as well, usually, and many employers who pay more than minimum wage as a rule and have no contracts with unions still pay on the basis of labor time. Salaried employees are also generally paid on the basis of time elapsed, though it may not be based on a precise number of hours worked or spent on some work site.

Quantity of labor, for Marx, was measured in labor time. Labor time is widely, if not universally, used in our day as a measure by which to quantify payment to workers. What is so strange about all this is that there is no necessary correlation between labor time—time spent at the labor site—and production. Marx tried to get around or at least obfuscate the difficulties in such a concept. He referred to "socially necessary labor." He defined this as the work provided by a "normal" workman possessed of the "normal" skill for producing particular goods, and so forth. He also claimed that what employers bought from workmen was "laboring power," whatever that might be taken to mean. But these terms are mental constructs which do not in the least dispose of the difficulty of relating payment to production or productivity.

It is possible to see the problem most clearly by examining a case where whatever amount of labor time might be spent there might be no resulting production. Whether the labor time was "socially necessary" is revealed for the empty phrase that it is. Let us illustrate this by asking a precise question. What is the socially necessary labor time to produce a fifty-pound watermelon? An agricultural question is posed rather than an industrial one because a whole range of problems are more dramatically apparent in farming than in manufacturing. It will help us to see, too, when we turn to manufacturing what is done to try to implement Marx's—or anyone else's—quantity theory of labor.

The first difficulty is that watermelons do not regularly and predictably come in fifty-pound sizes. Indeed, it might happen that in a large field which produced good sized watermelons, not a single one would weigh precisely fifty pounds. Yet a standard weight or size is necessary in order to arrive at a quantifiable socially necessary labor time. The difficulty can be overcome statistically, of course. All that would be necessary would be to weigh all the watermelons produced (in a field, on a farm, in an area, or whatever) and divide the total number of pounds by fifty.

That having been done, let us suppose, by way of example, that 1,000 fifty-pound watermelons were produced on a given acreage by 200 hours of labor time. We might then conclude that the socially necessary labor time to produce a fifty-pound watermelon was twelve minutes. We might go even further, if we were in a generous and unrestrained mood, to declare that a normal workman of normal skill, etc., could produce a fifty-pound watermelon in twelve minutes of labor time. It should be emphasized, however, that what we have actually arrived at are averages of aggregates, that there is nothing discernibly socially necessary about the time, nor do any norms necessarily rise from them. They are figures arrived at *after the fact* (as are all statistics dealing with actual things). Moreover, aside from possibly using these after-the-fact figures as some sort of basis for paying the laborers, they have no further application. (This is improbable, however, as Marx himself noted, since it is likely that any day-laborers have long since been paid before all the watermelons were weighed and harvested.) The next year, 200 hours of labor time applied to the same land might produce no watermelons at all. The whole crop might be destroyed by flood, by drought, by blight, or what not. The only thing that "socially necessary" could add to labor time would be that the labor was actually applied to the task at hand in a way calculated to accomplish it. Otherwise, labor time may signify nothing more than that workers put in so much time at the work site. But that is only a guess as to what Marx may have meant by "socially necessary," and we have no way of knowing that he would not have reckoned "featherbedding" to be "socially necessary," in which case there would be no safeguard against people putting in labor time at the work site but accomplishing nothing. In any case, it can be abundantly proved statistically that crop yields vary from year to year in the average per unit of land without regard to the labor time expended on them.

When production is moved into a factory setting, there are some changes of moment. Indeed, Marx's notions about labor time and the crucial role of labor were undoubtedly formed in connection with the factory system. Manufacturing in a factory setting does reduce and change some of the variables from what they are in farming. The weather is no longer so significant a variable, since the work is usually performed and materials housed under shelter. Quantity and quality can be much more effectively controlled than in farming. Indeed, one of the most significant features of the factory situation is that it is a controlled situation, ideally reflecting the decisions and commands from those in authority. Even so, there remain significant variables, and Marx's notions of "socially necessary labor time," "normal" workers, and "normal" conditions hardly yield the results he predicts. Whatever actual figures are arrived at are still after-the-fact. In manufacturing as in farming, it is still possible to match the labor time with the quantity of commodities produced in a particular instance. For example, 1,000 widgets might be produced during 200 hours of labor time. In which case, the average labor time to produce a widget was twelve minutes. But there is no way to transform that average of twelve minutes into a norm for particular workers, nor 200 hours of labor time into the "socially necessary" time to produce 1,000 widgets. It is only the amount of time it took "x" number of workers in a particular instance to produce what they did. The next time, they might produce 900 or 1,100 widgets, or whatever number they happened to produce. After all, the machinery might break down. Or the power—whether water, steam, gasoline-driven engine, or electricity—might not be available during all or some portion of the time. Above all, though, this now brings us to the variables involved in the quality and quantity of work.

In the first place, Marx has not, by his imaginary and vague qualifications, actually made clear what labor time is. Rather than defining it, he qualified it. Let us look much more directly at the matter. *Time* poses no particular problem for us, for we are not here concerned with its philosophical dimensions. The conventional measures of it are widely accepted, and its lapse in these terms can be reckoned with great precision. Not so, however, *labor* time. There are at least three different meanings which can be attached to "labor" in this context. First, it can be defined as the time spent at the job site and available to perform such tasks as may be assigned. That is surely the legal definition for the purposes of wages and hours legislation. The great advantage of this usage is that labor time can be measured with great precision. That is the case because it has been reduced to the lapse of time and has no other dimension.

Obviously, this measurement of labor time bears no necessary relation to production or productivity. How much time at the work site would be required to produce a widget? There is no way of knowing. It might be forever, if nothing were done, or twelve minutes with vigorous application.

Second, "labor" might conceivably be defined as the actual effort put forth or energy expended. Since the effort put forth cannot be measured, the thing resolves itself to the amount of energy expended. There may be ways of doing this, but it would almost certainly have no economic significance. The amount of energy expended would bear no necessary relation to producing anything that would be valued. Energy can be expended in all sorts of ways that produce no commodities or goods.

There is a third way to define "labor," however, which does get into the vicinity of the essence of its contribution to production. To do this, it may best be equated with work. Not "work" in the sense of exertion, but "work" as it is defined in physics or mechanics. "Work," in mechanics, is "the product of the force acting upon a body and the distance through which the point of application of force moves." There are two ingredients in this definition of work: there is not only the amount of the exertion but also how far the object is moved. The sum of this can be calculated as, for example, foot-pounds, which is defined as the "amount of work involved in lifting one pound one foot high."

It is not my purpose, however, to arrive at any such precise calculation as this, which is both impossible and unnecessary in defining work. I call attention to the mechanical definition because it defines work in terms of what is accomplished. I have sometimes called this definition to the attention of students who thought they ought to have a higher grade than they received because, or so they alleged, they had worked so hard at it or put in so much time on it. I pointed out that what counts is not how hard you pushed but how far you moved it. That is surely the case in production: it is how many and what quality commodities, or goods, that are produced that matters. With that in mind, labor is what work contributes to the production of goods.

It should be noticed, though, that this is a definition of labor, not labor time. An economic definition of labor does not include time. There is a reason for this. The *amount* of time spent at an undertaking is *incidental* to production. That is not to say that time can be eliminated from production. Any production entails time, but the quantity used in producing any particular commodity is incidental. It is easy to see why this is so. For example, a workman may ruin the materials on which he is working. Or, again, a workman may malinger, making little progress toward accomplishing what he has been sent to do. In any case, individuals differ one from the other, and among these differences there are those that will affect to some extent the amount of time they will take to perform a task or produce a commodity. One person may, for example, do work of the highest quality but take much time in doing so because he is meticulous, while another works rapidly but much of what he does is below standard. Indeed, the possible variations are as great as the number of people. In fact, the same person will at different times vary in the amount he can produce in a given time. In short, the amount of time it takes to produce goods is relative to persons and situations, hence incidental in production.

To base payment for workers on quantity of time worked, or labor time, is to base it on an incidental factor so far as production is concerned. It might be supposed, then, that such a practice would be very nearly unworkable. After all, it tends to place the emphasis upon time rather than accomplishment. The predictable results would be clock watching, lack of interest in the quality of what is produced, boredom on the job, malingering, and low productivity. So far as payment is based on time primarily, those do tend to be the results. There is little motive in that to produce goods in quantity or quality.

The history of labor and production for the past one hundred thirty-forty years could probably be written largely around two countervailing trends. One is to base compensation for work on labor time, and, increasingly, on the amount of time at the work site. The spread of socialist ideas, from Marx and others, has given impetus to this trend both ideologically and by way of government intervention in the marketplace. The countervailing development has been a massive and sustained effort to make this system work by modifying it toward the essential factor in production, namely, work or productivity. The factory, I have already noted, is a *controlled* situation. One of the functions it serves is to provide a setting for the supervision of workers. This is also true of office buildings, mines, mills, school buildings, and so forth. This is very nearly essential if payment is to be made on a time basis, for there has to be a means for seeing to it that workers are usually applying themselves constructively to their work. There are other means available, too, to bend the worker effort away from clock watching to productivity. Where machinery is involved, its pace can be set so as to speed up the work. Production quotas are often set so as to get the desired yield from workers. Where there is a minimum wage (or for other reasons such as the most efficient use of space or machinery) the worker may be required to "make production" in order to keep his job. Otherwise, workers may be given additional pay for production above a certain minimum. All sorts of techniques are employed to shift the emphasis away from time and toward productivity. Thus, a largely unworkable system of payment is made to work at least tolerably well, some of the time anyhow.

Payment by labor time, or, more precisely, payment for time at the work site, creates a large problem. It is basically a problem of motivation. Workmen are, of course, lured to the work site by such payment, but have to be dragooned into quantity and quality production if they are not rewarded for it by extra payment. The motivation problem was long apparent in Communist countries, where payment for being at the site not only set up the wrong motivation but also was inadequate to produce anything but the most minimal work effort. For decades, rulers used the force of the state to try to produce adequate production, with extremely poor results. Marx's quantity theory of labor simply did not work.

Payment by labor time, or time at the work site, works much better in lands where there is private ownership of capital goods and where rewards are more nearly apportioned to actual production by a variety of devices. That should not be taken to mean, however, that payment on the basis of so-called labor time is a desirable or appropriate means of rewarding work, achieving quantity and quality production, and bringing out the best that is in people. At best, payment for time at the work site is an expedient; at worst, it is a wasteful, inefficient, and possibly inhumane means of getting work done. Rather than being encouraged by public policy, it might better be discouraged.

Notes and References

1. Smith, Hedrick, *The Russians* (New York, NY: Quadrangle, 1976), p. 288.
2. Wright, David M., *The Trouble with Marx* (New Rochelle, NY: Arlington House, 1967), p. 64.
3. Marx, Karl and Engels, Friedrich, *Selected Works* (New York, NY: International Publishers, 1968), p. 204. Italics are Marx's.
4. Marx, Karl, "Wage Labour and Capital," Eugene C. Black, ed., *The Posture of Europe, 1815 - 1940: Readings in European Intellectual History* (Homewood, IL: The Dorsey Press, 1964), p. 303.
5. Böhm-Bawerk, Eugen von, *The Exploitation Theory of Socialism-Communism* (Spring Mills, PA: Libertarian Press, Inc., 1975), p. 56.
6. Quoted in *Ibid.*
7. Marx, "Wage Labour and Capital," p. 293.
8. Quoted in Sowell, Thomas, *Marxism: Philosophy and Economics* (New York, NY: Quill, William Morrow, 1985), p. 110.

8

ON SOME FORGOTTEN PASSAGES IN THE HISTORY OF LIBERTY

Camille P. Castorina*

As the past is prologue to the future, may all those who prize liberty be inspired by persons and events in the struggle for freedom. This essay will focus on selected historical passages.

The inalienable right of man to be free stems from his nature since creation—at the dawn of history—and so we begin there.

Sumeria

Around 4,000 B.C., what may be the first word for freedom, "amargi," appeared. While it actually meant "return to the mother," it perhaps indicated in an age of political despotism a sense of the naturalness of liberty. Urukagina, an unusual ruler for his time, reversed many government infringements on the economy and liberty, which may explain why so many clay tablets from his era are business records.

Egypt

Egypt, land of the pharaohs, provides the setting for another ancient struggle for freedom. Recorded alike in the Old Testament and certain secular sources is the story of God's command to Moses to liberate the Hebrew slaves from bondage. God then

*Dr. Castorina is Associate Professor of Economics at Florida Institute of Technology. She travels throughout the world as an independent economist, lecturer, and writer, and is an advisor to several international research institutes and publications. She also serves as public policy expert for the Heritage Foundation in Washington, DC.

delivered to Moses a set of laws—the Ten Commandments—to live by and thus to protect their new freedoms. When the Israelites refused to live by these natural spiritual and economic laws, Moses destroyed the Decalogue (although later it was re-given). History has recorded much suffering because governments do not know or do not obey the laws of a moral economy. Ludwig von Mises in his twentieth-century masterpiece, *Human Action,* has this to say regarding the natural laws of economics:

> The body of economic knowledge is an essential element in the structure of human civilization; it is the foundation upon which modern industrialism, and all the moral, intellectual, technological, and therapeutical achievements of the last centuries have been built. It rests with men whether they will make the proper use of the rich treasure with which this knowledge provides them or whether they will leave it unused. But if they fail to take the best advantage of it and disregard its teachings and warnings, they will not annul economics. They will stamp out society and the human race.[1]

One additional episode from the story of Moses is his statement on leading the Israelites to freedom: "Proclaim liberty throughout all the land, and to all the inhabitants thereof." This quotation was inscribed on the famed American "Liberty Bell."

Israel

Also recorded in both secular and Biblical sources are the histories of Kings David and Solomon. In the period immediately preceding their rule, Israel was governed by judges.

Wanting to be like the other ancient empires, however, the Israelites demanded kings. The judges told them they did not need kings and princes—but they wanted them anyway. They got them—and it destroyed Israel. We focus on the story of King David and his son Solomon in building the famed temple in Jerusalem. David, believing the best architects in the world then were from Phoenicia, arranged with Phoenicia's King Hiram to use these artists. In exchange David gave Hiram several cities in the part of Israel closest to Phoenicia. However, the Israelites were forced to work on the temple *without compensation.*

Eventually, Babylon invaded Israel and carried the Israelites into captivity. Giuseppi Verdi immortalized this loss of freedom in his opera, "Nabucco" (for Nebuchadnezzar, king of Babylon).

Verdi, elected to the first free parliament of Italy, was a member of the Italian classical economic liberals who greatly admired the Physiocrats (of whom, more later) and were friends of Richard Cobden, for example. Verdi closes his opera with the "Chorus of the Hebrew Slaves," who were in chains and lamenting their failure to guard their freedoms. This chorus became the rallying cry for the forces of classical economic liberalism in Italy.

Greece

Much is known about the profound intellectual battle between Plato, "Father of Socialism," and Aristotle, "Father of Natural Law Philosophy" and free market economics. We will not dwell upon that here except to note that for the 2,000 years since then, economists have been fighting the same battle.

Not widely known, however, is that Plato, who wished a benevolent "philosopher-king" to plan men's lives to the smallest detail, may have reversed his position later in life. Plato's *Republic* is the model for a government-controlled state. His lesser-known *The Laws* indicates he may have been mistaken. Why so? Plato as a noted philosopher of his time was asked by the Greek ruler of Syracuse, an ancient city state, to become an economic advisor. Honored, Plato accepted. The problem was that the tyrant of Syracuse differed with Plato on some points, and Plato fled in order to "save his neck."

Another well-known Greek deserves some notice. The dramatist Aristophanes' play *Women in Parliament* ridiculed socialism, and his comedy *The Frogs* anticipated Gresham's Law by more than 1,700 years.

Greek history has particular tales of special courage. One such is the story of Thermopolyae, where Leonidas and 300 Spartans knowingly fought to their death defending the idea of Greek freedom (however imperfect) from the onslaughts of Persian despotism. One of the most poignant reminders of Thermopolyae is from the great poet George Gordon, Lord Byron. In a poem written about Thermopolyae, Byron writes:

> Earth! render back from out thy breast
> A remnant of our Spartan dead!
> Of the three hundred grant but three
> To make a new Thermopolyae.

Continuing, Byron speaks also about George Washington's struggles of centuries later:

Leonidas and Washington
Whose every battle field is holy ground
Which breathes of nations saved, not
worlds undone."[2]

Rome: On Pertinax

Publius Helvius Pertinax (126–193), the son of a freed slave and earthy teacher of philosophy, became a statesman, general and emperor. But this student of ideas wished to reform the corruption that was Rome. When his cutting of government expenditure infringed on too many vested interests, even his own guard turned against him. Pertinax knew it, but (like the brave Socrates) he went to meet and admonish his detractors. Though shamed momentarily, they drew their swords against him and he was decapitated. And so there developed the "Pertinax Syndrome," with countless examples through all of history.

China

As the Chinese were the first to invent paper, so they were the first to employ paper money. Paper being easier to devalue than metals, the government engaged in an early inflation. Around the time of Marco Polo—long before the West even had paper—two Chinese philosophers Yeh Shih (1150–1223) and Yuan Hsieh (*Ca.* 1223) realized that perhaps government should prohibit the use of paper money (at least without specie backing).

Medieval Islam:

The Saracens

When in the Dark Ages a good part of Europe was subsisting miserably in a uniform grayness of squalor, ignorance, and hopeless apathy; when one of her greatest kings, Charlemagne, could not write,[3] and intellectual thought was rare, there existed another civilization which was vibrant, prosperous and tolerant. Its intellectual world crystallized ideas which would have a profound and lasting influence. Three and one-half centuries before Columbus, a prodigy of this culture could write: "The earth is round like a sphere and the waters adhere to it through natural equilibrium which suffers no variation."[4] This was the Saracen civilization, which at its height extended from southern France and Switzerland to the Congo, and from the Atlantic to India.

It was a civilization with thriving cities. Cordova bustled with 1 million inhabitants, 260,000 buildings and shops, 4,300 markets, 700 bathing establishments, 500 mosques, countless public and private libraries, 28 suburbs, the greatest center of Arabic book trade in the west,[5] and a business metropolis which exported glassware, bound books, and rugs throughout East and West.[6] Marrakesh in the middle of the Sahara boasted over 200 bookstores.[7] Cities were lighted at night for many miles by public oil lamps on asphalt paved streets.[8] It seems almost anticlimactic to note the greatness of Baghdad at this time, where men and women discussed Aristotle, and the pleasures described in *The Arabian Nights* were shared by multitudes.

Its society offered Moslem, Christian, Jew, man or woman the chance to rise as far as talent and luck would allow. Its golden age lasted about six centuries, from 700 to 1300 A.D. No less spectacular were the economic achievements of the Saracens.

In the areas of economic history and the history of economic theory, the Saracens deserve a critical place. It was no mere coincidence that the economic renaissance of Europe, which began in the twelfth-century Italian towns of Venice, Lucca and Florence, had its origins in cities to which the medieval Moors of Sicily, Spain, and the near East traded their commodities and ideas.

Saracen Economic Thought

Among the Saracens were many thinkers; they generally knew the works of Aristotle but not Plato, and furthered the idea of a free market. These included Al Dimisqui, Al Idrisi, Al Farabi, Ibn Battula, Ibn Khurradbah, and Ibn Sina (Avicenna in the West). But by far their greatest thinker and philosopher economist was Ibn Khaldun (A.D. 1332-1406).[9]

Robert Flint claims, "Plato, Aristotle were not his peers and all others were unworthy of being mentioned with him."[10]

Interestingly enough, he wrote during the declining period of their civilization. Tired of what he saw around him, he returned with his family to the castle of Qalat Ibn Salana near Oman, Tunisia and for four years worked on *The Mugaidimah*, which means introduction in Arabic. Also called *Prologemna* in the West, it is an analysis of the forces that bring rises and declines of civilizations. It is a masterful work, predating by many centuries ideas of Adam Smith and others. In his earlier life he tried politics and, disgusted with its corruption by that time, eventually became a professor of jurisprudence at the University of Qambiyah. He did then rise to being the Grand Cadi (Chief Justice of the Courts) in Cairo.

Khaldun's major work, *Prologemna*, written in 1377, realized that land, labor, capital, and entrepreneurship were the factors of economic development. Man did best when unfettered by government. Profit was not exploitation but a reward for industry which benefited all. He despised the practice of the government debasing money (which formerly had been pure). Centuries before John Locke and David Hume, he understood the sophistication of an international gold standard and wrote that free trade without tariffs is the best trade practice to follow. Free trade would insure that countries which did not have gold would prosper and that countries which had gold would nonetheless be poor if they did not use free trade and free enterprise. Five hundred years before Adam Smith, he discussed the division of labor and the harmony of interests in a free market.

Ibn Khaldun warned against high taxation—it had been low in the earlier periods of their civilization. He said he saw his civilization crumbling and would write so the world would know why. In the final stages:

> Famine and deaths begin to increase towards the end of the state, Famines increase because many people begin to give up cultivation owing to the increased burden of taxation and the insecurity of property; owing also to the widespread rebellions and troubles...[11]

Ibn Khaldun implied that if the medieval Arabs did not understand their free roots and curtail the power of the state and certain religious fanatics, their civilization would become nothing but "sand blowing in the wind" and no one would remember them.

One of his translators said, "Ibn Khaldun remained for five centuries a prophet without honor in either his own country or abroad."[12]

Some Events in the Middle Ages

One lesser-known but nonetheless colorful event of the Middle Ages was the origin of the phrase "Business is business." This was coined by an heir of a medieval banking family, one Jacob Fugger (who, unusually, was not an Italian but a German). It seems he lent money to a prince (a prerequisite for getting a government banking license, which eventually ruined most bankers) who refused to repay the loan to his bank. Fugger shocked the world when he wrote the prince and asked him to repay, please, because after all...business is business.

Governments for centuries accorded monopoly privilege to various groups, and usually took a cut of the monopoly action, causing the masses to live lives which were in the words of the philosopher Thomas Hobbes, "nasty, brutish and short." Eventually, however, even this monopoly trade brought about demands for some freedoms, and the government sometimes realized it should not kill the goose that laid the golden eggs.

The Physiocrats

Any follower of the history of economic thought will know of the profound work of the Physiocrats, mostly French, in paving the way for the economic liberty following the Enlightenment.

What is slightly less known are their methods of drawing attention to their ideas. Their dilemma was one many followers of reform had faced before and faced after. Who should be trusted to change society—should there be a revolution "from above" or from the masses "below" (who held no power and were then greatly illiterate or superstitious or both). However, the masses were not totally hopeless, even then. After all there had been at least three famous peasant revolts in the Middle Ages (England, Germany and Sicily) proving that somehow the desire for freedom is innate regardless of societal position. Those revolts were thwarted cruelly.

So what were the Physiocrats to do? Surely, they had heard of Plato's "benevolent despot" who would lead their country to great things, but they wanted the great thing to be freedom and not Plato's socialism. Because of the realities of Versailles and the age in which they lived, they chose to influence those at the top. Perhaps the king (if not his corrupt courtiers) had some feeling for his people. His ego could be bolstered by his becoming "benevolent."

In addition, the Physiocrats cultivated a fantastic wit, if only to amuse the aristocrats and gain their attention. This they did so well that duchesses galore invited them to parties in the grand salons. Anne Robert Jacques Turgot even became Minister of Finance to the French king. A couple of years thereafter, he was thrown out when too many realized their privileges were to be taken away. So was the revolution to be from below?

Many Physiocrats knew some of the American Founding Fathers and saw in a young American the chances for success. A very young Physiocrat follower, the Marquis de Lafayette, used his own fortune to offer his services to a beleaguered George Washington, and just when he most needed help. Benjamin Franklin, also a consummate wit, eventually was able to get the French to aid the Americans using the same subtle diplomacy that gave the Physiocrats an early hearing.

Early Economic Thought in Russia

Many wrongly assume that Russia in the eighteenth and nineteenth centuries either produced no economic thought or had Marx and other socialists only. Virtually unknown today is the story of a Russian woman, Princess Dashkova, who furthered economics. She befriended a young Catherine the Great and began The Philosophical Society of St. Petersburg. Also, Princess Dashkova's son studied in Scotland directly under Adam Smith. In fact, Dashkova travelled to Scotland from St. Petersburg to try to steal Adam Smith for a part in the intellectual scene of St. Petersburg. She felt however that even though Smith was brilliant, he did not have much "skill with the ladies" and could not "fit in" with the life there—as the Physiocrats had done earlier in Paris. Who knows but that the history of the world might have been different had Smith been more of a *bon vivant*.[13]

Two Forgotten Female Market Economists

In the history of feminist literature, the work of Mary Wollstonecraft (later the wife of philosopher William Godwin) is the early paradigm. Her 1792 *A Vindication of the Rights of Women* inspired many women to brave writing on "serious matters." The voluminous works of two British women, Jane Haldimand Marcet and Harriet Martineau, command the attention of all those who wish to popularize the ideas of economic liberty. Their works are among the most masterful expositions of the basic realities of natural law economics.[14]

Jane Haldimand Marcet (1769-1858) came from a business family. Her brother became a director of the bank of England and a member of Parliament. Jane was given an education similar to her brothers (but unusual for a woman then). She married a Swiss physician, and they retired to Switzerland, where they counted among their friends the great British economist David Ricardo.

Marcet wrote books in Socratic dialogue fashion. These, remarkably, were meant for children, or at least the publisher was led to believe such so he would print a woman's work on economics. She told her publisher that if children and adolescents were educated properly in economics, there would be no need to "unlearn" them at the university level. What professor today of free market economics has not spent hundreds of hours on lectures designed to "unlearn" their students' unsound notions of economics. Yet these stories with attractive names like "The Three Giants" were subliminally extremely sophisticated. She even challenged some of what she considered Ricardo's mistaken notions of value theory in them.

Marcet penned many books—*Conversations on Political Economy* (1816), *John Hopkins Notions on Political Economy* (1833), and *Rich and Poor* (1851), and Marcet was highly praised by great men in the field. The renowned Jean Baptiste Say said of Jane Marcet that she was "the only woman who has written on political economy and shown herself superior even to men." Economist J. R. McCullough wrote that her work was "on the whole perhaps the best introduction to the science of political economy that has yet appeared." Lord Macauley wrote "Every girl who has read Mrs.

Marcet's little dialogues on political economy could teach Montague or Walpole many lessons in finance."

Harriet Martineau (1802-76) also came from a business family; but due to a family financial crisis and her father's early death, she was left to her own resources. She had to overcome an incredible handicap after becoming deaf at age fourteen. Martineau turned to doing needlework for subsistence, but she eventually rose to pen *Illustrations in Political Economy* (1834). She was keenly aware of the importance of the accumulation of capital, and wrote dramatic fables to illustrate her points.

As with Marcet, Martineau knew many economists of her time. She was a great help to Richard Cobden and his colleagues in their battle to repeal the Corn Laws in 1846—a symbolic victory in the struggle for liberty. Though Cobden and his colleagues wrote more sophisticated treatises, they used Martineau's work to acquaint many with free market ideas.

Liberty in the Music of Romanticism

Another woman Ayn Rand, the twentieth-century model of capitalism, wrote a work entitled *The Romantic Manifesto.* She argues that romanticism had many free market routes, and there is a psycho-epistemology to art. Some of liberty's champions are found among great composers whose works include many pleas for liberty which could not be made directly for fear of severe political reprisals. Many took the risk anyway. In Mozart's opera, *The Marriage of Figaro*, Figaro, a barber to the court, sings to a count during the time of the French Revolution: "If you wish to dance now, Mr. Count, you will dance to my tune!"

Beethoven used Schiller's *Ode to Joy* in the chorus section of his Ninth Symphony. The Ode was originally entitled, *Ode to Freedom,* but censors considered celebrating freedom too controversial. Beethoven had dedicated another masterpiece to Napoleon but withdrew the dedication when Napoleon betrayed his ideal of freedom.

Even the ballet master Adolph Adam of Paris made a statement. His greatest ballet *Giselle* tells the story of an innocent peasant girl who is betrayed by a prince, and the plea is made in the ballet to treat women with more respect and kindness. Adolph Adam corresponded with the great British classical liberal Richard Cobden and made explicit his ideas of respect for women.

A great opera composer, Verdi, was previously cited for his opera *Nabucco* about ancient Israel, and the Hebrew longing for freedom.

Finally, even the "waltz-king" Johann Strauss Jr., who was active in the Revolution of 1848 in Vienna, wrote *Die Fledermaus* ridiculing governments which raise taxes and the people who pay them. One Adele, a maid, goes to a masquerade ball, dressed as a queen. She sings:

> Born to the purple, I will walk erect,
> While the people genuflect,
> And when they hear that their taxes are increased,
> They will laugh to say the least!
> Tra la la la la.

Cobden and the Manchester Liberals

Those familiar with free market economics are familiar with the name of Richard Cobden. What they may not realize, however, is the immensity of his work, the sophistication, the wide-ranging work of his intellectual colleagues, and the international following they had. Professor Friedrich von Hayek has stated in his preface to this author's book manuscript on Cobden, that the Manchester School of Economics was more sophisticated than any had believed and that Cobden and his colleagues, many almost unremembered or unknown, now are "justly resurrected."[15] Cobden's colleagues included among others, Thomas Perronet Thompson and John Bowring. Thompson's life mirrors all that is good about free market ideas. In the early 1800s he led the fight in the British military to stop brutal flogging and other draconian measures for discipline. Later he helped lead the anti-slavery movement. Thompson later joined John Bowring in establishing a seminal journal, *The Westminster Review.*

As early as 1832, 16 years before the *Communist Manifesto,* Thompson in *The Westminster Review* critiques Saint Simons's doctrine of the "Grand Deputy" to supervise all economic activity:

> And here it is impossible to maintain a staid countenance any longer, and not to break out into the assertion that this is the shallowest plot ever begotten of human love of power or human imbecility. As if one great

lesson which the experience of all ages has impressed upon mankind, the mighty moral which failure and misfortune in every direction has been whipping into the world since the creation, though it appears without ultimate success, was not, that whoever has brains so unwashen as to give up the guidance of himself and his concerns to any man or collection of men, call it Pope, Papa, Priest, Parliament, Parish-Officer, in the confidence that they, in their superior wisdom and prodigious virtue are to do better for him than he can compass for himself—is as sure to be cheated as fatlings to be eaten.

Thompson continues, responding to one of Saint Simon's notions:

Things will never go right till [sic] select vestries rule the world ... This is a "cock and bull" story to attract the working classes by promises which with half an eye may be seen to be impossible... The Saint Simonians are not in the Middle Ages, but they will be as like [them] as they can. They are a reproduction of the fallacy "Give us all power and you shall see how happy we will make you"[16]

Sir John Bowring, another Cobden colleague, was also a "romantic" figure with a colorful international life. In the early nineteenth century Bowring was active in financing "The Greek Committee" with the poet Lord Byron, which raised a volunteer force of internationals who wished to "liberate" Greece from eastern oppression under the Turks. Bowring, who knew an incredible 23 languages, introduced free thought to the King of Siam and tried to convert the Pasha of Egypt to free enterprise. The Pasha's family later paved the way for the Suez Canal, built by Frenchman Ferdinand de Lesseps, a member of the international "Cobden Club of Political Economy."

When Cobden died, he was mourned all over the world as if he had been a citizen of people's own nations. Cobden was called "The International Man" and known as "The Apostle of Free Trade." As Wilhelm Röpke wrote of the Cobden Club just after the horrors of World War II:

Free Trade, Peace, Goodwill Among Nations—that was Cobden's battle-cry, and its nobility stifles any attempt to smile it off with the sophistication of one above such naïveties. We have heard other battle-cries since then which have wiped the smiles off our faces.[17]

Notes and References

1. Mises, Ludwig von, *Human Action,* 3rd ed. (New York, NY: Regnery, 1963), p. 885.
2. Gordon, George, (Lord Byron); *Don Juan Canto III,* stanza 86 & 87; *Canto IV,* stanza 5.
3. See discussion of Charlemagne in Asimov, Isaac, *The Dark Ages* (Boston, MA: Houghton Mifflin, 1963), pp. 168-69.
4. al Idrisi, *The Book of Roger or The Vocation of a Man Desirous of a Full Knowledge of the Different Countries of the World.* Translated from Arabic and quoted in Norwich, John Julius, *The Kingdom in the Sun, (Sicily 1130-1194)* (New York, NY: Harper & Row, 1970), p. 102.
5. It was the Saracens who devised the concept "book", as we know it, pages bound at one side with a separate cover and a flap to protect the edges.
6. For statistics, see Descola, Jean, *A History of Spain* (New York, NY: Knopf, 1967), pp. 110-111.
7. Welch, Galbraith, *North African Prelude* (New York, NY: Morrow, 1949), p. 291.
8. See description of Saracen daily life in Lane, Rose Wilder, *The Discovery of Freedom,* 2nd Edition (New York, NY: Arno Press and the New York Times, 1972), part 2, Ch. 2. Also Weaver, Henry Grady, *The Mainspring of Human Progress* (Irvington, NY: Foundation for Economic Education, 1953).
9. Castorina, Camille, "The Economic Thought of the Saracens," unpublished manuscript.
10. Flint, Robert, "History of the Philosophy of History," in Charles Issawi ed., *An Arab Philosophy of History: Selections from the Prolegomena of Ibn Khaldun of Tunis* (London: Murray, 1963).
11. Issawi edition (Quatremere edition, Vol II, p. 24), p. 96.
12. *Ibid.,* p. 25.
13. See the pathfinding work on Dashkova and the Philosophical Society in the work of Professor Glenn Alexandrin, unpublished manuscripts, Villanova University, Villanova, PA.
14. For a brief introduction to their works (as well as some women socialists) see Thompson, Dorothy Lampen, *Adam Smith's Daughters* (New York, NY: Exposition Press, 1973).
15. Hayek, Friedrich, preface to Castorina, Camille, *Cobden and the Manchester Liberals,* (book under review). See also Castorina, Camille, *Richard Cobden and the Intellectual Development and Influence the*

Manchester School of Economics, Dissertation (University of Manchester, England, 1976).
16. Thompson, Thomas Perronet, "St. Simonianism." *The Westminster Review* 1 (April, 1832). Also reprinted in Thompson Exercises. See quotation in Castorina, Camille, "Cobdenism for the 1980s." *Economic Affairs* (London) Mar-April 1985.
17. Röpke, Wilhelm, *Against the Tide*, "The Centenary of British Free Trade," trans. Elizabeth Henderson. Orig. publ. for *Neue Zurcher Zeitung,* 17 July 1946 (Chicago, IL: Regnery 1969), p. 103.

9

OUR COMMON ROAD TO THE MARKET*

Edwin G. Dolan**

I have been invited here at the end of a year living and teaching in Moscow to address the question, "Is a transition to a market economy possible in the Soviet Union?" I will be happy to address this question, but permit me please to expand it to include also the question, "Is a transition to a market economy possible in the United States?" I wish to address this expanded version of the question to emphasize that the common struggle of our two countries to move toward a market economy is an element that unites us.

So, then, is a transition to a market economy possible for either of our countries? Yes, I think so. In recent years, we have both achieved significant successes in this direction. Of course, the road is a long one. Both of us are far from the end of it. But there is hope, provided we understand clearly where we are going and just what is the nature of our common goal.

Perhaps this whole way of posing the question seems strange to you. What am I talking about? A transition of the American economy to a market system? Isn't that exactly what we already have?

No. A market economy—capitalism, if you prefer that eminently proper term—is an *ideal* that neither we nor you have yet achieved. Maybe to go all the way to this ideal is impossible for either of us. But to make progress in that direction certainly is

*Note: This paper was originally presented as a lecture in Russian at Moscow State University in May 1991, at the invitation of the Moscow University Club of Liberal Economists. The following text is a translation by the author, slightly edited for inclusion in this volume.

**Dr. Dolan is affiliated with Gettysburg College and The Russian-American University (Moscow).

possible—if, as I have said, we understand just where we are going.

What, then, is a market economy? Such a system, in my view, is based on three principles.

First, private property in all things that can be owned—industrial capital, land, natural resources, housing—including, of course, not just formal title to these things but also the right to buy and sell them. Especially important is the property right of each person in his or her own self—nothing other than the absence of slavery.

Second, freedom of contract. This includes the right to buy or sell any good or service for any mutually agreeable price; the right to refuse to enter into any transaction that is not to your liking; the right to produce any good if you can manage to conclude the necessary voluntary contracts with suppliers and customers; and the right to work for anyone you want and to hire anyone you want at any mutually agreeable rate of pay.

Third, freedom of international trade and travel, including the right to establish permanent or temporary residence wherever you choose. But in fact, this is nothing but freedom of contract extended to contracts between residents of separate countries, and in that sense, is not really a separate issue. So in that sense, there are only two conditions that define a market economy: private property and freedom of contract.

That is our common goal. We, like you, are far from it. In our country as in yours, there is a massive number of governmental interventions in the economy, of barriers to free enterprise. In our country, although you may not realize it, more than a third of all land belongs to the government. (Granted, that's better than 100 percent, as here.) We, like you, have many controls on prices, many restrictions on trade. We, like you, are struggling to free ourselves from these nonmarket elements of our economy. How exactly can we do so? I think a first requirement is that we free ourselves from certain widespread myths.

The first is the myth of *convergence*—the notion that our two systems are moving toward each other in the direction of some central point. I remember this myth as a powerful article of faith during my graduate school days in the 1960s. But the facts do not bear out this myth. Not only would such a convergence be highly undesirable—it is not taking place. In recent years we have been moving decisively in the opposite direction, away from the middle ground—away from it and toward the market. By "we," I mean not only we in the United States, but also the major countries of Western Europe, the new industrial powerhouses of Asia, and even a majority of countries of the third world. This general movement toward the market is taking place along three broad fronts: privatization, deregulation, and increasing openness of international trade.

In the area of privatization, the lead role was taken by the Thatcher government in Great Britain, which sold a national airline, gas company, telephone company and many other state enterprises. But privatization in Europe has been no conservative monopoly. Across the English channel, French socialists, led by President Francois Mitterand, were busily at work selling nationalized banks and industrial companies. Elsewhere in the world, Japan has privatized its telephone company, Mexico has sold nationalized banks and sold or closed many money-losing industrial concerns. In the United States, where relatively few firms had ever been nationalized, the most important direction of privatization has been contracting out the provision of services formerly provided by government, such as garbage collection, prison operation, and park management.

On the deregulation front, the United States has led the way. As recently as fifteen years ago, there existed pervasive price controls and barriers to competition in such industries as transportation (trucking, airlines, railroads, buses), finance (banking, brokerage services), and long-distance telephone service. Today all of these sectors are characterized by extensive competition and freedom of price formation. The result? Lower prices on the average, a broadening of the range of service options for consumers, the entry of numerous new firms, and the disappearance of old ones that could not adapt to the new competitive circumstances. Even in areas where the government continues to play an active regulatory role, such as protection of the environment, market-oriented methods of regulation are gaining credibility relative to the traditional administrative-command methods.

As for the opening of international trade, some simple figures show what has been accomplished. Twenty years ago, the sum of imports plus exports relative to Gross National Product in the United States was only about 12 percent. Today it is approaching

30 percent. The result—a distinct improvement in living standards, especially with regard to the quality and range of choice of consumer goods. The movement toward the creation of European and North American trade zones free of internal barriers is an especially encouraging sign. Even greater results will follow if the newly democratic counties of Eastern Europe and the third world can be brought into such free trade areas, and if free movement of goods between, as well as within, zones can be achieved.

To be sure, much remains to be done. But the direction of movement is clear. There is no convergence. We are moving toward the market, and you, we hope, are headed in the same direction.

Now the second myth—the myth of the mixed economy. This is the idea that the best of all possible economic systems is one that somehow combines features of capitalism and socialism, thus achieving all the proclaimed benefits of both. Yet the middle turns out to be not the firmest ground to build on, but rather, a treacherous swamp.

Unfortunately, the myth of the mixed economy remains a seductive one. How many times, reading the Soviet press today, do we not encounter the following primitive syllogism?

Major premise: In the West, all is well—prosperity is everywhere.

Minor premise: In the West, we see such-and-such examples of intervention in the market, or state monopolies, or price controls, or trade barriers—all sorts of things.

Conclusion: If we, too, include those interventions, monopolies, controls and barriers in the market system we are building, we, too, will prosper.

We could laugh at this, if it weren't so tragic. Sometimes your policy makers remind me of the cargo cults that sprang up in the South Pacific during World War II. The war brought many new things to the native islanders—beer, for example. They carefully watched how the American fliers opened their refrigerators and extracted this wonderful new beverage. If only they had such refrigerators! After the war, when the fliers went home, the islanders carefully built their own wooden refrigerators complete with all the details—knobs, handles, a vine for a power cord—but when they opened them, there was no beer.

To speak seriously, at the heart of the myth of the mixed economy is a simple failure to understand that the interventions, monopolies and controls that are so widespread in the West are not our virtues, but our vices. The West is prosperous not because of such policies, but in spite of them. We are doing everything we can to rid ourselves of these policies as fast as possible—and you want to copy them?

The third myth I want to address is the myth of the cautious transition. Suppose we are convinced that the territory between the administrative-command economy and the market is indeed dangerous. Does it not follow that we should make the transition slowly, cautiously, pausing at each step like a tightrope walker? But in the sphere of economics, the saying, "Slow and steady wins the race," is not always applicable. If we want to borrow a metaphor from the circus, the correct one is not the tightrope walker, but the daredevil who dashes through a corridor of fire. If he runs full speed, he makes it. If he slows down, that's the end of him.

Won't a rapid transition lead to chaos? Of course it will. But there's chaos, and then there's chaos. Either there's that destructive chaos that exists already, the chaos of a collapsing economy, of hyperinflation, of civil conflicts, or there's an entirely different, constructive chaos, out of which can be born a new spontaneous order. In what lies the difference? It lies in the fact that in the destructive chaos—the chaos of collapsing socialism—people can save themselves only at the expense of their neighbors. But in the chaos of the market, people can advance their own interests only on the basis of voluntary, mutually beneficial cooperation with their neighbors. Adam Smith saw this clearly enough more than 200 years ago. Isn't it about time for economic thought in this country to advance to the eighteenth century?

And don't think that chaos is a property only of the transitional period. A fully developed market economy is chaotic in many ways. That, in fact, is the source of the market's adaptability and creativity. The most orderly of all economic systems is, no doubt, the Soviet-style administrative-command economy. In such a system there is nothing unpredictable—because there is nothing free, nothing human. If that kind of order (stagnation might be a better word) is what you want, the choice is open to you.

Now we come to the last of our myths—the myth of the saving angel. I know this myth has a long tradition in Russian culture, from Pushkin's Tatyana to the peasants who waited patiently for the arrival of a good tsar. The modern version of the saving angel is help from the West. As in Marx's day, a specter is stalking Europe. But instead of the specter of communism, this specter is a minister of the Soviet government, stalking from capital to capital, hat in hand, begging a billion francs here, a billion marks there.

It reminds me of the old story about the believer whose home was threatened by a flood. The water was already three feet deep in the street when the driver of the last truck out of town saw him praying on his porch. "Come with me, I'm the last truck," he calls.

"No, I'll stay and pray. God will save me," answers our believer.

Soon the water is as high as the second floor window. The pilot of the last boat to leave town sees our friend standing at the window, praying. "Come with me, I'm the last boat," he calls.

"No, I'll stay and pray, God will save me."

Now the water is up to the rooftop. The pilot of the last helicopter sees our friend praying on the roof, already up to his knees in water. He offers help, but again our believer refuses. He continues to pray. In a few minutes, the water rises a bit more and he is swept away and drowns.

A short time later he finds himself standing before St. Peter's throne. As St. Peter hands him the keys of heaven, our friend risks a question. "I don't mean to criticize, he says, but I prayed, I had faith—and yet you let me drown. There's something here I just don't understand."

"Ah," says St. Peter. "An interesting point. There's something here we don't understand either. First, we sent you a truck, then we sent you a boat, then we sent you a helicopter. Exactly what more did you want us to do?"

The moral of the story, of course, is that God helps those who help themselves. And we in the West also are prepared to help those who take on themselves the responsibility of removing the barriers to effective aid. I'm not speaking so much of government-to-government aid, which has a limited role to play, at best, but of real aid in the form of private capital and know-how. Who wants to build a factory in a country where you can't own the ground the factory stands on? Who wants to sign a contract when there is no working legal system through which to enforce it? Who wants to seek out opportunities for profit in a country where the activity of earning a profit is defined in the criminal code as "speculation" and subject to the strictest penalties? The basic legal reforms needed to attract Western capital don't require billions of dollars in government aid—they require only a willingness to assume responsibility, to decide, and to act.

So here's my advice to you. It's time to decide. You can decisively begin a transition to a market economy, introducing the basic institutions of private property, freedom of contract, and free trade. In that case, we're your partners, your traveling companions, because we're headed along that same road, and we'll share our supper with you on the way. Or you can decide to remain in that treacherous swamp between two systems—and we'll pray for the salvation of your souls as we float by in our boat.

10

VARIATIONS ON THE DEMAND FOR MONEY THEME: Ludwig von Mises and Some Twentieth-Century Views

Richard M. Ebeling*

The generally recognized centerpiece of Austrian monetary theory is its emphasis on the non-neutrality of money. In contrast to the predominant focus of macroeconomic theory during the last fifty years, Austrians have been reluctant to pursue an analysis of economy-wide economic fluctuations that fails to ground the investigation in a microeconomic sequence-analysis. Their rationale for this has been based on two arguments. The first rests upon the postulate of *methodological individualism*: all changes in market demand and supply, including the demand for or supply of money, originate in either a change in the preferences or the endowments of the individual market participants whose choices and actions are the foundation of all economic activity. Therefore, any theory that fails to base its conclusions thoroughly upon an analysis that begins with and follows through the decisions of the individual actors whose behavior generates all "macro" outcomes is constructed in a manner inconsistent with the discipline's "first principles."

The second argument is based upon the idea of *theoretical sufficiency,* i.e., no analysis of market phenomena should be reduced in terms of conceptual simplification beyond that level consistent with the nature of the problems requiring explanation. The Austrian critique of macroeconomics centers on this point more than on anything else. The standard analysis of output and employment *as a whole* treats an economy as if it were a single production unit. The "price level" is juxtaposed to the "wage

*Mr. Ebeling is Professor of Economics, Hillsdale College, Hillsdale, Michigan.

level" to evaluate profits "in general," and, therefore, to the amount of total or aggregate employment and output it is lucrative for employers "in general" to generate. To the Austrian, such an approach not only involves excessive simplification, but is also, in fact, simplistic. It subsumes under the heading of aggregate supply and demand all of the interdependent and relative price relationships between industries and sectors of the economy that are the core of understanding the reasons and motives for the hiring of particular amounts of labor and resources, and their distribution among alternative uses, in the economy *as a whole.*

This also explains why there is often misunderstanding between Austrians and macroeconomists when the former accuse the latter of ignoring the non-neutral effects of money's impact on market outcomes. For the macroeconomist money is non-neutral when changes in "total spending" bring forth "real effects," i.e., an increase or decrease in the level of *total* employment and output. For the Austrian, money is non-neutral when a change in the supply of money deflects the *structure of relative prices* from the pattern they would have followed if the monetary change had not occurred. Hence, for the Austrian, money can be non-neutral even if the total level of employment and output over the analytical period under consideration does not change. The non-neutrality of money, in the Austrian perspective, refers to modifications in relative price relationships and resource allocation and not, *per se,* to changes in aggregated quantities. For the Austrian, if the latter occurs, it is a *special case* of the more general phenomenon of money's impact on market decisions and activities.

As has often been pointed out, an understanding of how changes in the supply of money can influence the relative price structure goes back at least to Richard Cantillon in the eighteenth century.[1] But its development among the Austrians had its beginning with Ludwig von Mises's *The Theory of Money and Credit,* originally published in German in 1912.[2] It is this work, more than any other, that has served as the general framework for what has become known as the "Austrian monetary theory of the trade cycle." But Mises's analysis contained more than a theory of the effects of variations in the quantity of money. This part of his book was, in fact, an extension of his theory of the demand for money. In the history of economic theory Mises usually is credited with being one of the first to apply the concept of marginality to the theory of the demand for money. Following in the footsteps of Carl Menger,[3] Mises is seen as having developed a monetary theory that escaped from the "Austrian Circle" (through use of the regression theorem) and which pioneered what has come to be called the "cash balance" approach to the demand for money.[4] He also formulated an original method for defining money and its various component elements.[5]

What we shall attempt to do in this paper is to contrast Mises's theory of the demand for money—as a choice-theoretic, microeconomic theory—with a number of alternative formulations in the twentieth century. First, we shall compare Mises's theory with that of A. C. Pigou, who usually is credited with having been a founder of the Cambridge cash balance approach. Then we shall compare Mises's theory with the two leading macroeconomic theories, the Keynesian and the Monetarist.

The Cambridge and Austrian Cash Balance Approaches to the Demand for Money

Formulation of the Cambridge theory is usually attributed to Alfred Marshall, but its influence was felt predominantly through "oral tradition" since he did not present it in published form until 1923, when his *Money, Credit and Commerce* appeared in print.[6] The first rigorous published appearance was in 1917, with Arthur C. Pigou's 1917 article, "The Value of Money."[7]

Pigou saw his analysis of the demand for money as not a denial or refutation of Irving Fisher's equation of exchange approach but an alternative way of dealing with the same question. The superiority that Pigou saw in his formulation was not that his was "truer" than Fisher's, but rather that instead of focusing on the flow of transactions (the velocity of circulation of money), "...it brings us at once into relation with volition—an ultimate cause of demand.... It focuses attention on the proportion of their resources that people choose to keep in the form of titles to legal tender."[8]

The choice facing members of a community, Pigou said, was between holding their resources in the form of consumption items, means of production for future consumption, and sums of money holdings. All three uses operate under the principle of diminishing marginal utility. But he sets aside the question of the trade-off between consumption and cash balances and sees the critical alternative between cash holdings and the future return of investing in resources transformable into future consumption.[9]

> [T]he curves that represent the desire for resources to be used in production and in money respectively both slope downward; and resources will be devoted to the two uses up to the point at which the last unit of resources devoted to each of them yields the same quantity of satisfaction.[10]

Why would community members bother to hold any portion of their resources in money form? Pigou argues that this arises from two causes: a lack of simultaneous cancellation of obligations and claims (that can result in a financial shortfall) and the uncertainty of unexpected demands for which sums of money will be required for consumption of desired transactions.[11]

How much of the community's resources will be convenient to hold in cash form is determined by two factors, Pigou argues: the purchasing power, or exchange value, of a unit of money, and the institutional setting under which financial obligations must be fulfilled and the form under which they may be extinguished. For "convenience," Pigou postulates that the relative values of commodities are determined independent of the value of money. The relative values of those commodities are expressible in terms of any one of them serving as a *numeraire* ("wheat"), and the purchasing power of a unit of money is then expressed in terms of how many bushels of wheat it can purchase. The higher the exchange value of a unit of money the fewer units will be required to facilitate a given number of desired transactions, and vice versa. Thus, the quantity of money demanded moves inversely with its purchasing power.[12]

While the demand for money is demonstrated to be a downward sloping function, its "position" is dictated by the institutional circumstances under which transactions are conducted. Among them are: the frequency of payment; the extent to which payments may be made in the form of checks instead of cash; and the degree to which financial intermediaries have developed mechanisms to economize on cash transfers, etc. These constitute the "constraints" on the economizing and use of cash holdings, and the latter changes with modifications over time in these institutional constraints.[13]

Pigou wished not to bury Fisher's equation of exchange, but to restate it in a fashion he believed more consistent with the logic of marginal choice. But by confining his exposition to the framework of Fisher's equation it can be seen as having fallen short in at least three ways. First, Pigou's demand for money is a tautology and not an explanation. If the velocity of circulation is the number of times a sum of money "turns over" during a period of time to facilitate a set of transactions, then the "demand for money" must arithmetically be its reciprocal, or that sum of money held on average by members of the community to consummate those transactions during that period of time.

Secondly, why that average demand for money is what it is, is not *explained but described.* Given the relative prices of goods (and therefore the quantities of these goods a unit of money can purchase) and given the institutional structure under which exchanges are transacted, then a certain amount of money *must* be held on average, given the frequency and number of transactions "the community" wishes to complete during a set period of time. In Pigou's formulation it remains (as in Fisher's framework) a *residual* element and not a causal one.

And, finally, Pigou's theory remains subject to the "classical dichotomy," i.e., money and the "real" economy remain compartmentalized and separate. The relative prices of goods are assumed to be formed independently of the supply and demand for money. Money, in other words, is not integrated into the market pricing process. Furthermore, money is not *directly* linked into an exchange relationship with the individual commodities against which it trades. Rather, money's value is expressed as a composite in the form of bushels of wheat serving as the *numeraire.*

Mises's formulation of the demand for money stands in stark contrast to Pigou's in certain essential ways. To begin with, the Austrian version is free from the classical dichotomy. Like Menger, Mises asks why and how money arises in the first place. And following Menger, Mises sees its origin in the inconveniences of barter with, over time, one or a few commodities possessing the characteristics most useful for the facilitation of transactions becoming the money good(s). But this means that the exchange value of the money good is inseparable from the structure of relative prices, because money begins as one of the "real" economy goods and merely extends its exchange relationship with other commodities as its role as the general medium of exchange results, at the limit, in its being on one side of every exchange.[14]

This also means that Mises's conception of the purchasing power, or exchange value, of money is different from Pigou's. Instead of that value being expressed in terms of an index of some sort (or Pigou's wheat value), the value of money is expressed as the *array of individual exchange ratios* between money and each of the individual commodities against which it trades. Hence, *changes* in money's value result from and originate in variations in those individual money-commodity exchange ratios rather than modifications in money's exchange ratio in terms of an aggregate index of goods. Indeed, Mises's formulation establishes a *direct* connection between "micro" variations and a "macro" change. The macro shift in the "general" purchasing power of money arises from the cumulative individual changes in money's exchange value against those other goods that more or less all move (though not necessarily simultaneously) in the same direction.[15]

While Pigou argued that his formulation's advantage was that it focused on "volition," i.e., choice behind the demand for a commodity, we saw that in fact it remained a residual element as a proportion of the community's resources that the community "chose" to hold as cash balances. Mises argued that such an approach was insufficient:[16]

> It is inadmissible to begin with the demand for money of the community. The individualistic economic community as such, which is the only sort of community in which there is a demand for money, is not an economic agent. It demands money only insofar as its individual members demand money. The demand for money of the economic community is nothing but the sum of the demands for money of the individual economic agents composing it.

The individual demands for money, Mises admits, are influenced by custom, habits, institutional arrangements of production and exchange—but they are not determined by them. "[A]ll these objective factors always affect the matter only as motivation of the individual," he says. "They are never capable of a direct influence upon the actual amount of the demand for money. Here, as in all departments of economic life, it is the subjective valuations of the separate economic agents that alone are decisive." And these subjective valuations potentially vary from individual to individual.[17]

The demand for money arises from the desire to take advantage of exchange opportunities, the consummation of which would be either impossible or extremely difficult without possession of sums of the general medium of exchange. Yet, possession of money balances at any time excludes the immediate possession of either consumer goods or means of production for future consumption. Thus, there are opportunity costs of holding money, that are weighed at the margin. Cash balances held, therefore, are not a residual but an active choice made by the individual for purposes of desired transactions in the future.[18]

The weighing by each individual of the marginal utility of a sum of money in relation to a quantity of each commodity that could be bought with money compositely generates the market money prices of those goods, and at the same time, by implication, the relative price structure among all goods as reflected in the amounts of money offered for each one. The establishment of the array of money prices also determines the purchasing power of a unit of the money good, and then acts as a feedback influence on each individual's valuation of the sum of cash balances worth holding at the margin. The interaction between the individual's demands for money and the existing supply of money produces a monetary equilibrium that determines the general purchasing power of money and the accompanying structure of relative prices expressed through money. And the same analytical framework served Mises as a foundation for his theory of changes in the value of money arising from changes in the supply of or demand for money.

The value of this approach was expressed by Joseph Schumpeter in his *History of Economic Analysis:*[19]

> ...the Austrian way of emphasizing the behavior or decision of individuals and of defining exchange value of money with respect to individual commodities rather than with respect to a price level of one kind or another has its merits, particularly in the analysis of an inflationary process: it tends to replace a simple but inadequate picture by one which is less clear-cut but more realistic and richer in results.

The Keynesian and Monetarist Debate over the Demand for Money and the Misesian Perspective

For almost thirty-five years the Keynesian and monetarist debate has revolved around two questions: What are the relevant arguments in the demand for money function; and, is the money demand function "stable"?

The debate seems to have been more or less won by the monetarists. Keynes had argued, in *The General Theory,* that consumption was basically insensitive to changes in the rate of interest. Out of a given income a certain proportion was devoted to consumption expenditures (as explained by the "propensity to consume"). The residual unspent was "saved." In what form that unspent margin was saved was determined by the opportunity cost of holding idle (or "speculative") balances—the rate of interest to be earned on bonds.[20]

In Keynes's analysis, the demand for money when viewed as a proportion of income is potentially an extremely unstable function. Since a decline in the quantity demanded for bonds when interest rates fall cannot be offset by a redirection of spending toward consumption, the proceeds from the bond sales can only flow into additional holdings of cash balances. Hence, the proportion of income held as cash balances rises, and "total spending" in the economy tends to be significantly less.

The logical shortcoming in this conception of the opportunity cost of holding was pointed out as early as 1940 by Dennis Robertson:[21]

> Such phrases as that interest is not the reward of not-spending, but the reward of not-hoarding seem to indicate a curious inhibition against visualizing more than two margins at once. A small boy at school is told that if he wins a race he may have either an apple or an orange. He wins the race and chooses the orange. When his mother asks him how he got it, must he reply "I got it for not eating an apple"? May he not say proudly "I got it for not losing a race"?

The case against Keynes's formulation was made in the strongest form in the years after the Second World War by Milton Friedman in his essay, "The Quantity Theory of Money—A Restatement."[22] What Friedman did, in fact, was to emphasize all the multiple margins that enter into the decision concerning what proportion of one's "wealth" one will hold in the form of cash balances. The demand for money is "stable" for the monetarists, as captured in Friedman's theory, in two meanings. First, it is stable as a proportion of income; a decrease in bond holdings from a decrease in the rate of interest results in the proceeds being redirected to many marginally attractive alternatives, so that in general only a small fraction will find its way into additional cash balances. Second, it is claimed to be stable as a predictable function of a set of empirically relevant variables.

Whether analyzed as a proportion of income, spending, or wealth, the demand for money is evaluated in purely aggregated terms by both Keynesians and monetarists. Thus for both no direct connection is made with the micro economy underlying the macro magnitudes. In general, Keynesians have viewed the structure of relative prices as an institutionally determined "datum." Monetarists, in general, postulate that the price and wage structure is competitive and fairly rapid in adjusting to change. For Keynesians, an unstable demand for money with a wage structure rigid downwards lays the seeds for fluctuations in unemployment. For monetarists, a flexible wage structure with a stable money demand function assures a stable "price level" with the capacity for requisite shifts in relative prices to assure a redistribution of labor and resources for maintenance of "full employment."

In Mises's theory there exists no counterpart of a stable money demand function, and this for two reasons. First, Mises was suspicious of all attempts to discover fixed or stable empirical relationships in a social science such as economics. All market relationships and patterns originate in the actions of individual men; and men are open to re-evaluation and change, both concerning their beliefs and their preferences:[23]

> Exchange ratios are subject to perpetual change because the conditions which produce them are perpetually changing. The value that an individual attaches both to money and to various goods and services is the outcome of a moment's choice. Every later instant may generate something new and bring about other considerations and valuations.

While money possesses unique qualities that distinguish it from other goods traded on markets and, therefore, influence the magnitude of fluctuations in the demand for it, it remains in its essentials bound by the same "laws of economics" as all other commodities and, hence, open to the same changes in demand as all the rest.

Secondly, and more importantly from Mises's perspective, it is inappropriate to speak about *the* demand for money and *its* stability. There are as many demands for money as transactors entering the nexus of exchange in the money-using economy. *The* demand for money is a statistical illusion created by the quantitatively minded economic historian investigating a specific period of economic history. Why is it not legitimate to refer to *the* demand for money in the same manner as the economist considers it legitimate to speak of the demand for eggs relative to that commodity's price?

First, there exists no single market or single price for money. Money has as many markets and prices as commodities against which money trades. The relevant markets and prices for some users of money are not necessarily the same for others—or if they overlap, they do not perfectly coincide. Second, every change in the relative demands for goods also modified the general purchasing power of money (expressed as the array of individual exchange ratios between money and other goods); and every change in the purchasing power of money resulted in the re-evaluation of money versus goods on the part of the multitude of market participants. Likewise, any change in the individual demands for money not only modified the general purchasing power of the monetary unit, but also varied the structure of relative prices as reflected in the change in spending patterns for various goods arising from the change in monetary demand. Every change in relative prices brought in its wake shifts in relative income positions that would become reflected in changes in the individual demands for money on the part of those affected by the relative price changes throughout the system of division of labor. Monetary relationships and relative price relationships were elements in one process that only worked through the actions of the transactors and their demands for various goods, of which money is the one commodity used for transacting all the others.[24]

Conclusion

The Austrian emphasis on the non-neutrality of money follows from the "Misesian" concept of the demand for money and money's exchange relationship to the commodities against which it trades. Grounded in an "individualistic" method of analysis, changes in the demand for money or in its supply are seen as originating only in the preference or endowment positions of the separate market participants. They demonstrate their changed circumstances through modification in their spending patterns for the particular commodities they wish to or have purchased. The composite outcome of the general purchasing power of money changing in one direction or another results from the cumulative changes in the individual ratios of exchange between money and various goods and services traded on the market.

As a consequence, to speak of the community's "aggregate demand for money" is not only methodologically unsound, but analytically incomplete. It ignores the fact of money's unique exchange quality of possessing no single market or single price. Rather, there are as many markets and prices for money as are reflected in exchange relations between money and goods. Which of these markets and prices are relevant at the margin for individuals in evaluating desirable cash balance holdings will vary from individual to individual, depending upon the agent's preferences, goals, and perceived opportunity costs in terms of what are viewed as substitutable alternatives, given ends in mind and means considered appropriate for their fulfillment.

The standard macroeconomic formulation aggregates the individual money demand and supply relationships underlying any statistical computations of economy-wide money demand and supply relationships. Furthermore, from the Misesian perspective the aggregate approach can easily create the impression of macroeconomic money-demand stability when, in fact, the demands for money may have been shifting significantly among individuals in various sectors of the economy. Each of these individual money-demand changes will set in motion specific required shifts in relative prices, resource and labor redistribution among alternative uses and income shares that will be hidden easily under the appearance of stable aggregate magnitudes.

The Austrian approach also highlights the fact that if unemployment of idle resources materialize in sizable amounts in the economy, the source of the problem is not a deficiency in "aggregate demand" due to an excessive demand for ("speculative") cash balances at the prevailing "price and wage levels." Rather, it is due to a failure of adjustment in the structure of relative money wages and prices, given changes in the demands for money balances as manifested in changed patterns of spending streams by the individual market participants. Unemployment is a microeconomic problem in the setting of the Austrian point of view.

Notes and References

1. Hayek, F. A., *Prices and Production* (New York, NY: Augustus M. Kelly, 2nd ed., 1935), pp. 1-31.
2. Mises, Ludwig von, *The Theory of Money and Credit* [1912] (New Haven, CT: Yale University Press [2nd revised ed., 1924], 1953).
3. Menger, Carl, "Geld" in *Grundsätze der Volkswirtschaftslehre* [1891] (Vienna: Holder-Pichler-Tempsky A.G., 2nd., 1923).
4. See, Ebeling, Richard M., "Ludwig von Mises and the Gold Standard," *The Gold Standard: An Austrian Perspective* (Lexington, MA: Lexington Books, 1985), p. 53, n. 13.
5. Mises, *op. cit.*, pp. 50-67.
6. Marshal, Alfred, *Money, Credit and Commerce* (London: Macmillan and Co., Ltd., 1923), pp. 38-50.
7. Pigou, Arthur C., "The Value of Money" [1917] in *Readings in Monetary Theory* (Homewood, IL: Richard D. Irwin, Inc., 1951), pp. 162-183.
8. *Loc. cit.*, p. 174.
9. *Loc. cit.*, pp. 166-167.
10. *Loc. cit.*, p. 168.
11. *Loc. cit.*, p. 164.
12. *Loc. cit.*, p. 163.
13. *Loc. cit.*, pp. 170-173.
14. Mises, *op. cit.*, pp. 30-34.
15. *Loc. cit.*, pp. 187-194.
16. *Loc. cit.*, pp. 131-132.
17. *Loc. cit.*, p. 132.
18. Mises, Ludwig von, *Human Action, A Treatise on Economics* [1949] (Chicago, IL: Henry Regnery Co., 3rd rev. ed., 1966), pp. 404, 430.
19. Schumpeter, Joseph A., *History of Economic Analysis* (New York, NY: Oxford University Press, 1954), p. 1090.
20. Keynes, John Maynard, *The General Theory of Employment, Interest and Money* (New York, NY: Harcourt, Brace & World, Inc., 1936).
21. Robertson, Dennis H., "Mr. Keynes and the Rate of Interest," *Essays in Monetary Theory* (Bombay: Asia Publishing House, 1940), p. 27.
22. Friedman, Milton, "The Quantity Theory of Money—A Restatement," *Studies in the Quantity Theory of Money,* ed. by Milton Friedman (Chicago, IL: University of Chicago Press, 1956), pp. 3-21.
23. Mises, *Human Action, op. cit.*, p. 217.
24. *Loc. cit.*, p. 418.

11

THE ANONYMOUS LIFE

Ridgway K. Foley, Jr.

To the extent that they consider the human right to and yearning for freedom at all, Americans display a striking tendency to concentrate upon the active aspects of liberty. A review of some of those cherished and transcendent freedoms supposedly guaranteed by the First Amendment—speech, press, religion, expression, association and petition—affords both an apt example of this trend and a starting point for analysis of another, even more precious, incorporated set of human rights, the right to be left alone, to be passive, to live an anonymous life if you will. Myopic focus upon the active sense solely will do more than obscure the entire spectrum of proper human moral choice; left unchecked, it will devour the whole, leaving useless skeletal remains in the place of something once vital and vigorous.

Return to yesteryear, and review a synopsis of First Amendment history as a backdrop for this commentary.

Most of the men who constructed the Constitution in that fateful summer of 1787 saw neither need nor reason for explication of the rights now expressed in the First Amendment.[1] They presupposed the existence of those rights from both the context of the Constitution and the ideological history just past. Further, although ardent Federalists such as Alexander Hamilton may have harbored suppressed intentions regarding a more powerful national government, most of the draftsmen assumed both the existence of rights of press, expression, religion and association, and their protection by virtue of the constitutions of the thirteen former colonies. After all, at least in theory, these framers were constructing a federation of *sovereign* states, a federal union of strictly limited powers, and each such state retained all the undelegated powers and privileges

*Dr. Foley is an author and an attorney in private practice.

tant and then-novel obligation to protect the God-granted liberties of its citizens.

Nonetheless, many of the former colonists and not a few of the delegates to the convention at Philadelphia had serious misgivings. They suspected and greatly feared the essential tyranny imbedded in *any* government: Supposition was fine, but English constitutional history was littered with the trials and travails of those subjects residing in a nation which relied upon an unwritten constitution, one which tended to expand and contract across the centuries. Further, the monarchical and aristocratic excesses in other European states increased this basic concern and heightened the desire for something enduring and precise in regard to those particular freedoms which had been trampled recently and repeatedly. Thus, in order to secure ratification of this new Constitution, ten amendments spelling out a number of express rights relevant to the then recent past were added to the proposed draft; then, and only then, could ratification ensue. First among these ten additions was the promise that the federal government would neither establish nor interfere with the exercise of religious belief, a free press, or personal association, petition and expression.

During the United States's first century of life, scant gloss appeared upon these transcendent values. Men understood such basic rights. Their fathers and grandfathers had fought for them and they were clear and very special. Often these rights were expressed in even greater detail in state constitutions. The Civil War amendments, specifically referencing only the right to due process of law, made no patent mention of other fundamental rights; these mid-nineteenth century accretions prohibited involuntary servitude, created a federal citizenship, and assured all citizens of equal privileges and immunities, due process and equal protection of the laws. It remained for the twentieth-century Supreme Court to concoct an *inclusive* theory whereby the Fourteenth Amendment was said to selectively "incorporate" the essence of our celebrated Bill of Rights.[2] Until Reconstruction and the Granger movement at least, a consensus clearly understood and agreed that governments ought to leave men and women alone and free to speak, write, think, believe and associate as they pleased, so long as they did no harm to their neighbors. Indeed, America became haven and home to all manner of disbelievers, strange believers, and ardent believers, all of whom found space in a society open of texture and generally tolerant of difference. The genius of the nation arose from the contributions great and small produced by men and women unshackled to the bondage of enforced orthodoxy and incipient fascism.

As the nation matured and the Instrumentalist Revolution e-roded the basic juridical fabric of the United States, the First Amendment freedoms took on a positive or activist cast which re-mains dominant today. Litigants and courts concentrated upon the right of all manner of folk to speak their piece, no matter how dis-tasteful it might appear to others. Hence, syndicalists could utter their extreme social theories in public places; Jehovah's Witnesses could refuse to salute the flag in wartime; draft protestors could march on public ways with obscene signs. Seemingly few restric-tions crept in, ordinarily under the guise of some "Rule of Neces-sity" or need for order, but the emphasis upon openness prevailed.

No one should disparage whatever openness remains in the United States today. Sages such as John Milton early made the case that truth best tends to surface in a society where few re-straints curb diverse opinions. In the grand old English common law, the cherished rights of confrontation and cross-examination of adverse witnesses rests upon a substantially similar premise, a be-lief proved in the fire of experience over the centuries. Today's goofiness may well be tomorrow's gospel. Even if nonsense re-mains nonsensical, it does precious little harm in the absence of force; very few people in America put much credence in its home-grown national socialists of the 1930s; the corporate fascism im-posed upon us by Franklin Delano Roosevelt and his Brain Trust (*e.g.*, the National Recovery Act) caused infinitely greater and more lasting damage. A society tolerant of dissenting belief and diversity of opinion is a far happier and more advanced society than the typical mandate state of narrow consensus. The right to be wrong—and even wildly wrong—seems counterproductive of order and growth but that assumption is myth; the spontaneous society of creative individuals produces its own spontaneous order in the realm of ideas and faith as well as in the arena of production and reason. No one can fully explain why or how this works; it just does.

Nonetheless, despite the more prominent emphasis upon the ac-tive aspects of the freedoms ensconced in our Bill of Rights, the unheard and unseen facets of our basic liberties merit attention, explanation and protection. It is all too easy to overlook the distinction between the positive and negative concepts of liberty so cogently analyzed by philosophers such as Isaiah Berlin,[3] and by attention and overemphasis to subordinate or forget the importance of anonymity and withdrawal from the positive battles of the day.

A more perfect freedom results when the right to speak (or write, believe, think, assemble, associate) freely necessarily includes an equally protected right to refrain from speaking at all. Chief Justice Warren Burger put the matter plainly and persuasively when he declared that: "The right to speak and the right to refrain from speaking are complementary components of the broader concept of 'individual freedom of mind.'"[4]

Unfortunately, such high-sounding declarations of principle seldom find their way into protectable practice. Consider the continuing confrontation at the purported intersection of the First and Fifth Amendments, a multi-act drama frequently played out on the concourse and in the stores of the modern shopping mall. Customarily, a private party constructs a convenient and pleasant center or mall attractive to shoppers by virtue of free and easy parking, secure premises, clean and pleasant surroundings, and a variety of separate shops and services. The owner sells or leases space in the mall to selected shop owners or tenants who contract to purvey their goods and services and to abide by the standards of the center. Thoughtful and coordinated unitary advertising, and the lure of convenient, one-stop shopping, reduces individual tenant expense and enables the smaller enterprise to compete more favorably in the market place than if it had to "go it alone." The practical problem arises when the quiet commercial atmosphere of the mall is invaded by ideologues who do not wish to shop, and who merely seek to push petitions, stage protests, collect donations, promote religions and generally engage in their personal variety of exhortatory free speech—on the private property of the owners and tenants.

At this point, by the very nature of our highly political society, the issues set forth often contain explosively charged and emotional overtones: legalization of prostitution, marijuana, or abortion; institution or removal of the death penalty for major crimes; denunciation of American foreign or war policy; exhortation to espouse or to protest, unpopular or strange sociopolitical theories and the like. Obviously, this attempted conversion of the modern day shopping center into a replica of Hyde Park brings into conflict the desires of the owners and tenants to engage in commerce in a proper atmosphere; of the customers who wish to shop in pleasant surroundings without being subject to harangue; and of the interlopers who want to reach the greatest audience with the least effort in the shortest time in order to disseminate the message which they consider both appropriate and valuable.

This common context, a germane example of several parties asserting supposedly conflicting rights, demonstrates how a fundamental right to be left alone may be shouted down and trampled upon in the process of apparent "protection" of the narrow positive aspects of transcendent rights. After all, in a highly emotional atmosphere, the seller of shoes or doughnuts often prefers to sell shoes or doughnuts; he does not want to take a position—in either direction—on controversial issues for fear of personal harm, loss of business, community misunderstanding and a host of other concerns including his personal lack of interest in the whole matter.

Nevertheless, the Supreme Court of the United States has been loathe to recognize and sustain the rights of non-participants to avoid the political, practical and philosophical battlefield altogether. Only Justices Lewis Powell and Byron White countenanced this seminal issue in the leading case of *Pruneyard Shopping Center v. Robins.*[5] Taking as his text the principle that "the State may not compel a person to affirm a belief he does not hold,"[6] Justice Powell observed in his concurring opinion that:

> The property owner or proprietor would be faced with a choice: he either could permit his customers to receive a mistaken impression or he could disavow the messages. Should he take the first course, he effectively has been compelled to affirm someone else's belief. Should he choose the second, he has been forced to speak when he would prefer to remain silent. In short, he has lost control over his freedom to speak or not to speak on certain issues. The mere fact that he is free to disassociate himself from the views expressed on his property...cannot restore his "right to refrain from speaking at all."[7]

For Justice Powell, then, "To require the owner to specify the particular ideas he finds objectionable enough to compel a response would force him to relinquish his 'freedom to maintain his own beliefs without public disclosure,'[8] and would thus deprive the commercial property owner or lessor of his First and Fourteenth Amendment rights to refrain from speaking at all.[9]

The majority opinion in *Pruneyard* disappoints. Justice Rehnquist—classically and wrongly considered the epitome of judicial conservatism—dismissed any suggestion that a private property owner enjoys a First Amendment right to be free from any state's compulsion to use his property as a forum for the speech of others. Instead, the majority asserted that a state may exercise its police power or its sovereignty to adopt more expansive individual liberties in its own constitution than those conferred by the United States Constitution.

The majority rationale demonstrates the very problem perplexing us: Whose liberties are to be "more expansively" set forth in a state constitution? Must the private person desiring his privacy inviolate succumb to the shrill shriek of all manner of interventionists and demonstrators? State constitutions indeed ought to provide a safe harbor for individual rights but, as the wisest draftsmen of 1787 discerned, so should a national constitution; else, why have a Bill of Rights at all? It is all well and good that the current crop of Supreme Court Justices has decided that private commercial property owners need not admit those who wish to speak rather than shop under the Federal Constitution, but that is small solace to a tradesman who merely wants to trade, not talk, in a state with an "expansive" state constitution which creates "rights" for other people to come into his store and march, picket, dance, or exhort. A robbery victim doesn't really care whether his transgressor is authorized by national or local law. And, of course, to propound "police power" or some vague and unarticulated notion of "sovereignty" as a justifying rubric for the obliteration of human rights must be dismissed as either patronizing or downright addlepated. Either the First Amendment transported to the states by the Fourteenth grandly protects the transcendent rights to free expression for all (including dissenters and non-participants), or it provides an ephemeral fortification for the favored few who fit within an ever-shifting consensus. There appears to be no middle way and certainly only one correct choice.

The right to live an anonymous life partakes of the much flaunted and vaunted "right of privacy" currently in vogue. Yet, we find troubling discontinuities in this talisman, discrepancies reminiscent of those apparent in the *Pruneyard* majority. Legal historians often trace the modern right of privacy to a century-old dissertation by Samuel D. Warren and Supreme Court Justice-to-be Louis D. Brandeis.[10] In fact, Brandeis and Warren synthesized existing Anglo-American case law for their exposition concerning the existence and roots of the right of an individual to enjoy a private life unsullied by commercial exploitation. They surmised that such a right flows from the fundamental right to life and to enjoy that life, a right which inheres in an "inviolate personality." Many of the early judicial decisions sustaining such a right to privacy repudiated the non-consensual commercial use of a person's features, works, likeness, or other identifying essence; for example, one whose photograph was employed without his permission to promote a product might have a cause of action against the unauthorized user.[11]

It required no leap of logic or faith to enable the Brandeis and Warren rationale to encompass the counterfeit use of an individual's name, reputation, standing or essential being for or against an idea or an ideology. For example, a large department store contained an optical department. In 1939, the Oregon Legislative Assembly passed a bill which barred retail mercantile establishments from fitting and selling eyeglasses to the public. Mr. Hinish, a federal civil servant unconnected with the department store, sued when the store, without his knowledge or consent, dispatched a telegram over his name to the governor urging a veto of the bill as unnecessary and unwise. The Oregon Supreme Court upheld Mr. Hinish's right to recover damages from the store for this invasion of his right to be left alone.[12]

Whatever the form of the embryonic right to privacy, however well and broadly conceived, its metamorphosis has revealed a quite different creature. For example, in the name of free speech, legislators introduce bills to ban punishment or expulsion of students by private colleges for violation of codes limiting the form and content of expression and governing civil behavior. Applicants or job holders seek state inhibition of the employer's power to test (and refuse to hire, or to terminate) for the use and abuse of various harmful substances, citing some vague "privacy" concept and ignoring the employer's vicarious *(respondeat superior)* responsibility for injuries occasioned by the "stoned" worker, either to himself or to third parties. Or, further, compulsory union laws command membership in, or payment to, labor organizations at least to the extent that such mandated dues or agency shop fees are employed for collective bargaining and grievance procedures under some nebulous "free rider" concept.

These intrusions and their prolific kindred overlook the essential nature and value of true liberty: that the absence of restraints upon creative human endeavor unleashes the most moral and productive society possible. Conversely, each needless intrusion rots the fabric of freedom in exponential fashion, for it not only destroys the particular instance but also serves as precedent for succeeding and ever-increasing inroads into what should remain a personal sanctuary.

Assume the sincerity of those who believe that their design, message or program is of such importance that it ought to be imparted to and acted favorably upon by a vast audience. That is, assume that the person who enters the shopping mall to deliver a speech or push a petition does so in the fervent belief that his concern ought to be a concern of all mankind. Assume the conviction of the legislator who believes in mandatory open forums upon all issues on all campuses, public and private, without limit (even by the rules of manners and morals) upon content or comment. Assume the honesty of the union official in his supposition that failure of all members (voluntary and dissenting) to pull as one portends failure for the entire movement. The existence of these and analogical assumptions does not alter the existence and propriety of the right to privacy. Either privacy constitutes a good and desirable end, in which case it should remain consistent, complete and inviolate; or it is a limited favor, to be bestowed by the powerful and persuasive upon the special few, and subject to recapture at the bestower's whim.

No reasonable middle ground exists. Human predilection includes the natural belief in the primacy of "my way": Each of us rates our beliefs, desires, interests, and goals above those of our neighbors and friends, let alone those of some stranger. Left to our own devices, we are prone to decide that our particular idea, notion, or plan of the moment merits the breach, or at least the extension, of an otherwise good and just rule. Unfortunately, in that process we forget the brilliant aphorism of Baldy Harper that "principles break; they do not bend."[13]

Albert Jay Nock observed the intrusions of his day and foretold of invasions yet to come:

In a society like ours, bitterly resentful of privacy, the integrity of one's personality is constantly under attack from all sides; not only under direct frontal attack, but, which is worse, it is always exposed to insidious influences which will infect it and rot it down. To the individualist, the integrity thus menaced is the most precious thing on earth; and the dangers to it being what they are, they beget a corresponding extreme of sensitiveness and caution which in time becomes a sort of secondary instinct. "Hide thy life," said Epicurus, and the individualist is the one who most diligently lays that invaluable advice to heart.[14]

The siege on individualism continues unabated one-half century later. *Pruneyard* proves that legal institutions offer scant armor against the assaults of intrusion. My father perceived that tide of intrusion in a long-ago speech when he admonished that "this is the Age of the Busybody." Busybodies have now multiplied and run amok. In short, one committed to Epicurus's dictum faces truly daunting barriers.

Dislocations of freedom take place for several reasons. Tiny deteriorations of principle go unnoticed, misunderstood or unheeded. Disturbances of a consistent liberty find justification by some "greater good" argument. Malevolent men and women simply sweep away dissenters and individualists who stand in their path to power. The myriad variants that exist all fit within these three broad categories.

The right to live an anonymous life suffers greatly from those tiny assaults which, seemingly harmless standing alone, coalesce into a rapacious force fully capable of toppling the sturdiest edifice. These petty intrusions, often occurring unnoticed and with the best of superficial intentions, produce the unexpected, unobserved, and unheeded results one has come to expect from an interloper or busybody. While wickedness all too often plays a role, the more subtle deviltry of the well-meaning invasion casts a greater pall upon the right to a private life.

Several vignettes, some public, others private, should illustrate areas along the penumbra of the problem of privacy. Genealogy—the study of family history—is an increasingly popular hobby. The nascent genealogist soon learns that even our recent ancestors left precious few traces. The mere demands of survival and daily living often commandeered all available time and resources; few records were considered essential and most were maintained in a haphazard and perishable fashion; and, not a few of our forefathers feared and disliked Nosy Nellies—after all, a large number of immigrants escaped to the New World to avoid conscription, serfdom, and other forms of medieval servitude. Consequently, even such official records as a nineteenth-century federal census may show a 20 percent error rate.

Hypothesize a genealogist anxious to learn of her ancestry; she seeks the minimal essentials—dates and places of birth, marriage, and death, together with nominal information about the collateral family—and perhaps something more substantive about the person of the past. She frets when her ancestors disappear in the mists of time without a trace. She curses the ill-informed immigration officer who likely misspelled the ancestor's odd-sounding foreign name. She mourns the fire which destroyed the county courthouse and its mother lode of places, dates, and persons. She laments the ancient kinswoman who did not see fit to maintain a detailed diary which would erect road signs to her earthly sojourn. Sooner or later, every family researcher reaches a dead end caused by this manner of barrier.

Since Frédéric Bastiat and Henry Hazlitt reminded us to recognize both the "Seen and the Unseen," consider the desires of the elusive ancestor. Should she not be allowed to leave no trace of her existence? At the very least, may not *any* person (most of us will be ancestors someday) select the proverbial footprints she chooses to leave on the clichéd "sands of time," and to erase those which we disfavor? One can conjure up many good reasons for anonymity: a battered spouse or abused child may drop out of a dangerous life and surface with a new, fictitious identity as the only likely means of survival; the youthful, pregnant victim of rape or incest may possess strong physical, emotional, and psychological reasons to use a pseudonym when giving up her child for a private adoption; an individual haunted by earlier indiscretions may find a more effective forgiveness by obliterating his past and substituting a chronicle more in keeping with his mature present.

Like all other human values, reasons to leave no, little, or a fictitious trace are necessarily subjective and distinctly personal. Should a child, grandchild or other descendant enjoy the right to interfere with some earlier person's right to privacy? One could argue for recording an elementary and accurate medical history for the protection of posterity. On reflection even that contention crumbles. Among other things, it assumes a static state of medical knowledge, the certainty of genetic predisposition and, more pertinently, a limitation upon one's most essential right—the right to his person. The recent imbroglio concerning the cause and circumstance of President Zachary Taylor's death demonstrates one current boundary of this silly invasion of personal rights. Unchecked, the trend would lead to a detailed national or even worldwide system of human registration, complete with identity cards, enrollment questionnaires and all of the trappings of the omnipotent state foreseen and feared by Ayn Rand in *Anthem* and George Orwell in *1984*. Simply stated, while subjective arguments for personal record keeping abound, none justify intrusion into that sacred domain called inviolate, personal and individual.

Consider another illustration which enjoyed temporary currency several years ago. A hobo in an Eastern metropolis constructed living quarters in a solitary jury-rigged hut on an unused corner of the local common. In a society obsessed with the plight of the homeless, predictable patterns emerged: The well-meaning weak brains, intent on imposing their own brand of goodness upon the world, willing or not, closed down the hobo's lair and tried to force him into some plastic public housing, "for his own good."

At this point, the pattern disintegrated: While ordinarily the perceived beneficiaries of do-good largess are unable or unwilling to resist, this particular fellow proved to be much sturdier and less submissive than the run of the mill. He did more than merely protest and resist the benevolent advances; he persisted in his determination to live his life as he pleased. He met every compelled relocation effort with a dedicated return to residence in the public park. He did not mug or steal; he only sought to live as before, rudely sheltered on the lonely common and sustained by odd jobs and occasional panhandling. He broke no fundamental common laws, only those needless ones directed at channeling conduct into a Procrustean mode.

Of course, the illiberal consensus cannot stomach a loner or an individualist—after all, it would not do to allow people to think for themselves—so the ardent advocates of anti-homelessness sought their ultimate refuge in the law, that contemporary bastion of proper nonsense. The hovel was destroyed, the eviction made permanent by a judicial restraining order, and the tale lost its newsworthiness. While no one knows, some harbor the hope that this modern descendant of the mountain men has found a new hut in some other park, far from the clutches of those who would deny him his way of life. But, for the purposes of this essay, the persistent and resilient hobo provides another illustration of an enforced orthodoxy which not only destroys elemental individualism but also obliterates the true right to privacy, to be left alone, to live an anonymous life.

The hypothetical genealogist and the anonymous park dweller represent categories of private persons whose freedom from compelled expression seems manifest, but what of more public men, those who have sought and claimed the spotlight for some reason? Do they forfeit their privacy forever? Is there some nook or cranny of the life of the public man which must remain sacrosanct? As the following examples and tidbits display, even the famous deserve protection from busybodies prying into the corners of their lives where the individual seeks quietude and exclusion.

The magnificent and prolific H. L. Mencken left his private papers and personal diary on deposit with the Pratt Library in Baltimore with the express direction that the latter "remain sealed and inaccessible for twenty-five years after his death. Even then it wasn't clear that he intended it [the diary] to be published, for he stipulated that it be accessible only to scholars."[15] William Manchester tartly commented: "Now the diary of his later years... is being published—he had expressly prohibited publication, but the lawyers found a way to thwart his instruction...."[16] Certain precognitive reviewers reacted with what Mr. Manchester aptly describes as "generational chauvinism," and excoriated the powerful, profound, and insightful writer and critic thirty-four years after his demise and forty-two years after a stroke ended his productive career, leading his late-life friend to observe:

> But as one who cherishes accuracy in literary history, I am appalled by the distortion of his considerable role in it. And I am deeply offended by the smearing of my old friend by ignorant liberal bigots.[17]

Compare the fate of the correspondence of Lucia Joyce, the daughter of that esteemed and very public Irish man of letters, James Joyce. As Dr. Walter Block recently chronicled,[18] Stephen Joyce, the novelist's grandson, consigned dozens of these family missives to the flames in order to salvage a semblance of privacy for his late aunt who had suffered the torments of mental illness during her life. Dr. Block deftly demolishes the pleas of "the public's right to know" posited by would-be scholars and other intruders who delight in other people's problems. Simply put, no such generalized "right to know" can, should, or does exist in a truly free society: property rights entail the right to save, consume, alter, exchange, and destroy; the owner need not answer for his choice unless he employs his property for purposes of initiated aggression.

H. L. Mencken and James Joyce were public men. They became so volitionally, by a concatenation of God-given talent and a willingness to set forth some of the fruits of that talent for all the world to see and, incidentally, in exchange for fame and fortune; but no civilized legal system nor sound moral system can torture that public part of their existence into a blanket forfeiture of all vestiges of privacy for all time and in all spheres, much less (in the case of Lucia Joyce) extend such a forfeiture to encompass other individuals fortuitously related to them. By their very nature, diaries, correspondence, and unpublished journals are private; in most instances, if the author or recipient intended publication, that intention could be manifested in simple fashion. Absent manifestation of that intention, private papers like private lives do not belong in the public domain.

Contrast the Mencken and Joyce events with a very different case. Suppose that a Victorian scholar possessed a lesser-known sideline, the composition of bawdy tales of considerable literary merit. The tenor of the times and the notions of family propriety suppress publication against the wishes of the writer. He saves his putatively prurient work for his literary executors to publish in a more liberal era. Nevertheless, at his sudden death the scholar's spouse hurriedly burns his "bad books" to preserve her concept of the reputation of her husband and, of course, "the family." This hypothesis, rooted in the reality of various times and places, represents the counterpoint to the actions of Stephen Joyce: Stephen Joyce destroyed private writings intended by the author to remain private; the Victorian wife burned work intended by the writer to be preserved, disseminated and considered by the public of the future. In the one case, the descendant preserved a right of privacy; in the other, the successor contravened the creator's wishes, destroyed private property, and in so doing invaded another discrete aspect of the writer's essential humanity, the right to leave an undefiled record of the past.

Albert Jay Nock understood that even public men deserve private lives. He wrote of Thomas Jefferson:

> But if all Mr. Jefferson's family correspondence lay open to view, no doubt it would have value only for its implications. *Hide thy life,* said Epicurus; and no one ever succeeded better than Thomas Jefferson at hiding his inner springs of sentiment. He was the most approachable and the most impenetrable of men, easy and delightful of acquaintance, impossible of knowledge. In matters of opinion, principle, or public policy he was always ready to speak out, and did speak out, with a frankness sometimes astonishing; but in more intimate matters, especially in matters of affection and feeling, he never spoke out. Undoubtedly he had great regard for his father and mother, but he seldom mentions either. His memoirs say nothing of his mother, beyond giving record of her name and family; and the few words about his father are quite impersonal....[19]

Privacy resembles other fundamental aspects of liberty in many features. It is not comprehended nor well understood by most of mankind, even those who prattle about it with the greatest assurance. It is often viewed too narrowly, with the kind of myopia which sees the Seen and ignores the Unseen. It is contemplated by those who recognize it at all through the haze of bias inherent in each of us. Its features are distorted by our own emphases, goals, and motives. It is often discarded as unnecessary, unachievable or contradictory to some presupposed public interest, but it is a precept of essential beauty, absolutely necessary for a truly free and tolerant society.

Notes and References

1. Seventy-two Representatives were invited to consider "reform" of the Articles of Confederation; 55 (from twelve former colonies) eventually showed up; 42 stayed to the end; and 39 signed the Constitution in September 1787. George Mason, Elbridge Gerry, and Edmund Randolph declined to endorse the document; these men thought that fundamental rights deserved more explicit protection from a Federal government.
2. For example *Gideon v. Wainwright,* 372 U.S. 339, 83 S.Ct. 792, 9 L.Ed 2d 799 (1963); *Pointer v. State of Texas,* 380 U.S. 400, 85 S.Ct. 1065, 13 L. Ed. 2d 923 (1965). Until the advent of the Fourteenth Amendment, the First Amendment was considered inapplicable to the several states. See *Wallace v. Jaffree,* 473 U.S. 38, 49, 105 S.Ct. 2479, 2485-6, 86 L.Ed. 2d 29 (1985); *Permoli v. Municipality No. 1 of the City of New Orleans,* 3 How 588, 609, 11 L.Ed. 739 (1845).
3. See for example Berlin, Isaiah, *Two Concepts of Liberty* (Oxford University Press, 1958), p. 6.
4. *Wooley v. Maynard,* 430 U.S. 705, 714, 97 S.Ct. 1428, 51 L.Ed. 2d 752 (1977).
5. 447 U.S. 74, 100 S.Ct. 2035, 64 L.Ed. 2d 741 (1980).
6. *Ibid.,* 447 U.S. at 97. Justice Powell here echoed the forceful words of a fellow Virginian, Thomas Jefferson, in 1786: "To compel a man to furnish contributions of money for the propagation of opinions which he disbelieves is sinful and tyrannical."
7. *Ibid.,* 447 U.S. at 99.
8. *Ibid.,* 447 U.S. at 100.
9. *Ibid.,* 447 U.S. at 100-1.
10. Brandeis, Louis D. and Warren, Samuel D., "The Right To Privacy," 4 *Harvard Law Review* 193 (1890) ("Brandeis and Warren").
11. Compare *Roberson v. Rochester Folding Box Co.,* 171 NY 538, 64 NE 442 (1902) (declining, by a 4 to 3 vote, to find and enforce a right of privacy) with *Pavesich v. New England Life Ins. Co.,* 122 GA 190, 50 SE 68, 70 (1905) (unanimous decision finding a natural law right of privacy; "...Liberty includes the right to live as one will so long as that will does not interfere with the rights of another or of the public. One may desire to live a life of seclusion; another may desire to live a life of publicity; still another may wish to live a life of privacy as to certain matters, and of publicity as to others.... Each is entitled to a liberty of choice as to his manner of life, and neither an individual nor the public has a right to arbitrarily take away from him this liberty....").
12. *Hinish v. Meier & Frank Co.,* 166 OR 482, 113 P2d 438 (1941).

13. Harper, Floyd A., "Morals and Liberty," 2 *Writings of F.A. Harper,* 579, 583 (Institute For Humane Studies, Inc., 1979).
14. Nock, Albert Jay, "Autobiographical Sketch" reprinted in *The State of the Union. [Essays in Social Criticism]* (Charles H. Hamilton, ed.) (Indianapolis, IN: Liberty Press, 1991), p. 28.
15. Childs, Roy A., from his review of *The Diary of H. L. Mencken,* Laissez Faire Books, January 1990, page 4.
16. Manchester, William, Letter to the Editor, *The New York Times Book Review,* January 1990, page 33.
17. *Ibid.*
18. Block, Walter, "Old Letters and Old Buildings," *The Freeman* March 1991.
19. Nock, Albert Jay, *Mr. Jefferson* (Delvan, WI: Hallberg Publishing Company, 1983), p. 28.

12

MISES'S NEW YORK UNIVERSITY SEMINAR AND THE AUSTRIAN SCHOOL OF ECONOMICS IN THE UNITED STATES

Bettina Bien Greaves*

Dark clouds of economic and social disorder are gathering on the horizon. Most Americans refuse to see them, but are uneasily aware that a storm is coming.... A few courageous men and women are sounding the alarm. To the limit of their ability and strength they are engaging in a bitter intellectual struggle with the forces of disorder. Addressing every important economic and social issue, they are writing books, essays, and articles and lecturing fervently on the furies of debt [and] capital consumption .

Sennholz, *Debts and Deficits,* (p. 101)

If liberal principles once again are allowed to guide the policies of great nations, if a revolution in public opinion could once more give capitalism free rein, the world will be able gradually to raise itself from the condition into which the policies of the combined anticapitalist factions have plunged it. There is no other way out of the political and social chaos of the present age.

Mises, *Liberalism,* (p. 156–157)

One of the fundamental themes of Ludwig von Mises's teachings was that ideas are powerful; that the only way to change the world is to change the ideas. The best way to learn may be one-on-one, or in a small class or seminar. But for those who do not have the opportunity to study with a master, books are a good

*Dr. Greaves is a senior staff member of the Foundation for Economic Education.

substitute. Thus, at every opportunity Mises stressed the importance of books for the transmission of ideas. Mises said it was a book, Menger's *Principles of Economics,* that "made an 'economist'" of him.[1] Sylvester Petro, lawyer, serious scholar, specialist on labor law, and close personal friend of Mises, first ran across Mises's *Human Action* in a library card catalog. "Life has never been the same for me," he wrote. "Books are not passive."[2] Moreover, books expand the reach of a scholar. As Guatemalan businessman Ulysses S. Dent pointed out: "Originators like Mises influence more through the writings of their followers than they seem to do directly."[3] Nevertheless, there is no substitute for the stimulus that may come from personal contact. To be sure, Ludwig von Mises has influenced many through his books. But he has also had a profound impact through his teaching, both in Vienna and in the United States.

Ludwig von Mises and the Austrian School

In 1912, Ludwig von Mises, a promising young economist living in Austria-Hungary, wrote and published his first major book, *The Theory of Money and Credit.* Ten years later, in 1922, his masterful critique of socialism came out. These two books, and the others he wrote during this same period, were in the tradition of his intellectual predecessors, Carl Menger and Eugen von Böhm-Bawerk, the progenitors of the Austrian school of economics. For decades thereafter, the Austrian school of economics and Ludwig von Mises were practically synonymous. When war came to Europe, Mises and his students scattered to the far corners of the earth. Yet the Austrian school continued to live through the works of Mises and his students from Vienna. Now Mises has gone. Yet the Austrian school survives, and is expanding, thanks to Mises's American students and a still younger generation of Austrian economists.

Just what is the Austrian school of economics? It stemmed originally from the writings of Carl Menger, who set forth the subjective value theory, the cornerstone of Austrian school teachings. Böhm-Bawerk applied subjective value theory to interest. Mises built on their work. By explaining the operations of the free market economy and how government intervention threatened individual freedom, the Austrian school provided the scientific basis for classical liberalism.

Judging from Mises's writings during his Vienna years, he explained to students in his lectures that economics was the science of human action, the study of the actions of individuals. To understand any economic phenomenon, even the most complex phenomenon, one must trace it back to the actions of individuals, their ideas, preferences, values and choices. The entrepreneur was the prime mover. But if he wanted to succeed, he could not simply pursue his own goals; he had to satisfy consumers. The consumers were in the driver's seat; they were sovereign. The entrepreneur was guided by prices that evolved from consumer bids and asks; he was persuaded to satisfy consumers by the lure of profits and the desire to avoid losses. Money, too, was a market phenomenon; it evolved, like any other market phenomenon, out of the actions, and transactions, the bids and asks of market participants. "Cyclical" economic booms and busts stem from government interferences with money and credit, interferences that distort the bids and asks of market participants. Because of the nature of man and society, Mises pointed out, there were economic laws that could not be violated with impunity.

The Austrian brand of economics was not popular with the "establishment" during the years when Mises was teaching and writing in Vienna. Academicians, as well as politicians, wanted to believe that they could revamp the economy as they chose. Politicians resented being reminded by Austrian economists that there were inviolable economic laws and that they, the politicians, were not omnipotent. Nevertheless, Austrian theory had a few loyal supporters, most of them students of Mises.

The English-speaking world began to learn of the Austrian school when Mises and his students fled Europe as the Nazi tide threatened academic freedom. Mises had moved to Switzerland in 1934, because he foresaw trouble in Austria. One by one, his students also left Austria as Hitler's armies started rolling across Europe. Friedrich A. Hayek migrated to England; Fritz Machlup, Gottfried Haberler, Oskar Morgenstern, Felix Kaufmann, Alfred Schuetz, Erich Vögelin, and others, came to the United States. Through these émigré scholars, the world learned something about Mises, his writings, his university teaching, his founding of the

Austrian Institute for Business Cycle Research, his private economic seminar, and his contributions to true liberalism through the Austrian school of economics.

Hayek, at the University of London, was already writing economic books in English. Several of the others who had come to the United States became professors at prestigious universities and wrote scholarly books. Thus, the Austrian school of economics migrated. When Mises reached the United States in 1940, knowledge of the Austrian school here was based largely on what was known from Mises's Viennese students. Now, fifty years later, it seems high time to talk about the next generation of "Austrians" who were influenced by Mises after his arrival in the United States. Most histories of economic thought include brief references to the Austrian school, the development of the subjective theory of value and marginal utility by Carl Menger in his *Principles of Economics* (1871), Böhm-Bawerk's analysis of interest theory in *Capital and Interest,* and sometimes Ludwig von Mises's path breaking 1922 work on socialism. But Austrian economics has not yet penetrated most U. S. colleges and universities.

Mises's Influence in the United States

Mises was quiet and unobtrusive, but determined. As a young high school student he adopted as his motto a verse by Virgil: "Do not yield to the bad, but always oppose it with courage." With this as his inspiration, he vowed that he "would do everything an economist could do. [He] would not tire in professing what [he] knew to be right."[4] His persistence in the pursuit of truth made him friends, but it also made him enemies. In spite of intellectual differences, his socialist and interventionist antagonists came to respect his honesty and integrity. His writings and active participation in economic meetings earned him respect, if not affection, and international recognition in Europe. Even Hans Mayer, his arch rival for many years who had received the University of Vienna professorship many thought should have gone to Mises, and who, as President of the Nationalökonomie Gesellschaft (Economic Society), went along with the Nazis[5] after Hitler's occupation of Austria in 1938, came to respect Mises. When Mises turned seventy in 1951, Mayer wrote of Mises's "courage in the advocacy of his convictions and—what must have been a source of special pride to him: he is one of the few Austrian émigré economists to the United States...who did not simply adapt passively to the new scientific milieu" but remained active and "sought successfully to spread the ideas of the Austrian School, to work for its further development and for its utilization in solving actual economic problems."[6] It was precisely because Mises continued to teach and to write "to spread the ideas of the Austrian School" that he has been influential in this country.

The New York University Seminar

Most of Mises's books were available only in German before World War II—only two had been translated into English. Thus, when he came to the United States, he was practically unknown here. As a refugee in a strange land, he had to begin anew to build his reputation.

In 1945, Mises began teaching at New York University, Graduate School of Business Administration. At first he gave only one lecture class each week; then in 1948, a weekly graduate seminar was added. His lecture class was usually full. The weekly seminar was small, averaging only ten-twenty participants an evening. But many attended faithfully, some year after year, until the spring of 1969 when Mises retired. There were a few businessmen (H. M. Boettinger, Herbert S. Bracey, Wayne J. Holman, Jr. among others), an accountant (Ronald Hertz), a Catholic priest (Rev. John F. Davis), a Navy captain (Richard Fruin), and a restaurateur (I. Hodes). But the majority of the regular attendees were students, writers, or prospective teachers. Among the faithful attendees were—in alphabetical order—Robert G. Anderson, Bettina Bien [Greaves], M. Stanton Evans, Percy L. Greaves, Jr., Henry Hazlitt, Mary Homan [Sennholz], Joseph Keckeissen, Israel M. Kirzner, Beverly Kline [Anderson], George Koether, Toshio Murata, William H. Peterson, George Reisman, Murray N. Rothbard, and Hans F. Sennholz. As professors, writers, speakers, and lecturers, these seminar participants have helped to spread the teachings of Mises and the Austrian school, each in his own way, according to his own aptitude, temperament, disposition, and inclination.[7]

By far the most prolific alumni of Mises's NYU seminar have been Hans F. Sennholz, Israel M. Kirzner, and Murray N. Rothbard. Each has found a particular niche in which he has been effective; each has advanced the teachings of the Austrian school of economics and each has developed a new and younger generation of American "Austrians."

Hans F. Sennholz

Hans Sennholz, a pilot in the German air force during World War II, was shot down and became a P.O.W. in the United States. After returning to Germany he went back to college at Marburg University. Money and banking was taught there by a student of an old socialist antagonist of Mises, Othmar Spann. The students at Marburg could make neither head nor tail out of his course. However, the word among Marburg students was that if they wanted to understand money, they should read Mises's *Theorie des Geldes und der Umlaufsmittel* (now translated into English as *The Theory of Money and Credit*). "Mises," they said, "is the only one who makes any sense on the subject." Sennholz read Mises's book on money at that time. He went on to earn a doctorate from Köln University. Then in 1949, he migrated to the United States.

In the fall of 1950, Sennholz was working on Wall Street. Being ambitious and energetic, he enrolled at nearby New York University, Graduate School of Business Administration, where Ludwig von Mises, whose book he had read when at Marburg, was teaching. When he arrived to register, the only class he had intended to take that was still open to students was Mises's seminar, so he registered for that. He continued his studies and in time received a second doctorate, this one from NYU-GBA with Mises as his adviser. In his doctoral thesis, published as *How Can Europe Survive?* (1955), Sennholz analyzed from the Austrian viewpoint the various proposals for European political and social reform. Sennholz continued to attend Mises's seminar until he moved out of New York State to take a position as Professor of Economics and Department Chairman at Grove City College in western Pennsylvania. His classes have always been among the most popular at the college. In addition to teaching, he has written books, hundreds of articles, and given countless lectures all around the United States, Central and South America, and in Europe. He has been an especially effective spokesman for Austrian economics among businessmen and professionals.

Money (1975) which he edited, *Death and Taxes* (1976/1982) which dealt with taxation in principle and estate taxation in particular, *Age of Inflation* (1979), *Money and Freedom* (1985), *Politics of Unemployment* (1987), and *Debts and Deficits* (1987). He also translated into English from the German several books by Mises and the three volumes of Böhm-Bawerk's *Capital and Interest.* He has written about banking, credit expansion, and economic depression, and he has strongly criticized monetarism and mathematical economics. Sennholz has been strong in his criticism of government interventions. He has fearlessly attacked many "sacred cows"—business subsidies, tariff protection, Social Security, public schools, unemployment insurance, and on and on.

The need for a moral revival is a frequent Sennholz theme. In a piece criticizing the "transfer society," government subsidies and "entitlements," he wrote: "An important spring of action for the transfer society is the desire by most people to *get even* in the redistribution struggle. 'I have been victimized in the past by taxation, inflation, regulation, or other devices,' so the argument goes, 'therefore I am entitled to partake in this particular benefit....'

"Surely getting back that which is rightfully and morally our own is a principle that is rooted in our inalienable right to our lives.... It is a specific right to recovery or compensation from those who are wronging us or have injured us in the past.

"This right to restoration does not beget the right to commit the very immoral act from which we seek restoration, to imitate others in acting immorally, or to seek revenge against the trespassers or innocent bystanders. But this is precisely what the 'get-even' advisors urge us to do....

"A free society is the offspring of morality which guides the actions and policies of its members. To effect a rebirth of such a society is to revive the moral principles that gave it birth in the beginning."[8]

Sennholz has contributed liberally to the Austrian school through his books, translations, articles and lectures which interpret current affairs and political problems in the light of Austrian principles. He has been a powerful force in the advancement of the "Austrian" tradition through his students also, many of whom are themselves now passing along the Austrian torch in various ways.

Murray N. Rothbard

Murray Rothbard was working for his doctorate at Columbia University when he learned of Mises's NYU seminar. He began attending in 1949. Rothbard was one of the most active participants; he presented more papers to the class than anyone else. Judging from his prodigious output over the years, one can only conclude that he is blessed with boundless energy. Not only has he taught most of his life—he is now at the University of Nevada (Las Vegas)—but he has written extensively on a wide range of subjects—economics, history, politics.

One could describe Rothbard as having two personalities—a Dr. Jekyl and a Mr. Hyde. As Jekyl, he writes serious and profound economic studies. As Hyde, he is fearless, polemical, holds nothing sacred, engages in political combat, and attacks unmercifully all socialists, collectivists, and interventionists.

He hadn't been attending Mises's seminar for very long when he realized that he differed with Mises on several points. One was government. Mises held that government was necessary to protect private property and peaceful social cooperation. Rothbard calls himself an anarchist. Another difference between Mises and Rothbard concerned monopoly. Mises held that under certain conditions it was *possible* for a monopolist to receive a higher income, by holding off the market some of a monopolized factor and selling fewer items at a higher price, than by increasing his output in response to consumer demand and selling more. Mises said it was important to analyze this situation because it was the *only* case in a free market where consumers were not supreme. Rothbard holds that *every* seller wants to increase his earnings as much as possible and that the monopolist who reduces output and raises his asking price is no different in this respect from any other businessman. When Mises revised *Human Action* for its second edition, he responded to the questions Rothbard had raised by expanding the sections on government and monopoly.

Mises and Rothbard also differed with respect to monetary reform. Mises favored free banking, that is, he held banks should be accountable, like any other business on the market, for fulfilling commitments and contracts entered into; Mises maintained that to fix by law the reserves a bank must hold as security for paper money or credit issued opens a Pandora's box; in effect it grants legislators the authority to revise the required reserves—upward or downward. Rothbard, on the other hand, maintains that banks should be *required* to hold one hundred percent reserves for all paper money or credit issued, and that any deviation from this could be prosecuted as fraud or mislabeling.[9]

Rothbard has defended Mises's apriorism,[10] but Rothbard himself holds a natural rights philosophy.[11] Rothbard also denies that economists, as scientists, can, or even should, remain "value-free" as Mises believes they can, and as Mises believes, as scientists, they should. As Rothbard put it, he would "cast out the hobgoblins of *Wertfreiheit.*"[12]

Israel M. Kirzner

A third Austrian strain that has come from Mises's NYU seminar has been sparked by Israel M. Kirzner. Kirzner, born in England and raised in South Africa, came to the United States and received a B.A. from Brooklyn College in 1954. He then went to NYU, earned an M.B.A. and in 1957 a Ph.D. under Mises. His doctoral thesis, *The Economic Point of View* (1960), dealt with the shift in the subject matter of economics from business, commerce, trade, and money under the classical economists, to actions, choices, and preferences of individuals under the Austrian economists.

Kirzner teaches at New York University. He has written many articles and books, primarily about various aspects of entrepreneurship. For Mises, the entrepreneur was a speculator who seeks to cope with the uncertain future. Kirzner has expanded and elaborated on that concept, analyzing in detail the entrepreneur's role with respect to competition, perception, opportunity, discovery, distribution, justice, etc.

Percy L. Greaves, Jr.

Percy Greaves attended the Mises seminar more faithfully and longer than any other participant—from the fall of 1950 to the spring of 1969. His early career had been as newspaper reporter, businessman, and researcher for the Republican National Committee and congressional committees. He became an expert on the background, investigations and coverup of the Roosevelt Administration's role in inciting the Japanese attack on Pearl Harbor. Disillusioned by the direction New Deal and welfare state policies were taking the nation, he turned to economics and full-time freelancing. He applied the teachings of Mises and the Austrian school to everything he did. He wrote, lectured, gave seminars, and taught—for the Foundation for Economic Education, for Robert LeFevre's Freedom School, and at Plano University in Texas. As the American Party's candidate for United States President in 1980, he even presented Austrian arguments on the hustings.

For many years Greaves wrote for *Christian Economics,* a paper distributed to Protestant ministers throughout the United States. When writing for ministers, his general theme was:

> There is a perfect system. It is the free market system, sometimes called capitalism. It is *laissez faire* capitalism. It is not that mutilated form of capitalism in which government, or those clothed with political privileges, interfere with those actions of men that are moral in the sight of God. Capitalism, the free market system, is the Christian economic way of life.[13]

Greaves's writings followed closely in the vein of Mises. His *Understanding the Dollar Crisis* (1973) explains Austrian fundamentals in simple terms—the principles of human action, money, inflation, and the cause of the "great depression" of the 1930s. His *Mises Made Easier: A Glossary for Ludwig von Mises's "Human Action"* is a valuable aid to reading and understanding Mises.

Henry Hazlitt

Because of Henry Hazlitt's favorable review in the *New York Times* of the English translation (1936) of Mises's *Socialism,* Mises and Hazlitt had been in touch with each other before Mises came to this country. Therefore, Hazlitt was one of the first persons Mises contacted upon his arrival in the United States in 1940. The two men became close friends. Although older than most of the seminar participants and already well established as an economic journalist, editor, and writer, Hazlitt frequently attended Mises's seminar. He said he always learned something or was led to some new insight by Mises's remarks. Hazlitt is surely entitled to recognition as a Mises seminar alumnus who has contributed significantly to the Austrian revival in this country. Many thousands of readers have benefited from his critique of government intervention and his simple explanations of economic principles in *Economics in One Lesson* (1946). For several years he edited the free-market magazine, *The Freeman.* For two decades in *Newsweek* he dealt with current events from an Austrian perspective, often speaking out against the government's inflationist policies. His book, *The Failure of the "New Economics"* (1959) was a detailed Austrian critique of John Maynard Keynes's *The General Theory of Employment, Interest, and Money.* Also, in *The Foundations of Morality* (1964), Hazlitt elaborated on Mises's statement that the "rightness" or "justness" of an action depends on whether it fosters or hampers social cooperation. Thus he gave utilitarianism a sympathetic hearing.

Conclusion

As Mises wrote, "Ideas and only ideas can light the darkness. These ideas must be brought to the public in such a way that they persuade people. . . . Our civilization will and must survive. And it will survive through better ideas than those which now govern most of the world today, and these better ideas will be developed by the rising generation."[14]

The Austrian school of economics has marshalled the theories on which a truly liberal free market society must be based. As people come to understand these principles and adopt government policies based on them, individual rights, private property, savings and investment will be protected and a truly liberal society will evolve. The students of Mises's seminar in the United States have furthered these free market Austrian ideas. One hopes that the "rising generation," among whom are numbered many followers of these seminar participants, will bring these ideas to the public "in such a way that they persuade people."

Notes and References

1. Mises, Ludwig von, *Notes and Recollections* (Spring Mills, PA: Libertarian Press, Inc., 1978), p. 33.
2. Sylvester Petro, a serious Mises student though not himself a participant in the NYU seminar, has written, "It has taken me a long time fully to absorb the meaning and implications of Mises's frequent exhortation: 'write books!' A solid scholarly work on an important subject has a much longer life and greater influence than any living person has.... Any decent scholarly work will be purchased by all the great universities and public libraries. If it is really good, it will find its way into smaller university, public, and private libraries. Its presence will be signalled for ages to come in the library's card-catalogue.... I believe that what libertarianism *must* have now...is an extensive literature of heavyweight, exhaustive, thoroughly documented books demonstrating the fallacies and the destructive consequences of the anticapitalist policies which are now ruling the world.... The only way to reach those [coming] generations is by planting on library shelves books that document definitively the theoretical blunders and the historical calamities associated with the syndicalist mess we are in.... As Mises said, 'write books!'—or encourage others to do so" (Petro, "A Strategy for the War of Ideas," *The Freeman,* June 1979, pp. 323–333).
3. Dent, Ulysses, "The Need to Make Cognizance Available," *Toward Liberty,* I (Menlo Park, CA: Institute for Humane Studies, 1981), pp. 258ff.
4. Mises, *op. cit.,* p. 70.
5. Mayer wrote: "In consideration of the changed situation in German Austria I am informing you that under the respective laws now applicable also to this state, all non-Aryan members are leaving the Economic Society." Quoted in Mises, *op. cit.,* p. 99.
6. "Consistency in the pursuit of his scientific goals, unyielding rejection of any compromise, courage in the advocacy of his convictions—and what must have been a source of special pride to him: he is one of the few Austrian émigré economists to the United States...who did not simply adapt passively to the new scientific milieu. Professor Mises has been active and has sought successfully to spread the ideas of the Austrian School, to work for its further development and for its utilization in solving actual economic problems." (Translated from the German) Hans Mayer, *Die Presse* (Vienna), September 30, 1951, pp. 513–516.
7. Anderson became a college teacher, then Executive Secretary of the Foundation for Economic Education, and an eloquent lecturer. Evans wrote several books and founded a school to teach economics and

writing skills to young journalists. Keckeissen earned a doctorate from NYU and then went to Guatemala where he has been teaching for many years at the Austrian oriented Universidad Francisco Marroquin, founded by Mises student, Manuel Ayau. Koether commissioned the sculpting of a bronze head of Mises, a copy of which he has now donated to the University of Warsaw (Poland), where it stands next door to a room dedicated to Oskar Lange, a prominent socialist antagonist of Mises. Peterson and Reisman became college professors and have written books, as have Bettina Bien Greaves and Mary Homan Sennholz. Toshio Murata earned a Masters degree under Mises, returned to Japan, where he has had a successful career of college teaching and writing; he has translated into Japanese several books including *Human Action.* Concerning Greaves, Hazlitt, Kirzner, Rothbard, and Sennholz, see the text.

8. Sennholz, Hans F. "You Can't Get Even," *The Freeman,* June 1978, pp. 335-338.

9. Rothbard, Murray N. "The Case for a 100 Per Cent Gold Dollar," *In Search of a Monetary Constitution.* Leland B. Yeager, ed. (Harvard University Press, 1962), pp. 94-136.

10. Rothbard, Murray N. "In Defense of Extreme Apriorism," *Southern Economic Journal,* (January 1957), pp. 314-320.

11. Rothbard, Murray N. *For a New Liberty* (New York, NY: Macmillan, 1973/1978), Chapter 2 in both editions.

12. Rothbard, Murray N., *The Ethics of Liberty,* (Atlantic Highlands, NJ: Humanities Press, 1982), p. 26.

13. Greaves, "Is There a Christian Economic Way of Life?" *Christian Economics,* December 10, 1957. Also, "[F]ree market economics is the only system of the division of labor that advances the general welfare of all the people. It is in accordance with the Golden Rule. We advance ourselves as we help others. The more we help others, the more we receive in return." Greaves, *Understanding the Dollar Crisis* (1973, 1984), p. 62.

14. Mises, *Economic Policy: Thoughts for Today and Tomorrow* (South Bend, IN: Regnery/Gateway, 1979), p. 105.

13

CAPITALISM AND WOMEN: Some Principles of Political Economy of Special Interest to Women

Robert L. Guarnieri*

Introduction

In her book entitled *Sexual Politics*, feminist author Kate Millett says that it is "possible that women now represent a very crucial element capable of swinging the national mood, poised at this moment between the alternative of progress or political repression, toward meaningful change. As the largest alienated element in our society, and because of their numbers, passion and length of oppression, its largest revolutionary base, women might come to play a leadership part in social revolution, quite unknown before in history."[1] While her interpretation of female alienation and oppression can be challenged, women certainly are "a crucial element capable of swinging the national mood."

American society is poised in a critical balance between the continuation of more interventionism (socialism), or a rediscovery and resurgence of the market economy (capitalism). During the last half of the century, freedom and free enterprise have been so severely undermined by so many forms of opposition that we are leaning towards complete destruction of the market economy.

While no single pressure group will stand out with certainty as responsible for pushing us "over the edge," their combined effects

*Dr. Guarnieri was one of the first students of Dr. Sennholz, and one of the last of Ludwig von Mises. Formerly Vice President and Chief Economist of International Investors, Inc., he is now a free-lance writer and high-tech marketing consultant in California.

can certainly do it. This is what makes the feminists' movement important at this point in time, because its leaders have already proven their ability to swing thought towards more interventionism.

Consider these comments by Germaine Greer, another of the feminists' leading spokeswomen. She says:

> Women's revolution is necessarily situationist: we cannot argue that all will be well when the socialists have succeeded in abolishing private property and restoring public ownership of the means of production. We cannot wait that long. Women's liberation, if it abolishes the patriarchal family, will abolish a necessary substructure of the authoritarian state, and once that withers away, Marx will have come true willy-nilly, so let's get on with it.[2]

When capitalism has done so much for people (including women), why should the feminists be siding with the "leftists" all the time? The benefits of the capitalistic system have been important to women, from the material comforts in unprecedented variety, quantity, and quality, to the creation of unbounded opportunity.

But if feminist leaders join with other political groups clamoring for more and more government control, taxation, and spending, the capitalist economy will be crippled and cease to function despite its resiliency. When the market system ceases to function, the government, in the process, will have become authoritarian.

We have waged expensive, meaningless wars fighting communists and socialists in places like Vietnam, while few resources have been spent challenging *communism* and *socialism* here in the United States.

Collectivism is an idea, and we cannot shoot an idea. It must be fought with another idea. Reasoning must point to the superiority of freedom and free enterprise. The capitalistic system of social organization, not socialism or communism, has brought about the economic emancipation of women. Indeed, the unhampered free market economy, not political intervention, has elevated the economic status of *both* sexes. Capitalism has delivered the goods, while the collectivists have only supplied propaganda.

In the past, there were economic fallacies that hurt women and that hurt men. The feminist writers are fond of holding up and burning their straw man, the "male chauvinist pig," but the real enemy has been ignorance. There really is no "battle of the sexes."

Erroneous economic doctrines prevailing in the past have hurt the whole human race, not just women.

The membership of the so-called women's movement is varied. There are the journalists who have found a gold mine in producing the literature of what is euphemistically called "women's liberation." There are the "activists," who have made lucrative careers as speakers, organizers, etc. Some enjoy defiance for its own sake. Others are driven by hate, seeking destruction for the sake of destruction. Finally, there are those who really do mean well. They act sincerely and almost consistently, but lack a clear economic perspective.

Whatever the variation in motives, the main thrust of the political and economic position of the feminist movement is collectivist and anti-capitalistic, whether or not they themselves realize or acknowledge it. Most feminists would object to being called a socialist or communist, but their actions, their comments, and their thoughts, nonetheless, embrace the substance of such doctrines. Few advocate the nationalization of private property. They advocate the preservation of private enterprise, but with all-encompassing government control over its operation. However, that is simply a form of fascism or control-socialism.

Only if we understand how government intervention in the economy tends to impair, rather than enhance, economic progress can we hope to avoid undesirable results. This essay is intended as a contribution toward increasing that understanding, and is especially addressed to reasonable women with open minds who may realize that their economic success hinges on capitalism.

Capital and Productivity

We must wonder which means have proven more successful for women in advancing their standings in society. How beneficial has been the political agitation and rabble-rousing of the feminist interventionists? Likely, more effective have been the women who have simply chosen to compete, perform jobs, and demonstrate their values in the market place, rather than enlisting in political militance and lawsuits. Women have liberated themselves more by seizing the opportunities of capitalism than by wasting energies on political action.

For real emancipation in their individual life styles, women must first be freed from basic material wants. The impact of economic development on the whole of one's life is often underestimated, while the effects of laws and political activities are overrated.

The use of "law" to achieve economic goals, or any aim for that matter, is really the use of intimidation and force to achieve said ends. We cannot overemphasize that the way to succeed in business is by eliciting the voluntary cooperation of those with whom one deals. Resorting to force fails. The history of government intervention shows that the more restrictive the laws become, the more ingenious the ways of circumventing them become. The existence of all the hostile agitation and the passage of unfavorable laws only serve to discourage employers from hiring women. So, one of the results of feminist agitation is higher unemployment among women. Women really need to find ways to make their services more appealing to employers, not less so.

The crucial question is what environment will enable women to create work arrangements compatible with their personal lives, be it the life of a spouse, parent, or a single woman.

Only when capital and labor markets are left free can individuals and companies experiment, take risks, and evaluate results. Only the flexibility of the free market economy allows for such shifts to be made freely and spontaneously in an orderly, step-by-step fashion at the initiative of the individuals involved. Creative solutions, however, are stifled in a planned economy where every individual case has to be settled and directed by a central planning board. Government intervention, control, and regulation will necessarily make the labor market more rigid and is today restricting opportunities for women. If the freedom of nineteenth-century capitalism prevailed, women could enter the work force much more rapidly than they are now able to do.

The passage of time does not necessarily bring progress. While we are accustomed to thinking "modern is better," we would be mistaken to overlook the truths of a previous age simply because time passes. For example, the political environment that existed in the late eighteenth century and early nineteenth century was a much better environment in which to create a vigorous economy than is the twentieth century. That older environment of competition has been replaced by a political environment that is anti-commerce.

The way to "get more" in the market economy is to produce more. Men have traditionally made more money than women only because they could perform more jobs characteristic of an earlier age. Physical strength and exertion were the main ingredients of almost every task, including housework.

In the beginning of human existence, the struggle for survival depended almost solely on strength and physical toughness. There were no tools. There was no capital and no division of labor. Because of women's relative physical weakness, they were the first to perish in times of scarcity. They were deliberately rejected from tribal societies because of their inability to hunt, fight, or do productive labor under primitive conditions. Among those societies which practiced infanticide, baby girls were abandoned much more often than boys. Luckier females were sold as slaves or concubines, while a young male was highly prized for his future abilities as a hunter or warrior. Children were left to starve, and slavery was common. Countless generations lived and died under such conditions in the centuries preceding capitalism and the Industrial Revolution. With the coming of tools, agriculture, and the division of labor, substantial changes began to occur. Division of labor and specialization made possible a level of productivity which was otherwise not possible.

In pre-capitalistic times, a family's economic well-being was limited to what they themselves could produce with homemade tools. Enormous amounts of time had to be spent to produce the basic necessities, and the standard of living was at the subsistence level. The human condition then was literally a daily struggle for survival characterized by back-breaking work from dawn to dusk under unpleasant and often dangerous working conditions, and included occasional famines, plagues and wars. About half of all the infants then born died before the age of ten.

Mortality rates for all age groups, not only children, were many times higher than they are today. The average life span was forty years of age compared with seventy-five in the United States today. People rarely ate meat, and were happy to have a piece of cheese once in a while. Their staples consisted of bread, potatoes and oatmeal. Coffee, tea, and sugar were considered luxuries.

Plumbing was scarce, sewer systems were non-existent, and soap was a rare and expensive item. Clothing was anything but plentiful, and the emphasis was on durability rather than on style. Laundering was minimal in an effort to keep clothes from wearing out, and everyone wore hand-me-downs (whenever they could get them). How could a typical woman think about looking her best under those conditions?

But the Industrial Revolution changed all that. The mass production of the factories replaced the making of clothes by hand. Textiles became more abundant, and dresses no longer had to last for decades; they could be changed even for the sake of style. Improvements in quality made fabrics wear longer and launder better. Eventually came the invention of dry cleaning, and innovative garments made of rubber and plastic.

Commercial interest in the garment industry stimulated the activities of fashion designers and helped to develop style beyond practicality into an art form as well. After centuries of being subject to economic constraints, feminine fashion was free to express independence and originality. There was a general upgrading of taste because it now became possible to indulge it. Women could be daring in a positive way. Western women, especially American women, became the best-dressed and best-groomed women the world had ever seen.

The introduction of capitalistic methods of production brought an ever-improving standard of living and made possible the survival of millions of people whom the world's productivity simply could not support in earlier states of development. From the cave man to the medieval serf, to the modern worker in industrial society, the main reason for the great differences in standards of living is the existence of differing amounts of capital. These material improvements were the basis for the development of the arts and the humanities, sciences, etc., which were impossible at the subsistence level. Further refinements of political and sociological development, such as the upgrading of the life styles of women, had to await capitalism.

The feminists think that women were held back by traditions of European patriarchy, but it was not so. It was the traditions of feudalism, guilds and caste systems, not patriarchy. Working men were subjected to these also, and the caste system restricted everybody. It was only after the free labor markets of capitalism were established that men could make their move and women could follow.

Women acquired the right to vote in all elections in the United States in 1920, but this was not really "emancipation." It had to be completed socially and economically before it was real. A sudden change in political status could not change the deeply ingrained behavior patterns of the whole population, nor could it create the many material things, including job opportunities, that were necessary for increased independence of the female. It had taken the Industrial Revolution to begin changing the old patterns of behavior.

Under capitalism, men or women are not held to the status of their family or caste, or class. They can choose with whom they will associate and into what kind of relationships they will enter. In liberating man from medieval regulation and authority, and destroying the rigidity of the feudal system, capitalism raised all individuals to an unsurpassed level of freedom. Unprecedented goodwill and respect developed among people, as did a regard for the individual value of each human being.

Conversely, in the Middle Ages, for example, human relationships were filled with mutual suspicion and fear. Every man regarded his neighbor as a potential enemy, and treachery and violence were common in men's dealings with each other.

Many of the nobility, born into wealth, were haughty and vain, contemptuous of any kind of work and of anybody outside their own class. They were the so-called gentlemen who spent most of their time in idleness or the leisurely pursuit of pleasure. The advent of the Industrial Revolution gave the masses new hope.

A lack of control over one's own life, curbs on all forms of individual initiative, and a suppression of intellectual development were characteristics of the Middle Ages. The capitalist period finally put an end to slavery and serfdom. In the free market economy's society, human life was valued more highly than ever before.

With the improvement of tools, and the division of labor, substantial changes began to occur. Jobs began to appear which a woman could perform and so produce enough to support her existence. As the primitive society advanced economically, the marginal product of the weakest person was increased. Thus, a female was no longer considered unproductive, but became a valued member of economic life.

Economic advancement has resulted in increased cooperation between the sexes. Deep, fundamental economic developments, not political agitation, lobbying and legislation, have brought changing roles for men and women in their work places. Less time and energy is consumed by burdensome material problems.

Indeed, it seems that women benefit more from productivity gains than do men. In today's modern economy, physical strength is not a crucial factor. Anyone strong enough to use a pencil can win a top-flight position. This is capitalism's greatest contribution to women.

As government intervention wastes capital resources, women suffer more than men. They are first to become "marginal workers" as capital is lost. Seemingly, all women should be staunch supporters of capitalism. But, alas, many of them are not. They are unwittingly cutting their own throats by helping to undermine free enterprise.

The Industrial Revolution

Following the Renaissance, capitalism spread from the commercial cities of northern Italy through France and Germany to Britain, where it enjoyed its fullest development without despotic political power to suppress it. It spread again from there, in its more fully developed form, to the rest of Europe and to America in the seventeenth and eighteenth centuries.

One of the characteristic developments of this period was the freeing of individuals from traditionally prescribed ways of making a living. Prior to that time, the rigid views of the authorities in charge of education and employment stifled incentives, inventiveness, and industrial development. When the free enterprise system eliminated authoritarian imposed boundaries to creativity, the great strides in industrial development and productivity of the last two hundred years were made possible.

However, the great economic achievements of the United States in the past two centuries were really the unforeseen by-product of the emphasis on political freedom and individual liberty. That the uncontrolled efforts of individuals cooperating with each other would result in a system of economic activity that would function efficiently and harmoniously was unforeseen. The classical economists (such as Adam Smith and David Ricardo in England) observed the consequences of economic freedom and set forth a consistent explanation of this fortunate phenomenon. They analyzed systematically what had been happening sporadically, and spread the idea from England over most of the European continent and to the New World.

The fundamental principle of classical economics is to base the economy upon a division of labor, maximizing use of the spontaneous forces in society and resorting as little as possible to coercion. This is the principle of *laissez faire*. The idea is to create an environment in which competition and self-interest will work as beneficially as possible. The first society in history which was not dominated by church or state was that of the United States. The political principles embodied in its constitution provided for a check on government power rather than for its exercise. The unparalleled system of social organization that resulted from this political environment was capitalism, or free enterprise, and it set a shining example in the eighteenth century that spread to all the countries of the civilized world in the nineteenth and twentieth centuries.

It was not a totally consistent, completely unregulated form of *laissez faire*, but this was the first and only time in history it had ever come close. The degree of political freedom and its corollary, economic freedom, is reflected in a country's industrial, agricultural, and commercial progress. This is why the United States made the most economic progress and not because its land was blessed with the richest natural resources.

Along with a general lack of understanding of free market processes, there exists a great lack of appreciation that so much which we value depends heavily upon their preservation. The economic growth that resulted from capitalism exceeded all expectations. Its success surpassed mankind's wildest dreams, and by the twentieth century, the average working man in the western world had reached a degree of comfort and security which would have been thought impossible a hundred years earlier. People achieved a standard of living that could only be enjoyed by the "nobility" in the pre-capitalist world. Along with this came a new sense of independence and of control over one's life. For the first time, men and women began to believe in the great possibilities of improving their own lot in life.

The Industrial Revolution is an underrated event in human history. The Renaissance brought a rebirth of man's mind, but the process was not completed until the Industrial Revolution finished this liberation of thought. For the first time in history men had gained an extensive mastery over the physical forces found in nature and were able to harness them in productive ways. It was no longer necessary to rely solely on the muscle power of men or animals. The Industrial Revolution encouraged the application of scientific knowledge to the methods of production.

The engineers were able to take the scientific discoveries of the physicists into the industrial plants and use them to design the capital equipment and methods that revolutionized human life. Mass production created mass markets, and made for more and better products at every income level of society.

The new plants and equipment increased the productivity of human labor, and made it possible for workers to enjoy greater rewards. The entrepreneurs, with their uncanny talent for organizing productive enterprises, created employment for unlimited numbers of men and women. Through the Industrial Revolution, in about one half a century, they relieved men from the depressing drudgery of working strenuously from sunup to sunset just to survive. The words "pursuit of happiness" took on a new meaning as the masses for the first time aimed at more than an "escape from misery."

The earlier successes of capitalism have so spoiled us today that in our impatience for quick results, we are too often led to choose methods which, although they may accomplish some short-run goal, are not compatible with the preservation of free enterprise. The increasing tendency to rely on government intervention in economic matters, and to resort to direct controls, is a legacy of the socialist influences in our midst, and it is leading us down the road to a totally controlled economy. The previous achievements of free enterprise have mistakenly come to be regarded as secure, regardless of the interference from government.

Slowly, in small steps, our economic system has been changed, and the sum of all this change amounts to a complete reversal of the trends which accounted for the building of our nation. It is almost a complete abandonment of the American principles as set forth in the Declaration of Independence and the Constitution.

Perhaps the most important change among all these developments is the change in the philosophical outlook of the people. In particular, over the last two or three generations, people's attitudes towards self-reliance and authority have changed greatly. Only if our traditional individualism reasserts itself in time can we succeed in defeating the forces that are leading us further and further in the direction of totalitarianism.

And such changes can take a long time. The economic conditions of the twentieth century are the results of the thinking of the eighteenth and nineteenth centuries. The existence of free enterprise was the result of what occurred mainly in the eighteenth century, and the rise of collectivism started in the nineteenth century. The capitalism that was practiced in the nineteenth century emanated from ideas espoused during the eighteenth century, and the thinking of the nineteenth-century socialists (Karl Marx, *et al.*) gave rise to most of the collectivism that exists today.

Over the centuries, transportation technology has progressed from the horse and buggy to the jet plane, for example. One can easily make the mistake of thinking that all other features of a society would somehow be determined by the state of technology of the period. To some, all the changes in technology seem to require some sort of change in other institutions. The implication is that the Constitution of the United States, for example, was all right for the horse and buggy era in which it was written, but today's jet age requires something else. But why should a change in the technological ambiance require a change in the form of government? There is no reason or need for political philosophy to change every time technology advances. The basic needs of humans and their fundamental relationships to each other are the same today as they were two or three thousand years ago.

The socialists in our midst like to refer to themselves as "liberal" or "progressive" and to libertarians as "reactionaries," but in reality it is otherwise. The "liberals" are fond of associating the ideas of limited government with the horse and buggy, and they imply that socialism and state interventionism are compatible with the jet age. But, instead, just the opposite is true. The ideas of collectivism and government control over people are many centuries old, while the ideas of freedom and the supremacy of the individual are rather recent developments in history.

The "creeping socialism" of today, while being hailed as the wave of the future, in reality threatens to plunge us back into the suppression of the past. For technology to continue to advance, men need complete freedom to study scientific truth and to develop new ideas. Only a free economic system encourages this kind of technological development. When that freedom disappears, science too will wither and decay as the whole of society reverts toward the barbarism of the Dark Ages.

It is not surprising that many people, observing socialism and prosperity advancing at the same time during this century, think that interventionism has not interfered with economic growth. Quite simply, we are "coasting" on the fruits of the capital accumulation and the technology developed in the past two centuries here.

To think we can coast indefinitely is to be fooled by an illusion, and the effects of capital dissipation will become all too painfully obvious in the years ahead. The time lag between the institution of an unsound economic policy and the manifestation of the undesired effect does not in any way alter the certainty of its occurring.

Before women went into the expanded factory system of the Industrial Revolution, manufacturing was a "domestic industry" where goods like textiles, for example, were made at home with a whole family participating. The parents were the "managers" controlling both earnings and expenditures (including those of their children). There was nothing cozy or quaint about a family living and working crowded together in a little cottage. In sharp contrast to this, the factory system afforded each individual member of the family his or her own pay. Young women applied themselves in places outside the home. The Industrial Revolution was the powerful fundamental force that brought the beginning of the end of the notion that the only constructive thing a woman could do with her life was to keep house and raise children.

The factories, drawing young women away from the family and the restraint imposed by their parents, discouraged the idea of female subordination. As unpleasant and hazardous as industrial conditions were at that time, factories were still more attractive to women than the other alternatives, such as becoming a domestic servant or rushing into an early marriage.

There is a popular but mistaken notion that without political intervention, such as minimum wage laws, child labor laws, and special rules for women and children, the difficult conditions of the past would still exist. Many people think that the legislators of a century or two ago could have prohibited child labor, instituted the forty-hour work week, and otherwise improved working conditions by passing laws. They think that safety and health standards could have been raised by law.

But the truth is that legislators were powerless to change economic conditions. They could neither legislate higher productivity nor abolish poverty for the people. If it were that simple, then governments the world over would have abolished poverty many centuries ago. The real reason that children no longer must work for low wages from dawn to dusk, under poor conditions, is the very same reason that adults can avoid such grueling conditions in an advanced industrial society. Earning a living is made easier by the use of tools and machines acquired with capital accumulated by personal saving and investment.

The "emancipators" of the child laborers were not the politicians of the day, but rather were the entrepreneurs, the savers, and the investors. Capital accumulation brought enormous improvements in the lot of women and children when compared with their precapitalist conditions. Mass production led to a rise in the general standard of living, and effected a dramatic decrease in infant mortality and the lengthening of life spans.

Before the Industrial Revolution, the children's alternatives were not to work or to play, but rather, to work or to starve. Whole families were destitute and starving. The factory system saved them by providing a means of rising above the level of bare subsistence. Children usually went to work under the supervision of their parents and were given light jobs. Child labor ended when it became unnecessary for children to be productive. With the general advancement of productivity, the parents themselves, and eventually the father alone, could earn enough to support a whole family.

But capital is not accumulated rapidly, and industrialization does not occur in a short span of time. On the contrary, it is a slow, difficult process, and in its early stages one is likely to find women and children trying to increase their chances for survival by working in the fields or factories. To pass a law against their doing this in any poor country would be the same thing as condemning many of them to death by starvation.

Men and women took their children out of the "sweatshops" as soon as they could afford it, and the opportunity came about as the supply of capital increased and technology advanced. The only laws necessary for this purpose were those designed to protect private property and to encourage personal saving and investment. The much-touted labor legislation was superfluous.

Capitalism's philosophical and moral foundations preclude the taking of wealth by force, and acknowledge only the producer of wealth as its owner. *Laissez faire* expects the best of human nature and rewards people accordingly. It lets men and women choose their own careers and to go as far as their abilities will take them. In a market economy, the best product or best performance wins the competition.

Socialists accuse capitalism of being a harsh system, but a true capitalist system is the most benign and gentle economic environment. Even a physically weak person, an unintelligent person, an old person or a child can get more if he or she is working in a productive, rich society rather than in an inefficient collective. The collectivist economies limp along in comparison with capitalism, and their low productivity and economic failures incite more and harsher political intervention.

Just because the socialists say they are going to elevate women doesn't mean they are able to do so. It takes something much broader, more fundamental and more powerful than political proclamations and legislation. The Soviets can pass all the laws they want, but to no avail economically. They struggle with the same basic problem as everyone in the world, i.e., the accumulation of capital and the raising of productivity; but unfortunately, their system is designed to discourage both.

On a personal basis, an individual has more dignity in the private enterprise society, where the individual is considered supreme. In an authoritarian society everyone is subject to orders, and the whole society is organized along the lines of an army. What makes anyone think that a woman is going to be treated more like a whole human being? Women are not consulted there. No one is. Everyone is expected just to follow directives.

A woman working in a capitalist economy has more control over the fruits of her own labor. How can the socialists claim to do more for women when even the men do not have command over their own resources under socialism? How can they possibly talk about giving women more "rights" and more "opportunity" when all persons, of both sexes, are more enslaved by authoritarian governments?

Collectivist concepts are drawing us ever away from individual freedom and the opportunities of capitalism. Each of us must advance our understanding of the free society. But if we remain confused and complacent, we are going to lose the ideological struggle that has become the hallmark of the twentieth century. Like it or not, we are all involved in this struggle, and women are going to play a more important role than ever before in determining whether or not free enterprise will be saved, or if the United States will succumb to socialism.

Notes and References

1. Millett, Kate, *Sexual Politics* (Garden City, NY: Doubleday, 1970), p. 363.
2. Greer, Germaine, *The Female Eunuch* (New York, NY: McGraw-Hill, 1971), p. 326.

14

THE KEY QUESTION

Mark W. Hendrickson*

Aleksandr Solzhenitsyn once wrote, "Tell me what you think of Stalin, and I will tell you who you are"—meaning that the individual Russian's thoughts about Stalin would define both his moral code and his political affinities. Similarly, if you ask someone what the most important economic question is, the answer will be equally definitive—it will reveal the school of thought which colors that person's perspective, and perhaps even disclose whether that person is, in fact, an economist.

What, then, is the key economic question? If someone answers, "How much will Gross National Product (GNP) grow during a certain period of time?", you have encountered someone whose economic viewpoint has been derived from that of John Maynard Keynes (1883-1946). If you are told, "What is the rate of increase in the country's supply of money?", you are hearing echoes of monetarist theories. If the response is, "What can be done to stimulate production—the [so-called] 'supply side' of the economy?", you have met someone whose orientation is that of supply-side economics.

Keynesian, monetarist, and supply-side are the three major contemporary schools of macroeconomic thought. Macroeconomists reify the economic activity of an entire country as an actual unitary entity, the components of which they formalize as statistical data, from which basis they purport to calculate the proper mixture of government policies.

In fact, the very epistemological assumptions which underlie macroeconomics beg for implementation via public policy. All three mainstream macroeconomic schools accept the fundamental

*Dr. Hendrickson is a businessman in New Wilmington, PA. He is also an author, and has taught at Grove City College.

premise that the government is an essential, integral factor in the economic life of a country, and that government officials should design policies that steer economic activity in the direction suggested by the particular macroeconomic model favored by those in power. Thus, the Keynesians' key economic question—how much is GNP increasing?—strongly suggests a normative corollary: "What policies should government implement to boost GNP and improve on the performance of the private economy?" The monetarist's fixation on money supply implies the normative equivalent, "Would an expansive or restrictive monetary policy by the central bank best contribute to stable economic growth?" The supply-sider's concern with stimulating production has its normative counterpart in the question, "What policy changes can be made that will reduce disincentives and barriers to production, and so promote growth in the national economy?"

There is another active contemporary school of economic thought—the Austrian school—which has a radically different concept of the key economic question. Their key question is: "How free are the individual members of society?" The Austrians reject the holistic methodology of the macroeconomic schools.[1] They do not focus on aggregate statistical data or regard the "national economy" as an actual entity, but approach all economic problems from the starting point of individual action.

Just as they reject the macroeconomic framework of economic analysis, so, too, the Austrians differ from the macroeconomists in their normative prescriptions. The normative dimension of the question, "How free are we?" is the presumption that individuals should be free to seek economic betterment free from government interference; that Government's legitimate role is to defend property rather than to redistribute it; that government should act as a night-watchman who protects property rather than as a thief who plunders it.[2]

Why do Austrian economists view freedom rather than economic growth as primary? It isn't that they desire economic growth any less than do the macroeconomists. Rather, it's because they see freedom as the necessary precondition for growth. They know that economic progress is inevitable if it is not squelched by government intervention. They reject as spurious all claims that government policies are capable of producing more wealth in a country than citizens interacting in a free market would. Those who oppose a truly free enterprise system (i.e., an unadulterated private property order) are quick to dismiss the question "How free are we?" as hopelessly generalized, unscientific, and more suited to a political ideologue than to an economist. Let's examine the merits of these criticisms.

To say that "How free are we?" is a "hopelessly generalized" question is specious. Yes, undeniably, it is a broad, sweeping question. Its immense scope seems jarringly radical to the macroeconomists. Whereas the Keynesians, monetarists, and supply-siders, seeking to "fine-tune the economy," call for incremental changes within the existing constellation of public policies, the Austrian economist has a far more ambitious vision: he categorically denies the very legitimacy of the transfer state. He unequivocally opposes all government programs that channel economic activity away from where free people would direct it, thereby redistributing wealth among citizens. The Austrian economist wishes not to fine-tune the elaborate maze of government intervention, but to abolish it.

What the critics of the Austrian school really object to, and try to dismiss as a trite generality, is the utter consistency of the Austrian position. Recognizing that government intervention into economic activity is the disease, not the cure, the Austrians refuse to temporize with it. They consistently denounce such intervention no matter how pervasive it may be.

It is quite illuminating to contrast the Austrian economists' consistency with that of the macroeconomic schools. The Keynesians claim a need for the government to adopt fiscal policies designed to compensate for what they believe are the inherent defects of free markets. Keynesians believe that necessary adjustments of price, supply, and demand don't take place in a free market—in short, that markets don't work. If markets don't work, then why do the Keynesians temporize by trying to fine-tune them? Why don't they follow their premise that government intervention is superior to free markets to its logical conclusion: that government planning should supplant the private property order?

The monetarists, who, to their great credit, often are found in the vanguard of those calling for a free market in most economic goods, indulge in the flagrant inconsistency of advocating a government-sponsored monopoly for the most universal economic good of all—money. And the supply-siders, who are acutely aware of the disincentives to productive economic activities which government policies cause, nonetheless recommend policy changes—such as reducing the tax on capital gains or the top marginal rate on the individual income tax—that are designed to maximize government revenue. It is a glaring inconsistency to attempt to increase the production of wealth while also working to increase the size of the very agent—government—that hinders production.

The second criticism of "How free are we?" is that it is not a scientific question. The positivists who predominate in the macroeconomic mainstream aver this, because they equate science with mathematical precision and quantifiable prediction. Honest seekers for truth, though, are justified in asking, "What rational basis exists for the macroeconomic positivists' assertions of mathematical precision in measuring human behavior?" Where is proof that human satisfaction can be quantified and that human action can be reduced to meaningful numbers from which the future may be extrapolated? No such proof exists, of course, and even the proverbial man on the street intuitively knows that life is not a numbers game and that there is no formula for peering into the future.

The spuriousness of the positivist macroeconomic methodology is increasingly coming to light, especially among those who have had close experience with it. Many large corporations and financial institutions are scaling back or completely eliminating their mathematically oriented economic forecasting departments. Having spent millions to obtain forecasts which have been no more accurate than those provided by the reading of tea leaves, business leaders are cutting the losses accruing from macroeconomic "expertise."[3]

The evidence that positivistic macroeconomics is not scientific economics is substantial. One of the principal pillars of the Keynesian paradigm was the so-called "Phillips curve" which purported to give scientific proof that high inflation and high unemployment could not exist concurrently. This was shown to be a scientific error, as well as a public policy fraud, during the "stagflationary" 1970s, when the two phenomena coincided.[4] The fallaciousness of the monetarist paradigm became apparent in the 1980s, when their confident predictions about price inflation—based upon supposedly mechanistic relationships between various measures of the supply and "velocity" of money—erred abysmally. The supply-side paradigm is, *prima facie*, a political program rather than scientific economics. It is no more scientific to speak of a "supply-side economist" than a "left-side physician."

The positivist notion that science must be mathematical is unduly narrow, contrived, and ultimately erroneous. Science in the broadest sense has always been the study of cause and effect relationships and their underlying principles. Science is forever the search for truths that explain and make comprehensible the phenomena of this world.

Seen in this light, the Austrian school of economics is eminently scientific. In fact, the founder of the Austrian school of thought, Carl Menger (1840-1921), made one of the seminal contributions to the development of economic science when, in 1871, he published his discovery of the "missing link" in economic science: a valid explanation of value. Menger showed that value is subjective—that is, that value is not inherent in economic goods, but rather, each individual imputes value to an economic good according to its perceived contribution to his sense of well-being.[5]

Value is the primary concept in economic analysis. All other subjects of economic analysis—prices, costs, profits, wages, interest, etc.—are derivatives of value. Any economic analysis that proceeds from any basis other than individual valuation is fundamentally flawed. Economics without individual valuation is no more scientific than physics without energy or biology without cell structure.

In economics, as elsewhere, to begin rightly is to end rightly. How can valid conclusions be drawn when the elementary premise is absent from the reasoning process? Thus, the macroeconomist, whose analysis deals in aggregate statistical data and totally ignores individual valuation, is not truly an economist, but rather a public policy statistician.

Menger's brilliant breakthrough lifted economics out of the vague realm of conjecture and mysticism, and made possible the development of economics as a logical, *a priori* science. Proceeding from the foundation laid out by Menger, Ludwig von Mises (1881-1973) developed a comprehensive superstructure of rational, scientific economics, known as "praxeology" (the study of human action) in the broader sense and "catallactics" (the science of exchange of economic goods) in the narrower sense.[6]

The link between economic science and freedom is fundamental and unbreakable. People are free when their ownership and control of property is intact and unabridged. Private property, in turn, is the necessary precondition for economic valuation, for the inescapable reason that value exists only in the minds of individuals, for there are only individual minds. There is no such thing as a collective mind, which is why collective valuation is chimerical, and, consequently, why collective ownership is impracticable. Nor is there a happy medium between free enterprise and a command economy.[7] Whenever government intervenes in economic activity—distorting prices by imposing a tax, doling out a subsidy, decreeing a minimum or maximum price or wage, imposing costly regulations, etc.—then economic goods are diverted from where they are most highly valued, and economic value is correspondingly obliterated. In short, government intervention reduces wealth as it suppresses free markets (i.e., the ability to exchange one's property in line with one's own valuations and not at prices artificially raised or lowered by the direct or indirect influence of government programs). Therefore, the question, "How free are we?" is a profoundly economic one.

Finally, the critics scoff at this key question as being a matter of political ideology rather than of economics. This is certainly no more true for the Austrian school than for the other three. They are all political, in that their ideas have extensive political ramifications. Likewise, all four are ideological, in the primary sense of dealing with ideas and theories. The word "ideology," however, also has a strongly negative connotation, which signifies stubborn adherence to dogma in the face of contrary evidence. In public debate, it is common for one to describe his own tenets as "principles," while denigrating the tenets of opponents as "ideological." It is in that pejorative sense that the critics of Austrian economics invoke the phrase "political ideology."

Once again, it is helpful to turn the spotlight on the accusers. An honest comparison of the four schools will best answer the charge that the Austrians are mere political ideologues.

A central canon in the Keynesian liturgy was that government macroeconomic management would smooth out the booms and busts of the business cycle while reducing unemployment and inflation. However, even though Keynesianism has been the reigning economic doctrine in the United States for most of the past half-century, neither the frequency nor the severity of recessions has lessened from historical norms, but inflation and unemployment have become more severe and chronic than had been the case in the pre-Keynesian era. In spite of that dismal record, many Keynesians and post-Keynesians persist in trumpeting the virtues of government macroeconomic management. Now, who is the ideologue—the Keynesian who says, "Let's have government keep trying to manage the economy?", or the Austrian who suggests, "Let's try freedom"?

A main monetarist doctrine has been the need for centralized control over money. The U.S. dollar has lost over 95 percent of its purchasing power since the Federal Reserve started operations in 1914. This wretched performance stands in stark contrast to the pre-Fed era: the purchasing power of a dollar in 1913 was virtually unchanged from 1813. Still the monetarist clings to his faith in a politically centralized system of money and banking. Who is the real ideologue, the Austrian who contends that government monopolies of money are injurious to the economic well-being of the people, or the monetarist who says, "Let's refine the operations of the Federal Reserve, and our monetary problems will be over"?

The thought of reining in government spending has never been near the top of the supply-side agenda. Supply-siders have generally downplayed the significance of government debts and deficits, arguing that the economy would grow out of them under a supply-side policy regimen. Even today, as the government debt swells by a billion dollars per day, most supply-siders remain silent about the economic necessity of reducing government spending. Who, then, is the ideologue, the supply-sider who fails to sound the alarm about runaway government spending, or the Austrian who declares that government must desist from devouring the economic substance of the people?

In order to dismiss the Austrian school's assertion that political intervention is, by its very nature, antieconomic as the ravings of a political ideologue, this assertion must first be shown to be false. One of the boldest declarations ever made by an Austrian economist was Mises's statement that socialism was inherently impracticable. Mises first propounded this thesis in a 1920 essay, "Economic Calculation in the Socialist Commonwealth," and developed it more fully in his 1922 book, *Socialism*,[8] in which he logically demonstrated that collective ownership makes economic calculation impossible and severely retards economic progress. It is important to realize that Mises advanced these arguments against socialism at the dawn of the age of socialist experimentation, when such ideas were widely regarded as unfashionable by the intelligentsia. Today, some seven decades later, the truth of Mises's assessment is irrefutable. The evidence that lack of freedom leads to economic catastrophe is massive. Those who have lived under it testify that socialism creates a hell on earth. Even the American socialist, Robert Heilbroner, has admitted that "Mises was right" about socialism.[9]

It is not Mises and his successors, then, who are ideologues, but those apologists for socialism whose blind adherence to a monstrously irrational ideology inflicted incalculable human misery upon millions of innocent victims.

Some (Heilbroner, for example) will concede that the Austrians have been right about socialism, but still assert that some government intervention is preferable to the free-market capitalism which Austrians "ideologues" endorse. However, interventionism is partial socialism, still inimical to economic progress, though admittedly less so than full socialism. Where socialism utterly devastates, interventionism cripples. Interventionism is not some sort of happy medium between socialism and capitalism as it advocates glibly assert. The tradition of compromise runs strong in the United States, but a compromise between capitalism and socialism is a compromise between the economic and the antieconomic, the true and the untrue. To say that socialism is bad, but some intervention is good, is no more logical than to say that while a full-body cast will immobilize a person, a lower-body cast is no more restrictive than wearing no cast at all.

Since the Misesian paradigm has not been disproved, should not honest thinkers give it the benefit of the doubt? Dr. Yuri Maltsev thinks so. He was an economic advisor to the Central Committee of the Communist Party of the Soviet Union until he defected in 1989. Maltsev has said, "After decades of enslavement, almost no one in the Soviet Union is interested, for example, in the views of John Maynard Keynes. People...are looking for freedom, not an alternative method of government control....Mises is far more respected in the Soviet Union than Paul Samuelson or J.K. Galbraith."[10] Those who have lived under radical government control know from bitter experience that only a market economy can help them climb out of poverty. There are many telltale indications that people are gradually coming to the realization that Mises was right in making freedom the paramount economic question. Backward countries around the world are taking their first shaky steps away from various command systems toward a market economy while there is a discernible global trend toward privatization and lower taxation in many of the more economically developed countries. Freedom is the dimly perceived ideal that the peoples of the world are instinctively groping toward. Clearly, the Austrian economist can't be dismissed as a mere ideologue just for having been the first to see that the key economic question is, "How free are we?"

Ludwig von Mises deserves great credit for making plain that freedom is the key economic question, and that lack of freedom has been the economic error that has enshrouded most of human history. Yet, Mises's treatment of that question was not completely satisfactory. The shortcoming has nothing to do with its validity, but rather with its orientation and epistemological basis.

Influenced by the German sociologist, Max Weber (1881-1961), Mises strove to develop a *wertfrei* (value-free) mode of economic analysis that would be purely scientific—i.e., totally uninfluenced by normative or ethical notions of right and wrong. In this he succeeded grandly. He proved beyond all doubt that if one's desire was to maximize production, a private property order was the appropriate social order for achieving that end. Taking the utilitarian approach pioneered by Jeremy Bentham (1748-1832), Mises proved that capitalism provides the greatest good for the greatest number, and in so doing, disproved Karl Marx's (1818-1883) assertion that socialism would achieve that utilitarian goal.

The problem with basing the case for freedom on utilitarian grounds alone is that freedom is ineluctably an ethical question as well as an economic one. Man is essentially a moral creature. Not many will study advanced economics, but virtually everyone has notions of right and wrong. "How free are we?" is indeed the key economic question, but a full treatment of that question requires going beyond the field of economic science. By hewing to the utilitarian approach and eschewing the moral dimension, Mises ceded the moral high ground to his opponents by default.

Mises was by no means blind to the moral evil of government despotism, which he showed to be economically destructive. He showed a well developed humanistic awareness of the dehumanizing effects of tyranny—for example, when he wrote, "Where the authoritarian system is fully established, as was for instance the case in the empire of the Inca in pre-Columbian America, the subjects are merely in a zoological sense human; virtually they are deprived of their specifically human faculty of choosing and acting..."[11] He even disclosed a poignant awareness of the enervating stagnation suffered by the bureaucrats employed by the interventionistic state, who in some ways are even less free than the citizens whose lives they regulate.[12]

Still, by not defending freedom on ethical grounds, Mises left economic freedom defenseless against assaults (however spurious) by those claiming moral superiority for government intervention. For example, it long has been clear to many opponents of capitalism that capitalism is the superior social order in terms of sheer productive capacity (even Marx conceded the great productivity of the system that he despised), but these opponents have been able to win support for socialistic or interventionistic policies on such grounds as social justice. Capitalism, to these critics, may be more productive and efficient, but it isn't as fair as, say, a welfare state.

In an age when intellectual rigor and integrity have declined to the point where a Harvard University graduate with a major in economics may never have heard of Ludwig von Mises; when the economics profession has degenerated into a priesthood lording it over a bewildered people with its abstruse, esoteric pseudo-scientific mumbo-jumbo; when economists themselves persist in convenient illusions rather than searching for inconvenient truths, not because they are venal, but because they desire to be fashionable—in such an age freedom needs to be advocated on the grounds that it is the morally right choice. Mises's praxeology may be perfectly true, but will his dispassionate, *wertfrei* utilitarianism be able to inspire a new generation of thought leaders or mobilize the masses as effectively as impassioned appeals to justice, kindness, and brotherly love? Many people choose to do what they believe to be right, but they have better-developed notions of what is morally right than what is scientifically right (i.e., correct, true).

Because the key economic question, "How free are we?", is also an ethical one, economics and ethics are inseparable. Thus, the economist of today must address ethical matters as part of his work. Mises advanced economics as far as is possible on a utilitarian basis. What remained for Mises's successors to accomplish was to develop a synthesis of the ethical with purely scientific economics—to elucidate the ethical as well as economic imperatives of freedom.

This requirement should neither surprise nor daunt us. After all, the modern study of economics was inaugurated by the Scottish moral philosopher, Adam Smith (1723–1790). We should remember that Smith's descriptive treatise on political economy, *The Wealth of Nations,* was preceded by his prescriptive treatise on ethics, *The Theory of Moral Sentiments.* In *Theory*, Smith propounded the principle that "each individual is naturally, and antecedent to the institution of civil government, regarded as having a right...to defend himself from injuries..." and that "The most sacred laws of justice...are the laws which guard the life and person of our neighbor; the next are those which guard his property and possessions...."[13] In these statements, we hear echoes of John Locke's (1632–1704) natural law theory: individuals have the right to be safe in the enjoyment of their life, liberty, and property. These Enlightenment ideals were derived from the Judeo-Christian tradition, in which God's commandments explicitly forbade the taking of the life or *property* of others.

Indeed, the idea of freedom is what inspired the founding of the American republic. The Declaration of Independence boldly proclaimed that all men have God-given rights to "life, liberty, and the pursuit of happiness," and that governments are properly established for the sole purpose of guarding those rights. Thus, the Bill of Rights appended to the Constitution of the United States explicitly guarantees government protection of the individual's rights to "life, liberty, and property." The Founding Fathers of the United States had a clear moral vision that the only legitimate use of force by government is to preserve rights, and that any use of force by government to infringe on individual rights is illegitimate and morally indistinguishable from the deed of a common criminal. Thus, a tax to pay for the defense of the country against foreign invasion would be legitimate, but for government to tax wealth away from Citizen "A" in order to direct it toward the private, privileged benefit of Citizen "B" would be no more morally defensible than if "B" had simply walked up to "A" and taken the money at gunpoint.

Viewed in this light, it becomes apparent that the social order which Karl Marx sneeringly dubbed "capitalism" is that social order which embodies the moral code set forth in the Mosaic Decalogue. We also see the grandeur of the intellectual feat performed by Mises who, through human reason and logic alone, demonstrated that the social order which would bless mankind the most was that one that was most consistent with God's law. Indeed, what intellectual achievement can possibly be greater than confirming, through the highest exercise of human reason, the wisdom, validity, and truth of the divine laws that God revealed to mankind on Mount Sinai several millennia ago?

The needed infusion of an ethical afflatus into the paradigm of Misesian praxeology has come from the first of the four Ph.D. graduates who studied under Mises during his decades at New York University, Hans F. Sennholz (1922–). Unlike so many of Mises's students, who, like Galileo, have found it politic to recant at least part of the truth they have learned for the sake of popularity or career advancement, Sennholz has been as stalwart as Mises in proclaiming the unadulterated truth of economics without making the slightest concession to the intellectual fashion of the day.

Furthermore, in addition to standing foursquare for scientific truth, Sennholz has championed the cause of human freedom on the basis of Judeo-Christian precepts. Knowing that human life is a moral journey, he never shrinks from affirming that no person has a right to the property of another because that would be wrong—contrary to God's Eighth Commandment and Christ's Golden Rule. By injecting the religiously-inspired moral basis for private property into his economic writings, an important reversal has taken place. In the utilitarian context of Mises, the implication was drawn that capitalism is good because it produces the most wealth. In the Judeo-Christian context which Sennholz has brought to this same issue, we see that capitalism produces the most wealth because it is good. It is because capitalism is the social order which comes closest to embodying God's law in the fabric of daily life that it brings the blessing of abundance.

Throughout his prolific publications, Hans Sennholz has always kept the grand question of human liberty before the minds of his students, his public audiences, and his legions of readers. He has been an indefatigable champion of freedom, both as scientific and moral truth. He has decried the Keynesian tactic of trying to deceive workers by advocating inflationary policies by the central bank as a means of raising nominal wages while actually lowering real wages.[14] With uncommon eloquence he has implored, "To spearhead a rebirth of our free society, let us rededicate ourselves to a new covenant of redemption, which is a simple restatement of public morality," and then he enumerated for us eight principled standards of self-control, such as "No matter how the transfer state may victimize me, I shall seek no transfer payments, nor accept any."[15] In arguing for the return of money and banking to the market place, he has reminded us that "in the hands of politicians and endowed with monopolistic privileges, money becomes dishonest and despotic, violates contracts, sanctions legal fraud, and takes property without compensation."[16] This is wrong because it denies "individual freedom as an inalienable right."[17] In another book, he has explicitly reminded us of the ethical dimension of economics by writing: "No matter how tragic the economic effects may be on certain groups of victims, [of unemployment artificially caused by increases in the minimum wage] we must not overlook the psychological harm and the moral wrong that are inflicted on them."[18] Elsewhere: "Significant reforms, in the final analysis, are moral reforms."[19] Nowhere has the moral basis for human liberty been more explicitly linked with economic science than in Sennholz's monograph *Three Economic Commandments*.[20]

The visible fruit of Sennholz's tireless efforts in promoting freedom is this: whereas in the 1950s there were but a few hardy pioneers toiling in the wilderness for the cause of freedom in America, today collectivistic ideologies are on the defensive; the freedom philosophy is staging a magnificent comeback in America and around the world; even the economics profession itself is experiencing a renaissance, as the realization gradually spreads that freedom is indeed the key economic question.

Surely, the Lord who judges all will reward the brave pilgrims who, in a secular age, dared to apply the truth of His law to economics far beyond the capacity of this material world. As the world heeds the priceless message of these voices of wisdom, it, too, will be blessed. To the extent that economists and Judeo-Christian thought-leaders follow the trail blazed by Menger, Mises, and Sennholz, they will enable future generations to grasp the vital importance of the key economic and moral question—"How free are we?" As we do so, the damage that has resulted from mankind's seduction by the false idols of spurious ideologies—the false prophets promising an illusory salvation if one would only bow down and serve them—will be healed, and the human race will be a step closer to entering into the heritage of good which the Father of all has promised to them that love and obey Him.

Notes and References

1. All three schools perform microeconomic analyses, too, but the key question with which each of them is associated reflects their macroeconomic orientation.
2. A few so-called Austrians define freedom as anarchy. This is an aberration. Ludwig von Mises, whose voluminous works define what Austrian economics is, repeatedly rejects anarchy as a viable option. Cf. Ludwig von Mises, *The Ultimate Foundation of Economic Science*, 2nd ed., with forward by Israel M. Kirzner, (Kansas City: Sheed Andrews & McMeel, Inc., 1978), p. 98-99; *Idem, Liberalism: A Socio-Economic Exposition*, 2nd ed., with forward by Louis Spadaro, (Kansas City: Sheed Andrews & McMeel, Inc., 1978), p. 36-37; *Idem, Omnipotent Government*, [1914] (New Rochelle, NY: Arlington House, 1969), p. 48.
3. Wechsler, Dana, "Dreary Days in the Dismal Science," Forbes, 21 (January, 1991), pp. 68-71.
4. For the definitive exegetical rebuttal of Keynesian quackery, see: Hazlitt, Henry, *The Failure of the "New Economics"* (Princeton, NJ: D. Van Nostrand Company, Inc., 1959), p. 458.
5. Menger, Carl, *Principles of Economics*, [1871] trans. by J. Dingwall and B. F. Hoselitz, with intro. by F. A. Hayek, (New York, NY: New York University Press, 1981), p. 116 et seq..
6. See: Mises, Ludwig von, *Human Action*, 3rd rev. ed., (Chicago, IL: Contemporary Books, Inc.,), p. 907, for the definitive exposition of praxeology.
7. Mises, Ludwig von, "Middle-of-the-Road Policy Leads to Socialism," *Planning for Freedom*, 4th ed. enlarged, (Spring Mills, PA: Libertarian Press, 1980), pp. 18-35.
8. Mises, Ludwig von, *Socialism: An Economic and Sociological Analysis,* trans. J. Kahane, (Indianapolis, IN: Liberty Classics), p. 567.
9. Heilbroner, Robert, "Reflections After Communism," The New Yorker, 10 (September, 1991), p. 92.
10. Quoted in Tucker, Jeffrey A., "Mises in Moscow! An Interview with an Austrian Economist from the U.S.S.R.," *The Free Market*, (Auburn, AL: The Ludwig von Mises Institute, Vol. 8, No. 3, March 1990), pp. 1, 6.
11. Mises, Ludwig von, "Liberty and its Antithesis," in *Planning for Freedom*, op. cit., p. 216.
12. *Idem, Bureaucracy* (New Rochelle, NY: Arlington House, 1969), p.94.
13. Smith, Adam, *The Theory of Moral Sentiments,* [1759], (Indianapolis, IN: Liberty Classics, 1969), pp. 158, 163.

14. Sennholz, Hans F., *Age of Inflation,* (Belmont, MA: Western Islands, 1979), pp. 32–33.
15. *Ibid.,* p. 77.
16. *Idem, Money and Freedom*, (Spring Mills, PA: Libertarian Press, Inc., 1985), p. 78.
17. *Ibid.,* p. 77.
18. *Idem, The Politics of Unemployment*, (Spring Mills, PA: Libertarian Press, Inc., 1987), p. 52.
19. *Idem, Debts and Deficits,* (Spring Mills, PA: Libertarian Press, Inc., 1987), p. 163.
20. *Idem, Three Economic Commandments,* (Spring Mills, PA: Libertarian Press, Inc., 1990), p. 42.

15

THE DYNAMICS OF GOVERNMENT INTERVENTION: Theory and Implications

Sanford Ikeda*

The middle system of property that is hampered, guided, and regulated by government is in itself contradictory and illogical. Any attempt to introduce it in earnest must lead to a crisis from which either socialism or capitalism alone can emerge.

Ludwig von Mises, *Critique of Interventionism*

As historians begin to chronicle the monumental failure of socialism in practice as well as theory, social scientists need now to examine more closely than ever the nature of the system toward which many formerly socialist countries are starting to turn, namely, government intervention or the so-called "mixed economy." Any such undertaking must build on the work of the Austrian economists, whose contributions to this area have been pioneering and consistently critical.

Hans F. Sennholz, an economist in the Austrian tradition, not only has written prolifically against statism, but has undertaken translations proven valuable to the scholarly community.[1] In particular, his translation of Ludwig von Mises's *Critique of Interventionism* made accessible a valuable and long-awaited essay to the English-speaking world. Here Mises points out the instability and illogicallity of what threatens to become, after the demise of socialism, the ruling doctrine of our times. Sennholz's assertion in 1977 that *Critique* "is as pertinent and timely today as

*Dr. Ikeda is Assistant Professor of Economics, State University of New York at Purchase. He is a contributor to the forthcoming *The Handbook of Austrian Economics,* and is writing a book about the dynamics of mixed economies.

it was half a century ago," rings even truer in these days of revolutionary change.

Mises in this and several other studies has offered a splendid argument for the futility of interventionism as a doctrine, but what may be necessary in a world where most countries have (more or less) mixed economies in transition is a more systematic theory of what can be called the "interventionist process." For example, Mises's and F. A. Hayek's brilliant theory of the trade cycle is but one aspect of a more general phenomenon whose framework has yet to be fully elaborated.[2]

This essay does not present a complete version of such a study but will outline its general features and give a few examples drawn from recent experience. After discussing the meaning of intervention as an unintended process, this writer will examine the nature of interventionist dynamics, extending the Hayekian "knowledge problem" to the governmental sphere and explaining how such an unstable system could nevertheless persist for a very long time. The final paragraphs will offer some concluding remarks about the relation between the implications of the framework outlined here and recent observations.

Intervention as a Process

Economists are fond of pointing out the unexpected and frequently unwanted effects of a given public policy. It is our stock in trade. Adam Smith, for example, devoted Book IV of his *Wealth of Nations* to debunking mercantilism, which claimed, among other things, that tariffs and boycotts will bring prosperity to a nation.[3] Smith argued, however, that international trade restrictions will have precisely the opposite effect of that intended by protectionist governments, worsening conditions for citizens of all nations. Today, we who in some sense follow in Smith's footsteps continue to point out that rent controls make housing costlier rather than cheaper, that minimum wage laws perpetuate rather then alleviate unemployment among the unskilled, and that deliberate central-bank credit expansion weakens rather than strengthens the economy.

What is almost always missing from such analyses, however, is a description of the principles underlying the process by which one government intervention leads to another, or by which partial deregulation establishes forces that can push toward either re-regulation or further deregulation. In short, we lack at present a theory, based on Mises's critique of interventionism, of this ebb and flow of government growth—a theory of the "interventionist process."

Examples of Intervention

Rent control in New York City, for example, has not only created shortages of affordable housing—this much, standard theory explains well—but it has also led to the substitution in many instances of ruthless landlords who do not hesitate to use intimidation or even coercion for more humane landlords who would never resort to such methods. In addition, the government-created shortage of lower-priced housing has led activists to call for the government to provide even more housing for the poor, including an ever-growing population of homeless persons.[4] Thus, renters have called for further regulation to protect themselves against unscrupulous landlords, and the poor or their representatives (often self-appointed) advocate a larger role for government in the housing market.

Another example is the partial deregulation of the airline industry, which stopped short of reducing government control in sectors that provide complementary services, such as air-traffic controllers and municipal airports. While there have been no shortages of pilots, attendants, airplanes, and flights in the deregulated sector, serious congestion and safety problems persist in the still regulated complementary sectors. Politicians responding to public concern have once again raised the issue of re-regulating the airlines or (more radically but less often) of further deregulating the air transport system.

As a final example, recent efforts in Eastern Europe and the People's Republic of China to decentralize politico-economic power have resulted in serious bottlenecks in those areas of their respective economies that have not kept pace with free market reforms made elsewhere in the system. In the case of China in particular, inflation and economic disruption were the unintended consequences of partial reform, which led to the public discontent so brutally crushed in the summer of 1989. Unless further economic decentralization occurs, however, serious social and economic dislocation and deterioration are inevitable.

The Interventionist Process and Rent Seeking

Let us define a *process* as "change subject to order."[5] In Austrian economics both social change and social order are the result of human action, especially that aspect of human action that effects the discovery of new knowledge, or what Israel M. Kirzner has called "entrepreneurship."[6] Entrepreneurship is crucial for this analysis because the exploitation of previously undiscovered errors and opportunities which result from regulation or deregulation forms the basis from which arises the spontaneous order[7] that constitutes the interventionist process.

"Intervention as a process" could also refer to the actions of special-interest groups, politicians, and bureaucrats which go on "behind the scenes" of a regulation; that is, it could refer simply to "rent-seeking" activity.[8] As fascinating and complex as the wheelings and dealings of lobbyists and politicians may be behind a particular piece of legislation, and as important as the study of such behavior is for a complete understanding of the politico-economic world, this is not what this essay means by intervention as a process. This approach does indeed increase our understanding of political dynamics as far as it goes but ignores the broader question of how disparate pieces of legislation or seemingly isolated political acts may be linked to a much larger process. The very nature of traditional rent-seeking analysis, however, seems to preclude inquiry into this larger process.

The problems of rent-seeking occur, in a sense, because agents who use political means to achieve their ends get what they want. That is, rent-seeking models endow their agents with some version of "perfect knowledge," which allows them to calculate precisely the expected costs and expected benefits of their actions. Since they possess, at a minimum, the ability to forecast all of the probable outcomes of any particular action, there are no unforeseen consequences arising from such an action that would require the exercise of entrepreneurial alertness for their discovery, and thus a crucial piece of the Misesian interventionist dynamic is missing from the beginning.

Intervention as an Unintended Process

What does it mean, exactly, to say that the process of intervention, the growth and contraction of government, is an *unintended* process? To fully understand this phenomenon, we need to invoke Hayek's concept of the "knowledge problem."[9] This refers to the fact that information relevant for decision making (regarding tastes, expectations, resource availability, and technology) is dispersed among individuals in society who may not be the ones who currently place the highest value on it. For example, I may be able and willing to pay $50 for a special pair of running shoes. Someone else may be able and willing to sell such a pair of shoes for $40. Hence, each of us possesses information that is relevant to the other; however, if neither of us knows about the other's information there is a "gap in knowledge." This is the knowledge problem, and we each would be better off if at least one of us possessed the other's relevant information. Entrepreneurship is the power to uncover these gaps for profit (e.g., by buying at $40 or selling at $50). Thus, entrepreneurship satisfies the urge to better one's perceived condition and it also serves a social function by (unintentionally) solving the knowledge problem.

Entrepreneurship creates net benefits or surpluses when it successfully reveals profit opportunities. This surplus represents newly created value that agents can then use to increase the capital stock and the wealth-increasing capacity of society. In this way, the entrepreneurial market process, of which Kirzner has written so eloquently, is a *self-sustaining* spontaneous order. The question that arises here is whether the interventionist process is also such an order. The next section will argue that it is indeed self-sustaining.

The Dynamics of Intervention

A free market order may start on the path toward socialism by accident as well as by design. That is, the *initial* impetus that nudges the system away from a limited government order onto the path may very well be unintentional and non-ideological.[10] But attitudes toward intervention do play a key role at each of the subsequent steps toward socialism in two ways.

First, social rules and conventions that constrain the use of coercive political means (versus voluntary economic means) may be overcome "at the margin." If the various agents in the market order manifest a diversity of attitudes toward the use of political means, being disposed in different degrees to letting the government intervene, then unforeseen problems created by prior intervention may induce those at the margin (between government and private action) to look more favorably upon further intervention as they perceive a rise in the ratio of the benefits to the cost of intervention. Suffering the unintended hardships of an intervention might raise the propensity of agents already so inclined to use political means to ease these hardships.

Second, a certain "statist" mentality that looks hopefully upon collectivist ownership of the means of production as a more attractive alternative to private property and *laissez faire* may gain progressive acceptance as a direct consequence of the level of government intervention itself. In other words, each restriction of individual choice might make the next seem less onerous, fostering a disposition on the part of the public to accept further intervention, and a proclivity on the part of the government to create it. Moreover, a new regulation might itself create previously unimagined opportunities for political entrepreneurs that would not otherwise have existed.[11] Today, for example, a growing number make their living as full-time "political activists."

Hence, there are two attitudinal forces operating in the direction of further intervention: Interventions that change the relative costs and benefits of further intervention result in *marginal changes in attitude*; this acceptance at the margin may set into motion a process that induces *changes in the preference for intervention* itself. These, along with the force of unpredictable errors resulting from the interventions themselves, drive the mixed economy toward socialism.

Against these, however, operates an opposing tendency. We would expect agents' enthusiasm for further intervention to cool as they become aware of "government failure"—the persistent errors and disruptions that accompany each attempt to address an alleged market failure.[12] But two factors impede the acquisition of the knowledge that would reveal the illogic of interventionism.

First, as a rule, we would expect the regulatory framework to grow in *complexity* as it grows in scope. This greater complexity presents agents with "bounded-rationality" problems.[13] Each additional intervention adds to the computational complexity of the regulatory framework, which in turn creates further problems. Taken as a whole, the entire set of problems so created will be of enormous complexity. Thus, as the process evolves, the computational complexity raises the costs too much for the public to be informed of the full magnitude of the overall problem for them to pressure policy makers to change.[14]

More fundamentally, as noted earlier, each intervention creates *gaps in knowledge* owing to outcomes that were not foreseen by its proponents. It seems reasonable to expect that as the regulatory framework grows in scope, the incidence of these gaps and the resulting errors will grow apace. The upshot of these two considerations (complexity and ignorance) is that *a long time* might pass before sufficient numbers of those in a position to influence public policy and public opinion discover in the internal contradictions of interventionism. In the meantime the system could have moved quite close to socialism.

Thus, we would expect that as the interventionist system approaches full central planning, the increasing benefits of deregulation and decentralization are for some time offset by the enormous information costs owing to complexity and ignorance generated by spreading intervention. While in the market process ignorance and error create profit opportunities, the sort of "profit opportunities" created in this process lead only to further intervention, complexity, and error as long as the statist mentality prevails. Eventually, problems will grow so widespread that the public will be affected directly by specific incidences of the overall problem and indirectly through the impact of systemic failure.

The Knowledge Problem In The Public Sector

In the Misesian analysis, after each episode of intervention with its accompanying unintended consequences, policy makers face a choice: Remove the regulation that produced the undesirable outcome or intervene further to try to mitigate it. As we have just seen, ideology and beliefs, on the one hand, and the agents' entrepreneurial ability to discover the futility of prevailing policy, on the other, both influence the direction of policy makers.[15] But in a mature mixed economy, the overall picture may be hard for anyone to see, including public authorities.

It is well known for example that those who make policy with respect to tax matters are not necessarily the same people who decide the budget for, say, funding for the arts, even though tax changes will have important ramifications for arts funding. In a modern interventionist democracy no single individual or group is simultaneously aware of the overall policy of the government and all of its consequences. Within the United States Congress are dozens of committees and subcommittees that oversee the myriad functions of the federal government; there is a profusion of bureaus in the executive branch each with a responsibility that may either conflict or overlap with that of another; within the federal judicial system are scores of courts in which the legal interpretation of legislative statutes often differ or even contradict one another. Under these circumstances, it is not too far-fetched to imagine that a "knowledge problem" of some kind exists in the government. This public-sector knowledge problem, combined with the cognate phenomenon in the private sector, make the discovery of and solution to the interventionist quandary even more difficult.

The Reserve Fund and Crises

The two prongs of Mises's criticism of interventionism are (1) the impossibility of rational socialist calculation and (2) the irrationality of a mixed economy. Although Mises himself did not state it this way, the reasoning underlying his critiques of both socialism and interventionism are the same—the existence of the knowledge problem makes the consequences of government intervention nasty and unexpected. And as the interventionist process drives the economic system closer to socialism, ever more of the problems that plague socialism reveal themselves progressively.

In order to sustain itself against the waste that these problems cause, the interventionist process feeds off what Mises referred to as the "reserve fund," the exploitable social surpluses that are created by entrepreneurial alertness in the market process.[16] When the market order is no longer able to replenish the reserve fund quickly enough to sustain the interventionist process, the system approaches a *crisis*, at which point the authorities must consciously decide whether to continue on toward socialism or to embrace free market reforms. As noted earlier, however, by the time public opinion in an interventionist democracy finally turns against interventionism, centralized planning ("constructivism" to use Hayek's apt term) may have considerably replaced the market order and the price system that guides it.

Is the Interventionist Process Self-Sustaining?

If we accept the Mises-Hayek analysis, the process of the centralization of decisions (though spontaneous in Hayek's sense) clearly reduces the social surplus or reserve fund and is therefore not, by itself, self-sustaining. The process of decentralization, however, is both spontaneous and adds to the social surplus as impediments to the discovery of socially beneficial profit opportunities are removed. Taken together, this means that if the system cycles between more and less intervention, the overall process, including the ebb and flow of government growth, may be a self-sustaining spontaneous order. Understood in this sense, rather than being transient (as one interpretation of Mises's analysis might suggest), it is easy to imagine that the interventionist process could continue indefinitely.

Conclusions

There are roughly three kinds of economic systems in the world today: Economies in transition that have rejected central planning to one degree or another apparently in favor of "mixed economies" (Eastern Europe and the Soviet Union); highly centralized economies that are on the verge of similar radical change (the remaining communist regimes); and interventionist systems in which, despite modest backtracking from time to time, the secular trend is toward more rather than less intervention (the United States and the rest of the world). These facts are fully consistent with the analysis outlined here.

This writer has argued that mixed economies are self-sustaining processes that possess a powerful internal dynamic that tends to drive them persistently toward centralized decision making (socialism) and inevitable crises. Furthermore, these crises often represent turning points (as in Eastern Europe today) at which the widespread realization of the inner contradictions of all varieties of constructivism has generated pressure for dramatic change. However, anything less than a radical dismantling of the central decision-making apparatus and its replacement with a genuine market order with private property rights well-defined and protected will not offer a stable middle ground, but will only mean severe and unpredictable hardships for the unfortunate inhabitants of those economies. It will only make more difficult the inevitable choice between further decentralization or a return to socialist methods. A perpetual cycle of intervention, followed by disaster, followed by more intervention, and so on, is a highly unpleasant prospect, but one which may be inescapable without radical change and the ideas and courage to support it. A better understanding of the dynamics of mixed economies would help us to seize the moment for radical change when it arises.

The moral and intellectual framework that teachers and students of the free society help to build will play a significant role in guiding all economies toward establishing the institutions essential for the market order. Continuing our efforts is critical in order to spare the West the magnitude of the crisis that has so shaken the socialist economies, for such a collapse here would be a disaster from which the world might never fully recover.

Notes and References

1. These include Böhm-Bawerk, Eugen von, *Capital and Interest*, in 3 vols. Trans. by Sennholz, Hans F., with Huncke, George D. (Spring Mills, PA: Libertarian Press, 1959), and Mises, Ludwig von, *Notes and Recollections*, Trans. by Sennholz, Hans F. (Spring Mills, PA: Libertarian Press, 1978).
2. For the most systematic treatment to date of the inner dynamics of political capitalism along with the lines of this essay, see Grinder, Walter and Hagel, John III, "Toward a Theory of State Capitalism: Ultimate Decision-Making and Class Structure." *Journal of Libertarian Studies*, vol. 1(1):59-79, 1977; and Hagel, John III, "From Laissez Faire to Zwangswirtschaft: The Dynamics of Intervention," presented at a Symposium on Austrian Economics, June, 1975.
3. Smith, Adam, *An Inquiry into the Nature and Causes of the Wealth of Nations,* in two volumes, ed. by Campbell, R. H. and Skinner, A. S., (Indianapolis, IN: Liberty Classics, 1979 (1776).
4. For an intriguing article on the roots of homelessness in government urban-renewal programs, see Husock, Howard, "The Roots of Homelessness," *Critical Review*, Vol. 4(4):505-521, 1990.
5. Hayek, Friedrich A., *Rules and Order*, Vol. 1 of *Law, Legislation and Liberty* (Chicago, IL: University of Chicago Press, 1973), p. 36, defines "order" as "a state of affairs in which a multiplicity of elements of various kinds are so related to each other that we may learn from our acquaintance with some spatial or temporal part of the whole to form correct expectations concerning the rest, or at least expectations which have a good chance of proving correct."
6. Kirzner, Israel M., *Competition and Entrepreneurship* (Chicago, IL: University of Chicago Press, 1973).
7. A "spontaneous order" is an order that is the result of human action but not of human design. See Hayek, Friedrich A., *Studies in Philosophy, Politics and Economics* (Chicago, IL: University of Chicago Press, 1967).
8. Rent-seeking, as contrasted with profit-seeking, activity involves the use of scarce resources (labor, time, capital, etc.) to capture a position (usually government-created) from which to reap monopoly rents. Since rent-seekers spend resources to produce nothing that consumers demand, such expenditures are considered socially wasteful. For a survey of this topic, see Mueller, Dennis C., *Public Choice II: A Revised Edition of*

Public Choice (New York, NY: Cambridge University Press, 1989), Chap. 13.

9. See, for example, Hayek (1967).

10. The question of the stability of such an order is logically distinct and I will not address it in this essay.

11. Mises, Ludwig von, *A Critique of Intervention (Kritik des Interventionismus)*, Trans. by Sennholz, Hans F. (New Rochelle, NY: Arlington House, 1977(1929), p. 30, describes another aspect of this process when he says that the "very failure of interventionism reinforces the layman's conviction that private property must be controlled severely. The corruption of the regulatory bodies does not shake his blind confidence in the infallibility and perfection of the state; it merely fills him with moral aversion to entrepreneurs and capitalists."

12. One reason for government failure lies in the public-sector knowledge problem discussed below.

13. Traditional neo-classical economic theory views agents as finding the constrained optimal solution when the ends and means they face are fully known. Herbert A. Simon provides one alternative to this approach, his "bounded rationality." According to Simon, Herbert A., "Bounded Rationality," in *The New Palgrave's Dictionary of Economics*, vol 1, ed. by John Eatwell, Murray Milgate, and Peter Newman (London: Macmillan, 1977), p. 266, "the term 'bounded rationality' is used to designate rational choice that takes into account the cognitive limitations of the decision-maker—limitations of both knowledge and computational capacity." See also Simon, Herbert A., "Theories of Bounded Rationality," in *Decision and Organization*, ed. by G. B. Radner, and R. Radner (Amsterdam: North-Holland Publishing Co., 1972).

14. I am assuming that in a representative democracy legislators can take no effective action without the support of a sufficient number of their constituents.

15. According to Mises, Ludwig von, *Human Action: A Treatise on Economics*, Third revised ed. (Chicago, IL: Henry Regnery, 1966 (1949)). p 860, "neither a low standard of living nor progressive impoverishment automatically liquidates an economic system. It gives way to a more efficient system only if people themselves are intelligent enough to comprehend the advantages such a change might bring them."

16. For a discussion of this fund and its role in the process of intervention see *Ibid.*, pp. 855–858.

16

THE LEGAL STATUS OF MONEY

Bruce W. Ketler*

Most traditional and popular monetary theories claim that government can appoint any economic good it wants as money and, furthermore, can even dictate the laws of exchange. These notions are false. Nonetheless, the historical landscape is littered with examples of governments that harbor these notions. Government's tampering with money carries important economic considerations. For instance, legal-tender legislation is a form of economic interference. Such legislation directly impairs contracts and interferes with private property rights.

Money is not the creation of government. Nor can government guarantee its value. Money is a market phenomenon. The habits, customs, and practices of individuals determine what economic goods serve as money. Money has value because it serves as a useful medium of exchange and, in turn, as an acceptable medium of payment. Of all economic goods, money is the easiest to exchange. The usefulness of money rests on its value in exchange. Money does not require legal-tender legislation or any other form of government management. Economic exchange governs the acceptance of the most marketable of all economic goods.

The United States Supreme Court did not recognize the importance of this basic principle of exchange. Instead, the Court saw money as a creature of law. The judiciary agreed that the primary purpose of money was to serve as a medium of payment. Positive law determined the legal, or debt satisfying, value of money. As for transactions spanning time, the Court only addressed what constituted legal tender at the time of payment. The Court ignored

*Dr. Ketler is Chairman of the Department of Industrial Management and Associate Professor of Business at Grove City College, Grove City, PA.

what was acceptable means of payment when entering into contracts. In the United States, the federal government's journey down the road to a fiat money standard based on irredeemable paper required "assistance," which the Supreme Court provided amply to Congress and the executive branch.

Federal Sovereignty

The United States Supreme Court often reviews federal laws. The Court determines the extent of the executive branch's authority to execute specific laws according to the Constitution. The landmark case, *McCulloch v. Maryland,* established the practice of judicial review.[1] *McCulloch v. Maryland* dealt with the right of an individual state to tax a federal agency, namely, the State of Maryland and the Second National Bank of the United States. Maryland claimed the right to tax any banking association, including national banks, operating within Maryland's area of jurisdiction.

Chief Justice John Marshall, writing the majority opinion for the Court, stated that the implied powers of Congress provided the legal structure of the United States. Marshall's influence caused the Court to reassess its duties. Interpreting the Constitution became its primary task. But how was the Court to interpret this basic political document? It had two choices. The Court could interpret the Constitution strictly to the letter of the law or it could explore the broader intent of the document. The Court adopted the latter, feeling that a changing society requires a wide latitude.

The Court's right to review legislative activity preoccupied Marshall's mind until his death in 1835. The last words he ever uttered as Chief Justice reflected his thoughts on the subject.[2] "In the excitement produced by ardent controversy, gentlemen view the same object through such different media that minds not infrequently receive therefrom precisely opposite impressions. The Court, however, must see with its own eyes, and exercise its own judgment, guided by its own reason." Marshall's conviction had a lasting influence on the Court.

Few could dispute the effect Marshall's briefs had on the evolution of law in the United States. In turn, the ideology of Federalism helped forge Marshall's ideas on governance.[3] Marshall based his interpretation of the Court's responsibilities squarely on the principle of a strong national government. The Federalist position was quite clear. The central government must be strong enough to protect the liberties and advance the welfare of the people it governed. Historian Henry Steele Commager noted that the underlying philosophy of federalism was one that trusted human intelligence, eschewed the theoretical for the practical, was prepared to compromise, recognized the role of human nature in politics, and proposed to achieve reform by evolution rather than by revolution.[4] Marshall, as did his Federalist colleagues, felt that the individual states were a threat to individual liberty and economic freedom.[5] Only a strong central government could check the powers of the individual state governments.

However, the federal government's efforts to exceed its authority rarely went undisputed. This was certainly true with regard to the regulation of money, and the Supreme Court listened to opinions addressing four major questions of federal authority over money. The Court used the McCulloch case to rule on the extent of federal jurisdiction. Later cases addressed legal tender, the right to exchange precious-metal coins, and contracts containing gold clauses.

Ruling on the latter three questions hinged on how the Court responded to discussions about federal authority. Marshall's response to *McCulloch v. Maryland* upheld the federal government's position. His conclusion confirmed the legal relationship between the individual state governments and the federal government.

Marshall outlined the extent of the federal government's authority as implied by the Constitution. "The very nature of a constitution requires that only its great outlines should be marked, its important objects be deduced from the nature of the objects themselves.... This being true, the power of Congress to establish a bank is undeniable—it flows from the great powers to lay and collect taxes; to borrow money; to regulate commerce; to declare and conduct war; to raise and support armies and navies."[6]

Marshall's position was clear. Congress had the right to ensure the survival and prosperity of the Republic. Its legislative responsibility was especially important during unduly trying times for the nation. Marshall concluded his McCulloch opinion with these words: "The Congress may perform the high duties assigned to it, in the manner most beneficial to the people. Let the end be legitimate, let it be within the scope of the Constitution, and all means which are appropriate, which are plainly to that end, which are not prohibited but consistent with the letter and spirit of the Constitution, are constitutional."[7]

The balance of power between the individual states and the central government permanently shifted. The Supreme Court, in effect, lowered the constitutional barriers for the executive and legislative branches of the federal government. Marshall's words bear repeating. Any legislative act, as long as it reflected "the letter and spirit of the Constitution" was constitutional.

This particular passage became a familiar theme. *McCulloch v. Maryland* advanced the monetary authority of the federal government more than any other case presented before the Court. It served as a reference for the high Court's opinions in all the cases dealing with monetary jurisdiction. It is true, *McCulloch v. Maryland* did not address any specific aspect of monetary authority. The importance of the case was its effect on federal jurisdiction and sovereignty.[8]

The Constitution and Money

Beginning during the Civil War, the executive branch signed into law several legislative bills pertaining to money and issued related orders. The United States Constitution, however, does not explicitly state that the executive branch or the legislature has such authority. Nevertheless, upholding the government's position in these statutes, the Court claimed the right to set monetary policy was an implied power.

The Currency Acts of 1862, 1863, and 1878 permitted the federal government to issue paper money. Often called greenbacks, paper money had the same legal value as gold coins. However, the market value of greenbacks to gold coin was not the same. Gold coins had a higher exchange value than the government-issued paper money. During the 1930s, the executive branch enacted laws that made it illegal to tender gold coins as payment. Legislation denying the use of gold coins as money applied to future as well as existing gold clauses.

The Currency Acts and the restrictions placed on the use of gold as money raised questions of constitutional and contract law. Did the federal government exceed its authority? Was there a suitable reason to declare paper money at par with full-bodied gold coin? Could the federal government decree that mutually agreed-upon means of payment were void? Did the government have the right to require creditors to accept an alternative means of payment? The implications were significant. The Supreme Court responded to these questions about contract law, money, and government authority.

The opinions of Marshall and Roger Taney, Marshall's replacement as Chief Justice, were partly responsible for the Court's agreement on the need to regulate money. The Supreme Court, despite two minor exceptions, remained consistent. It continued to approve of government's implied monetary powers. Neither *Bronson v. Rodes* nor *Hepburn v. Griswold* deterred the Court's support of the government's right to set monetary policy and regulate the value of money.[9]

Changing Contractual Relationships

Any attempt to regulate the value of money runs contrary to the basic principles of economic exchange. There is no such economic condition as perfect price stability.[10] The exchange value of one good to another changes over time. It is market preferences that determine rates of exchange. This is true of the voluntary exchange of all goods, including money.

In a contract, the involved parties agree to a particular rate of exchange. However, at the time of payment, the exchange value of money itself may shift to favor one party over the other. This is a risk contracting parties must be willing to bear. No one, including an omnipotent government, can guarantee perfect price stability.

Changes in contractual relationships due to direct government interference is another matter. In keeping with the U.S. Constitution, what level of government had the right to regulate commerce? The Marshall Court was true to its Federalistic heritage. The obligation-of-contracts provision limited a state government's power to regulate economic activity *(Fletcher v. Peck).*[11] In addition, the contracts clause secured freedom of contract from interference by the state governments *(Ogden v. Saunders).*

Marshall's opinion in the Ogden case set forth words to that effect. Marshall used Ogden to uphold the economic liberties of the individual. "Individuals do not derive from government the right to contract, but bring that right with them into society....The obligation is not conferred by positive law, but rather is intrinsic and conferred by the act of the parties. The obligation of contract is confined to that which is actually written into the instrument."[12]

For Marshall, the contract clause was part of the American scheme of government. Marshall concluded his Ogden opinion with these words: "The power of changing the relative situation of debtor to creditor, of interfering with contracts, a power which comes home to every man, touches the interest of all, and controls the conduct of every individual in those things which he supposes to be proper for his own exclusive management."

Marshall was warning that if one law, such as a legal-tender law, becomes part of all contracts, so does every other law affecting contracts. Thus, a legislature could decide that all contracts should be subject to its authority. The Supreme Court did not heed Marshall's advice. Cases concerning legal tender and gold clauses made it possible for the federal government to dictate the payment medium for contracts.

The Taney Court

The Supreme Court did not heed Marshall's advice in part because of Roger Taney, a Jacksonian democrat. Taney, replacing Marshall as Chief Justice, did not identify with his predecessor's position. Taney correlated the public interest with government authority. He envisioned an authoritative central government. There was to be no question about the superiority of public authority over individual rights. Taney believed that private economic arrangements were a potential menace to the welfare of the people.[13]

Throughout his tenure, Taney seized opportunities to maintain the authority of the federal government. The Court followed Taney's lead, especially on questions about money. One finds the Taney Court's opinions on money in two cases: *Gwen v. Breedlove* and *United States v. Marigold.*[14]

Gwen v. Breedlove focused attention on proper tender in the payment of debts. James W. Breedlove had received a judgment in a Circuit Court of the United States against a debtor owing Breedlove $12,976 plus interest. Mississippi law required Gwen, a state marshall, to collect the sum due Breedlove. Gwen collected $5,000 in specie and the balance in bank notes. Breedlove accepted the coins but refused the bank notes. He claimed the bank notes were not *bona fide* legal tender.

The Supreme Court upheld Breedlove's position. Only gold and silver coin could serve as legal tender. The Court said that a state marshall may receive bank notes in satisfaction of an execution. However, he must account to the plaintiff in specie.

Justice John Catron delivered the Court's opinion. Catron based his opinion on Article I, Section 10 of the United State Constitution. Debtors can only tender gold or silver coin made current by law in payment of debts. Nevertheless, creditors still had a choice. A creditor could voluntarily receive bank notes in discharge of a contract. The law considers payment the same as specie. Thus, a creditor may, if he so chooses, accept any form of payment. He also reserves the right to demand payment as stated in contract or in what the law recognizes as current money.

One concept in particular influenced the Court's opinion on monetary authority. Government, not commercial trading practices, created the means of exchange. Six years later in the case *United States v. Marigold*, the Taney Court implied that money was a creation of law. Congress, in turn, was responsible for protecting that creation.

The Circuit Court (Northern District of New York) indicted Peter Marigold. Marigold's crime was importing foreign specie that resembled certain gold and silver coins made by the United States Mint. This was in violation of a law Congress passed on March 3, 1825 (4 Statutes at Large, 121). The law made it illegal to import coins with the intent to use the coins as money.

The Taney Court upheld the law as being within the spirit and intent of the Constitution. Under the power to regulate commerce, Congress can prohibit any activity falling within the legitimate sphere of commercial regulation, and the power to coin money and regulate its value fell within that sphere. In effect, the Supreme Court authorized Congress to protect the creation and object of that power.

A New Standard

Based upon Marshall's concept of judicial review and Taney's ideas concerning the sovereignty of the federal government, judicial guidelines for those who were to sit on the bench of the Supreme Court were firmly established. All that Congress and the president had to do was act in order to consolidate monetary authority in the hands of the federal government. All such acts would eventually have the blessing of the Court.

It would take eighty-five years to establish a money monopoly. The point of departure was a common law standard favoring precious metal coins. The new destination was a fiat standard of irredeemable paper money. Money based on politics replaced the economic goods the market chose as mediums of payment. Along the way to a fiat standard, the Supreme Court provided support when asked for directions. The Court gave federal government notes legal-tender status.[15] It upheld the government's authority to limit an individual's right to exchange money for other goods.[16] The Supreme Court also sustained the federal government's right to interfere with contract clauses specifying the means of payment.[17] In the end, the Supreme Court erected a barricade blocking the once heavily traveled path of freedom in money.

Notes and References

1. *McCulloch v. Maryland,* 1 Cranch 137 (1819).
2. *Mitchell v. United States,* 9 Peters 723 (1835).
3. Beveridge, Albert J., *The Life of John Marshall,* vol. 4 (Boston, MA: Houghton Mifflin Company, 1919).
4. Commager, Henry Steele, ed., *Hamilton, Madison, Jay Selections From the Federalist* (New York, NY: Meridith Corporation, 1949).
5. *Fletcher v. Peck,* (1810); *Ogden v. Saunders,* 25 U. S. (12 Wheaton) 334 (1827).
6. *McCulloch v. Maryland.*
7. *Ibid.*
8. Holzer, Henry Mark, *Government's Money Monopoly* (New York, NY: Books In Focus, 1981).
9. *Bronson v. Rodes,* (7 Wallace) 229 (1868); *Hepburn v. Griswold,* 75 U.S. (8 Wallace) 603 (1870).
10. Sennholz, Hans F., *Money and Freedom* (Spring Mills, PA: Libertarian Press, Inc., 1985).
11. *Fletcher v. Peck,* 6 Cranch 87 (1810).
12. *Ogden v. Saunders* (1827).
13. Smith, Charles W. Jr., *Roger B. Taney: Jacksonian Jurist* (New York, NY: Da Capo Press, 1973).
11. *Gwen v. Breedlove,* 2 Howard 38 (1844); *United States v. Marigold,* 9 Howard 560 (1850).
15. *Julliard v. Greenman,* 110 U. S. 421 (1884).
16. *Ling Su Fan v. United States,* 218 U.S. 302 (1910).
17. *Nortz v. United States,* 294 U. S. 317 (1935).

17

TAX, BORROW, AND SPEND:
The Dilemma of Federal Budget Reform

Matthew B. Kibbe*

The federal budget process, as it now exists, is symbolic of all that is wrong with government. It is tyrannical and coercive, blindly destructive, and seemingly uncontrollable. It serves as an arbitrary, faceless mechanism which steals from all, but benefits few. The federal budget is, in a very real sense, like a dead albatross hanging around the necks of the American people—slowly choking every individual under the weight of its swollen corpse.

The problem with the federal budget process, like government in general, is not so much born of corrupt individuals but of corrupting institutions, where power is so unlimited that its only real restraint comes from the moral sensibilities of individual members of Congress and their constituents. Such self-imposed limits typically give way to the allure of authority. "The state," notes Joseph Sobran, "is a devilishly convenient instrument for delegating otherwise criminal behavior: most people wouldn't kill or rob someone else, but if the state will do it for them, under the forms of legality, they will accept the spoils.... Both [Alexander Hamilton and James Madison] had hoped for a stronger central government than the Constitution had finally established, but they would have been appalled by the limitless and many-tentacled monster Americans take for granted in 1991."[1]

Clearly, the federal appropriations process that today consumes over one fourth of total income is not that which was originally

*Mr. Kibbe is Director of Federal Budget Policy for the United States Chamber of Commerce in Washington, DC. His articles, editorials, and reviews have appeared in *The Wall Street Journal, The Washington Times, Reason, The Freeman,* and *Market Process.*

envisioned by Hamilton, Madison, Thomas Jefferson and the other Founding Fathers. They had sought to limit severely the federal government's ability to redistribute wealth, and also to limit the transfer of power from individuals to government, which flows logically from that redistributive process.

The hope for change persists, as does the dire need for an ultimate realization of the limits on government power originally intended by the Constitution's authors. But the road to reform remains elusive.

A Lesson From History

In the fall of 1990, confronted with a growing federal budget deficit and a feeble economy, President George Bush signed into law the Omnibus Budget Reconciliation Act. That legislation imposed five years and $165 billion of new and higher taxes—the largest tax increase in the history of the United States—just as the economy was sliding into the dark waters of recession.

President Bush, encouraged by his fellow country-club Republicans and the Democratic leadership in Congress, personally defended this so-called "deficit reduction" package, at great personal political cost. He promised the American people the budget agreement would eliminate, once and for all, the deficit "cancer gnawing away at [the] nation's health." And he warned of the dire consequences of opposing the new taxes, predicting that "if we fail to act, next year alone we will face a federal budget deficit of more than $300 billion, a deficit that could weaken our economy further and cost us thousands of precious jobs."[2]

To economists and historians alike, the whole political debate that culminated in the tax and spending hikes of 1990 sounded sadly familiar. In his annual budget address on December 7, 1931, President Herbert Hoover similarly expressed concern about a growing budget deficit. According to that president, the federal government was then "face to face with a situation where for a time the current revenues of the government under our existing laws have fallen below the amounts required to meet the absolutely necessary expenses." Like Bush's, Hoover's solution to what he perceived to be a deficit crisis was higher taxes. "We cannot," he reasoned, "maintain public confidence nor stability of the federal government without undertaking some temporary tax increases."[3]

Less than a week later, then Secretary of the Treasury and close presidential advisor Andrew Mellon, further fanned the flames of political hysteria surrounding the deficit in a statement before the House Ways and Means Committee. "Under existing conditions," said Mellon, "the task of bringing our budget into balance is by no means an easy one, and involves not only self-denial but some measure of sacrifice."[4]

Faced with a shrinking economy and an estimated $2.1 billion budget deficit for 1932, President Hoover and Secretary Mellon proposed a host of destructive new and higher taxes, including higher income tax rates, higher taxes on gasoline, and other excise taxes.

In the wake of Hoover's proposed tax increase, a grassroots tax rebellion erupted across the nation. "Wherever you go you run into mass meetings called to protest against taxes," wrote Anne O'Hare McCormick. "Opposition has seldom been so spontaneous, so universal, so determined. The nearest thing to a political revolution in this country is the tax revolt."[5] Echoing the general mood of the people, Representative Claude Parsons entered the following into the *Congressional Record*:

> He was taxed on boots, was taxed on shoes, was taxed on suits and
> taxed on booze,
> Was taxed on socks, was taxed on hose, was taxed on everything
> that grows.
> A tax attacked him when he was born, attacked him 'til he
> felt forlorn.
> If they increase, as in this bill, it won't be long until they will
> Impose a tax on growing corn and on the toots of Gabriel's horn.[6]

Despite public opposition, Congress went on to pass what was one of the largest peacetime tax increases in the history of the United States as the Revenue Act of 1932. The Democratic leadership in Congress, particularly Speaker of the House of Representatives, John Garner, was instrumental in passing the final tax bill.

Compounding the effects of years of inflationary Federal Reserve policies, the Smoot-Hawley Tariff Act and other regulatory burdens, this massive tax increase was the Hoover Administration's swan song. As economist Hans F. Sennholz observes, "It does not matter whether [this tax increase] was conceived in malice or benevolence—it shattered all hope of recovery."[7] Gross National Product fell from $75.8 billion in 1931 to $58 billion in 1932, and bottomed out at $55.6 billion in 1933.[8] Already high civilian unemployment skyrocketed from 15.9 percent in 1931 to 23.6 percent in 1932, and peaked at 24.9 percent in 1933.[9]

Ironically, the federal budget deficit which had concerned the Hoover Administration increased dramatically, even with (or because of) the 1932 tax increase. Due to a collapsing economy, actual government revenues fell from $3.1 billion in 1931 to $1.9 billion in 1932.[10] Combined with higher spending, the lagging tax revenues resulted in a deficit of over $2.7 billion, up from $461 million in 1931. The deficit remained high at $2.6 billion in 1933.[11] Based on Secretary Mellon's original projections, the 1932 budget deficit would have actually been $600 million lower if the tax increases had never occurred.

Herbert Hoover was defeated by Franklin Delano Roosevelt in 1932. As Roosevelt's running mate and Vice Presidential candidate in late 1932, former Speaker John Garner, the key Congressional proponent of higher taxes, blamed Hoover and his Administration for "their failure to balance the budget of a family of 120,000,000 people [which] is at the very bottom of the economic troubles from which we are suffering."[12]

Higher Spending, Higher Deficits

History is cruel in its insistence, but affords new opportunities to learn from past mistakes. As Herbert Hoover discovered, and as much as it irks big-spending politicians on both sides of the congressional aisle, the *only* way to achieve genuine and lasting deficit reduction is through spending restraint and spending cuts. Raising taxes, particularly during periods of economic malaise, only exacerbates the deficit by further reducing the size of the economic pie. George Bush, then a candidate for president, himself recognized this simple economic truth in 1988, when he argued that "the surest way to kill recovery is to raise taxes. That will stifle everything from investment and personal savings to consumer spending."[13]

Bush had it right the first time. A little over one year after his cherished budget agreement was first implemented, the economy remains listless, unable to move forward, devastated by a recession that has lasted far longer, and cut far deeper, than the self-anointed "experts" within the Washington establishment had predicted. The budget deficit, the *raison d'etre* behind the budget agreement, has nearly doubled in size, from what was expected to be a $179 billion deficit in fiscal year 1991, to an unprecedented $362 billion expected in fiscal year 1992. Projected out at its current rate of growth, the *annual* budget deficit will exceed $1 trillion by the year 2000.

As a result of the budget agreement, federal spending will consume over $1.5 trillion of the nation's total wealth in 1992—up from 23 percent of Gross National Product in 1990 to over 25 percent in 1992, a post-World War II record. Total federal spending will rise by nearly 17 percent, from $1.25 trillion in 1990 to over $1.5 trillion in 1992.

The budget agreement of 1990 is but one, albeit extreme, example of how the federal budget process operates, one fiscal year after another. Higher tax revenues are continually outrun by new spending as established entitlements grow uncontrolled and new spending programs are enacted. On average, Congress increases federal spending by $1.59 for every $1.00 of new taxes raised.[14]

The problem, then, is not the deficit itself, but rather the total burden of government on the private economy.

A Vicious Cycle of Taxing and Spending

Unfortunately, that burden of government continues to grow, nourished by higher taxes and encouraged by a political culture of redistribution. The result is much more than the expected outcome of pork-barrel politics, where legislators divide up the expropriated wealth of government as best benefits their political constituents, and in turn are re-elected to do so again and again. For with the transfer of wealth comes a relinquishing of freedom from the people to the government. Wanting to expand their influence and control, politicians profit from increasing unemployment benefits, food stamps, and other welfare programs, ostensibly intended to help the unemployed and downtrodden, but simply add to their ranks (and continue to build the power base of politicians). The individual becomes trapped in a spiral of government-generated "crisis" and "solution," where Uncle Sam knocks down with a left hook and extends a helping hand with his right.

But individuals typically seem willing to consent to this process by re-electing their own representatives in the appropriations process. Or, at very least, a simple majority of that portion of the population which votes tends to re-elect those same legislators who are responsible for the continuation of the process. Why?

The very nature of our government's institutions forces constituents to maintain the entrenched power of well-placed and experienced legislators and, through them, an ability to manipulate the federal appropriations process to their relative advantage. Constituents saddled with higher and higher tax burdens have every incentive to elect and support legislators who bring back a lion's share of the federal plunder. Likewise, legislators who want to be reelected have every incentive to raise spending, and will typically choose to borrow or raise taxes on all Americans rather than cut spending earmarked for their congressional district. This, in large part, explains the predominance of legislators whose official ideology is one of bigger, "better" government and higher government spending.

This vicious cycle of taxing and spending is a classic example of what public choice economists refer to as a "prisoners' dilemma." As the story goes, two captured partners in crime, both prisoners, could go free if neither cops a plea by admitting guilt. But if only one cops a plea, the other will receive a lifetime sentence. Since neither prisoner can trust the other not to squeal, each cuts a deal, and both go to jail. Even though cooperation would have freed both prisoners ultimately, each must settle for a sub-optimal, shorter jail term in order to avoid a life sentence.

In this particular case, most citizens want the federal government to live within limited means, and everyone would benefit from the lower tax burden which would result from limited government. But it is in no one's interest to make the first move in that direction, and the process of taxing and spending continues, unchecked, even though almost everyone's situation is worsened.

This "voters' dilemma" explains why widespread public dissatisfaction with higher taxes, record spending levels and swollen deficits does not typically translate well at the polls. And it also explains away the apparent paradox of an electorate which simultaneously wants less government interference in their lives but more government money in their pockets.

One always hopes that a certain public-spiritedness, and perhaps even a sense of moral courage, will prevail at the voting booth. But unless an individual derives unusually high psychic benefits from not feeding at the public trough, he must inevitably vote to sustain the process that steals more and more of his income.

The Death of Gramm-Rudman

The taxing and spending cycle goes a long way in explaining why legislators continue to choose higher taxes and deficits over spending cuts. And it explains why both Congress and the White House rushed forward with a budget agreement which effectively eliminated the one remaining constraint on that process: the Gramm-Rudman-Hollings budget law, the Balanced Budget and Emergency Deficit Control Act of 1985.

Gramm-Rudman set deficit reduction targets, and required across-the-board cuts in spending, referred to as sequesters, if those deficit targets were not met. The law had many loopholes, particularly the exemption of most bloated entitlement programs from sequester. But by 1989, it had actually reduced the deficit as a share of Gross National Product, from 5.4 percent in 1985 to 2.9 percent.[15]

Not surprisingly, Gramm-Rudman was almost unanimously rejected by official Washington the moment it became a genuine constraint upon the spending behavior of the federal legislature. Indeed, Professor Hans F. Sennholz predicted that very result in 1987, arguing that "even if the Act should reflect political honesty and sincerity, which are rare virtues in the world of politics, it lacks wide intellectual support and, above all, the moral foundation on which it can endure.... Obviously, the Act will be a favorite target of political criticism until it is repealed, declared unconstitutional, or merely circumvented and evaded."[16] In that year, the Gramm-Rudman deficit targets were revised significantly upward, as part of the Balanced Budget and Emergency Deficit Control Reaffirmation Act of 1987. One year before the deficit originally was to be eliminated, Gramm-Rudman was jettisoned completely in favor of the Budget Enforcement Act of 1990.

In fact, the specter of the Gramm-Rudman sequester was used as a bludgeon to ram the Omnibus Budget Reconciliation Act, higher taxes and all, down the throats of the American people. At that time, the Congress faced a fiscal 1991 budget deficit of between $179 billion and $205.8 billion, well over the $64 billion deficit target mandated by Gramm-Rudman. The potential of a $120 billion cut from a $1.12 trillion budget was a full-blown political crisis, the latest perennial budget crisis in a town that generates crises, and then feeds off them. The headlines and soundbites spoke of a government starved for revenues and a bare-bones federal budget lacking sufficient funds to support the most fundamental government functions. Everything from air traffic control, to federal meat inspection, to "infrastructure" (read: anything and everything the government wants to spend money on) would have bled under the arbitrary steel of the Gramm-Rudman knife.

The conclusion was inevitable before the "crisis" ever occurred. A *Newsweek* headline matter-of-factly observed: "An Out-of-Control Deficit is Forcing Both Parties to Confront the Awful Necessity of New Taxes."[17] Unless the administration struck a budget deal with Congress, unexempt federal spending programs would have been cut automatically to meet the Gramm-Rudman target.

Cut federal government spending? Not likely. Richard Darman, the Bush Administration's top budget advisor as Director of the Office of Management and Budget, warned that "clearly, the sequester alternative is unattractive. It is, therefore, all the more reason to seek to reach prompt agreement on a responsible, multi-year deficit reduction program."[18] "It [across-the-board spending cuts] would have a chilling effect on our way of life in the United States," shuddered Republican Representative Silvio Conte.[19]

The Charade of Budget Reform

A deal was struck, taxes were raised and, as is the pattern, the new taxes came with new budget reforms and a vague promise of spending control in the future. For example, while many proponents of the Omnibus Budget Reconciliation Act of 1990, including President Bush, openly acknowledged the potential for these excessive new taxes and spending to cause some short-run harm to economic growth, they pointed to the fundamental changes in the budget process also included in the agreement as reason enough to support the package. These changes, so it was claimed, would finally provide tough and enforceable constraints on the federal government's future ability to tax and spend. Ostensibly, higher taxes and engorged spending programs were the ransom to be paid for reform. But, it was claimed, future benefits would far outweigh the short-term costs.

These so-called reforms became the Budget Enforcement Act of 1990. This supposedly tough and enforceable strait jacket on the growth of federal spending and taxes is nothing of the sort. A careful examination of its provisions shows that the new budget reforms actually enforce automatically *higher* spending levels and *higher* taxes.

The Act eliminates what little spending restraint was provided for by the Gramm-Rudman-Hollings deficit reduction law. Unlike the fixed deficit targets which characterized Gramm-Rudman before, the new deficit targets automatically adjust upward to accommodate higher deficits. As such, these targets no longer provide budget discipline. Instead, the new budget enforcement relies on two separate mechanisms: discretionary outlays are subject to spending caps, while entitlements and revenues are required to meet a new "pay-as-you-go" requirement.

An important point to note is that the spending caps are "rubber" caps, not real limits. They are subject to automatic adjustment for up to nine separate factors, particularly for changes in either economic conditions or technical assumptions. As official economic assumptions are adjusted to meet reality, and as other unanticipated spending increases are "held harmless" under the new budget enforcement system, the caps will continue to rise to accommodate higher spending.

The pay-as-you-go provision accomplishes two things. First, it shields automatic entitlement increases, such as Social Security COLAs, from sequester. And it mandates that any future tax or entitlement legislation which either reduces revenues or increases outlays must be offset with either equivalent tax increases or spending cuts or both. This effectively eliminates the possibility of tax cuts by linking them to politically sensitive cuts in Social Security, Medicare, or other special entitlements. It also means that new entitlement programs will necessarily be financed with higher taxes, and not spending cuts from discretionary accounts.

In the long-run, the most damaging aspect of the 1990 budget agreement may not be the record tax and spending increases, but these changes in budget enforcement, which effectively prevent the correct tax and spending policies from being adopted in the future.

The Need For Institutional Change

This should be a fundamental lesson for all those interested in real and lasting reforms in government institutions: Unless you change the rules of the game at the constitutional level, the outcome of the game will remain the same. As the game now exists, legislators have little incentive either to impose limits on their own behavior or, if they do, to adhere to those limits.

Strict constitutional limits on the federal government's ability to tax, borrow, and spend would change the rules of the game and, more importantly, would break the upward spiral of taxes and spending. The need for constitutional reform is premised on two historical events. The first was an explicit change in the Constitution itself, when Congress passed the 16th Amendment to permit a national income tax in 1913. With this, Congress successfully stripped away an important constitutional barrier to excessive taxation. The second was the more subtle, progressive erosion of moral constraints on government behavior. Culturally imposed limits had previously kept federal spending in check. Their deterioration precipitated the passage of the 16th Amendment, which in turn unleashed government to expand virtually unchecked.

Nobel laureate economist James Buchanan argues that new changes to the Constitution are necessary, "as substitutes for the eroded moral rules." According to him, "balanced budgets that were dictated once by moral standards were never explicitly mentioned in formal constitutional documents. Without such standards, however, balanced budget constraints must be explicitly chosen, imposed, and enforced."[20] Strict limits on the legislature's ability to levy new taxes and to appropriate those monies would alter the rules of the game, forcing Congress, like every individual household, to allocate scarce means among unlimited wants.

Unfortunately, in their bipartisan frenzy to do something about the deficit, many balanced-budget advocates in Congress seem to have lost sight of the ultimate cause of budget deficits and the real problem—namely, excessive government spending. Like almost everything that emerges from the political process, the constitutional reforms that do enjoy the solid support of Congress would in fact cause more harm than good, would do nothing to limit the overall size of government, and would actually fuel the tax and spending cycle by forcing ever higher taxes.

On Capitol Hill, the most popular of such balanced budget proposals would strictly limit the ability of government to finance new spending through debt. S.J. Res. 18, a Senate resolution that would amend the Constitution to require a balanced budget, is an excellent case in point. Senator Paul Simon, a liberal Democrat from Illinois, is the author of this proposal, and a leading advocate of this approach. The language in the Simon resolution requires that "total outlays for that year shall not exceed the level of estimated receipts set forth...unless three-fifths of the total membership of each house of Congress shall provide, by roll call vote, for a specific excess of outlays over estimated receipts." Unfortunately, it also allows for tax increases with the approval of a mere constitutional majority. "No bill to increase revenue shall become law unless approved by a majority of the total membership of each House by a roll call vote."

The problem with S.J. Res. 18, and other similar approaches, is its almost singular emphasis on deficit reduction *per se*. It would actually encourage more of both taxes and spending by increasing the already substantial federal bias toward new taxes. A bias is created because, while strictly limiting the government's ability to borrow, it would leave virtually unchanged Congress' ability to levy new taxes. This asymmetrical structuring of the rules would allow, even encourage, a constant upward ratcheting of both federal tax receipts as a percentage of national income and total government spending.

Some proponents of this balanced budget amendment argue that requiring a constitutional majority vote to raise new revenues offers a sufficiently strong restraint against higher taxes. Any vote for higher taxes is an onerous one for members of Congress, it is claimed, and it is always difficult to find majority support for higher taxes. Historically, this has not been the case. During the past four full sessions of Congress, for example, an average of 96.3 percent of all tax and revenue bills passed the House of Representatives by more than a constitutional majority. In the Senate, an average of 99.1 percent of all tax bills passed by more than a constitutional majority. In practice, the decision to finance new spending programs with new tax dollars seems to be rote for the vast majority of federal legislators. What Congress could not borrow it would continue to extract through new and higher taxes. As Hans F. Sennholz observes:

> A Constitutional mandate to balance the budget could be interpreted to mandate higher taxes and more government intervention. Most politicians, including the amendment advocates, are likely to opt for boosting revenue rather than reducing expenditures. After all, they themselves launched the expenditures and created the entitlements; they would be rather reluctant to rescind them as long as they can raise revenues through new taxation.... Under the strictures of a balanced budget amendment, Congress undoubtedly would boost taxes significantly, no matter how they would depress the economy.[21]

Amending the U.S. Constitution is serious business. Any proposed changes in the rules must be carefully scrutinized by the advocates of those changes. Hasty fundamental alterations in the federal budget process may well produce unwanted and even destructive behavior on the part of Congress.

Still, a properly constructed balanced-budget amendment that has an effective limit on taxes and spending is possibly the only *direct* budget process reform that could restore lasting fiscal integrity and stem the steady encroachment of government upon the private economy. Needless to say, there is little sincere support for such an amendment in Congress itself.

Public support for constitutional reform remains strong. Across America, 30 states have passed legislation calling for a constitutional convention to adopt a balanced-budget amendment. Many citizens want to curb the overall growth of government spending because they understand that government impedes economic prosperity by taxing productive resources, and by spending on the basis of special and parochial interests rather than on the basis of economic efficiency. But the "voters' dilemma" still looms: in order to recoup something in exchange for the taxes they pay, Americans continue to support their representation in the entrenched legislature, and with it the spending programs they directly benefit from.

Is Real Fiscal Discipline Possible?

Out of anger and frustration, many citizens have begun calling for congressional term limits as the only means of breaking out of this vicious cycle. Across the nation, state term limitation initiatives are beginning to appear on ballots. Colorado's voters have already approved such a measure, and many more states will have congressional term limits on their ballots in 1992.

Across-the-board limits on congressional terms might finally break the process of taxing and spending that entraps constituents and nourishes the arrogance of an entrenched, incumbent legislature. James Miller III, chairman of Citizens for a Sound Economy and former Director of the Office of Management and Budget, has concluded that term limits would significantly reduce federal spending.[22] Among other things, he finds a strong positive empirical relationship between the length of time a legislator spends in office and the amount that legislator votes to spend each year. Eliminate the privilege of incumbency, Dr. Miller concludes, and the size of government will be reduced, perhaps by one third.

He is right. Still, his analysis attributes too great an effect to term limits themselves on the appropriations process. The positive relationship between congressional experience and spending more likely reflects the relative power, in terms of leadership positions and committee chairmanships held, which logically follows from seniority. Term limits would eliminate the advantage of incumbency, but the potential number of taxpayer dollars to be divided up among legislators would remain, and would most likely be spent. Simply limiting terms would not alter fundamentally the short-run incentives of elected officials. Even limited in their tenure, legislators would still attempt to engorge their particular constituents at the expense of the public at large.

The most powerful positive effect of term limits on the federal budget process is more subtle, but no less important. In the long-run, term limits would indeed break the vicious cycle of tax-and-spend because it would alter legislators' long-run incentives. A politician limited to two terms would in a very real sense be a citizen legislator, with a career outside of a shorter stint in politics. By shortening a legislator's tenure in power, term limits would lengthen his perspective on particular policy decisions.

While in power, members would still be tax consumers, but they would also look to the day when they would once again become taxpayers. Presumably, this would make them much more receptive to long-run, fundamental changes in the rules of the game itself—to tough constitutional constraints on the budget process. A Congress limited in tenure just might pass a line-item veto, or even a strong tax limitation/balanced budget amendment to the Constitution.

Unfortunately, as a recent vote against term limits in Washington state demonstrated, implementing such limits will be difficult. Initiative 553, a federal term limit measure which early polls suggested had the overwhelming support of voters, ultimately failed by a margin of eight percentage points. Only 46 percent of Washington's voters actually pulled the lever that would have "thrown the bums out."

The vote against term limitation in Washington state was certainly frustrating, but not wholly surprising. Initiative 553 would have placed retroactive limits on federal public service, forcing the entire Washington delegation out by 1994. In effect, voters were asked to give up the skilled and well-placed representation of their own interests in the federal appropriations process almost immediately, with absolutely no promise of fundamental change in the budget process itself. Other, entrenched congressional delegations, unhindered by term limits, presumably would move in and devour Washington's share of the take.

For one thing, the state would have lost a powerful voice in Representative Thomas Foley. As Speaker of the House of Representatives, Foley has the political power to determine single-handedly the entire agenda for the House of Representatives. He is arguably one of the most influential men in the federal government. Had Initiative 553 passed, Foley would have been replaced in 1994 with someone with little or no experience in the federal appropriations process, and no means of obtaining the power necessary to compete for federal tax dollars. Washington state's new citizen legislators would face the likes of Representative Jamie Whitten, the Potentate/Chairman of the House Appropriations Committee who was elected to Congress in 1941, presumably before most members of the freshman delegation would have been born.

Indeed, these implicit costs to the citizens of Washington state were made very explicit by the entrenched political machine that actively campaigned against the measure. Foley personally lead the campaign against term limits, warning that "it would in every way weaken our state's ability to serve the people of this state."[23] This amounted to a thinly veiled threat of lost pork-barrel dollars to the state. According to one *Los Angeles Times* report published just days before the vote, "the federal government is hugely influential in the economics of Washington, both through the management of forest resources and through the U.S. Bonneville Power Administration, which provides some of the cheapest electricity rates in America from hydro-electric generators on the Columbia River. Safeguarding this low-cost power is a job for a congressional delegation with clout, opponents of the initiative say."[24] By 1992, the federal government will have incurred obligations totaling $3.23 billion in the operations of the Bonneville Power Administration, including both spending outlays and direct federal loans.[25]

Voters got the message. According to a *Seattle Times* poll taken just prior to the vote, 52 percent of registered voters asked feared the loss of their congressional delegation's clout in Washington, D.C.

Where Do We Go From Here?

A constitutional amendment that limits congressional terms *nationwide* would not create a disadvantage for any one state which otherwise might alone be sacrificing its delegation's incumbency. With an across-the-board reduction in congressional power, voters might also reasonably expect some relief from higher taxes down the road. Unfortunately, term limitation has few supporters in Congress itself. But, like constitutional limits on taxes and spending, there is almost no likelihood that the beneficiaries of government power would choose to constrain their own authority through limits on legislative tenure.

Or perhaps state-by-state term-limit initiatives will ultimately succeed. After all, an impressive 46 percent of Washington's voters did choose term limitation, despite the potential costs. Term limitation succeeded in Colorado because the costs associated with the loss of congressional seniority were pushed back past the year 2000. But if piecemeal term-limit initiatives do sweep the nation, it will signify more than voter dissatisfaction with their representation in the federal government. It will symbolize an intellectual revolution among the governed, a modern-day Tea Party.

Short of that revolution, there is little hope for fundamental change.

Notes and References

1. Sobran, Joseph "Beyond Delegated Powers?" *The Washington Times* (October 21, 1991).
2. *The Washington Post* (October 3, 1990).
3. *Report of the Special Committee on Federal Taxation*, No. 60 (Washington, DC: U.S. Chamber of Commerce, 1932), p. 5.
4. *Ibid.*
5. McCormick, Anne O'Hare, *The World At Home* (New York, NY: 1956), p. 93.
6. *Congressional Record*, 1932, p. 6379.
7. Sennholz, Hans F., *The Great Depression: Will We Repeat It?* (Spring Mills, PA: Libertarian Press, 1988), p. 15.
8. *Historical Statistics of the United States*, Volume I (Washington, DC: Department of Commerce, Bureau of the Census, 1975), p. 224.
9. *Ibid.*, p. 135.
10. *Historical Statistics of the United States*, Volume II (Washington, DC: Department of Commerce, Bureau of the Census, 1975), p. 1104.
11. *Ibid.*
12. Herbert Hoover quoting John Garner in *Memoirs: The Great Depression*, p. 142.
13. *George Bush: Leadership on the Issues* (Washington, DC: Republican National Committee, December 1988), p. 65.
14. Vedder, Richard, Gallaway, Lowell, and Frenze, Christopher, "Taxes and Deficits: New Evidence," Joint Economic Committee document (October 30, 1991).
15. *Budget of The United States Government, Fiscal Year 1991*, p. A-283.
16. Sennholz, Hans F., *Debts and Deficits* (Spring Mills, PA: Libertarian Press, Inc., 1987), pp. 134-135.
17. *Newsweek*, (May 21, 1990), p. 18.
18. *Mid-Session Review of the Budget* (Washington, DC: Office of Management and Budget, 1990), p. 1.
19. "Desire to Avoid Gramm-Rudman Cuts May Determine Course of Budget Talks," *The Wall Street Journal*, (May 15, 1990).
20. Buchanan, James, "The Moral Dimension of Debt Financing," in *Liberty, Market, and the State* (New York, NY: New York University Press, 1985), p. 190.
21. *Debts and Deficits*, pp. 122-123.

22. Miller, James C. III, "Cut Federal Spending—Limit Congressional Terms," *The Wall Street Journal*, (August 19, 1991).
23. "Foley Calls Term Initiative 'Anti-People,'" *Seattle Times*, (November 3, 1991).
24. "Push for Term Limits May Rob Washington State of Its Clout," *Los Angeles Times*, (October 29, 1991).
25. *Budget of the United States Government, Fiscal Year 1992*, Part Four, p. 620.

18

HUMAN ACTION, FREEDOM, AND ECONOMIC SCIENCE

Israel M. Kirzner*

I

In pondering which topic to choose for a paper in a volume honoring Professor Hans Sennholz, a scholar who has devoted his long and fruitful career to the dissemination of the ideas of his teacher, Ludwig von Mises, with such distinction, my memory took me back to my first meeting, at New York University, with Hans in the mid-fifties. This was, in fact, in the Mises seminar held each Thursday evening in a palatial room in a townhouse on Washington Square North. It is this trip down memory lane which has, indirectly, indeed suggested the topic for this paper.

I was a very green young graduate student at the time I first met Hans, who had just completed his doctoral dissertation under Mises. It was a short time later (early 1956, I believe) that Mises suggested to me a topic for my own dissertation. I have often thought back to my sheer good fortune not only in being able to study under Mises, but, in particular, to have been guided by him from that early stage in my work, to think intensively about the foundations of economic science. What has brought me to the topic of this paper is my recent realization that it has taken me some thirty-five years to appreciate fully what I now believe to be the uniqueness of Mises's own position in the topic which he suggested for my research. Let me explain.

Mises suggested that I explore the changing views about individual behavior which economists had, since the time of Adam Smith, adopted in order for them to grasp the possibility of a science of economics. Given the apparent unpredictability of indi-

*Dr. Kirzner is Professor of Economics at New York University.

vidual behavior it is intuitively difficult to account for the economic regularities which seem to occur. It was necessary somehow to "understand" individual behavior in a way consistent with the possibility of "scientific laws." The classical economists had seen economics as a science of wealth, made possible by the notion of selfish, materialistic, economic man. Neoclassical economics had escaped this view and (as ultimately made clear by Lionel Robbins) was able to see economics as an abstract science rooted in allocative, maximizing, economizing individual behavior. Mises saw his own system as going beyond the Robbinsian view, permitting us to see economic science as made possible by *human action,* the decisions made by purposeful, reasoning human beings intent on improving their situations. I learned a very great deal by pursuing this suggestion of Mises, a great deal of the history of economic doctrines, and a great deal concerning the epistemological foundations of economics. This research enabled me to complete a doctoral dissertation which matured, several years later, into my first book, *The Economic Point of View* (1960). I burden the reader with these autobiographical details in order to provide the background for the present paper. It is my present opinion that the concluding chapter in that book, the chapter discussing the Misesian system, does not do full justice to Mises's understanding of the role of human action in serving as the foundation for economic science.

In the following section, I briefly outline the relevant portion of my 1960 discussion of Mises's notion of human action and its implications, and contrast that discussion with my present understanding of the implications of Misesian human action. In section III, I place this deepened appreciation for "what Mises really meant,"[1] in the context of broader twentieth-century developments within the Austrian economics tradition. I also draw attention to the implications of this deepened understanding, for appreciating the role of individual freedom in inspiring the efficiencies of the market process.

II

The difference between my 1960 understanding of Misesian human action and my 1991 appreciation of it can be expressed as follows: In 1960 I had understood Misesian economics as proceeding by logically tracing through the consequences of interacting individual human decisions—each of which was governed by reason—in pursuit of respective individual purposes. It is this purposefulness of action which characterizes "conduct that is accompanied by the consciousness of volition, of something more than a bundle of reflexes responding to specific stimuli. The nature of these various stimuli and the directions towards which they variously tend to guide action are completely independent of the desires and will of the actor.... But because man possesses the power to reject one course of action for another..., the physical, physiological, and psychological sciences do not exhaust the facts of action that are capable of scientific explanation.... Sciences of human action will be distinct from other sciences in that the former begin where the latter end, *viz.* in the implications of the rationality that governs purposeful behavior."[2]

The possibility of a science of economics, explaining the emergence of market regularities out of the freely made decisions of autonomous individuals, rested not on any fictitious reduction of man to the classical caricature of selfish *homo oeconomicus* single-mindedly pursuing material wealth. Nor did it rest on the neoclassical view of man as lightning calculator of mathematical problems of utility maximization in the context of given ends and means. Instead the Misesian system (as interpreted in my 1960 chapter) rested simply on the "praxeological" insight that the action taken by a purposeful human being will be one reflecting his rationality, his reasoned assessment of the possibilities for and consequences of alternative attempts at improving his situation. (Optimal, economizing, allocation of given scarce means among competing given ends might well be one possible consequence of this rational assessment. But what renders a science of economics possible is this latter rationality, rather than the particular allocative pattern which has monopolized the attention of neoclassical economics.)

There is nothing in this 1960 discussion which draws attention to the role of entrepreneurial discovery in generating the systematic results which economic science is able to explain. And, from my perspective of 1991, it is this which seems the major inadequacy of the earlier treatment.

I should perhaps emphasize that the characteristic Austrian emphasis on market *processes* (as distinct from the exclusive neoclassical preoccupation with market states of equilibrium) was well known to me in 1960.[3] Although (as will be made clear in section III) I was not yet sufficiently aware of the cardinal role of entrepreneurial discovery in Mises's system. I certainly did appreciate the sense in which Mises saw the market as a *process* (possibly pointing in the direction of equilibrium). There is no discussion of market process in my 1960 chapter not because I was unaware of its central role in Mises's understanding of the operation of the market, but because (as I then thought) the process character of the market had no bearing on the definition of the "economic" side of social phenomena (which my 1960 book was devoted to explore). What made economic science possible, I understood Mises to argue, was the rationality, the purposefulness of human action. Market processes emerge in systematic fashion because of this rationality, of this purposefulness. The critics who had attacked the validity of economics because it depended upon the view of man as unrealistically selfish, or as mechanically maximizing, were wrong; economics does not depend (and, in Mises's eyes, never did really depend) on these caricatures. The theorems of economics depend only on the power of reason to guide purposeful behavior, that is all. It was thus not necessary to emphasize the process nature of markets in order to identify the unique " point of view" which economics expresses. So I believed in 1960.

What I wish now to emphasize is that, from my 1991 perspective, this earlier way of understanding Mises is inadequate. When Mises identified the concept of human action as the essential building block for a praxeological economic science, it is now clear to me that this implies far more than simply the importance of purposefulness for the analysis *of decisions made in given situations.* The concept of human action, it is now clear to me, is important in the Misesian system because of its fruitfulness in explaining how *economic agents discover changes that have occurred in their very market situations,* and generate, as a consequence, those systematic market process which are so central to Misesian economics.

Critics of economics have, for close to two hundred years, criticized it for depending upon some variant of the idea of universal human selfishness. In 1960 I understood the Misesian response to this criticism to consist simply in identifying the essential key to human behavior *in given situations* as purposefulness rather than selfishness. I now understand the proper Misesian response to this criticism to consist in showing how the purposefulness of human action (without any necessary selfish motivations) is the essential key to the discovery by agents that they are in fact *not* in the "given situations" which they had hitherto assumed to be relevant.

For my 1960 understanding, the entrepreneurial element in Misesian human action is not important for the distillation of an analytically unique economic point of view. For my present understanding matters appear rather differently. What sets Mises's conception of human action (as the foundation of economics) apart from the mainstream neoclassical conception of the rational, economizing decision (in that same role) is, as I now see, that, unlike the latter, the concept of human action illuminates directly those dynamic processes through which the market absorbs and responds to exogenous changes. When we challenge the erroneous belief that the efficiency of market outcomes depends upon selfishness, we are able to do so by showing how the flexibility and responsiveness of market adjustments is rooted, not necessarily in man's passion for material wealth, (and certainly not in any programmed pattern of allocative maximization) but in man's entrepreneurial propensity to discover changes which can redound to his benefit (i.e., to the more successful attainment of his goals, *whatever* they may be). If we are able to recognize that possibility for understanding social phenomena which is not covered by the most complete imaginable application of the physical, physiological, and psychological sciences, we are inevitably drawn to recognize also that this possibility transcends the narrow scope of static decision making. That uniquely economic element which enables us, in Misesian fashion, to understand the economic rationale of the human decision, inevitably illuminates for us at the same time the manner in which that rationale extends to the dynamics of discovery in the context of change, and hence to the dynamic processes which are thus generated.

Whereas my 1960 exposition implied, in effect, that the entrepreneurial element in Misesian human action is not essential for the identification of what constitutes, for Mises, the economic point of view, I now believe this to be incorrect. A Misesian appreciation for the existence of a uniquely economic point of view rests, it now seems to me, squarely on that understanding of the discovery-potential in human action which constitutes its entrepreneurial aspect. Let me, in section III, now turn to place my new appreciation of "what Mises really meant," in the context of some of the more fundamental changes in the core of Austrian economics which have occurred during the past three quarters of a century.

III

During the nineteen-twenties the Austrian economists enjoyed considerable reputation within the profession. Economists visiting the Continent, whether from England or from the U.S., would almost invariably make it their business to visit Vienna. The subjectivist approach of the Austrians was widely recognized and respected as one of the key traditions in contemporary economic thinking. Yet it seems fair to state that the understanding which Austrians had of their own subjectivism and of the theory of markets which it was able to support was, from today's perspective, quite limited.

When Lionel (later Lord) Robbins wrote his *Nature and Significance of Economic Science* in 1932, there can be no doubt that he accurately reflected the Austrian thinking which he had learned from his visits to Vienna.[4] That thinking enabled Robbins to formulate the economic decision in narrowly allocative terms. And it was Robbins's formulation which led subsequent microeconomic thought to see the market not as an unfolding discovery process, but as an equilibrium network of perfectly dovetailing individual allocative decisions.[5] There was nothing in the post-World War II work of prominent Austrians such as Rosenstein-Rodan and Machlup—whose Austrianism was rather narrowly rooted in the doctrines dominant in Vienna in the twenties—to indicate that these developments were in any way inconsistent with Austrian doctrines. Yet the writings of Mises and Hayek (especially those subsequent to World War II) enable us to see these developments sparked by Robbins's 1932 book as gravely flawed.

From our present day perspective we can see how Mises and Hayek were able to advance Austrian understanding of markets significantly beyond the limited subjectivism of the inter-war

Austrian tradition. It becomes clear that Mises was, already in the 'thirties, if not earlier, articulating a view of market processes which emphasized human action as a driving force for change, and which saw market processes themselves as systematic processes propelled by human action. Hayek came to emphasize the role of knowledge and the discovery processes needed to overcome the gaps in knowledge attributable to the phenomenon of dispersed information.

Although Mises never did employ Hayek's terminology drawing attention to the discovery of existing but dispersed information, there is every reason to interpret Mises's entrepreneurial market process in terms of such mutual discovery by market participants. In my 1963 book, *Market Theory and the Price System,* I attempted to present a Misesian statement of the core body of price theory in precisely such terms. However I did not, at that time, see the importance of the *entrepreneurial* element in human action, for the generation of such market learning processes.

When, ten years later, I published *Competition and Entrepreneurship,* I certainly did understand the importance of this entrepreneurial element in human action. But I have not, until quite recently,[6] recognized how this element was integral not only to Mises's theory of the market process, but also to his perception of how it is only this element that makes at all possible a uniquely economic chain of causation in social phenomena, a chain which only economic science can explain.

Late twentieth-century Austrian economics has consistently paid at least lip service to the idea that economics is a science of human action. But we have perhaps not paid sufficient attention to what Mises meant by this insight. We can now see, I believe, that human action drives the market in a sense that is quite distinct from any of the implications of the maximizing rationality which governs Robbinsian equilibrium economics. Human action drives the market, more fundamentally, in that it expresses the changes in agents' awareness of their environment and of their visions of the future—changes which are inspired by their "entrepreneurial" alertness to the dynamic world in which we live. This alertness is motivated by the purposefulness which defines and identifies conscious human action. If we are to understand the world in which we live—the world of disequilibrium as distinct from the analytical-model world of equilibrium—we must recognize how the decisions taken during any given span of time reflect this aspect of human action. It is the systematic market process of mutual discovery so generated, which constitutes the core of Misesian economics. Our understanding of what causes *these* facts of the market process is not exhausted by the fullest application of the physical, physiological and psychological sciences; for the fullest possible understanding we can draw, in addition, upon the explanatory power of the science of economics, the science of human action. The systematic changes in bids, offers, and completed transactions, which constitute the competitive market process, can be grasped by understanding how initial errors generate profitable opportunities which come to be perceived and exploited by alert, purposeful market participants. One cannot identify the economic side of life without drawing attention to this feature of human action and its implications for social processes.

It is worthy of notice that our deepened understanding of the manner in which human action inspires the market process and identifies the economic aspect of social phenomena affords us a correspondingly deeper appreciation for the role of individual freedom in Misesian economics. Individual freedom, quite apart from its ethical or philosophical appeal, is important, of course, for all schools of microeconomics, as a prerequisite for the beneficial operation of the market system. But for a science of human action this observation means more than the simple insight that free individuals can be relied upon to squeeze maximum benefits from any given situation. For the science of human action, freedom is the circumstance which permits and inspires market participants *to become aware* of beneficial (or other) *changes* in their circumstances. An environment in which human freedom is limited, in which profitably exploited opportunities invoke confiscatory social reactions, is an environment in which beneficial changes may never be noticed in the first place. An understanding of Misesian economics thus permits us to see directly how it points unerringly to the social usefulness of political institutions which guarantee individual liberties and the security of individual rights to life and property.

Notes and References

1. Although Mises wrote a commendatory Foreword to my 1960 book, and never did suggest that I had failed to grasp his position, I do not see this as inconsistent with the thesis that my earlier treatment was inadequate. The fact is that, despite my present interpretation of the Misesian system, it must be acknowledged that this interpretation of Mises's views argues for insights which Mises himself did *not* explicitly articulate. Possibly he took them as obvious; it is not then implausible that he took them as obviously implicit also in the more superficial exposition of Mises's position which I offered in 1960. Or it is possible that my present understanding of Mises's views incorporates insights which, even for Mises himself, were never more than implicit in his understanding of the workings of the market. Either way, there is no great difficulty in explaining why Mises did not critically identify what I now see as the inadequacies in my 1960 discussion.
2. Kirzner, Israel M., *The Economic Point of View* (Princeton, NJ: Van Nostrand, 1960), p. 151.
3. See also Kirzner, Israel M., *Market Theory and the Price System* (Princeton, NJ: Van Nostrand, 1963), pp. 22-31.
4. For further discussion of the matters dealt with in this section, see Kirzner, Israel M., "Ludwig von Mises and Friedrich von Hayek: The Modern Extension of Austrian Subjectivism," in Norbert Leser, editor, *Die Wiener Schule der Nationalökonomie* (Wien: Hermann Bohlau, 1986), together with the references cited in that paper.
5. On this see Walsh, Vivian C., *Introduction to Contemporary Microeconomics* (New York, NY: McGraw-Hill, 1970), p. 17.
6. For an expression of my recently learned insights, see Kirzner, Israel M., "Self-Interest and the New Bashing of Economics," *Critical Review* (Winter-Spring, 1990) Volume 4, numbers 1-2, especially pp. 33-39.

19

EQUALITY AND THE BIBLE

Charles S. MacKenzie*

Egalitarianism is a social philosophy which calls for an equalizing and leveling of people. In the halls of Congress, on college campuses, in union halls, and in many pulpits, voices call for the government to redistribute and to equalize wealth, power, and status. Many Americans sense something amiss in such advocacy. They have an uneasy feeling that modern egalitarianism is at variance with the notions of equality, freedom, and justice which gave birth to the United States. Many Christians have an uncomfortable feeling that egalitarianism contradicts both Biblical teachings and traditional American values. In this volume, we salute Professor Hans Sennholz who has been courageous in exposing the fallacies of egalitarianism.

Today's egalitarians would make equality the ultimate and normative value.[1] Equality of condition is to be imposed upon all people even if freedom is jeopardized. This is a radical departure from those perspectives which have shaped American life for over two hundred years. Contemporary egalitarianism threatens the future of the freedoms to which generations of Americans have been committed. In its pursuit of total and unlimited equality it threatens to destroy a free society.

Many Americans have been influenced by Biblical teaching. Therefore, we will examine a Biblical perspective on equality. In particular, a Trinitarian perspective throws special light upon this social value. *It views human life against the backdrop of the community of persons in the Trinity.*

Notions of equality seldom were voiced before the coming of Christ. Inequality ruled the world. The slave-master relationship

*Dr. MacKenzie is Chancellor and former President of Grove City College, Grove City, PA.

permeated most societies. Even the ancient Greeks endorsed and justified inequality. Plato's *Republic* perpetuated inequality by espousing an elite class of philosopher kings to rule ordinary mortals. Aristotle maintained that slaves and manual workers did not possess sufficient reason to share in the decisions of government.[2] Occasionally, intimations of equality surfaced but they were short-lived. The Sophists of fifth-century Athens went counter to popular thought when they suggested that all men had some low degree of equality by virtue of their possessing the faculty of reason. Stoics and Epicureans intimated a very limited equality when they said all men were capable of experiencing virtue and happiness. Yet such suggestions of equality were rare and exceptional. They did not challenge the widely held belief that superior people should rule the inferior.

Even in the Bible, equality is scarcely mentioned. On the other hand, natural inequality is acknowledged by Biblical writers. The very existence of the Triune God as the infinite, omniscient, omnipotent source of all reality represents the ultimate inequality. Everything in creation is inferior to the sovereign Creator.

Ever since creation, the Creator has continued to demonstrate a differentiation within Himself as He goes outside Himself to undergird the cosmos and all it contains, "...upholding the universe by his word of power" (Hebrew 1:3). Without His power, all that exists would cease to exist and go over into non-being. "In him [Christ] all things hold together" (Colossians 1:17). God, the Spirit, as the "ground of all being," undergirds both that which is according to His will and that which opposes His will. His power gives existence both to the equalities and inequalities of life. The divine power which is diffused throughout all of creation undergirds and upholds a universe which is permeated with inequalities.

As the omnipotent, omniscient Creator of all that is, God created a universe replete with differentiations and distinctions. The universe He created thrives on contrarieties. Venus is larger than Mars. A tree is taller than a stone. Oxygen is not hydrogen. Rain is not sunlight. Creation is dynamic and in constant flux because of the existence and interaction of diverse elements. Diversity is part of the richness and vitality of the cosmos. Diversity implies inequality.

The diversity, differentiations, and what people call "inequalities" in creation reflect something of the nature and character of God Himself. That is why Paul could write, "Ever since the creation of the world His invisible nature, namely His eternal power and deity, has been clearly perceived in the things that have been made" (Romans 1:20).

The Triune God, though dynamically one in an infinitely loving relationship, is eternally differentiated as Father, Son, and Holy Spirit. The Father, Son, and Spirit in their inner life of love are sublimely one and equal. In their outward relations with created reality, their diversity and differentiations become visible and apparent. Both unity and diversity characterize the Triune God and His creation. God is three eternal and equal "persons" in the sublime one-ness of the divine community of love. *Their equality arises from the one-ness of love, mind, and spirit,* which is the essence of true community. In a differentiated God, the ancient questions of one-ness and many-ness, being and becoming, equality and inequality find their resolution. Equality of three persons in the sublime unity of true community, as well as an inequality which results because each person is less than the whole, characterizes the source of all existence and is reflected into existence itself. Equality and inequality are united in God.

Diversity also is seen amidst the masses of humanity. There are aesthetes and philistines, geniuses and the mentally deficient, strong and weak. No two snowflakes, fingerprints, or people are alike. Each person is unique, different, unduplicated, though each shares a common humanity. Each is born with a unique capacity. There are two-talented, five-talented, and ten-talented people. People are not born equal in their abilities or natural gifts. The God of creation has brought into being a multi-colored, richly diverse universe. Emil Brunner expressed it: "Now the Creation simply means an incomprehensible inequality, conditions for which we cannot account."[3]

Against the backdrop of a differentiated God and His differentiated universe, God created humankind as man (Adam) and as woman (Eve). Each was different from the other, yet they shared a common humanity. God created woman not from man's feet which would have suggested she was inferior to him, nor from his head to indicate her superiority, but from his side to symbolize their essential one-ness and equality in God. The fact that all humanity has descended from primal parents also suggests that unity, community, and complementarity was intended at the beginning.

The story of creation describes the awareness of equality and inequality as it came into human consciousness. God created man (Adam) and woman (Eve) in the midst of a magnificently differentiated universe which God viewed as "good" (Genesis 1:31). Adam recognized differences in creation when he named the creatures (Genesis 2:19). Yet a sublime harmony, unity, and community pervaded Eden before the fall. In the harmony, unity, and community of Eden, God's presence merged all differentiations into a primal spiritual unity and equality.

Reinhold Niebuhr once pointed out that only in such a setting is equality a possibility. After pointing out that "Differences of need or of social function make the attainment of complete equality in society impossible," he said, "Equality belongs to the golden age or the perfection before the fall."[4] Only when everything is in harmony and one-ness with God is equality really possible. Only when people participate in the community of the Divine Three-in-One do they begin to know the deep one-ness and community which can give rise to genuine human equality. Even then, equality is essentially a deep, spiritual one-ness amidst vast differentiation.

But the prototypal woman and man fell away from God. They ate of the forbidden fruit. They became autonomous individuals. They ruptured the harmony and communion with God by their exaltation of themselves above God. Suddenly, they experienced the distinction between God and that which is not of God, the difference between good and evil. Having a new knowledge of good and evil, they began to make moral comparisons. *Differentiations came to be viewed as inequalities by the fallen pair.* The yardstick and standard of reference became individualized man who placed himself at the center of his universe. God was no longer the standard against which everything was to be measured. Man became the measure. Ever since, man has measured himself against man and has tended to view differences as inequalities.

Adam and Eve exalted their own wills above God's will. The curving back of the ego upon itself shattered the image of God which they once had possessed equally and alienated them from God. Only a remnant of the image of God remained. Their descendants now possess only remnants of the image of God. So they are unequal in both their humanness and their brutishness. Brunner once observed, "As created in the image of God all men are equal; created as individuals, they are unequal."[5]

Ever since Eden, a dream has lingered in the archetypal, collective consciousness of humanity. The dream, which is really an Edenic memory, is of a utopian world where all things are one in God and where equality and inequality are unified in God. That dream lingers in the psyche of society inspiring egalitarians and other utopians. But it exists in tension with the actual inequalities of life.

Men always have sought to discern whether or not there is any meaning underlying the inequalities of existence. In the ancient world, Stoic philosophers suggested that there is an impersonal type of providence (fate) permeating the circumstances of life. Biblical writers insisted that there is a divine purpose unfolding amidst the pain, poverty, and inequalities of life. They saw God's providence in all that happens. "...His kingdom ruleth over all." (Psalm 103:19). "The Lord maketh poor, and maketh rich; he bringeth low, and lifteth up" (I Samuel 2:7). He "maketh all things after the counsel of his own will" (Ephesians 1:11).

John Calvin expressed the doctrine of providence thus: "But faith ought to penetrate more deeply, namely, having found Him Creator of all, herewith to conclude He is also everlasting Governor and Preserver not only in that He drives the celestial frame as well as its several parts by a universal motion, but also in that He sustains, nourishes, and cares for everything He had made, even to the least sparrow" (*Institutes*, Book I, ch. XVI, 1,1). ". . . even though the rich are mingled with the poor in this world while to each his condition is divinely assigned . . .";". . . it is by His secret plan that some distinguish themselves, while others remain contemptible" (I, XVI, 1,6). "Job recognizes that he was divinely stripped of all his property, and made a poor man, because it so pleased God" (I, XVIII, 1). In the living tapestry which is humankind, God has woven threads of poverty and prosperity, deprivation and plenty, pain and joy. Historically, many Christians have believed that the inequalities of life reflect a mysterious plan in the mind of God which may only be understood fully on the other side of death.

The natural inequalities in the world serve to fulfill God's plan for a fallen world. They produce magnificent diversity, richness, and creativity in society. Creativity prospers amidst diversity. Inequality fosters a sense of human interdependence and community, which reflects something of the divine community in the Trinity. Those who work with their hands on an assembly line and those who furnish the capital to build the assembly line mutually need each other. A great society is achieved only by the interweaving of people's unequal talents, functions, and wealth. Inequality can be an energizer in society motivating the poor and powerless to strive upward. Brunner put it: "Woven through the inequalities of existence are many such intimations of divine purpose."[6] God-ordained, natural inequalities stimulate the development of community.

Another insight, given by Scripture on inequality and equality, derives from Biblical teaching on the holiness or transcendence of the Triune God. The divine holiness reflects itself into the human scene as God's revealed laws. All people are judged equally by His laws. As one Adamic, corporate personality or community, all people are equally guilty before God's holy law. "...all have sinned and come short of the glory of God" (Romans 3:23). "There is no partiality with him" (Ephesians 6:9).

But God's holiness, which judges all humanity equally, has produced disparate and unequal results when applied to individuals. Individual reactions to God's law vary. People differ both in their understanding of the law and in their responses to it. Consequently, they are unequal in the extent of their disobedience and will be punished unequally. Some will be punished with few stripes, others with many stripes (Luke 12:47,48). The law results in unequal rewards and retribution, which are represented by the ultimate inequalities, heaven and hell. The law, when applied to individuals, discriminates and separates. R. J. Rushdoony summed it up, "The law cannot favor equality without ceasing to be law."[7] Emil Brunner put it: "The element of equality which is decisive in all human justice has no validity in the divine justice."[8]

Just as divine holiness, interacting with humanity, results in equality when it is applied to corporate humankind and inequality when it is applied to individuals, so God's love produces both equality and inequality. God's redemptive love is like an infinite fountain which will never run dry. He loves all people with a love that is infinite. All people are equally dependent upon His love, both for their existence and for their redemption.

Yet God has chosen to ensure that some will respond to His love. He has focused His love in a special way upon some individuals and some nations. He chose to single out Israel and to establish a special, covenant relation with her. There was nothing egalitarian in God's choice of Israel above all the other nations of the ancient world.

In a similar manner, God has gone outside Himself to touch certain individuals and to influence them in ways which ensure their freely responding to His love. The Apostle Paul pointed out that God exerted such an influence upon Jacob, but not his brother Esau (Romans 9:6-13). Is such an unequal application of God's love favoritism? Paul answered that we must trust that what God does is just and right, even though by fallen man's standards it may seem unequal. The Triune God knows in advance who will choose to respond to His love. If He chooses to focus special influences upon them, that is His sovereign prerogative. Eventually the glory of His sovereign purpose and love, when fully understood, will provide the answers to humankind's questions about equality and inequality. Meanwhile, fallen men still complain that He who loves all people has treated individuals unequally by applying His love with special force to some and not to others.

A Biblical perspective, then, faces squarely the vast inequalities in life. It shows (1) that differences among people reflect dimly the differentiations in the Triune God; (2) that some inequalities are God-ordained as a stimulus to developing a sense of human complementarity and community paralleling the community in the Triune God; (3) that some inequalities result from human fallenness, sin, and selfishness as people strive to exert control over others; and (4) that some inequalities result from God's holiness and love as they touch people in conformity with His providence.

The Bible also indicates that there is an *ideal* of equality which has been revealed to humanity and which serves to restrain the man-made inequalities which are the fruit of sin. It is spiritual, not material. It is not inherent in the nature of things but rather is a gift given to humanity by God's grace. It emerges when people are deeply one in a corporate personality or spiritual community which reflects the Triune community. It is an ideal to be received, not a fact to be measured. It is a goal which will be realized in eternity when equal and unequal will be unified completely in perfect community with God. Like the North Star, the ideal of equality guides men and nations though it is unattainable on earth. It saves society from shipwrecking on the shoals of selfishness and greed.

Such equality must be abstract, ideational, and spiritual, transcending the material conditions of life. Emil Brunner expressed it: "The idea of equalization is not a constitutive principle but a regulative idea."[9] Equality according to the Bible is not an actual, historical, empirically quantifiable reality. It is a transcendent yardstick, a theoretical ideal derived from God Himself.

It becomes real to those who experience the Triune God. They realize a sublime one-ness and spiritual equality with others in God. It is manifest in those who identify with God and with each other. It is a gift of grace given along with the gift of human unity and spiritual community. A pre-condition to the Biblical awareness of equality is the unity which comes when people deeply identify with each other in a divinely given corporate personality.[10] The equality of people, according to a Biblical perspective, is in proportion to the degree and the depth of their community with each other in the Triune God.

This was the experience of the early church. God's Spirit made believers one. As men and women were identified with God and with each other in the body of Christ, a spiritual equality became visible. Though they remained unequal in intelligence, talent, poverty, and dedication, a spiritual one-ness and concomitant equality before God was apparent. Though there were inequalities of individual talents and functions, i.e., elders, deacons, etc., all believers were corporately one both as sinners and as saints and experienced a beautiful, spiritual communion and equality before God.

Yet the sublime spiritual unity of those early Christians did not equalize them materially. Egalitarians within the Church today are quick to point to Paul's words: "There is neither Jew nor Greek, there is neither slave nor free, there is neither male or female; for you are all one in Christ Jesus" (Galatians 3:28). They seem blind to the fact that Paul was emphasizing the believers' spiritual unity in the Triune God, not material, social equality. They also refer to the church in the Book of Acts. "And all who believed were together and had all things in common" (Acts 2:44). They seem to ignore the obvious fact that the passage emphasizes the spiritual unity of those who had faith. Their sharing of "all things" was entirely voluntary and spiritually motivated. It certainly was not normative for all Christians and churches. The early church did not attempt to impose the ethic of some Jerusalem believers upon the whole church. Nor did they demand that the pagan world adopt an ethic which compelled sharing all their material possessions. In that day and in ours, it would be naive and cruel to try to force the radical ethic of some Christians upon a pagan society which lacks the grace of sharing.

The early church fathers frequently referred to the equality of the primitive community before the fall.[11] Though some yearned to see a restoration of an Edenic equality to the human situation, most recognized that it was not possible in the secular world as it is. Therefore, many voluntarily sought unity and equality in a monastic community. St. John Chrysostom longed to transform Constantinople and Antioch into fellowships of love and equality following the monastic ideal, but he acknowledged that such an ideal would be impossible to put into practice both because of the actual inequalities in life and because the masses lacked spiritual community.

In the Middle Ages the notion of God's calling people to unequal places of work and service was recognized by Christian thinkers. St. Augustine saw inequality as part of God's ordering of a fallen world. "Surely now, this example teaches plainly enough for anyone that it is for the good of some to be in an inferior position, and that it is good for all without exception to be subject to God."[12]

St. Thomas Aquinas clearly described inequalities as belonging to the very nature of human existence. Predestination, divine Providence, and divine calling were seen as playing parts in establishing human differences. Thomas also warned against turning natural inequalities into unnatural, man-made injustices by human sin and passion. At the same time, he acknowledged the existence of a "religious" equality in the face of massive inequalities.

Later, Meister Eckhardt described the spiritual equality in God. He declared that in God no creature is more noble than another.[13] The divine love in every creature requires that all be loved equally.

The basis for Eckhardt's understanding of inequality was the different capacities humans have for receiving God's love.

Calvinism taught that, in themselves, equality and inequality are of little significance in comparison to the glory and sovereignty of God who overshadows them. Before God all men are corporately and spiritually equal since all are sinners, since all are equally dependent on God's grace, and since all are equally obligated to obey Him. Yet, in actual relation to each other, people as individuals are unequal since God has providentially ordained differences which are part of the very fabric of human existence. Their inequalities impose an obligation of service, particularly upon those who are the elect. But for Calvinism the equalities and inequalities of life were of relative unimportance when seen in the light of the sovereignty, holiness, wisdom, and glory of the Triune God.

Calvinism profoundly influenced the thinking of Americans in colonial days. As the Founding Fathers sought to translate a transcendent vision of equality into social reality, they sought a society which would express the ideal of *equality before God and His law.* They recognized the natural inequalities of intelligence, ability, motivation, and industry. When Jefferson penned the words "all men are created equal," he was not saying that all men had been created with equal natural endowments. Rather, he meant that Americans were born with the same rights which belonged to Englishmen.[14] The Founding Fathers sought to build a nation on the principle that all men are born to be equally free.

As the years of American history unfolded, however, the vision of equality expanded and contracted. Slaves were set free by a bloody civil war. Women were given suffrage. Yet, the egalitarian dream continued to be elusive because it contradicted nature. Then the role of the central government changed. During Franklin Roosevelt's New Deal and continuing to this day, the federal government incrementally has taken to itself increasing power to redistribute wealth. Government more and more has become the chief instrument of social policy. The increasingly centralized and powerful federal government has imposed an equality of outcomes upon all segments of American life. The transcendent ideal of equality before God and the law spoken of by the Founding Fathers has metamorphosed into an equality of outcomes. And so today millions have the vain dream of a utopia in which everyone is economically equal.

In a world where egalitarian principles are trumpeted by many politicians, preachers, academicians, and labor leaders, how should the average citizen evaluate egalitarianism? How should people, whose views have been shaped by those traditional American perspectives which were derived from Christian values, react to egalitarianism?

First, it should be understood that today's egalitarianism materializes the Christian spiritual ideal of equality in the Triune community. It despiritualizes and materializes equality. It concentrates its efforts on equalizing material power and wealth. It advocates the state's shifting material wealth from those who have to those who have not by a variety of government transfer schemes. In materializing the notion of equality, it seeks to seize the property of some and to give it to others.

Yet the commandment, "Thou shalt not steal," (Exodus 20:15) assumes that a person has a divine right to possess his own property. The state defies God's commandment when it "steals" from its citizens what they have a right to possess. All property comes from God. "The earth is the Lord's..." (Psalm 24:1). Man's stewardship of property for God as well as his responsibility to care for the poor is clearly taught in Scripture. "Beware that thou forget not the Lord thy God . . . for it is He that giveth thee power to get wealth" (Deuteronomy 8:11–18) With the right of property comes the responsibility and the right of disposal. God has commanded that individuals give of their substance to the less fortunate. Yet, if egalitarianism disallows private ownership, how shall individuals give away what they do not possess? Man was destined to work, to cultivate, to develop the created order and to use the fruits of his labor to the glory of God. The right to property, the necessity of work, and the obligation of stewardship all are Biblical mandates. No one, not even government, has the right to take people's property. "Thou shall not steal." Neither does it have the right to deprive people of the joyful experience of stewardship and of a personal caring for the poor.

Schemes for the forced redistribution of property violate basic Biblical principles. The egalitarian movement, whether of Marxist, humanist, or Christian persuasion, denies people the right to retain the property they possess. Each would compel a governmental redistribution of wealth and would destroy people's sense of stewardship and personal responsibility for their neighbors. This would be a betrayal of real community since compulsion is a denial of love. Love is the mortar of community. Egalitarianism also gives priority to the collective rather than to the individual. It inhibits freedom in its quest for justice. It dehumanizes and disregards the nature of fallen man. It also fails to answer the question: "Who is wise enough to make a fully equitable redistribution?" As Henry Hazlitt has said, "Who is going to decide on people's true moral worth or 'real' merit? . . . But little thought would convince us that only someone with the omniscience and impartiality of God would be able to decide on the relative merit and deserts of each of us."[15] Egalitarianism fails to recognize that the emergence of some oligarchy to enforce redistribution becomes a necessity in man's drive for power. It robs people both of the experience of stewardship and of the gratitude which wells up in the hearts of those whom God has blessed. It also aborts man's aspirations to garner riches in order to serve society. It destroys the initiative and ambition without which humanity cannot fulfill its potential. It assumes that the destruction of private property will guarantee an equalization of power but fails to recognize that property is not the only form of power. The egalitarian concept is inimical to the Biblical teaching of man's right to hold property.

A second criticism of egalitarianism is that it is an ethic of rebellion. Failure to accept God's providential ordering of the world is unbelief. To try to eliminate the inequalities of life imposed by nature is obstinate, self-induced blindness to the facts of life. It is ridiculous naivete to pretend that differences in ability, intelligence, and physical energy do not exist. Social planners who challenge the human inequality set by nature assume the divine prerogative and play God by sitting in judgment on the order God has created. Emil Brunner declared, "The egalitarian idea does not arise out of reverence for the Creator, but out of the desire to dictate to the Creator how things ought to be, on the presupposition that the Creator ought to treat everyone alike. Hence, because this idea opposes the Divine order in creation, it also works out destructively in life."[16] Giovanni Sartori aptly described the demand for equality as a "protest ideal."[17] As an ethic driven by envy, it defies and denies the natural inequalities of God's creation.

Thirdly, egalitarianism is antagonistic to a Biblical perspective because it absolutizes equality and downgrades other Biblical values such as freedom and justice. It fails to acknowledge the interrelatedness and mutual dependence of those values which characterize the Godhead and true community. It tends to isolate equality from the rest of reality.

The vision of equality will turn into a dreadful nightmare if, as modern egalitarians insist, equality becomes an end in itself. When equality becomes the ultimate value, it becomes absolutized and deified. It tends to become concretized and materialized. But equality, if it is to be humanizing, requires an ideal, indestructible, transcendent framework. From a Biblical perspective and from the viewpoint of those who laid the foundations of America, the notion of equality must be subordinate to the higher ethical values of freedom and justice. Equality is a means to freedom and justice, but equality without its God-ordained linkage to higher values ultimately will destroy all the values which have been cherished in Judeo-Christian culture. By destroying human incentives, it will smother hope which is a mainspring of human advancement. By destroying freedom, it will destroy love and the possibility of true community in God.

A fourth criticism of egalitarianism is that the attempt to equalize everybody eventually will result in horrible new inequalities. Its demand for an omnipowerful, omnicompetent superstate to enforce social and economic equalization will result in an enormous new inequality—a huge gap between the masses of people and the elite government enforcers. The inevitable creation of a superstate to enforce material equality will destroy freedom, love, and justice.

Fifthly, egalitarianism will result in the dehumanization of people. Personhood, exalted by the persons of the Trinity, will be diminished by egalitarianism. Citizens who allow themselves to be coerced into a society where everyone has the same level of power, prestige, and possessions will be dehumanized as they lose incentive, ambition, creativity, and hope. The vast majority of people will be equalized to a lowest common denominator of both income and powerlessness. Coercive egalitarianism will shift power from the people to the central government and will level the masses into dehumanizing conformity. Dehumanization and forced equalization go hand in hand.

Sixthly, in comparison with Biblical teaching, egalitarianism is not radical enough. The Biblical ethic goes far beyond an egalitarian redistribution of wealth. It calls for those who own private property to use it to the glory of God and for the blessing of humanity. It reflects the divine self-giving of the Triune community. Believers are to be stewards, using their possessions in ways which accord with the purposes of Him who owns all things. Those with wealth to invest should invest with an eye either to the creation of jobs or to benefit society in some other way. What is evil is the holding of riches simply for one's own gratification. The Biblical ethic is positive in its view of the possession of property, whereas, egalitarianism is primarily negative.

A Biblical ethic also is more radical than egalitarianism because it does not stop with a vision of equality. It goes beyond equality by insisting that all God's people should treat others as *better* than themselves. "In humility count others better than yourselves" (Philippians 2:3). Just as the persons of the Trinity are eternally self-giving, i.e., begetting, proceeding, so believers are called to give and to share for the sake of community. The Biblical ethic calls for a beneficial inequality. Each believer should, like the servant Lord, be willing to kneel and to wash the feet of others. He should put their interests before his own. He should work and pray and act toward others in ways which will enrich their lives even though that may humble and cost him. This suggests that the Christian man should esteem women better than himself, that the Christian white should regard black, brown, red, and yellow people as his superiors, that the rich Christian should treat the poor as nobler than himself, that the Christian employer should consider his employees as more worthy than himself, and vice versa. All Christians should esteem others better than themselves. The Christian ethic is not egalitarian. Though it offers a vision of spiritual equality, it goes far beyond that vision by calling for a radical inequality of esteem and action which builds the divine community. "In humility count others better than yourselves."

A seventh reason egalitarianism ought to be unacceptable to those with a Biblical commitment is that it is inimical to love and to the community of love which has its source in the Trinity. Love must be freely given. When an impersonal government coerces an equalizing of people, the state becomes the destroyer of love. It becomes an instrument of envy. Its weapons become power and force which inevitably destroy love. On the other hand, a Biblical ethic derives its motivation and direction from love-in-community freely shared. There is spiritual equality in love; but apart from love freely given and freely received, equality becomes an inhuman, coerced uniformity.

Still another objection (the eighth) to egalitarianism is that it fosters dishonesty and alienation. In actual practice, a forced equalization of income by the state prompts men and women to rely on personal influence, bribery, and the black market to secure goods which they otherwise could not afford. In egalitarian societies, desirable apartments, better cars, furnishings, and clothes are reserved either for government officials or for those who by bribery, by the black market, or by personal influence can secure them. Such a society becomes permeated with dishonesty. True community is dissolved. Two leading egalitarian economists, Assar Lindbeck and Gunnar Myrdal, have observed that the erosion of honesty is one of egalitarian Sweden's most pressing problems.[18]

Egalitarianism tends to breed alienation. Though it loudly advocates social solidarity, it actually has increased the social strains in most societies which follow an equalitarian ideal. Equalization of the wages of skilled and non-skilled workers causes resentment, tension, and alienation. It simply is not true that egalitarianism creates a new type of person who is less acquisitive and competitive. The history of egalitarian societies in the 20th century explodes this myth. Human nature is basically the same everywhere.

The choice, then, before the world is not between equality and inequality. Rather, it is a choice between different views of equality. Which will it be? Equality before God and the law, a guiding, spiritual ideal, comes from God. It is motivated by faith and love. It derives from a spiritual sense of community and aims to build community. It inspires and liberates humanity. It is a means to freedom and justice, but is subordinate to both. It is expressed in society as equality before the law and as equal freedom to pursue one's destiny.

On the other hand, equality, when it is absolutized, demands a total equalization and leveling of people, goes against natural differences, materializes the notion of equality, requires a centralization of state power, brings about a dehumanizing enslavement of the masses, destroys the possibility of the community of love and results in a massive loss of freedom. It seeks a material equality of condition, outcomes, power, riches, and/or poverty. It begins as mild redistribution of wealth and power and proceeds until it becomes that equalization wherein the state controls all wealth, power and people. Above all, it goes counter to the impulses of the Trinitarian God which are humanizing, unifying, liberating, spiritual, and which produce the community of love. It ignores the Trinitarian principles of spiritual unity and of complementarity (the interrelatedness of values).

Which vision of equality will dominate the future of humanity? One offers "life, liberty, and the pursuit of happiness." The other leads to bondage, despair and spiritual death.

Notes and References

1. Compare Frankel, Charles, "The New Egalitarianism and the Old," *Commentary*, LVI, September 1973, pp. 54-61. Frankel pointed out the difference between equality as the ultimate human value (the newer egalitarian view) and equality as one value among "a larger scheme of values" (the traditional view).
2. Aristotle, *Politics,* Book VII, ix, l I, v. 8.
3. Brunner, Emil, *The Divine Imperative* (Philadelphia, PA: Westminster Press, 1947), p. 407.
4. Niebuhr, Reinhold, *The Nature and Destiny of Man* (New York, NY: Charles Scribner's Sons, 1949), V. II, p. 255.
5. Brunner, Emil, *The Christian Doctrine of Creation and Redemption* (Philadelphia, PA: Westminster Press, 1952), p. 66.
6. *Ibid.*
7. Rushdoony, Rousas John, *The Institutes of Biblical Law* (Nutley, NJ: The Craig Press, 1973), p. 60.
8. Brunner, *Christian Doctrine,* V.2, p. 185.
9. Brunner, *The Divine Imperative*, pp. 408-409. Compare also Niebuhr, R., *The Nature and Destiny of Man,* V.2, ch. ix, III, p. 254. Niebuhr also pointed out the transcendent nature of equality.
10. H. Wheeler Robinson recognized in Scripture an awareness of "corporate personality" which symbolized people's solidarity when they share certain essential characteristics in common. For example, ancient Israel and the early church each had a unique "corporate personality" which described and defined a whole group of individuals. Compare Robinson, H. Wheeler, *Corporate Personality In Ancient Israel,* (Philadelphia, PA: Fortress Press, 1980), p. 25ff.
11. The Stoic doctrine of the "Primitive State" influenced the early church fathers significantly.
12. Compare Augustine, *City of God*, Book XIX, ch. 21 (New York, NY: Image Books, Doubleday and Co., 1958) p. 470.
13. Eckhardt, Meister, *Breakthrough* (New York, NY: Image Books, 1980), pp. 523-530.
14. David Lovejoy has shown convincingly that the equality sought by the colonists was equality before the laws of the British empire. Compare Lovejoy, David S., *The Glorious Revolution in America* (New York, NY: W. W. Norton and Co., 1972).
15. Hazlitt, Henry, *The Foundation of Morality* (Los Angeles, CA: Nash Publishing, 1972), p. 337. Reinhold Niebuhr observed that "Nations are even more incapable than individuals" of fully understanding the rights

and claims of people. Compare Niebuhr, R. *The Irony of American History* (New York, NY: Charles Scribner's Sons, 1952), p. 138.
16. Brunner, *The Divine Imperative,* pp. 408-409.
17. Sartori, Giovanni, *Democratic Theory* (Detroit, MI: Wayne State University Press, 1962), pp. 326-327.
18. *Wall Street Journal*, Feb. 1, 1980, p. 16. Article by Melvyn Krauss.

20

FREE MARKET ENVIRONMENTALISM

Luisa Zorraquin de Marcos*

The noisy attention that environmental problems is receiving from both specialists and lay people has grown over the last twenty years and now has reached a loud crescendo. Popular beliefs include:

- People are trashing the earth.
- Pollution is growing and is much worse under market economies than with government controlled or command economies.
- Global warming, depletion of the ozone layer, the killing of thousands of species, acid rain, the end of the tropical forests, and the like are real dangers that must be solved now if planet earth is to survive the next century.
- Raw materials, especially for energy and food, are becoming scarce in the face of a growing population.
- Through controls and regulations, government is the only institution capable of ending the trashing of the planet.

Growing concern for these issues has led to the rise of "environmentalism," meaning the growing political movement favoring government command and control over environmental problems. There are three intellectual aspects of this movement: scientific, philosophic, and economic. This essay focuses mainly on the economic aspect.

*Mrs. de Marcos is currently teaching institutional economics at ESEADE in Buenos Aires, Argentina. She is also Executive Vice President of Fundación Concordia, a foundation dedicated to the advancement of free market economics.

The Intellectual Roots of Environmental Movement

Science and Environmentalism

The scientific findings in the natural sciences (*i.e.*, biology, chemistry, physics, meteorology, demography, etc.) provide the factual foundation for the other two intellectual aspects of this movement. The fact which dominates the media is that the earth is in danger of not surviving through the next century.[1] Millions of deaths are being predicted in the short-run by starving, flooding, and pollution.[2]

Looking closer at these "facts," we are surprised that they are still hotly debated issues even in the serious scientific community. On the issue of global warming there is no agreement among scientists as to its existence, let alone causes. Seventy-one percent of 1,500 scientists polled by *Nature* magazine said that recorded temperature changes have been "within the range of natural fluctuation" and that most scientific journals treat the forecasts of global warming with contempt.[3] This lack of consensus deters environmentalists neither from spreading the news that carbon dioxide emissions cause global warming nor from lobbying for government restrictions.[4] The situation is similar for other issues such as ozone depletion,[5] acid rain,[6] and the extinction of species.[7] Standards of truth appear to be less strict when the concern is environmental facts.

Malthusianism

The theories of Thomas Malthus are espoused in his *Essay on the Principles of Population as it Affects the Future Improvement of Society* (2nd edition, 1803), where he warns of population pressure on the scarcity of resources. His famous thesis purports that production grows arithmetically while population grows geometrically.[8] Therefore, in 225 years, populations would grow about 512 times while food production would grow only ten times. The results are poverty and famine. At the heart of Malthus's proposition is the idea that additional workers must necessarily mean less output per worker given a fixed supply of land and other resources (including capital). This is the theory of diminishing returns (which is only true in the absence of technological change).

Even though Malthus's thesis has been proven false by statistics, economic theory, and demographic studies, it is alive and well as we approach the end of the twentieth century. The Club of Rome resurrected it in *The Limits of Growth* in 1975,[9] which was followed by a long list of similar writings. One of the most widely read is the 1980 *Global 2000 Report to the President*, which summarized its findings as follows:

> If the present trends continue, the world in 2000 will be more crowded, more polluted, less stable ecologically, and more vulnerable to disruption than the world we live in now. Serious stresses involving population, resources and environment are clearly visible ahead. Despite greater material output, the world's people will be poorer in many ways than they are today.
>
> For hundreds of millions of the desperately poor, the outlook for food and other necessities of life will be no better. For many it will be worse. Barring revolutionary advances in technology, life for most people on earth will be more precarious in 2000 than it is now—unless the nations of the world act decisively to alter current trends.[10]

These views are a milder version of the more radical ones, such as those maintained by Stanford Professor Paul Ehrlich, who already made headlines in 1968 with his *The Population Bomb*. The opening phrase summarizes his thesis: "The battle to feed all humanity is over. In the 1970s the world will undergo famines—hundreds of millions of people are going to starve to death."

The Allocation of Resources

The tenets of environmentalism view resources as fixed and the environment as a grand public good. For them, use of resources always produces externalities which end in market failure. The solution is political allocation of resources instead of market allocation through the functioning of prices. Thus government agencies are created to represent the "public interest"; they employ technical experts to determine scientifically the "socially optimal" use of resources.[11] As Jo Kwong Echard explains:

> However much environmental activist organizations may seem to differ from each other in their philosophies, strategies, or programs, they possess one shared characteristic: the consistent reliance on governmental 'solutions' to environmental problems. The environmental agenda focuses primarily on securing greater government control over natural

and environmental resources: more taxpayers' dollars, more regulations, more agencies and more government ownership.[12]

Sustainability

Some analysts of global trends have defined sustained development as a process of change oriented to satisfy people's needs without diminishing the possibilities of defining their future needs or those of other societies or of future generations.[13] There are as many different versions of sustainability as there are persons who sustain it. The most extreme requires "maintenance of resources," meaning that no resource stocks should be diminished. That goal is impossible, however, if there is to be any present consumption of nonrenewable resources.

A more moderate version calls for "maximizing subject to constraints." The constraints usually involve population growth, rapid industrialization, mounting urbanization, energy consumption, and food supplies. The combined result of these human pressures is a range of complex, interconnected impacts on the environment. One measurement has estimated that people now consume, control, or destroy almost 40% of plant energy.[14] According to this moderate version, the cause of unsustainability stems from *incomplete models of development.* They advocate a new model of development where all ecological principles and environmental ethics will be included in the institutions that govern development. But the question always is *who* will decide *which* model of development is "right."

Public Opinion

Given the current mixture of scientific facts and economic theory, it is not surprising that solutions offered by environmentalists require government intervention in almost all cases. In 1979, Professor Hans F. Sennholz wrote:

> All free societies are governed by public opinion, and the quality of this public opinion shapes the character of government and its policies. If public opinion favors individual freedom and self-reliance and is suspicious of political authority, it brings forth a system that governs least. If, on the other hand, public opinion favors political governance and chooses to allocate income and wealth by force, it gives birth to a system of authority and conflict; it creates authority, *i.e.*, government

force, that is commensurate to the political objectives desired, and generates economic and social conflict, not only between the beneficiaries and victims of the political process, but also among the beneficiaries themselves.[15]

This statement, though written years ago, could well be the most accurate description of what is happening today with environmentalism. Public opinion seems to know little more than begging for government intervention and political control. A case for free market environmentalism must be made better known to help shape more desirable policies for the future.

Free Market Environmentalism

The debate between those who urge a political approach and those who support market solutions to environmental problems usually centers on these issues: Does economic growth continuously and universally increase environmental disruption? Does population growth accelerate this process? Do government intervention and non-capitalist economies offer better safeguards for the environment than market economies?

Understanding the Pollution Problem

During the "Limits to Growth" debate of the 1970s, the main concern was the depletion of nonrenewable resources. Today the attention of environmentalism has shifted to the possible overloading of the environment's capacity to absorb waste products and maintain essential life-support functions (such as a stable climate).

Although different types of pollution problems are discussed under different names (air pollution, water pollution, global warming, *etc.*), scientists and environmentalists point to a common fact that increasing industrialization leads to environmental disruption. But is this a real fact? A recent study by Mikhail S. Bernstam of the Hoover Institute shows just the opposite. Let us consider his opening remarks:

...growing evidence shows that high levels of economic development and continuing economic growth in some countries, namely those with open competitive market economies, have recently reversed the relationship between expansion and pollution from positive to negative.[16]

Bernstam's study shows that as economies grow, discharges to the environment increase rapidly, then decelerate and eventually decline.[17] He claims this occurs because of *a secular increase in the productivity of resource use in Western market economies which eventually produces absolute declines in resource throughput and pollution.* He also remarks that the extent of government environmental regulation and environmentalist movements across countries *does not* correlate with the depths of pollution declines. If anything, there is a slightly negative correlation.[18]

Thus, to understand the nature of the problem, we should note that pollution is a consequence of resource use,[19] and reduced discharge of pollution is explained by the increased productivity which is the predominant feature of market economies[20] and results in the *decline* of resource and material inputs per unit of output in production chains (for instance, more meat with fewer heads of livestock, requiring less feed grain, produced with fewer tractors, produced from less steel, using less pig iron from less iron ore).

Economic growth can occur in market economies simultaneously with pollution decline for a *technological* reason: *the growth in resource productivity in excess of the growth of resource input.* Thus, Bernstam concludes, economic growth under open competitive markets offers a better choice for both the economy and the environment.[21]

Bernstam also reveals that trends in resource use and pollution in the decades of the 1970s and 1980s showed an amazing divergence between Western market economies and the socialist economies of the Soviet Union and Eastern Europe. While in Western economies pollution declined both proportionally and absolutely, *the exact opposite occurred in socialist economies.* The fall of the Iron Curtain has unveiled environmental devastation far exceeding the alleged excesses of present-day market economies. The dismal economic performance of socialist and communist economies has been achieved at high costs to the environment and the health of their citizens.[22]

Rent-Seeking and Political Allocation of Resources

In a market economy, rents or extraordinary profits—that is, profits in excess of opportunity costs—set entrepreneurs in motion.

Profit-seeking entrepreneurs will engage in innovative processes and keep the whole economic process dynamic. The search for profits or rents leads them to allocate resources to the most productive uses. In time these rents send signals to other potential producers who will imitate the entrepreneurs and enter the same markets in the absence of barriers. In normal competitive markets, *freedom of entry* guarantees that rents will dissipate and consumers will benefit from lower prices. At the same time, resources are efficiently allocated and the economy remains dynamic.[23]

Environmentalists, however, favor the political allocation of resources. What they fail to see is that such an allocation is in effect a granting of monopoly rights to individuals. If supply is arbitrarily restricted and price is then allowed to rise to market-clearing levels, rents accrue to those who secure the rights to engage in the activity. Government licenses, quotas, permits, approvals, or franchise assignments each imply arbitrary or artificial scarcity created by government,[24] which will cause rents to emerge and attract rent seekers. But artificial barriers of entry will prevent these rents from dissipating and thereby induce persons to invest genuinely scarce resources in attempts to secure the initial assignment of rights or to oust others from privileged positions. The outcome is inefficient allocations of scarce resources. As economist James Buchanan notes, it would be absurd to think that a politically determined allocation of resources could be frozen once and for all and that resource owners and entrepreneurs would not continually seek more profitable opportunities in politics as they do in the markets.[25]

Rent-Seeking and the Environmental Movement

Government planning is based on the notion that officials act on behalf of the "public interest" and that they have better information to determine the "optimal allocation of resources" and the pattern of use that best meets standards of efficiency and environmental control.[26] In reality, government allocation of resources by means of regulations motivates environmental groups to engage in active rent-seeking.

The United States abounds with examples in which these groups have profited from political policy. Through their tax-exempt status, environmentalist groups are subsidized indirectly by

American taxpayers.[27] They have discovered more direct subsidies through "fee shifting," where it is "lucrative to file lawsuits against the government and other alleged violators of environmental statutes."[28] Because environmental organizations claim to be acting on behalf of the public, the courts have decided these groups should not have to bear the costs of lawsuits which are paid instead with taxpayer money. Consequently, the government pays for lawsuits against itself. This is one activity in which rent-seekers are assured of no risk of losses. Other federally supported activities are government contracts or even direct grants.[29] These types of intervention imply barriers to free entry and, therefore, provide rents to those who can capture them. We should not be surprised to find environmentalists deeply involved in politics, from lobbying to confirming or removing officials in charge of environmental politics.

The Free Market Price System

The price system is essentially an information system. Hans F. Sennholz explains, "The pricing process thus reveals itself as a social process in which all members of society participate. Through buying or abstaining from buying, through cooperation and competition, the millions of consumers ultimately determine the price structure of the market and the allocation of the income of each individual."[30] He continues, "Without the price yardstick, ... he [the economic planner] may calculate in kind, but such a calculation permits no value comparison between the costs of production and its yield."[31] This understanding is important when viewing the problem of nonrenewable resources such as copper, oil, and others.

Environmentalists tout the "finiteness" of these resources, and advocates of "sustainability" wish to impose political restrictions on the supply and demand of these resources, which prevents the functioning of the price system and hinders the creation of substitutes. Spot and futures markets for nonrenewable resources work in a way unrivalled by central planning. Economic agents, anticipating changes in market conditions (supply and demand), buy and sell in these markets. The resulting changes in spot and futures prices automatically "regulate" the allocation of commodities. Therefore, when environmentalists relentlessly push to eliminate markets in nonrenewable resources, they are really barring the higher future prices which conserve resources and signal entrepreneurs to find substitute supplies.

The paradox of sustainability policies is that historical, long-term trends show falling prices and increasing availability of resources[32] (which suggests an inability to measure finiteness). Nevertheless, environmentalists (and, alas, businessmen) interpret these falling prices as market failures. A 1991 document prepared by international business representatives reads: "In the absence of any effective price discipline, individuals will tend to maximize the resource in the short-term while abusing it in the long-term, leading to the well known 'tragedy of the commons.' Markets can only work with information. In the case of the environment, not only is there great uncertainty regarding the carrying capacity of various natural resources, but often information about possible improvements fails to reach the market (*e.g.*, energy conservation)."[33]

Strengthening Property Rights

Seven centuries ago, St. Thomas Aquinas explained the main benefits derived from private property ownership. Although nowadays emphasis is placed on efficiency and costs,[34] St. Thomas' powerful exposition of human nature is still relevant and is the real explanation of the so-called "tragedy of the commons."

Private property, he said, is "necessary to human life for three reasons:

> First, because every man is more careful to procure what is for himself alone than that which is common to many or to all since each one would shirk the labor and leave to another that which concerns the community as happens when there is a great number or servants;
>
> Secondly, because human affairs are conducted in more orderly fashion if each man is charged with taking care of some particular thing himself whereas there would be confusion if everyone had to look after any one thing indeterminated;
>
> Thirdly, because a more peaceful state is ensured to man if each one is contented with his own. Hence it is to be observed that quarrels arise more frequently where there is no division of the things possessed.[35]

Thus the three reasons are: to assure efficiency, to avoid confusion and, especially, to promote peace among men.

An example taken from contemporary life shows that these three conditions are still the relevant issues today. Anderson and Leal tell of the problems that arise with the Yellowstone bison in Yellowstone National Park:

> Because Yellowstone National Park officials are not liable for the potential damages from brucellosis carried by the bison, the responsibility falls on someone else's shoulder. In this case, the owner has never been identified. The Montana Legislature instituted a hunting season on bison who wandered from the park into Montana. Once the animals cross the park boundary, they become fair game for hunters who carry bison permits. But it is still unclear who owns the bison. If the Park Service owned the bison, then it would be responsible for trespassing animals and it would have an incentive to find innovative ways of controlling their movement or eliminating the virus they carry. If the state owned the bison, then it would have the authority to manage the herd size both inside and outside the park and would be responsible for any damage the animals might cause. But neither situation holds. Our purpose is not to propose a definitive solution to the bison problem but to explain why the door to property rights would always be kept open for addressing such problems.... Admittedly, it is difficult to imagine a mechanism for establishing clear property rights to the bison, and fencing the perimeter of a 2.2 million acre national park seems impossible. By examining the evolution of property rights in the American West, however, *we can see that changing economic and technological conditions do generate innovative property right solutions* [emphasis added].[36]

The establishment of property rights is a key issue in solving most of the problems of the environment. Environmentalists point out that most of the damage stemming from environmental hazard is the result of public goods, which generate externalities. In many cases, however, these "public goods" can become private goods in which all costs and benefits are internalized. Some of the best examples are found in the protection of endangered species, such as the African elephant.[37]

The African elephant population has diminished by half in eight years, dropping from 1.2 million to 600,000. At this rate, extinction could occur by the year 2010. In the Green literature, this killing of one of nature's most splendid creatures is treated as the classic example of market failure because of a flourishing trade in ivory, the price of which has risen from a 55 a kilo in 1983 to $150 a kilo in 1988. Unfortunately, elephants were being killed faster than they can reproduce. Older bull elephants were killed first and then the smaller females. In the end herds became unbalanced, and baby elephants died without their mothers.

However, the ivory export trade produces a mere $35 million a year. The elephant is much more valuable as a tourist attraction and even more for its ecological role in diversifying savannah and forest ecosystems (dispersing seeds that reduce bushlands, expand grasslands and curtail the incidence of the tsetse fly). Why elephants are not raised as cattle is then a puzzling question.

The answer is found in the lack of property rights for these animals. The elephants belong to nobody in particular but are simply asserted to be state property. Therefore, neighborhood tribes have no incentive to preserve them but instead to kill them for the quick cash yield of their ivory. Thus poachers are willing to assume all kinds of risks to hunt and sell the ivory in the black market. (A huge gap exists between the Japanese price of $85 to $99 a kilo and the $7 a kilo which ivory producers receive in the controlled market.) Each African country was given an ivory quota, which was monitored by the issuance of permits. This approach has totally failed as the elephants are approaching extinction. A notable exception to this history of repeated failures is Zimbabwe, which (like South Africa and Botswana) has systematically farmed the elephants, and the herds there are either growing or stable. The revenue obtained from exports provides the money for the expensive upkeep of game parks, game wardens and suppression of poachers.

Furthermore, Zimbabwe has given property rights to the tribes in the neighborhood, while making a modest charge on the final sale to go into the state treasury. The economic rent is then fully realized by the owners of the resource, and cost and benefits are internalized.

As Anderson and Leal point out, property rights are not static; the social arrangements, laws and customs that govern asset ownership and allocation are continually evolving. Technological innovations, for instance, have enabled the imprinting of salmon to facilitate their return to the farms where they were bred. Private salmon ranches currently catch approximately 70 percent of its released fish. So rather than privatizing the rivers, technology increasingly permits ways to define ownership of specific resources.[38]

As long as the benefits of establishing ownership claims are low relative to costs, little incentive exists for individuals to define and enforce private property rights. On the contrary, the higher the value of an asset and the higher the probability of losing the right to use that asset, the greater the incentive will be for "institutional entrepreneurs" to devise a mechanism to establish property rights.

Population Growth and Environmental Damage

In the nineteenth century only one billion human beings could sustain themselves on the earth. Ten thousand years ago, the number was only four million. Now, five billion people are living on average longer and healthier lives than ever before. This extraordinary increase in the world's population represents man's battle against death and famine.[39] By devoting itself to improving the lot of the living, each generation transmits a more productive world to those who follow.

Throughout history, however, concern over limited resources has always led to outcries for population control. The World Bank has been among the most prominent institutions that call for population control. Others include the United Nations Fund for Population Activities and the International Planned Parenthood Federation. Their rationale is simple enough: because the quantity of available resources is limited, more population means less quantities of resources available to each individual. This, as we have seen, is nothing less than Malthusianism in its purest form, which has been proved wrong both in theory and in practice.

The data clearly show *that natural resource scarcity as measured by the economically meaningful indicator of price has been decreasing rather then increasing in the long run for all raw materials with only temporary exceptions from time to time.* For example, copper prices have fallen over hundreds of years. In the eighteenth century B.C. in Babylonia, under Hammurabi—almost 4,000 years ago—the price of copper was about 1,200 times its price in the United States relative to wages.[40] There is, however, one important resource which has shown a trend of increasing scarcity rather then increasing abundance. That resource is the most important of all—human beings. As economist Julian Simon puts it, "the two appropriate price measures—wages and income—both clearly show that the average price of labor has recently been going up everywhere in the world, except in a few exceptional situations. The logic is inescapable: Despite the rising numbers of people, human beings have been getting scarcer."[41]

Though evidence shows that wages and income *per capita* are rising, there is a mounting choir of voices both from international organizations and the scientific community to promote population control. One such organization has maintained that the combined weight of an increasing population, a rapidly growing economy, and an environmentally intensive pattern of development threatens to breach a number of environmental "safety limits" (whatever that means). They surmise, however, that the intensity of human activities can be reduced over time by slowing the rate of population growth and transforming the quality of economic development. Their goal, which is the same for all these organizations, is "stabilization." They presume that governments can handle these tasks better than individual choices. A tragic example of government intervention in these matters, however, is the case of China, whose family planning program has virtually led to infanticide.[42]

The truth, which these international organizations either fail to see or are unwilling to acknowledge is that market-oriented economies have performed much better than centrally planned economies. In the former, wages are higher, and income *per capita* continues to rise. As the recent fall of the Berlin Wall has shown, the condition of these government-controlled economies is one of poverty, food scarcity, and in many cases impending famine—regardless of population growth. Moreover, the environmental conditions in East Europe are appalling. Jo Kwong Echard reveals that, according to Western ecology groups, rivers, lands, and forests are so contaminated that many are biologically dead, no longer capable of repairing the damage without aid.[43] Nevertheless, the international business and scientific community sustains the myth of the "population explosion" and fails to see the inefficiencies of politically controlled economies.

Environmentalism Where People Matter

This brief essay has tried to show that the cause of environmental mismanagement is neither a high industrialization rate nor an increasing population, but rather the political, economical, and social institutions which various nations adopt. Surely, all is not well with the environment. But the solution to the problems lies not in government intervention but rather in creating institutions which will allow individuals to care for the environment in a way that is respectful both to nature and to humanity.

Theologian Michael Novak recently noted that when economists (and, we may add, environmentalists) read that a pig is born in Peru, they raise that nation's per capita income. When a child is born, they lower it by the same amount. They do not realize that wealth can be created only in a real sense by man's productivity. Even though resources may exist, only man's creativity can utilize them. Oil has existed for millenia. Its use as an energy source, however, was not discovered until the last century. And the same is true for other resources or new materials.

When God created man, He said:

> Let us make man to our own image and likeness: and let him have dominion over the fishes of the sea, and the fowls of the air, and all the living creatures that move upon earth...
>
> And God blessed them, saying: Increase and multiply, and fill the earth, and subdue it, and rule over the fishes of the sea, and the fowls of the air, and all living creatures that move upon the earth.[44]

God made man co-creator and gave him dominion over nature. Man's dignity stems precisely from his being in the image and likeness of God. His place in creation then is above other creatures. His intelligence and freedom make him unique among other creatures. Thus, the Judeo-Christian idea of man and creation is incompatible with that of the "Greens," whose core value is *status quo* ("sustainability" in the approved jargon). Their ideal is of an earth without change, that shows little or no impact from human activity.[45] In the extreme green ideology, man has little or no place in creation.

Some writers even suggest that environmentalists would be genuinely unhappy if technological advances refuted their apocalyptical claims. David M. Graber, National Park Service research biologist, has expressed their contempt for humanity in a breathtaking way: "Human happiness, and certainly human fecundity, are not as important as a wild and healthy planet. I know social scientists who remind me that people are part of nature, but it isn't true. Somewhere along the line—at about a billion years ago, maybe half that—we quit the contract and became a cancer.

We have become a plague upon ourselves and upon the Earth .... Until such time as Homo sapiens should decide to rejoin nature, some of us can only hope for the right virus to come along."[46]

In contrast, free market environmentalism is rooted in an understanding of human nature: that man is naturally inclined to take care of what is his own and, as St. Thomas Aquinas expressed it, is more careful to procure what is for himself alone than that which is common to all. New scientific research attempting to protect the environment should be based on these premises and search for a better definition of property rights.

Recently the newly elected deputy prime minister of Russia, whose political career began with the campaign to save lake Baikal, (one of the world's largest fresh water lakes) has said "the efficient use of resources is possible only when a real master of those resources appears. As long as decisions affecting the future of Siberia were made by some bureaucrat in Moscow, mismanagement was inevitable."[47] The Russians have learned the lesson the hard way, but in the Western world the disastrous effects of government solutions are only beginning to show its fundamental flaw. We still have to learn our lesson, but as Hans F. Sennholz once noted "even in evil we can discern the rays of light and hope; man may gradually come to see, through suffering and misery, the error of his ways."[48] The environmental movement represents a great challenge for intellectuals who value man's dignity and freedom; it is an incentive to search for new ways of expressing old truths. Free market environmentalism is environmentalism where people matter.

Notes and References

1. The world famous *National Geographic* dedicated its entire centennial issue to the topic, "Can Man Save This Fragile Earth?" (December 1988).
2. In his best selling book *The Population Bomb*, Paul Ehrlich, Stanford's Bing Professor of Demographic Studies, makes a famous opening statement: "The battle to feed all humanity is over. In the 1970s the world will undergo famine—hundreds of millions of people are going to starve to death."
3. Lewis, Russell, "Global Hysteria," *Economic Affairs* (February 1991), p. 4. See also Ellsaesser, Hugh W., "The Threat of Global Warming is Maintained by Ignoring Much of What We Know." Paper written in preparation for attending the hearing by the California Energy Commission, Los Angeles, California, July 30-31 1990. Elsewhere Ellsaesser makes the following statement: "After 48 years of studying the atmosphere and how it behaves, including 30 years of trying to model it on computers and 15 years of pondering over the greenhouse effect itself, I strongly believe that greenhouse warming has been greatly exaggerated and its effects distorted largely for the same purpose that motivated the tailors of The Emperor's new clothes." Ellsaesser, Hugh W, "Planet Earth: Are Scientists Undertakers or Caretakers." Arkansas, 1990, p. 7. He also states that "...independent of its climatic effects, increased carbon dioxide will exert primarily beneficial effects on the biosphere, both acting as a fertilizer for plants and improving their efficiency in the use of water. Carbon dioxide, after all, is by far the main food of most, if not all plants." *Ibid.*, pp. 7-8.
4. In the United States, for example, this led to President Bush's 1990 proposal for amending the Clean Air Act of 1970.
5. See Ellsaesser, *op. cit.*, pp. 5-7.
6. *Cf.* Krug, Edward C., "The Acid Rain Hoax," *Fact Sheet,* Washington, 1990.
7. Edward O. Wilson of Harvard University declares that "Virtually all students of the extinction process agree that biological diversity is in the midst of its sixth great crisis, this time precipitated entirely by man," *National Geographic* (December 1988), p. 822. One of the main voices among believers of this extinction process is the World Wildlife Fund (United States) which, as reported by Julian Simon, "[Informed] Congress that some scientists believe that up to 1 million species of life will become extinct by the end of this century unless governments do

something. The proximate source of WWF's forecast is the 1979 book, *The Sinking Ark*, by Norman Myers. Mr. Myers gives these two statistics: the estimated extinction rate of known species between the years 1600 and 1900 was about one every four years. And the estimated rate from 1900 to the present was about one a year. Mr. Myers gives no sources for these estimates, but let us assume they are valid.... Mr. Myers then departs spectacularly from the modest evidence. He goes on to say that some scientists have hazarded a guess that the extinction rate could now have reached 100 species a year.... In brief, this extinction rate is nothing but pure guesswork. The forecast is a thousand times greater than the present, yet it has been published in the newspapers and understood as a scientific statement." Simon, Julian L., *Population Matters*, (Transaction Publishers, 1990), pp. 146-7.

8. The series he presents for a period of 200 years can be visualized as follows:

population	1	2	4	8	16	32	64	128	256
production	1	2	3	4	5	6	7	8	9

9. The most surprising fact is that *The Limits to Growth* was repudiated by the sponsoring Club of Rome itself. Four years after its publication (four million copies were sold), the Club of Rome "reversed its position" and "came out for more growth." Julian Simon quotes this report from *Time*, labeling it "as a masterpiece for double talk": The Club's founder, Italian industrialist Aurelio Peccei, says that *Limits* was intended to jolt people from the comfortable idea that present growth trends could continue indefinitely. That done, he says, the Club could then seek ways to close the widening gap between rich and poor nations—inequities that if they continue, could all too easily lead to famine, pollution and war. The Club's startling shift, Peccei says, is thus not so much a turnabout as part of an evolving strategy. Simon, *op. cit.,* p. 324.

10. Quoted by Simon, *op. cit.,* p. 337.

11. Echard, Jo Kwong, *Protecting the Environment: Old Rhetoric, New Imperatives* (1990).

12. *Ibid.*, p. 35. She also states: "In the United States environmentalists have worked to secure passage of sweeping laws for the regulation of just about every natural and environmental resource imaginable: the Clean Water Act; Federal Insecticide, Fungicide, and Rodenticide Act of 1972; Endangered Species Act; Federal Water Pollution Control Act; Forest and Rangelands Renewable Resources Planning Act; Federal Land Policy and Management Act; and so on." *Ibid.*, p. 37.

13. Myers, Norman, "Natural Resource Systems and Human Exploitation Systems: Physobiotic and Ecological Linkages," Environment

Department Working Paper N. 12, The World Bank Policy Planning and Research Staff, Washington, D.C.
14. "Caring for the World," IUCN, UNEP & WWF, 2nd. draft, (1990).
15. Sennholz, Hans F., *Age of Inflation*, Western Islands, (1979), p. 1.
16. Bernstam, Mikhail, S., *The Wealth of Nations and the Environment*, Institute of Economic Affairs, (1991), p. 11.
17. The available long-term data suggest not only non-proportionality of pollution with respect to economic growth but also that it eventually falls. The evidence strongly suggests that pollution levels grow at a decreasing rate and then fall increasingly during decades of rapid economic growth." *Ibid.*, p. 19.
18. *Ibid.*, p. 18.
19. When the technical efficiency of resource use grows, wastes and input/output ratios decline over the production cycle. Inversely, productivity of resources, defined as the ratio of economically useful resource outputs to total resource inputs, increases. *Ibid.*, p. 31.
20. *Ibid.*, p. 27.
21. *Ibid.*, p. 59.
22. For data, see Bernstam, *op. cit.,* pp. 20-29.
23. For a complete explanation of this process see Buchanan, James, "Rent Seeking and Profit Seeking," in Buchanan, Tollison and Tullock, *Towards a Theory of the Rent-seeking Society*, (1980).
24. Buchanan, *op. cit.,* p. 9.
25. *Ibid.*, p. 11.
26. *Cf.* Jo Kwong Echard, *op. cit.,* p. 93ff.
27. "The Internal Revenue Service has established a nonprofit status under Section 501 (c)(3) of the Internal Revenue Code according to which most environmental groups are classified in part because of their 'charitable,' 'educational' and 'scientific' purposes, and pursuant to which they receive such benefits as tax-deductibility of donor contributions, exemption from federal corporate income taxes and local property taxes, and a choice of options with regard to payroll taxes and unemployment insurance contributions." Echard, *op. cit.,* p. 60.
28. *Ibid.*, p. 62.
29. "It should be noted that even though these federal grants are funded with tax dollars, there frequently is little information available as to their specific purposes." *Ibid.*, p. 63. For a complete discussion see, Echard, *op. cit.,* pp. 62-64.
30. Sennholz, Hans F., "The Formation and Function of Prices," *The Freeman*, (February 1965), p. 383.
31. *Ibid.*, p. 385.

32. "Even such doomsayers as Paul Ehrlich and Garret Herdin now agree that man's history has been one of increasing availability of resources (as measured by falling prices)" Simon, *op. cit.,* p. 433.
33. *La Nación*, Buenos Aires, Marzo 6 de 1991. Remarks added.
34. There is vast technical literature on the property rights issue, starting with Ronald Coase's classical article "The Problem of Social Cost," *Journal of Law and Economics*, 3:1-44, (1960); Harold Demsetz's article "Towards a Theory of Property Rights," *American Economic Review*, 57(2):347-359, (1967) is also a classic. For a complete list on the theory of property rights and its institutional implications, the reader may consult Libecapp, Gary D., "Property Rights in Economic History: Implications for Research," *Explorations in Economic History*, 23:227-252, (1986).
35 St. Thomas Aquinas, *Summa Theologica*, II-IIae, Q. 66 a.2.
36. Anderson and Leal, emphasis added.
37. Information about the African elephant problem is found in *Elephants, Economics and Ivory*, by Barbier, E. B., Burgess, J. C., Swanson, T. M., and Pearce, D. W., Earthscan Publications, London, (1990). The following information is condensed from *Economic Affairs*, (February, 1991), pp. 44-45.
38. *Cf.* Echard, Jo Kwong, "Report on Free Market Environmentalism," *Atlas Economic Research Foundation*, Mimeo, (November, 1990), p. 9.
39. *Cf.* Simon, Julian, "Too Few People? Too Many Trees?" *Crisis*, (February, 1991), p. 19.
40. *Cf. Ibid.*, p. 20. One of the best lessons in this respect is the bet Julian Simon offered Paul Ehrlich: $1000 that the price of any raw material would indefinitely decline, adjusted by the consumer price level for inflation. Ehrlich chose a date ten years from October 6, 1980, and specified five metals: copper, chrome, nickel, tin and Tungsten. He finally lost the bet and ended paying Simon $576.07.
41. Simon, Julian, *Population Matters*, *op. cit.,* p. 196. All this section relies heavily on his work.
42. "Compare China with Singapore. China's coercive population policy including forced abortions is often called 'pragmatic' because its economic development supposedly requires population control. Singapore despite its very high population density, now suffers from a labor shortage and imports workers. It is even considering incentives for middle-class families to have more children." Simon, *op. cit.,* p. 179.
43. Echard, Jo Kwong, "Report on Free Market Environmentalism," Atlas Economic Research Foundation, Mimeo, p. 3.

44. Genesis, 1, 26 and 28. "Increase and multiply" is not a precept but a blessing, rendering them fruitful; for God has said the same words to the fishes and the birds (1, 22) who were incapable of receiving a precept.
45. *Cf.* Postrel, Virginia, "The Green Road to Serfdom," *Reason*, (April, 1990), p. 25.
46. Quoted in Postrel, *op. cit.,* p. 28.
47. Quoted in Echard, Jo Kwong, *op. cit.,* p. 3.
48. Sennholz, Hans F., *Age of Inflation*, p. 178.

21

SUPPLY-SIDE ECONOMICS: A Critique

Robert H. Miller*

The failure of the Reagan Revolution to reduce the scope and burden of government hardly requires documenting. A tripling of the federal debt to nearly $3 trillion dollars speaks volumes to the failure of his administration to challenge the idea that government can and should be all things to all people.

Ronald Reagan's domestic agenda—centerpiece of the 1980 GOP platform, the subsequent campaign, and the marching orders given to appointees in the new administration—called for lower taxes, reduced spending, balanced budgets, a rollback of regulatory interventions, and a return to sound money. Only tax rate reduction (arguably beneficial by itself) was achieved.

In part, perhaps decidedly, the revolution was pre-empted by traditional Beltway politics. It ran headlong into the personal rivalries and special interests of the entrenched liberal orthodoxy. Appointees were neither intellectually prepared, nor personally inclined to confrontation. They came to manage and were soon captured by the insatiable appetites of departments and agencies for more resources and expanded missions, and a Congress anxious to accommodate.

This part of the failed revolution is recounted thoroughly and candidly by David Stockman in his book, *Triumph of Politics.*[1] After five years as point man for President Reagan's economic agenda, he concluded that the welfare state had been constructed brick by brick as much by the duplicity of Republicans and

*Mr. Miller is an economist, investor, and entrepreneur living near Pittsburgh. He has written for *National Review* and *Journal of Commerce,* among others, and was a Reagan appointee.

conservatives as by the initiation of Democrats and liberals. And they were not about to help Ronald Reagan dismantle it. So much for the "power that corrupts."

But what about ideas? The world would change dramatically because of this president's willingness to confront authoritarian rule and to inspire millions to know that the blessings of liberty could be theirs. Surely, the compelling case for freedom and free enterprise would change the course of domestic governance as well. Keynesianism failed to deliver on its promises and was on the run; the liberal dogma of social and economic engineering that it accommodated was in disarray. The power of free enterprise ideas and the drumbeat of articulate supporters of free markets in every congressional hearing room, in the media, and at every public forum would restore America's belief in limited government.

This would be the task of "supply-side" economics, a designation which by January 20, 1981, was synonymous with the Reagan Revolution. And it is here that one finds the real reason that the nation missed the opportunity to turn from what Hayek has called "The Road to Serfdom"—permitting Stockman his final indictment: "The Reaganites were, in the final analysis, just plain welfare state politicians like everybody else."[2]

Ronald Reagan's ideas about our political, social, and economic arrangements were well positioned before the wave of supply-side economics surfaced in the mid 1970s. His ideas emerged from a healthy appetite for reading and the diverse experiences of an economics major, broadcaster, actor, guild leader, corporate spokesman, radio columnist, after-dinner speaker, and politician.

Two months into his first term as president, columnists Evans and Novak asked him who had influenced his ideas most. "Mises, and Hayek, and Say," was his response.[3] Reagan had also acknowledged drawing for his radio broadcasts and speeches from the singularly forceful and prolific writings of Professor Hans Sennholz. Although more anecdotal than intellectual, Reagan's presentation rarely strayed from views consistent with Austrian economics—from individual freedom to property rights, to unhampered markets, free trade, and the gold standard.

Radical? Yes, and yet some marveled that only two other radicals were named to high level positions—James Watt as Secretary of Interior and David Stockman as Director of OMB.[4] Austrian?

Yes, and yet not a single Austrian economist was given an influential role in promoting and implementing the domestic agenda. Still and all—Austrian, Reagan, Supply-Side—the common wisdom would have thought them interchangeable. Indeed, a bright young conservative scholar, Gregory Wolfe, has authored an outstanding source book on conservative thought. He offers the following in making the point that conservatism, while seeking political expression, is grounded in principal, not pragmatism:

> For example, whereas some journalistic observers may think that 'supply-side' economics burst on the scene from nowhere, it actually rests on decades of work done by Ludwig von Mises, and the Austrian economists,...[5]

But this is emphatically wrong and goes directly to the real reason that the Reagan agenda was not effectively pursued. The explicit principles of supply-side economics are in almost every instance antithetical to the work of Mises and the Austrians. Except for Stockman and Lewis Lehrman, who remained outside the administration, supply-siders were philosophically incapable of embracing a policy agenda consistent with free market principles. While a thorough critique of supply-side theory and derivative policy conclusions requires a more comprehensive treatment, a brief inquiry may be sufficient to support the conclusion expressed above.

Supply-Side Economics

Professor Sennholz was among the first to question supply-side concepts from a free enterprise perspective. Acknowledging its valuable contribution in challenging the aggregate demand orthodoxy driving Keynesian economics, he found supply-side to be a "curious blend of old virtues and modern temptations." And he cautioned:

> ...this economist cannot escape the strong suspicion that the supply-side advocates merely want to replace the Keynesian blueprint with theirs, and the demand-side tinkerers in Washington with a new team of supply-side tinkerers who are waiting to take their place.[6]

Supply-side, a name coined by Keynesian economist Herbert Stein, emerged in the mid-seventies when Congressman Jack Kemp proposed a 30 percent across-the-board reduction of individual tax rates on the premise that if people just had enough incentive, prosperity was inevitable. He was soon joined by Arthur Laffer—often called the father of supply-side—and journalist Jude Wanniski, soon to publish his widely acclaimed book, *The Way The World Works.*[7] They were joined by Stockman and conservative businessman-economist Lehrman, and eventually by George Gilder who would produce another influential supply-side treatise in 1981.[8]

They shared revolutionary temperaments, spirited discussions of ideas in search of a grand design for governance, a first priority commitment to tax cuts, and a loosely defined common interest in returning to the gold standard. But strong differences emerged as well. Stockman and Lehrman questioned Laffer's contention that tax cuts would be self-funding and insisted on slashing the scope and expenditures of government with a balanced budget goal. There were deep divisions on monetary policy as well. While Stockman and Lehrman never retreated, the others grew increasingly hostile and accused them of practicing "root canal economics" and wasting political capital by "imposing societal pain and sacrifice" which would only undermine support for tax reduction.[9]

Moreover, the Stockman-Lehrman position became increasingly isolated and insignificant, as the nomination and election of Ronald Reagan brought everyone scurrying to get under the supply-side umbrella where the prevailing view held only one litmus test, tax reduction.

The Laffer Curve

The archives of supply-side economics are littered with napkins, the most famous from a Georgetown restaurant where Laffer first sketched "the curve" for Richard Cheney, then a staffer at the Ford White House. The Laffer curve graphically portrays the principal tenet of supply-side, i.e., that at two rates of taxation—0 percent and 100 percent—revenues will be zero. Somewhere in between as rates rise from 0 percent and then turn again toward 100 percent, there lies an optimum revenue-generating tax rate.

At rates above this point, revenues are lost due to the tax disincentive to work, save and invest. And, conversely, rates to the lower side would generate less revenue than the optimum rate.

Reducing taxes, thus lowering the disincentive to produce (supply-siders call this the "wedge") was singularly and vigorously pursued without regard to other consequences.

In pressing for the Reagan tax cut passed in July, 1981, Laffer and Wanniski held out the promise that the tax cut would generate sufficient short-term economic growth to be self-funding. Of course, it was not. Much was written about the Coolidge-Mellon and Kennedy cuts and subsequent higher revenues. The Treasury supply-siders, Paul Craig Roberts and Norm Ture, had urged a projection of nearly 8 percent real growth for GNP in 1982 as the president's new team was preparing his first economic message to the Congress (actual growth for the year was negative).[10]

And many who were more concerned about the level of the deficit than the level of taxes nonetheless supported the Reagan tax cuts in the hope that reduced revenues would force the Congress to cut spending. They were certainly disappointed. Ten years later the supply-siders are taking credit for a 24.8 percent gain (in real terms) in income taxes paid in 1988 over 1980. But of course, it is impossible to know the extent to which this gain in revenue was due to higher incomes influenced by the reduced "wedge."

As Wanniski made clear, the goal was increasing revenues without concern for spending levels or reigning in the activities of the bureaucracy:

> We have no interest in cutting taxes but rather we believe that in current circumstances taxes can be raised with lower rates. We don't believe in lower spending, except where economies can be had by the elimination of waste and fraud. Indeed, we believe correct supply-side monetary and fiscal policies would yield greater national output, with an increasing share going to the public sector for goods and services.[11]

By its own admission, supply-side economics supports even more government and, as noted by Thomas Hazlett, "of the interventionist, central planning variety."[12] Moreover, supply-side reaches this position by ignoring or denying tenets basic to Austrian economics—marginal utility in price determination, consumer sovereignty, the spontaneous order of market processes, and problems of calculation and rational resource allocation under socialism.

Both Gilder and Wanniski ignore the contribution of Austrian Carl Menger who launched with Jevons the marginalist revolution changing the way which all economists have addressed questions of value and price for over a hundred years. Wanniski, having announced that all human decisions are made "at the margin," proceeds to describe the market determination of price without recognizing marginal utility.

Assuming Smith and Jones agree to an exchange of one fish for two coconuts, price is simply the ratio of one quantity to the other, Wanniski assures us. He then proceeds to indirect exchange and the introduction and definition of money as follows:

> Up until now, mother and child have been bartering. Now mother is offering to trade an ice cream for a 'good' that must first be manufactured by the child, i.e., dinner must first be eaten. The child must invest in production on mother's promise to pay ice cream. Thus, the concept of money is introduced, in this case money being the mother's credit, the medium of exchange in this transaction.... Money is a credit instrument just as, in the example, mother's verbal promise is a credit instrument.[13]

The obvious confusion between money and fiduciary money, the absence of savings necessary to a credit transaction, the reference to a promise as money itself, and defining the exchange of two present goods as a credit transaction are troublesome. A shallow and untrained approach to theory leads to an equally undisciplined development of policy expressions.

Gilder errs with greater clarity, beginning with a labor theory of value and a premarginalist view that price is determined by cost. Addressing the role of buyers in the market, Gilder observes: "He values his money because his expenditure of funds is psychologically rooted in his earlier expenditure of effort,"[14] and later, "...the basic price of each marketable good is ... the sum of its own intermediate costs plus a share of other costs passed on in its price."[15]

Of course such ideas have long been discredited. Both value and price are driven by consumer evaluations. The individual acts to bring about an improvement in his condition, to achieve higher levels of satisfaction than would be the case without action. Goods and services offered through exchange are valued for their utility in providing such satisfactions, totally without concern on the part of the buyer for costs incurred by producers in bringing the good to market.

Moreover, the individual subjectively ranks from higher to lower order the wants which he will satisfy as his available resources permit. It is this array of demands which the market addresses with reference to supply to determine price at the point of marginal utility, i.e., price is determined with reference to the lowest-ranked demand which would go unsatisfied in the absence of the last unit of supply. A higher price would create a product shortage, inducing sellers to compete by lowering the price; conversely, a lower price would cause buyers to bid higher in response to a shortage of the good or service.

In turn, demand for consumer goods determines the demand for intermediate goods as producers compete for the resources needed for production. It is this enormously complex process subject to continuous change which generates market prices, determines profit and loss, and allocates all scarce resources to the end of improving the condition of the consumer.

But supply-side economics emphatically denies the central role of the consumer, and with most mischievous results. Listen to Gilder:

> Capitalist creativity is guided not by any invisible hand, but by the quite visible and aggressive hand of management and entrepreneurship.[16]

And to John Kenneth Galbraith's assertion that for production to increase, "the wants must be effectively contrived," Gilder responds:

> Exactly. The quality of capitalist society depends not on automatic mechanisms, but on the quality, creativity, and leadership of the capitalists.[17]

Thus, it is not freedom, not free enterprise, nor any invisible hand, nor market process which rewards producers in accordance with their contribution to bettering the consumer condition—not from the supply-side perspective. Rather, the central figure of progress is the producer, and he is the one that supply-side must favor. Like Keynesianism, this is the economics of social conflict.

Finally, to what economic standard can supply-side look in asking the question: What is the appropriate role of government in the economic life of the nation? Unable to accept a free enterprise standard, Gilder opens the door to unrestrained statism:

> If the American government could make itself more productive than the private sector throughout the spectrum of needed economic activity, the public would gladly surrender its earnings to the state.... Far more than private services, government must be made to become productive.[18]

Mises's extraordinary contribution to the science of economics in demonstrating the failure of economic calculation under socialism was conspicuously ignored by the intellectual leadership of supply-side.[19] It is not in the nature of government to be efficient in the performance of economic tasks. And this is fortunately the case. When the only agency in the community which enjoys a monopoly on the right to use force adopts efficiency as its standard, then the protection to life, liberty, and property will surely be compromised.

Deficits and the Wedge

Having little concern for the size of government, and fearful that budget-cutting would undermine support for the tax cut, supply-siders advanced the idea that the deficit was of little consequence.[20] And as the economy improved, this reactionary view became more fashionable.

Warming up to the supply-side view that "deficits don't matter," Paul Craig Roberts (chief architect of the original Kemp-Roth tax-cut proposal and Treasury Assistant Secretary for economic policy during the first year of the Reagan administration) opened his comments to a small group gathered at lunch in early 1986 with the observation that "there is no empirical evidence that interest rates are responsive to deficits."[21] After all, the current deficit surging above $200 billion was three times larger than the record Carter shortfall, and yet higher deficits were accompanied by economic growth and sharply lower inflation and interest rates.

This writer challenged his conclusions, pointing out that in the interim, particularly with respect to the capital markets, events were being influenced by more than just the supply-side tax cuts of 1981.

Eight years earlier, the federal deficit coincided with equally large state and local government credit demands, leaving only about a third of a stagnating supply of new capital to meet the needs of the private sector. And in November of 1989, the Federal Reserve (under Paul Volker's leadership) shifted to restraint in monetary policy and focused on money growth rather than fine-tuning.

Conditions by the mid-1980s were significantly different. The nonfederal public sector reduced its annual burden on the capital markets by $100 billion. Also, higher real rates of return triggered a massive reflux of dollars from overseas (estimated as high as $200 billion annually, including substantial purchases of long-term treasury bonds by Japan). And (admittedly due in part to tax reduction), the economy was generating significantly higher rates of capital formation including gains in savings, retained corporate earnings, and paid-up annuities. But fortuitous circumstances, e.g., the dollar's reflux, will not indefinitely mask the crushing effects of growing deficits.

And there remain more serious objections. Supply-siders fail to see that their "wedge" is more meaningfully defined at the level of government spending rather than revenues. Government at any level constitutes an expense to be born by the output of the private economy. Government allocates and consumes resources in response to political forces, and not economic ones. To reduce revenues without a corresponding reduction in expenditures simply transfers part of the wedge to the capital markets and to those who will bear the terrible costs of inflation and credit expansion.

In the first instance, increased government borrowing directly reduces the availability of capital for private borrowers. Moreover, interest rates—even when declining—will be higher than would be the case in the absence of the additional demand from the public treasury. And one ignores history and human nature to venture the hope that government will not embark on additional inflation and credit expansion—the most destructive of taxes—to further accommodate higher deficits.

Sound Money

The idea that inflation is a monetary phenomenon is today more generally accepted. Thus, discussion of monetary policy focuses most often on discipline and the most feasible design of a monetary system which both meets the "needs" of the market place and insulates the supply of money from the vagaries of politics. And here, the advocates of sound money break into two camps—monetarists advocating the continued reliance on fiat money subject to a constant rate of growth, and gold advocates proposing a return to some form of gold standard. Leading supply-siders were advocates for gold (Roberts and Ture being notable exceptions).

Ronald Reagan rarely spoke of his goals without mention of sound money, and prior to the 1980 convention added occasional reference to gold and to "undoing the Nixon action of 1971."[22] During the 1980 primary campaign, Reagan made a TV commercial endorsing the gold standard, but it was withdrawn after several local showings due to poor voter response. Frankly, one-minute spots do not lend themselves to educating the electorate.

Arriving in Detroit for the GOP convention, the supply-side "central committee" including Kemp, Stockman, Wanniski, Jeff Bell and others, decided over lunch that the one weak section in the draft platform was inflation.

Kemp grabbed another napkin and, after much debate, penned a statement reading in part as follows:

> The severing of the dollar link with real commodities in the 1960s and 1970s ... has unleashed hyperinflationary forces at home and monetary disorder abroad, without bringing any of the desired economic benefits. One of the most urgent tasks in the period ahead will be restoration of a dependable monetary standard—that is, an end to inflation.[23]

While gold was clearly implied, Stockman prevailed in omitting the emotive word on the grounds that drawing attention to gold would require the candidate to deal with a widespread negative reaction including that from many of his closest advisors. Besides, much else needed to be accomplished before taking up a radical reform of monetary policy.[24]

An Austrian criticism of supply-side views on money is reserved essentially for those holding the monetarist position. First, however, it may be useful to note rather important differences with the gold supply-siders, to look at the "velocity" debate which separates both supply-side and monetarists from the Austrian school, and to comment on the Gold Commission appointed to explore the potential future role of gold in the monetary system.

Wanniski is no doubt the most outspoken and insistent of the gold supply-siders—yet, his discussions of money are the most confused and convoluted. As noted earlier, he gives new meaning to *reductio ad absurdum* in defining money. Later, in the book which Laffer calls "the best on economics ever written," he espouses a quantity theory of money. However, he concludes erroneously that prices on average will respond proportionately to an increase of money supply.[25]

Still later he reverses the causal money-price relationship. He suggests that money supply simply responds to the price and transaction volume requirements of the "electorate." Referring to the 1930-33 price and monetary contraction, he writes, "This fall in the real incomes and output brought with it a reduction in the demand for money at the going level of prices." (But this would produce rising, not falling prices.) "The electorate simply had need of one-third less money."[26]

Here, too, in his only reference to Austrian economics, he identifies Austrian scholar Murray Rothbard as a "monetarist" who cannot explain the causes of the Great Depression. Rothbard of course wrote what free enterprise economists regard as the definitive work on this subject.

Laffer writes with clarity on the issue of money, but constructs a proposed gold standard having little actual discipline. Convertibility would be reestablished at an official price, and the Federal Reserve would acquire gold reserves at 40 percent of its liabilities. The Fed would then be free to conduct monetary policies, expanding or contracting money supply so long as reserves were maintained within a range of 25 percent (higher and lower) of this 40 percent "targeted reserve requirement." When reserves persistently exceed the range, further flexibility is provided by a temporary suspension of convertibility, allowing the price of gold to adjust. Sophisticated—yes; well-intentioned—yes; a gold standard—hardly!

Velocity Controversy

According to economist Manuel H. Johnson, who succeeded Roberts as Treasury Assistant Secretary for Economic Affairs, the controversy between monetarists and supply-siders over the question of the "velocity" of money significantly impacted the development of fiscal and monetary policy and objectives in the early Reagan presidency.

By itself the velocity issue is not of great moment. But, it is valuable in 1) contrasting the Austrian perspective with that of both monetarism and supply-side, and 2) recognizing that if wrong methodology leads us to misunderstand the real world, our attempts to address its needs will not produce the desired results.

The economic assumptions and objectives of the Reagan administration were outlined in February, 1981.[27] The forecast of three key statistics, money growth, price inflation, and real gross national product, are shown in Table I below for each year to 1986. The data are expressed as a percentage change from the previous year. Column two is derived from the other three, velocity being determined by dividing nominal GNP by money supply.

Further, the sum of the columns one and two is equal to the sum of columns three and four as the Table corresponds to the so-called "Equation of Exchange." This device, put forward by Irving Fisher in search of price stability, has since been adopted almost universally by economists. And, more than just an expository device, it is employed as an analytical construct implying a statement of cause and effect relationships.

The controversy arose because monetarists insist that statistical inquiry shows velocity to be stable around a trend of 3.2 percent, and that any significant variation will quickly return to trend.[28] But administration objectives would (as Table I indicates) result in velocity going from an actual 2.5 percent in 1980 to a level of 6.3 percent in 1981, then remaining at this higher plateau through 1986.

Supply-siders, in turn, marshalled evidence to suggest that the current trend of velocity growth is much higher and argue that velocity would be further influenced by higher growth rates and after-tax yields. While the argument was not settled, policy targets continually shifted to accommodate differing conclusions.[29] In the meantime, it is interesting to note how actual results for this period differed from the 1981 consensus forecast:

Table I
ECONOMIC FORECAST
(annual percent change)

Year	Money*	Velocity	Prices	Real GNP	Actual Velocity
1980	6.4	2.5	9.0	-0.1	2.5
1981	5.9	6.3	9.6	2.6	5.1
1982	5.4	6.0	8.0	3.4	-4.6
1983	4.9	7.1	7.0	5.0	-2.1
1984	4.4	6.1	6.0	4.5	4.8

1985	3.9	5.7	5.4	4.2	-6.0
1986	3.4	5.7	4.9	4.2	-11.5

* M1-B

Velocity proved both unstable and quite unpredictable over this period. But the problem with empirical macroeconomic exercises (this one being fairly typical) is not with the reliability of forecasts. It is a question of whether the data and their arrangement is meaningful.

Austrian economic analysis finds this construct to be both meaningless and exemplary of the mischief resulting from the inappropriateness of empiricism as the method for inquiry in economics.

The equation of exchange, generally stated as Money Supply x Velocity = Price x Quantity, is not an equation at all. It is simply an identity. It says no more than that the value of purchases equals the value of sales. This identity can tell us nothing of reality nor of causation, but it would hold true by definition even if money supply were to drop by 90 percent while GNP grew tenfold.

Nor does velocity itself have a causal relationship to inflation or output. To measure velocity suggests that one is observing the number of times money changes hands through transactions for a given period. But this is not the case. GNP (and thus velocity) measures only final sales, i.e., the value of current production adjusted for inventories.

The value of all transactions—each affecting the well-being of the individuals involved—exceeds by an unknown (but certainly huge) factor the value indicated by macroeconomic data. The data, for example, ignore all intermediate transactions involved in making goods and services available to the final consumer.

Similarly, if you purchase a used car or invest in a used lathe, their is no impact on GNP, velocity, or other national income account totals. Transfer payments, gifts, taxes, and the payment of principal or interest on loans have no impact on velocity. The sale of securities or other assets resulting in a capital gain is captured in the national income accounts neither as savings, nor income, nor GNP, nor of course, velocity.

Inherently wrong constructs themselves act as a wedge denying the essential clarity and force of argument necessary to a revolution of ideas.

In other instances, supply-siders carried the debate brilliantly by abandoning the empirical trappings of conventional economics in favor of logically deduced reasoning from self-evident principles of human action. Paul Craig Roberts, for example, is compelling in his argument that the "substitution effect" would dominate the "income effect" as individuals responded to the higher "take home pay" following tax rate reductions.[30] The substitution effect relies on a shift of preference to work from leisure as the marginal cost of leisure increases.

Keynesian economists Alice Rivlin, Director of the Congressional Budget Office, and Lester Thurow argue that the income effect would result as individuals opted for more leisure preferring to simply maintain their current levels of spendable income. Rivlin's position rests on such tenuous empirical evidence as that of a study from her office indicating that lower corporate taxes would result in less corporate production. And Thurow argues that lower marginal tax rates present a disincentive to the wealthy.

Roberts, in turn, demonstrates that the perverse logic of the Rivlin-Thurow case renders all goods and services to be "inferior goods," which is to say that as incomes rise a lesser amount of such goods will be purchased. The insistence among conventional economists to apply the method of inquiry appropriate only to the natural sciences most often results in error similar to that of Rivlin-Thurow thesis.

The Gold Commission

The Commission on the Role of Gold in the Domestic and International Monetary Systems included seventeen members appointed in June, 1981, by Treasury Secretary Donald Regan. Only two, Lewis Lehrman and Congressman Ron Paul, were recognized gold advocates. Monetarists prevailed among both members and staff, which was directed by Dr. Anna Schwartz, well known for her collaboration with Milton Friedman in their major study of monetary history.

Among two dozen witnesses—most supporting a return to gold—Hans Sennholz and Murray Rothbard represented Austrian economics. Strangely, the supply-siders absented themselves from this unique opportunity.

Except for a "sleeper" recommendation discussed below, the results might easily have been anticipated. The Commission issued its report to the Congress in June, 1982, noting that most members "believe that a return to the gold standard is not desirable," and proposed a number of recommendations including, most significantly, the continuation of flexible exchange rates, and an indirect endorsement of a fixed rate of monetary growth.[31]

Expressing dissenting views, Lehrman joined by Congressman Paul penned a brilliant essay of nearly 300 pages presenting the historical and theoretical case for gold.[32] Interestingly, Rothbard, Lehrman, and Schwartz all drew attention to the positive experience of price stability under the gold standard. Edward Bernstein in a commissioned study for the Gold Commission argued the more conventional case of instability. He failed as others have to acknowledge that crises identified with the history of the gold standard actually arose during periods of temporary suspension or abandonment of gold convertibility.[33]

In addition to his testimony, Dr. Sennholz submitted a paper calling for the privatization of federal gold stocks and detailing the enormous benefits to all concerned.[34] This is likely to have influenced the thinking of members when they later passed a resolution calling on the Congress to authorize:

> ...the issue of gold bullion coins of specific weights, and without dollar denomination or legal tender status ... to be sold at a small markup over market value of the gold content ... Furthermore, we recommend that the coins be exempt from capital gains taxes, and ... from sales taxes.[35]

A coin issued with these additional provisions could provide the market with a commodity money alternative—a point no doubt overlooked by the Commission's members. However, it drew immediate response from the Congress. Without waiting for the report of the Commission, the House Banking Committee adopted a statement condemning this recommendation and saying it had no purpose "other than to appease the gold lobby."[36]

Gold or Monetarism

The Federal Reserve, Treasury, and Council of Economic Advisors in the Reagan administration became bastions of monetarism. Their views on money (though not always in other areas) were shaped by the Chicago School of economics.

The rejection of gold—the money of the unhampered market—comes mostly from those holding the market system itself in contempt; to them, monetary intervention is a necessary tool for rechanneling market resources to achieve socio-economic arrangements more to their own liking.

The Chicago School of Henry Simon, Lloyd Mints, and Milton Friedman is an exception to this statement. On the one hand, they propose a pure fiat standard of money, referring to the gold standard as a "19th Century myth" and a "cultural lag."[37] On the other hand, they claim allegiance to libertarian doctrines of limited government and free markets.[38]

Early in his book, *A Program for Monetary Stability*, Friedman seriously questions the role of government in monetary matters:

> Control over monetary and banking arrangements is a particularly dangerous power to entrust to government because of its far reaching effects on the economic activity at large—as numerous episodes from ancient times to the present and over the whole of the globe tragically demonstrate. In consequence, one question that a liberal must answer is whether monetary and banking arrangements cannot be left to the market, subject only to the general rules applying to all other economic activity. I am by no means certain that the answer is indubitably in the negative.[39]

Nevertheless, the remainder of his book is spent rationalizing an answer "indubitably in the negative." Friedman points out that production of the monetary commodity requires resources which are, therefore, denied from employment in producing other goods and services destined for consumption. This allegedly creates a strong incentive for issuing fiduciary money not fully covered with specie reserves. Thus, government has a proper and necessary function in limiting its supply.[40]

The first error here reveals a shortcoming in the Chicago School's understanding of the libertarian view of fractional reserves and the inexorable economic forces at work in the free market. Fiduciary media is not an instrument of the market system. It is incompatible with the legal protection of private property against theft.[41] On the other hand, a so-called "free banking" system permitting fractional reserves with the knowledge and contractual concurrence of depositors is an option which would employ competitive market forces (i.e., the desire of issuing banks to attract depositors) and is defended by Mises.[42]

As for the costs of production of the monetary commodity, it must be remembered that choice and value are rooted in utility no less than with other goods destined for consumption. To legislate the adoption of paper money on the basis of its cost of production is no less arbitrary than to legislate the use of construction material X in place of the market's choice of material Y because government officials have decided that X will provide similar service at less cost.

Moreover, it is naive in the extreme to assert that government will long observe any "monetary rule" such as Friedman's proposed 4 percent rule. Recent congressional spending "rules"—Gramm-Rudman and the 1990 Budget Accord—testify to the sanctity of such commitments.

It is true that removing the monetary demand for gold increases its use as an industrial metal, but it also invalidates the essential service of the gold standard—the gold standard renders the determination of purchasing power independent of the policies of governments and protects citizens from the disastrous consequences of inflation and credit expansion.[43]

Austrian economist and Nobel Laureate F. A. Hayek observes:

> There is no justification in history for the existing position of a government monopoly of issuing money.... To put it into the hands of an institution which is protected against competition, which can force us to accept the money, which is subject to incessant political pressure, such an authority will not ever again give us good money."[44]

Freedom and free enterprise suffered a great disservice from those who captured the Reagan Administration agenda, embracing little more than the narrow goal of tax reduction. And it is difficult to say the president was served well by those who insisted on accommodating that agenda to conventional Beltway demands in the interest of acceptance.

The Reagan revolution in the hearts of millions of those who carried it to January, 1980, was meant to confront wrong ideas, misguided goodwill, and the greed of special interests. Perhaps it would have lost, but the taste of battle would be sweet still.

Notes and References

1. Stockman, David A., *The Triumph of Politics* (New York, NY: Harper and Row, 1986).
2. *Ibid.*, p. 385.
3. Evans, Rowland, and Novak, Robert, *The Reagan Revolution* (New York, NY: E.P. Dutton, 1981), p. 229.
4. *Ibid.*, p. 242.
5. Wolfe, Gregory, *Right Minds* (Washington, DC: Regnery Gateway, 1987), p. 14.
6. Sennholz, Hans F., "Supply-Side Economics" (Unpublished manuscript, Foundation For Economic Education, June, 1980), p. 2.
7. Wanniski, Jude, *The Way the World Works* (New York, NY: Simon and Schuster, 1978).
8. Gilder, George, *Wealth and Poverty* (New York, NY: Basic Books, 1981).
9. Stockman, *op. cit.*, p. 75.
10. *Ibid.*, Chapter 3.
11. Wanniski, Jude, "Letter to the Editor," *The New Republic* (December 14, 1981), p. 6.
12. Hazlett, Thomas W., "The Supply-Side's Weak Side," *Supply-Side Economics*, Richard H. Fink, Ed. (Frederick, MD: University Publications, 1982), p. 113.
13. Wanniski, *The Way the World Works*, p. 48.
14. Gilder, *op. cit.*, Chapter 4.
15. *Ibid.*, p. 202.
16. *Ibid.*, p. 34.
17. *Ibid.*, p. 35.
18. *Ibid.*, p. 216.
19. Mises, Ludwig von, *Human Action*, Rev. Ed. (New Haven, CT: Yale University Press, 1963), pp. 698-715.
20. Stockman, *op. cit.*, Chapter 3.
21. Informal remarks before a small group in Washington.
22. Evans and Novak, *op. cit.*, pp. 105-108.
23. Stockman, *op. cit.*, pp. 62-63.
24. *Ibid.*
25. Wanniski, *op. cit.*, p. 113.
26. *Ibid.*, pp. 164-165.
27. "America's New Beginning: A Program for Economic Recovery," (The White House, Office of the Press Secretary, February 18, 1981).

28. *Cf.* Tobin, James "The Reagan Economic Plan," *Economic Review*, April, 1981.
29. Stockman, *op. cit.*, Chapter 3.
30. Roberts, Paul Craig, "The Breakdown of the Keynesian Model," *The Public Interest*, No. 52 (Summer, 1978), pp. 20-33.
31. *Report to the Congress of the Commission on the Role of Gold in the Domestic and International Monetary Systems* (Washington, DC, March, 1982) Vol. I, pp. 16-20.
32. *Ibid.*, Vol. II, Annex B, pp. 9-303.
33. *Ibid.*, Vol. II, Annex B, pp. 310-365.
34. Sennholz, Hans F., "Federal Gold Must be Employed Productively," *Gold Commission Report*, Vol. II, Annex E.
35. *Gold Commission Report*, Vol. II, Annex B, pp. 304-305.
36. *Ibid.*
37. Friedman, Milton, *A Program for Monetary Stability* (New York, NY: Fordham University Press, 1959), p. 81.
38. Friedman, Milton, "Real and Pseudo Gold Standards," *The Journal of Law and Economics*, Vol. IV (October, 1961).
39. Friedman, *A Program for Monetary Stability*, p. 4.
40. *Ibid.*, pp. 4-9.
41. Rothbard, Murray N., *Man, Economy, and State* (New York, NY: D. Van Nostrand Company, Inc., 1962), Chapter 11.
42. Mises, *Human Action*, pp. 440-445.
43. Mises, *Theory of Money and Credit* (New Haven, CT: Yale University Press, 1953), p. 416ff.
44. Hayek, F.A., "Toward a Free Market Monetary System," *Journal of Libertarian Studies,* 3, No. 1 (1979) p. 7.

22

THE INSEPARABLE LINK BETWEEN MORALITY AND ECONOMICS

Judd W. Patton*

What do modern day economists do? What procedures and methods do they employ? The standard textbook response is that economists formulate economic principles which are useful in establishing policies designed to solve economic problems. To discover these principles, also known as generalizations, economists engage in positive economics, that is, they hypothesize and theorize about empirical observations, strictly limiting themselves to describing reality; and they avoid issues or questions of "what ought to be." The latter is called normative economics.

In this positivist approach there is an impassable line of distinction between morality and economic science. Morality is a "non-fact" for positive theory and analysis. To suggest that moral principles could be relevant "empirical data" within the positivistic episteme clearly would be a serious breach of scientific analysis and purity.

Yet a little reflection, according to Henry Hazlitt, reveals that economics and ethics:

> ...are, in fact, intimately related. Both are concerned with human action, human conduct, human decision, human choice.... There is hardly an ethical problem, in fact, without its economic aspect. Our daily ethical decisions are in the main economic decisions, and nearly all our daily economic decisions have, in turn, an ethical aspect.[1]

The subject matter of both morality and economics is human action. Economic inquiry wants to know the cause and conse-

*Dr. Patton is Associate Professor of Economics at Bellevue College, Bellevue, NE. He is also director of the Entrepreneurial Leadership Center, which publishes the newsletter, *The Bottom Line.*

quences of human actions. Morality purports to show which human actions are right or wrong. Clearly human action is the common denominator, suggesting a possible link between moral principles and economic principles. Thus, could it be possible that a moral principle has its counterpart in the economic realm? Could both moral and economic principles be a part of an inseparable body of thought? Could the economic and moral realms be, in fact, in harmony with one another as opposed to being hermetically sealed, unrelated areas of human knowledge as required by positivism?

The positivistic episteme rejects such questions out of hand. Positive economics excludes the possibility of ineluctable economic principles and it excludes ethical or moral principles as relevant knowledge in explaining the consequences of human action in the economic realm. To repeat, morality is a "non-fact" for contemporary economic science.

To consider these questions, then, a new episteme is required—one that can investigate a possible link between economic events and moral and immoral human actions. The purpose of this essay is to demonstrate that such an episteme not only exists but reveals a necessary connection between ethical decisions and economic results. Its analysis will address the basic premises of this world view, its methodology, and some of its magnificent economic and moral laws, and it will demonstrate the interconnection of these two areas of human action by analyzing some important economic issues of our day.

Historical Development

The science of economics is generally recognized to have begun with the 1776 publication, *An Inquiry into the Nature and Causes of the Wealth of Nations,* by the Scottish moral philosopher, Adam Smith. Unlike his predecessors in previous centuries, he systematically deduced many cause and effect principles that operate in a market economy. For this accomplishment he is rightly recognized as the "Father of Economics." Adam Smith's efforts led to the rise of a tradition known today as the "Classical School of Economics." It lasted nearly one hundred years and was developed by such great thinkers as Jean Baptiste Say, David Ricardo, John Stuart Mill, James Mill, Nassau Senior, and Frederic

Bastiat. Together, their ideas were a major force in ushering in the age of capitalism in the eighteenth and nineteenth centuries.

For Adam Smith and most of the classical economists, economic science (or, in their words, political economy) was a branch of moral philosophy built on a moral base. Adam Smith himself believed in the existence of a moral order which he called natural liberty or natural law. Using this framework, he logically demonstrated that free markets were not only vastly more productive than any other alternatives, but free markets were also in harmony with the God-ordained order of natural liberty. To paraphrase Adam Smith, individuals within a capitalistic system of private property acting in their own self-interest are led by an "invisible hand" to promote the general well-being of society.

In the 1870s three economists working independently revolutionized classical economic science by discovering the subjective theory of value as the basis for market prices and phenomena. Carl Menger at the University of Vienna, William Jevons at Cambridge University, and Leon Walras at the University of Lausanne each perceived that it is acting, preferring, and valuing individuals who are the source of market prices, not labor times as most classical economists had assumed. And thus, neoclassical economics was born.

Another equally revolutionary idea emerged during the nineteenth century. The idea was that economics should become an exact science, like the natural sciences, by adopting its trial and error approach. The impetus given to this experimental or empirical method was due in large part to the notable successes and progress of Newtonian physics, biology, and astronomy. A corollary to this development was that science should not have a moral foundation, as did the work of Adam Smith and other classicalists. Science should be value-free.

Undoubtedly, no scientist should inject his opinions, prejudices, and judgments into his analysis or work. Scientists by definition are unbiased researchers. Nevertheless, a general understanding exists today that all science is based on a foundation or paradigm that shades thinking and theorizing.[2] To exclude God or revealed knowledge from their "starting point" in the study of economic phenomena in an effort to be unbiased is to make man and his reasoning the sole source of knowledge. This latter position is known as humanism. Humanistic trial and error science has no place for absolute, universal principles. Clearly, they would claim, the testing process in economics is never-ending. Economic theories are not universal but they evolve and change continually.

This virtually unheralded revolution changed the scope of economic science from a morally based, deductive science revealing universal principles of human action, to a non-moral, humanistic, experimental science producing principles that are relative to time and place, continually open to refinement or refutation. As one well-recognized scientific empiricist said, "truth may exist in the universe, but science can never know for sure if it has discovered it." Only one neoclassical school of economics has not followed the humanist, no-truth, empirical methodology. Founded by Austrian Carl Menger at the University of Vienna, and developed most notably by Ludwig von Mises (1881-1973), this tradition has developed a body of economic principles based on the self-evident axiom that mankind acts purposefully. Reminiscent of Adam Smith's work, these economic laws or principles are true and timeless because they have been deduced by the rules of logic from a true axiom. Unless a logical error is made, Austrian theory is true and correct, providing mankind with essential knowledge of relationships in the economic sphere. Austrian principles reveal the necessary means to the attainment of economic goals.

Within this Austrian tradition a group of economists has endeavored to expand the Austrian episteme to include the moral dimension. For the most part, this episteme was developed in a fortnightly journal entitled *Christian Economics* that spanned two decades, 1950-1970.[3]

Gary North is most emphatic about the Judeo-Christian foundation or episteme for economic science. "I am not arguing that Christians should develop a better approach to economics, both theoretical and practical, but that Christians are required to work out the Biblical principles of the only kind of economics that there can ever be, revelational economics."[4] Let us examine North's assertion.

Two Kinds of Economics

The Bible informs mankind that the fear (awe) of the Lord is a foundational premise for all knowledge (Proverbs 1:7). Christians take seriously this admonition: "...and lean not to your own understanding. In all your ways acknowledge Him, and He shall direct your paths" (Proverbs 3:5-6). Indeed, the Apostle Paul warns against the paradigm of humanism—man and his reasoning as the sole source of knowledge—as the basis for any science: "See to it that no one takes you captive through hollow and deceptive philosophy, which depends on human tradition and the basic principles of this world rather than on Christ" (Colossians 2:8, New International Version). The Greek word for "basic principles" means "primary and fundamental principles of any art, science or discipline."[5]

Thus, the Bible reveals that there are only two broad world views or paradigms—God's and man's. In terms of economic knowledge, there can be only revelational or Biblical economics and man's economics. Mankind either develops economic knowledge on the foundation God has revealed in His word, or mankind does not. In the book of beginnings, *Genesis,* the Creator God explained how man's "alternative" view came about. God explained personally to Adam and Eve that they could eat of every tree in the Garden of Eden except the tree of knowledge of good and evil. It was strictly forbidden. If they chose to eat of it, they would surely die (Genesis 2:16–17). Adam and Eve disbelieved and disobeyed God. They ate fruit from this forbidden tree and took unto themselves, and for all mankind afterward, the discovery of knowledge apart from God (Genesis 3:22). Humanism was born.

Economically speaking, man has constructed his own economic systems and generated his own diverse and numerous schools of thought that seem right or good to him (Proverbs 14:12). Our point is that the Judeo-Christian tradition must begin its quest for economic knowledge, understanding, and wisdom—as well as for all areas of knowledge—within the revealed episteme of the Bible (Matthew 4:4). According to Gary North, this episteme and the substance of Biblical economics is an almost untouched field for academic work.

Biblical Economic Paradigm

The Bible addresses a wide range of economic topics. For example, the parables of the pounds (Luke 19:12–26), of the hired servants (Matthew 20:1–16), and of the talents (Matthew 25:14–

30) are essentially economic in substance. They deal with money, interest (usury), profit and loss, wages, entrepreneurship, and contractual relations. The Bible does not directly expound principles of economics. It does, however, provide the essential framework for the systematic development of economic science.

The Bible identifies four paradigmatic premises for economic science. The first premise mentioned previously is that God's word (the Bible) is the foundation for all knowledge. Christian wisdom, knowledge, and understanding originate from fearing (respecting) God by striving to keep His commandments, hating evil, and living by His every word (Ecclesiastes 12:13; Proverbs 8:13; Matthew 4:4). All other knowledge and wisdom is prophesied to come to naught (I Corinthians 1:19-20).

The second premise central to economic methodology is that man is a purposeful being endowed with a spiritual essence that gives him a mind and free will. Man is not an animal programmed with instinct but is, instead, made in the very likeness and image of God (Genesis 1:26). Man has a spiritual essence that imparts intellect (I Corinthians 2:12). This spirit, working within man, gives him mind power—something not possessed by animals or other living organisms. When Adam and Eve sinned, their descendants—humankind—were simply cut off from access to God's Spirit (Genesis 3:22-24) until Christ's atoning sacrifice and resurrection. Man is special and unique in God's creation. Man alone possesses an inner self of volition, self-awareness, and the ability to choose goals and the means to fulfill these goals. He also has the capacity to build Godly character, assisted by the Holy Spirit in choosing the right and resisting the wrong (II Corinthians 4:16; 10:4-5). Man acts; he values and prefers. He is a purposeful being.

A third premise is that God as Creator and Lawgiver (James 4:12; Isaiah 33:22) has set in motion inexorable laws governing human action—in the social, economic, and political realms—generating "...life and prosperity" (Deuteronomy 30:15-20; Exodus 20:3-17). These spiritual laws reveal to humankind how to love God (the first table of four laws) and how to love neighbor (the second table of six laws, as summarized in Matthew 22:37-38). To obey and live within these eternal principles of human action or conduct is to bring about harmony, peace, economic prosperity, and liberty (James 1:25). As Michael Novak put it:

"Virtue can hardly help bearing material fruit.... The relation of Creator to creation would otherwise seem odd."[6] Many verses attest to a relationship between moral law and economic well-being (Job 36:11; Psalms 1:1–3; Joshua 1:8). Living in defiance of these moral laws is the definition of sin: "...for sin is the transgression of the law." (I John 3:4). Moreover, sin entails penalties. God's eternal principles invariably exact a price for all offenses. Since much of human activity is economic in nature, it follows that many penalties will be in the economic realm as well.

The fourth premise is that God has given mankind a stewardship role on the earth (Genesis 1:28; Hebrew 2:6–8). Indeed, the Greek word for economy, *oikonomia,* which translates literally as "law of the household," means stewardship. God has given man the responsibility to care for the earth, though God still retains ownership of all the earth (Psalms 24:1). According to North, the Hebrew conception of property rights was covenantal. It set boundaries on the power of individuals and the state to administer property. God delegates to mankind the responsibility of acting as stewards of His property.[7]

However, wise stewards need more than moral laws to carry out their responsibilities. They need to possess a knowledge and understanding of economic cause and effect. For example, would abolishing private property in the means of production (socialism) be an appropriate means to a more productive, efficient economy? Would protective tariffs or quotas reduce a nation's unemployment rate or balance of trade deficit? Would higher minimum wage legislation be an effective policy to raise labor income? Would increasing the quantity of money be a proper means for a central bank to lower interest rates and thereby "fight" recession? A knowledge of the Ten Commandments does not directly answer these questions. Godly wise stewards must also understand the intimate relationship between moral laws and economic cause and effect. Otherwise their economic behavior or advocacy of public policy may contradict their moral standard. Biblical or Christian *oikonomia,* then, is the administration of God's way of life on earth. How can these economic laws or principles be discovered?

Economic Methodology

The key to understanding Christian economics and the generation of economic principles lies in the second paradigmatic premise. Mankind acts purposefully. The Bible clearly shows through numerous examples that when dealing with human action, the scientific method of hypothesis and controlled experimentation is inadequate. It cannot assess the facts of reality. Empiricism is appropriate for the purposeless realm of the natural sciences. It is misleading, however, in the realm of purposeful human action, that is, in economics.

In brief, the scientific method alone cannot make the economic world understandable in terms of either human purposes or God's purposes. Thus, it cannot establish the "facts of reality." Here are a few Biblical proofs. As noted above, Adam and Eve observed that the forbidden fruit looked good to eat. They ignored God's directive and purpose. It was not good to eat, regardless of sensory perception. Their observation, apart from a knowledge of God's command, was incapable of determining the facts of the situation.

Another example is Job. In fact, the whole book of Job is a study in the failure of empiricism. Job was righteous. God even said so. But Job's problem was self-righteousness. After Job finally lost everything, his friends pointed to his calamity as evidence that had committed some horrible sins. Since they did not grasp that God's purpose in afflicting Job was to overcome his pride, their comments were misdirected, not factual. In the end, Job's friends were chastised by God (Job 42:7).

The exodus from Egypt provides yet another example of the inadequacy of the scientific method to deal with human action. God purposefully led the Israelites into a box canyon, trapped between the mountain ranges and the Red Sea. Pharaoh thought the Israelites had trapped themselves (Exodus 14:3). But Pharaoh's observation—without a knowledge of God's purpose—was faulty. God was working out a great purpose: to deliver His people miraculously. Had Pharaoh known that, his course of action would likely have been different. Again, empirical observation alone was incapable of discovering the truth of the circumstances.

By excluding God's purposes from economic analysis, it is impossible to either grasp the facts of reality or existing relationships. Humanistic economic science, for example, could never discover that individuals who tithe will receive economic blessings and those who do not will be cursed (Malachi 3:8–10). Indeed, how can empiricists ever discover that failure to tithe is robbing God? How could they test the tithing law or the following economic relationship: "He who has pity on the poor lends to the Lord. And He will pay back what he has given" (Proverbs 19:17)?

Likewise, it is just as important to base economic analysis on human purposes. A classic illustration is given by Israel Kirzner. Suppose an economist from Mars focuses his telescope on earth. Being an avowed proponent of the scientific method, he proceeds to observe an interesting regularity. He observes that at a specific time each day a moving box stops at a fixed box. In a matter of moments some tiny objects move from the fixed box and disappear into the moving box. Further, he observes that this occurs five out of every seven days. As he continues his research, he observes that sometimes the moving box stops and leaves without any objects disappearing into it. At other times he observes the tiny objects moving at a rapid rate, arriving just in time at the fixed box to be swallowed up by the moving box. After extensive empirical research, our Martian scientist may be able to establish a tentative principle about moving boxes and objects. His theory may even provide excellent predictability as to when any tiny object is going to miss or catch the moving box. Nevertheless, our Martian economist will have developed an incomplete picture of what is actually happening—people catching a bus for work each morning.[8]

Through numerous examples, the Bible shows clearly that the scientific method, by itself, is an incomplete methodology for economic science. In summary the problems are: (1) empiricism's inability to identify and discriminate facts from non-facts due to its abstraction from human purposes and God's purposes as revealed in the Bible; (2) its inability to perform controlled, replicatable experiments; and (3) the inappropriateness of its goal to attempt to discover and measure quantitative relationships that do not exist in the realm of human action due to subjective human values.[9]

As Murray Rothbard has stated, "To ignore this primordial fact about the nature of man—to ignore his volition, his free will—is to misconstrue the facts of reality and therefore to be profoundly and radically unscientific."[10] Rothbard and other Austrian theorists identify the ordinary use of the scientific method for economic theorizing as scientism—the unscientific attempt to transfer the methodology of the physical sciences to the study of human action.

Since its inception, the Austrian tradition in general has been keenly aware of epistemological issues for economic science, most notably by Ludwig von Mises. The founder of the tradition, Carl Menger, concluded that universal causal economic laws (which he called *verites de raison*) could be discovered by logical deduction by relating external events to human plans, purposes, and values.[11] As Rothbard expressed it, "economic theory consists of the elaborations of the logical implications of the concept of action."[12] But it was Mises who developed most of this phenomenal body of economic principles or laws in his magnum opus, *Human Action.*[13] From the Biblical paradigm and perspective, Mises and the Austrian school have developed, by means of a "borrowed premise," a major portion of Biblical economics; that is, they have logically deduced inexorable, universal laws of economics starting from the axiom that man acts purposefully. While the Austrians outside the "Christian economic" tradition have made the world understandable in terms of human purposes, their framework and analysis, however, do not include making the world understandable in terms of God's purposes as revealed in the Bible. These Austrians thus fail to perceive the inextricable relationship between moral laws and economic laws, i.e., that violating moral laws also violates economic laws. Nevertheless, they have provided necessary economic knowledge and understanding for Biblical economics.

Seven Economic Laws

The following are some of the major laws of cause and effect derived from and consistent with the axiom that humankind acts purposefully:

1. *Law of Supply and Demand:* Harmony and balance between producers and consumers is only attainable through market-

clearing prices that reflect the actual supply of, and demand for, a particular product or service.

2. *Say's Law:* Supply creates demand, or salable production is the source of demand.
3. *Law of Comparative Advantage:* Income or production is maximized when each individual and nation specialize in producing goods and services in which they have a cost advantage, that is, in which they are more efficient or profitable than others.
4. *Law of Employment:* There is always work to be done and, therefore, no fixed number of jobs, but to be employable individuals must accept wages and salaries (including fringe benefits) that correspond to the market value of their service.
5. *Law of the Quantity of Money:* There is no economic benefit from increasing the quantity of money. Prices and costs adjust to the available supply. More money means higher prices and less money means lower prices.
6. *Law of Time Preference:* Mankind prefers a present good or satisfaction to the same good or satisfaction in the future. That is, time is valuable; it commands a price (the interest rate).
7. *Gresham's Law:* "Bad" money drives "good" money out of circulation. More precisely, money artificially overvalued by government will drive money artificially undervalued by government out of circulation.

Modern day positivist economists would, of course, deny and reject the above seven propositions as eternal principles. But to Austrians and Biblical economists, these laws are deducible from the axiom that mankind acts purposefully. They are principles to be learned and used to understand the causal relationships in the economy. Specifically, they are essential components for Christian stewardship. For example, from these laws Christian stewards know that persistent shortages and surpluses are the consequences of legal price ceilings and price supports which fail to "obey" the law of supply and demand. Price inflation and business cycles are the consequence of ignoring the law of the quantity of money. Unemployment, especially for the young and unskilled, is a consequence of minimum wage legislation that violates the law of employment. Lower standards of living are a consequence of protective tariffs and barriers, that is, a failure to get in step with the law of comparative advantage. Government deficit spending to "create demand" and thereby restore full employment is perverse since it contradicts Say's Law.[14] Loss of American silver coinage in 1964 was the consequence of ignoring Gresham's Law.

Now we come to a key insight of the Biblical economic episteme. The economic difficulties listed in the preceding paragraph are the consequences of not only "disobeying" economic laws, but the consequence of disobeying moral precepts. Truth is consistent. Stated differently, these negative economic consequences are the result of employing inappropriate economic means initiated by immoral human actions. Thus, every breach of the Ten Commandments by individuals, businesses, or governments in the economy simultaneously leads them to breach economic laws or sound stewardship principles! There is an interconnection and unity of the moral realm and the economic realm.

One Indivisible Body of Science—Examples

Consider the issue of economic systems, capitalism versus socialism. Is socialism—where government owns and centrally directs all of the factors of production—a system based on economic and moral principles? Absolutely not!

Economically, socialism contradicts the law of economic calculation. Rational, efficient allocation of economic resources is impossible without a price system that accurately communicates to producers the relative scarcities and demands in the economy. Socialism contains an economic paradox: the economy is planned but planners have no mechanism or means to assess the profitability of any endeavor. Therefore, unbalanced production, shortages and unusable surpluses, duplication, time lags, inefficiency, and appalling economic waste are guaranteed. Mises labeled socialism "planned chaos."[15]

In the moral realm socialism violates the First and Eighth Commandments against idolatry and stealing. In a centrally planned economy, the state becomes omnipotent and pretends to omniscience, in place of the true Creator God. Individual freedom is suppressed contrary to God's will (Isaiah 61:1; James 1:25). The state and its leaders become substitute gods. Moreover, the Eighth Commandment, "Thou shalt not steal," implies private ownership. How can an individual not steal when all resources are owned in common? Thus, socialism defies at least two moral laws.

The Bible makes it plain that private property (Micah 4:1-4) and free markets, along with entrepreneurial profit and loss (Matthew 25:14-30), are the means He has created for mankind to carry out the assigned stewardship role on earth. Stewardship requires economic calculation (Luke 14:28) in "counting the cost," something a socialist economy can never perform because it has no genuine price system. Thus, while Christians can live under any economic system, only a free market economy is consistent with moral and economic laws. Socialism as an economic system is immoral. To embark upon its realization is to violate simultaneously both economic and moral precepts.

Protective tariffs or other trade barriers also violate economic and moral precepts. Trade restrictions are contrary to God's way of love toward neighbor. Christians should even love their enemies (Matthew 5:44). They should not be biased against other nationalities (Acts 10:34). Tariffs and trade barriers are sought based on motives of coveting, greed, selfishness, or even hatred. These motives break God's laws. And the breaking of eternal moral principles necessarily causes mankind—via the tariff or trade barrier—to violate a vital economic principle of stewardship, the law of comparative advantage. Tariffs bear false witness in that they misdirect and limit entrepreneurial opportunities. Economic progress is thwarted.

The most shocking example of the immorality of protective tariffs was the Smoot-Hawley Tariff Act of 1930. The sponsors wanted to force Americans to "Buy American" to eliminate the historically high unemployment rate. But foreign nations retaliated in kind. The result was a disintegration of the whole world economy. The worldwide division of labor collapsed. The Great Depression was the result. Hans Sennholz noted the true causes: "Social and economic decline is facilitated by moral decay. Surely the Great Depression would be inconceivable without the growth of covetousness and envy of great personal wealth and income, the mounting desire for public assistance and favors."[16]

Minimum wage legislation—a legal price "floor"—is contrary to moral and economic precepts. As such it is an inappropriate and ineffective policy to raise labor income, regardless of the "good intentions" of its sponsors. Why? Because the legislation falsifies the market worth of some labor. Many laborers, notably young and unskilled people, are legally priced out of a job. Unemployment and disemployment result for all laborers whose services are worth less than the minimum prescribed by the legislation.

Once again it can be seen that moral and economic laws are tied together. Minimum wage laws simultaneously break the Ninth Commandment against false witness and the economic law of employment. Thus minimum wage laws are not in synchronization with the harmony designed by God in the economic realm.

What if the economy is in a recession? Should the United States monetary authority, the Federal Reserve, stimulate the economy by lowering interest rates through expanding the quantity of money? From the Biblical perspective, such an "easy money" policy is immoral and economically counterproductive. Hazlitt candidly explains why: "When modern governments inflate by increasing the paper-money supply, directly or indirectly, they do in principle what kings once did when they clipped the coins. Diluting the money supply with paper is the moral equivalent of diluting the milk supply with water."[17]

An "easy money" policy, morally considered, entails false witness and theft. Not surprisingly, it also breaks an economic law—the law of the quantity of money. Moreover, inflation's false witness causes a business cycle, since inflation—or more precisely credit expansion—disorients and falsifies business decisions. The credit expansion appears to increase the supply of savings in the loan market. In reality, there are no additional real savings or physical goods available for entrepreneurial activity. Nevertheless, this artificial expansion of monetary savings will move interest rates lower than they otherwise would have been. A key economic signal is distorted. This results in desynchronizing entrepreneurial plans from consumer saving-spending preferences. The inevitable result must be malinvestment. A recession is the painful but necessary means whereby misallocated resources are liquidated and returned eventually to profitable employments.[18]

Morally, Biblical economics understands inflation or monetary debasement as equivalent to legalized counterfeiting. Like a counterfeiter, inflation does not increase a nation's real wealth and, therefore, must redistribute income in a wanton fashion to favored individuals or groups. The Bible defines money as a specific weight of either gold, silver, copper, or brass. God's law condemns the debasing of money (Isaiah 1:27; Amos 8:4-6; Micah 6:11). As shown in Haggai (1:6-7), generally higher prices are a consequence of monetary debasement, "and he who earns wages, earns wages to put into a bag with holes." It should not be surprising, then, that inflation, as false witness and theft in economic action, also violates an economic law—the law of the quantity of money. From this law a Judeo-Christian steward knows that there is no social or economic benefit from increasing the money supply. Inflation demonstrates, once again, that every immoral action or policy has adverse consequences, violating economic laws, that is, applying wrong means to chosen ends.

Finally, let us consider redistributive transfer payments. Are food stamps, public housing, farm subsidies, Medicare, Medicaid, Aid to Families with Dependent Children, and Social Security programs consistent with moral and economic laws? Absolutely not! Each of these transfer payments (often deemed entitlements) is contrary to the Eighth Commandment against stealing. Of course, many, if not most, people believe these programs are acts of charity for some social good. Actually, these programs take income by political force from those who have earned it and give it to those who have not earned it. Charity is voluntary; it is not expressed through government transfer payments which is stealing. The economic consequences of redistribution is to destroy or crowd out real charity and thereby weaken individual concern for fellowman. It diminishes productive expenditure in favor of consumptive spending. The inevitable consequence is capital consumption and lower living standards for all.[19] Again, morality and economic results are seen to be tied together.

Conclusion

To accept the premise that the fear of the Creator God is the beginning or foundation of all knowledge, implied by Proverbs 1:7, is to admit to the possibility of a science of Biblical economics. An attempt has been made to demonstrate that there can be a unique, if controversial, distinctive science of revelational or Biblical economics. It consists of an episteme of four foundational premises that produce a body of immutable economic laws tied to moral laws. Together, they provide mankind with the stewardship principles and wisdom to allocate and manage the earth's resources successfully for God's glory.

Undoubtedly, one of the most controversial features of Biblical economics is its methodology. By superseding the scientific method, as required by Scripture, and adopting the method of logical deduction from the Biblical axiom that mankind acts purposefully, economic principles that are timeless and universal may be discovered. This procedure might puzzle some economists and other scholars. Yet these conclusions follow from the premises. Thus, there is no positive-normative dichotomy. Economic principles reveal cause and effect relationships and simultaneously "tell" mankind what he ought to do or advocate because they are in harmony with moral precepts—the Ten Commandments. Our conclusion is that morality and economics are components in one indivisible body of science. Dr. Sennholz said it best: "In God's world, causes and consequences are connected logically. To offend against an economic principle, or to disobey an ethical commandment is to suffer the inexorable consequences of our action.... His eternal laws and principles invariably exact a price for all offenses."[20]

Notes and References

1. Hazlitt, Henry, *The Foundations of Morality* (Los Angeles, CA: Nash Publishing, 1964), p. 301.
2. Kuhn, Thomas S., *The Structure of Scientific Revolutions* (Chicago, IL: University of Chicago Press, 1962), p. 2.
3. Major thought leaders included Hans Sennholz, Percy Greaves, Howard Kershner, R.J. Rushdoony, and Tom Rose. For a textbook on Christian economics, see Rose, Tom, *Economics: Principles and Policy from a Christian Perspective* (Melford, CT: Mott Media, 1977). For other developments of a systematic Biblical economic body of thought, see Sennholz, Hans F., *Three Economic Commandments,* (Spring Mills, PA: Libertarian Press, 1990), and North, Gary, *An Introduction to Christian Economics,* (Nutley, NJ: Craig Press, 1973), and *The Dominion Covenant,* (Tyler, TX: Institute for Christian Economics, 1982), p. ix.
4. North, Gary, *The Dominion Covenant,* p. ix.
5. Thayer, Joseph H., *Greek English Lexicon of the New Testament* (Grand Rapids, MI: Baker Book House, 1977), p. 589.
6. Novak, Michael, *The Spirit of Democratic Capitalism* (New York, NY: Simon & Schuster, 1982), p. 34.
7. North, Gary, *An Introduction to Christian Economics* (Nutley, NJ: Craig Press, 1973), pp. 212-213.
8. Kirzner, Israel M., "On the Method of Austrian Economics", Edwin G. Dolan, ed., in *The Foundations of Modern Austrian Economics,* (Kansas City, MO: Sheed & Ward, 1976), pp. 45-46.
9. Patton, Judd W., *An Inquiry Into Some Economic Effects of Government Spending,* (Ph.D. thesis on file at Grove City, PA: Grove City College Library, 1981), p. 137.
10. Rothbard, Murray N., *Individualism and the Philosophy of the Social Sciences,* (San Francisco, CA: Cato Institute, 1979), p. 3.
11. White, Lawrence, *Methodology of the Austrian School* (New York, NY: Center for Libertarian Studies, 1977), p. 3.
12. Rothbard, Murray N., *Man, Economy and State,* (Los Angeles, CA: Nash, 1970), p. 63.
13. Rothbard, Murray N., *The Essential von Mises,* (Auburn, AL: Ludwig von Mises Institute, 1980), p. 29.
14. Rothbard, Murray N., *America's Great Depression,* (Los Angeles, CA: Nash, 1972), pp. 11-38.

15. Ludwig Mises von, *Human Action,* (Chicago, IL: Henry Regnery, 1966), pp. 679-80.
16. Sennholz, Hans F., *The Truth About the Great Depression,* (Lansing, MI: Constitutional Alliance, Inc., 1969), p. 27.
17. Hazlitt, Henry, *What You Should Know About Inflation,* (New York, NY: Funk and Wagnalls, 1968), pp. 131-132.
18. Rothbard, Murray N., *The Essential von Mises,* (Auburn, AL: Ludwig Von Mises Institute, 1980), pp. 18-20.
19. Sennholz, Hans F., *Three Economic Commandments,* (Spring Mills, PA: Libertarian Press, 1990), p. 13.
20. *Ibid.,* p.42.

23

AMERICA'S SECOND DEMOCRACY

William H. Peterson*

Dr. George Roche, president of Hillsdale College, tells the story of two buddies exchanging pleasantries during the Christmas Season and each asking the other: How's business? "Great," says one, who works at a department store, "the place is crowded from morning to night." "Awful," says the other, who works at the post office, "the place is crowded from morning to night."

The story bears on perception and public policy. And on America's second democracy, with its enormous second empowerment of the people, with its sovereignty in the individual American citizen. This second democracy is one of the country's best-kept secrets, even after the collapse of communism in Eastern Europe with the once-"superpower" of the Soviet Union an economic basket-case begging alms from the West.

Consider that this second democracy, this second government, this second dominion within a dominion, comes without taxation, without political parties, without corruption, politics and politicians, at least as far as those terms are commonly understood, and even without a second bureaucracy spinning out red tape and telling the citizen what he can or cannot do.

Moreover, in the light that the first democracy necessarily involves compulsion—its laws and taxation are cases in point—this second democracy is, to the nth degree, voluntary; and, what is more, it is a lot more moral than the first democracy.

Now, just where is this Shangri-La, this Eden, this happy land? Why, it is right under our noses, it is all around us. For it is none other than our common, ordinary, everyday, taken-for-granted market place.[1]

*Dr. Peterson occupies the Lundy Chair of Business Philosophy at Campbell University, Buies Creek, NC.

Let us compare and contrast these two democracies and the kind of undeclared Cold War raging between them. In this second democracy, note that every day is Election Day, a daily plebiscite, that the market constitutes a giant, never-ending auction, that every producer-candidate runs scared, that he is held strictly accountable, that every market "shortage" or "surplus" soon gets wiped out, that every consumer becomes sovereign, King or Queen Customer, a dictator ruling with an iron hand, ordering this, ordering that, literally.[2]

So talk about democratic empowerment: here is free democracy in which vast power, the power of economic life-and-death, is in the hands of the consumer, indeed in those of all consumers, i.e., the people. Thus market place democracy is truly of the people, for the people, and by the people, again, far more so than in the first democracy.

Here, too, democracy is reflected in its strict counterpart, free enterprise, and in its broader voluntary area, the private sector, with each subservient to, and directed by, the consumer. Here are, then, consent galore, continual agreement among parties, and widespread social cooperation. Here is our far-flung global market system at work from sea to shining sea, from one continent to another, strangers cooperating with strangers, serving each other, helping each other, caring for each other, almost loving each other, most of the time unknowingly.

Here, for example, is the farmer feeding the city dweller, the doctor prescribing for the sick, the clergyman ministering to his parish, the banker extending credit to finance a crop or build a home, the city dweller or suburbanite working in factory, store, office, bakery, warehouse, school, hospital or mill; everyone working not only for one's self, inexorably following his self-interest, but in effect working for everyone else, for the public interest, the national interest, for the mutual advancement of virtually everybody, all driven by that inner dynamo undergirded by private property rights.

So as Adam Smith taught us, self-interest sparks drive, incentive, productivity, and advancement on behalf of self, of course, but also, inadvertently, on behalf of a much larger group: "Every individual necessarily labors to render the annual revenue of the society as great as he can. He generally, indeed, neither intends to promote the public interest, nor knows how much he is promoting it.... He intends only his own gain, and he is in this, as in many other cases, led by an invisible hand to promote an end which was no part of his intention."[3]

Self-interest, undergirded by private property, also promotes peace. For here in this second democracy are infinite peaceful relations in society, extensive social harmony, vast ongoing two-way exchanges of goods and services, constructive division of labor at home and abroad, friendly person-to-person and people-to-people contacts around the globe—all captured neatly in IBM's slogan, "World Peace Through World Trade."

Drink tea, for instance, and you give a friendly pat on the back to the people of India or Sri Lanka. Eat a banana and you stroke the people of Ecuador or Costa Rica. Bite on a bar of chocolate and you help add dignity to the people of Ghana or the Ivory Coast. Buy a Daewoo or Hyundai automobile and you strengthen our relations with South Korea. Fly Lufthansa, Alitalia or Japan Air and you advance our relations with our former adversaries, Germany, Italy, and Japan.

Even local frictions and antagonisms tend to be smoothed over and calmed down through market place voting. Catholics and Protestants trade with each other, i.e., vote for each other in Belfast; Hindus and Moslems in Bombay; Arabs and Jews in Jerusalem; Malays and Chinese in Kuala Lampur; blacks and whites in Johannesburg. To a very great extent, the market place is color-blind and bias-free in a global meeting of minds.

To be sure, market place motivation is more love of money than love of neighbor, and the Roman rule of *caveat emptor*—let the buyer beware—has been anything but repealed. But the upshot of market place democracy is nonetheless service to the trading partner, improvement of mutual understanding, enhancement of social amity, a growing realization that through exchange the other fellow, whoever and wherever he is, is vital to an individual's health, happiness, and prosperity, a realization thereby knitting society closer together.

This realization is reinforced again and again in the ubiquitous market place. There the vote is not once every few years but many times a day, in fact, every time an individual picks up a telephone even when talking to a friend. And on some days that individual casts votes by the dozen as he buys in a supermarket, shopping mall or department store. In other words, on a vast macro scale billions of votes are cast daily across the nation; across the world, billions more.

Moreover, as Ludwig von Mises points out, comparing economic with political democracy is imperfect in the sense that minority voting in the market place "has the power to work on the production process."[4] For example, the processed food industry not only prepares packaged food for the masses but esoteric health food for a relatively tiny minority. Publishers not only put out spy novels for the majority but unrhymed poetry for the minority. Automotive producers seek niches and cater to all sorts of car preferences. In our first democracy, on the other hand, generally only the votes cast for the majority candidate play a role in deciding the course of political events. Voters in the minority column have no say.

In addition, not even the weather, which can sometimes upset the political strategists on Election Day in the first democracy, poses much of a problem. No need to get out the vote rain or shine. Voting in the market place can be as convenient as a telephone for a consumer to order pizza, buy sheets and pillow cases, call a plumber or electrician, or purchase travel or theater tickets.

Contrast the first and second democracies further. Note that most political paraphernalia and impedimenta disappear in America's second democracy. Voter registration is unnecessary. Residency requirements don't apply. Party affiliation is unessential. Absentee ballots are needless. Minimum voting ages are not binding. Poll challengers are superfluous. Primary elections are redundant. Run-off elections are needless. National political conventions and electoral colleges serve no purpose. America's Election Day, the Tuesday after the first Monday in November in biennial or quadrennial years, is meaningless in the context of the market place where every day is Election Day.

In the ubiquitous market place nobody is really absent. Observe, for example, that the Bavarian can vote locally in Schleswig-Holstein, the New Englander in Florida, the British Columbian in Ontario. But, for that matter, in the global market place the Bavarian can vote in France, the New Englander in Morocco, the British Columbian in California. Also observe that making voting in the market place even easier and doing away with local currencies is the ubiquitous credit card—plastic money—a practically universal instantaneous ballot, good anywhere, no questions asked, from Australia to Zimbabwe.

Too, look at market place voting hours. In political polling places, voting hours are restricted, typically 7:00 a.m. to 7:00 p.m. or 8:00 a.m. to 8:00 p.m. and, as noted, only once every few years. In the democratic market place, on the other hand, most producer-candidates are open for business daily from morning to night, with many open on weekends and some even on a twenty-four hour, seven-days-a-week basis, including quite a few convenience stores, gasoline stations, telephone companies, newspapers, airlines, and radio and TV stations.

In sum on this point, voting in the second democracy is a snap; in the first democracy it poses something of a problem.

What of persuasion in the two democracies? Granted, advertising and salesmanship are strong in the market place, even garish, with billboards, blinking neon-lights, and scents wafting from magazine perfume ads. Yes, buy this perfume. See this show. Tour this land. Purchase this mouthwash. This beer. This soap. This anything. Scores of messages bombard the consumer daily, hourly, and then some, from newspapers, magazines, radio, television, telephone, billboards, direct mail, and sometimes, door-to-door salespeople.

Yet even so, does the market place reflect as much pressure as the first democracy? There, persuasion not infrequently borders on propaganda, on official disinformation. After all, no need in the market place for outright provocation, for placards, parades, petitions, gerrymandering, logrolling, bribery, lobbying, campaign buttons, poll-watching, doling out political action committee (PAC) money, underwriting candidates or causes, wearing armbands or headbands, engaging in street demonstrations, writing to your representative, giving testimony before legislative committees, demanding special privileges or exemptions, or participating in political movements or agitation of any kind, least of all in the occasional violence amidst our democratic brethren the world over—the Slovenians in Yugoslavia, the Tamils in Sri Lanka, the Tigres in Ethiopia, the Walloons in Belgium, the Catholics in Northern Ireland, and so forth.

So, in America's second democracy, forget advocacy. No need to tell the world that you are pro-South African sanctions or anti-South African sanctions, pro-lottery or anti-lottery, pro-abortion or anti-abortion, pro-United Nations or anti-United Nations, pro-this or anti-that. You're sovereign, period. If you like it, buy it; if you don't, don't.

Nor is there a problem of your not participating in the market place. Here, by definition, participation is always, in a very real sense, 100 percent, as consumers weigh available resources and seek to optimize returns from myriad choices.

Not so in our first political democracy. There participation is a problem, and politicians and political scientists concede it. The 1988 Presidential election in the United States, for example, recorded but 50.2 percent of eligible voters actually voting, according to the *U.S. Statistical Abstract*. Think of that: only one out of every two American voters bothered to vote, despite all the hoopla about voting as a sacred duty. The U.S. Congressional election of 1986 was even worse. Then the voter turnout was down to 33.4 percent, or, but one eligible voter out of every three actually cast a ballot.

Why this disinterest, this growing loss of voter incentive in political democracy, our first democracy? Well, it is important to see that political issues are often complex, involved, confusing. Moreover, history demonstrates that quite a few political candidates dissemble, denigrate opponents, muddy issues.

On any given issue, can the typical American citizen on Main Street, U.S.A., readily marshal data, make arrangements with the appropriate Congressional committee or Executive department or agency, incur the cost of travel to Washington, and testify against organized interests, interests which already maintain expensive Washington suites, interests which hand out PAC money, monitor data, and engage high-priced "experts" who regularly mount sophisticated arguments in hearings before congressional committees or federal regulators, experts who perhaps know the chairman on a first-name basis? Hardly.

Let us illustrate this situation with the case of sugar. Why is it that the American housewife or candy producer has to pay more than twice as much for domestic sugar than the housewife or candy producer abroad who is unencumbered by sugar protection? Well, it turns out that the Washington-based American Sugar Alliance, an organization of 15,000 cane and beet sugar producers, in recent years augmented by corn-fructose syrup producers, is well organized and represented in the nation's capital. Proclaims the

Alliance, never mentioning the consumer nor his right of free market access:

> The American Sugar Alliance strives to assure that farmers and workers in the U.S. sweetener industry survive in a world of heavily subsidized sugar. Only through a united effort can a plentiful and secure domestic supply of sweeteners continue to be offered. The Alliance is committed to meeting this national need.[5]

Little wonder, then, that the American Sugar Alliance has a cozy arrangement with the Congress. The Alliance sweetens the deal with generous PAC campaign contributions. For its part, a compliant Congress legislates a sugar import quota system allocating, in the five years beginning in 1991, 27 percent of the American market to low-cost Third World sugar producers including Haiti, Mexico, Jamaica, Brazil, Madagascar, and the Philippines. (Guess who gets the remaining 73 percent of the market?)

Congress has similar deals with literally hundreds if not thousands of other trade associations, unions, professions, veterans' organizations, ethnic groups, and other special interest organizations that trade money or votes for deals, for cozy arrangements. So it follows that Congress eases into iniquity, that Will Rogers had a point in noting that every Congress opens with a prayer and closes with an investigation, that the knowing consumer can only shrug his shoulders and say: "You can't fight City Hall."

No wonder, then, that the individual citizen wonders if his vote counts when he sees free-spending Democrat and Republican incumbents in the U.S. House of Representatives win reelection in 1986 by an incredible 98 percent and win bigger in 1988 by just under 99 percent under the cynical rule of spend and spend, elect and elect.

Alas, something went wrong in 1990. Perhaps it was talk of term limitation. Anyway, the spendthrift incumbents slumped to a 96 percent reelection rate.[6] The situation reminds one of the remark of President Reagan that it's unfair to compare Congress to drunken sailors on shore leave...the sailors are at least spending their own money.

In contrast, in America's second democracy, the individual consumer's choice works. All he has to do is relate price and quality to cast a ballot. Here his ballot works because, again, he has every producer-candidate in the market place running scared. Not just in election years, but daily, hourly.

Here his vote cannot be taken for granted. Here his money talks. Why? Because repeat business is crucial, business reputation is ever at stake, competition is tough, courtesy, service, innovation, value, cost control, quality maintenance and upgrading have to prevail, or else. Or else entrepreneurs who drag their feet get sacked; sacked by the sovereign consumer. Witness defunct Eastern Air Lines. Witness Ford's abandoned Edsel.

On the other hand, entrepreneurs who produce higher quality products or lower prices are rewarded with profits. Rewarded by the sovereign consumer. Witness growing Sony. Witness growing Wal-Mart.

Under economic democracy, then, entrepreneurship, personified in the producer-candidate, is ever seeking the consumer's approval, his consent, his vote, his dollar. Entrepreneurship, in terms of new strategies, new technologies, is at work, even if the Ivan Boeskys, "Diamond Jim" Bradys, and other con artists occasionally foul the nest and warrant the retribution of the courts.[7]

And, to be sure, the entrepreneurial motive is to maximize profits, but this means having, without respite, to win, retain, and expand consumer patronage, to fend off competition. This means further: give the customer more for less—as Adam Smith taught. For the pharmaceutical companies, this means more life-saving drugs. For the auto companies: more safety features, more styling, better economy and reliability. For the food companies: more flavor, more convenience, less cholesterol, less cost, etc.

Of course, critics of economic democracy, of our second democracy, may protest: the consumer may be sovereign, but doesn't this process of one-dollar-one-vote confer more votes on the rich than on the non-rich?

True. But these critics should be reminded that it is wiser to dwell, not on the rich or non-rich, but rather on the successful and less successful in the market place. Also, these critics ought to dwell on the fact that the rich are few in number. The non-rich have by far the bulk of buying power.

Moreover, critics should also consider that riches generally, and necessarily, reflect the greater contribution of the successful, the talented, to the joint productive effort. America's second democracy thus becomes a meritocracy or what Jefferson called "a natural aristocracy." Hence, critics should take into account that income inequality under economic democracy is almost wholly the result of the previous pattern of consumer voting. For the consumer determines, really dictates, the distribution of income to all members of society; he votes to make some members, including sports-, rock- and movie-stars, rich, just as the consumer votes to make others less rich.

But soon the consumer votes again, starting a new cycle of income distribution, making some rich people poorer and some poorer people rich. The entrepreneurs and all other market producers, then, are ever at the consumer's bidding. The scorecard of income winners and losers is always changing. Some historians see this democratic phenomenon of wealth on the move as "from shirt-sleeves to shirt-sleeves in three generations." Gertrude Stein saw it this way: "Money is money. Only the pockets change."

Besides, it is important to observe in this second democracy that the rich, the successful, the talented, are part of Adam Smith's Invisible Hand idea of self-interest serving the public interest, of harnessing mighty private incentives to advance the common good. Service is the name of the game. In America's economic democracy, rich can preserve their riches only by continuing to serve the consumer. The slogan of Burrows T. Lundy, the founder of Lundy Packing Company and the donor of the Lundy Chair to Campbell University, "Service above all. He profits most who serves best,"[8] explains the situation perfectly.

Accordingly, in America's second democracy, the successful, the talented, by serving more, earning more, saving more and committing their resources to entrepreneurial ventures, or by investing their money in stocks, bonds, or real estate, add to social capital (the nation's productive tools).

In other words, the successful, in pursuit of further gain, put up their capital for use by society and, however unintentionally, thereby advance a nation's competitiveness, boost its national productivity, and provide for cultural development. And, it follows that the successful thereby serve to boost the personal income of all Americans, including the poor. In the famous words of President John F. Kennedy defending his big all-brackets tax cut proposal in 1963: "A rising tide lifts all boats."

This is why, in the light of consumer sovereignty, the title of this paper, "America's Second Democracy," is, perhaps, a misnomer. Government is unquestionably a necessity, but not quite as

Thomas Paine put it in his *Common Sense* in 1776, "a necessary evil."[9]

Evil intrudes as limited government becomes unlimited, as in the American Republic, as the state becomes Frederic Bastiat's fiction by which everyone seeks to live at the expense of everyone else, as majoritarianism converts an election into what H. L. Mencken described as an advance auction of stolen goods, as the citizen-consumer or his representative in government advertently or inadvertently votes for programs, including inflation, detrimental to the consumer interest. In effect, the citizen votes to do in the consumer, i.e., himself. Hence, the observation at the outset of this paper that, in America, we witness a kind of undeclared Cold War between the two democracies.

So, perhaps a more apt title for this paper may be "America's First Democracy." In other words, the economic democracy is a kind of political democracy in the form of limited government which is the secondary, albeit still critical, institution supporting the morality, individual freedom, social cooperation, and consumer sovereignty implicit in our first democracy—the market place.

Notes and References

1. Compare Mises, Ludwig von, *Human Action*, New Haven: Yale University Press, 1949, p. 271.
2. *Ibid.*, p. 270. Mises, along with W. H. Hutt, seems to have pioneered the concept of consumer sovereignty.
3. See Smith, Adam, *The Wealth of Nations*, Modern Library ed., p. 423.
4. Mises, *op. cit.*, p. 271.
5. From a 1991 brochure issued by American Sugar Alliance, 1155 Connecticut Ave., N.W., Washington, DC 20036. Material here on the sugar lobby is supplied by the Alliance.
6. *1991 World Almanac and Book of Facts*, New York, NY: Scripps Howard, 1990, p. 40.
7. Compare Mises, *op. cit.*, p. 149. "The state is essentially an institution for the preservation of peaceful interhuman relations. However, for the preservation of peace it must be prepared to crush the onslaughts of the peace-breakers."
8. Lundy Packing Company literature.
9. *Bartlett's Quotations*, 15th ed., p. 384.

24

CAPITALISM, DEMOCRACY, AND ELECTIONS

Sylvester Petro*

The dissolution of the Soviet Empire after the fiasco of August 1991 should be less an occasion for self-congratulation than for self-examination by the western capitalist countries, especially America. In respect of the basic institutions of a free, orderly, and prosperous society, we ourselves are none too secure. And while the Soviet dissolution was a global blessing, an American breakdown would be a global catastrophe, especially because the media which regard the Soviet breakdown as a blow to conservatives would undoubtedly interpret one in America as a predictable consequence of its *laissez faire capitalism!*

This country is remarkably resilient, with abundant human and material resources. It has displayed a capacity to survive generations of misgovernment equalled only by the English and exceeded only by the Italians. Yet merely listing the present ills of American society, of American government, and of the American economy, would consume most of the space I have been allotted for this essay. Some of those ills, I fear, despite our capitalist resilience, could become terminal.

The cure for our private problems lies in prayer, self-discipline, and patience; in sum, a renewal of private virtue. But the worst and most seminal of our equally, perhaps *more*, serious *public* problems of government and economy, I hold, is a distorting excess of "democracy," and more particularly of its characteristic method of choosing its rulers, elections and re-elections. To remedy those excesses will require public virtue of a high order. The required therapy is rigorous.

*Dr. Petro is Director of the Institute for Law and Policy Analysis, Winston-Salem, North Carolina.

It is more likely, I believe, that the American Union will break down from a surfeit of political elections than that the Soviet Union broke down from a scarcity of such elections. Convinced of this, I shall propose as a measure to buy time for capitalism, until our ruling majority learns to trust *laissez faire* more than it does interventionist government, that political elections be severely limited and that re-election to political office be strictly forbidden.

First, however, let us see what we can learn from the recent events in what used to be called the Soviet Union.

The Decline and Fall of the Soviet Empire and the Effect on Cuba

Although I have just used the term, I believe that "breakdown" is not the best way to describe what happened in the Soviet Union. Reflection on its seventy-odd years of repression has led me to believe it more accurate and more instructive to say that a fake society, a society that never was in any proper sense, a thing more like a concentration camp, finally revealed itself for what it was, and just gave up the ghost. Having lost their will to terrorize, the Communists had nothing left. They just quit, faded away, or went back into the woodwork. Moreover, the people did not seem to have been as upset about the emptiness of their elections as they were about the emptiness of their bellies, their shops, their prospects, and their hopes of being admitted into the well-stocked stores reserved for the *Nomenklatura.*

The Communist apparatus gave up the ghost, it seems to me, precisely because the people were so hungry and unhappy, because the usual bitter Soviet "winter of discontent" was coming, because all the world was aware of the looming tragedy, and because its elite had not the foggiest notion of what to do about it. The Soviet Union was never an economy, let alone a society, in any proper sense, any more than the Mafia or any other gang of thugs is properly called a society or an economy. Adept only in thuggery and terror, incompetent to respond to consumer demands, unsure whether or not the army tanks would roll over the people and kill for them, the ruling Soviet elite, when it saw that the game was up, simply abdicated.

In running for cover, they left to the politicians of the capitalist world the stupendous job of validating, enabling, and financing the follies of all those who believe in the fables of Cockaigne, socialism, and anticapitalist redistributionism.

Revolution by "the people" is, I believe, as chimerical as democracy is, if by democracy we mean government actually by the people *en masse*; or for that matter as "communism" is, if we mean by *that*, ownership and operation of the means of production by the proletariat, and equality in the distribution of wealth. All such romantic nonsense is exploded at this moment of history by the persistence in Cuba of the outrageous abuse of the masses by the thuggery called Communism after the coup-makers in Russia abdicated and the Soviet Empire was dissolved. A noncommunist Cuban journalist, Sergio Lopez-Miro, wrote in September 1991 that:

> Cuba, by any rational standard, is an economic basket case. General scarcity and deprivation are the order of the day....Fidel Castro...continues demanding eternal sacrifice, while he and his cohorts reside in magnificent splendor.[1]

The end of Communism in Cuba, if that is what we choose to call the travesty of that once lovely land, is certain. But I feel confident that when the end comes it will be because Fidel Castro loses heart, dies, or another gang of thieves supplants him. The people who have remained there with America just ninety miles away will not unseat him.

Communism has dissolved in Russia in part because of Boris Yeltsin's leadership (with no help from George Bush), but mainly because the Communist leadership of Mikhail Gorbachev and his ilk lost their will to terrorize. It, whatever it is, survives in Cuba because "El Loco," as some Cubans call Castro, has not yet lost his will to terrorize. The people? Listen again to Lopez-Miro:

> Cubans' frustration and resentment are evident in the endless bread lines and packed buses, where the slightest altercation can turn instantly into a fist fight. On the other hand, 32 years of repression combined with emotional dependence on *Papa Fidel* thus far continue to keep such frustration from boiling over. ....[I]t is extremely difficult to predict how or when the end of Castroism will come about....How long Castro can continue successfully to employ demagogy and persuasion to sustain himself in power, not even the aging dictator can know for sure. If he did, he would not create fascist-style rapid-action brigades, such as the one used against peaceful protesters on Friday [September 6, 1991]....I came away [from Cuba] convinced that the need for [peaceful] change is

greater than ever, but that with Castro in power, it will never come about.[2]

There are surely more than a few solid citizens in the former Iron Curtain countries who believe in private property, free contract, and capitalism as the cure for their ills. But from all I have been able to gather, the masses and their followers, sometimes called the leaders, still prefer, as does Gorbachev, the so-called Swedish model, the dubious mish-mash fatuously called "capitalism with a human face"—capitalism in the form of a Mercedes Benz in every garage, without tears, compliments of the West Germans by way of Helmut Kohl—with Willy Brandt and the Social Democrats in the wings, ready to take power if and when things get rough as a result of the prodigious challenge, grandly grasped by Kohl and the West Germans, to rebuild the East German economy devastated by fifty years of government of the thugs, by the thugs, and for the thugs.

Properly understood, the dissolution of the Soviet Empire teaches a profoundly useful lesson. Interpreted as a consequence of the absence of democracy, it teaches nothing, because the absence of democracy had nothing to do with it. I say again, "Democracy" is as purely illusory in the existential sense as "Communism" is. The mass can no more govern than it can collectively own and operate the means of production.

Yet, interpreted as a demonstration that without rights of private property and freedom of contract and capitalism, their naturally resulting economic form, no society in any meaningful sense is possible, it can teach everything. And in doing so, it may help avert the greatest tragedy of human history, the breakdown of the great and good world society that capitalism has been trying to build ever since the merchant traders described by Herodotus began roaming the Mediterranean for profit, without help or hindrance of government.

The most serious question facing the capitalist world has to do with capitalism itself in its current political framework, the so-called democratic welfare state. That question is: Can capitalism survive the curbs, restrictions, burdens, and drains on it by our own political "system," this indescribably contradictory delusion called "democracy"?

The Decline and Fall of Democracies: Of Gorbachev, Brandt, Mises, Maine, and Taxing and Looting

Milking is one thing, desanguinating, another. If democracies could permanently confine themselves to taxing away a modest part of the wealth generated by capitalist fecundity, like, say, the Mafia does, or like old-fashioned ward-heeling politicians used to do, a partnership between capitalism and democracy could go on in mutual prosperity forever, especially if democracy spent a bit of the plunder maintaining an institutional framework which encouraged the growth of capital. A tiny bit of ward-heeling corruption such as went on in eighteenth-century aristocratic England or in nineteenth-century limited-democracy America never hurt anyone. However, the best thinkers of the nineteenth century concluded with Aristotle, the best thinker of any century, that of all forms of government, a full-blown, universal-suffrage, unlimited democracy was the worst and most dangerous, promising the most freedom and delivering the worst tyranny.

Writing just as rule by the many in the form of universal suffrage was beginning to supplant rule by the one or by the few, these thinkers saw as the basic defect of popular government the scarcity of intelligent, informed, skeptical, and sophisticated citizens among the majority who select the necessarily small number of rulers in all "democracies." In the approximately one hundred years of popular government since the great analyses of the nineteenth century, new defects of equal or near-equal gravity have emerged. Some of them, sad to say, are aggravated by capitalism's own productivity.

With no intention to do so, capitalism has provided for its enemies, the crowd-gulling interventionist politicians, and the wicked with whom they consort, unprecedented wealth and miraculous means with which the more greedily to loot and plunder. The fabulous means of transportation, of communications, of vote-purchasing bribery and subsidy thus provided by capitalism have made it possible for the political plundering of its fruits to grow to dimensions that Aristotle and his great epigoni of the nineteenth century could not have begun to imagine. Imagine the unimaginable plunder of a government, or, more relevantly, of the small minority who govern, who take for themselves, at a minimum, one-fourth of what the productive many produce: well over a trillion dollars to squander year after year!

And that is not all, nor even the worst of what is going on.

As is ever the doom of plunderers, our current politicians and their adjuncts, not satisfied with absorbing the lion's share of *its fruits,* are also in their unbridled greed digging up the very *roots* of capitalism. For even with well over a trillion dollars a year to squander, the needs of the greedy remain limitless, so our federal government will run deficits of hundreds of billions of dollars a year—forever. Crack-up inflation is the inevitable end of this process, and, unchecked, of the society which permits it to continue.

Mikhail Gorbachev said in his September 1991 TV show with Boris Yeltsin that despite the Communist fiasco he remains a socialist but has now developed a great interest in the capitalist form of socialism, namely the welfare state, thus coming thirty years or so later to the insight that burst upon Willy Brandt in the sixties. Brandt, it will be remembered, realized then that socialism could never compete with capitalism in producing wealth, hence, that socialist leaders could never hope under socialism to enjoy such perquisites as the fleet of airplanes which the American president has at his beck and call (just as General Motors, strangled by the United Automobile Workers Union, cannot compete with Toyota). And so Herr Brandt induced the German Social Democrat Party to abandon the straightforwardly socialist nationalization plank in its platform and to adopt the wealth redistribution program which seemed to be working so well for the social democrat party of the United States: tolerate capitalism but milk it—tax, spend, inflate, and elect and elect and elect.

The renunciation of straightforward socialism by such politicians as Brandt and Gorbachev is not something which should cheer anyone with any sense. By itself it is no more heartening than the flight of the coup makers of August 1991. All depends on what happens next.

Committed socialist politicians who abandon socialism only because they can think of no way to prosper other than by milking capitalism are unlikely to be restrained in the milking. Indeed, they will have to milk ever more frantically in order to retain the power they have gained by promises of loot and plunder. There is in vote-buying interventionism a servo-mechanism that quits functioning in its mad robotic way only when there is no more to loot.

Besides, committed socialists are that way because they are deadly enemies of freedom (for others) and of the individual rights, private property, and freedom of contract which are the soul as well as the operating principles of capitalism. Capitalism, it must be remembered, delivers the goods for all human beings in the best possible mix, and supplies the conditions in which human beings flourish, essentially because it rewards, handsomely, the persons gifted in best combining the factors of production—the entrepreneurs. No committed socialist, no matter how well-treated by capitalism, can view with approval the freedom of entrepreneurs who command more goods and exercise more real authority than he does. The well-spring of socialism is consuming, uncontrollable envy of one's betters.

The survival of capitalism, which is a matter of the survival of civilization, as Ludwig von Mises has said, cannot be trusted to committed socialists such as Gorbachev and Brandt, or to their counterparts sitting at present in the Congress of the United States and in its myriad bureaus. Many hard choices must be made day in and day out if capitalism is to survive in a world full of stupidity, envy, greed, and over-zealous environmentalists, choices so hard that they can be trusted only to persons committed firmly enough to freedom to refuse to intervene when, in political office, they are asked if they are going to let children starve and watch California kangaroo rats perish just to protect the profits of the lumber industry.

Enough of Gorbachev and Brandt, and, in fact, of all committed socialists. Securing the survival of capitalism in a democratic political setting is difficult enough without them, as anyone familiar with the Congress of the United States knows.

Ludwig von Mises wrote in the twenties, when communism was the darling of the intellectuals here and abroad, that government ownership and operation of the means of production could not possibly satisfy human wants optimally, as does a market economy, all things considered; and that socialism constituted a deadly onslaught on all the institutions the western world had created over the centuries, the institutions that constituted its society, the ones that made it tick.[3]

Still earlier, in 1885, a superb English scholar, an economist-historian-lawyer of comparable learning and intellect, Sir Henry Sumner Maine, reviewed and evaluated the then-current movement toward universal suffrage in a book of great power and scope called, *Popular Government.*[4] In it, he came to almost as grim a conclusion about democracy as Mises was later to come to about socialism.

Impressed by the remarkable progress of the United States as of 1885, Maine thought that popular government, "democracy," had a bare chance of working here, provided that it remained as narrowly circumscribed as the framers of the original United States Constitution, the one written in 1787, had made it. Unless thus rigidly and rigorously confined, Maine thought, the socialist-populist forces inherent in "democracy," or "popular government," as he called it, would stifle the energies set free by the institutions of private property and free contract. Because Maine's work has gone virtually unnoticed even in England, as well as in the United States, I quote it liberally here, especially since it is what I want to say, and would be saying without quotation marks, if he had not said it sooner and more elegantly.

"[I]f," Maine wrote in *Popular Government,* "the mass of mankind were to make an attempt at redividing the common stock of good things, they would resemble, not a number of claimants insisting on the fair division of a fund, but a mutinous crew, feasting on a ship's provisions, gorging themselves on the meat and intoxicating themselves with the liquors, but refusing to navigate the vessel to port. It is among the simplest of economical truths, that far the largest part of the wealth of the world is constantly perishing by consumption, and that, if it be not renewed by perpetual toil and adventure, either the human race, or the particular community making the experiment..., will be extinguished or brought to the very verge of extinction."[5]

A little later, Maine said, "Wealth may come very near to perishing through diminished energy in the motives of the men who reproduce it. You may, so to speak, take the heart and spirit out of the labourers to such an extent that they do not care to work. Jeremy Bentham observed about a century ago that the Turkish Government had in his day impoverished some of the richest countries in the world far more by its action on motives than by its positive exactions; and it has always appeared to me that the destruction of the vast wealth accumulated under the Roman Empire...and the decline of Western Europe into the squalor and poverty of the Middle Ages, can only be accounted for on the same principle."[6]

Mises in *Human Action* expressed the same opinion about the breakdown of the Roman Empire, in more detail. He said:

> The interference of the [Roman] authorities [in the grain trade] upset the adjustment of supply to the rising demand...The showdown came when in the political troubles of the third and fourth centuries the emperors resorted to currency debasement. With the system of maximum prices the practice of debasement completely paralyzed both the production and the marketing of the vital foodstuffs and disintegrated society's economic organization. The more eagerness the authorities displayed in enforcing the maximum prices, the more desperate became the conditions of the urban masses dependent on the purchase of food. Commerce in grain and other necessities vanished altogether. To avoid starving, people deserted the cities, settled on the countryside, and tried to grow grain, oil, wine, and other necessities for themselves.[7]

Mises's account continues more circumstantially in this extraordinary vignette, so characteristic of his genius, entitled, modestly, "Observations on the Causes of the Decline of Ancient Civilization." He then sums up: "The marvelous civilization of antiquity perished because it did not adjust its moral code and its legal system to the requirements of the market economy. A social order is doomed if the actions which its normal functioning requires are rejected by the standards of morality, are declared illegal by the laws of the country, and are prosecuted as criminal by the courts and the police. The Roman Empire crumbled to dust because it lacked the spirit of liberalism and free enterprise. The policy of interventionism and its political corollary, the Fuhrer principle, decomposed the mighty empire as they will by necessity always disintegrate and destroy any social cntity."[8]

Just as Mises here identified the anti-capitalistic, anti-private-property spirit now inhibiting the American economy, Maine likewise called attention, from another temporal and intellectual point of view, to the factors which cause the rise and fall of democracy. What he had to say about the reasons for American well-being in the nineteenth century is especially relevant. He began:

> Here then, is the great question about democratic legislation, when carried to more than moderate length. How will it affect human

motives?...The motives which at present impel mankind to the labour and pain which produce the resuscitation of wealth in ever-increasing quantities, are such as infallibly to entail inequality in the distribution of wealth.

...The United States have justly been called the home of the disinherited of the earth; but, if those vanquished under one sky in the struggle for existence had not continued under another the same battle in which they had been worsted, there would have been no such exploit performed as the cultivation of the vast American territory....There could be no greater delusion than to suppose this result to have been attained by democratic legislation...The Government of the United States...is [one] under which coercive restraint...is reduced to a minimum. There has hardly ever before been a community in which the weak have been pushed so pitilessly to the wall, in which those who have succeeded have so uniformly been the strong, and in which in so short a time there has arisen so great an inequality of fortune and...luxury. And at the same time, there has never been a country in which, on the whole, the persons distanced in the race have suffered so little....All this beneficent prosperity...reposes on the sacredness of contract and the stability of private property, the first the implement, and the last the reward, of success in the universal competition....[9]

Maine's conclusion, like the one quoted above from Mises, leads directly to our own inquiry:

The Americans are still [as of 1885] of the opinion that more is to be got for human happiness by private energy than by public legislation. The Irish, however [of 1885, remember], even in the United States, are of another opinion, and the Irish opinion is manifestly rising into favour here. But on the question, whether future democratic legislation will follow the new opinion, the prospects of popular government to a great extent depend.[10]

The experience of England between Maine's time and Margaret Thatcher's, an experience of almost one hundred years, tends to bear out Maine's fears. With universal suffrage which Maine warned against, England did fall from being the leader of the developed world to a second-rank country at best, and perhaps even third-rank, after World War II, out-ranked by recrudescent, powerfully capitalist Germany and Japan. Its current revival is, however, as encouraging as its decline was ominous in terms of the future of American society. For our political and social and even our biological genes, to a considerable extent, are English, and our destiny has been tied to it since our beginnings.

Capitalism: Violated and Desanguinated

No non-communist country in the world has been as over-governed and wrong-headedly mis-governed as the United States has been since the 1930s. No country, including the Communist countries, *could* have been so *over*-governed. As I have pointed out above, no other country has had the capitalist-created wealth to squander on counterproductive programs and huge bureaucracies that our governments have had. What other country could have produced, let alone afforded, a Congress as profligate as ours? All our governments and all our branches of government have had a bread machine to plunder such as no other country in world history has ever had. Sad to say, that is a big, and irremediable, part of the problem. For who would abandon capitalism and settle for poverty in order to keep the people awake to the problems of over-government?

Consider what our governments have done for and to this country over the last sixty years or so:

- gold standard abandoned and replaced with fiat money and the profligacy that fiat money permits and encourages;
- extravagant, imagination-defying deficit-spending, inflationary over-government and mis-government, a national debt the mere servicing of which consumes all the exiguous savings of our desanguinated economy, crowding out other borrowers and further stultifying our capital-starved capitalism;
- saving discouraged and even punished by inflation on the one hand and heavy taxation on the other, while borrowing, until recently, was encouraged by tax deductions;
- a hypocritical free trade policy contradicted by dollar-devaluating protectionism in return for political support by trade unions and the companies so debilitated by them that they cannot compete;
- unique excrescences such as "special prosecutors" established by Congress, accepted by an ill-advised Reagan administration, and approved by a Supreme Court (Scalia, J., honorably dissenting) which habitually ignores the Judiciary Article of the Constitution and the Separation of Powers principle which happens to be the Constitution's most important check on Congressional tyranny, democracy's fatal flaw;

- federal judges who think they know better than businessmen how to run companies;
- state judges who encourage punitive-damages excesses and deep-pocket-liability perversions of justice;
- jurors who believe that corporate treasuries are stocked by Martians with infinite resources;
- "Naders" and anti-nuclear-power fanatics who force companies into bankruptcy and with the connivance of complacent judges have made the construction of nuclear-power plants so prohibitively difficult and expensive that none is being planned, let alone built, even though nuclear power is the cheapest, and environmentally friendliest form of power available, and abandoning it leaves only fossil fuels which the environmentalists are also putting off limits to production here, compelling our embroilment in the millennial quarrels of the Middle East;
- congressionally subsidized ecological hypochondriacs who prefer the welfare of spotted owls, snail darters, California kangaroo rats, coastal gnatcatchers, and a vast assortment of other such denizens of the earth to the welfare of mankind, and who undoubtedly stay awake nights brooding over the extinction of Tyrannosaurus Rex, certain that the lumber industry was somehow responsible for that tragic loss;
- war of all-against-all for job preference brought about by affirmative action programs designed to compensate black or other "minorities" for wrongs presumed to have been done to their remote ancestors by the presumed ancestors of white males, some of whom came to this country recently and were themselves victims of discrimination, long after slavery was abolished and employers were forbidden to discriminate on the basis of race, color, creed, or national origin; affirmative action programs which bear no rational relationship whatsoever to the merits of the particular human beings—female, male, black, red, white, yellow, or Hispanic, competing for a particular job or promotion; person needlessly pitted against person in society-fracturing tension;
- conflict between the young and those of the old who are out for all they can get in the form of "social security" benefits based on payroll deductions long-since squandered by the profligate Congress, so that the heavily taxed young and their

employers have an additional, back-breaking tax burden to carry;

- socialized medicine called "Medicare" and "Medicaid" which, at the rate of its increase in cost since Lyndon Johnson and a profligate, permanently electioneering Congress established it, will, indubitably, bankrupt the country in another generation or less unless it is cut back by a Congress which, also, indubitably, is politically incapable of doing so; a disoriented Congress which in fact is being pressured by "welfare" client groups and some business groups, terrified by the skyrocketing costs of their health-care fringe-benefits, to load the already overloaded general economy (taxpayers, businesses, anyone else not already desanguinated) to extend this disastrous socialized medicine to the whole population!
- Keatings, Keating Fives, Metzenbaums, Bidens, Kennedys, Wrights, Lyndon Johnsons, and all the other plunderers who have been bleeding capitalism while whipping it with scorpions....

Having written the foregoing catalogue of over-government and mis-government from the top of my head, I suppose it may be deficient, but it is certainly not an exaggeration or overstatement of the ominous evils loose in this country. I have not even mentioned the failure of public education; the drinking and drugging delinquency of so much of our youth, owing in no small part to the breakdown of the family, in turn, brought about by inflationary interventionism (by a process too complicated for development here); the mockery of "higher education" of students who come to college almost illiterate; the incompetence of our youth compared with the youth of other developed nations; and the sad state of our economic infrastructures.

Regard, for example, the wreck of our transportation system caused by interventionist government's saddling it with destructive unions while refusing to permit non-polluting surface and subway railway companies to charge even the modest fares which would permit them to operate profitably, thus profoundly damaging the economy and even the face of the earth by forcing on both, as the only possible alternative means of transportation, the vast and super-expensive, pollution-prone, automobile and trucking industries. Socialized transportation, as shown by the shoddy and heavily subsidized New York subway system and the federal railroad fiascoes, could no more do the job of transportation than our socialist school systems or medical care systems can do theirs.

It is the stuff of tragicomedy, the way our "democracy" is working, I mean. Now our geniuses in government and the "environmental" movement are up in arms about the polluting internal combustion engine forced on a transportation-hungry economy by fumbling interventions.

It all comes together in an insanely coherent way. Interventionists tend to dislike industry and lean toward what they think of as the "environment," the "unspoiled" environment, that is. If we are to believe the head of Jacobs Engineering Group, a firm which has become prosperous mainly because it specializes in environmental cleanup projects inspired by the environmental movement, those same environmentalists will succeed in returning us to a state of unspoiled nature if they get what they are demanding from Congress. Referring to the vast cleanup program they have submitted piece by piece to Congress, Mr. Joseph Jacobs, founder and CEO of the company, and therefore a qualified witness, was quoted recently in a *Wall Street Journal* article as saying:

> The Congress cannot resist these individual things as they come along. I am certain as I am sitting here that if you took them all and added them up, we'd be broke. We couldn't produce enough to pay for them. And there are a bunch of them, such as asbestos remediation, that are a joke.[11]

If they have their way, the "environmentalists" will bankrupt us, and if the "health" industry, physicians, nurses, hospitals, welfare and social workers, druggists, medical workers, National Institute of Health, etc., has its way, *it* is even more likely to bankrupt us. Then we shall have no industrial pollution. "Environmentalists" will be happier, with only horse-droppings littering the environment, and the "health" lobby will have all the work it could ever want, for in primitive societies, germs prosper mightily. Germs and horses. Some future!

I do not wish to be understood as one who believes that the interventionists act from a good-faith confidence in the omnicompetence of government. Quite the contrary, I am of the opinion that, all unaware perhaps, they are, in going to government for the satisfaction of their desires, moved down deep by the same primal impulse that moves ruffians and thieves to gain their hearts' desires by forcible means.

Whatever interventionists may think, government is not art, not industry, not science, not reason, not persuasion. Webster defines the verb "to govern" as "to direct and control...actions or conduct..., either by established laws or by arbitrary will." There is nothing in the definition, or in the existential reality of government, about doing good, spreading welfare, or increasing knowledge or any of the other blessings associated with the good-and-free-society. The real-world meaning of government, as well as all human experience of it, means, *at best,* command by law, which means, at bottom, by force. A run-in with the Internal Revenue Service, a creature of law, perhaps the first that government sets up, will teach anyone (capable of learning) just what government is about.

There are those, of course, who reject out-of-hand what I have just said. They believe that one cannot justly accuse of criminal thuggery the membership of the Sierra Club and the Audubon Society, or the professionals who promote our welfare scams, or the scientists who every day find, with taxpayer money spread around by the National Institutes of Health, a new cause of cancer.

Perhaps you can't without more information. Of course, there is a difference between them and the run-of-the-mill mugger. *They* do not extort directly, and they do not use their own hands in the mugging. But then neither do Mafia chiefs or con men. The members of special-interest pressure groups who aggressively seek special privileges and subsidies for their purposes, whatever they may be, (but most definitely *not* those who are in Washington to defend themselves against such aggression) get Congressmen, by way of political contributions of money or other kinds of help, to do their dirty work for them. But what they fail to see is the bayonet and the freedom-denying incarceration, which are the hidden but still the only means by which Congress is able to give them what they seek. They get Congress to do *their* dirty work, Congress gets the IRS to do *its,* and the IRS gets the courts and the federal marshals and jails to do *its. Quod erat demonstrandum.*

Outraged by this demonstration, the special interests will contend that they are acting for the public good, that they are simply going to government to get it to do what governments exist to do. This, however, is not argument; it is flim-flam. They are not asking Congress to do good; they are asking Congress to redistribute wealth, to rob Peter in order to provide Paul with the means of satisfying *his* desire out of Peter's pocket, not his own. Congress will deny that it is in the business of robbing, of course, but calling theft "doing good" does not change it. It will not wash. A common thief does good for himself, but he remains a thief, and his act, a theft.

Let us call down again the first principles hovering over this essay. All history, logically arranged, agreeing with Webster, demonstrates that government is force and violence, not creation. Tanks do not create; guns produce death and destruction. Jails cancel freedom for those who abuse it, or are supposed to do that. The goods of life come only from persons peaceably going about doing *their own* things. There is a role for government, one as valuable and as important to the good life as the free enterprise, free-market system is. In fact, it is logically, though not always existentially, prior to both. Straight thinking gives government a monopoly of physical force in order to ensure the domestic tranquility, and the system of irresistible justice in disputes between man and man, without which the rights of private property and freedom of contract which constitute the market economy cannot achieve existential reality.

Absent these powers which provide a semblance of rightness to wealth-redistribution, the state would be indistinguishable from the Mafia.

Interventionists who honestly believe that it is the job of government to do good directly, and not solely indirectly, by keeping the peace, ignore the fact that government—force—is a blunt and awkward special-purpose instrument, something like a hammer, ill-adapted to the production of anything but punishment, and has a hard time doing even that. They must grasp also the fact that, producing nothing, government is not in a position to finance the doing of good except by taking from someone else the means of doing that good. The result of such redistribution is always, and inexorably, a reduction in the amount of good that can be done: a reduction equal, at least, to the cost of the redistributive machinery, but in fact much more because, to some degree, the capacity also of the expropriated persons to produce is reduced. Concretely, if a corporation and its shareholders are desanguinated, as they are, pitifully, they may retain the will to produce, but the capital which enhances production is diminished by *at least* the amount taken from them by force.

Human needs and wants are to all intents and purposes infinite. Goods provided gratis by nature are inadequate. Human production is all we have available to satisfy human needs. If we have learned nothing else in the past three hundred years, and especially, the last five years, we have learned that freedom, by which I mean, essentially, economic freedom—private property, freedom of contract, and the free-market capitalism which is their natural product—is the best means available for the service of human welfare in the broadest sense. We have learned also that government is incompetent toward that end. Finally, the events in East Europe of the last few years should have taught the whole world what the Misesian Austrians, and first among them, Hans Sennholz, have always known: That the further government intervenes in the economy, the worse the mess it makes. Knowing nothing about production itself, it violates and desanguinates the production machine, capitalism, to the great and lasting sorrow of mankind.

The more the government intervenes, the weaker the economy; for each intervention reduces the capacity of the producing sectors to fill needs.

We reach here the climax of our analysis. I referred earlier to the servo-mechanism which in vote-buying interventionism shuts off only after it has bankrupted society. Here is how it works. Every intervention by government in the working of an economy at once benefits some person or persons and injures others. The only intervention by government which is an advantage to everyone is the absolutely equal rule of law. One tires of coping with the vulgar technique of evading this truth by derision and not by argument. The differing conditions of the rich and the poor, not all to the advantage of the rich, by the way, have no bearing on the truths just uttered. It is irrelevant that the rich are less likely than the poor to sleep under the bridges of Paris. It does not matter who sleeps where, or under what constraints.

The fact remains that economic intervention by governments, which produces nothing but more government, always works to the disadvantage of someone; that in the long run, government intervention provides lasting benefits to no one at all does not change the fact that, in the meanwhile, the intervention harms someone. And no matter how much this fact is ignored, it will assert itself.

Once again, then, let us recognize that each time government takes from A to subsidize B, A is to some extent impoverished or debilitated, either as a consumer or as a producer, or possibly both. Moreover, once government has thus favored B, it has set a precedent establishing itself as a source of such handouts. In an unlimited, universal-suffrage "democracy" such as ours, especially one in which the supreme power rests in a body such as our House of Representatives, composed of persons who run for office continually, even *continuously;* and a Senate composed in practically the same way, the rest, as the saying goes, is history. The subsidy for B, at the expense of A, sets the servo-mechanism going in two ways. It activates A, C, D, E, and all the rest, inducing and justifying them also to go to government when they have an appetite which they are unable to satisfy any other way. At the same time, it activates candidates to solicit votes on the strength of promises to "look after constituent interests," a current euphemism for vote-buying. And with what does the candidate propose to purchase the votes? Of course, since government produces nothing, it can buy the votes only with resources taken from somewhere else.

Ruinous taxation or even more ruinous inflation, or both, as long as the process continues are the *only* possible outcomes. And the process must continue as long as the causes which started it continue to exist.

We have, roughly, a five trillion dollar Gross National Product, according to the *Statistical Abstract of the United States (1990).* Of this, all governments spent *in 1987*, $1,810 billion, or almost two trillion. The federal government accounted for 63.5 percent, or $1,149 billion. Any one with the patience to track down the freakish things included in these sums must agree with my "automated-interventionism" theorem of governmental expenditures in the democratic-welfare state, the system in which the ruling majority believe that it is the role of government to take care of all human problems, all human insecurities, all human inequalities and preoccupations.

For quite a while now, in fact something like a year (as of September 1991), the country has been in a recession, with considerable unemployment. Well over seven million persons, supposedly, are looking for work and cannot find it. The main source of jobs is capital, invested by firms and persons who expect to produce things that people want badly enough to pay what it costs to produce them, and, after taxes, to have left a little profit with which to compensate the savers who have sacrificed in order to supply the things they want or need. This recession is proving sticky, apparently. I heard on the news September 17, 1991, that the Federal Reserve has eased interest rates for the eleventh straight time in the last six months, but that no increases in the money supply have yet occurred, or not enough to crank up the economy.

Is it so strange, when more than a third of the Gross National Product is being drained by governments, governments which are spending only a minor fraction of their take on legitimate governmental functions and the rest on redistributionist vote-buying, that the economy is sluggish? We are so heavily taxed, and the federal deficit and the "funny money" have produced such inflated prices, that consumers have little money to throw around, and personal savings are virtually nil. And savings, it must be remembered, are the source of capital. Without savings, no capital; no capital growth, no jobs, and a sluggish economy, which is what we have.

The remarkable thing is not that the economy is sluggish. A starving swimmer with his arms and legs tied will break no speed records. Like our starved and hampered economy, the swimmer simply has all he can do to stay afloat. That our economy and those of the European welfare states are surviving at all is the remarkable phenomenon, violated and desanguinated as they are.

Henry Maine said in one of the excerpts quoted above, that one of the heartening features of the limited democracy of nineteenth-century, ruggedly individualist, vigorously competitive America, was that "the persons distanced in the race have suffered so little."[12] He was referring, far in advance of Lyndon Johnson's fakery, to the real war on poverty, the only effectively waged war on poverty known to this world, that is, the one waged by free-market capitalism. While government at best provides internal tranquility, only savers and investors and entrepreneurs can carry on that war by ever-increasing productivity. Redistributing their wealth will never reduce poverty. On the contrary, the only effect that redistributing wealth can have is to negate capitalism's war on poverty. Twenty-five years ago Lyndon Johnson began *his* war on poverty. He should have called it a war *for* poverty, or a war *on* the poor, for we have all become poorer since then, and in many ways.

It is impossible to believe, at this time in history, that the members of the House of Representatives and of the Senate of the United States are unaware of these simple, now uncontroversial truths. What then drives them so inexorably, session after session, to expand the federal budget and the federal deficit, despite the resolutions, the statutes, the expenditure-control agreements that pour from the halls of Congress so continuously? The answer, it seems to me, is simple. They are running for office all the time, and the only way they think they can keep the votes they have and replace attrition is to buy them with promises of government largess. Perhaps they should take note of the last election in Sweden, the paragon of welfare states. Finally sick of the socialists who have been in power there so long, and burdened by taxes that take 70 percent of their pay, with their economy in consequence even more sluggish than ours, the people of Sweden have voted them out.

Must we, too, go through the wringer as Sweden and the misgoverned countries of Eastern Europe have done? This country is in serious trouble, morally and socially, as well as politically and economically. Its troubles run deep, but it is pointless to resign ourselves to imbecility, although that is our destiny if we continue in our present course of tax and tax, inflate and inflate, spend and spend, and elect and elect. We shall "go out not with a bang, but with a whimper," a dull, dispirited mendicant country whose politicians will have to travel in ragged clothes, seeking handouts from our betters, instead of jetting around the world showering largess extorted from the American people and enterprises they are now violating and desanguinating.

I said at the beginning of this essay that I was going to propose a way of buying time, until our ruling majority learn that only free enterprise, left to pursue its productive objectives, can deliver the goods and services that all seek. Here is the plan.

Six Million Dollar Congressmen and No Re-Elections

I propose that we pay members of the House of Representatives and of the Senate $6 million dollars a year, with no more strings attached than our laws place upon all other workers: no special privileges for our representatives, no exemptions from the laws they pass for the country at large, and no immunities for them which are denied to private citizens. While in office, the members must be required to forego all other income not produced by their own wealth. Their income should be taxable in the same way, at the same rates, subject to only the same deductions and exemptions as other citizens have.

The Congress should be provided with no other goods or services, human or material. While the present Senate and House Buildings stand, the government might continue to allow their use for offices, hearing rooms, restrooms and so on. Better yet, the buildings might be leased or sold to private investors or companies. Those purchasers should be required to charge the members market rents, to be paid out of their own pockets, not by drafts on the federal treasury.

If the members wish to hire office help, research assistants, and the like, they should be required to compensate them out of their $6 million salaries. And the employment relations between the members and their help, if any, should be subject to whatever labor laws all other employers are subject to.

Tenure of office should be different for House and Senate. Members of the House should be limited to one twelve-year term, with no re-elections permitted. Senators should hold office for life. Either, of course, may resign at will. In no event should members of either House be allowed to run for, hold, or be appointed to any other federal office.

The objective of the foregoing proposals is to make the government of the United States respectable once more, aristocratic in quality, but democratically elected. There is no going backward in human history. We cannot return to the limited kind of democracy we had in the beginning, when voting was to some extent tied to property qualifications, and senators and presidents were indirectly selected. But handsome salaries and freedom from running for office every minute of their lives should make it possible for the members to develop some genuine self-esteem. With self-esteem, they will come to scorn cheap politicking, although to expect an end to all politicking would be infantile.

Those who think the salaries I propose are too high should study carefully the present cost of the legislative branch of our federal government. As nearly as I can figure it, that cost, counting everything, comes to about $6 million dollars per head. We might as well pay them that amount directly, instead of inducing them to sneak around as they do, loading themselves with staff, research assistance, boondoggling trips, constituent services, special dining rooms, gymnasiums, etc.. Apropos, there should be *no* other allotments: not for travel, or housing, hospitalization, pensions—nothing. With $6 million a year for twelve years, members of the House should provide for themselves; and with such a stipend for life, senators need ask the taxpayers for nothing else.

Just as the proposed stipends will cost the taxpayers no more than they are paying now, so, too, the tenures proposed do not change things very much, except definitely for the better, from the point of view of the public good. At present, almost every incumbent who runs for re-election wins in both the House and the Senate. Thus, for House members, the twelve-year terms constitute, in fact, a reduction in tenure. As for the Senate, once upon a time it was called the greatest deliberative body in the world, and that was not absurd hyperbole. If our country still has capacity to produce the greatness that it once had, the plan I propose would certainly establish the most propitious possible conditions for the restoration of the Senate to its erstwhile glory.

Present opinion on congressional stature, pay, and tenure is, I believe, wrong and wrong-headed. It is wrong to blame Congress for our plight when the pay and tenure of members virtually force them to abuse the country in order to survive. Blame low pay and precarious tenure. Blame voters. Don't blame the servant for doing what his masters virtually force him to do.

If one pays peanuts to persons to whom one entrusts "the keys of the kingdom" and its treasury and then tells them that they are subject to being fired at whim, what can one rationally expect?

The ultimate power of our government rests, by the Constitution, in Congress. If Congress is governing for the benefit of special interests, as I have been at pains to establish in this essay, and not for the general welfare, as the Constitution requires, it is because, conditions of congressional employment and human nature being what they are, that is inevitable. Like everyone else, members of Congress act in their own perceived interests. That is Nature's plan, the method of ensuring the survival of the species. By making each individual a passionate agent of his own survival and advancement, Nature, as is so often the case, came to a solution as supremely elegant and self-sustaining for the survival problem as it did with the reproduction objective.

Conclusion

The pay of Congressmen, even now, after the last furtive raise, is less than that of some freshmen lawyers and physicians; and their terms of office are nasty and short, akin to those of Roman gladiators. Such policies on the terms and conditions of congressional employment are absurd and ridiculous, well-designed to produce only the terrible public problems I have summarized above. Let us abandon the romantic concept of public service as its own reward for men of noble character and unblemished virtue. We are not made that way, none of us. The heads of large companies are about as good and as incorruptible as human beings get. They are not corrupted by their good pay. More probably, it helps keep them virtuous. Why should politicians be expected to assume responsibility for even vaster affairs purely out of the goodness of their hearts? Candidates for public office often say that they do so in order to "serve." Others believe that they seek public office out of mixed motives, varying from person to person, among which may be a desire to serve. It is neither necessary nor serviceable to be cynical about this. What counts is how we as a nation set up public office, its terms and conditions of employment, especially.

It is preposterous to say, as some do, that as a general rule congressmen inherently prefer the good of the few over the good of the many. I am confident that the crassest among them resents the kind of kowtowing that serving special interests must involve. Give him a strong incentive to serve the public interest exclusively, as handsome salaries and secure tenure in office for a reasonable period are likely to do, and I believe we shall get as good government as the country is capable of producing. It won't be any better than that. It can't be.

There will be members who will never amount to much, some who will be positively evil. Yet the legislative branch cannot but improve under the plan I have sketched. Legislation is bound to be conceived and crafted better when legislators are not permanently under the gun. It should be both improved in quality and reduced in quantity when members are not compelled by their instinct of self-preservation to produce and market it by the ton.

Notes and References

1. *The Wall Street Journal*, September 13, 1991, p. A11.
2. *Ibid.*
3. *Socialism* by Ludwig von Mises first appeared in 1922 and has been republished most recently by the Liberty Fund (Indianapolis, IN), in the Liberty Classics series in 1981.
4. *Popular Government* by Sir Henry Sumner Maine was first published by John Murray, Albemarle Street, London, 1885. Liberty Fund (Indianapolis, IN) reprinted this book in 1976.
5. 1885 edition at 45.
6. *Id.* at 48.
7. Mises, Ludwig von, *Human Action* (New Haven, CT: Yale University Press, 1949), p. 762.
8. *Id.* at 763.
9. 1885 ed. at 50–52.
10. *Id.* at 52.
11. *The Wall Street Journal,* September 17, 1991, p. A17.
12. Text *supra* at note 9.

25

THE PERILS OF FORECASTING

Lawrence W. Reed*

In the field of forecasting, we might rely just as well on the economists to predict the weather and meteorologists to predict the economy.

Economists have made notoriously faulty forecasts throughout the history of the discipline. Indeed, if economists really knew as much about the future as some of their finely detailed predictions would suggest, they would routinely reap vast fortunes in the stock and commodity markets. We must wonder if those forecasters who are financially "healthy" make more money *making* their predictions than actually *investing* in them.

The dismal record of the economic forecasting profession led one economist at the State University of New York to conclude a few years ago that *non-economists* on balance are better at seeing the future than are the professional forecasters. Perhaps that's what financier Bernard Baruch had in mind when he said, "An economist is a guy who thinks he knows more about money that those of us who have it."

Tomorrow's economy will always be less understood today than most soothsayers will admit—a major reason for faulty predictions. Additionally, the theories which form the bases for interpreting economic statistics are often flawed and the statistics themselves frequently defective. This essay develops those points and suggests strongly that most of today's "crystal ball economics" is little more than a fancy pretense to knowledge.

*Mr. Reed, a former professor at Northwood Institute, is President of The Mackinac Center, a free market public policy institute located in Midland, MI. He writes a syndicated newspaper column weekly, and is the co-author of several books.

The Uncertainty of the Future

Why is the future so hard to describe now? The answer is at once both simple and profound: *it hasn't happened yet*.

The existence of *uncertainty* pervades the nature of the human condition itself. Human hindsight is "20/20" but the focus of foresight has limited precision in the ever-changing world of human values and actions. Forecasting the future will never be an exact science as long as fallible, volatile mortals interacting with each other and with the elements of nature are the main ingredients in economic life as we know it.

To say that the future is uncertain, however, does not end the matter. Surely, *investors* are but one prominent category of market participants who must learn to fly by more than the seat of their pants, or investing could never be more than a toss of the dice.

Equally apparent is the fact that *entrepreneurs* who assemble the tools of production today must make decisions based upon what they *think* the future will bring. Their business is to grapple with such questions as: What will the general state of the economy be next year or the year thereafter? How much will materials cost and will they be available? What wage rates will be required to attract and keep the kind of employees we need? What will be the effect on sales if we change our prices? What are our competitors likely to do? Where will the best markets for our products be? Is this a good time to seek outside financing or will interest rates decline in coming months? Should we be reducing our inventories? What will the politicians do that might affect our business?

To the point, what can we reasonably say about tomorrow and what methods enable us to say it? A glance at the more prominent methodologies employed in economic forecasting is in order.

Simple Trend Projection

Simple trend projection is an approach relying upon pure extrapolation of previous trends in some economic activity and, as such, offers little more than a pretense to being scientific. It works only so long as those trends continue and cannot begin to account for any significant changes or turning points, let alone anticipate them.

The predictor may, for instance, estimate that next year's income will equal this year's plus 4 percent. What rationale beyond pure inductive reasoning explains the forecast? Simply assuming that past trends and past relationships will persist is a primitive and rather limited forecasting tool.

This problem has plagued even the most renowned forecasters, producing some embarrassingly bad forecasts in recent years. The entire profession of economic soothsayers failed to call the 1982 recession, and later in the 1980s failed to anticipate the attraction of foreign investors to the United States, and its implications. Earlier in the 1970s, they failed to foresee the tremendous surge of price inflation and the two recessions that were to follow.

Thomas Malthus, early in the nineteenth century, used a kind of simple trend projection to forecast over-population and starvation. In the 1970s, the "Club of Rome" made the same prediction with the same approach. In Malthus's case, capitalism's heroic Industrial Revolution interfered with his prediction rather decisively; the Club of Rome did not foresee the dramatic decline in birth rates, now a reality in the industrialized countries.

Forecasters who rely on simple trend projection (and many do), are walking on ice so thin one can hear it cracking as they go. They assume that humans are robots unable to change their behavior.

Gross National Product Models

The concept of Gross National Product (GNP) purports to express the total value of all goods and services produced during a specific period of time (a real leap of faith, given the fact that value is a purely subjective phenomenon and that prices are merely exchange ratios, not measurements of value).

GNP is the consummation of what the mathematical economists call "national income accounting"—the process of identifying and adding all the components which comprise the material economy. It is one of the most widely quoted yardsticks of "aggregate economic activity" and is the statistic which most conventional analysts use to express their predictions of business performance. Its many components supposedly form a "model" of the economy which can be a foundation for economic forecasting.

But this concept, appearing on the surface to be profound, happens to be a shallow trap. GNP, being the most "aggregate" of statistical aggregates, is riddled with problems and errors and, what's worse, *problems and errors of unknown magnitude*.

Simon Kuznets himself, the "father" of GNP, once suggested that to assume an average margin of error of about 10 percent for the principal components of GNP would be reasonable. Yet, some economists routinely predict quarterly GNP figures in tenths of 1 percent. Congress often makes public policy based upon those computations which, even if accurate, conjure up what Professor Roger Garrison describes as "the vision of a dietician who weighs a locomotive both before and after the crew boards it, then uses the difference between the two weighings as the basis for prescribing a diet for the whole crew."

Additionally, no account is made for the tremendous value of activities in the "subterranean economy," those transactions which for various reasons escape the tax and data collectors. Likewise, non-monetary exchanges are not counted. The value of *your* work is ignored, for instance, if you paint your own house but the wages paid to a painter *are included.*

The changing quality of goods remains unreflected in GNP. The measure does not rise if an improvement in a product does not result in a higher price. Excluded also is the "commodity" we call "leisure," an economic good which people often freely opt to "consume" more of in exchange for consuming fewer traditional goods and services.

Finally, GNP statistics are constantly subjected to revision. Those adjustments are often significant and sometimes come months or years after the initial calculation. In short, by the time we have a statistic which we can reasonably assume is "final," it may have long since lost any forecasting value, if indeed it had any in the first place.

GNP will always suffer serious deficiencies as a forecasting tool if for no other reason than its dealing with the economy essentially as a single faceless lump, rather than as the intricate and dynamic outcome of the decisions and actions of tens of millions of real and specific people.

Econometrics

Many of the problems of simple trend projection and GNP models are present in the more sophisticated, heavily quantitative econometric models. These artificial constructs, which many economists once thought to be quite promising, comprise hundreds of mathematical equations that purport to represent relationships among the major aspects of economic activity. Expensive, high-speed computers churn out the meticulous forecasts of the econometrician.

The record of these models has been dismal at best. Mistakes in econometric forecasts often have been so bad that merely changing their signs (from + to - or - to +) would have put them significantly closer to the mark. They are no more accurate in calling an oncoming recession, for instance, than most economists' intuition.

"Macroeconomic theory," says economist William Niskanen, "is in absolute shambles. The standard models, used to predict the economy for decades, have been discredited." Another economist, John Rutledge, adds, "It's like Beirut. Fourteen different armies are vying for control, and no one seems to be winning."[1]

Certainly these erroneous forecasts occur not because the practitioners lack effort. They are simply employing inappropriate assumptions—assumptions that if rejected would lead to the virtual termination of econometric models as we know them.

Economists of the "Austrian" school have demonstrated that economics—the science of *human* action—is best analyzed *qualitatively*, not *quantitatively*. The values which drive human action are neither constant nor measurable, which means that most of the relationships postulated in the static equations of econometric models are tenuous at best. "Garbage in, garbage out," as they say in computerese. Even if the econometrician could construct a perfect "picture" of the economy, he would have no more basis for prediction than the person who snaps a photo of a dog at the very height of a jump over a fence. That snapshot tells you nothing about where the dog is headed, why he's going there, or what he's going to do when he gets there.

Robert J. Samuelson expressed it well in a *Newsweek* column in early 1988:

> At a recent conference, a well-known and respected economist exclaimed: the equations don't work. In the contest between

economists' computers and the real world, the computers have been creamed. The story of economics over the past 15 years is a junkyard full of discarded equations. The computers project past patterns into the future, but new technologies, government policies, business practices, and popular beliefs constantly invent a future that isn't like the past. The equations for exchange rates are the latest additions to the scrap heap. They join battered formulas for inflation, interest rates, trade deficits, and many others.[2]

The equations of econometric models profess complexity, yet they really represent a feeble, simplistic, and futile effort to mirror the infinitely more complex network of human actions we collectively call "the economy." They make little effort to recognize the full breadth of interaction between economic and non-economic variables. They fail to account for any number of unforeseeable elements, including those enumerated in Samuelson's remarks above. Attempts to quantify such elements in advance or to attach numerical significance to the subjective judgments of entrepreneurs in the marketplace are intellectually shoddy, if not dishonest. They are ordained to suffer the failure which springs from gross simplicity and imprecision.

It is ironic that econometrics strives for the exactness of numbers and yet bogs down in static equations which necessarily cannot begin to account for all the relevant factors and their interrelationships. Henry Hazlitt tells us that if a mathematical equation is not precise, it is worse than worthless; it is a fraud:

> It gives our results a merely spurious precision. It's an illusion of knowledge in place of the candid confession of ignorance, vagueness, or uncertainty which is the beginning of wisdom.[3]

Statistical Indicators

Statistical indicators are measurements of economic activity which supposedly "lead," "coincide with," or "lag" the business cycle.

A list of "leading indicators" generally includes the money supply, housing permits, stock prices, raw materials prices, inventories, and corporate profits.

"Coincident indicators" include industrial production, factory capacity, retail sales, and personal income.

Unemployment, bank interest rates on short-term business loans, labor cost per unit of output in manufacturing, and new capital appropriations are considered key "lagging indicators."

Much attention is paid each month to the government's Index of Leading Economic Indicators, widely regarded as the measure of the most important future-telling signals. The facts are, however, that the ILEI is out-of-date and inaccurate.

It overweights the influence of the stock market and undervalues the role of global economic developments. It does not account for the growth of the service sector in the United States or the declining role of manufacturing. The figures which go into computation of the Index do not take inflation into full account.

The Index's lead time in signalling the onset of recessions has ranged from four months to nearly two years, which makes it a shaky guide for anyone trying to plan for economic swings. Its performance in calling the upturns is only marginally better. On several occasions, it has signalled booms or busts which never materialized.

A quick sampling of other statistical indicators reveals serious weaknesses: The unemployment rate does not accurately reflect joblessness in the inner cities, in distressed rural areas, or among migrant workers and illegal immigrants, and the official rate includes people as unemployed who are just voluntarily moving from one job to another; retail sales reports are routinely based on a woefully inadequate sampling; the Federal Reserve's figures on factory utilization fail to consider the capacity of firms to increase output by using more efficient machinery; and revisions in most government economic statistics are common, sometimes massive, and often very belated.

Little wonder then, that we can read in the popular press so many assessments such as this one: "More and more, thc art of economic planning appears to be degenerating from astral navigation to something closer to astrology." [4]

Assuming that statistics could be assembled accurately and indicate what they purport to and do not require later substantial revision, we might have a sketchy picture of where "the economy" *was* or perhaps even where it *presently is*. But still we couldn't say, with much certainty at all, *where it is headed.*

Educated Speculation

Nonetheless, having said all that, reason indicates that if we can say anything at all about the economic future, we probably should know something about the economic *present* and *past*. That's where reliable statistics might play some part, not as a basis for simple trend projection, but merely as descriptions of economic activity already behind us or underway.

Even the finest and most reliable numbers should only be ingredients in a more fundamental approach to proper economic forecasting. For want of a better descriptive title, I call it "educated speculation." It is characterized by the following:

1. A clear recognition of the uncertainty of the future with no leaps of logic or mindless extrapolations.
2. Careful use of only the most meaningful and dependable statistics, understanding all of the limitations of such aggregates discussed above. This implies a task of "de-aggregating" aggregates—of analyzing-economic activity as it results from acting, decision-making, welfare-maximizing individuals.
3. A sound grasp of basic principles and of the political process. Understanding the political process is vital in an economy where government looms as large as it does in ours. It's also a quandary. Politicians throw their weight around like "bulls in a china shop," and predicting their next moves is like trying to forecast which vases the witless bulls will break next.
4. A thorough understanding of the causes and consequences of the business cycle. Cycle theories abound, but the one which fully integrates an explanation of boom-and-bust with an analysis of the entire economic system is the "Austrian malinvestment theory."

Propounded first by Ludwig von Mises and later elaborated by Nobel laureate F. A. Hayek, the Austrian theory holds that the source of the cycle lies in money and credit expansion by central banking authorities. It is the theory which enabled Mises during the subtle inflation of the 1920s to warn of a coming depression.

In the final analysis, the art of *entrepreneurship* is the art of "educated speculation." Upon the shoulders of the entrepreneur in the market economy rests a special burden of forecasting. For him, it is, in the words of Murray Rothbard, "a matter of intuition, 'hunch,' and deep insight into the slice of the market that the entrepreneur knows and is dealing with." That, plus the tools listed above allow an entrepreneur, an economist, or an investor to say something about the future and have some reasonable grounds for saying it. He must always be wary, though, of the severe limitations which proscribe any human's ability to see tomorrow. Brian McAndrew clarifies this point:

> If forecasters recognized the limitations of economic theory and empirical information, they would realize that the most an economist can hope to do is explain the likely consequences of different policies. An economist can show, for instance, that a minimum wage tends to cause unemployment because it alters supply and demand conditions in the labor market. An economist cannot say exactly when, where, and by how much unemployment will rise (i.e., he cannot forecast the unemployment rate), but he can say that if a minimum wage law is instituted unemployment will tend to increase. In addition, he can, by combining theory with empirical information, get a rough idea of the amount of unemployment caused by the minimum wage at different times in the past, but he cannot say what this amount will be in the future.[5]

"Educated speculation" is really economics brought down to earth. It may not be as fancy as econometrics or GNP, but neither is it as pretentious. It says simply that an economist should be an economist, not an aspiring prophet.

The reader who began this essay hoping to discover a crystal ball may be disappointed to find nothing of the kind. Instead, what has been shown is that much of what is commonly referred to today as "economic forecasting" goes far beyond the real abilities of economists to predict the future. When it comes to soothsaying, the old maxim still holds: "The beginning of wisdom is to admit that there's much we just don't know."

Notes and References

1. Brock, David, "Seeing the Economy's Future with a Shattered Crystal Ball," *Insight,* June 30, 1986, p. 42.
2. Samuelson, Robert J., "Speculating about 1988," *Newsweek,* January 11, 1988, p. 41.
3. Hazlitt, Henry, *The Failure of the New Economics*, (Princeton, NJ: D. Van Nostrand Company, Inc., 1959), p. 99.
4. Benjamin, David, "A Mess of Leading Indicators," *Time,* June 13, 1988, p. 49.
5. McAndrew, Brian, "The Failure of Econometric Forecasting," *Policy Review,* November, 1981, p. 6.

26

FREEDOM OF OPPORTUNITY, NOT EQUALITY OF OPPORTUNITY*

George Reisman**

The advocates of economic equality have a fallback position, which they also frequently use as a camouflage, namely, the doctrine of equality of opportunity. They do not, they say, advocate anything so foolish or so extreme as the imposition of actual economic equality. All they advocate, they say, is that everyone have an equal chance, that, as they put it, all the runners begin the race from the same starting line. On this basis, they feel free to advocate the confiscation of inheritances, public education through the postgraduate level, and laws preventing private discrimination on the basis not only of such factors as race, religion or national origin, but also age, medical condition, and physical handicap.

The supporters of the equality of opportunity doctrine view opportunities as fundamentally external to the individual, in effect, as various dishes carried by waiters on trays, which, under capitalism, are arbitrarily served to some and withheld from others. They want the government to seize control, they say, not of the distribution of wealth and income, but merely of the distribution of these dishes, as it were, that is, of the opportunities to earn wealth and income, and so give everyone an equal chance.

**Dr. Reisman is Professor of Economics at Pepperdine University's School of Business and Management in Los Angeles, and is the author of *The Government Against the Economy* (Ottawa, Illinois: Jameson Books, 1979). This essay is excerpted from his forthcoming book *Capitalism: A Treatise on Economics.*

To most people, the equality-of-opportunity doctrine sounds eminently fair and reasonable. But, in fact, it is as much against the nature of reality as is the doctrine of the out-and-out equality of wealth and income. This becomes clear as soon as we look beyond the inheritance of wealth and begin to consider other external factors that affect the opportunities an individual has.

For example, consider such factors as the intelligence of a child's parents, their education and vocabulary, their system of values, and their love for him and treatment of him, not to mention their level of income and the kind of material life they lead and thereby expose him to while he is growing up. It is certainly arguable that differences in these factors confront a child with differences in opportunities that are of no less significance for his future life, including his ability to earn wealth and income, than those which are based on the wealth he may or may not inherit.

To create equality of opportunity with respect to these factors, nothing less would be necessary than to abolish the institution of the family and to raise all children in government orphanages, where they could all be brought up in exactly the same way. This, of course, was the idea of Plato, and it was supported by many socialists in the nineteenth century and earlier in this century.

But even this would not be enough to achieve equality of opportunity. Because even if all these environmental factors could be made the same, there would still remain enormous differences in the intellectual and physical endowment of the child himself, based on his genetic inheritance. A highly intelligent, strong, and beautiful child, for example, automatically has enormous advantages over a stupid, weak, and ugly child that is given the same upbringing. How can such different children, and the adults they later become, be given equality of opportunity?

One possible answer to this question is that the government should concentrate more heavily on the upbringing of the less fortunate, thus perhaps raising their intelligence, improving their strength, and possibly even their looks. But no amount of such extra effort by the government can significantly make up for what nature has denied. Thus, another possible answer is that the government should insist that such differences simply be disregarded. The first answer manifests itself today in large-scale government support for special programs for the education of the retarded; the second, in those anti-discrimination laws, such as California's, which prohibit discrimination in employment based on medical condition or physical handicap.

A third possible answer is that, failing the government's ability to create equality of opportunity by raising up the less fortunate, it should tear down the more fortunate. If it cannot make the stupid intelligent, the weak strong, and the ugly beautiful, it can find a way to hamper or destroy intelligence, strength, and beauty, and so achieve equality of opportunity by making everyone stupid, weak, and ugly. It may be difficult to find anyone who would openly advocate such a policy, but it does follow logically from the goal of equality of opportunity.

There is a fourth conceivable answer: The government should attempt to determine the genetic endowment of children. It could enact a program of eugenics, and attempt to breed children who would all possess the same characteristics at birth. Then, with the same upbringing as well, the demand for equality of opportunity could, apparently, at last be satisfied.

These absurd and vicious implications of the equality of opportunity doctrine should make one begin to wonder what kind of ideal equality of opportunity really is. In reality, it is not a legitimate ideal at all. It appears to represent justice only on the basis of a thoroughly confused view of the nature of opportunities and the causes of human success.

Let us consider what opportunities actually are, and then establish some important facts about them.

An opportunity is merely *an occasion on which successful action is possible.* It is a situation that an individual can take advantage of to his gain.

What needs to be realized about opportunities is, first of all, that there is no scarcity of them; they arise again and again. The second thing that needs to be understood is that what is important in connection with them and deserves to be fought for, as a matter both of justice and universal self-interest, is not that vicious absurdity—the equality of opportunity—but *the freedom of opportunity.* What the freedom of opportunity means and why it is so important will be explained shortly. Finally, what needs to be understood about opportunities is that they can be and regularly are *created* by individuals. Indeed, opportunities are themselves products of human thought and action. Just how they are is something that will also be explained shortly.

Let us consider the abundance of opportunities. An opportunity exists every time there is the possibility of improving oneself in any way. If one is penniless and there is an unfilled job available that one has the ability to fill, one has the opportunity of ending one's pennilessness. If one has a job, and there is any better job available that one has the ability to fill, one has the opportunity to improve one's position further. If there is any skill that one does not possess, but is capable of learning, then one has the opportunity of adding to one's skills.

In fact, in the nature of the case, the economic opportunities potentially open to the individual far exceed his ability to exploit them, with the result that he must *choose* among them, selecting some and rejecting others. This follows from the fact that there is always room for improvement in the satisfaction of man's wants, and that the basis for carrying out such improvement is the performance of either more labor or more productive labor. In other words, built into the fact that man's wants can always be satisfied more fully or better is the opportunity for the performance of more labor as the means of satisfying them more fully or better, and the opportunity for improving the productivity of his labor.

Indeed, in the nature of things there are potentially limitless opportunities both for increasing employment and for raising the productivity of labor, for there are virtually limitless possibilities for improvement in the satisfaction of man's wants. The potential opportunities for employment always dwarf man's ability actually to work, which is the major reason that he must be concerned with raising the productivity of his labor.

The fundamental scarcity of labor is manifest in the fact that virtually everyone would always like to enjoy an income many times greater than the income he is presently capable of earning. For example, today an average worker may earn $20,000 per year for working forty hours a week. If such a worker had it in his power to earn $100,000 per year, he would have no difficulty in finding ways to live up to such an income. Unfortunately, to earn such an income at his present rate of pay, he would have to work more hours than there are in the week. His maximum actual ability to work is obviously vastly less than corresponds to the income he would like to have. But this is only another way of saying that the utmost goods and services he is capable of *producing* are far less than the goods and services he would like to consume. For, taken collectively, our desire to be able to spend five or ten times more than we now can afford to spend is an indication that we would like five or ten times more work performed than is now performed. In the present state of technology and productivity of labor, this is how much additional labor would need to be performed to produce the larger volume of output we would like to be able to buy.

Thus, people can work themselves to the point of utter exhaustion, and still they cannot produce more than a small fraction of all that it would be useful and desirable for them to produce. As a result, the supply of labor that people can provide falls radically short of the supply of products they would like to have. In other words, labor is inherently scarce.

People may wonder how it can be true that there are virtually limitless employment opportunities and yet, at the same time, the world in which we live is characterized by chronic mass unemployment and the experience of millions is that they have no opportunity for work. There is a simple reconciliation of these facts. Namely, although there is never any metaphysical reason for the existence of unemployment, that is to say, any reason for it by virtue of the necessary, inescapable nature of things, *misguided laws* can easily deny man the freedom of exploiting the opportunities for employment that the nature of reality offers him and so force unemployment upon him. The problem of unemployment is thus the result of the violation of the freedom of opportunity, that is, the violation of man's freedom to exploit the opportunities that reality offers him. The freedom of opportunity means, to be precise, *the ability to exploit the opportunities afforded by reality without being stopped by the initiation of physical force.*

People are unable to find work not because there is no work for them to do in the nature of things, but because government and labor union interference, based on the initiation of physical force, prices their labor beyond the reach of potential employers. This interference is, specifically, the inflation of the money supply coupled with so-called prolabor legislation. The inflation of the money supply first entices business firms into a state of illiquidity, a state in which, in the feverish expectation of taking in more and more money, they lend or invest too heavily in relation to the funds at their disposal and thus leave themselves with dangerously low levels of cash in relation to the bloated volume of financial activity they are carrying on. Then, as soon as the inflation is stopped or significantly slowed, or even merely fails to accelerate sufficiently, they need to rebuild their cash holdings; they cut back their spending and lending, and a financial contraction ensues. The resulting fall in wage payments and sales revenues of all kinds leads to widespread business insolvencies and bankruptcies, which causes bank failures and possibly, as a further result, an actual decline in the quantity of money, which causes still further reductions in spending and an intensification of the financial contraction and ensuing depression.

In an environment of financial contraction, government efforts to maintain or increase wage rates, through such measures as minimum wage laws, prounion legislation, or other forms of pressure on businessmen to maintain or increase wages, necessarily result in mass unemployment. For the government's action deranges the relationship between the ability of business firms to spend for labor, on the one side, and wage rates, on the other. It is not possible to have full employment when the government causes a cut in payroll spending and yet insists that each worker receive as much pay as before. Reduced payrolls could employ as many workers as larger payrolls, but only at correspondingly reduced wages per worker. This last is precisely what labor legislation and similar government interference prevent.

Thus, unemployment and the lack of employment opportunity are not the result of any fundamental or metaphysical lack of employment opportunity, but of the government's violation of the freedom of opportunity with respect to employment. That is, first the government creates the boom-bust cycle, and then, when the bust comes, it prohibits businessmen and wage earners from offering and accepting the wage rates that would enable them to exploit the limitless employment opportunities that reality offers to the point of establishing full employment.

The violation of freedom of opportunity is also what underlies the problems described under the head of racial discrimination. Their solution, too, would follow from the establishment of freedom of opportunity. For example, under the freedom of opportunity an impoverished black youth would be able to take a low-paying job, if that is the best he can find, and then with the experience and skill he gains from that job go on to something better. It means that he would be able to keep the income he earns from that job and, if he wishes, save it to buy a taxicab or any other kind of business he can afford and so further increase his ability to earn money. By the same token, his potential employers and customers would be free to exploit the opportunities afforded by his willingness to work and then go into business for himself. No one would be debarred from taking advantage of the opportunities reality offers either by so-called prolabor legislation, by licensing laws, or by any other laws representing the initiation of physical force.[1]

I stated that opportunities are themselves products. In any given instance an opportunity is the result of a combination of external circumstances and the skills and abilities an individual possesses, such that he is able to exploit the circumstances to his advantage. An opportunity is a product in the sense that the skills and abilities an individual possesses are the result of his successful exploitation of previous opportunities.

It must be realized that opportunities are never a matter merely of external circumstances that are served up on a plate, as it were. They always depend on what the individual himself brings to the external circumstances in the way of skills and abilities. These skills and abilities in turn are never the automatic result of the individual's genetic inheritance and or upbringing. They are the cumulative product of what the individual has done with his life up to that point. They reflect his initial choices to use his genetic inheritance to deal with external circumstances in ways that developed certain skills and abilities, and then further choices to use those skills and abilities to deal with further external circumstances in ways that developed also further skills and abilities, and so on up to the present moment.

For example, a child who chooses to use his mind to learn arithmetic thereby creates an indispensable precondition for the potential opportunity to learn algebra. Unless and until he learns arithmetic, there can be no possibility of any opportunity for him to learn algebra. If he does learn arithmetic and then, when he is confronted with the opportunity of learning algebra, successfully exploits it too, he creates a necessary internal basis for the further opportunity of learning calculus. And so on.

It is similar with regard to employment. The individual who exploits the opportunity to become a worker in a factory thereby creates a possible basis for his later on becoming a foreman there. If he becomes a foreman, he creates a possible basis for later promotion to a higher managerial position, and so on. Of course, he will have to expand his abilities in each of these jobs and possibly acquire other skills off the job, as well, perhaps by going to night school, for example. The principle is that opportunity presents itself as the rungs of a ladder. Each rung is open only to those who have climbed within reach by ascending the previous rungs.

Once things are viewed in this light, the notion of the advocates of equality of opportunity that opportunities are a matter of environmental circumstances, or environmental circumstances combined with genetic inheritance, appears absurdly inadequate. It is actually ludicrous to think that what a person does is the outcome merely of his environment and genes. In between the environment and the genes are a lifetime of choices, each of which has a vital bearing on the individual's ability to deal with his environment and to make further choices. In between the environment and the genes is the whole life of the person as a being who functions on a level above that of an automaton.

It is not necessary that people make the choices that develop their skills and abilities at any precise moment. There is considerable leeway. And it is never completely too late to start. For example, someone can learn to read even in old age and then begin rapidly to build on that foundation.

In a free society, with its abundance of opportunities, with no fixed deadline on the process of developing one's skills to better exploit them, all talk of inequality of opportunity must be judged as just so much whining and excuse-making. In such a society, everyone, whatever his starting point in life, is able to raise himself very far, if that is what he chooses to do. He can miss many, many opportunities, and still there will be more. He can begin improving his ability to exploit them at any time, and start moving up from that moment.

It is true that in such a society if two individuals were born equal in every respect, except that one had richer parents than the other, and if they both actively and consistently chose to develop their skills and abilities from birth on, the one with the richer parents would probably always be ahead of the one with the poorer parents. But far from representing any kind of embarrassment to a free society, it is perfectly just that things be this way. The advantages of the individual with the richer parents would not prevent the one with the poorer parents from rising, and rising not only very high, but without any fixed limit. It is simply the case that wealth *is* beneficial, and if everything else is *in fact* the same, it makes a difference. But what else is wealth for, if not to provide benefits? (And, more fundamentally, what are parents for, if not to provide every possible benefit to their children? One of the ugliest consequences of the equality-of-opportunity doctrine is that it actually causes some parents deliberately to do less for their children than they otherwise would, on the grounds that other parents are unable to do as much, and thereby willfully to default on their responsibilities as parents.) Furthermore, everyone, non-heirs as well as heirs, benefits from the capital that is accumulated in order to be passed on to heirs. The nonheir is thus able to achieve more than he would have in the absence of the institution of inheritance, even if that is less than what someone else can achieve who is both equally capable in every respect and has the benefit of an inheritance.

The way this principle applies in the present instance is not only that the nonheir has the benefit of a more abundant supply of products and a greater demand for his labor by virtue of the existence of capital accumulated because of the institution of inheritance, but also that he can benefit specifically in his potential capacity as a businessman and capitalist himself. In the case of the two boys who grow up with equal ability while one has the advantage of money, that advantage can enable the one without the money to make his own fortune, even if it is a smaller fortune than the one who begins with the money. For example, suppose the two of them become partners in business. If neither of them had capital, both would be equal partners, because they are equally talented. But neither of them would be able to get very far, or at least not nearly as soon, because of their lack of capital. If one of them has the necessary capital to contribute to their business, he will have more than a fifty percent share in their partnership, but the one with the smaller share will also be better off now. He will have, say, forty percent or thirty percent of a business that now earns two, three, or five times more profits because of the capital contributed to it, with the result that his absolute share is greater. He must have more than he otherwise would have had, or he will not enter into the partnership.

Now, of course, the real fact is that individuals are not born perfectly equal in all respects but the wealth of their parents, and they do not make the same choices in connection with developing their skills and abilities. Time and again, there are individuals born to poorer parents, to parents badly deficient not only in wealth, but in education, knowledge, and even character; individuals whose own endowment at birth or in childhood is not only not exceptional, but possibly deficient in some important respects. Yet, over the course of their lives, these individuals manage to far outstrip in their accomplishments practically everyone else, despite their having begun under such seemingly insuperable disadvantages.

What enables them to do this is making the choice and the effort to exploit as far as they can whatever opportunities present themselves for self-improvement. Once they begin to do this, they actually do begin to improve themselves. And now, when they face the world, they are better equipped than before. And because they are better equipped, there are more opportunities for self-improvement open to them than there were before. They seize these further opportunities, thereby further improving themselves and their subsequent ability to act and to seize opportunities. And so on, year after year.

What happens is that these individuals engage in a personal, internal process very similar to capital formation in the economy of a country. They use the means at their disposal to *build* the personal attributes—intellectual, psychological, moral, and physical—required for further success. And then they use the personal attributes they have constructed thus far to further construct such attributes. It is similar in principle to the process of a poor farmer scrimping and straining to obtain an additional supply of seed; of then using the larger supply of seed to produce a bigger crop the following year, from which a much greater supply of seed can be obtained for the year after that, and so on. It is similar to the economy of a whole country working very hard and saving very heavily to be able to make iron and steel available for the construction of the first railroads and steel mills, and then with the aid of those first railroads and steel mills being able to produce more of practically everything, including more and better railroads and steel mills.

Concentration on building up the means of further action, whether internal and personal or external and material, produces exponentially increasing results. Each success serves to increase the capabilities for further action, which makes possible still greater success. Those who concentrate heavily on these efforts rapidly improve, while those who neglect them stagnate or decline. It is on these principles that we can understand both such things as how Japan, so poor and backward a generation or two ago, can now be within sight of economically overtaking the United States, and how Demosthenes, the ancient Athenian who began as a stutterer, could become a great orator, and how, again and again, in a free society poor boys grow up to become rich and famous.

The secret of the success of the poor boys is contained in that old but very accurate expression that is so seldom heard today: *the self-made man.* Those poor boys build themselves into the kind of men capable of achieving great success. (While custom and tradition apply the principle to boys and men, it should go without saying that the principle applies no less to girls and women. There are self-made women, as well as men.)

The following example, perhaps, can help in understanding how by building themselves into the right kind of men such poor boys ultimately outstrip even those with the greatest advantages at birth. Thus, imagine two boys, one the newborn son of a highly educated millionaire; the other, the newborn son of a poor, uneducated coal miner. To most people, it seems that the millionaire's son has such great advantages that he can never be overtaken. But this is not so. And the reason why not can be seen in terms of a few conceptual snapshots, as it were, of the two boys at different stages of their development.

At birth, neither of them is capable of very much of anything. All of their capabilities remain to be developed. The millionaire's son is not capable of jumping out of his crib and using his father's millions to make more millions. If he is ever to have that ability, he will first have to develop it.

By age six or seven, say, the two boys have developed certain attitudes toward acquiring knowledge, and other important attributes, too, of course. But, for simplicity's sake, we will focus just on this aspect and its possible ramifications. If the poorer boy recognizes the value of knowledge and the necessity of making his best effort to acquire it, while the richer boy does not, the poorer boy has gained an advantage that can become of growing significance over the years. By age fourteen or fifteen, perhaps, the poorer boy has acquired an important body of knowledge that the richer boy has not. He understands algebra, trigonometry, and something of physics and chemistry. The richer boy has no real understanding of these subjects. By age twenty or twenty-two, the poorer boy is capable of working as an engineer, say, and making a significant contribution to the profits of anyone who employs him. The richer boy, on the other hand, can only be employed either in a menial capacity or at the expense of his father, who must continue to support him under the guise of giving him a salary, or who must provide for some associate to pay a fictitious salary, and compensate that associate in some form.

By age thirty, if he is really talented, the poorer boy has developed some significant ideas which have earned him some significant sums of money and have enabled him to start his own business. He now possesses a capacity for earning money which exceeds the richer boy's. The richer boy may still have vastly more money and earn a larger absolute amount, but the poorer boy is in a position to earn it now at a much faster rate. For the poorer boy's money is under his own, intelligent control and can earn a high rate of profit. The richer boy's money is either in his own, incompetent hands, in which case he can rapidly lose it, or it is in the hands of others who are more competent but who pay him only a relatively modest rate of interest or dividends. As the years go by, with the poorer boy earning a fifty, seventy-five, or one hundred percent annual rate of profit, and plowing back almost all of it, while the richer boy earns a three, four, or five percent rate of interest or dividends and consumes almost all of it, the poorer boy becomes the richer man.

This, in briefest essence, is how it actually happens that in a free society penniless newcomers are able to overtake and surpass even those with the greatest inherited wealth.

It cannot be stressed too strongly in this connection how critical is the element of freedom of opportunity. In order to succeed, the poorer boys must have the freedom to earn the highest rates of profit they can and to keep those profits. They must also be free of government controls and regulations, which can easily prevent them from ever getting started, by placing innumerable bureaucratic obstacles in their way, such as causing unnecessary delays, requiring unnecessary staffs of lawyers, accountants, and clerks that they are unable to afford, and by diverting their valuable time and efforts from serious work to contending with the arbitrary power and sheltered incompetence of government officials.

Now it is also true that the success of the poorer boys depends on their being able to obtain education. But this certainly does not mean that a case is made for public education of any kind. The kind of men and boys I have described grasp very early the value of acquiring knowledge and make it their business to find opportunities for acquiring it. Public education, on the other hand, by removing all incentives of profit and loss and all possibility of genuine competition in education, and by thus sheltering inefficiency and incompetence along with making improvement almost impossible, creates a system of instruction so poor that compulsion is the only means of keeping most of the students in attendance. And because people, including children, are not automatons programmed by a combination of genes and their environment, the system of forcing books and lectures on unwilling minds just does not work.

For the kind of men and boys I have described, public education is unnecessary. What is necessary, or, more correctly, would be extremely helpful to them, and would be far more efficient and effective for everyone, is *the freedom of education,* combined with the availability of private, voluntarily supported merit scholarships, and also the freedom of working and earning money to pay for education. People do not generally realize the extent to which the present system of public education destroys the freedom of opportunity with respect to education. By making educational innovations virtually impossible through government controls on curricula, faculty qualifications, and teaching methods, and requiring that competition take place against a subsidized competitor who does not charge, countless educational innovations that might have been made have not been made. People have been prohibited or prevented from exploiting the opportunities they perceive for improvement in education. The further opportunities that those improvements would have made possible for students have thus been prevented from coming into being.

We have a situation today where the law both prevents better, more economical forms of education from being offered and prevents students from earning the means of paying for education, by making it almost impossible for anyone under the age of eighteen to obtain any kind of meaningful job. Our present system is one of almost systematic opposition to the freedom of opportunity with respect both to education and to the subsequent achievement of prosperity. On an increasing scale, it prevents people from exploiting the opportunities open to them, and thereby prevents the creation of further opportunities that would be available not only to them but to those with whom they dealt. In preventing the development of a better, more efficient educational system, it prevents the opportunities that such a system would have afforded to students from coming into existence. In preventing the acquisition of fortunes, it prevents the opportunities that those fortunes would have afforded to workers and suppliers in the form of a demand for labor and capital goods, and to customers, in the form of more and better products produced.

These last observations bring out a further important principle pertaining to opportunities that is consistent with the whole nature of economic inequality under capitalism and with the synergistic nature of a division-of-labor society: namely, each person's successful exploitation of the opportunities open to him creates further opportunities not only for himself, but for those with whom he deals. In other words, with respect to opportunities one man's gain is the gain of others. The losses caused by the violation of freedom of opportunity represent losses to everyone.

Summary

The notion of equality of opportunity, however innocent it may sound at first, is actually vicious and absurd. In its logically consistent form, it implies the destruction of the institution of the family, the implementation of a governmental program of eugenics, and the elimination or destruction of every personal attribute that represents an advantage of one person over others.

In a positive vein, what has been shown is that what is actually important in connection with opportunities is the establishment of a free society and its corollary the freedom of opportunity. In such a society, the individual is free to exploit the virtually limitless opportunities offered by the combination of his nature and the nature of the world. He must pick and choose among them. And he progressively creates better and better opportunities for himself by successfully exploiting the best of the opportunities available to him at any given time.

In such a society, the notion of equality of opportunity reveals itself as absurdly irrelevant, as nothing more than an excuse for not taking advantage of the opportunities one has and for not creating better ones. In such a society, everyone can rise no matter what his starting point or present position, and again and again people of the most humble origins overtake and surpass those who begin with seemingly insuperable advantages.

What is required for everyone to be able to succeed and, at the same time, represents full justice, is not equality of opportunity, but freedom of opportunity. The successful exploitation of opportunities that freedom makes possible is the basis of each individual's being able to rise and create better opportunities not only for himself, but also for those with whom he deals.

Notes and References

1. See Reisman, George, "Capitalism: The Cure for Racism," *The Intellectual Activist,* Vol. II, nos. 15–17, 20; Vol. III, nos. 1, 2 (March, April, May, September, October, November 1982). Reprinted as a pamphlet (New York, NY: *The Intellectual Activist,* 1982.)

27

THE *SINE QUA NON* OF ENDURING FREEDOM

John W. Robbins*

Hans Sennholz is a greater defender of freedom and free enterprise than most of his teachers, peers, and students. The reason is simple, though little mentioned in polite society: A logically competent defense of a free society requires divinely revealed information; all other defenses fail. Sennholz, almost alone among eminent free enterprise economists, rests his defense of a free society on revelation.

Failed Defenses

There are four principal methods of defending a free society: economics, natural law, utilitarianism, and Biblical revelation. In this essay, I shall briefly point out some of the fallacies in the first three defenses, beginning with economics.

Economics. A competent defense of freedom and free enterprise cannot rest on Austrian economics, Chicagoan economics, Keynesian economics, or any other body of economic theory. The reason is quite simple: *Wertfreiheit.* Economics, as a value-free science, simply is not and cannot be a source of values. Like physics, economics describes (or purports to describe) what is, not what ought to be. An economist *qua* economist, even (or especially) if he be the purest Austrian, cannot logically say that free markets, wealth, and increasing productivity are good, or that price controls, shortages, and unemployment are bad; at best he can only point out the consequences of price controls and free markets. An Austrian economist cannot logically say that John Maynard Keynes was

*Dr. Robbins is president of the Trinity Foundation and the author of several books.

wrong in preferring the short run to the long run. An economist cannot even say that economics is good. Economics can establish no values, including its own. An economist, *qua* economist, can make no ethical statements whatever. He can, however, give technical advice; and the better the economist, the better the advice. If a ruler wishes to impoverish a people, he would do well to listen to his Austrian advisers: they would be able to advise him how best to do it.

Utilitarianism. Since economics is a descriptive science, those interested in defending a free society must find their means of defense elsewhere. Ludwig von Mises chose utilitarianism. It was an odd choice for a refugee from totalitarianism, for if utilitarianism could justify any political regime, it would surely be totalitarianism. The "greatest good of the greatest number" is a slogan that has been used to justify all sorts of (at the time) politically correct murders and depredations in the twentieth century. But utilitarianism, though it purports to offer ethical guidance, is an ethical failure. It can provide no ethical guidance, for the calculations of pains and pleasures that it requires are simply impossible.[1] Utilitarianism commits the naturalistic fallacy as well, for the fact that men are motivated to act by pain and pleasure does not imply that they ought to.

Natural law. Other students of Mises have chosen some form of natural law theory as the basis for their defense of a free society. But natural law, whether in its Aristotelian, Stoic, Thomistic, or Lockean form, rests on a logical blunder of the first order, first pointed out by David Hume: Natural law theory violates the rule that conclusions of arguments can contain no more than the premises.

John Locke unwittingly illustrated the naturalistic fallacy when he wrote that persons in the state of nature, "being all equal and independent, no one ought to harm another in his Life, Health, Liberty, or Possessions."[2] If the premises of an argument are descriptive (as in Locke's statement), the conclusion must also be descriptive. *Ought* cannot be derived from *is.* The Marquis de Sade illustrated what happens when one tries to base ethics on nature. It is not surprising that natural law has been used by various natural lawyers to reach various conclusions on such issues as the rights of women, children, and animals; slavery, abortion, infanticide, and marriage. Natural law, being unwritten, is very much a wax nosc that can be used to "justify" any conclusion one prefers.[3] Actually, of course, it justifies no action and offers no ethical guidance. Natural law is not a logically competent defense of a free society.

A Logically Competent Defense

In contrast to his secular colleagues, Sennholz rests his defense of a free society on information revealed by God. In that, he has displayed far more perspicacity than most other contemporary apologists for freedom.

In a 1987 book, *Debts and Deficits,* he wrote, "A [political and economic] reform ... would have to restore the harmony of interests and repair moral standards. It would have to rebuild the economic order on the old foundation of the Eighth Commandment—Thou shalt not steal—and the Tenth—Thou shalt not covet anything that is thy neighbor's."[4] In a discussion of Social Security, he wrote: "When public assistance seems to be called for, the children of a retired worker should be given an opportunity to contribute to the support of their parents. As parents are responsible for their children, so are children responsible for their parents. No Social Security System should eradicate this moral law and Biblical Commandment."[5]

Discussing the burden that AIDS is placing on government and health and welfare programs, Sennholz has written: "In ages gone, when moral obligations meant conformity to the will of God, carriers of contagious diseases who knowingly and willingly infected other individuals, and thereby inflicted great suffering and early death on others, would have been treated as criminals, yea, even as murderers, and been promptly quarantined from the healthy community...."[6]

Sennholz uses Christ's story of the Good Samaritan to make another point: "A helper and benefactor to the unfortunate and poor, the Good Samaritan binds the wounds, nurses the sick, and helps them get back on their feet. He *does not* call for government programs that make poverty a permanent social institution playing a central role in politics. He *does not* favor progressive income taxation, nor depend on poverty administrators consuming the lion's share of the poverty budget, or poverty politicians enacting minimum wage laws, occupational licensing, and union power or privilege. To be a helper indeed is to lend a friendly hand to a needy person; it is personal effort and sacrifice."[7]

In one of his most recent works, *Three Economic Commandments,* Sennholz asserts that "Both economic systems [capitalism and socialism] rest on the foundation of an ethical order that provides answers to questions such as: Why and when is an economic act called 'good' or 'bad', 'right' or 'wrong?' What standard of conduct is acceptable and commendable or distasteful and repugnant? What is virtue in economic life?

> The market order or capitalism finds its answers in the Judeo-Christian code of morality. Private ownership in production is squarely based on the Ten Commandments. It obviously rests on the Eighth commandment: Thou shalt not steal. The private-ownership system also builds on the solid foundation of the Sixth commandment: Thou shalt not kill, which includes every form of coercion and violence.... To freely exchange goods and services, the contracting parties must not deceive each other. They must not bear false witness, which is the Ninth commandment of the Decalogue.[8]

These quotations from Sennholz's writings—and there are many more—clearly teach that it is information revealed in the Bible that forms the basis for capitalism and freedom. It is the purpose of this essay to summarize some of the Biblical information on the nature, power, and limits of government; specifically, what role government should play in money, banking, and foreign affairs.

The Hebrew Republic

The Old Testament, in particular the book of I Samuel, is the oldest textbook in political freedom. Absent from its pages are the communism of Plato, the fascism of Aristotle, and the democratic totalitarianism of Rousseau. Written about 1000 B.C., the book of I Samuel may be the first handbook in republican political theory.

God established a model government in ancient Israel, and it is the only government for which he gave explicit rules. While many of those rules applied solely to ancient Israel, cities of refuge, for example, others apply to all governments. The judicial laws of Israel expired with that nation, but it may be possible to discern general principles in the Old Testament laws that may be applied to modern governments.

As for the form of government, God established a republic in Israel. The nation was divided into twelve tribes, much as the United States is divided into fifty states. Each tribe had its own territory and border; each had its own local government; and the nation as a whole had a national government. There was no king; there was no powerful central government. The government consisted mostly of judges; there was no legislature to create new laws each year, only judges to settle disputes in accord with the laws that God had already given.[9] There was no standing army. There was no military draft or national service. Education was not a function of government but of parents, schools, and synagogue. Charity was handled privately. Taxes were extremely low. Money, gold and silver, was provided by private merchants, not the government.

The remarkable thing about this political arrangement is that it apparently was unique in ancient times, at least in the Middle East. This very uniqueness became an objection to it during the time of the prophet Samuel. The people of Israel rebelled against their model government. The story is told in I Samuel 8:1-18:

> Now it came to pass when Samuel was old that he made his sons judges over Israel. The name of his firstborn was Joel, and the name of his second, Abijah; they were judges in Beersheba. But his sons did not walk in his ways; they turned aside after dishonest gain, took bribes, and perverted justice.
>
> Then all the elders of Israel gathered together and came to Samuel at Ramah, and said to him, "Look, you are old, and your sons do not walk in your ways. Now make for us a king to judge us like all the nations."
>
> But the thing displeased Samuel when they said, "Give us a king to judge us." So Samuel prayed to the Lord. And the Lord said to Samuel, "Heed the voice of the people in all that they say to you; for they have not rejected you, but they have rejected me, that I should not reign over them.... Now therefore, heed their voice. However, you shall solemnly forewarn them, show them the behavior of the king who will reign over them."
>
> So Samuel told all the words of the Lord to the people who asked him for a king. And he said, "This will be the behavior of the king who will reign over you: He will take your sons and appoint them for his own chariots and to be his horsemen, and some will run before his chariots. He will appoint captains over his thousands and captains over his fifties, he will set some to plow his ground and reap his harvest, and some to make his weapons of war and equipment for his chariots."

"He will take your daughters to be perfumers, cooks, and bakers. And he will take the best of your fields, your vineyards, and your olive groves, and give them to his servants. He will take a tenth of your grain and your vintage, and give it to his officers and servants. And he will take your menservants and your maidservants and your finest young men and your donkeys, and put them to his work. He will take a tenth of your sheep. And you will be his servants. And you will cry out in that day because of your king whom you have chosen for yourselves, and the Lord will not hear you in that day."

Despite this detailed and explicit warning from God, the people of Israel persisted in their demand to have a king "like all the nations." So God instructed Samuel to give them what they wanted. In Augustinian terms, big government is both the result of, and the punishment for, sin.

God's warning against monarchy makes it clear that God despises all monarchies: The people of Israel rejected God as their invisible king in favor of a visible, human king. This account in I Samuel makes it clear that human kings, powerful governments, are ersatz gods; they are idols of a wayward people. Subsequent verses in I Samuel repeat God's disapproval of monarchy: "But you have today rejected your God, who himself saved you out of all your adversities and your tribulations, and you have said to him, 'No, but set a king over us!'"(10:19). "'Is today not the wheat harvest? I will call to the Lord, and he will send thunder and rain, that you may perceive and see that your wickedness is great, which you have done in the sight of the Lord, in asking a king for yourselves.' So Samuel called to the Lord, and the Lord sent thunder and rain that day.... And all the people said to Samuel, 'Pray for your servants to the Lord your God, that we may not die; for we have added to all our sins the evil of asking a king for ourselves'"(12:17-19).

But God's warning was directed at more than monarchy: It is a warning against big government generally, a warning of what happens when God's model government, a republic of limited powers, is rejected. Rather than the governors being servants of the people, the people become servants of the governors. There is an echo of I Samuel in the New Testament:

But there was also rivalry among them [Christ's disciples] as to which of them should be considered the greatest. And He said to them, "The kings of the Gentiles exercise dominion over them, and those who exercise authority over them are called 'benefactors.' But not so among you; on the contrary, he who is greatest among you let him be as the younger, and he who governs as he who serves." (Luke 22:24-26).

The American notion that government ought to the servant of the people, not exercise dominion over them, may be traced directly to I Samuel 8 and Luke 22.

Taking

In the warning God gives the Israelites through the prophet Samuel he uses the phrase "he will take" six times. The monarchy, the strong central government demanded by the people, will be a tyrannical government. The king will take:

...their sons and their daughters; their best fields, vineyards and olive groves; a tenth of their grain and vintage; their menservants, their maidservants, their finest young men and their donkeys; a tenth of their sheep; and the people themselves to be his servants.

Through this warning we can understand more clearly what the Hebrew republic was like, for none of the evils about which God warned the Israelites characterized the republic. I Samuel is the earliest historical account that contains such a detailed analysis of the overweening powers of big government and explains the powers of such a government as the result of a defection from the divinely revealed model government.

Notice that the people of Israel demanded a change in the form of their government because of corruption among Samuel's sons. Rather than eliminating the corrupt officials, as they ought to have done, they blamed the system of government itself and exchanged their unique republic for the pagan system of monarchy.

The king they demanded would take their sons for himself, for his chariots, to run before his chariots, to be captains in his armies, and to work for him growing food and making weapons. The primary difference between the Hebrew republic and the later monarchy was what we have come to call a military-industrial complex. The growth of this establishment would begin with a draft and national service, for the king would need enormous quantities of cheap labor to sustain his war machine.

The draftees would be the servants of the king. Some would work closely with him; others would be part of his personal entourage and palace guard. A standing army would be established for the first time—there would be captains of thousands and captains of fifties. Chariots, which at that time were offensive weapons, would be added for the first time to Israel's defense forces. Other draftees would work to support this military machine, tending the crops in the fields the king had taken from the people, reaping the harvests for the army and the bureaucracy, and making weapons of war and equipment for the king's chariots.

The first warning that God gives to the Israelites who were demanding a king is a warning against the militarism of the king. Militarism is not an exclusive characteristic of monarchies but it is a trait of all large governments, whether they be called monarchies, people's democracies, or welfare states. The military draft, a standing army, weapons factories, a large government bureaucracy, large government farms—all these were absent from the Hebrew republic, and all were disapproved by God.

But this military-agricultural-industrial complex was merely the first of the oppressions the king would impose on the people. He would compel their sons to serve him, and he would take their daughters as well. They would feed his troops, his bureaucracy, his weapons makers, and his own appetites: "He will take your daughters to be perfumers, cooks, and bakers." The taking of both sons and daughters for the king's service would be the monarchy's version of national service.

Forced labor, however, would not be enough to support the new central government. There are three factors of production, and the new king would take all of them: labor, land, and capital; land and capital in the form of fields, vineyards, groves, and grain. Eminent domain, the right of the ruler to take private property for public use, became, for the first time, a policy of the government of ancient Israel.

After the king had taken all this property from the people of Israel he would give it to his favorites: "He will take a tenth of your grain and your vintage, and give it to his officers and servants" (I Samuel 8:15). Today we might call such a program a transfer or entitlement program, redistributing the wealth, or, echoing Bastiat, legalized theft. The last phrase is the most accurate, for God regarded these actions of the king as violations of the Eighth Commandment, "You shall not steal."

But the king, God warns, will take more. In addition to their children, land, and capital, he will take their servants, their servants' children, and even their farm animals "and put them to his work." When this massive program of compulsory labor and taxation is finally in place, God continues, "You will be his servants. And you will cry out in that day because of your king whom you have chosen for yourselves, and the Lord will not hear you in that day." The kind of government that God had created for ancient Israel, a government in which the governors were the servants of the governed, would be changed into a pagan form of government in which the rulers would exercise dominion over the people.

In his detailed warning to the ancient Israelites God explains, by way of contrast, the kind of things governors are not supposed to do. Rulers exceed their authority if they:

1. Use compulsory labor, either for their armies, bureaucracies, or households.
2. Establish standing armies.
3. Establish government production facilities.
4. Redistribute property.
5. Impose taxes of ten percent or more.
6. Nationalize the means of production.

From this warning we can see how far the United States has moved from the Biblical model: Our taxes are far higher than ten percent; they are closer to forty percent. Our government, although it is not drafting anyone at the moment, is registering young men for the draft, and it asserts its right to compel them to serve at any time. We have an enormous standing army of more than 2.5 million. There is an even larger federal bureaucracy, to say nothing of the state bureaucracies. Altogether, nearly twenty million people work for the local, state, and federal governments. The federal government owns factories, power plants, banks, and one-third of the land in the United States. More than half of the federal budget consists of transfer programs by which the government takes property from taxpayers and gives it to tax consumers. Our kind of government, in brief, is the one about which God warned the ancient Israelites.

The Hebrew Constitution

While I Samuel 8 establishes the limits of governmental power in a negative way by warning against the consequences of rejecting a republic and establishing a monarchy, Exodus 21-23 and some other important passages establish the limits of governmental power in another way, by telling rulers what they are permitted and required to do. As one examines these chapters, one is struck by the preponderance of laws about domestic and internal affairs. There are laws about murder, accidental killing, kidnapping, assaulting and cursing one's parents, negligence, stealing, trespass, seduction and rape, witchcraft, idolatry, lying, bribery, and the treatment of foreigners. There is little mention of either foreign or commercial relations.

This dearth of information is in itself important. It means, first of all, that the Hebrew republic was to be primarily concerned with its own affairs, not with either economic or foreign interventionism. It was supposed to mind its own business. Its business was to see that justice be done within its own borders. The judges of the republic were not to be concerned with establishing similar governments elsewhere, even in neighboring states, nor with rectifying the enormous injustices that must have occurred daily in the pagan nations that surrounded the republic. The borders of Israel were the limits of the jurisdiction of the republic. Even within those borders, government was not to concern itself with commercial regulations; its primary interest in commerce was to punish fraudulent weights and measures.

The State and Money

In his book *Honest Money, The Biblical Blueprint for Money and Banking,* Gary North makes an excellent point: "There is nothing in the Bible that indicates that gold and silver became money metals because Abraham, Moses, David, or any other political leader announced one afternoon: 'From now on, gold is money!' ...the State didn't create money."[10] This is quite true. The Bible is the oldest and most reliable history book we have, and there is nothing in it to indicate that the State originally created money. Rather, the evidence is that money originated in the market, when merchants offered their own coins and weights of metal in trade.

Those who think that the use of gold or silver as money evolved relatively late in human history might learn something from the history of Abraham. About two thousand years before Christ, he paid for a field by weighing out 400 shekels of silver. The account is given in Genesis 23.[11]

Honesty. From this example of Abraham we see that money in the Bible is a weight of metal. *Talents* were certain weights of silver. Now this historical fact does not require modern money to be a weight of silver or even of metal. But it does lead to another major teaching of the Bible on money: If money consists of weights, and throughout history it usually has, then the money must be full-bodied; less than honest weight constitutes fraud. There are several passages on this point in the Bible:

> You shall do no injustice in judgment, in measurement of length, weight, or volume. You shall have just balances, just weights, a just ephah, and a just hin: I am the Lord your God, who brought you out of the land of Egypt (Leviticus 19:35-36). The Lord abhors dishonest scales, but accurate weights are his delight (Proverbs 11:1).
>
> The Lord detests differing weights, and dishonest scales do not please him (Proverbs 20:23).
>
> Do not have two differing weights in your bag—one heavy, one light. Do not have two differing measures in your house—one large, one small. You must have accurate and honest weights and measures, so that you may live long in the land the Lord your God is giving you. (Deuteronomy 25:13-15).

Any use of fraudulent weights was subject to the penalties imposed for theft: at least double restitution, with the ultimate penalty being required for recidivism. The dishonesty of fraudulent weights is a case of the broader principle that nothing is to be misrepresented.

Fractional Reserves. If modern money does not consist of weights of metal, and it need not, it must nevertheless not misrepresent itself. The Biblical requirement is not for metal money and one hundred percent gold reserves, but for honesty. So long as private (not government) paper money is not misrepresented by its owners, it is clearly acceptable. Government paper money, on the other hand, even when backed by gold or silver, is always wrong, for government has no authority to print money.

Retribution, not Regulation. There is another principle besides honesty underlying these rules. It would seem that there were no regulatory police in ancient Israel; the buyers and sellers were responsible for making sure that they were not being cheated, and if detected in fraud, a person was subject to stiff penalties. Biblical law follows the principle of punishing wrongdoers rather than trying to regulate everyone in the hope of preventing wrong-doing. That is why Paul writes in Romans 13 that the sole purpose of civil government is to punish evil-doers.

Legal Tender. Another thing that follows from the restricted Biblical role of government with regard to money and banking is the absence of legal tender laws. I wish to make clear what I mean by "legal tender," since it seems to have at least two different meanings. Of course, if a government is to collect taxes or payments of any sort, it must specify acceptable forms of payment. This is one meaning of "legal tender." In the early years of the American republic, this problem was solved by the government publishing a list of monies in which it would accept payment. It did not restrict payment to one form of money, but published a broad list of acceptable means of payment. The constitutionality of this form of legal tender was not challenged.

But there is another meaning of the phrase "legal tender": Usually it means that a creditor is compelled to accept whatever the government has declared to be tender as payment for outstanding debts. Each Federal Reserve note bears the words, "This note is legal tender for all debts public and private." Those words mean that a private creditor must accept them in payment for a debt. It makes little difference that the creditor may have a contract calling for payment in something else, for the courts do not, as a rule, order specific performance of contracts. Perhaps at one time they did. But today a creditor is compelled to accept the government paper as payment.

There is no warrant for this sort of legal tender in the Bible. Rather, the clear implication is that the parties to a contract may set the terms of the contract, so long as they are not illegal in themselves, and those terms must be obeyed. The Bible praises the man who makes a promise and keeps it, even though he might be injured by keeping it. It condemns the man who defaults on a deal, or seeks to substitute something of lesser value for that which he promised to deliver. Legal tender laws are an institutionalized form of defaulting on debts.

Mammon. Finally, there is another aspect of money and the Bible that we ought to consider: money as mammon. Everyone knows that the Bible strongly condemns mammon, and many people equate mammon with money. The two, however, are not the same. Mammon is money worshipped. That is why Christ said, "You cannot serve God and mammon." Mammon is money become an idol, and even beneficial things can become instruments of destruction if they are regarded more highly than they ought to be. The Bible condemns all forms of idolatry, including the idolatry of money. Ayn Rand did not understand this when she wrote her books, but I am sure that she has a better understanding of it now.

This Biblical view of money and banking is reflected in Hans Sennholz's 1985 book, *Money and Freedom,* in which he advocates the repeal of compulsory tender laws and concludes:

> Sound money and free banking are not impossible, they are merely illegal. That is why money must be deregulated.... In freedom, the money and banking industry can create sound and honest currencies, just as other free industries can provide efficient and reliable products.[12]

The State and Foreign Policy

Any adequate discussion of the foreign policy of ancient Israel must deal with several subjects: treaties, alliances, diplomacy, colonialism, espionage, and war. I shall discuss each of these briefly.

Treaties. In Exodus 23:20-33 there is an explicit command to Israel not to make treaties with the nations of Canaan: "You shall make no covenant with them, nor with their gods" (verse 32). God intended to destroy those nations, and he did not want Israel fraternizing with them. The command does not imply that all treaties are wrong, only that it was wrong for Israel to make treaties with the nations God was about to destroy. It was a command intended only for ancient Israel.

When treaties are made, however, they are to be kept, even if one is tricked into making the agreement. A treaty negotiated by Joshua with the Gibeonites resulted from his failure to follow God's instruction ("The men of Israel...did not ask counsel of the Lord," Joshua 9:14), and Joshua was deceived by the clever Gibeonites. Nevertheless, because the Israelites had sworn an oath, they were bound to keep it: "But the children of Israel did not attack them [the Gibeonites] because the rulers of the congregation had sworn to them by the Lord God of Israel. And all the congregation murmured against the rulers. Then all the rulers said to all the congregation, 'We have sworn to them by the Lord God of Israel; now therefore we may not touch them'" (Joshua 9:18–19).

Alliances. God's command to ancient Israel not to make treaties with its neighbors does, however, raise the question of the legitimacy of making treaties and forming alliances. On alliances the Bible seems to speak quite clearly: "Woe to those who go down to Egypt for help, and rely on horses, who trust in chariots because they are many, and in horsemen because they are very strong, but who do not look to the Holy One of Israel, nor seek the Lord.... Now the Egyptians are men, and not God; and their horses are flesh and not spirit. When the Lord stretches out his hand, both he who helps will fall, and he who is helped will fall down; they all will perish together" (Isaiah 31:1, 3). This seems to be a general condemnation of alliances and of trust in armies and weapons. The Bible disapproves of political and military alliances because they are acts of faith in weapons and soldiers, and not in God; and it discourages treaties because they are serious agreements that must be performed.

Diplomacy. The limitation on government-to-government contact in the Bible is so restrictive that embassies and permanent diplomatic missions were not authorized for the Hebrew republic. Rather, when the necessity arose, an emissary was dispatched for the specific purpose of carrying a message or discussing a problem. For example, after the Israelites had escaped from Egypt, Moses sent out emissaries to the King of Edom asking permission to pass through Edom: "Please let us pass through your country. We will not pass through fields or vineyards, nor will we drink water from wells; we will go along the king's highway; we will not turn aside to the right hand or to the left until we have passed through your territory" (Numbers 20:17). The king of Edom refused Moses's request, and "Thus Edom refused to give Israel passage through his territory; so Israel turned away from him" (verse 21).

There are two things that ought to be noticed about this account: the use of emissaries for specific and unavoidable negotiations, and the refusal of Moses as the leader of God's chosen people to cross the border of Edom without the Edomites' permission.

Even when ancient Israel was a monarchy, it seems that it had no ambassadors or embassies abroad: "Now Hiram king of Tyre sent his servants to Solomon, because he heard that they had anointed him king in place of his father, for Hiram had always loved David. Then Solomon sent word to Hiram" (I Kings 5:1-2). Even between friends, Hiram and David, there apparently were no permanent ambassadors. King Hiram had helped David build his house, but he sent messengers to Solomon. There were no permanent ambassadors even under the monarchy.

No provision was made for resident ambassadors and embassies in the model government, the Hebrew republic, and even the monarchy, apparently, did not enlarge its meddling in foreign affairs to the point of sending and receiving permanent representatives.

Espionage. A related foreign policy question is the matter of spies, for perhaps the predominant function of embassies today (and perhaps whenever they have been used) is espionage. Ancient Israel used spies, but only during war and for short periods of time. Just as there was no standing army, so there were no standing armies of spies and diplomats. God commanded Moses to "Send men to spy out the land of Canaan," one from each tribe (Numbers 13:2). Ten of the spies were worthless; two were useful. I suspect the same ratio has always held. Moses also sent spies to Jazer (Numbers 21:32), a Canaanite city. Joshua sent two spies to Jericho (Joshua 2:1).

Some of this spying was commanded by God, and perhaps all of it was, but we are not told that all of it was done at God's express command. But spying was used exclusively during wartime. Spying on other nations was not a normal, peacetime practice of either the Hebrew republic or the monarchy. It seems clear that spying on one's neighboring governments during peacetime, even more than maintaining embassies that harbor spies, is a form of prohibited foreign intervention. It can hardly be argued that God's command to Moses justifies the regular use of spies, for the command was very specific: Spy out the land of Canaan. Espionage, except during wartime, is not a proper function of government.

Colonialism. In the nineteenth century the phrase "white man's burden" was used to justify the colonial policies of the European nations. Because of his superior culture, intelligence, race, and learning, so the argument went, the white man has the burden of ruling the lesser breeds. Ancient Israel, by contrast, had no burden to rule over the benighted nations of the world. God's foreign policy, even when he was establishing a political state in the Middle East, was very limited in scope.

This was as it had to be: A government of limited domestic powers must also be a government of limited international powers. The proper concerns of foreign policy cannot exceed the proper concerns of government in general: the safety and freedom of the territory and people within its borders. Israel, though it was the only nation specially chosen by God, had no authority to liberate Egypt from the Pharaohs. If ancient Israel did not have such authority, even though it had specific commands from God and occupied a unique place in human history, far less does any modern nation have such authority.

War. God commanded the ancient Israelites at different times both to refrain from war as well as to attack certain nations. In Deuteronomy 2:5 God says, "Do not meddle with them [the children of Esau who lived in Seir], for I will not give you any of their land, no, not so much as one footstep.... You shall buy food from them with money, that you may eat; and you shall also buy water from them with money, that you may drink.... Do not harass Moab, nor contend with them in battle, for I will not give you any of their land" (verses 5, 6, 9). Continuing commercial relations are not forbidden, but continuing military and political relations are. Borders were instituted for the purpose of separating rulers, not peoples, from each other.

From all these considerations it is clear that the people, not the governors, play the major role in foreign relations. The governors are to settle disputes by negotiation, if possible, and by war if necessary and justifiable. Free trade and travel between nations is the rule. The absence of both resident ambassadors and spies is the norm.

In foreign policy, the role of government in ancient Israel was not to make the world, or even the Middle East, safe for theocracy. The nation was simply to occupy the land that God had given them. Had God not commanded them to do so, in specific detail, they would have had no authority to act even as they did.

Conclusion

It is not to Plato's *Republic* nor to Aristotle's *Politics*, not to the Greek city-states, nor the city and empire of Rome, and not to the

Code of Hammurabi or Solon that we must look for a model of good government and a competent defense of a free society, but to the Bible and the Hebrew republic. Because the Bible is divinely revealed information, it furnishes us with the principles we need to defend a free society.

Notes and References

1. See Clark, Gordon H., *A Christian View of Men and Things* (Jefferson, Maryland: The Trinity Foundation, 1991 [1952]); *Religion, Reason and Revelation* (Jefferson, Maryland: The Trinity Foundation, 1986 [1961]); and *Thales to Dewey: A History of Philosophy* (Jefferson, Maryland: The Trinity Foundation, 1989 [1957]) for some destructive analyses of utilitarianism and other ethical systems. It is remarkable that Ludwig von Mises, the economic genius who pointed out the impossibility of economic calculation under socialism, accepted utilitarianism and the possibility of hedonic calculation. Utilitarian calculation is even more absurd than socialist economic calculation.
2. *Two Treatises of Government,* Peter Laslett, editor (New York: New American Library, 1965), p. 31. John Locke tries to save his argument by appealing to Scripture. Modern natural lawyers generally make no such attempt.
3. The recent revival of natural law theory is more than remarkable; not only does it fly in the face of David Hume and logic, it ignores Charles Darwin and biology as well. If one accepts some variety of the theory of evolution (as many natural lawyers do), one has adopted a view of nature that undermines natural law theory: nature and nature's laws are constantly changing.
4. Sennholz, Hans F., *Debts and Deficits* (Spring Mills, PA: Libertarian Press, 1987), p. 164. See also page 44.
5. *Ibid.,* p. 166.
6. *Ibid.,* p. 170.
7. *Ibid.,* pp. 44-45.
8. Sennholz, Hans F., *Three Economic Commandments* (Spring Mills, PA: Libertarian Press, 1990), pp. 1-2.
9. Compare Leoni, Bruno, *Freedom and the Law* (Los Angeles, CA: Nash Publishing, 1972).
10. North, Gary, *Honest Money, The Biblical Blueprint for Money and Banking* (Tyler, TX: Institute for Christian Economics, 1986), page 22. For a review of this book, see "Money, Freedom, and the Bible," *The Trinity Review,* November/December 1989.
11. It is bizarre but not surprising that secular economists rely on fables about the origin of money while ignoring a reliable history book like the Bible.
12. Sennholz, Hans F., *Money and Freedom* (Spring Mills, PA: Libertarian Press, 1985), p. 83.

28

CHRISTIANITY AND FREEDOM

Rousas John Rushdoony*

We live in an age of illusions and fiction. At no other time in history have men given more time to fiction and myth. By means of films, television, novels, theater, and the media generally, we are now immersed in fiction. From time to time, we are told how many hours children and adults sit in front of a television set watching unreality masked as reality.

As a result, shadows have come to replace substance and reality for most people, something the news media exploits. For example, it is commonplace to equate the right to vote with freedom. The peoples of the Soviet Union and other tyrant states have had the "privilege" of voting all these years, but they have not been free. The forms of freedom, voting, legislative bodies, and other like "democratic" things mark many of the third world tyrannies, even as they did ancient Athens and republican Rome. Because of this, many assume that free societies existed then, and that they exist now in various parts of the world.

But our very definition of freedom has changed. Red China is a free country in that it is not under the rule of a foreign state, but the people are not free. The freedom of the state does not necessarily mean the freedom of the people, and it may in fact contradict it. The Founding Fathers of the United States hoped that its Constitution would be a chain binding down the power of the federal government. By means of court decisions, it is now being increasingly used to chain the people.

The word *totalitarian* is new, but the fact of totalitarianism is an old one. It was universal in pagan antiquity, and it is a central aspect of our reviving paganism. In the ancient state, there was no area of freedom; all kinds of activities were controlled by the state.

*Rev. Rushdoony is President of the Chalcedon Foundation.

There was no free economic activity; there were no unlicensed assemblies; there were no dissenters from the policies of state allowed outside the narrow ruling clique. The state was the ultimate order, man's only true society. In some ancient documents, it becomes apparent that a stateless man was a non-person. Moreover, a state license was required for any approved activity. Torture was routinely used; it disappeared in medieval law to re-appear with the Renaissance tyrants.

The state as the ultimate order was thus in some sense god on earth. In some instances, the person of the ruler was divine; in others, it was the office, and, with still others, the ruling class or race. Logically, there is no dissent where a god is concerned. As a result, no activity apart from his control or governance was possible or permitted.

Our English word *liturgy* comes from the Greek *leitourgia*, a public work. It had then as now reference to religion, but religion then was seen as a branch of state control; the Romans used religion, any religion in their case, as social cement, as a means of keeping the various peoples of the empire controlled and contented. No unlicensed cult could exist, and a necessary step toward gaining a license was to appear before the proper authority and testify, "Caesar is Lord," i.e., the ultimate god over us all.

It was at this point that Rome and the early church came into conflict. Christians refused to be licensed and were imprisoned and killed for refusing. In effect, they were guilty of treason. The Christian position was clearly stated by St. Paul, who, in Philippians 2:9-11, speaking of Jesus Christ, declared:

> 9. Wherefore God also hath highly exalted him, and given him a name which is above every name:
>
> 10. That at the name of Jesus every knee should bow, of things in heaven, and things in earth, and things under the earth;
>
> 11. And that every tongue should confess that Jesus Christ is Lord, to the glory of God the Father.

At this distance, it is hard for us to appreciate how radical and revolutionary this statement was and still is. Jesus Christ is a name, or a power, "which is above every name," above all earthly rulers. He is the cosmic emperor. In I Timothy 6:15, St. Paul describes Jesus Christ as "the blessed and only Potentate, the King of kings, and Lord of lords." Every king, Caesar, and emperor is below Him and under Him. The goal of history is then plainly stated: *every* knee is to bow to this divine King, and *every* tongue shall in due time confess that He is the cosmic ruler and Lord.

The implications of this were far-reaching. *First,* the Christian Church was an empire within the empire which declared its destiny to be the conqueror of the whole world for Christ (Matt. 28:18-20), and therefore more important than Rome and Caesar. The audacity of this faith appears, for example, in I Timothy 2:1-2:

> 1. I exhort, therefore, that first of all, supplications, prayers, and intercessions, and giving of thanks, be made for all men:
>
> 2. For kings, and for all that are in authority; that we may lead a quiet and peaceable life in all godliness and honesty.

In the Roman doctrine, intercessions and prayers, as well as thanks, were addressed to the emperor. Now these Christians were placing themselves above or on a footing with the emperor by praying for him. This was an unprecedented step, and it made clear that Christ was and is King indeed over all kings. Rome saw the church as an empire within the empire that had to be smashed. Moreover, St. Paul describes himself in I Corinthians 5:20, together with other Christian leaders, as "ambassadors for Christ." This was an assertion of a status beyond Roman law; one of the first words applied to the Christian community still remains in our English word *parish.* In its Latin original, *parochia* could mean the residence or area of a foreign embassy.

Second, while the Christian community sought to be law-abiding without declaring Caesar to be lord, they moved in terms of another law, God's law, and the whole Bible was seen as the law-word of the Creator-Sovereign. This meant that, while Christians could tell their oppressors, as Tertullian later did, that they were Caesar's most honest citizens and honest taxpayers, they were viewed as worse than other men because their faith, Lord, and law by-passed and in effect subverted the Roman Empire. Then as now the best citizens are the chosen victims of statism! (After all, who can pay more taxes than honest, hard-working men?) To believe in another king and another law was subversive to the Roman Empire.

Third, the early church was actually a government within the empire. It cared for the sick and needy, for widows and orphans, and for helpless aliens. It educated its own. In terms of I Corinthians 6, independent Christian courts, in which both parties contracted to abide by the decision, were established, and even pagans turned to them for justice. Captives were ransomed, abandoned babies picked up and reared, and so on and on. The church was governing better than Rome. Constantine the Great, on assuming sole power, ordered all bishops to wear in public the garb of a Roman magistrate so that people could appeal to them for justice. Bishops to this day retain variations of this official garb.

Fourth, this meant that the idea of a unitary state controlling all things, i.e., totalitarianism, was negated. This was a difficult lesson for converts to learn. Newly converted peoples and states in Europe and elsewhere wanted to restore the old pagan model of a unitary state. This included control of the church, against which the medieval church fought. Slowly and with difficulty, the idea that the state is not the umbrella under which all spheres of life had to exist began to take root. The state usually fought back bitterly, as witness the pretensions and claims of the Holy Roman Emperor, Frederick II. There have been numerous revivals of paganism over the centuries, during the medieval, Renaissance, and modern eras; all seek to establish again a unitary state controlling every sphere of life and thought.

All the same, a new order was developing. Very early, after the fall of Rome, merchants began to develop and determine their own rules of operation, merchants' law. At times, rulers intervened; at other times, the merchants paid protection money to rulers. Freedom to a degree was gained, although in the seventeenth century the monarchies gained exclusive jurisdiction. This was a step in line with the doctrine of the divine right of kings.

But the centuries-old battles for control and for freedom have not had a straight-line history. On the one hand, the Christian influence has militated against the unitary state. The starting phase of the rebellion against the Soviet power in Armenia was priest-inspired. In Romania, it was a Reformed pastor.

More importantly, the moral world has been turned upside down. The good state is not now Plato's radically totalitarian order; it is, however naively held, the belief in a free society. In this long history, the *church* has at times played a cowardly role, but the *faith* has maintained the subordinate status of the state to the triune God.

Fifth, many of the radically statist measures are increasingly openly pagan. The cult of Gaia, the earth mother, environmental paganism, and like movements are working to destroy freedom. In Australia, mining operations are being shut down by non-Christian, and anti-Christian groups, as violations of the holy ground and the sacred places of the Australian aborigines. In New Zealand, the Maoris and their friends are busily turning one area after another into holy ground. Paganism stresses man as a consumer and destroyer, not as a producer and creator under God. One of the initial environmental and anti-industrial manifestos in the United States has Christianity as the villain.

It was, however, Christians who, very early in the Christian era, began to reclaim the sea in the Netherlands and vastly increase the land area. It was also Christians who eliminated many desert and useless areas of Europe and made them successful agricultural and livestock areas. Some lords would give such useless lands to the monks to reclaim, and then take back the lands. Such activities were seen as a religious mandate to exercise dominion, and such texts as Isaiah 35:1–2 were used:

1. The wilderness and the solitary place shall be glad for them; and the desert shall rejoice, and blossom as the rose.

2. It shall blossom abundantly, and rejoice even with joy and singing: the glory of Lebanon shall be given unto it, the excellence of Carmel and Sharon, they shall see the glory of the LORD, and the excellency of our God.

It is well known that the log kept by Christopher Columbus in 1492 had many references to Isaiah; he believed he was called to fulfill the prophecies with respect to the far-off places and islands.

Sixth, by placing the triune God above all human powers, including the state, the Christian faith undermined the supreme authority of the state. The state was no longer man's ultimate authority: God who sits in judgment on all men also judges all the nations. This did not sit well with Enlightenment kings, who actually forbade the use of Mary's Magnificat in churches because of these "revolutionary" sentences therein:

51. He hath shewed strength with his arm; he hath scattered the proud in the imagination of their hearts.

52. He hath put down the mighty from their seats, and exalted them of low degree.

53. He hath filled the hungry with good things; and the rich he hath sent empty away. (Luke 1:51–53)

Christianity has given to men a concept of truth and of freedom which transcend this world. No human ruler nor court can define truth and freedom: God is not only the Creator but also the Definer.

Richard Sennett, in *Authority* (1980), said, "The need for authority is basic." We can add that, when it is not sought for in God, it will be assumed by men. Johann Fichte, rejoicing in the French Revolution, wrote in 1793 that it meant to him the overthrow of all who refused to agree with his strange version of freedom. He wrote,

> And once I throw you down, I will insult you, dishonor you, trample you under. Since you can be of no use to me, I will profit by my right of conquest to seek your total destruction.

From the French Revolution to the present-day revolutions, this has been the "new freedom." A higher court being denied, whatever the revolutionary regime decides is truth and freedom then governs. Shortly after World War II, U.S. Chief Justice Frederick Moore Vinson denied the validity of any higher law of God and paved the way for the steady diminution of freedom. Pagan authority is destructive to freedom, because it allows no dissent from the dominant human authority, usually the state—now also the university—with its emphasis on being "politically correct." The authority of God is inseparable from His justice, love, mercy, wrath, and all His many attributes. God's nature being unchanging, there is no change in His justice, nor in the freedom He gives to go to hell or to heaven. The state has its own version of heaven; it is determined that we shall all go there or else, and its version of heaven very emphatically resembles hell.

Seventh, there are two old American proverbs which are relevant here:

1) If we lose our freedom we have nothing else to lose; and 2) the grouch is the guardian of our freedom.

Perhaps these are over-statements, but there is a hard grain of truth to them. The Christian who wars against the growing neo-paganism and its statist faith is called worse than grouch usually. One of the earliest charges by Roman citizens against Christians appears in Acts 17:6–7:

> 6. And when they found them not, they drew Jason and certain brethren unto the rulers of the city, crying, "These that have turned the world upside down are come hither also."

7. Whom Jason hath received: and these all do contrary to the decrees of Caesar, saying that there is another king, one Jesus.

The rabble-rousers in Thessalonia had quickly grasped the implications of Christianity: another King, another law, a freedom from the state as the ultimate authority, and a freedom to live under God primarily, not under the state. Christianity was indeed turning the world upside down, even though many of its adherents have still not grasped that fact. It cannot live in peace with statism. Moral controls in most areas must replace state controls. Freedom must be a moral fact, not a state grant.

In Germany, by law, work councils composed of representatives of all workers were formed in enterprises. Management was excluded, although the councils' concerns are "social issues" and working conditions. This is the kind of "freedom" increasingly promoted everywhere, and it is death to liberty. According to Sennett, in one study in Yugoslavia in 1965 it was found that workers in "self-managing bureaucracies were far more alienated from their jobs than workers in more traditional settings." Such concepts of freedom, which violate moral property rights, do harm, not good.

The revolutionary, anti-Christian doctrines of freedom are today leading to tyrannies and evils. Morality then becomes class domination, and justice is sacrificed. Christian freedom means moral responsibility and a respect for the God-given immunities of others. The neo-pagan doctrine of freedom separates liberty from God's moral law to make it a class privilege. The result is a "warfare" society, a constant conflict of interests. Freedom is more than a matter of law or license: it is a moral premise which rests on faith in God's governing and transcendent order and law.

The enemies of freedom have a problem. Christianity has left its mark on all the world. It provides men with a premise for resistance, and for the rebirth of faith and freedom. The resistance to this rebirth is intense, but the rebirth is coming, and it shall prevail.

29

DEPOSIT INSURANCE, THE USE OF INFORMATION, AND THE CURRENT CRISIS IN THE FINANCIAL INDUSTRY

Gary G. Short*

The recent savings and loan crisis has focused attention once again on one of Dr. Hans Sennholz's long-term interests, money and banking. There has been a great deal of discussion on the problems in the savings and loan industry, and, more broadly, in the financial industry itself. While much of the current discussion finds the partial deregulation of insured depository institutions responsible for the current crisis, this position is remarkably unpersuasive, particularly for those economists, such as Dr. Sennholz, who have spent a lifetime examining the market economy. The investigation into the recent crisis has led also to an examination of the underlying institutional structure, including the federal deposit insurance system. The crisis has drawn attention to the seemingly never-ending dispute over the appropriate role of market discipline and governmental controls in regulating financial markets.

This paper briefly examines the historical background of the current federal deposit insurance system and considers the perverse incentives that this system has created, particularly in light of the manner in which deposit insurance has actually been administered. The paper also explores the potential operation of private deposit insurance and whether reforms are likely to be introduced to allow markets to price risks in this arena.

*Dr. Short is a partner in the law firm, Vinson and Elkins in Dallas, TX.

Background

The current structure of the U.S. financial industry is, in large measure, an outgrowth of the legislation adopted in response to the Great Depression. The Banking Act of 1933, commonly known as the Glass-Steagall Act, created the federal deposit insurance system, separated commercial and investment banking, prohibited banks from paying interest on demand deposits, and regulated interest on time and savings deposits. Thus, the federal deposit insurance system was created as part of an effort to reduce excessive risk-taking on the part of banks and to preclude deposit runs on banks.

The rationale for federal deposit insurance was, in part, to prevent runs on "good banks." The general concern was that if a "bad bank" failed and individuals lost their deposits, depositors at otherwise sound banks would panic and attempt to withdraw funds from the "good banks." This "panic" could cause the failure of the good banks as well as the bad banks. With the presence of deposit insurance, however, the depositors in the good banks would have no incentive to panic and destroy the good banks. In fact, Milton Friedman has argued that deposit insurance made the lender of last resort function of the Federal Reserve unnecessary.[1]

Federal deposit insurance is the regulatory structure through which depositors in banks and savings and loans are guaranteed the return of their deposits, up to a specified maximum (currently, $100,000). There can be little doubt that federal deposit insurance "works," in the sense that it does reduce the likelihood of banking "panics." When individuals are confident that their deposits are safe, then the fact that other financial institutions fail generally will not cause them to remove their deposits from solvent institutions.

Criticism of federal deposit insurance focuses on the role that this insurance plays in distorting the market pricing mechanism. The existence of deposit insurance reduces the incentives that individuals have to monitor the soundness of the financial institutions in which they make their deposits. Because depositors are guaranteed the return of their deposit, they are far less likely to consider the riskiness of the financial institution's investment portfolio. In this sense, federal deposit insurance subsidizes risk-taking by financial institutions. It is ironic that the legislation which was designed to reduce excessive risk-taking created perverse incentives for insured depository institutions to engage in excessive risk-taking.

Markets and Information

Austrian economists have emphasized the critical role that prices play in conveying information to market participants and the distortions in this flow of information that are engendered by various regulatory schemes.[2] In the case of federal deposit insurance, such insurance not only causes financial institutions to undertake excessive risk intentionally, but it prevents the institutions from receiving the necessary information to assess risk adequately. Thus, the federal deposit insurance system is yet another example of price distortion caused by government regulation.

The effect of the Glass-Steagall Act was to substitute supervisory and regulatory oversight for market discipline. The regulatory structure precluded the price system from conveying appropriate information to market participants. As an example, studies have shown that interest rates paid on certificates of deposit at competing financial institutions were not proportional to the riskiness of the institutions. Abstracting from the admittedly difficult (if not impossible) task of adequately measuring risk, the data have shown that riskier institutions have not had to pay higher interest rates than their more financially sound competitors.

Consider the factors that a potential depositor must take into account when deciding which financial institution to use. While there are clearly numerous factors to be examined, from location to price to available services, two of the more significant factors are the interest (the return on the investment) and the likelihood of receiving the promised interest and return of principal (the riskiness of the investment). Other things being equal, an individual will require a higher expected return on an investment to compensate for greater perceived risk.

In a world without deposit insurance, depositors have a strong incentive to monitor the riskiness of a financial institution's assets. Clearly, if an institution has an extremely risky portfolio, the depositors's funds are at greater risk (absent deposit insurance). Thus, there is a market check on "excessive" risk taking by financial institutions. It is, of course, true that even without deposit insurance (and other financial regulations) some institutions would take greater risks than others. To the degree that information regarding the riskiness is available, such institutions would be able to attract depositors only by offering higher interest rates (or other services).

Without federal deposit insurance, depositors have an incentive to monitor the riskiness of a financial institution's assets because they face a potential loss if the institution fails. In such a world, depositors would withdraw or deposit additional funds based, in part, on the asset quality of the institution. A signaling mechanism would be created which assists institutions in assessing their risks. This signaling mechanism does not exist with federal deposit insurance. Thus, institutions are deprived of information necessary for them to adequately evaluate risks. In this sense, federal deposit insurance distorts market signals not simply by encouraging excessive risk, but also by eliminating market information.

Assuming a bank is attempting to maximize profits, the existence of federal deposit insurance encourages it to have a riskier portfolio. The riskier portfolio can take the form of investments in non-investment grade securities ("junk bonds"), loans to borrowers which are less well secured, etc. Since the depositor does not bear the cost of the riskier portfolio (due to the deposit insurance) banks are encouraged to take greater risks.

The existence of federal deposit insurance creates a textbook example of the moral hazard problem. Federally insured depository institutions pursue risks they would not otherwise take, and it is possible for them to do this because the depositors have little incentive to monitor the risks the institutions take.[3]

Under a fractional reserve banking system, the riskiness of a bank is primarily a function of what the bank does with the deposits it receives. Thus, the riskiness is related to the asset side of the bank's balance sheet. Historically, the principal options a bank has for non-reserve assets are to make loans or to purchase various investments such as bonds or government securities (all subject to various regulations).

Under the current deposit insurance structure in the U.S., banks are charged a flat "insurance premium" of $.25 per $100.00 of domestic deposits. This premium is completely unrelated to the riskiness of the bank. Banks on the verge of insolvency pay the same premium rate that the most sound banks pay. Indeed, it has been argued that the current system is not really insurance at all because insurance requires an actuarial analysis of risks, and federal deposit insurance premiums are not risk based.[4]

If federal deposit insurance premiums were tied to the riskiness of the institution, there would at least be some incentive for the institution to monitor risk. Similarly, if federal deposit insurance were effectively limited to a specified amount, with depositors at risk for deposits in excess of such limits, there would be some incentive for large depositors to monitor the soundness of financial institutions.

While legally the federal deposit insurance guarantee is limited to $100,000, in practice there has been virtually no limit on the amount of coverage provided. In part this is true because the law limits coverage to $100,000 *per account,* so virtually unlimited coverage can be obtained through the use of multiple accounts (whether at the same or a different financial institution). The use of brokered jumbo certificate of deposits has also enabled large investors to receive unlimited deposit insurance. Additionally, the doctrine of "too big to fail" has resulted in unlimited coverage, at least at large institutions. Under this doctrine, depositors are encouraged to place accounts that are larger than $100,000 in large institutions which the regulators have in practice deemed "too big to fail." When large institutions have failed, all depositors have been made whole, not simply those with accounts up to $100,000.

Recent data demonstrate the ironic result that the practice of removing the $100,000 limitation for institutions that are deemed "too big to fail" actually works to the advantage of large, weak banks and to the detriment of small, strong banks.[5] A perverse Gresham's Law is at work when individuals remove large deposits from small, sound banks and place them in large, weak banks.

One could imagine that while deposit insurance might discourage depositors generally from considering the riskiness of a financial institution's portfolio, in extreme cases, where an institution is near failure, deposit insurance might be insufficient to prevent a run on the institution. This could occur because even with deposit insurance there might be costs to a depositor when the institution fails, *e.g.*, delays in accessing funds and the general inconvenience involved when the institution is closed.

The actual practice of the federal deposit insurance system, however, has been to eliminate, or at least reduce, such costs. Regulators typically arrange for an institution's "purchase and assumption" by another institution so that depositors in the failed institution suffer virtually no inconvenience at all. All accounts of the failed institution are maintained and checks drawn on the old accounts are fully honored by the acquiring institution. Thus, even in extreme cases, the market mechanism which would otherwise cause depositors to remove funds from riskier institutions (or demand higher interest rates) is thwarted.

Edward Kane has argued that deposit guarantees allow financial institutions to finance operations at a lower cost and encourage a go-for-broke strategy. While uninsured depositors would not lend to "hell-bent-for-leather thrifts" (or, more accurately, would only do so for higher interest rates), deposit insurance cuts the link between the riskiness of an institution's assets and its ability to raise funding for the assets. An asymmetry in the outcome of high-risk investments arises where the institution keeps the profits of a successful investment but the government (taxpayers) bears the costs of failed investments.[6]

We previously saw that one reason for the creation of the federal deposit insurance system was to prevent runs on good banks. Query, however, whether it is likely that without deposit insurance the failure of a bad bank would cause a run on otherwise solvent banks, as opposed to a movement of funds from weaker banks to stronger banks. Indeed, there is a significant difference between a flight from banks into currency (a panic) and a movement of funds from weaker to stronger banks. The latter is simply part of the market discipline process and certainly not a cause for alarm. Just as with any other business enterprise, one would expect to see some banks fail. This is hardly a source of systemic risk or an appropriate rationale for further regulation.

The Market for Deposit Insurance and the Need for Reform

The current crisis with financial institutions has led to numerous proposals for reform. While there is a wide range of issues that could be addressed in any discussion of reforming the federal deposit insurance system (or financial institutions generally), fundamentally there are two divergent approaches to reform. One approach calls for increasing regulatory efforts to combat the "market failure" that is viewed as inherent in current financial markets. The other approach argues for decreased regulation and greater reliance on market discipline.

While it is beyond the scope of this paper to examine the fundamental issues of market discipline versus regulatory control, the evidence appears overwhelming that the federal deposit insurance system is part of the current problem. How one approaches the need to change this system—whether by roll-backs in federal deposit insurance coverage, elimination of the use of multiple accounts, or complete abolition of federal deposit insurance—ultimately depends on whether one trusts the market to discipline financial institutions, or, more precisely, whether one feels that market forces or governmental regulatory forces are more likely to appropriately control excessive risk taking. In any attempt to address such fundamental questions, there is clearly a great deal more at stake than simply whether or not there should be a federal deposit insurance system.

One aspect of reform is to consider how the market might provide deposit insurance. While it is impossible to know precisely how private deposit insurance might operate, several observations should be made.[7]

Perhaps the starting point should be that if deposit insurance provides a valuable service to healthy financial institutions (by preventing runs) then one would think there would be a market for such private deposit insurance. It does, however, seem extraordinarily unlikely that private deposit insurance could effectively compete with federal deposit insurance. Thus, if politically it is not possible to eliminate the role of the government in deposit insurance, it is not likely that private insurance will arise. The current federal deposit insurance system is not only not profitable, it is losing hundreds of billions of dollars. While most of these losses may be attributable to the extremely poor manner in which the system is structured, *e.g.*, *de facto* 100 percent coverage, no co-insurance or deductibles, insurance premiums that are unrelated to risk, etc., the fact that federal deposit insurance is backed by the government's power to tax (including printing money) puts potential private carriers at an extreme disadvantage.

Private deposit insurance would certainly not be provided in the same manner as is the current federal deposit insurance. In particular, it is inconceivable that private insurers would charge the same premiums to all institutions, regardless of the riskiness of the institution's portfolio. At a minimum, private insurers would charge higher premiums to reflect the greater risk associated with higher risk portfolios. Additionally, unlike governmental insurers, private carriers would not have the ability to issue money or draw on the Federal Reserve's "lender of last resort" function to bail out a run.

The very existence of a fractional reserve system with a central bank may inherently create a banking system which cannot be insured by private carriers. Indeed, it has been argued that such a banking system is subject to systemic risk which cannot be privately insured.[8] While it may be true that a fractional reserve world is subject to greater systemic risk, and it is certainly true that private carriers would not have the ability to issue currency, it does not follow that the market is not capable of providing private deposit insurance.

In a fractional reserve system, most banks would fail if all depositors simultaneously attempted to redeem their deposits, just as most insurance companies would fail if all insureds had an untoward event at the same time. Nevertheless, it should be possible for private carriers to evaluate the risk of runs—a risk which is presumably much greater for an institution with riskier investment portfolios—and set appropriate premiums for such deposit insurance. Assuming depositors prefer a bank with deposit insurance (and are willing to receive a lower return on their deposits in exchange for such coverage), there does not appear to be any obvious reason why this insurance could not be provided by private carriers.

The existence of private deposit insurance would not result in the same excessive risk-taking that characterizes governmental deposit insurance. Since the premiums that a private carrier would charge to banks would be, in part, a function of the riskiness of the bank, a bank's attempt to increase profits by taking additional risks on its assets would result in greater deposit insurance premiums, thus reducing the incentive to take the excessive risks.[9] While a depositor in a privately insured bank would also have a lack of incentive to monitor the riskiness of the bank's portfolio, the private carrier providing the insurance would have the incentive to consider the riskiness of that bank's portfolio.

As has been shown in countless different studies in various contexts, profit-maximizing businesses have a strong incentive to evaluate risks properly and set appropriate premiums. Government bureaucrats, however, face their own set of incentives, which are exceedingly unlikely to include properly evaluating risks in setting insurance premiums.

Even if we assume that the market could not (or would not) provide deposit insurance, the question arises as to whether this is an argument for retaining the current federal deposit insurance system. While concern has been raised that banks and savings and loans could not raise capital without federal deposit insurance, this argument seems unpersuasive. Financial institutions raise billions of dollars every day without the government protecting investors. In light of the fungible nature of capital and the increasingly diverse and interrelated global capital markets, the idea that U.S. banks and savings and loans can only exist with federal deposit insurance seems far-fetched.[10]

The real problem which is preventing reforms in financial markets, and particularly federal deposit insurance, is political. The current system subsidizes existing institutions, particularly large, weak banks, which gain enormously from the present deposit insurance system. Government-provided 100 percent guarantees to their depositors make it easier for them to raise capital.

Unfortunately, however, the current system has resulted in losses to the savings and loan industry in excess of $200 billion, losses greater than any experienced during the Great Depression. Additionally, losses in the banking industry are now showing ominous signs of paralleling those of the savings and loan industry. The FSLIC became insolvent and BIF (the new Bank Insurance Fund) is now either insolvent or on the verge of insolvency.

It is difficult to imagine how free markets in deposit insurance could possibly be worse than the current situation. The federal deposit insurance system does not work in theory and it has been a disaster in practice. Indeed, it is ironic that at this time in history when the Soviet Union and Eastern bloc countries have apparently rejected governmental controls and embraced the market (thus vindicating the work of Mises and Hayek), the United States is unwilling to abolish the federal deposit insurance system and give markets an opportunity to function efficiently.

The price of the short-term stability provided by the federal deposit insurance system (a lack of bank runs) has been a long-term disaster. By eliminating incentives for individuals to monitor the risk of depository institutions, a problem far in excess of the one designed to be prevented by federal deposit insurance has been created. It is time to free our financial markets from federal deposit insurance.

Notes and References

1. Friedman, Milton, *A Program for Monetary Stability* (New York, NY: Fordham University Press, 1960).
2. Hayek, Friedrich A., "The Use of Knowledge in Society," *American Economic Review,* (September 1945).
3. Selgin, George A., "Legal Restrictions, Financial Weakening, and the Lender of Last Resort," *CATO Journal* (Fall 1989), pp. 435-437.
4. Kane, Edward J., *The S&L Insurance Mess: How Did It Happen?* (Washington, DC: The Urban Institute Press, 1989), p. 4.
5. Short, Eugenie D., and Gunther, Jeffrey W., *The Texas Thrift Situation: Implications for the Texas Financial Industry*, Federal Reserve Bank of Dallas (1988).
6. Kane, *op. cit.,* pp. 4-6.
7. Short, Eugenie D., and O'Driscoll, Gerald P. Jr., "Deregulation and Deposit Insurance," *Economic Review*, Federal Reserve Bank of Dallas (September 1983).
8. Salsman, Richard M., *Breaking the Banks: Central Banking Problems and Free Banking Solutions* (Great Barrington, MA: American Institute for Economic Research, 1990), pp. 23-24.
9. In theory, governmental deposit insurance could also adopt risk sensitive premiums, although this has not occurred in practice. It may be worth noting that the federal pension insurance system run by the Pension Benefit Guaranty Corporation does, in fact, charge differential premiums based upon a measure of risk. In the case of pensions, the measure of risk is the extent to which the pension plan is underfunded.
10. It is beyond the scope of this paper to consider the fascinating issues relating to how these financial institutions are creatures of other regulations as well, and how financial institutions might operate absent governmental regulation.

30

CROWDING OUT

Mark Skousen*

At first, [federal debt] may consume only a small share of the individual savings coming to market, causing a slow-down in capital formation and economic development. In time, the share consumed by its apparatus of politics tends to grow until it depletes all savings and causes economic progress to grind to a halt. In a final frenzy of spending, it may actually consume capital accumulated by previous generations, and thus cause economic conditions to deteriorate.

Hans F. Sennholz[1]

An eerie complacency has enveloped the economics profession in the United States. Whether the issue is deficit spending, inflation, unemployment, savings, the stock market, the trade deficit, or the business cycle, mainstream economists are increasingly adopting a "don't care" attitude.

Robert Heilbroner and Peter Bernstein, representing the Keynesians, have long argued that the federal debt is not a net national liability, not the result of profligacy, and not a burden that will impoverish our grandchildren through higher taxes. The whole issue is a "false alarm."[2]

That the deficit and crowding out are a non-problem is to be expected of the Keynesians. But what about free-market economists? Milton Friedman, leader of the monetarists, asserts that the twin deficits—in trade and in government—are "scarecrows"; they are far from a curse, but a "blessing."[3] Friedman also maintains that a low savings rate in the United States is not a national disaster. What if nobody saved? "...[T]hat would mean no growth. Perhaps so, but what is wrong with that?"[4]

*Dr. Skousen is editor of *Forecasts and Strategies,* and Adjunct Professor of Economics and Finance at Rollins College, Winter Park, FL.

Paul Craig Roberts, leader of the supply-siders, sides with Friedman and Heilbroner. "The deficit hysteria is unjustified," he concedes.[5]

Robert J. Barro, exponent of the New Classical school—this is the school that argues that unemployment is never a problem because it's always "voluntary" and that the economy, no matter how bad off, is always in "equilibrium"—seems to take pride in his laid back attitude about the economy during a severe recession: "The questions I am asked most often these days are: Why is the economic recovery weaker than expected? How will the economy do over the next year? What should the government do to help? As a first approximation, the right answers to questions like these are: 'I don't know,' 'I don't know,' and 'nothing.'"[6]

This nihilistic "I don't know and I don't care" attitude seems to have spread like wildfire throughout academia. In researching my book, *The Structure of Production*, I came across an erudite work by economist Daniel Hausman on capital and interest. He made a remarkable admission: "Economists do not understand the phenomena of capital and interest. They do not understand why the rate of interest is positive (and thus how it is that capitalism can work). They do not know how large-scale technological changes will affect wages and interest or how changes in the rate of profits will affect innovation."[7] And he's a specialist!

Today's economists claim ignorance at every turn, perhaps fearing responsibility for their theories. On the first page of their thousand-page textbook, Ruffin and Gregory maintain that economists can't be held accountable: "Economics cannot teach you how to get rich. It doesn't supply magic formulas that tell you what stocks to pick, whether or not interest rates will rise, or if the dollar will fall. It doesn't predict which of today's new businesses are the IBMs of tomorrow."[8]

Most academic economists scorn those who try to predict the future and try to beat the market. The efficient market theory is gospel truth on ivory-tower campuses. Burton G. Malkiel expresses the orthodox view succinctly: "[The efficient market theory] means that short-run changes in stock prices cannot be predicted. Investment advisory services, earnings predictions, and complicated chart patterns are useless.... Taken to its logical extreme, it means that a blindfolded monkey throwing darts at a newspaper's financial pages could select a portfolio that would do just as well as one carefully selected by the experts."[9]

Economists as ignoramuses can best be summed up by John Maynard Keynes, the economist king of the twentieth century, who wrote: "The fact that our knowledge of the future is fluctuating, vague and uncertain, renders wealth a peculiarly unsuitable subject for the methods of classical economic theory.... There is no scientific basis on which to form any calculable probability whatever. We simply do not know."[10]

I am happy to see that Professor Hans F. Sennholz does not fit today's characterization of an economist. He has been in the forefront of declaring the ill effects of government intervention in the economy. Throughout his career as an economist, professor, writer, speaker, real estate investor and commodity speculator, he has raised a prophetic voice of warning. Now, more than ever, his sound, albeit heretical, views deserve the widest possible promulgation.

In the spirit of Hans Sennholz's long-time interest and experience in the investment markets, this paper focuses on one major example of where the economics profession has gone wrong—the federal debt. I will seek to demonstrate that uncontrolled federal deficits do in fact have a serious and growing debilitating effect on the U.S. economy and the private financial markets. First, I will show that the Treasury debt is growing at an alarming rate and has reached a dangerous level, in absolute and relative terms. Second, I will demonstrate that the manner in which the deficit is financed is extremely important: Deficit spending often leads to wasteful government spending, higher taxes, inflation, trade deficits, higher than expected interest rates, short-term business planning, crowding out of private capital investment, or a combination of all of the above. In sum, excessive deficit spending may not spell imminent bankruptcy, but it can seriously retard economic growth and, carried to the extreme, lower our standard of living. As a financial economist, I will focus primarily on the negative impact Treasury securities have had on the investment markets, which, I assert, is far more serious than most Wall Street analysts realize.

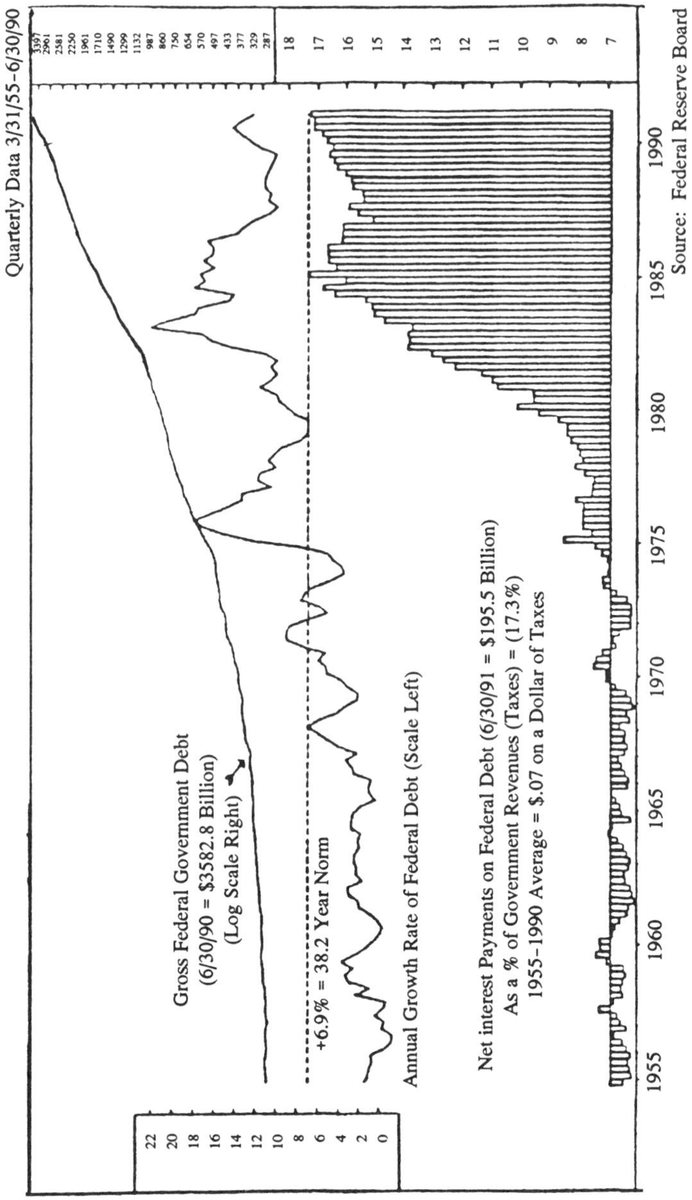

Growth of Federal Debt and Net Interest Payments, 1955–1990
Exhibit 1

How Big is the Federal Debt?

The debt obligations of the federal government have grown monstrously since the beginning of World War II, and have accelerated since 1973. As Exhibit 1 demonstrates, total Treasury debt has continually increased for the past 30 years. At the end of 1991, total Treasury debt reached $3.5 trillion.

Exhibit 1 also demonstrates that the rate of growth in federal debt is generally increasing. Note how the rate was around 2-3 percent during the late 1950s and the early 1960s, spurted up to 4-6 percent in the late 1960s and early 1970s, then rose sharply to 10-15 percent following the 1973-75 and 1980-82 recessions. Today the rate of federal debt growth is accelerating again in the midst of another recession.

The interest on the debt is also of deep concern. As Exhibit 1 shows, the interest on the debt was relatively unimportant until the late 1970s. Since then, when interest rates skyrocketed, the interest on the debt has taken up a larger and larger chunk of government revenues. Lower interest rates since 1982 have kept the interest payments within manageable proportions for now. Nevertheless, it is not comforting to know that the interest on the debt—now exceeding $200 billion a year—will soon be the largest item on the federal budget, exceeding military spending.

Today the federal deficit is at an all-time record high. The deficit for fiscal year 1992 could exceed $400 billion. (See Exhibit 2.)

Should we be alarmed? Are we facing a major fiscal crisis? Most economists apparently are unconcerned. Fortunately, Hans Sennholz is not one of them. He warns, "The federal debt...may be an inconvenience now, but is likely to become a calamity tomorrow. It may dissipate our levels of living, foster inflation, and cause millions of Americans to sink into poverty and despair."

In the fall of 1972, Dr. Sennholz estimated and projected the trend of official federal deficits and debt in a study entitled *Inflation or Gold Standard?* His calculations rested on a number of assumptions that have proven to be fairly accurate over the years. The final verdict can be rendered in the year 2003 (see Exhibit 3).[11]

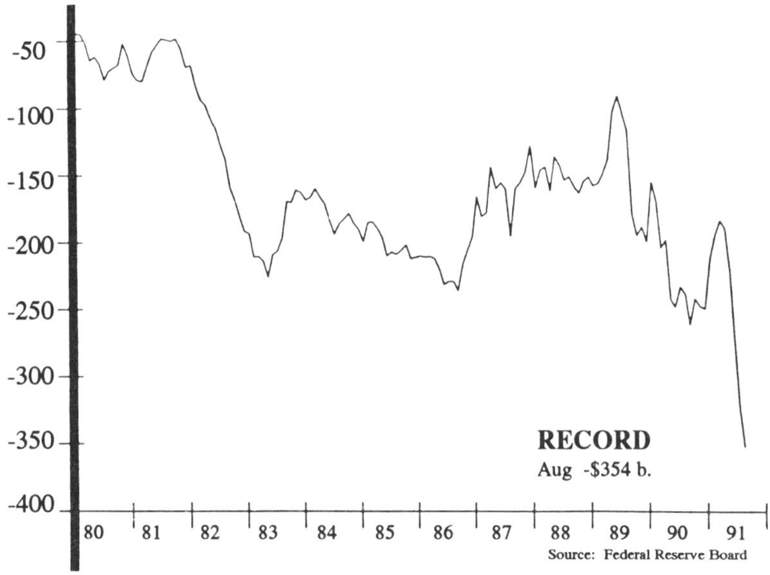

Federal Deficit, 1980–91
4 Month Average
Seasonally Adjusted Annual Rate

Exhibit 2

Political Fallout

There is a political fallout to this "don't care" attitude about the deficit: Politicians in Washington are happy to learn that they don't have to worry about the shortfall in revenues. They've even been told that they don't have to worry about the interest on the debt. They can run up a deficit as long as they think they can get away with it. Most members of Congress give lip service to a balanced budget and play a lot of games (placing programs "off budget," shifting funds from one fiscal year to another, etc.), but in the final analysis they feel very little responsibility to limit spending, especially on programs in their own state.

Friedman argues that it is the level of government spending, not the deficit, that matters.[12] He is half correct. The level of government spending is important. But if Congress does not recognize any significant limitations on the deficit, how can the budget be controlled? Surely a strongly held premise that the deficit can be expanded without any serious ill effects will lead to an ever-expanding budget.

Year	**Receipts**	**Expend-itures**	**Surplus/ Deficit**	**Year-End Public Debt**
1933	1,997	4,598	-2,602	22,539
1943	25,097	78,909	-53,812	140,796
1953	71,495	76,769	-5,274	266,123
1963	106,560	111,311	-4,751	310,800
1973 est.	224,984	249,796	-24,812	473,300
1973 actual	**232,225**	**246,526**	**-14,301**	**468,400**
1983 projected	700,000	825,000	-125,000	1,400,000
1983 actual	**600,562**	**808,327**	**-207,764**	**1,381,900**
1993 projected	3,000,000	4,000,000	-1,000,000	4,000,000
2003 projected in new currency	300,000	300,000	0	1,000,000

Source of 1933-1973 data: *The Budget of the United States Government,* 1974, pp. 370-371
Source of Table of Projections: *Debts and Deficits,* p. 75

Sennholz Projections for the Federal Budget and Debt
(in millions of dollars)

Exhibit 3

Friedman, in fact, believes that Congress recognizes serious limitations to the budget deficit and that, therefore, tax cuts are the best way to put real pressure on Congress to reduce government spending. The deficit, according to Friedman, "is currently preventing the imposition of a still larger and still worse tax."[13] But surely this is political fantasy. Today's congressional leaders are constantly opposing all tax cuts "unless they can be paid for" by closing loopholes or increasing taxes elsewhere. Moreover, growing deficits increase the likelihood that Congress will raise taxes in a vain attempt to close the deficit. George Bush's decision to reverse his "read my lips" stand against taxes was made precisely because of pressure by Congress to reduce the ever burgeoning deficit. As a result, we got a massive tax increase in 1990. Ironically, it did not close the deficit—it actually widened it. Apparently Congress saw the increase in revenues as an opportunity to spend more.

Suppose, on the other hand, that Congress was facing a surplus in the budget. I suspect that the White House and Capitol Hill would be falling all over each other to propose tax cuts to the American people. If ever we needed an environment favoring a tax cut, a nice big surplus would do the trick.

The Public Debt and Social Security

A common argument, made especially by Keynesians, is that the deficit does not matter because "we owe it to ourselves."[14] Heilbroner and Bernstein point out that approximately 21 percent of the Treasury obligations are owned by government agencies and trust funds, such as the Social Security Trust Fund.[15] "The part of the debt owned by agencies of the federal government is not a burden of any kind—it would be called on Wall Street a 'wash': whatever is paid out with one hand is taken in with the other."[16]

But is it a "wash"? Not really. Take, for example, the huge Social Security Trust Fund, now nearly $400 billion and expected to reach $12 trillion by the year 2033. By law, it is required to be invested entirely in government securities. It's a nice, tidy arrangement, but Heilbroner and Bernstein forget one thing: What if the Social Security Trust Fund (as well as other agency trust funds) could be invested in corporate stocks and bonds? That would be a tremendous boost to the stock market, adding billions to private capital. It would increase our rate of capital formation tremendously if billions were shifted from public consumption to private capital. The result would be a substantial increase in our standard of living over the long run.

As it stands, Social Security cannot be counted as legitimate "savings," even though it is viewed as such by employees and employers who pay into it. It is a great tragedy that the billions of dollars that Americans pay in payroll taxes each year are not really "savings" at all, but pure consumption—funds that are either transfer payments to Social Security recepients, or funds invested in government securities. Not a penny is invested directly in private enterprise. Contrast our policy with Chile's new Social Security system, whereby workers invest 10 percent of their wages in a wide variety of mutual funds, including corporate stocks and bonds.

Indexing the Debt for Inflation

After netting out U.S. agency borrowing from the Treasury, Heilbroner and Bernstein reduce the "real" deficit to practically zero by indexing the remaining deficit for inflation. For the 1988 fiscal year, they reduce the deficit from $255 billion to a "real" deficit of $3 billion—almost a surplus![17] Robert Eisner, former president of the American Economic Association, uses an inflation-adjusted measure of the deficit during the early 1970s and concludes that Washington actually ran surpluses during this inflationary period.[18]

But is it fair to index the deficit for inflation when the deficit may well be responsible for the inflation in the first place? If Washington's fiscal plan was to expand expenditures in order to achieve a "real" (after inflation) balanced budget, it may find itself increasing expenditures at an ever-increasing rate.

"We Owe It to Ourselves"

Keynesians argue another way in which we allegedly "owe it to ourselves." On a national scale, they reason, we are really taking money out of one pocket (the government borrowing money) and putting it into our other pocket (government paying interest to bondholders). Thus, the public debt is a public credit, except when foreigners own the bonds (representing about 13 percent of the Treasury debt), and there is no net loss.

But this sort of reasoning is an example of what Paul Samuelson calls the fallacy of composition. The question is, "Who are the *we* and who are the *ourselves*?" They are not the same person. Murray Rothbard was the first economist to raise this critical question. "For we might just as well say that taxes are unimportant for the same reason...."[19]

In reality, Treasury financing causes significant distribution changes within society. Wealth is transferred in two ways. Initially, buyers of government bonds transfer their savings from private sources (corporate bonds, bank certificates of deposit, etc.) to public sources. Over the long run, as deficits are paid through either inflation or taxes, wealth is transferred from taxpayers, who are primarily middle class income earners, to bondholders, who are generally well-endowed institutions and wealthy retirees seeking interest income. It is a serious mistake for economists to ignore these wealth transfers.

Empirical Studies on the Deficit

One of the reasons economists have considered the federal debt benign is a variety of studies showing no clear relationship between the size of U.S. government borrowings and interest rates, inflation, the money supply, and the trade balance.[20] For example, the deficit rose sharply in 1982-83 and 1989-91 when interest rates were falling. No strong correlation exists between the money supply, whether measured by the adjusted monetary base, M1, M2, or M3, and the rate of federal debt growth. Sometimes the Treasury debt is monetized, other times it is not. Studies have also found no automatic relationship between the size of government borrowings and the size of the trade deficit, or weakness in the dollar.

Does this mean that fears of the deficit are baseless, as many economists suggest? Again, economists have jumped the gun. As Roger Garrison pointed out, the problem with these empirical studies is that they fail to take into account the wide variety of options in the financing of the deficit, none of which follows a predictable pattern. A federal deficit can be accommodated in a number of ways: (1) It can be financed through domestic credit markets, which will tend to raise interest rates and crowd out private investment; (2) it can be financed by our trading partners, resulting in weakened export markets and a widening trade deficit as funds normally used to buy our goods are now used to buy Treasury securities; (3) it can be paid for through open market operations by the Federal Reserve, which will tend to increase the money supply and cause price inflation; and (4) it can be paid for eventually through tax increases which reduce the funds available to the private sector. Roger Garrison also makes the point that any one of these options can be used at any time, and there is no reason why one will always be selected over the other. "During the Carter administration, for instance, debt was monetized; during the Reagan administration, debt was sold abroad."[21] According to Garrison, the policy mix is largely unpredictable, which explains why the empirical evidence linking the deficit with one specific effect is weak or mixed.

The National Debt and GNP

Most economists contend that the deficit is not really large when compared to Gross National Product (GNP). They maintain that this relative measure is a more accurate way of looking at the deficit, because GNP is supposed to reflect the economic ability of a nation to pay its debts. (I wonder about the government portion of GNP, whether it reflects economic prowess or fiscal irresponsibility.) Exhibit 4 demonstrates how the total federal debt as a percentage of GNP has been rising recently to approximately 50 percent of GNP. This rate is certainly high by post-war standards, but substantially less than the high of 110 percent during World War II.

Apologists for the national debt also point out that many other industrialized nations, including Japan, Germany, England, and Italy, have a higher government debt as a percentage of GNP than the United States. Even Friedman is persuaded by this argument: "...the combined government deficit is considerably lower than in many past years and lower than in Japan, West Germany, and France—whose pundits have been among the loudest in decrying the U.S. debt."[22] But wait! These countries with a heavy debt burden apparently recognize the problem and are trying to do something about it. Recently, while the United States has been running up historically high deficits, other countries have made real progress in reducing theirs. In the late 1980s, for instance, Japan, Germany, and England *reduced* their national debt by running surpluses. Amazingly, Mexico, a nation infamous for its out-of-control fiscal policies, will produce a surplus in its budget for 1992, the first in this century! Does not this trend suggest that the United States is fiscally out of step with the rest of the world?

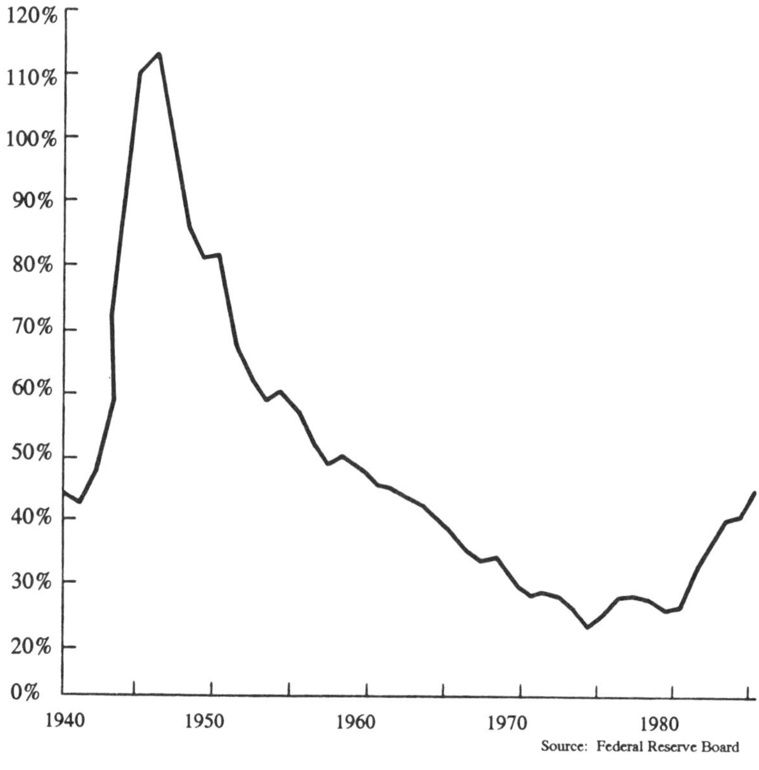

National Debt as Percentage of GNP

Exhibit 4

The Risk of Bankruptcy

Granted, inter-country comparisons regarding debt as a percentage of GNP confirm the position of the economics profession that the U.S. government is far from bankrupt. Certainly the Treasury was able to finance the huge World War II deficits fairly easily and at relatively low interest rates (2 percent throughout most of the war). Other countries have borrowed and inflated a lot more than we have without going under. The threat of federal bankruptcy at the present time is clearly remote.

This is not to say that bankruptcy is not impossible. Many countries have gone this route during the twentieth century—Germany in the 1920s, China in the 1940s, many Eastern European countries in the 1940s, several Latin American countries in the 1970s and 1980s. McConnell and Brue make the ridiculous claim that a nation can always avoid bankruptcy by inflating the money supply: "It is difficult to conceive of governmental bankruptcy when government has the power to create new money by running the printing presses."[23] But any government that has to resort to the printing press has already reached the point of *de facto* bankruptcy.

There are many forms of partial bankruptcy. As Roger Garrison points out, "The likelihood of the government's defaulting on its debt in the conventional sense is nil, but its defaulting in some other way is all but inevitable. It may partially default by inflating away the real values of outstanding debt. It may default on its promise not to raise taxes. It may default on its commitment to pay retirement or other benefits to government employees and participants in social programs."[24]

Interest on the Debt: Ponzi Finance

To get an idea of where the United States is headed, it's also important to consider the interest paid on the national debt as a proportion of GNP. In this case, alarm bells start ringing again. (See Exhibit 5.) The current rate, now over 3 percent of GNP, is substantially higher than the World War II period, and headed upward.

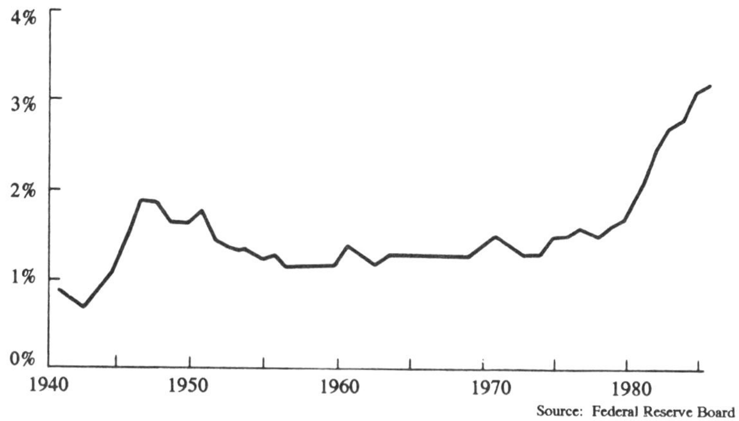

Net Interest on National Debt as a Percentage of GNP Exhibit 5

What appears to be happening is what economist Hyman Minsky (the only Keynesian I know who makes some sense) properly calls "Ponzi finance."[25] By not taking the national debt seriously, Washington has reached the point where they neither pay off the national debt nor the interest on the debt. It's a classic Ponzi scheme where the interest is added onto the debt rather than paid off. Such a condition spells disaster somewhere down the road, where the rate of federal debt growth skyrockets at a faster and faster pace.

What About "Crowding In"?

The relationship between debt and GNP may reflect the ability of the government to avoid bankruptcy, but it does not translate necessarily into the depth of potential harm the deficits can do to private investment, economic growth and our standard of living. In other words, the deficit may well be serviceable, but is it good for the economy?

Most Keynesians argue that deficits are actually good for business during a recession when idle resources exist. This is standard Keynesian fare. An autonomous increase in government expenditure and deficit financing will expand aggregate demand, put people and machines back to work, and therefore stimulate investment. In this sense, argue the Keynesians, deficits really cause "crowding in."[26]

This kind of standard Keynesianism raises some serious issues, however. What if an excessive fiscal and monetary policy brought about a bust and recession later on? Wouldn't more of the same just aggravate the problem? Moreover, where will the new federal funds be spent? To devout Keynesians, it may not matter, but if one accepts a time structure of production, deficit spending will probably favor the consumer goods industries rather than early stage capital projects, causing a shortening of the production structure and perhaps even capital consumption.[27]

To the extent that the deficit transfers savings from the private sector to the public sector, wherein wealth is in large measure systematically misused, wasted or merely consumed, the effects are clearly detrimental. Savings invested in Treasury securities, albeit voluntarily by institutions and individual investors, can no longer be treated as real savings when they are in the hands of the government. They are, in reality, a form of capital consumption.

But what if the federal budget allocated most of its funds to much-needed capital projects, such as roads, highways, high-speed trains, bridges, sewage and water systems, and other forms of public infrastructure? This is a much stronger argument for "crowding in" since it involves a direct form of investment and capital formation. Recently many economists, from Keynesians to free marketers, have complained about the failure to expand vitally needed public investment in the United States.[28]

There are two points to be made in this regard: First, if government through deficit spending engages in public works projects that everyone deems to be vital, then there is no reason why private enterprise could not finance these projects in a more efficient manner. Government financing of vital public works must therefore be regarded a second-best solution. The right kind of public investment may indeed increase a nation's productivity, but surely private investment would increase productivity even more.

Second, it is quite conceivable that many of the public works the deficit might finance would prove to be wasteful. What if expensive highways, schools, and dams were built and the demand for them turned out to be grossly overestimated? Cost-benefit analysis is helpful in public finance, but is no guarantee that public investment will be socially efficient.

Deficits as a Percentage of Savings

The best way to measure crowding out is to compare the annual federal deficit with the total amount of corporate and private savings created each year[29] (see Exhibit 6). According to this chart, two periods stand out in particular: the World War II era and the 1980s. World War II was clearly a period of crowding out. Private investment was relatively moribund during the war. The stock market and the corporate bond market were lackluster, and few new issues came on the market.

In the 1980s, corporate and individual savings grew significantly from $478.4 billion to $783.9 billion. During this decade, the deficits also climbed sharply. On average, the deficit equaled approximately one-fourth of all institutional and private savings. The percentage suddenly escalated during the recession of the 1990s, as it did during previous recessions—estimated at 32 percent in 1991 and, by my calculations, could exceed 50 percent in 1992.

New Classicist Robert Barro maintains that government borrowing does not reduce private saving, it actually increases it. The deficit induces individuals to save more in order to meet higher tax obligations in the future.[30] This is another one of those wrong-headed theories of the New Classical school that has just enough truth in it to lead economists astray. First of all, it is highly doubtful that Americans, who often fail to make rudimentary provisions for their estate upon death, will be farsighted enough to plan on higher taxes in the future. Second, insofar as they do plan for the future, they are more likely to expect higher inflation, which causes them to save less.

EXHIBIT 6

Federal Budget deficits (and surpluses) in comparison to corporate and private savings for the years 1940 through 1990

Economic Report of the President

Washington D.C. February 1991 page 318.

Year	Def-(Sur+)	Saving	Def/Sav
1940	**-1.3**	**14.3**	**-9.1**
1941	-5.1	22.6	-22.6
1942	-33.1	42.3	-78.3
1943	-46.6	50.0	-93.2
1944	-54.5	54.9	-99.3
1945	**-42.1**	**45.4**	**-92.7**
1946	3.5	30.3	11.6
1947	13.4	28.1	47.7
1948	8.3	42.4	19.6
1949	-2.6	39.9	-6.5
1950	**9.2**	**44.5**	**20.7**
1951	6.5	52.6	12.4
1952	-3.7	56.1	-6.6
1953	-7.1	58.0	-12.2
1954	-6.0	58.8	-10.2
1955	**4.4**	**65.2**	**6.7**
1956	6.1	72.1	8.5
1957	2.3	76.1	3.0
1958	-10.3	77.1	-13.4
1959	-1.1	82.1	-1.3
1960	**3.0**	**81.1**	**3.7**
1961	-3.9	86.8	-4.5
1962	-4.2	95.2	-4.4
1963	.3	97.9	.3
1964	-3.3	110.8	-3.0
1965	**.5**	**123.0**	**4.0**
1966	-1.8	131.6	-1.4
1967	-13.2	143.8	-9.8
1968	-6.0	145.7	-4.1
1969	-8.4	148.9	5.6
1970	**-12.4**	**164.5**	**-7.5**
1971	-22.0	190.6	-11.5
1972	-16.8	203.4	-8.2
1973	-5.6	244.0	-2.3
1974	-11.7	254.3	-4.6
1975	**-69.4**	**303.6**	**-22.9**
1976	-53.5	321.4	-16.6
1977	-46.0	354.5	-13.0
1978	-29.3	409.0	-7.1
1979	-16.1	445.8	-3.6
1980	**-61.3**	**478.4**	**-12.8**
1981	-63.8	550.5	-11.6
1982	-145.9	557.1	-26.2
1983	-176.0	592.2	-29.7
1984	-169.6	673.5	-25.9
1985	**-196.9**	**665.3**	**-29.6**
1986	-206.9	669.5	-30.9
1987	-158.2	662.6	-23.9
1988	-141.7	751.3	-18.9
1989	-134.3	779.3	-17.2
1990	**-161.3**	**783.9**	**-20.6**
1991 est.	-255.0	780.0	-32.0

Crowding Out and the Financial Markets

In the 1980s, there was deep concern about crowding out of private investment by a rapidly expanding public sector. However, the huge increase in Treasury offerings (bills, notes and bonds) was absorbed fairly easily by the financial markets in the 1980s because of heavy foreign buying. As Salomon Brothers reported recently, "The United States attracted massive inflows of foreign capital—in excess of $800 billion—to fill the shortfall of domestic savings."[31]

However, in the early 1990s, facing a worldwide slowdown and bear markets, the inflow of foreign capital has fallen significantly. At the same time, the domestic savings rate has declined again. Meanwhile, the budget deficits have skyrocketed.

In the bond market, U.S. Treasury bonds outstanding grew by an estimated 13 percent in 1991, 10 percent in 1990, and 8 percent in 1989. Clearly the trend is up. Salomon Brothers estimates that approximately 57 percent of the U.S. bond market goes into Treasury bonds, up from 47 percent in 1980.[32] If one adds in state and local government securities, clearly government issues dominate the long-term bond market (see Exhibit 7).

The impact of the Treasury and U.S. federal agency fundings on the long-term debt markets is significant. It is by far the largest debt market in the world. While corporate and municipal bonds trade relatively infrequently with substantial bid-ask spreads, the Treasury market is extremely active with extremely small bid-ask spreads. A look at the corporate bond section of the *Wall Street Journal* reveals that only a handful of corporate and municipal bonds trade hands each day. This lackluster market is due to a variety of factors: the Treasury's monopoly position, its high safety ratings, and its favorable marketing conditions. The public has been oversold by the financial media on the safety and convenience of Treasury bond funds and all-government money market funds. Even politically active investors who oppose deficit spending are, ironically, heavy buyers of government only funds.

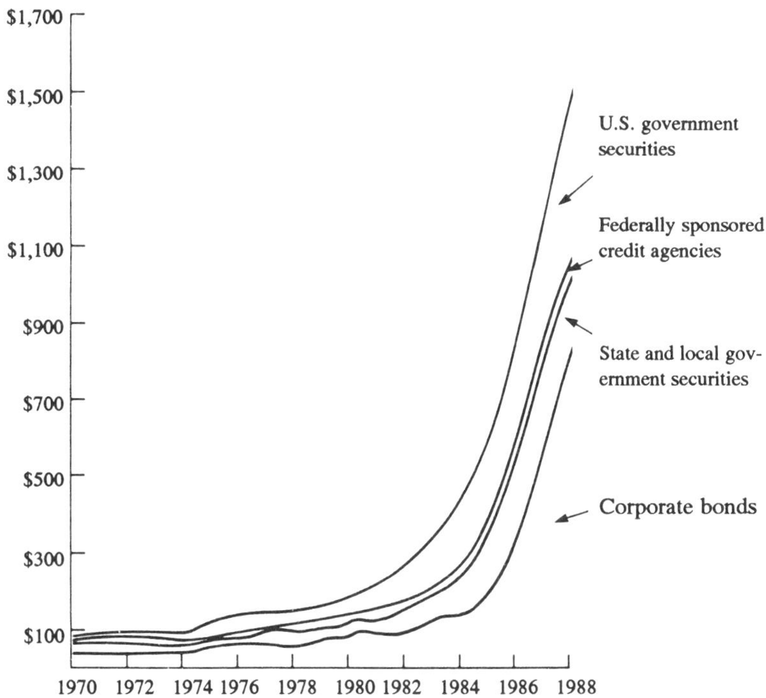

Source: Federal Reserve Board

Long-Term Debt Issued by Government and Business
Exhibit 7

Treasuries Versus Junk Bonds

While the Treasury is able to raise billions of dollars with long-term bonds at 8 percent, major corporations struggle to market new issues paying 10 percent or more. Interest on both types of securities is taxable, but Treasuries have a distinct advantage in liquidity and perceived safety. Commercial banks are discouraged from holding high-yielding corporate bonds and recently, due to the banking crisis, have been big buyers of Treasury securities. Many major and mid-sized corporations have had to issue above average high-yielding bonds (12-15 percent) is order to raise capital for their expanding businesses. These include such household names as Macy's, Safeway, RJR Nabisco, and Long Island Lighting. They have been dubbed "junk bonds," even though a recent exhaustive study by Glenn Yago demonstrated that "companies that raised funds in the junk bond market created jobs four times faster than the economy as a whole, experienced one-third greater growth in productivity, 50 percent faster growth in sales, and about three times faster growth in capital spending."[33] Can government bureaucrats make the same claim?

Despite the economic benefits of corporate financing, the yield spread continues to widen between corporate issues and Treasuries. Apparently, investors view Treasury securities as relatively more attractive, despite the high yield on corporates: Treasuries are more liquid, impose lower transaction costs, are less volatile, and are considered safer. The widening yield spread is an indication of the increasing difficulties facing long-term corporate financing in the United States.

Garrison even makes the claim that large deficits facilitate larger deficits by creating growing uncertainty in the market place. Given that investors continue to view Treasury securities as "risk free," if the risks in the market place increase in uncertainty, investors will shift their funds toward safety and Treasury securities: "That is, the more overextended the U.S. Treasury becomes, the *less* risky its debt becomes relative to private-sector debt. The relatively low and falling cost of borrowing encourages the government to borrow still more."[34] Indeed, T-bills are growing in demand in the early 1990s despite extremely low yields.

Short-Term America

Another characteristic of the debt market is the gradual shift away from long-term securities to shorter-term debt instruments. In the Treasury market, the shift toward shorter terms is apparent. Bonds used to dominate the Treasury market; now notes between 2-10 years are the biggest issue; short-term Treasury bills, maturing in less than a year, is the fastest growing sector.

The tendency to move away from long-term bonds is due to a general rise in real interest rates since 1980. Despite the fall in nominal interest rates during this time, real interest rates—after taking price inflation into account—remain at historically high levels. The cost of borrowing, especially for the long term, is heavily influenced by high interest rates. Throughout the 1980s, the cost of borrowing in Japan, Germany, and most other industrialized nations was substantially lower than in the United States. Among other things, this allowed foreign companies to be more long-term oriented and to invest more capital in long-run projects (such as research and development and technological advancement). As a result, the United States became less competitive in the world.[35]

Summary: The Coming Fiscal Crisis

In conclusion, most economists, representing the entire spectrum of thought, have made a serious mistake in underestimating the serious impact of the federal deficit. The main reason why the economics profession has missed the importance of the deficit crisis is due to an excessive emphasis on macroeconomic aggregates rather than microeconomic details.

For example, many free-market economists believe that the way the federal budget is financed is unimportant because of their interpretation of the so-called "Ricardian Equivalence Theorem." Ricardo argued that government borrowing eventually must be paid in taxes. Therefore, they contend, taxes and borrowing are essentially equivalent. Either the public pays now (taxes) or later (borrowing). When you discount the cost of borrowing by the interest the Treasury pays, it amounts to the same thing as taxation.[36]

Yet, as we have shown above, it does make a big difference *how* government finances its budget.

First, if the government finances the budget through taxation, it matters a lot what form the taxation takes (sales taxes, value-added taxes, income taxes, capital gains levies, import duties, etc.) and the marginal rate of taxation (progressive or regressive).

Second, if the government finances its budget by borrowing domestically, it keeps interest rates higher than what they would be otherwise and alters the structure of production toward the short term, making U.S. companies less competitive worldwide.

Third, if the state finances its budget by borrowing abroad, it reduces the demand for exports and increases the trade deficit.

Fourth, if the government finances its budget by expanding the money supply, it causes price inflation and an inevitable disco-ordination of the factors of production, creating a boom-bust cycle.

As the deficits have worsened over the past 30 years, we have witnessed all of the above ill effects from time to time. Economic and financial instability has been particularly evident since 1971, not coincidentally at the same time the world officially went off the gold exchange standard. (Gold is another topic about which Hans Sennholz has a sound, albeit heretical, opinion, but that's another subject.) Such instability has created incredible opportunities for speculators, but the majority of Americans are worse off because of it. "There is much ruin in a nation," Adam Smith once said. And the federal deficit is a reflection of Adam Smith's pronouncement.

What To Do

What needs to be done to get the government's finances in order? I recommend the following policy changes.

First, the tax burden should be sharply reduced through significant tax cuts, especially on savings and investment. Since taxes on savings and investment are a form of double taxation, Congress should exempt interest, dividends and capital gains from taxation. At the very minimum, each taxpayer should be given a sizable personal exemption on interest, dividends and capital gains. For starters, I recommend a $5,000 exemption on interest and dividends, and $20,000 on capital gains.

Such tax cuts would stimulate economic growth, create jobs, expand exports, and revitalize the nation's infrastructure. They would also expand the income tax base and thus increase government revenues, as the supply siders have argued.

Second, allow the Social Security Trust Fund and other agency funds to invest in the stock market rather than just government securities. Even better, Social Security should be privatized along the lines of the Chile plan.

Third, once the recession is over and a sound economy has been re-established, the president should forcefully demand an immediate budget surplus. This would require creative thinking by government leaders—cutting out the fat in government, adopting many of the Grace Commission recommendations, selling off unnecessary government assets and privatizing many government services. Such action would require a strong president who has the guts to stand firm against waste in government.

Is this wishful thinking? If it can happen in Mexico, it can happen here.

Notes and References

1. Sennholz, Hans F., *Debts and Deficits* (Spring Mills, PA: Libertarian Press, 1987), p. 76.
2. Heilbroner, Robert and Bernstein, Peter, *A Primer on Government Spending* (New York, NY: Random House, 1963); *The Debt and the Deficit* (New York, NY: W. W. Norton, 1989).
3. Friedman, Milton, "Why the Twin Deficits are a Blessing," *Wall Street Journal* (December 14, 1988).
4. Friedman, Milton, "What is the 'Right' Amount of Saving?" *National Revie,* (June 16, 1989).
5. Roberts, Paul Craig, "Why the Deficit Hysteria is Unjustified," in Richard H. Fink and Jack C. High, eds., *A Nation of Debt* (Frederick, MD: University Publications of America, 1987), pp. 83-86.
6. Barro, Robert, "Don't Fool With Money, Cut Taxes." *Wall Street Journal* (November 21, 1991).
7. Hausman, Daniel M., *Capital, Profits, and Prices* (New York, NY: Columbia University Press, 1981), p. 190.
8. Ruffin, Roy J., and Gregory, Paul R., *Principles of Economics,* 3rd ed. (Glenview, IL: Scott, Foresman & Co., 1988 [1983]), p. 2.
9. Malkiel, Burton G., *A Random Walk Down Wall Street,* 4th ed. (New York, NY: W. W. Norton, 1990), p. 24.
10. Keynes, John Maynard, "The General Theory of Employment," *Collected Writings of John Maynard Keynes,* edited by Donald Moggridge (London: Macmillan, 1973), p. 114. This essay originally appeared in *The Quarterly Journal of Economics* in 1937.
11. Sennholz, *Debts and Deficits*, pp. 74-75, 147.
12. Friedman, "Twin Deficits."
13. *Ibid.*
14. McConnell, Campbell R., and Brue, Stanley L., *Economics*, 11th ed. (New York, NY: McGraw Hill, 1990), p. 402.
15. Heilbroner, Robert and Bernstein, Peter, *The Debt and the Deficit* (New York, NY: W. W. Norton, 1989), p. 32.
16. *Ibid.*, p. 72.
18. Eisner, Robert, *How Real is the Federal Deficit?* (New York, NY: Free Press, 1986).
19. Rothbard, Murray N., *Man, Economy, and State* (Los Angeles, CA: Nash Publishing, 1970[1962]), p. 882.
20. Roberts, "Why the Deficit Hysteria is Unjustified" in Richard H. Fink and Jack C. High, eds., *A Nation of Debt,* pp. 83-86.
21. Garrison, Roger W., "Public-Sector Deficits and Private-Sector Performance," in Lawrence H. White, ed., *The Crisis in the Banking*

Industry (New York, NY: New York University Press, 1992), forthcoming.
22. Friedman, "Twin Deficits."
23. McConnell, and Brue, *Economics*, p. 296.
24. Garrison, in "Public-Sector Deficits and Private-Sector Performance," forthcoming.
25. Minsky, Hyman, "Review of The Debt and the Deficit," *Journal of Economic Literature* 28 (September 1990), pp. 1221-1222.
26. Woodford, Michael, "Public Debt as Private Liquidity," *American Economic Review* 80 (May 1990), pp. 382-388.
27. Skousen, Mark, *The Structure of Production* (New York, NY: New York University Press, 1990), pp. 335-343.
28. Aschauer, David Alan, "Infrastructure: America's Third Deficit," *Challenge* (March-April 1991), pp. 39-45.
29. Garrison, in "Public-Sector Deficits and Private-Sector Performance," forthcoming.
30. Barro, Robert J., "The Ricardian Approach to Budget Deficits," *Journal of Economic Perspectives* 3 (Spring 1989), pp. 37-54.
31. Shulman, David G., Sargen, Nicholas P., Berner, Richard B., DiClemente, Robert V., and Hering. Susan M., *Structural Change in a Capital-Short World* (New York, NY: Salomon Brothers, December 1990), p. 16.
32. Benavides, Rosario, *How Big is the World Bond Market* (New York, NY: Salomon Brothers, September 30).
33. Yago, Glenn, *Junk Bonds* (New York, NY: Oxford University Press, 1991), p. 1.
34. Garrison, in "Public-Sector Deficits and Private-Sector Performance," forthcoming.
35. Jacobs, Michael, *Short Term America* (New York, NY: Free Press, 1991).
36. Barro, "The Ricardian Approach to Budget Deficits," pp. 37-54.

31

BEHIND THE BOTTOM LINE

Mark Spangler*

Asking people what their accountants do conjures up an assortment of responses and notions. Accountants are mathematicians, who spend their days immersed in "number crunching." Accountants are "bean counters" who track the assets of a firm. Sometimes a person's only encounter with an accountant is each spring for the dreaded ritual of tabulating income taxes and preparing and filing returns for a consortium of taxing authorities. The accountant, in any case, is viewed as the scorekeeper of income and expenses, of profits or losses—the bottom line.

The accountant is essentially a linguist. Accountancy is simply a language which describes all the summarized economic transactions of a given entity in a meaningful way. The accountant tries to create a portrait of the asset base which an entity possesses for its ongoing affairs and how and why the base has changed over a given period. True, the accountant utilizes mathematics, but generally only basic algebra. The prevalence of *tax* accounting is a function of government policy.

To understand the accountant's primary purpose in society, we must turn to economics, because accountancy is rooted in and reflects the economic setting in which transactions occur. There are only two logically consistent systems of economic order: private enterprise where the means of production are privately owned and government is limited to protecting property rights, or socialism where the state reigns supreme and owns or controls all the economic means. Straddling the fence which divides the two orders are the mixed economies of government intervention. Contradictory and unstable in and of themselves, mixed economies

*Mr. Spangler, a CPA, is the senior financial manager of a manufacturing company located near Philadelphia.

must give way to private enterprise or gravitate towards full socialism.

The basic economic fact of life is the scarcity of resources relative to the unlimited wants of acting humans who must choose means to achieve their ends. Economics is the study of means; and the way in which an economic order allocates means to satisfy individuals' needs establishes the accountant's role in society.

Social Function of Profits and Losses

Free enterprise, private enterprise, market economy, profit-loss system, and capitalism are all terms used to describe the economies of a free society. Whatever label is used, the paramount feature of such economies is private ownership *and* control of the means of production (capital goods). Under such conditions, the free choices and voluntary exchanges of acting individuals form the market economy. When a common medium of exchange—money—is utilized, the resulting exchange ratios (*i.e.*, prices) of goods, services, and factors of production can be expressed on a comparable basis.

Price information is the guiding force in the market economy; the objective is to produce a good or service at costs (prices) below what customers are willing to spend. The comparison of costs to proceeds is the process of calculating profits or losses. Consumers, through their patterns of buying or abstention from buying, ultimately steer the course of the economy. Driven in their search for profits, entrepreneurs attempt to allocate resources to their most profitable uses, *i.e.*, the most urgently demanded uses where customers are willing to pay the highest prices.

The changing configuration of prices provides the coordinating fabric of the economy. To illustrate this point, economist Hans F. Sennholz often asked why potatoes grown in Idaho are found on the dinner tables of consumers in Pennsylvania. The prices Pennsylvanians are willing to pay for Idaho potatoes relative to supplies and the costs of farming and transportation provides a profit to the enterpriser who successfully "delivers the goods." An oversimplified example? Hardly! Consider the plight of potatoes in the Soviet Union:

> The last consumer of the potatoes from the Kokino State Farm is Ludmilla Kudriavtseva of Moscow. She gets the raw end of the deal.

She found herself last week in Vegetable and Fruit Store No. 9..., staring at five bins of squashed, bruised and blighted potatoes. "The quality is disgusting," [she] said. "One out of ten is decent."

A visitor following the potatoes from the fields to Moscow, 300 miles to the northeast, is left with one overriding image: waste. Potatoes lie in neglected mounds in fields, at sorting sites, at railway junctions, in storage rooms. ...a quarter to a half of the potatoes planted at the Kokino State Farm last spring will not make it to store shelves. They will perish along the way, victims of outdated technology, poor storage, backward transportation and—most of all—indifference. By contrast, Western farmers are upset if 5 percent of their potato crop is lost between farm and market.

"Potatoes have rotted in state storage places for as long as Soviet power has existed," said Yuri Chernechenko, an author, legislator, and expert on Soviet agriculture. "Potatoes are an indicator of property: If it is somebody's, it will keep—if it's nobody's, it will rot. Potatoes rot in state warehouses, yet keep in the cellars of country homes. That's the whole deal."[1]

The harsh realty of Soviet agriculture, lacking private ownership and free markets, stands in stark contrast to the coordinating power of the price system (too often taken for granted in the United States) and reveals the pivotal role of the profit system—a means of economic calculation:

Our knowledge of prices also discloses the most crucial shortcoming of socialism and the immense superiority of the market order. Without the yardstick of prices, economic calculation is impossible. Without prices, how is the economic planner to calculate the results of production? He cannot compare the vast number of different materials, kinds of labor, capital goods, land, and methods of production. Without the price yardstick, he cannot ascertain whether certain procedures actually increase the productivity and output of his system.[2]

The factors of production derive their prices from the value and prices of the ultimate goods of consumption which they create. Only a system of private ownership and enterprise enables the formation of price information for capital goods and the calculation of profits in monetary terms. In the absence of market prices, how can the central planners of socialist nations coordinate their economies? Apparently the potato planners are still searching for a means.

Capitalism is often condemned for being guided by profits. However, profits—and losses—do have a social role. They tend to channel capital and other economic factors to the most efficient producers; losses indicate misallocations and remove wasteful entrepreneurs from the economic scene. A private enterprise may be organized as a hierarchy of owners, directors, officers, middle managers, sales people, and so on. It may have many branches and departments. Regardless of the exact arrangement, in the last analysis the firm must deliver what consumers want at a price they will pay. The customers are not interested in the firm's organizational problems. They buy from whoever supplies them with what they desire on the best terms and at the best prices.

Consequently, managing the firm's operations revolves around the profit-loss statements. Designing and planning are based upon market prices. Past operations are examined for profitability, and plans for the future are evaluated in terms of anticipated prices and the opportunity for profits. The goal is to know how each transaction affects profitability. This allows the owners or hired managers to calculate profits or losses for each branch or business segment. The determination of profits and losses becomes the *single criterion* on which to base business decisions. "The virtue of commercial management lies precisely in the fact that it provides the manager with a method of surveying the whole and all its parts without being enmeshed in details and trifles."[3]

The existence of this single criterion encourages decentralized management. The owner or general manager of the enterprise directs his division managers to make a profit. The calculation of profit-loss not only becomes a measure of overall success but provides a measure of performance. Has the division manager expended more to make a product than customers are willing to pay? He who cannot produce at a profit is doomed to demotion or discharge. The value consumers place on goods or services becomes the constraint on costs of production.

The single measure of profit and loss allows innumerable and vastly different commercial projects to be compared on a common basis. Industrial engineers can create different recipes for manufacturing; only economic calculation can say which consumes the least-costly resources and fulfills the preferences of the ultimate buyers. The profit-loss calculation enables entrepreneurs to choose from among alternate courses of actions. In this sense, one is able to compare apples to oranges.

Within a limited sphere of activity, even the owners and hired managers of profit-seeking enterprises must coordinate a division of labor and knowledge in the absence of price information. In every private firm there exists a point where internal operations can no longer be segmented and grouped into separate profit-loss centers. Alternate criteria must be established for decision making. The single most challenging task confronting a general manager is the dissemination and feedback of information to maintain coordination and consistency among the departments and employees of the firm.

The purchasing department must know what materials to buy and when. Production schedules must be established. Sales orders must be communicated to warehouses and manufacturing facilities. Vendors must be paid, and the credit worthiness of customers verified. Engineering must be informed of design requirements. Workers with proper skills must be hired. And so on. Internal management, to some degree, utilizes policy manuals, written procedures, oral directives, memoranda, and computer programs in the never-ending process of internal coordination. Nonetheless, private firms overall are driven by profits and are directly dependent upon customers for ultimate financing of operations. A person needs only to imagine extrapolating the process of private administration over an entire population and totally eliminating price information to gain some insight into life without economic calculation. The result, as Mises said, is "planned chaos."

Yet, in a free society, where government is limited to protecting private property and maintaining peace, there is a role for management by directives rather than by profit and loss statements.

Social Function of Bureaucratic Management

In the early part of this century, Ludwig von Mises, masterful economist of the Austrian school, began to develop his explanation of the distinguishing features of profit management as contrasted to bureaucratic management.[4] In 1944 he devoted an entire book to the subject.[5] He introduced the subject by pointing out that the terms "bureaucrat, bureaucratic, and bureaucracy" have negative connotations. No one wants to be called a bureaucrat.[6]

Some associate the word with government regulators who are appointed rather than elected. For others, a huge organization intertwined with subdivisions and departments comes to mind.

Despite all this confusion and ambiguity surrounding the concept, Mises stated, "...there seems to be unanimity with regard to the distinction between two contrary methods of doing things: the private citizens' way and the way in which the offices of the government and municipalities are operated."[7] Mises's analysis comes to bear on the problems faced by accountants in characterizing organizations and accounting for their affairs.

Management is radically different in an organization which is financed in the absence of market prices and profits from direct users. Mises explained management of democratic governments:

> The two pillars of democratic government are the primacy of law and the budget.... Primacy of the law means that no judge or officeholder has the right to interfere with any individuals' affairs or conditions unless a valid law requires or empowers him to do so.
>
> The administration, in a democratic community, is not only bound by law but by the budget. Democratic control is budgetary control.... It is illegal to use public funds for any expenditure other than those for which parliament has allocated them.... Bureaucratic management means, under democracy, management in strict accordance with the law and the budget.[8]

With government expenditures, the providing of services is no longer concurrent with payments from the users (as is the case with voluntary exchanges of private property). The collection of resources is by taxes, assessments, fines—by force. Only periodically through the ballot box can constituents influence the composition of government and its activities.

Government services are not supplied through the market process of profits and losses, so public offices must be managed under totally different principles; namely, spending must comply with laws, regulations, and the offical budget:

> Now we are in a position to provide a definition of bureaucratic management: Bureaucratic management is the method applied in the conduct of administrative affairs the result of which has no cash value on the market. Remember: we do not say that a successful handling of public affairs has no value, but that it has no price on the market, that its value cannot be realized in a market transaction and consequently cannot be expressed in terms of money.[9]

Therefore, no common measure of value exists to compare services within a particular government or between governments. Cash values of courts are not compared to cash values of police departments. Indeed, justice is not something that can or should be bought and sold in the market to the highest bidder. The effectiveness of a governmental unit must be measured by other criteria.

Bureaucratic management is centralized management. Public administrators are not allocated public funds and told to make a profit, and neither can they be given funds and told simply to do something useful. So, the authorities must fix detailed rules and regulations for bureaucrats to spend public monies. "The criterion of good management is not the approval of the customers resulting in an excess of revenue over costs but the strict obedience to a set of bureaucratic rules."[10]

Accountants have developed and traditionally used "fund accounting" for government units. There are few students of accountancy who have not rued their courses in fund accounting, the nature of which is alien to more customary calculations of profits and losses. Yet, accountants should realize that fund accounting suitably reflects the preeminent need for government spending to comply with laws, budgets, and appropriations.

Gaining in momentum in the last several years in the United States has been the popularity of groups advocating the voting of all incumbents out of office. No longer tolerant of the inefficiencies and waste of government, this grassroots movement proclaims "throw the bums out." Other business groups are calling for a chief financial officer of the United States. Again, we must emphasize that different managers sitting in the government bureaucracy will not change the nature of bureaucratic management; it is what it is. A changing of the guard cannot accomplish what only a rollback in the scope of government can do.

A society based upon collective (*i.e.*, state) ownership of property, and the total abolition of private property and the profit system, requires bureaucratic management in every aspect of the social order. It is socialism, under which economic calculation is impossible. The socialist system may have capital assets, but no means of expressing their relative values. The fabric of the socialist society is the apparatus of coercion and intimidation imposed by an authoritarian government.

Lenin, leader of the communist revolution in Russia, failed to grasp the essence of economic calculation when he characterized accountants in his writings of 1917:

> Accounting and control—these are the *chief* things necessary for the organizing and correct functioning of the *first phase* of Communist Society. *All* citizens are here transformed into hired employees of the state... [and] become workers of *one* national state 'syndicate.' ...the accounting and control necessary for this have been *simplified* by capitalism to the utmost, till they have become the extraordinarily simple operations of watching, recording and issuing receipts, within the reach of anybody who can read and write and knows the first four rules of arithmetic. ...the whole of society will have become one office and one factory....[11]

Lenin's narrow view of perfunctory record-keeping prevented his grasping the economic substance behind accountancy. After nearly eight decades Soviet leaders have come to realize the irrationality of the communist economic order, to understand the chronic poverty it inflicts, and to appreciate the incentives of profit-seeking. In a dire effort to raise funds, Soviet officials—in an ironic and perverse twist of fate—have actually suggested auctioning Lenin's remains to the highest bidder!

Management Accounting

By far the predominant role of accountants in a free society of private enterprise is assisting entrepreneurs and their managers in the process of economic calculation—detecting the profits and losses which emanate from human action and reflect the magnitude of consumer preferences.

The exact balancing of double-entry bookkeeping does not imply exactness in economic calculation; human judgment is always present. While double-entry bookkeeping forms the basic internal control of recording transactions, the language of accountancy must transform the accounts into a meaningful picture of the financial position of productive facilities, the owners of which are exposing their material well-being to the market daily. The determination of past profits or losses becomes the basis for interpretation, strategic planning, and decisions for future actions. It is a retrospective comparison of anticipated results with their outcomes. The chief financial manager becomes a crucial "player" in overall business planning as profits and losses unrelentingly confirm or challenge the continuing existence of a firm. The essential social benefit of these mental tools of profits and losses was not expressed by an accountant but by the famous German writer, Goethe:

> The devices of bookkeeping and accountancy are so familiar to the businessman that he fails to observe what a marvelous instrument they are. It needed a great poet and writer to appreciate them at their true value. Goethe called bookkeeping by double-entry "one of the finest inventions of the human mind." By this means, he observed, the businessman can at any time survey the general whole, without needing to perplex himself with the details.[12]

Broadly speaking, the branch of accountancy which generally achieves the bases for economic calculation and business planning is "management accounting" (whereas "financial accounting" is the branch concerned with external users of a firm's financial data).

Management accountants concentrate on the accuracy of product costing methods. They are the ones who capture the profitability of operations by branches, business segments, and even product lines or customer demographics. They subject data to statistical methods and ratio analysis to reveal correlations among costs and revenues. Economists make a theoretical distinction between the fixed costs and marginal income of the short-run and the ultimate variability of costs in the long-run; management accountancy interprets actual results in a similar light.

H. Thomas Johnson and Robert S. Kaplan, in their book, *Relevance Lost: The Rise and Fall of Management Accounting*, have evaluated the twentieth-century accomplishments of this branch of accounting. "What have management accounting practitioners been doing for the past sixty years? If there has been much innovation between 1925 and 1980, ...the innovating practitioners have managed to keep it mostly secret. ...virtually no new ideas have affected the design and use of cost management systems."[13] They point out not only the lack of innovation, but maintain that methods used for product costing are profoundly flawed as well. Those authors properly assert that this stagnation resulted from the domination of financial reporting to the public and to taxing authorities. Accounting systems have satisfied the requirements of the Securities and Exchange Commission, the Internal Revenue Service, and the Financial Accounting Standards Board (which is the profession's standard-setting body and tends to be preoccupied by SEC concerns). The profession's own forum for costing issues, the Cost Accounting Standards Board, primarily devotes its attention to questions of product costing for government contracts (which still may be based upon cost-plus pricing—a throwback to an economic notion which was thoroughly refuted over a century ago). The Board itself currently operates out of the Office of Federal Procurement Policy.

With the rise of government interventionism throughout the twentieth century, it is not surprising to find that the accounting profession's attention is dominated by the needs of the state. In the extreme case of socialist societies, accountants serve an entirely different set of objectives. Their accounts must be designed to collect data necessary to enforce the official bureaucratic directives that infiltrate every aspect of everyday living. Production quotas, state-mandated allocations of supplies, and ration coupons are the bottom lines of socialist accountancy. Authors Paul Craig Roberts and Karen LaFollette, for instance, in their comprehensive account of economic life in the Soviet Union, have said:

> Soviet managers work to please the state agency with jurisdiction over their firms. ...the plan is all important, and the leadership extols it as law. The targets of the plan are expressed in terms of 'gross output'—goods measured by volume, surface area, weight, or number. The factory concentrates all production efforts on meeting gross output targets.[14]
>
> ...if one considers that no enterprise director in the Soviet Union is constrained by a bottom line, that no director faces the specter of bankruptcy if the cost of production consistently exceeds the value of the final product, and that all directors can obtain subsidies from the state banking system to bail out their operations, then it becomes obvious that waste is built into the system. There is no incentive to conserve resources, because the factory manager is determined to meet output targets at whatever the cost.[15]

Roberts and LaFollette describe the character of accountancy in such an environment:

> Soviet factory directors must report on the status of the firm's plan fulfillment monthly, quarterly, and annually. Key personnel of the firm spend much of their time preparing these reports. Since the firm's appearance on paper is crucial, the director enlists the aid of the chief accountant, the planning chief, and the chief engineer to manipulate

production figures as the deadline approaches and it is clear that the firm is nowhere near fulfilling its norms.[16]

> A shadowy character has arisen from the universal shortages: the *tolkach*, ...[who] are people who have a network of personal connections enabling them to locate a source for virtually any item. They extensively use the black market in stolen state goods and are provided with expense accounts to wine and dine and bribe anyone who can wrangle supplies. ...they are never officially on any company's payroll but are paid through ingenious juggling of accounts devised by the chief accountant.[17]

Socialist accountancy apparently does not want for creativity.

Tax Accounting

Popular notions that equate accountancy with the preparation of tax returns are somewhat disturbing. Surely they are related, but the determination of taxable income and tax liabilities serves purposes distinct from, and often unrelated to, the profit-loss determination of economic calculation.

Since its inception in 1913, the federal income tax has proven to be an insidious device of government planning as interventionism and welfarism have supplanted private enterprise and individual freedom. Taxes are used to restrict or influence consumption and to alter commercial practices; estate taxation confiscates and redistributes wealth for some vague notion of social justice; in the name of equality, government officials tax the earners of high wages or profits at greater rates. All these practices tend to promote disastrous results for the economy—often opposite of the intent of the political planners: the concentration of wealth, immobility and rigidity in the economy, capital consumption, disincentives to work, higher prices, and the elimination of competition from newcomers (which permits large corporations to become bureaucratic and unresponsive to consumers).[18]

Aside from pure economic effects of taxation, the sheer complexity of modern tax laws has imposed an enormous administrative burden on taxpayers and the economy. Consequently, taxpayers have turned to their accountants to sift through the labyrinth of laws. The rise of tax accounting is characteristic of a primitive age of mankind. Long before the eighteenth and nineteenth centuries—when relatively free markets and private ownership allowed profit calculations and economic planning to emerge in Western societies—accounting records were solely for taxing authorities:

> But not until 3200 B.C., with the rise of the first city-states in Mesopotamia, did rulers show a need for intricate records of taxation, tributes, and inventories—and for an elaborate system of symbols for communicating. [This] first writing was called cuneiform....
>
> Although cuneiform is the earliest known writing, several other systems sprouted up independently throughout the world.... The birth of most writing systems coincided with the rise of a state in which a dominating elite used written records to establish and conserve power. In Egypt, for example, early writings depicted a leader receiving tributes from the masses,....[19]

The complexity and magnitude of taxation in the United States has once again given tax accountants a prominent role in society:

> The present business taxes have created a new profession: the tax expert. They have withdrawn hundreds of thousands of men and women from productive employment and put them to work on tax matters. They have crowded not only government bureaus with thousands of tax agents assisted by large clerical staffs but also the accounting departments of our productive enterprises with an even larger number of tax accountants, tax counselors and advisors, tax lawyers, and the like.[20]

Thus, highly skilled people are attracted to lucrative careers in tax accounting to help steer taxpayers through the web of tax statutes. The original federal income tax return of 1913 consisted of merely a few pages. In 1990, the instructions alone for just the federal individual return occupied over sixty pages. Forms and instructions for all types of taxpayers range into the tens of thousands of pages. Graduate degrees conferred in taxation are not based upon theoretical knowledge of public financing but are granted to those who are capable of maneuvering through the maze of tax laws which the government has imposed. How can the United States consider itself a free society when citizens need college degrees to defend themselves against a convoluted and oppressive tax system?

And the trends show no sign of reversing. The Tax Reform Act of 1986, enacted under President Reagan, was touted as tax simplification but was nothing of the kind. It introduced a whole round of new complexities into the tax laws which boggled even the minds of tax professionals and merely reshuffled tax burdens. The frequency of major tax law changes was measured in decades, but now each new year brings with it major revisions adding complications and higher costs to tax compliance. Taking into account the fees of public accountants, the cost of tax departments maintained by private firms, legal fees to tax attorneys, charges by pension plan administrators, and the budgets of the IRS and U.S. Tax Courts, the national expenditures for tax services and administration of tax laws in 1991 will approach at least *$80 billion.*[21] As America has compromised its free society, it has built a tax structure entrenched with special interests, making the restoration of limited government a formidable challenge.

The Bottom Line

Accounting is the language of economic exchanges. It has many dialects which mirror the economic policies of a given society. As such, the focus of accountants can serve as a barometer of the economic freedom enjoyed by society's members.

Where we find accountants devoted to elaborate tax accounting, where we find accountants devising systems to maintain hiring and production quotas, where the costs of inventory are categorized by country of origin, where we hire accountants to perform statutory audits in compliance with federal agencies, where cost accounting is guided by the requirements of government contracting, we will find a society where government dominates at the expense of individual freedom and private property.

During the twentieth century the United States has experienced a steady rise of government intervention into the economy. It has been transformed into a welfare state of political entitlements. Condemned on moral grounds by anti-capitalists, "profits" has become a dirty word. But economic calculation—the determination of profits and losses—is an inseparable link in the free society and the indispensable guide to economic prosperity. When the primary focus of accountants is the refinement of profit calculations and systems of product costing, when management information is no longer secondary to other financial information, when accountants appreciate the social benefits of profits and losses and can rebuff the critics of the profit system, when the prominence of tax accountancy is once again relegated to history, we will have rediscovered the free society—that's the bottom line.

Notes and References

1. Montaigne, Fen, "Soviets' Blighted Food System," *The Philadelphia Inquirer,* (October 27, 1991), p. 1-A.
2. Sennholz, Hans F., "The Formation and Function of Prices," *The Freeman*, (February, 1965). Also, *cf.* Mises, Ludwig von, *Human Action*, 3rd edition, (Chicago: Henry Regnery Co., 1966), Hayek, Friedrich A., *Individualism and Economic Order,* (Chicago: Henry Regnery Company; Gateway Edition, 1972), and Hayek, Friedrich A., editor, *Collectivist Economic Planning,* (London: G. Routledge & Sons, Ltd., 1935), for lengthy analyses of economic calculation.
3. Mises, Ludwig von, *Bureaucracy,* (New Rochelle: Arlington House, 1969, Yale Press, 1944).
4. *Cf.* Mises, Ludwig von, *Liberalism: A Socio-Economic Exposition,* (Kansas City: Sheed Andrews and McNeel, Inc., 1978), (translation of *Liberalismus*, published in German, 1927).
5. *Cf. Idem*, *Bureaucracy*.
6. *Ibid.*, p. 1.
7. *Ibid.*, p. 19.
8. *Ibid.*, pp. 41-43.
9. *Ibid.*, p. 47.
10. *Ibid.*, p. 62.
11. Lenin, V. I., *State and Revolution*, 1917, in *Collected Works of V. I. Lenin*, Volume XXI, (New York: International Publishers, 1932), pp. 229-230.
12. Mises, *op. cit.*, p. 32, quoting Johann von Goethe, *Wilhelm Meister's Apprenticeship*, Book I, Chapter X.
13. Johnson, H. Thomas, and Kaplan, Robert S., *Relevance Lost: The Rise and Fall of Management Accounting,* (Boston, MA: Harvard Business School Press, 1987), p. 176.
14. Roberts, Paul Craig, and LaFollette, Karen, *Meltdown Inside the Soviet Economy,* (Washington, D.C.: Cato Institute, 1990), p. 8.
15. *Ibid.*, pp. 21-22.
16. *Ibid.*, p. 18.
17. *Ibid.*, p. 15.
18. For relevant, detailed discussions of taxation and its effects on the economy, *cf.* Rothbard, Murray N., *Power and Market: Government and the Economy,* (Menlo Park, CA: Institute for Humane Studies), 1970, Chapter 4, and Sennholz, Hans F., *Death & Taxes*, Second Revised Edition, (Cedar Falls, IA: Center for Futures Education, 1982).

19. Schrof, Joannie M., "From Tax Audits to Poetry," *U.S. News & World Report*, (November 5, 1990), p. 70.
20. Sennholz, Hans F., "Business Taxes Concern Everyone," *The Freeman*, (March, 1959), pp. 38-39.
21. Sources used for this calculation include Cole, Barbara, "Surviving the Rate Race," *Accounting Today*, (November 5, 1990), p. S4; U.S. Department of Commerce, "Professional Services," *U.S. Industrial Outlook 1991*, p. 52-1; and the Budget of the U.S. Government, Fiscal Year 1992.

32

PRIVATE PROPERTY, NON-OWNERSHIP, AND THE THIRD WORLD

John A. Sparks*

The new economic order that was built on individual freedom and private property...liberated working people from their inveterate lot.

Hans F. Sennholz, *The Politics of Unemployment*

In Defense of Property Rights

The private property rights of persons have long been protected by both the Roman civil law with its many devices and doctrines[1] and by the English common law with its "bundle of rights" formulation. In the latter, ownership or property rights are comprised of a group of rights which the owner of the good claims toward others.[2] When we say that Mr. Schmied "owns" a shirt, we are ascribing to him a certain list of rights.

First, he has a right to use the shirt for his own benefit and to retain possession of it. This is another way of saying that, in the usual case, he can insist upon others not using it. A second right included in ownership is the right to alienate the shirt, which simply means to sell it to another. Once again, the right of transfer is available to the owner, not to non-owners. It is an exclusive right. The third right is the right of the owner, Mr. Schmied, to give the shirt to someone else. Lawyers call this an *inter vivos* gift (*i.e.*, a gift made between two living persons). Similarly, the owner has a right to devise or bequeath the shirt (will it to another). In

*Dr. Sparks is Chairman of the Department of Business Administration and International Management, Grove City College, Grove City, PA. He is also President of Public Policy Education Fund, Inc., a nonprofit organization which issues reports on public policy questions.

addition, the owner can choose to lease or rent the good to someone else, thus giving up temporary possession of the good but not the right to have the good returned. Finally, although implied by the right to lease, the owner has a right to earn income from the shirt (such as selling advertising space on it). All these rights when amalgamated, constitute ownership. Taking away these incidents would deny Mr. Schmied ownership even though the good technically still may be titled in his name.

In addition to legal defenses, various ethical and religious arguments in favor of private property have been offered through the centuries. One of the oldest and clearest sources arguing in favor of ownership is the Bible. Holy Scriptures maintain the principle of ownership. First, the Scriptures give specific protection by providing punishment for those who commit crimes against the owners of real and personal property. Most obviously, theft of property is condemned by the Decalogue and punished by requiring restitution (the restoring of the good or its value), as well as "super-restitution" (a multiple of the value of the item stolen).[3] As the Reformational leader John Calvin said in summarizing the Eighth Commandment, "To sum up: we are forbidden to pant after the possessions of others, and consequently are commanded to strive faithfully to help every man to keep his own possessions."[4] Calvin also says that one function of civil government is, "[I]t provides that each man may keep his property safe and sound."[5] Real estate is accorded separate, more specific protection by Biblical law. The injunctions against moving landmarks were meant to make inviolate the boundary stones by which the Hebrews marked the limits of their holdings.[6] The moving of the stones, which was a common practice among land thieves, was hated by the Almighty.[7]

On the subject of inheritance, there are clear legal rules designed to protect the descent of property to family members.[8] Moreover, the Old Testament law contains provisions for the restoration of lost property,[9] reparation for damage or loss to property,[10] provisions for governing risk of loss in bailments,[11] and redemption regulations.[12] In conclusion, Holy Writ provides ample evidence of God's consistent recognition of ownership rights in property, His intention to maintain and protect these arrangements, and His extreme dissatisfaction with those who attempt to take lawful property from another by direct or indirect means.

Another commonly referenced moral defense for private property is provided by John Locke in his *Two Treatises of Government.* Locke's theoretical justification for private property begins with certain propositions about God and man. The first is that the world was intended by the Creator for the use of His creatures. Second, that God intended us to labor for our livelihood.[13] Third, that we have a kind of exclusive right to ourselves, which Locke calls a property in our own person (apparently meaning a right to one's own labor). Fourth, we have a right to mix our labor with other resources, and in so mixing we are entitled to own the resource.[14] Locke's conception can be understood by imagining a person taking land that was not previously owned by anybody else and cultivating it, thus producing an ownership right for himself. By his effort and work, he creates an historical entitlement which is superior to the claims of anyone else. One of the main purposes of civil government, if not *the* main purpose, is the preservation of property rights gained in the manner described above.[15] Because the original right which a person enjoys in his own labor is morally defensible, then its transference to "things" makes holding and owning property morally defensible.

Private property has also been defended based upon the beneficial results produced by private ownership. Hardly debatable any longer is that collectivist systems of economic organization will yield citizens meager, drab goods when contrasted with market systems based on private property. Recently, certain authors have tried to measure the disparity between politically open societies which subscribed to the rule of law, private property, and free markets and those societies which were otherwise. The study showed that the open, private property-based economies grew at three times the rate and were two and a half times as efficient as economies where freedoms were abridged.[16]

Some would say that an argument from results is not a *moral* argument; and yet, if one system repeatedly yields significantly better benefits to substantial numbers of citizens while another system produces poverty and stagnation for the mass of the citizens, then are not the opposers of the first system required to refute its superior performance before advocating the second? Nevertheless, with legal defenses, moral and religious support, the advocacy of philosophers, and even the testimony of beneficial economic results all on the side of private property, non-ownership systems still find considerable favor in the countries of the less-developed world today. What are these non-ownership systems, what theoretical features do they have, and how do they work in fact?

Systems Of Non-Ownership or Weakened Ownership

Two kinds of non-ownership systems primarily exist in the less-developed world. The first type is customary communalism or common property; the second is some variety of state socialism (often adopted after independence has been gained from a particular colonial power).[17] This essay turns first to communal forms.

Communalism

Communal systems contrast in several important ways with private property orders. First, and most fundamentally, communal systems do not recognize individual owners with exclusive rights to use and benefit from the property.[18] Jeremy Waldron writes that private property is really not a matter of the relationship between a person and a thing, but instead a legal relationship between the owner and all other persons trying to claim the thing.[19] The owner's rights in private property are best understood as recognized protections against appropriation by others. Of course, under common-property arrangements, the property belongs to all the community members, who have undivided non-exclusive interests in it. No member can lawfully keep another from use of the property. Further, this means that individuals can neither transfer (alienate) the property or its parts nor devise (will) the property. In short, most of the basic rights bundled in English common law are not recognized under traditional communal arrangements. Whereas "ownership" in the Anglo-American tradition usually means the right to exclude, to benefit from individual use, to sell and will the property, the absence of these fundamental attributes of ownership has led the writer to refer to communalism as a "non-ownership" system.

Economic science tells us that there are certain predictable results from such communitarian arrangements. The first undesirable outcome of communal property is the dwindling incentive to work on and improve the property. Individual community members have little incentive to work hard because all members have a community claim on the fruits of labor done on the common lands. Students of nineteenth-century American history are familiar with this effect from the various utopian communities such as New Harmony, Oneida, and others. The founders of such communities were often averse to private property and sought more "benign" modes of organization. Consequently, the communities frequently jettisoned private ownership and sought to operate on a communal basis. Disputes and dissensions invariably arose among the members because some did not work or work enough in the eyes of others, and yet these "slackers" were entitled to the same equal share as others who worked hard.[20] Historically, members of these communes grew preoccupied with the "fair" distribution of the ever *decreasing* "pie" and became disinterested in the production of a larger "pie." By contrast, private ownership *links* production and distribution, so to speak. If one produces, then one is entitled to receive a distribution. This tension, among others, led to the eventual dissolution of the communities.

Furthermore, with common property not only is there a dearth of incentive to produce immediate goods, but there is no natural impetus to make improvements in communal lands which will yield future benefits. Why should a community member invest his own scarce resources in clearing, fertilizing, and sowing common lands which are then used by any and all members or which may be abandoned by a community decision to relocate (nomadic communalism)?

Pure communalism tends to orient users to immediate gains from use rather than to more distant returns, which leads to yet another harmful result. Economists sometimes call it over usage, intense usage or failure to conserve. Let us take a nomadic tribe as our example. The tribal member has no compelling reason to control the grazing of his livestock. As DeMeza and Gould conclude in their analysis of hypothetical cattle graziers:

> Under free access [communalism] each grazier increases the size of his herd until the private net marginal benefit (marginal revenue product minus fixed price of input) is zero. In so doing he ignores the external diseconomy imposed on the other graziers .... Under private property, the externality is internalized. A private landlord would restrict the herd supervised by each grazier to the efficient size.[21]

As Burton says in less technical language:

> Every tribesman has the incentive to get to good pasture first, and to graze it to the point of denudation, without consideration of the external (social) costs. The result has been over-grazing, denudation of the tree and shrub cover, soil erosion and eventual 'desertification.'[22]

Individual efforts to conserve resources over the long run are best promoted by the establishment of private property, not the advocacy of communalism.

Communalism in Practice

African countries have held tightly to customs of communal land tenure or its variations. Commentator Nicholas Harman could say in 1987 that "private land ownership is common in only two African countries. They are Kenya and Zimbabwe..." Of course, South Africa should be included, although the economy there is highly regulated. Little has changed in the last four years. The contrast can be seen between two African countries, Nigeria and Kenya.

In Nigeria, except for land in and around Lagos, the capital, "...there is no such thing as a private sector ownership of farmland."[23] According to Harman, British colonial policy was to allow natives to retain their customary communal land laws other than around the capital where British colonials insisted on English common law tenures. When Great Britain granted independence to Nigeria in 1960, the system of communal ownership was understandably left in place, since it was the custom.

Today, if a farmer wishes to purchase a piece of land to farm, he must begin by negotiating with communal "owners." Typically, the village leaders or councils demand certain compensation if they agree to allow him to use the land at all. After additional approval from the state governor, the farmer may receive an "occupancy permit" with a nominal term of 99 years but, in fact, it can be revoked at any time. At best the "property right" is virtually a revocable short-term lease because the certificates of occupancy cannot be transferred or sold.[24] "What incentive is there under such a land tenure system for a private agricultural sector to develop? Why should a farmer invest in the land and attempt to improve it if it cannot be sold or inherited, if in effect the improvements made will not inure to the future benefit of that farmer or his heirs?"[25] At the time of independence, Nigeria enjoyed "a sturdy economy and an agricultural sector that produced enough food to feed the nation,"[26] but now is dependent on large quantities of imported food. The existence of communal property is an important factor.

In comparison one can look at the land tenure system of Kenya, also a former British colony. Here, for various historical and policy reasons, a system of private property ownership predominates (which is not to say that the Kenyan government has a perfect record in the protection of private property).

Worthy of note is that private property is traceable to the Kikuyu tribe, which had established a system of private land tenure in the Kenyan highlands prior to the European colonizers of the nineteenth century.[27] Furthermore, the British established a Western-style system of private ownership with individual land titles in portions of the Kenyan highlands to attract white settlers to these pieces of land. At the same time, in other parts of Kenya, African farmers still were laboring under communal systems of property and were even prohibited from cultivating export crops.[28] However, by the 1950s the colonial government began to encourage native Africans to convert communal land tenures to private ones by a process called "consolidation and registration."[29] One of the predicted benefits of this conversion was the increased ability of African farmers to pledge land as collateral for improvement loans. Since independence, the major thrust of Kenya's land policy has been to continue this process of what could be called the privatization of land holdings. Today, "most of the country's high-potential land area [has] ... been registered under individual title to more than 1.5 million households..."[30] As Michael Lofchie, one of the most astute commentators on developments in Africa says, "Officials believe that the individual ownership of land encourages landowners to invest in the development of their farms and that it facilitates private lending for agricultural development because land titles can be used as collateral for loans."[31] Kenya's liberation of farmers from communal land tenure systems has led to stable agricultural production, virtually no dependence on food aid, and a sturdy farming citizenry experienced in the responsibility of ownership.

We should note in passing that considerable pressure was placed upon the Jomo Kenyatta government at independence and at various subsequent junctures to engage in vast land redistribution programs. To its credit, that government resisted such sweeping programs. When in early years of independence it did concede some land distribution, the government purchased it from white highland owners and did not confiscate it. This program was completed by 1965, and since then privatization through registration has been the prime characteristic of Kenya land policy.[32] Communalism, to the extent that it remains the social pattern of property arrangements in the less-developed world, should be reduced by programs of registration like those adopted by Kenya. The state's only role should be to recognize private land titles as soon as individual claimants can show a valid claim to a parcel.

Socialism and Ownership in the Third World

Turning from the limitations of traditional communal land tenure systems, one finds that various Third World countries adopted socialist systems of collective property following independence (or more precisely, the highly controlled economies that were engendered by many colonial regimes prior to independence were continued by the new rulers). Although over time Third World countries produced unique versions of socialism, the same essential components are always found—state control and ownership of the means of production either through collectives or state enterprises and attempts at central planning of production. As with communal property, socialist property is the antithesis of the bundle of rights which Anglo-American law calls ownership. (Of course, in practice, even the most intensely socialist regimes seldom succeed in totally abolishing private ownership. Usually some remnants of the ownership of personal property remain, small legal markets are permitted to exist for privately produced goods, and the illegal or black markets flourish).

There are some differences between communal and socialist property. Communalism originated in customary practice, but state socialism is largely a product of ninteenth-century meliorist thought. Communalism does not arise out of a conscious effort to impose an equal distribution of wealth on a given group. Despite these differences, the idea of socialist property is quite similar to that of communal property in that ownership is to be exercised by society collectively and not by individual owners. Consequently, the effects produced by socialism on the production, exchange, and use of property are virtually the same as those effects produced by communal property. In summary, because the whole society is said to "own" socialist property, citizens as individuals have little incentive to work upon and improve the social property insofar as they have no exclusive claim to the fruits which their labor produces on the property (either immediately or in the future). This is not to say that such a system cannot be made to work at all. But, that which is produced will be meager compared with the product of true private ownership systems.

Socialism in the Less-Developed World—Africa

One African country which has undergone one of the longest socialist experiments is Tanzania. Julius Nyerere was president there from 1961 to 1985. Nyerere's famous Arusha declaration of 1967 put Tanzania on a socialist road patterned after Chinese central planning. Virtually the whole economy was nationalized, income was redistributed by heavy taxation, and communal agricultural villages (ujamaa) were established. Michael Lofchie, an Africa watcher, says thusly, "Tanzania has proved to be a bitter disappointment .... Once the hope of a generation of moderate as well as radical sympathizers, Tanzania is now regarded as the sick country of Africa.... Tanzanian people have suffered a drastic and possibly irreversible process of impoverishment."[33]

Collectivist agriculture was imposed from about 1969-1975 and produced discontent among the often-relocated native populations, passive resistance to working in the collective fields, and, consequently, a general decline in production of agricultural products.[34] Next came the parastatal enterprises—government-operated marketing entities through which farmers were required to sell export and certain food crops. The prices paid by the parastatals were much lower than free market prices. As a result, producers shifted their production away from the price-controlled crops; or if they continued to grow the controlled crops, the native farmers arranged to sell as much as possible across borders into other African countries at higher market (i.e., black market) prices.[35] In either case, the agricultural production for export or domestic consumption declined, producing shortages and further impoverishment of all Tanzanians.

Similar experiments in Ethiopia under the Stalinist agricultural policies of Mengistu Haile Mariam have led to widespread shortages of food, severe hunger, and outright famine. There, as in Tanzania, the governmental policies called for the collectivization of agriculture and discouraged private grain trading. And in war-torn Mozambique, the idea of full-fledged private ownership was dealt a serious blow. The original draft of the constitution eliminated state ownership of land but was revised finally to grant citizens only a limited right to "use land, which is owned and regulated by the state; the land may not be sold, mortgaged or alienated. A farmer may own a cashew tree, but not the land it grows on."[36] Once again, the state has stripped private ownership of its essential elements and has reduced the use of "property" to the pleasures of the government. Peter Berger summarizes the situation well when he says:

> The typical record of Third World socialism is one of economic stagnation, often perpetuating abject poverty if not outright starvation; the species of egalitarianism that prevails among the 'masses' is one of an equality among serfs, lorded over by a privileged elite of party bureaucrats and managers.[37]

Poorly Developed Recognition of Ownership—Peru

So far our examples have been of non-ownership systems. However, there are countries which recognize private property rights, but only after an arduous process—so much so that ownership is virtually precluded. An example of such a set of "discouraging legal arrangements" is found in Peru.

The pioneering work of Hernando de Soto and his Institute for Liberty and Democracy has given us insight into the multitude of problems created by the absence of easily recognized and established property rights. In Lima, Peru, de Soto investigated the difficulties faced by persons who invaded and occupied land that was, in 90% of the cases, owned by the state.[38] These "informals" (a term which de Soto uses to describe those who are claiming rights outside the formal, highly bureaucratized legal system) would unlawfully occupy a parcel of government land. They have, at first, no legally recognized property right. De Soto labels them as holders of an "expectative right" (that is, a right that is expected in the future but which has not as yet been fully recognized).[39] De Soto found that instead of immediately recognizing the right of the informals to the individual ownership of state land (as the U.S. government did historically with the cheap land policies in Western lands), instead of granting titles to owners, and instead of incorporating the development into the formal city, the local authorities refused and resisted such steps so that achieving legal property title took on average about 20 years!

During this "waiting period" informals suffered from all of the problems which non-owners experience. First, during this span of time of substandard legal rights, the informal "owners" made fewer and less substantial improvements in their dwellings than they would have if they had obtained clear title.[40] Secondly, the absence of good titles made the transfer of ownership extremely difficult (and once again diminished incentives to improve). Moreover, the clouded titles made the property highly questionable as collateral for a loan, for example.[41] Thirdly, leasing of the property was made extremely difficult since the owner's claim was based largely on continuing physical possession, which would have to be relinquished if a tenant was to make use of the premises.[42] Fortunately, as de Soto points out, the local authorities have improved—albeit reluctantly—the process by which titles can be obtained, thereby recognizing the validity of a property right and encouraging the improved and varied use of the property by the informals (who have in the process become formal members of the community). Of course, in the meantime, the deprivation of private property made the poorest of Peru's citizens less prosperous, less free, and less contented than they otherwise could have been had the state acknowledged rights earlier.

Today, the less-developed world awaits a further explanation and a clearer defense of private property. If leaders in these countries, or their Western advisors, continue to advocate the continuation of unproductive, non-ownership systems, then a heavy moral responsibility rests on them to answer the question: Why not try freedom? Why not try private property?

Notes and References

1. Sohm, Rudolph, *The Institutes of Roman Law* (Oxford: Clarendon Press, 1982), pp. 231-277.
2. Waldron, Jeremy, *The Right to Private Property* (Oxford: Clarendon Press, 1988), p. 27.
3. Exodus 20:15; 22:1-4; Deuteronomy 5:19; 23:24-25; Leviticus 19:11; 6:2-7.
4. Calvin, John, *Institutes of the Christian Religion*, Bk.II, Chpt.VIII, Sec. 45, (Philadelphia, PA: The Westminster Press, 1975), p. 408.
5. *Ibid.*, Bk. IV, Chpt. XX, Sec. 3, p. 1488.
6. Deuteronomy 19:14; 27:17.
7. Kent, Charles Foster, *Israel's Laws and Legal Precedents* (New York, NY: Charles Scribner's Sons, 1907), p. 120ff.; Hosea 5:10; Proverbs 22:28; 23:10 and Job 24:2.
8. Deuteronomy 21:15-17; 25:5-6; Numbers 27:1-11; 36:1-12.
9. Exodus 23:4-5; Deuteronomy 22:1-4.
10. Exodus 21:28-36; 22:7-15; Leviticus 24:18;21; 6:1-15.
11. Exodus 22:7,9,10,14,15.
12. Leviticus 25:24-27; 29-32.
13. Waldron, *op. cit.*, p. 143.
14. *Ibid.*, p. 177-184.
15. *Ibid.*, p. 137.
16. Scully, Gerald W., *Journal of Political Economy* (Vol. 96, June, 1988), pp. 661-662.
17. Gwartney, James, "Private Proerty, Freedom, and the West," *The Intercollegiate Review* (Spring/Summer, 1985), p. 29.
18. *Ibid.*, p. 40.
19. Waldron, *op. cit.*, p. 27.
20. Carson, Clarence B., *The Flight From Reality* (Irvington-On-Hudson, NY: The Foundation for Economic Education, 1969), pp. 78-81.
21. DeMeza, David, and Gould, J. R., "Free Access Versus Private Property in a Resource: Income Distribution Compared," *Journal of Political Economy* (Vol 95, No. 6, 1987), p. 1319.
22. "Epilogue" by John Burton in Cheung, Steven N. S., *The Myth of Social Costs* (London, England: Institute of Economic Affairs, 1978), pp. 85-86.
23. Harman, Nicholas, "After the Ball, A Survey of Nigeria," *The Economist* (May 3, 1986), Special Supplement, p. 35.
24. *Ibid.*

25. Sparks, John A., "Africa II—Political and Social Life," *Special Report #43*, September 1987, Public Policy Education Fund, Grove City, PA.
26. Lamb, David, *The Africans* (New York, NY: Vintage Books, 1985), p. 301.
27. Lofchie, Michael F., "Kenya: Still an Economic Miracle?" *Current History* (May, 1986), p. 223.
28. Lofchie, Michael F., "Kenya's Agricultural Success," *Current History* (May, 1986), p. 223.
29. *Ibid.*, p. 224.
30. *Ibid.*, p. 224.
31. *Ibid.*, p. 224.
32. Lofchie, Michael F., *Current History* (May, 1990), p. 211.
33. Lofchie, Michael F., "The Roots of Economic Crisis in Tanzania," *Current History* (April, 1985), pp. 159-160.
34. *Ibid.*, p. 162.
35. *Ibid.*, pp. 161-162.
36. Knight, Virginia Curtin, Mozambique's Search for Stability," *Current History* (May, 1991), p. 218.
37. Berger, Peter L., Speaking to the Third World, "*Commentary* (October, 1981), p. 33.
38. Soto, Hernando de, *The Other Path* (New York, NY: Harper & Row, 1989), p. 20.
39. *Ibid.*, p. 23.
40. *Ibid.*, p. 25.
41. *Ibid.*, p. 160.
42. *Ibid.*, p. 25.

33

HEALTH CARE IN THE TWENTIETH CENTURY: A History of Government Interference and Protection

Terree P. Wasley*

Health care costs and coverage have become a dominant force in almost everyone's life over the course of the last fifty years. One of the first questions young people entering the job market are taught to ask is, "What are the benefits with this job?" Before many workers change employment they must weigh the costs of changes in health coverage. Many people are left out of the insurance market, either because they cannot get it or cannot afford it.

Patients complain that doctors do not listen anymore, and are anxious to sue their physician for the slightest imperfection in care. Physicians are tired of struggling under mountains of paperwork from the government and insurance companies, when all they want to do is treat patients.

And the costs keep going up. With health care expenditures expected to reach $748 billion in 1991, a perplexed American public ponders the boundaries of health costs.[1] Many remember the good old days when costs were lower, coverage was better, and paperwork wasn't so complicated. Fingers are pointed at shady insurance companies, greedy doctors, and wasteful government, all at the same time. No one can figure out the answer, and all everyone knows is that costs are too high and too many people are falling through the cracks of the health care system.

*Ms. Wasley, an economist and consultant based in Washington, DC, specializes in health care issues. This essay is based upon material in her book forthcoming from the Cato Institute.

How have we in the United States come to find ourselves in this kind of "mess"? An investigation into the evolution of the medical industry in America will uncover clues to the predicament in which we find ourselves. It will expose *not* the competitive market that most Americans assume has been operating, but stifling regulation and government control, regulations originating from interest groups such as medical organizations and insurance companies, resulting in a chaotic system for both doctors and patients. What appears to be a free market operation is really an industry legislated and regulated from behind the scenes. As Ayn Rand once remarked, "The concept of *free* competition enforced by law is a grotesque contradiction in terms."

The Beginnings of Modern Medicine (1880-1930)

Health and the Federal Government

The federal government's involvement in health care started long before most would realize. As far back as 1863 Congress established the National Academy of Sciences. In 1878, it passed the National Quarantine Services Act, and in 1889, it appropriated a sum of $100,000 to aid victims of yellow fever, a figure which by 1893 had reached the million-dollar mark and had expanded to include other epidemic diseases. President Theodore Roosevelt created several commissions on health care and was instrumental in the passage of several pieces of legislation, such as the Pure Food and Drug Act and the Meat Inspection Act. From 1921-29 the Sheppard-Towner Act provided public health assistance to mothers and children.

In 1870 President Ulysses S. Grant appointed the first Surgeon General, Dr. John Woodworth. In 1879 Congress passed legislation creating a National Board of Health. From 1891 to 1911 Walter Wyman was Surgeon General of what came to be known as the U.S. Public Health Service. Congress established the United States Veterans Bureau in 1921, which became the Veterans Administration in 1929.

A Commission on Industrial Relations, created by President Woodrow Wilson in the wake of labor violence, recommended national health insurance in its final report. The labor committee of the House of Representatives held hearings on a resolution introduced by its sole Socialist member to create a national social insurance commission. Organizations of public health officers and nurses endorsed the proposal. And, although a national health plan was not enacted, the federal government continued its expansion into the health care arena with the advent of the New Deal programs of the 1930s and Lyndon Johnson's Great Society in the 1960s.

The American Medical Association (AMA) was first established as a national organization in 1847. The AMA stated as its goals raising the quality of care for patients and protecting consumers from the activities of charlatans. However, there was a concern expressed by many members to maintain the financial stability and superiority of the physician. Thus began the development of a relationship between the government and the AMA which has continued to the present day, a relationship that sometimes involved government protection of its status through legislation and regulation.[2]

Hospitals and Health Insurance

The growth in the number of hospitals during the period around the turn of the century was phenomenal. In 1873 there were only 149 hospitals in the United States In just 50 years, by 1923, the number had soared to 6,830. Most of the new hospitals built between 1890 and 1920 were financed by religious organizations and charities.

Prior to 1930, most Americans paid most of their medical expenses out of their own pockets, but as early as 1900 various employers, unions, and fraternal groups had begun to offer health insurance plans, and the "corporate doctor" began to appear in many companies. The first to appoint company doctors were railroad and mining companies. As accident rates rose in industry, steel makers and other manufacturers adopted the practice also.

By the 1920s organized medical departments with full-time physicians were common in larger companies. The railroads were the leading industry in developing extensive employee medical programs. For the mining and lumber industries, geographical considerations motivated extensive company involvement in medical care. Doctors were guaranteed a salary, usually out of mandatory deductions from workers' wages, as an inducement to move to isolated areas. By 1930, company medical services covered an estimated 540,000 workers in mining and lumbering and approximately 530,000 railway employees and their dependents.

Employee medical programs were also started in some companies as part of a movement known as "welfare capitalism." Employers provided a broad range of welfare services, including schools, housing, social and religious programs, and medical care.

Medical societies, such as the AMA, regarded the corporate doctor as a form of exploitation because it enabled companies to get doctors to bid against each other and drive down the price of their labor. Consequently, the opposition of the medical profession to the company doctor contributed to the reluctance of employers to expand medical services.

In the early part of this century prepaid medical insurance developed both in Oregon and in Washington, largely as a result of the hazardous working conditions in the lumber, railroad, and mining industries. Typical policies provided for comprehensive medical and hospital care for a fixed fee which was split between employer and employee. The insurance companies, called hospital associations, were originally begun by physicians but were later managed by non-medical personnel. Some associations owned their own hospitals and others used the facilities of community hospitals. Since many of the associations were profit-making institutions, they had excellent incentives to control medical costs.

In the late nineteenth century fraternal orders and benefits societies became extensively involved in providing life insurance and aiding the sick and disabled. By the early 1900s some eight million Americans belonged to fraternal orders. Doctors conducted examinations for the life insurance offered by the fraternal societies and began to accept contracts to care for the lodge membership. A 1917 survey in New York City listed thousands of health insurance funds, mostly branches of larger fraternal organizations.

The AMA opposed lodge practice, objecting to the unlimited service for limited pay and the "ruinous competition" it invariably introduced.[3] Many county medical societies refused membership to any doctor who contracted with a lodge.

The early years of health care in America saw the establishment of the medical profession, both through the expanded duties and formal education of the physician and the growth of the hospital system. The start of the twentieth century also witnessed the beginnings of health insurance as a method of pre-paying health care costs, and the AMA's growing control over the medical market place.

The Decade of the 1930s

Health Insurance During the Depression

By 1930, the United States had as many (or more) medical, nursing, dental schools, and hospital beds per unit of population as it has today. The Great Depression, however, slowed the expansion of health care facilities and personnel. Many Americans had experienced hardship paying for the medical care they needed. Doctors tried to make allowances for patients in financial straits, but hospitals, with higher fixed costs, had much less flexibility. Between 1929 and 1930 average hospital receipts plummeted from more than $200 per patient to less than $60. Spurred by the ravages of the Depression, patients and hospital administrators began to look for some way to pay and be paid. Hospitals then began to turn to insurance plans as a way to guarantee a steady cash flow by spreading the financial risk.

The first plan was introduced in 1929 at Baylor University Hospital in Dallas, Texas. By paying a monthly fee in advance, a group of 1,500 schoolteachers contracted with the hospital to provide care should they need it. The fee was paid whether or not the individual teacher ever used the services. By spreading the risk over a number of teachers the hospital could afford to provide care if and when it was needed.

The idea caught on and other hospitals established similar plans. Soon, groups of nonprofit hospitals in several cities organized multiple hospital insurance plans. These plans gave subscribers a choice of medical care providers and therefore attracted more patients, strengthening the income to the participating hospitals. This multiple hospital plan served as a model for Blue Cross, established in 1932 in Sacramento, California.

These hospital plans changed the concept of insurance and forever changed the American health care system. Unlike other forms of insurance, such as home or auto, the primary purpose of these hospital plans was not to protect consumers from large, unforeseen expenses, but rather to keep hospitals in business by guaranteeing them a regular income. While these plans benefited consumers by giving them a predictable method of paying for their medical care, they contained serious flaws that would become increasingly apparent as our health care system developed:

- The plans centered on "front-end" coverage. They would pay for initial hospitalization and then terminate coverage after a specified number of days, exposing patients to high out-of-pocket costs. This encouraged hospitalization and contributed to the rise in health care costs.
- The plans reinforced the public notion of hospitals as the primary providers of medical care. To take advantage of their hospital plan patients had to be treated in the hospital. This was a first step toward a medical care system biased in favor of specific providers or services.
- The plans established a method for paying health insurance benefits that was different from the way benefits were paid under other forms of insurance. Instead of providing indemnity coverage, hospital plans paid service benefits. Under indemnity plans, such as automobile insurance, the policyholder is directly reimbursed a specified amount to compensate for his loss. Under a services benefits policy, the insurance covers certain specified services, whatever their cost might be. Under this kind of policy, the policyholder has little incentive to get the best value for the money, and the service provider has every incentive to increase the cost of his services or continue recommending additional services of marginal benefit.

The Beginning of Blue Cross and Commercial Insurance

In 1932 a community-wide health plan was developed in California. Under it, participating hospitals in a given area agreed to provide services to subscribers who paid their premiums to the plan rather than to individual hospitals. This concept eliminated any competition between participating hospitals. Hospitals in other areas embraced such plans and marketed them on a not-for-profit basis. They became known as Blue Cross plans. By 1937 these plans had 800,000 subscribers, while competing plans set up by individual hospitals had only 125,000. By 1940 membership in Blue Cross plans had ballooned to six million.

In response to Blue Cross, commercial insurers began to offer health plans. They calculated rates based upon their experience related to differences in age and health. Commercial policies offered cash payments to individuals rather than paying hospitals directly, and coverage was provided for physician services. By 1940 commercial insurers covered 3.7 million people. In response to the expansion of commercial health insurance, doctors established Blue Shield plans to cover physician services.

In the mid-1930s, some state insurance commissions tried to subject multiple hospital plans to the same government regulations as other types of insurance. They wanted to require these new plans to maintain reserve funds—that is, to set aside a portion of their premium revenues to cover unexpectedly large claims. In response, hospitals and doctors, working with the American Hospital Association and the AMA promoted state legislation to exempt Blue Cross plans from normal insurance regulations. In exchange, Blue Cross plans were required to serve the entire community by providing insurance to anyone who wanted it and charging rates that were affordable to lower income people. Blue Cross plans also received federal tax exemption as charitable organizations and were often exempted from other taxes such as real estate taxes. In some states commercial insurance policies sold to individuals were required to meet minimum benefit and premium rates, whereas Blue Cross policies were not.

The combination of negotiated rates with providers and the regulatory exemptions gave Blue Cross plans enormous financial advantages over other insurers. Of the total population with hospital insurance in 1940, half were covered by Blue Cross, and until the 1980s, Blue Cross and Blue Shield never held less than 40 percent of the entire health insurance market.[4] Unlike other health insurance companies, Blue Cross and Blue Shield were never enemies of the medical community. In fact, many believed that they were created to represent and protect the hospitals and physicians. A majority of the governing boards of both Blue Cross and Blue Shield in 1959 were either hospital trustees or administrators and physicians. Hospital finance experts Berman and Weeks concluded, "Blue Cross was founded to save hospitals from financial ruin."[5]

Probably the most interesting and eventually devastating contribution made by the "Blues" to the health care system were the reimbursement procedures they adopted. It was a system that hospitals approved of, and because of the domination of the market by the "Blues," other commercial insurers were forced to adopt the same policies to remain competitive. This reimbursement procedure, known as *cost-plus*, has contributed significantly to the continued rise in health care costs.

Cost-Plus Reimbursement

Under the "Blues," physicians were reimbursed either according to a negotiated schedule of fees or on the basis of what insurers considered to be "reasonable and customary" charges. Hospitals were reimbursed based on the "cost-plus" method. For doctors, this meant that they would be paid whatever they charged, provided it was generally comparable to the fees charged by other doctors in their locality. For hospitals, cost-plus reimbursement meant that the insurer paid the hospital a percentage of its costs, according to the percentage of policyholders using the hospital's services, plus an additional percentage of the hospital's working and equity capital.

The consequence of this was to create a perverse incentive for hospitals to increase costs. Under a cost-plus system, increased costs meant additional income for a hospital, while reduced costs meant diminished income. The more a hospital improved its facilities, equipment, or services, the more revenue it received. In essence, under the cost-plus system, health insurance assumed the role of insuring that hospitals had enough income to cover their costs. In doing so they became the representatives for the suppliers of medical care and not the recipients. Since hospitals and physicians could increase their incomes by increasing their costs, the cost-plus system inevitably led to higher health care costs.

In the cost-plus system, pressures to increase spending on health care were relentless. Patients had no reason to show restraint, since the money they spent belonged not to them but to a third-party. The role of the insurance company in the system was to pay whatever bills were submitted with few questions asked. Cost increases were then passed along to policyholders in the form of higher health insurance premiums.

Cost-plus reimbursement, now entrenched in the health care system, is contradictory to the market, where prices and competition allocate resources. It frequently creates incentives which are the opposite of those created by the market.

Prepaid Health Plans

About the same time the first hospital insurance plan was instituted at Baylor University Hospital the idea of a "prepaid" health plan began to emerge. In 1929 employees of the Los Angeles Department of Water and Power arranged with two physicians to provide comprehensive services for about 2,000 workers and their families. The plan cost each subscriber $2 a month and provided hospital and medical care. Soon other employee groups joined the program, and by 1935 the Ross-Loos Clinic had enrolled more than 12,000 workers and 25,000 dependents.

Five years later Kaiser Industries asked Dr. Sidney Garfield to form a group practice to provide medical services for workers building the Grand Coulee Dam in the state of Washington. In Dallas a mutual benefit association of about 800 street railway workers contracted with a private clinic for medical services. The workers paid 85 cents a month, while the company contributed $100 monthly.

In rural America groups of consumers organized plans that hired physicians to provide medical care services on a fixed salary. These cooperatives charged their members a predetermined fixed fee. The first "medical cooperative" was formed in 1929 in Elk City, Oklahoma by Dr. Michael Shadid. Called the Farmers Union Hospital Association, the members owned the hospital, paid staff doctors a fixed salary, and received medical care on a prepaid basis.

The AMA was hostile to both the prepaid plans and the consumer cooperatives, and launched a campaign to enact legislation regulating and even outlawing these plans. Even when prepaid plans were controlled by physicians, the AMA disapproved of them as a form of "unethical" contract practice. The founders of the Ross-Loos clinic were expelled by their local medical societies. The local medical profession repeatedly tried to deprive Dr. Shadid of his medical license, frightening away physicians wanting to join the cooperative, and keeping the physicians that did join out of the local medical association. Shadid eventually triumphed in a lawsuit that charged the local medical association with restraint of trade, and physicians in the cooperative were then allowed in as members of the association.

The question of cooperative medicine finally came to a head when the AMA was indicted on charges of violating the Sherman Antitrust Act in its efforts to suppress the Group Health Association of Washington, D.C. GHA was organized in 1937 as a nonprofit cooperative by employees of the Federal Home Loan Bank, providing medical and hospital care through salaried physicians. Immediately the AMA called on government authorities to take legal action against what it regarded as unregulated health insurance and the corporate practice of medicine. Unsuccessful in enlisting the government's help, the AMA threatened retaliation against the plan's doctors, and persuaded Washington hospitals not to accept the plan. The Supreme Court upheld a conviction of the AMA on antitrust violations in 1943.

Beginning in 1939, medical associations successfully lobbied for state intervention to assure professional control of prepayment insurance plans. Within the next decade twenty-six states passed laws effectively barring consumer-run medical service plans. In these states, either the incorporators of a medical service plan had to be doctors, or a majority of directors had to be doctors, or the plan had to be approved by the state medical society.

Seventeen states required all plans to allow "free choice" of physician (i.e., unlimited choice). Free choice of physician effectively ruled out the prepaid group practice plans. It also prevented plans from including only those doctors and hospitals that might agree to charge a lower price or give better service. And since free choice was feasible in a plan only if the doctors accepted a definite fee schedule, and since only the medical society could provide such a fee schedule, the requirement for free choice conferred a monopoly in medical-service plans on the profession. All of the various state restrictions on prepaid medical plans were significant in retarding the growth of such plans and skewing the market toward fee-for-service medical care and indemnity insurance like Blue Cross/Blue Shield.

Government Health Care Programs

The government's role in providing health care to the public continued to expand during the 1930s. The Ransdell Act, signed in 1930, conferred on the National Institute of Health the mandate of ascertaining the cause, prevention, and cure of disease. In 1938, the Interdepartmental Technical Committee on Medical Care, whose members were from the Public Health Service, the Children's Bureau, and the Social Security Board, proposed a national health program that included expanded public medical care to all the medically needy; and a comprehensive program designed to increase and improve medical service for the entire population, financed by general taxation or by specific insurance contributions from the beneficiaries. In February, 1939, Senator Robert Wagner of New York introduced a "National Health Bill" which incorporated these provisions. But President Franklin Roosevelt never pushed for passage of a national health plan, stating that it was "impossible to go up against the medical societies."

The 1940s and 1950s

Employer-Provided Health Insurance

The major development in health care during the 1940s was the growth of employer-provided health insurance. World War II brought about a shortage of labor, and wartime wage and price controls prohibited employers from increasing salaries to attract workers. However, in 1942 the War Labor Board decided that fringe benefits up to 5 percent of wages would not be considered inflationary. Employers began to offer health benefits as a way of providing additional compensation. Total enrollment in group hospital plans grew from less than 7 to about 26 million subscribers.

Concurrently, the Internal Revenue Service ruled that the purchase of health insurance for workers was a legitimate cost of doing business and could be deducted from taxable business income. The IRS also ruled that workers did not have to include the value of health insurance benefits in calculating their taxable income. These rulings amounted to a giant tax incentive for both employers and taxpayers, and did much to institutionalize employer-provided health care into the system.

The unions soon recognized that employer-provided health care was a desirable benefit and began to negotiate for it in their contracts. In 1941 Chrysler agreed to set up a group health plan with its recently recognized union. The initial plan covered only hospitalization, and employees paid the entire cost through payroll deductions. The Committee for Industrial Organization (CIO) declared in 1946 that health insurance was a high priority, and by 1948 ten unions had negotiated health and welfare plans. That same year the National Labor Relations Board (NLRB) ruled that health benefits were a legitimate subject of collective bargaining, and this encouraged the spread of plans even after the end of the war.

In the *Inland Steel* case of 1949, The U.S. Supreme Court ruled that certain fringe benefits, including health care plans, were among the collective bargaining issues the Taft-Hartley Labor Relations Act gave unions the right to negotiate. The number of union workers covered by health plans went from 2.7 million to 12 million by 1955.[6] Unions, through collective bargaining, became a significant influence on the medical care system.

Collective bargaining agreements expanded the scope of coverage as well as employers' contributions. Coverage of medical expenses caught up with hospitalization coverage. By the end of 1954, over 60 percent of the population had some type of hospital insurance, 50 percent some type of surgical insurance, and 25 percent medical insurance.[7] In 1945 employers paid only 10 percent of health care expenses, but by 1950 collective bargaining agreements were requiring them to pay 37 percent. In 1959, the United Steelworkers ended a 116-day strike when a settlement was reached that required the steel companies to pay the entire premium for health insurance. General Motors, Ford, and Chrysler followed with similar agreements with the United Automobile Workers in 1961.

An entirely new system of health care financing was created during the decades of the 1940s and 1950s. Government encouraged the development and expansion of provider-oriented insurance plans that ultimately distorted the health care delivery system. Employer-provided plans offering first-dollar and routine care coverage contributed significantly to the rise in health care costs. The preponderance of employer-provided insurance worsened the position of those without health plans because third-party payments tend to increase demands for services significantly and fuel their rising costs. Pressure from those left out of the system resulted in intervention through government health programs.

First-Dollar Coverage

Health insurance policies that cover first-dollar expenses (front-end coverage) pay for routine care. The defect in these policies is that there is no coverage for the medical calamities that can wipe out economically a patient and his family. Interestingly, front-end health insurance operates contrary to all other forms of insurance. The most obvious example is auto insurance where a driver insures himself for catastrophic damages and loss but pays out-of-pocket for routine repairs and maintenance.

Policies that pay for routine care actually favor the interests of physicians and hospitals more than the patient. Under an acute-care (routine) policy, the more treatment a doctor or hospital provides, the more money he receives. Under these plans, doctors are encouraged to prescribe additional treatments up to the limit of the patient's insurance coverage, even though these treatments may improve the patient's health or well-being only slightly.

Why do people purchase first-dollar, routine care coverage for their health care when they wouldn't think of purchasing that coverage for their automobile? Simply stated, they do so because the tax code encourages them to do so. Health insurance plans are viewed as tax-free compensation, not as real insurance. Workers then favor coverage that pays for routine care, freeing up their discretionary income for other uses. Insurance is no longer used for its normal purpose of spreading risk but for tax avoidance.

This form of coverage influences patients to demand additional and possibly unnecessary medical services because they have no reason to question the costs. Doctors and hospitals do not have any financial incentives to control costs either, and therefore increase prices and the quantity of their services.

Besides enacting tax incentives that skewed the insurance market, government intervention generated another problem in the industry—"experience rating." Because the "Blues" were protected by government due to their exemption from taxes and reserve requirements, they had a competitive advantage over commercial insurers. Commercial insurers turned to "experience rating" their insurance plans as a way to compete against the "Blues."

Usually, insurance companies use some form of "community rating" to calculate a basic premium. The premium reflects the average frequency and cost of claims among all the policyholders in a given area. Under an "experience rating" system, the cost of the premium depends on the actual experience of the individual policyholder, based on the frequency and size of the claims he files. Commercial insurers began to sell insurance to employers with relatively healthy, low-risk employees at cheaper rates than the "Blues." Since the "Blues" often were required by law to use a "community rating" system, they responded to this competition by receiving permission to use a "modified" community rating to reflect experience.

A problem evolved that companies calculated premiums for group plans based on those working for a single employer. As a result, smaller companies that have fewer employees over whom to spread costs generally must pay more for insurance. Additionally, they face the risk of large premium increases or even cancellation if only one employee becomes seriously ill. Had the government not intervened on behalf of the "Blues" and provided them with legislative protection, the "experience rating" system may not have developed, a system that results in a significant portion of small businesses not being able to afford health insurance coverage for their employees.

Government Health Programs

World War II marked the beginning of a great expansion of the federal government's role in health care. There were really four major post-war health programs: medical research, mental health, the VA, and hospital construction.

The National Institutes of Health (NIH) budget swelled from $180,000 to $4 million from 1945 to 1947. By 1950 the budget had grown to $46.3 million. In 1948 Congress created a National Heart Institute, and soon five other institutes followed. In 1950 Congress established the National Science Foundation. In 1953

Congress created the Department of Health, Education, and Welfare (HEW). Between 1941 and 1951, the federal budget for medical research rose from $3 million to $76 million.[8] Between 1955 and 1960, the NIH budget exploded from $81 million to $400 million.[9]

Another area of government involvement following the war was hospital construction. In 1942 the American Hospital Association organized a commission to lobby for a national program for hospital construction. This Commission on Hospital Care recommended a huge program of construction: an additional 195,000 beds at an investment of $1.8 billion. In 1946 the Hospital Survey and Construction Act (Hill-Burton) was passed. By the time the law expired in 1978, the program had used $4.4 billion in federal money as leverage to get state and local governments to contribute an additional $9.1 billion, building 500,000 beds.

The 1960s

Government Health Legislation

The preponderance of employer-provided health care accentuated the medical needs of those without insurance, primarily the unemployed, poor, and elderly. As the 1960s began, pressures began to build for some sort of government health program that would provide care for these groups. In 1960 Congress responded to this urging by passing the legislation known as Kerr-Mills. It extended federal support for welfare medicine programs to the states, with the federal government providing between 50 and 80 percent of the funds. But by 1963 the five large industrial states with only 32 percent of the population over 65 was receiving 90 percent of the funds. Proponents began to look for a more effective alternative.

Dissatisfied with a piecemeal approach, champions of the New Deal programs of the 1930s began agitating anew for a national health plan, while groups such as the AMA, fearing adoption of such a program, advocated decentralized, state-administered programs which would maintain the autonomy of physicians and hospitals. A compromise was reached in 1965, and the Medicare program was born.

The largest portion of the program, Medicare Part A, was a slimmed-down version of the universal social insurance scheme advocated by proponents of national health insurance. The other section, Medicare Part B, was a voluntary program to cover physician services, paid for by a mixture of premiums and general federal revenues. Medicare, through an intermediary (usually Blue Cross), provided direct payment for care of the elderly individual. Medicaid was based on the alternative originally proposed by the AMA. It paid for medical care for the poor, regardless of age, financed by a combination of matching federal and state funds and administered by the states. In an instant, with the passage of Medicare and Medicaid, the government had become the largest single purchaser of health care.

With the adoption of Medicare and Medicaid, the third-party payment system dominated the health care industry. Most Americans were covered either by private health insurance or a government program for their hospital and physician costs. But Medicare and Medicaid brought the same defects found in the private insurance industry to the health care landscape, accelerating the rate of medical price inflation already set in motion by cost-plus reimbursement, lack of patient incentive to control costs, and first-dollar coverage.

The cost-plus reimbursement policies of private insurance were replicated in Medicare, and by many states in their Medicaid programs. Hospitals charged Medicare for the "reasonable cost" of treating patients and doctors were reimbursed for their "reasonable and customary" fees. According to Joseph Califano, federal adoption of the cost-based, fee-for-service reimbursement system became a blank check for American hospitals and doctors. The volume of hospital services reimbursed on a cost-plus basis rose 75 percent owing to Medicare and Medicaid. The rate of increase in hospital spending, which had averaged 8.8 percent between 1960 and 1965, almost doubled, approaching an average annual increase of 15 percent from 1965 to 1970. Sharp rises occurred in hospital staffing, wages, and purchase of new equipment and supplies.[10]

Medicare's benefit structure favored the same kind of first-dollar, acute-care coverage as private insurance. Under Part A patients were charged a small deductible but paid nothing else for a 60-day hospital stay. After 60 days Medicare paid a decreasing amount, saddling seriously ill patients with catastrophic costs.

The medical care provided to beneficiaries under Medicare and Medicaid was either free or greatly subsidized, and premiums were nonexistent or unrelated to individual or group usage. Consequently, beneficiaries had no incentive to question costs and every motivation to demand more services.

Following the passage of Medicare, the Johnson Administration was faced with threats from physicians and hospitals that they would not participate in the program. In response to White House pressure to get the plan off to a running start, the Department of Health, Education, and Welfare issued reimbursement regulations that were extremely beneficial to the medical industry. Not only were doctors granted the power to charge "reasonable" and "customary" fees, they also received significant control over the setting of Medicare fees.

Hospitals also succeeded in having reimbursements include the costs of interest on current and capital debt, and pressuring HEW to pay for depreciation on buildings and equipment that had been purchased with federal funds under the Hill-Burton Act. In addition, government officials agreed to give them a 2 percent add-on to their actual costs for treating Medicare patients. According to Joseph Califano, "the 2 percent was a bribe to get the hospital industry to cooperate with Medicare."[11] The decision to provide capital reimbursement under Medicare involved millions of dollars annually in federal expenditures over and above the monies spent through the Hill-Burton program.

The 1970s and 1980s

The Cost Explosion in Health Care

The eruption in health care costs over the past few decades has been staggering. Per capita personal health care expenditures have increased from $70 in 1950 to over $1,200 in 1982. By the year 2000 the health care bill is expected to top $2,600 for each man, woman, and child.

Spiraling medical costs have strained government programs. In the decade between 1978 and 1988, Medicare spending jumped from $25.2 billion to $87.6 billion, a growth in constant dollars of

99 percent. At the same time, total Medicaid program expenses rose from $18.9 billion in 1978 to $54.7 billion in 1988, a 65 percent increase in constant dollars.

The higher inflation rates of the 1970s exacerbated the weaknesses in the health care financing system. As prices increased, workers demanded higher wages, oftentimes pushing them into a higher tax bracket. Facing a rising tax liability made employer-provided non-taxable benefits, such as health care plans, increasingly more attractive. More companies began to offer health insurance plans to workers and unions demanded additional benefit coverage to make up for a loss in disposable income. For example, between 1970 and 1980 the number of Americans with dental insurance plans rose from 12 million to 80 million.[12] Corporations and small businesses alike began to see their health costs skyrocket.

The ability to exclude health insurance from taxable income encourages employees to purchase too much insurance for their needs. The tax law also encourages over-insurance by allowing doctor's fees to be paid by an employer with pre-tax dollars, whereas fees paid by employees must be expended with after-tax dollars. This encourages first-dollar 100 percent health coverage.

Corporations and small businesses alike began to see their health costs "shoot through the roof." A survey of *Fortune* 500 companies and the nation's 250 largest nonindustrial firms found that "from 1981 to 1983, the average rate of increase of health insurance premiums was a staggering 20 percent." Total health care costs for those firms, on the average, amounted to 24 percent of after-tax profits.[13] From 1983 to 1984 medical costs for many corporations jumped 20 to 25 percent.[14]

The Government's Response

As costs continued to escalate through the 1970s and 1980s, what did government do to rectify the situation? Did it rescind its protection of the third-party payment system? Did it remove the tax incentives that encouraged employer-provided insurance? Did it eliminate cost-plus reimbursement from the Medicare program? Did it pass legislation nullifying the many laws and restrictions imposed on the health care market? Did it attempt to remove the incentives that result in increased demand for medical care with little concern for the cost?

The answer to all these questions is no. Instead of removing the controls and restrictions that were hampering the market, the federal government attempted to stifle the outcome of bad policies with a whole host of new controls and regulations, like so many bandaids on a mortal wound. The focus of all the legislation in recent years has been to control medical prices and hold down costs, specifically by applying restrictions to physicians, hospitals, and even patients.

Health Maintenance Organizations (HMOs) were created and promoted by Congress in 1973 as the solution to rising costs. It included a significant amount of regulation, including requiring all companies with 25 or more employees to offer an HMO plan to their workers. As a result of the new legislation, the grants and loans, and employer interest in controlling health care costs, HMOs grew from 26 plans with about 3 million subscribers nationwide in the early 1970s to nearly 700 plans with 28 million enrollees in 1987.

Although the growth of HMOs has been astronomical, and there has been some cost containment achieved, some physicians are expressing dissatisfaction with HMOs and other managed-care plans, and are questioning the solvency of some of the plans. It must be remembered, too, that although the HMO has been touted as a market-type solution, it was created and financially encouraged by the government and continues to be heavily regulated.

Congress introduced "professional standards review organizations" (PSROs) in 1972. Doctors review their peers' work to ensure that services Medicare paid for were medically necessary, provided according to professional standards, and rendered at the appropriate level and length of hospital stay. Although there are numerous PSROs in effect today, they have done little to check the rise in doctors' fees or to trim the number or length of hospital stays.

The National Health Planning & Resources Development Act was passed in 1974 and attempted to prevent the duplication or overexpansion of health care facilities. The idea was to control the capital investment in new facilities and technological equipment, hoping that the limitation of resources would slow utilization and curb the escalation of costs. The law required states to enact certificate-of-need legislation to implement this kind of control. But the huge bureaucracy of health service agencies that resulted from the law created such a monster that the program ended up costing more than it saved. It was eliminated in 1986 by an act of Congress.

In 1983 a major effort at controlling Medicare costs was a provision within Social Security legislation that established a "prospective payment system" (PPS) for hospital reimbursement. Under this system Medicare establishes a fixed schedule of fees that it pays hospitals for the treatment of each of 475 "diagnostic related groups" (DRGs) of illnesses. If the actual cost to the hospital is less than the DRG fee, it keeps the difference; if more, it absorbs the loss. The purpose was to encourage price consciousness and competition among hospitals.

What may have looked good on paper, however, was disappointing in reality. The PPS was destined to cause the same shortages and misallocations that any price control system would cause, and did so by shifting costs to activities not covered by the controls. Not surprisingly, costs in the Medicare program continued to rise. In the five years since the introduction of PPS, the average annual rates of growth in Medicare spending have been 6.5 percent for the Hospital Insurance program and 13.8 percent for the Supplemental Medical Insurance program,[15] much higher than the overall rate of inflation.

Another piece of regulation that drives up the cost of health care is found in a number of states—mandated benefit laws. Enacted usually as the result of lobbying from health care providers and advocates seeking coverage for various diseases, mandated benefit laws require insurance companies to pay for specific medical services. In 1970 there were only 30 state-mandated benefit laws in the entire country; today there are at least 800.[16] These laws provide a secure market for the providers of the mandated benefits, with the usual result of increasing demand for the service, increasing providers of the service, and increasing prices.

They are also a major reason that many people lack health insurance—state-mandated benefits increase the cost of insurance and price many people out of the insurance market. According to a study by the National Center for Policy Analysis, as many as one out of every four uninsured people lack health insurance because state regulations have increased the price. This means that as many as 9.3 million people lack health insurance because of current government policies.[17]

Regulations involving the approval of drugs and medical devices by the FDA have been a contributor to increased health care costs. In 1962, amendments to the Food, Drug and Cosmetic Act mandated that new drugs had to be tested and shown to be safe and effective before they were allowed on the market. Since then the process by which a new drug receives approval from the FDA has become increasingly complicated, lengthy, and costly. In 1965 it took approximately two years for FDA approval, by 1989 it had risen to three, and the cost had increased from about $4 million to over $231 million.[18] In July, 1980 the Medical Device Amendments applied some of the same standards to medical devices.

Conclusion

Despite the best efforts of business and the presumably good intentions of government, health care costs are still out of control and rising. The problem remains: until we change the fundamental defects in the system, no amount of tinkering will result in a significant slowing or reversal in the direction of increased costs. The government's hodgepodge of health care programs, its continual interference in the market, and the protection of its (and the medical community's) preferred methods of care, has distorted the market and created a built-in structure of cost escalation. It is swiftly bringing this country's health care system to the brink of disaster.

The solution to the health care crisis is to allow a system based on the market, one that offers citizens maximum freedom of choice in purchasing their health care. Only then will we see a health care system that offers sufficient coverage and good quality care at costs that all Americans can afford.

Notes and References

1. Source: Health Care Financing Administration.
2. For a more detailed account of the relationship between the AMA and government, see Goodman, John C., *The Regulation of Medical Care: Is the Price Too High?* (Washington, DC: The Cato Institute, 1980).
3. "Contract Practice," Journal of American Medical Association (49: 14 December, 1907), pp. 2028-29; "Contract Practice," *JAMA* (57: 8 July, 1911), pp. 145-46.
4. Health Insurance Association of America, Sourcebook of Health Insurance Data, 1984-1985, Tables 1.2, 1.3, 1.4, and 1.5.
5. Berman, Howard J. and Weeks, Lewis B., *The Financial Management of Hospitals,* 5th ed. (Washington, DC: Health Administration Press, 1982), p. 147.
6. Garbarino, Joseph W., *Health Plans and Collective Bargaining* (Berkeley, CA: University of California Press, 1960), pp. 19-20.
7. Anderson, Odin W. and Feldman, Jacob J., *Family Medical Costs and Voluntary Health Insurance: A Nationwide Survey* (New York, NY: McGraw-Hill, 1956), p. 11.
8. Endicott, Kenneth M. and Allen, Ernest M., "The Growth of Medical Research 1941-1953 and the Role of the Public Health Service Research Grants," *Science* (118: 25 September 1953), p. 337.
9. Congressional Quarterly Service, Congress and the Nation, 1132.
10. Califano, Joseph, Secretary of HEW.
11. *Ibid.*
12. Health Insurance Association of America, Sourcebook of Health Insurance Data, 1984-1985, Table 1.8.
13. Herzlinger, Regina E. and Schwartz, Jeffrey, "How Companies Tackle Health Care Costs: Part I," *Harvard Business Review* (July-August 1985), p. 69.
14. Califano, Joseph.
15. Based on data from the Committee on Ways and Means, U.S. House of Representatives, Background Material and Data on Programs within the Jurisdiction of the Committee on Ways and Means, 1989 edition, 15 March 1989, p. 152.
16. Goodman, John C., "An Agenda for Solving America's Health Care Crisis," National Center for Policy Analysis, Task Force Report, 1990, p. 19.

17. Goodman, John C. and Musgrave, Gerald L., "Freedom of Choice in Health Insurance," National Center for Policy Analysis, Policy Report No. 134, November 1988, p. 20.
18. Figures from the Pharmaceutical Manufacturers Association.

34

ARE UNIONS ALL THAT GOOD?

Walter J. Wessels*

Labor unions are monopolies. Most economists know monopolies are "bad." Yet, they sometimes develop models suggesting that unions really are not so bad.

Two such models have received a great deal of attention in recent years. The first is the "efficient bargain model" in which unions bargain not only for higher wages, but for more jobs as well. As a result, unions should reduce employment less than some might otherwise predict. The second is the "exit-voice model" where unions allow workers to voice complaints and thereby create a happier and more productive work force.

In this paper, we examine both the underlying reasoning and the evidence supporting these two models. We show the reasoning to be seriously flawed and the evidence unsupportive. With some simple modifications, both models can be made to substantiate their *opposite* conclusions.

The Efficient Bargain Model

The efficient bargain model (or contract curve model)[1] assumes basically that unions value higher wages and more employment (or, at least, more employment for its current members). If the union bargains only over wages and lets employers set employment, an employer's demand curve for labor will determine employment, that is, employers hire workers until the last worker hired adds just enough revenue to cover the worker's cost. But if

*Dr. Wessels is Associate Professor of Economics at North Carolina State University. His articles have appeared in the *Journal of Labor Economics, Southern Economic Journal, Journal of Labor Research,* and others.

the union bargains over *both* wages and employment, it can be shown that the union will bargain for even more employment in exchange for reduced wage demands. This effectively adds to the demand for labor. So the firm hires until the marginal worker's revenue *plus* the union's payment for more employment *equals* the worker's cost.[2]

The resulting contract improves the situation of both the union and the employer (or, at a minimum, neither is worsened). Hence, this model is called "the efficient bargain model."

In this model, then, employers hire more labor than standard labor demand theory suggests: the efficient bargain is *above* the demand curve for labor. Or stated another way, at the *same* wage, the unionized firm hires *more* workers than would a non-union firm. This result has serious consequences. No longer can economists use standard demand theory and all its tools to analyze the effects of unions. With the efficient bargain theory, any results from standard economic analysis is suspect.

However, the model is seriously flawed; it makes a significant theoretical error.[3] The model assumes a single state that focuses only on permanent changes in labor demand (in particular, those decreases in employment caused by higher union wages). Permanent changes in demand are those that affect the long-run growth or decline in union employment. However, union members with seniority do care mainly about what economists call transitory changes in labor demand, those changes in employment due to the business cycle. Yet, the efficient bargain model ignores transitory changes!

A more realistic model allowing for transitory changes in demand assumes that when the union makes its contract, there are several possible states of the economy (for example, expansion or recession). It also assumes that the union can bargain over employment and wages for all these possible future states. The resulting "efficient" bargain is likely to be what economists call an implicit contract. For these contracts, *average* employment is *on* the labor demand curve.[4] In the implicit contract, unions give up some jobs in good times in order to get more jobs in bad times. The implicit contract is adopted primarily because it addresses the union's concerns about transitory employment changes better than the efficient bargain model does.

Several articles[5] claim to have shown that unions bargain for more employment than the standard labor demand curve would predict. Certain papers focus on unions in the public sector, showing that unions sacrifice lower wages for more jobs. But what is the public sector's "demand for labor"? Quite possibly the demand for labor results in part from the desire for politicians to secure more votes. As a consequence, we should not be surprised to find that public sector jobs have excess employment and need not have anything to do with efficient bargains. The remaining articles focus on the private sector. But they also suffer a flaw as they only examine union firms. They show that union firms employ more workers than standard labor economic models imply. But even non-union firms might employ more workers than standard labor demand analysis suggests. For example, they may want to employ sufficient workers to handle any peak-load periods and to provide their workers with greater job stability.

The only way to test the assumption that unions bargain for added employment is to *compare* union with non-union firms. At the same wage, do union firms employ more than non-union firms?[6] Elsewhere, the author has performed this test on three data sets.[7] In every case, controlling for worker quality and the relevant economic variables, there is no evidence that unions bargained for added employment. In some cases, we found the opposite: unions had significantly fewer workers.

The Exit-Voice Model

A second model favorable to unions is the exit-voice model, developed by Freeman from Hirschman.[8] It posits that unions allow workers to voice their grievances.[9] Consequently, dissatisfied workers can "voice" their desires instead of having to quit or "exit." This voice supposedly creates more satisfied workers, thereby reducing quit rates and saving the firm considerable turnover costs, and raising the productivity of the work force.[10]

According to this model, unions are better able to elicit workers complaints because non-union workers who voice their dissatisfaction may fear retaliation by supervisors. Union members on the other hand are protected by the union and so can voice their grievances.

The model makes two key predictions: union workers will be more satisfied and union workers will be more productive. We will examine each of these in turn.

Unions and Job Satisfaction

Are union workers more satisfied? Of course union workers will be more satisfied when they receive higher wages and benefits. But the exit-voice model asserts that if union workers and non-union workers receive the same wage and have similar jobs, union workers would still be *more* satisfied.

Is this true? The answer is no. When the job satisfaction of union workers is compared with that of non-union workers, almost every article shows that union members are *less* satisfied. Union workers, while more satisfied about compensation and fringe benefits, are more *dissatisfied* about working conditions. Furthermore, they often have less overall job satisfaction.[11]

But the exit-voice literature itself cites these results as proof that unions allow workers to have a greater voice![12] The argument states that because more dissatisfied workers are retained by union firms, union workers are on average more dissatisfied. Also, workers allowed to voice complaints are more sensitive to working conditions and thus are less satisfied. But this counters the overwhelming evidence for the "Hawthorne" effect found in the organizational behavior literature. When employers allow workers to voice their complaints, workers become more satisfied, especially if the complaints are acted upon. This writer has yet to find a human resources article with the prescription, "Want More Satisfied Workers? Tell 'em: 'Shut Up!'"

We will now modify the exit-voice model to show why union workers are less satisfied with working conditions. Assume, as the exit-voice model, that non-union firms only care about the preferences of marginal workers (*i.e.*, workers who are on the margin of quitting because they have the least relative preference for the job). And assume the union firm bargains for the median intramarginal worker (workers with the highest full wage preference for the firm). Further assume that the intramarginal workers (those with seniority) control the union. In this case, if more senior workers care more about fringe benefits, for example, we can then show that union workers will bargain for more fringe benefits.

The exit-voice literature argues that senior workers want better working conditions due to their having a higher income, but this argument is questionable. Both new and senior workers have about the same lifetime wealth (the only difference is that new workers have a higher chance of being temporarily laid off). With similar lifetime wealth, they should both have similar demand for better working conditions. So an "income" effect is doubtful.

Let us examine a more likely difference between new and senior workers. Of first importance to note is that union jobs tend to have more undesirable working conditions, including less safe jobs, longer hours, and shift work.[13] Second, if the work force is heterogeneous in preferences for working conditions, then those workers who place the *least* value on good working conditions will be more likely attracted to union jobs and to stay in the job. This selectivity effect argues that intramarginal (i.e., senior) workers will place *less* value on good working conditions than do marginal workers. In this case unionized firms, listening to the "voice" of their workers, will provide *poorer* working conditions. Correspondingly, non-union firms (who care more about the marginal worker) will provide better working conditions than union firms. A simple example illustrates this.

Suppose the union can choose between $500 more in wages or $500 more per worker spent on safety. And assume the marginal worker values this added safety by $800 a year while a senior worker values it by only $200 a year. The union will select $500 more in wages, making the marginal worker's situation worse. Even if the safety were free, the senior workers may not want it. For example, suppose the firm wants to pay a full wage premium to all workers of at least $1,000 (say, to keep workers from striking, to reduce turnover cost, or to motivate workers not to shirk). Suppose the marginal worker just gets this premium and all intramarginal workers get much more. If the job were made safe, the firm could reduce its wage by $800, making the marginal worker no worse and the intramarginal workers $600 worse (they gain $200 in safety but lose $800 in wages). Therefore, the senior workers will oppose this improvement in working conditions. Of course, union wages are not this flexible, (the senior workers might fear that the firm will extract the $800 in the form of an increased work pace or in future wage concessions).

The result will be that union workers will, on average, be less satisfied with working conditions but more satisfied with wages, fringe benefits, and the job security that unions provide. In turn, this selectivity effect may explain why union firms have lower quit rates and longer job tenure even when they are paid the same as non-union workers.

The Effect of Unions on Productivity

Many articles have predicted that unions increase worker productivity. Some of these early articles claimed that unions increased productivity so much that it offset the increase in wage costs caused by unions. If this were true, as shown by Wessels,[14] unions would throw more workers out of a job than they actually do. For example, if unions increase wages by 15% and increase worker productivity by 15% such that costs are unchanged, then total output will remain unchanged (because it costs the same, and its price and therefore its demand remains unchanged). But the firm will need 15% fewer workers. However the evidence suggests that unions do not cause this many workers to lose work; more likely, we would observe 5% of the workers losing jobs. The conclusion must be that unions raise wages more than productivity (if they raise productivity at all).

More recent articles, especially those looking at longitudinal data, found far smaller increases in productivity or none or decreases.[15] In particular, economists have found that unions reduce spending for research, development, and investment in the firms they have unionized.

I suspect any productivity effect found for unions has more to do with *which* firms are unionized. For example, if unions organize the more productive firms in an industry, then they would appear to have increased productivity even when they did not. This is an obvious case. But consider an alternative reason. Unions tend to be in firms that have longer and more shift work. Why this is so may be for the selectivity reason given above. But for now, let us just take this as a given fact. What does this imply? Suppose it takes one worker working one shift and one machine to make one widget. And suppose a nonunion firm only has a single shift, say with 20 workers and 20 machines producing 20 widgets a day. On the other hand, a union firm with two shifts has 40 workers and 20 machines producing 40 widgets. If a researcher ignored the added shifts, the research would conclude that "unionization" makes the firm more productive. But of course, it does not. Union firms are more productive because they use capital more intensely. Whether this type of explanation holds true or not needs, of course, to be tested.

Summary

What do unions do? They monopolize the supply of labor. By constraining its supply, they raise wages of their members at the expense of those disemployed and at the expense of the public who have to pay more for union-made goods.

The idea that unions also fight to increase employment is not supported by theory or evidence.

The idea that unions may give voice to all members may be true, but in a way that makes working conditions worse for union workers.

Finally, that idea that unions raise productivity to offset the effect of higher wages finds little support.

Notes and References

1. The efficient bargain model was first presented in Leontief, Wassily W., "The Pure Theory of the Guaranteed Annual Wage Contract," *Journal of Political Economy,* 54:76-79 (February, 1946), and extended by Hall, Robert E. and Lillien, David M., "Efficient Wage Bargains Under Certain Supply and Demand," *American Economic Review,* 69:868-879 (December, 1979), and by McDonald, I.M. and Solow, Robert M., "Wage Bargaining and Employment," 71:896-908 (December 1981).
2. If the union utility function is U(W, L), where W is the annual wage and L is the number of workers, then holding the firm's profits (Total Revenue—WL—Other costs) constant, the marginal condition in the efficient bargain contract can be shown to be:

$$W = \text{Marginal Revenue Product} + LU_L/U_W,$$

where U_L is the first derivative of the union utility function with respect to employment and U_W, with respect to wages. The marginal revenue product reflects a point on the standard demand for labor curve. The second term reflects what the union is willing to pay (in reduced wage demands), per worker, for more employment.
3. Wessels, Walter J., "Contract Curve or Implicit Contract: Which Will a Union Choose?" *Journal of Labor Research,* 12:73-9, (Winter 1991).
4. An exception occurs in firms with declining labor demand. Then, an efficient bargain is likely to hold. While unions have of late been often in declining industries, for most of their history they have been in industries with rising employment and so this exception has not been the usual case. Cf. *Ibid.*
5. These include Brown, James N., and Ashenfelter, Orley, "Testing the Efficiency of Employment Contracts," *Journal of Political Economy,* 94:355-71 (June, 1986); McCurdy, Thomas E., and Pencavel, John H., "Testing Between Competing Models of Wage and Employment Determination in Unionized Markets," *Journal of Political Economy,* 94:S3-S39 (June, 1986); Svejnar, Jan, "Bargaining Power, Fear of Disagreement, and Wage Settlements: Theory of Evidence for U.S. Industry," *Econometria,* 62:1055-8 (September, 1986); Ebert, Randall W., and Stone, Joe A., "On the Contract Curve: A Test of Alternative Models of Collective Bargaining," *Journal of Labor Economics,* 4:66-81 (January, 1986); and Bean, C. R., and Turnbull, P. J., "Employment in

the British Coal Industry: A Test of the Labour Demand Model," *The Economic Journal,* 98:1092-1104 (December, 1988).
6. Note that unions on net may still employ fewer workers as they still will have higher wages than non-union workers.
7. Wessels, Walter J., "Do Unions Contract for More Employment," *Industrial Labor Relations Review,* forthcoming.
8. Cf. Freeman, A., "Individual Mobility and Union Voice in the Labor Market," *American Economic Review,* 64:361-8 (May 1976); and Hirschman, A., *Exit, Voice, and Loyalty* (Cambridge, MA: Harvard University Press, 1970).
9. Freeman, R., and Medoff, James, in *What do Unions Do?* (New York, NY: Basic Books, 1984), survey this literature.
10. Cf. Brown, C. and Medoff, James, "Trade Unions in the Production Process," *Journal of Political Economy,* 1978.
11. Meng, Ronald, "The Relationship Between Unions and Job Satisfaction," *Applied Economics,* 22:1635-1648 (1990) summarizes this literature and very carefully tests these results in various ways.
12. According to Freeman, R., *Labor Markets In Action* (Cambridge, MA: Harvard University Press, 1989), p. 290, the inverse relationship between unionization and job satisfaction "might reflect the role of unions as a 'voice' institution, encouraging workers to express discontent during contract negotiations and to make formal grievances rather than to quit, which would keep the dissatisfied from leaving the employer."
13. Kostiuk, Peter F., "Compensating Differentials for Shift Work," *Journal of Political Economy,* 98:1054-75 (October 1990). presents evidence that one-third of the union wage premium is due to the onerousness of shift work. Duncan, Greg J., and Strafford, Frank P., "Do Union Members Receive Compensating Wage Differentials," *American Economic Review,* 70:355-378 (June 1980), also examine the poorer working conditions faced by union workers.
14. Wessels, Walter J., "The Effects of Unions on Employment and Productivity: An Unresolved Conflict," *Journal of Labor Economics,* 3:101-8 (January 1985).
15. See in particular Addison, John T., and Hirsch, Barry T., "Union Effects on Productivity, Profits, and Growth: Has the Long Run Arrived?", *Journal of Labor Economics,* 7:72-105 (January 1989), and the summary table they present.

35

MISES ON FREE BANKING AND FRACTIONAL RESERVES

Lawrence H. White*

Professor Hans F. Sennholz has long been an outstanding exponent of the monetary economics of Ludwig von Mises (1881-1973), whom Sennholz has justly called "the late dean of monetary theory."[1] Another leading Misesian monetary economist is Murray N. Rothbard. Both Sennholz and Rothbard attended Mises's seminar at New York University, both share Mises's appreciation for the gold standard, and both cite his work frequently in their own contributions. It is therefore noteworthy that Sennholz and Rothbard appear to differ on a fundamental point concerning the proper banking policy for a free society.

In the eloquent concluding paragraph to *Money and Freedom,* Sennholz advocates free banking, that is, banking subject only to the ordinary law of contract and not to any special legal restrictions:

> Sound money and free banking are not impossible; they are merely illegal. This is why money must be deregulated. All financial institutions must be free again to issue their notes based on ordinary contract. In a free society, individuals are free to establish note-issuing banks and create private clearinghouses. In freedom, the money and banking industry can create sound and honest currencies, just as other free industries can provide efficient and reliable products. Freedom of money and freedom of banking, these are the principles that must guide our steps.[2]

Rothbard, by contrast, advocates limiting the freedom of the banking industry by outlawing fractional-reserve banking. Near the end of *The Mystery of Banking,* he proposes "that each bank be

*Dr. White is Associate Professor of Economics at the University of Georgia, and a prolific author.

legally required, on the basis of the general law against fraud, to keep 100% of gold to its demand liabilities."[3] Rothbard believes that the practice of holding fractional reserves against demand liabilities is inherently or *per se* fraudulent, so that in his view outlawing fractional reserves would be consistent with upholding the law of contract.[4] He also views mandatory 100 percent reserves as a desirable restriction on the balance sheets of banks: "At last, each commercial bank's loan operations will be separated from its demand deposits."[5]

Observing this contrast in views between two of Mises's leading students, one is led to ask: where did Mises himself stand on the desirability of free banking, and in particular on the issue of fractional versus 100 percent reserves? The present essay seeks answers by examining Mises's relevant writings on banking policy.[6] An exposition of Mises's own arguments is especially pertinent in light of Rothbard's reading of Mises. While he rightly credits Mises with having explained how free banking would limit and closely regulate the creation of bank-issued money, Rothbard has stated that "Mises's sole argument against 100 percent gold banking is that this would admit the unfortunate precedent of government control of the banking system."[7] We will find that in fact Mises offered several other arguments in favor of free banking and against 100 percent reserves.

Mises on the Feasibility of Fractional Reserves

In his pioneering work *The Theory of Money and Credit,* the first edition of which was published in 1912, Mises considered in detail the role of banks as issuers of fractional-reserve substitutes for basic money. He first faced the task of explaining how fractional-reserve banking is feasible. Mises noted that claims to basic money are unlike claims to ordinary goods (for example, bread) in an important economic respect. An individual who sells a thousand one-loaf tickets for bread must keep a thousand loaves at his disposal to avoid default. All the tickets will ordinarily be redeemed, because bread tickets are ultimately demanded for a service they render (enabling the acquisition of bread to be consumed) only when they are redeemed.[8] Money, by contrast to bread, is acquired not to be consumed, but to be passed on as a medium of exchange. Claims to basic money, such as banknotes and checkable deposits, can themselves serve as media of exchange. Because they can render this service without being redeemed, all the claims will not ordinarily be redeemed in any given period. The banker who issues them:

> ...can expect that these claims will remain in circulation for so long as their holders do not lose confidence in their prompt convertibility or transfer them to persons who have not this confidence. He is therefore in a position to undertake greater obligations than he would ever be able to fulfill; it is enough if he takes sufficient precautions to ensure his ability to satisfy promptly that proportion of the claims that is actually enforced against him.[9]

Mises added that the banker, in estimating the proportion of his claims that will actually be redeemed, "has to rely upon an uncertain empirical procedure which may easily lead to mistakes. Nevertheless, prudent and experienced bank directors—and most bank directors are prudent and experienced—usually manage pretty well with it."[10]

Mises's Critique of a Ban on Fractional-Reserve Banking

Mises devoted a section of *The Theory of Money and Credit* specifically to analyzing "The Case Against the Issue of Fiduciary Media." (In Mises's terminology, "fiduciary media" are redeemable liabilities, like banknotes and checkable deposits, that can be used as money and that are issued in excess of basic-money reserves.)[11] He correctly noted that a bank holding fractional reserves against demand liabilities is always vulnerable to a run: "Any bank that issues fiduciary media is forced to suspend payments if *everybody* begins to present notes for redemption or to withdraw deposits." For this reason "many writers" had called for the prohibition of fractional reserves.[12] But Mises cited several reasons why such a prohibition had not been imposed.

In a growing world economy, the real demand for media of exchange grows. If that demand can be met only by gold produced at increasing marginal cost, or bank liabilities backed 100 percent by gold, the purchasing power of gold must increase substantially over time. In Mises's view such an increase in gold's value has at least two major undesirable consequences. An economy which economizes on the use of gold by using fractional-reserve bank liabilities avoids these consequences.

1. An appreciating monetary unit can disrupt the economy: "The issue of fiduciary media has made it possible to avoid the convulsions that would be involved in an increase in the objective exchange-value of money." Mises unfortunately did not completely spell out his argument here. It appears that he rejected the view that the demand for money would grow only gradually, leading only to a gradual and secular increase in the value of money (or in other words to a gently falling price level), in favor of the view that the demand for money grows rapidly and unexpectedly at times. Such money demand shocks, in the face of a relatively fixed money stock, would indeed involve "convulsions" because of the sudden need for rapid declines in prices.[13] This interpretation is supported by a passage from a later essay by Mises:

> If all further expansion of fiduciary media had been forbidden in any form...prices would have declined sharply, especially at times when the increased demand for money surpassed the increase in its quantity. The economy...would also have suffered from the consequences of a rise in the monetary unit's purchasing power.[14]

It should be noted that a fractional reserve ratio as such does not prevent a fixed stock of gold from appreciating when real money demand grows; only a *falling* average reserve ratio does so.

2. A high purchasing power of gold makes the stock of media of exchange more costly: "Fiduciary media tap a lucrative source of revenue for their issuer; they enrich both the person that issues them and the community that employs them."[15] Here Mises's argument is clear and correct. The voluntary use of fiduciary media allows a community to substitute less expensive (paper or account-entry) media of exchange for more expensive (precious metallic) media, as Adam Smith had long ago argued.[16] Mises spelled out this point in an important passage that deserves to be quoted at length:

> If metallic money is employed, then the advantages of a diminution of the demand for money due to the extension of such other means of payment are obvious. In fact the development of the clearing system and of fiduciary media has at least kept pace with the potential increase of the demand for money brought about by the extension of the Money Economy, so that the tremendous increase in the exchange value of money, which otherwise would have occurred as a consequence of the extension of the use of money, has been completely avoided, together with its

undesirable consequences. If it had not been for this, the increase in the exchange value of money, and so also of the monetary metal, would have given an increased impetus to the production of the metal. Capital and labor would have been diverted from other branches of production to the production of the monetary metal. This would undoubtedly have meant increased returns to certain individual undertakings but the welfare of the community would have suffered. The increase in the stock of precious metals which serve monetary purposes would not have improved the position of the individual members of the community, would not have increased the satisfaction of their wants, for the monetary function could also have been fulfilled by a smaller stock. And, on the other hand, a smaller quantity of economic goods would have been available for the direct satisfaction of human wants if a part of the capital and labor power that otherwise would have been used for their production had been diverted to mining precious metals. Even apart from the diversion of production, a decrease of prosperity would result from the fact that as a consequence of the rise in value of the precious metals caused by the use for monetary purposes, the stock available for industrial employment would decrease, since certain quantities would be transferred from the latter employment to the former.[17]

The welfare gain from fractional reserve banking which Mises noted here can be conceived in purely individualistic and subjective terms: it is the benefit to an individual who chooses the interest income and services of fractional-reserve bank liabilities over the expensive security of 100 percent reserve liabilities. The additional productive capital, owned by the community that uses fiduciary media, is represented by additional earning assets on the balance sheets of banks. The amount of such assets corresponds to the difference between the banks' demand liabilities and their gold reserves. In a *competitive* banking system, the income from these assets is not retained as a windfall by the banks, but is passed on to the individuals who hold fractional-reserve bank liabilities in the form of interest and services on their demand deposits and banknotes.

Under 100 percent reserves, Mises pointed out, a private bank would have to charge fees to its customers to cover the costs of issuing notes and administering checking accounts. In some circumstances customers would be willing to pay these fees to avoid the physical transfer and storage of gold. But overall the prohibition of fractional-reserve banking "would mean almost completely suppressing the note-issue and almost strangling the check-and-clearing system."[18]

3. Mises also mentioned a third benefit historically conveyed by fiduciary media, the stimulus their issue gave to the development of banking: "In the early days of the modern banking system they [fiduciary media] played a further part still by strengthening the credit-negotiating activities of the banks (which in those times could hardly have proved profitable if carried on for their own sake alone) and so brought the system safely past those obstacles which obstructed its beginnings."[19] That is, the ability of banks to intermediate was aided by their ability to issue demand liabilities suitable for use as media of exchange, i.e. checkable deposits and banknotes, rather than only time deposits and dated notes.

In summary, although he recognized the risk that a fractional-reserve bank might at some time fail to meet its redemption demands, either through mismanagement of its reserves or through the occurrence of a run, Mises appeared to view that risk as a small disadvantage to be set against larger advantages. He viewed fractional-reserve banking as a natural and desirable development in a free society, most importantly because it reduced the resource costs associated with the payments system.[20]

Mises on Free Banking

In the first edition of *The Theory of Money and Credit* Mises endorsed free banking mostly by implication. An important passage analyzing the workings of a free banking system appears at the conclusion of his critique of the real-bills doctrine. The real-bills doctrine held that the quantity of bank-issued money would be automatically limited to the appropriate amount (the quantity demanded) if the banks would issue money only in exchange for the right kind of assets, namely, short-term commercial IOUs financing goods in process ("real bills") or loans similarly secured. Mises showed that the doctrine was fallacious because the banks could always expand their issues by lowering their discount rate on bills or interest rate on loans. Mises concluded, contrary to the real-bills doctrine and related views, that "the quantity of fiduciary media in circulation has no natural limits."[21]

He then immediately added that this is true only if the issue of banknotes and demand deposits is monopolized or cartelized, so that a uniform discount-rate policy can be followed. Under free banking, the competitive rivalry among banks of issue prevents their acting in concert to lower their discount or interest rates, and so the banks *cannot* arbitrarily expand the quantity of money in circulation.[22] There *is* a natural limit to the circulation of each bank set by the demands of its customers:

> A single bank carrying on its business in competition with numerous others is not in a position to enter upon an independent discount policy. If regard to the behavior of its competitors prevents it from further reducing the rate of interest in bank-credit transactions, then—apart from an extension of its clientele—it will be able to circulate more fiduciary media only if there is a demand for them even when the rate of interest charged is not lower than that charged by the banks competing with it.

The consequence is that a free banking system *does* automatically adjust the quantity of money to the quantity demanded, and thereby dampens movements in the purchasing power of money:

> Thus the banks may be seen to pay a certain amount of attention to the periodical fluctuations in the demand for money. They increase and decrease their circulation *pari passu* with the variations in the demand for money, so far as the lack of a uniform procedure makes it impossible for them to follow an independent interest policy. But in so doing, they help stabilize the objective exchange value of money.

Though Mises did not go on to indicate the benefits from the banks acting in this way, it is worth indicating them here. By promptly meeting seasonal and other short-run variations in the demand for money, a free banking system spares the economy the problems associated with alternative responses to monetary disequilibrium. An open economy with 100 percent reserves (or a similar reserve requirement at the margin) would face the expenses of promptly importing and exporting gold as money demand varied. A closed economy with a fixed money stock would confront the difficulties of adjusting the price level promptly. Free banking spares the economy from these unnecessary expenses or difficulties.[23]

In a section of his 1924 addendum to *The Theory of Money and Credit,* Mises directly addressed "The Problem of the Freedom of the Banks." Mises believed that the free banking debate of the mid-nineteenth century should be reopened. Recent experience had shown, he argued, that a free banking system's occasional bank failures were a trivial problem compared to the disasters produced by state regulation or monopoly of note issue: "What do all the failures of banks-of-issue and clearing banks known to history matter in comparison with the complete collapse of the banking system in Germany?"[24]

Mises then criticized the theoretical argument for note regulation made during the earlier debate by the Currency School. This passage bears quoting for the contrast it provides to Rothbard's largely positive appraisal of the School's arguments. In Rothbard's view, the Currency School "put forth a caustic and trenchant analysis of fractional reserve banking and central banking" similar to his own. He adds: "The Currency School was the first group of economists to show how expansion of bank credit and bank notes generated inflations and business cycle booms, paving the way for the inevitable contraction and attendant collapse of business and banks." Though he faults its execution in Peel's Act of 1844, Rothbard speaks of the School's "praiseworthy attempt to end fractional reserve banking and institute 100% money."[25]

Mises, by contrast, faulted the Currency School writers for failing to recognize that a free banking system does not have a central bank's dangerous capacity to generate a boom-bust cycle through credit expansion. He praised their "quite correct explanation" of how over-expansions led by the Bank of England had produced the British business crises of the 1830s and 1940s, but added:

> Unfortunately, the Currency School erred in two respects. It never realized that the remedy it suggested, namely strict limitation of the amount of banknotes issued beyond the specie reserve, was not the only one. It never gave a thought to the idea of free banking.[26]

The School's "second fault" was failing to recognize that checking accounts were also a "vehicle of credit expansion."

In Mises's view the Currency School's fear of cycle-generating expansions of credit was groundless in the case of a free banking system, because competing banks of issue would be unable to expand in concert.[27] The "Currency Principle" (the Currency School's argument for a 100 percent marginal reserve requirement) therefore proposed an unwarranted interference with the freedom of banks. Referring to the mid-nineteenth-century arguments against freedom of banking, Mises wrote:

> The argument, however, that was then supposed to be the decisive one was provided by the Currency Principle. From the point of view of this doctrine, any note issue that is not covered by gold is dangerous, and so, in order to obviate the recurrence of economic crisis, such issues must be restricted. ...We have already shown that the dangers envisioned by the Currency Principle exist only when there is uniform procedure on the

part of all credit-issuing banks, not merely within a given country, but throughout the world.[28]

A central bank can generate disequilibrating over-expansions of credit, and in fact (Mises would later argue) will be politically pressured to do so. A free banking system, left alone by the authorities, will *not* tend to over-expand. Mises had pointed out in 1912, in a passage quoted above, that competition will instead drive the banks to "increase and decrease their circulation *pari passu* with the variations in the demand for money."[29]

In the sections of *Human Action* entitled "Limitations on the Issuance of Fiduciary Media" and "Observations of the Discussions Concerning Free Banking," Mises spelled out the process by which a free banking system would limit and regulate the issues of banks. His key insight was that "credit expansion in itself does not expand a bank's clientele."[30] That is, each bank faces a limited demand to hold its particular brand of notes and deposits. It is one thing for a bank to *issue* more notes and create more checking deposits by granting more loans, but it is quite another thing for the bank to *keep* a greater volume in circulation. As Mises put it:

> It is very easy for a bank to increase the number of people who are ready to accept loans granted by credit expansion and paid out in an amount of money-substitutes. But it is very difficult for any bank to enlarge its clientele, that is, the number of people who are ready to consider these claims as money-substitutes and to keep them as such in their cash holdings.[31]

If a bank does not bear the expense of expanding its clientele (or of inducing its existing clientele to want to hold more of its notes and deposits), any increased volume of its notes and deposits will necessarily come into the hands of people who prefer not to hold (or to hold more of) its brand of money. Those people will redeem the notes and deposits directly, or deposit them into other banks which will redeem them at the next interbank clearing session. Redemption takes the excess out of circulation, and depletes the over-issuing bank's reserves. Faced with insufficient reserves, the bank "must abandon its expansionist methods," reducing its swollen loan portfolio to replenish its reserves.[32]

Mises emphasized that a competitive bank of issue would have to be very conservative, very careful to maintain adequate reserves, in order to safeguard the reputation for trustworthiness on which its circulation depends. If governments had not intervened to prop them up, imprudent banks would not have survived:

> Considerations of its own solvency would have forced every bank to cautious restraint in issuing fiduciary media. Those banks which would not have observed these indispensable rules would have gone bankrupt, and the public, warned through damage, would have become doubly suspicious and reserved.[33]

Mises quoted the French economist Henri Cernushi, an extreme proponent of the argument that the public would be cautious in taking banknotes, who proclaimed that "freedom of banking would result in a total suppression of banknotes in France." This quote should *not* be read as a prediction *by Mises* that free banking would automatically lead to 100 percent reserve banking.[34] Rather, Mises quoted Cernushi's statement as an expression of the idea that, in Mises's words, "freedom in the issuance of banknotes would have narrowed down the use of bank-notes considerably, if it had not entirely suppressed it," because the public would have accepted only notes issued by banks of the highest repute.

Later Writings on Banking Policy

In his 1928 essay on "Monetary Stabilization and Cyclical Policy," Mises reiterated many of these points. In a free banking system the banks would soon learn that their own self-interest required them to avoid over-issuing. They would have to exercise "extreme restraint in the issue of fiduciary media." State control of banking, by contrast, has led to inflations and breakdowns far more severe than could ever occur under free banking.

In this essay, however, Mises expressed a profound pessimism concerning the political prospects for free banking.[35] Four years earlier he had written that recent events had reopened the free banking question: "...it is no longer possible to consider it completely settled as it must have been considered for decades now."[36] He now indicated that the question was in fact settled for all practical purposes:

> It may be that a final solution of the problem can be arrived at only through the establishment of completely free banking. However, the credit structure which has been developed by the continued effort of many generations cannot be transformed with one blow. Future generations, who will have recognized the basic absurdity of all

interventionist attempts, will have to deal with this question also. However, the time is not yet ripe—not now nor in the immediate future.[37]

As a result of his pessimism over the political prospects for limiting credit expansion through free banking, Mises now called for a "second-best" interventionist policy. Much like the Currency School, he proposed to prevent future credit expansion through a 100 percent marginal reserve requirement, that is, 100 percent gold reserves against all future issues of notes and checking deposits.[38] Mises later explained the rationale for such a policy: "Government interference with the present state of banking affairs could be justified if its aim were to liquidate the unsatisfactory conditions by preventing or at least seriously restricting any further credit expansions." He reiterated the proposal in an epilogue on "Monetary Reconstruction" appended in 1952 to a new edition of *The Theory of Money and Credit,* there making it clear that his objective was not to limit private banking, but rather to block governments from attempting to generate revenue or to promote "full employment" by printing money.[39]

Mises continued to endorse the principle of free banking as first-best. In his 1952 essay, after noting that nineteenth-century governments had forced banks to lend to them, and had allowed those banks to suspend payments, Mises added:

> The logical conclusion to be drawn from these facts would have been to do away with privileged banks altogether and to subject all banks to the rule of common law and the commercial codes that oblige everybody to perform contracts in full faithfulness to the pledged word. Free banking would have spared the world many crises and catastrophes.[40]

Mises still preferred free banking to any policy of legislated reserve requirements:

> It must be emphasized that the problem of legal restrictions upon the issuance of fiduciary media could emerge only because governments had granted special privileges to one or several banks and had thus prevented the free evolution of banking. If the governments had never interfered...[t]he limits which are drawn to credit expansion would have worked effectively.[41]

As Rothbard has noted, Mises believed that a 100 percent reserve requirement constituted a government interference with banking, and could therefore serve as the precedent for other, more inflationary, interferences. Such an artificial rule would not prove durable against a government eager to resort to printing-press finance.[42] Ironically, Mises had previously (in 1924) noted a similar vulnerability on the part of free banking. European governments in 1914 "overthrew the whole system of bank legislation with a stroke of the pen, and they could have done just the same if the banks had been uncontrolled."[43] By the time of writing *Human Action,* Mises had evidently become convinced that free banking provided the most reliable way to block governments from expanding credit for fiscal purposes:

> Free banking is the only method available for the prevention of the dangers inherent in credit expansion. It would, it is true, not hinder a slow credit expansion, kept within very narrow limits, on the part of cautious banks which provide the public with all information required about their financial status. But under free banking it would have been impossible for credit expansion with all its inevitable consequences to have developed into a regular—one is tempted to say normal—feature of the economic system. Only free banking would have rendered the market economy secure against crises and depressions.[44]

The last sentence of this quote—denying by implication that a 100 percent reserve policy would eliminate crises and depressions—can be read as a reminder of Mises's argument that a 100 percent reserve policy exposes the economy to disturbances from increases in the demand for money.

Conclusion

Ludwig von Mises argued against a legal ban on fractional-reserve banking in the context of a gold standard, primarily on the grounds that such a ban (1) would make the economy more vulnerable to money demand shocks, and (2) would needlessly increase the cost of supplying the economy with media of exchange. In contrast to the Currency School, he argued that a ban on the future issue of fractional-reserve bank money was not necessary in order to prevent over-expansion by banks. Over-expansion would be most effectively prevented by allowing competitive banking and note-issue, free from any interference that would release banks from their contractual obligations to redeem their liabilities in gold. Free banking would compel banks to behave cautiously, and to limit the volume of their liabilities to the amount demanded by the public at the existing purchasing power of money. Mises concluded that monetary freedom, and not any program of restrictions or privileges, offers the only real remedy for the monetary upheavals the world has known. In reaffirming this conclusion, Hans F. Sennholz has followed in the best Misesian tradition.

Notes and References

1. Sennholz, Hans F., *Age of Inflation* (Spring Mills, PA: Libertarian Press, 1979), p. 365.
2. Sennholz, Hans F., *Money and Freedom* (Spring Mills, PA: Libertarian Press, 1985), p. 83.
3. Rothbard, Murray N., *The Mystery of Banking* (New York, NY: Richardson and Snyder, 1983), p. 265.
4. In my view no breach of contract or fraud is involved in holding fractional reserves unless the bank contractually obligates or represents itself to hold 100 percent reserves. White, Lawrence H., "Free Banking and The Gold Standard." Llewellyn H. Rockwell, Jr., ed., *The Gold Standard: An Austrian Perspective* (Lexington, MA: Lexington Books, 1985), pp. 120-121.
5. Rothbard, *The Mystery of Banking,* p. 265.
6. Ebeling, Richard, "Ludwig von Mises and the Gold Standard" in *The Gold Standard: An Austrian Perspective,* ably surveys Mises's views on monetary policy, with particular reference to his defense of the gold standard. James Rolph Edwards, in his 1985 study of Mises's monetary thought, is also useful; he touches on the issues discussed here in a footnote, *The Economist of the Country: Ludwig von Mises in the History of Monetary Thought* (New York, NY: Carlton Press, 1985), p. 127, note 4.
7. Rothbard, Murray N., "The Case for a 100 Percent Gold Dollar," in Leland B. Yeager, ed., *In Search of a Monetary Constitution* (Cambridge, MA: Harvard University Press, 1962), p. 119.
8. Mises, Ludwig von, *The Theory of Money and Credit* (Indianapolis, IN: Liberty Classics, 1981), pp. 299-300.
9. Block, Walter, "Fractional Reserve Banking: An Interdisciplinary Perspective," Walter Block and Llewellyn H. Rockwell, Jr., eds., *Man, Economy, and Liberty: Essays in Honor of Murray N. Rothbard,* (Auburn, AL: Ludwig von Mises Institute, 1988), pp. 30-31, in arguing that honest fractional-reserve banking is the economic equivalent of a lottery, appears to neglect this distinction. All claims against a lottery will be liquidated each period; all banknotes will not. Block actually qualifies his argument in an important way when he states that a 20 percent-reserve banknote "is only offering (*under certain conditions*) a 1 to 5 chance of receiving money" [emphasis altered]. The banknote is unlike a lottery ticket precisely because those "certain conditions"—the event of a run on the bank—are exceptional.
10. Mises, *The Theory of Money and Credit,* p. 362.
11. *Ibid.*

12. Here Mises cites the German economists Tellkampf and Geyer. To my knowledge, Mises never explicitly addressed the view that fractional reserves are inherently fraudulent. But he implied disagreement with that view when he indicated that a bank lives up to its contractual obligations so long as it meets the redemption demands that are actually made. In Mises, *Human Action: A Treatise on Economics,* 3rd. rev. ed., (Chicago, IL: Henry Regnery, 1966), p. 439, he stated that a bank wishing to retain its clientele "must never permit any doubt about its ability and readiness to discharge all it liabilities *in due compliance with the terms of the contract.* A reserve must be kept large enough to redeem all banknotes which a holder may submit for redemption" [emphasis added].
13. Mises, *The Theory of Money and Credit,* p. 359.
14. Mises, Ludwig von, *On the Manipulation of Money and Credit*, trans. Bettina Bien Greaves (Dobbs Ferry, NY: Free Market Books, 1978), p. 145.
15. Mises, *The Theory of Money and Credit,* p. 359.
16. Smith, Adam, *An Inquiry into the Nature and Causes of the Wealth of Nations,* ed. R. H. Campbell, A. S. Skinner, and W. B. Todd (Indianapolis, IN: Liberty Classics, 1981), pp. 292, 321.
17. Mises, *The Theory of Money and Credit,* p. 333.
18. Mises, in his *The Theory of Money and Credit,* pp. 359-360, added that the near-suppression of banknotes and checking accounts would "by no means imply a death sentence for the banking system," as banks would still intermediate between borrowers and placers of time deposits.
19. *Ibid.*, p. 359.
20. Thus I am puzzled by Percy Greaves's statement that Mises "considered [fractional reserve banking] a deviation from capitalism which free banking would have eliminated, if governments had not intervened...." Greaves, Percy L., "Introduction" to Ludwig von Mises, *On the Manipulation of Money and Credit,* (Dobbs Ferry, NY: Free Market Books, 1978), p. xlvii. Greaves's statement appears in his introduction to a collection of Mises's essays, in one of which Mises plainly stated: "Even if governments had never concerned themselves with the issue of fiduciary media, there would still be banks of issue and fiduciary media in the form of notes as well as checking accounts."
21. Mises, *The Theory of Money and Credit,* p. 346.
22. No single bank can expand ahead of the others because it would suffer adverse clearings against them and lose its reserves. Over-expansion must proceed in concert.
23. On the importance of monetary disequilibrium and the difficulties of adjusting the price level promptly see Leland B. Yeager, "The Significance of Monetary Disequilibrium" *Cato Journal* 6 (Fall 1986),

pp. 369-99. On the responsiveness of the stock of bank-issued money to variations in demand under free banking, see George A. Selgin, *The Theory of Free Banking: Money Supply Under Competitive Note Issue* (Totowa, NJ: Rowman and Littlefield, 1988), chs. 4-6.
24. On this debate see Vera Smith (1990) and Lawrence H. White, "Free Banking and the Gold Standard," Llewellyn H. Rockwell, Jr., ed., *The Gold Standard: An Austrian Perspective,* Chs. 3-4.
25. Actually, the Currency School never attempted to "end fractional reserve banking" or to "institute 100% money." The School argued for a 100 percent reserve requirement to be applied only to *additional* banknote issues. Under Peel's Act the Bank of England retained an authorized *uncovered* note issue of some £14 million.
26. Mises, Ludwig von, *Human Action: A Treatise on Economics,* p. 440.
27. *Ibid.,* p. 447. "But some people ask, what about a cartel of the commercial banks? Could not the banks collude for the sake of a boundless expansion of their issuance of fiduciary media? The objection is preposterous. As long as the public is not, by government interference, deprived of the right of withdrawing its deposits, no bank can risk its own good will by collusion with banks whose good will is not so high as its own." Murray N. Rothbard in "The Austrian Theory of Money," Edwin G. Dolan, ed., *The Foundations of Modern Austrian Economics* (Kansas City, MO: Sheed and Ward, 1976), p. 179, has expressed doubts about Mises's arguments on this matter: "Perhaps Mises underestimated the possibility of a successful bank cartel for the promotion of credit expansion."
28. Mises, *The Theory of Money and Credit,* p. 437.
29. One who holds the views (a) that free banks will expand to meet increases in the demand for money, and (b) that free banks will not generate disequilibrating *over*-expansions, should logically hold the view (c) that a demand-matched expansion in the quantity of bank-issued money is not disequilibrating. In one footnote, however, Mises, in *Human Action: A Treatise on Economics,* p. 442, note 17, suggested that any expansion is disequilibrating. For critical discussion see Selgin, George A., *The Theory of Free Banking: Money Supply Under Competitive Note Issue* (Totowa, NJ: Rowman and Littlefield, 1988), pp. 60-63.
30. Mises, *Human Action: A Treatise on Economics,* 3rd rev. ed., pp. 434-48.
31. *Ibid.,* p. 439.
32. *Ibid.,* pp. 437-438.
33. *Ibid.,*pp. 439, 441, 447.

34. Contrast Selgin, George A., *The Theory of Free Banking: Money Supply Under Competitive Note Issue,* p. 62, who cites the Cernushi quote to support an interpretation much likes Greaves's (see footnote 20). Mises, in *Human Action: A Treatise of Economics,* p. 443, plainly stated that free banking would "not hinder a slow credit expansion," though it would limit it to cautious banks staying within narrow bounds.
35. Mises, *On the Manipulation of Money and Credit,* pp. 138-140, 145-146.
36. Mises, *The Theory of Money and Credit*, p. 434.
37. Mises, *On the Manipulation of Money and Credit,* p. 156.
38. *Ibid.*, pp. 167-68.
39. Mises, *Human Action: A Treatise on Economics,* p. 448.
40. Mises, *The Theory of Money and Credit*, p. 482.
41. Mises, *Human Action: A Treatise on Economics,* pp. 440-441.
42. Mises, *Human Action: A Treatise on Economics,* p. 443.
43. Mises, *The Theory of Money and Credit,* p. 436.
44. Mises, *Human Action: A Treatise on Economics,* p. 443.

36

THE ETHICAL SETTING OF THE MARKET: The Perspective of Röpke

Richard A. White*

Wilhelm Röpke has been recognized by both libertarians and traditional conservatives as a profound scholar and an unswerving advocate of a free society. He is perhaps best known as the intellectual author of Germany's economic recovery following World War II.[1]

Röpke left Germany in 1933, and taught at the Graduate Institute of International Studies in Geneva from 1937 until his death in 1966. He was a prolific author, writing articles and books on economic theory, political science, and social philosophy.[2]

Along with eminent thinkers such as Alexander Rüstow and Walter Eucken, Röpke is often referred to as an "Ordo" or "neo-liberal."[3] He differs from his allies on the economic right, the "classical liberals," in his belief that the market, at least to a small degree, must be controlled and regulated.[4] A more profound difference exits, however, between Röpke and many modern representatives of classical liberalism concerning the ethical foundation (or lack thereof) of the market economy. Is the unhampered market even in need of moral prerequisites? If so, does the market generate these morals (as many libertarian thinkers would contend), or do they come from outside the market? In this essay, we will examine these questions, focusing in particular on Röpke's presentation of the problem.

*Mr. White is a doctoral candidate in theology at Marquette University in Milwaukee, WI. He was introduced to the ideas of Röpke at Grove City College.

Röpke and the Invisible Hand

For years, opponents of free enterprise have delighted in attacking the supposed immorality of the market. Left unattended, they contend, the market place fosters unbridled greed and self-interest, drowning all morality in "the icy water of egotistical calculation," as Marx put it.

Classical liberals, of course, have long challenged this line of thinking. True, the market is driven by the enlightened self-interest of individuals competing in the market place. But proponents of the market order point out that these self-interests work toward the good and not the detriment of the community. Indeed, entrepreneurs must yield and respond to consumer demand in order to succeed. They can expect profits only to the extent that they effectively and efficiently satisfy the wants and needs of others. Individuals who gain the largest profits, therefore, are those who serve the consumer better than their competition. This unseen subordination of the producer to the consumer is called the "invisible hand" of the market place, and, according to classical liberals, bears witness to the *inherent* morality of the unhampered market economy.

But a question arises. If the market is fueled by individual self-interest, then is appealing to this same self-interest sufficient to make individuals "realize that they serve their own best advantage by submitting to the discipline of the market and of competition?"[5] Or, expressed another way, does an appeal to the "invisible hand" alone constitute an adequate response to the challenge that the free market system is an immoral socio-economic order?

Here is where Röpke parts ways with what he terms "liberal immanentism".[6] The latter refuses to look outside the market for any moral prerequisites, whereas Röpke sees the market as one facet of a larger social structure, and "must find its place in a higher order of things which is not ruled by supply and demand, free prices, and competition."[7]

To be sure, Röpke is one with classical liberals in recognizing the positive and indispensable role of enlightened self-interest in the market place. "The 'liberal' economic system," Röpke writes, "delivers to useful ends the extraordinary force inherent in individual self-assertion, whereas the socialist economy suppresses this force and wears itself out in the struggle against it."[8] The market economy, therefore, is morally superior to all kinds of collectivism, leading Röpke to comment, "I would stand for a free economic order even if it implied material sacrifice and if socialism gave the certain prospect of material increase. It is our undeserved luck that the exact opposite is true."[9]

Röpke has no patience with the popular and naive moralism which would condemn self-interest in the name of a "higher" economic morality. He also points out that the "motives which drive people toward economic success are as varied as the human soul itself"[10] and are not necessarily related to a craving for material advantage. But even the latter should not be derided, for we must not forget that "the man who decently provides for himself and his family by his own effort and his own responsibility is doing no small or mean thing."[11]

In the final analysis, Röpke compares the ethics of the market place to "the ethical level of average man."[12] He explains:

> To put it briefly, we move on an intermediate plane. It is not the summit of heroes and saints, of simon-pure altruism, selfless dedication, and contemplative calm, but neither is it the lowlands of open or concealed struggle in which force and cunning determine the victor and the vanquished.... It is true that in our middle plateau of everyday economic life there is, fortunately, as much room for elevations into the higher sphere of true devotion as there is for depressions of violence and fraud; nevertheless, it will generally be granted that the world in which we do business, bargain, calculate, speculate, compare bids, and explore markets ethically corresponds by and large to that middle level at which the whole of everyday life goes on.... (I)t is a climate which, while not particularly nourishing to the soul, at least does not necessarily poison it.[13]

Röpke thus locates the "invisible hand" of the market place at this middle ethical level. As we have seen, however, he does not stop at the realm of supply and demand; rather, he looks beyond it to address the question of the market's moral foundation.

To begin, Röpke points out that the market is made up of "a constantly renewed texture of more or less short-lived contractual relations."[14] Contracts are limited arrangements, motivated out of self-interest, and conditional upon a set of terms previously accepted by both parties. There is nothing within them, however, to ensure the integrity of the contracting individuals. Röpke concludes, therefore, that the market can "have no permanence unless the confidence which any contract presupposes rests on a broad and solid ethical base in all market parties."[15]

Moreover, this ethical base must come from outside the market because self-interest is not always best served (in the short-run at least) by following the rules of the market. As Röpke forthrightly states:

> ...if one tells the various group interests nothing else than that loyal observance of the rules of the competitive price mechanism is in the interest of all and if no strong moral forces are at the same time working to curb their appetites, one must not be surprised by the disappointing results. Honesty is undoubtedly the best kind of ethics, but unfortunately it is doubtful whether, within certain limits, it is always the best policy.[16]

In the absence of moral norms, the "invisible hand" of enlightened self-interest can quickly degenerate into the visible hand of pressure groups, labor unions, and big government and result in unfair competition. Clearly, as Röpke observes, "economic life does not take place in a moral vacuum. Rather, it runs the permanent risk of losing its middle ethical line if not underpinned by strong moral supports, which must exist and be continually reinforced."[17]

Moral Foundations

Röpke never tires of describing these "moral supports." At the most fundamental level they consist of:

> a minimum of mutual trust, confidence in the stability of the legal-institutional framework of the economic process (including money), contractual loyalty, honesty, fair play, professional honor, and that pride which considers it beneath one to cheat, bribe or misuse the authority of the state for one's own egoistic purposes.[18]

As we have seen, the market does not generate these qualities, but presupposes them. They stem from what Röpke refers to as an unwritten creed, "a belief in a definite scale of ultimate values giving sense and purpose to the ordinary doings of all participating in the economic process...."[19]

According to Röpke, these values come from "family, church, genuine communities, and tradition...."[20] They provide the individual a sense of solidarity with the community, "civilizing" in effect, the elementary drive of self-interest.[21] This is accomplished primarily through the family, the "original and imperishable basis of every higher community."[22] Within this framework, "self-interest becomes family interest," and the individual develops the capacity "to serve ends that do not look to his own immediate betterment."[23]

The balance between the individual and the community is an important one for Röpke, and reveals his distrust of a "questionable form of individualism" which treats the individual as "an isolated, atomized entity who could as such be made the basis of the economy."[24] It is precisely such individualism, Röpke maintains, which goes hand in hand with the phenomena of "*Vermassung*" or "enmassment," the process of intellectual, moral, and social disintegration.[25]

Röpke describes this process in meticulous detail throughout his writings.[26] He mentions, among other things, the "agglomeration of people" in large cities and factories,[27] the increasing concentration of "economic and social power beside and under the state,"[28] and the "progressive disappearance of the difference between town and country."[29] The result is "a sand-heap of individuals who are more dependent than ever, less sharply defined and more depersonalized than ever, and at the same time more isolated, uprooted, abandoned, and socially disintegrated than ever."[30]

According to Röpke, the decline of the family, the decay of traditional values and norms, and the dissolution of a genuine sense of community are the end-products of this process. What Edmund Burke described as the "unbought graces of life" give way to a kind of crass consumerism. Better and cheaper material products, however, cannot fill the void left by mass society: "Dissatisfaction and discontent," Röpke writes, "seem only to grow with the profusion of goods designed for creature comforts and in inverse proportion to the happiness expected of those goods."[31] This passage from *A Humane Economy* summarizes the matter well:

> Of what avail is any amount of well-being if, at the same time, we steadily render the world more vulgar, uglier, noisier, and drearier and if men lose the moral and spiritual foundations of their existence? Man simply does not live by radio, automobiles, and refrigerators alone, but by the whole unpurchasable world of dignity, beauty, poetry, grace, chivalry, love, and friendship, the world of community, variety of life, freedom, and fullness of personality.[32]

These non-economic "unbought graces" do not stem from the market, but come from outside it.

We return now to the original question: "Does the free market create its own moral climate?" Röpke answers no. "Market economy, price mechanism, and competition are fine," he states, "but they are not enough. They may be associated with a sound or unsound structure of society."[33] To be sure, the laws of supply and demand work the same in both; but only in the former, Röpke would argue, do they work toward the happiness of men and, in the long run, toward the perpetuation and prosperity of the market place itself. "The decision on the ultimate destiny of the market economy...lies, in other words, beyond supply and demand."[34]

Conclusion

There is a famous story oft repeated in Röpke's writings.[35] He tells of an "old-time liberal" to whom a friend of his was showing some workers' allotments in Rotterdam. The liberal commented, "What an irrational form of vegetable production!" Röpke responds that while cultivating a piece of garden may indeed be an irrational way of producing vegetables, "it is certainly a very rational means of creating happiness, and we are old-fashioned enough to think that this is what really matters in the final analysis."[36]

The story, though seemingly a bit trivial, epitomizes the legacy of Wilhelm Röpke. He constantly sought to forge a middle path between an idealistic moralism on the one hand, and a false economism on the other. A representative of the former would relegate the sphere of economic activity to a lesser, even unimportant realm, focusing only on the moral and intellectual order of our existence. A representative of the latter, unable to think in terms other than money and costs, would raise the autonomous market machine to such lofty heights that it becomes an end in and of itself. Röpke rejected both extremes, noting that "we need a combination of supreme moral sensitivity and economic knowledge."[37]

As we have seen, this eclecticism is well exemplified in Röpke's treatment of the ethical framework of the market order. He affirms the importance of enlightened self-interest and free competition but at the same time recognizes that these forces alone do not ensure a moral socio-economic environment. Such an environment must be created by forces outside of the market itself—by principles, motivations, and a sense of obligations forged beyond the realm of profits and turnover figures—encompassing, as Röpke states, "all the things which anchor a community in the hearts of men."[38]

That Röpke's emphasis on extra-market moral reserves stems ultimately from his embrace of theism and natural law should come as little surprise. Moral norms are not generated by the market but are transcendent and absolute, their ultimate source being divine.[39] Indeed, he defends his vision of social order as something intrinsically desirable. And while a system of free exchange is absolutely necessary, it is "proper to a definite social structure and to a definite spiritual and moral setting."[40]

One need only to pick up the daily paper to realize how timely Röpke's message is for us today. The moral forces he so boldly described and defended are fast evaporating today. Furthermore, burgeoning government continues to choke the productive force of the market with unnecessary regulation, manipulation, and intervention. Heeding Röpke's teaching, we must not forget that these phenomena are interrelated. Indeed, to seek a "purer" free market without curing society's moral (and essentially spiritual) malaise would be entirely naive because moral supports from outside the market are absolutely necessary to ensure the long-term prosperity of the market order (not to mention the ultimate happiness of the human soul). Given the interrelationship of ethics and economics, Röpke's prescribed role for economists is unusual by contemporary standards:

> We, beyond all others, are representatives of the social sciences and are under the duty to make up our minds at the great cross-roads of our civilization. It is not enough for us merely to decipher the roadmarkers; we must know whether we are sending society along the road to freedom, to humane living, to unalterable truth, or in the opposite direction and toward slavery, the prostitution of man, and crassest falsehood.[41]

Notes and References

1. Röpke influenced the Minister of Economic affairs, Ludwig Erhard, who after the War was instrumental in dismantling Germany's planned economy. Writing in 1966, Ludwig von Mises stated that "most of what is reasonable and beneficial in present-day Germany's monetary and commercial policy credit is to be attributed to Röpke's influence." Mises, "Wilhelm Röpke, RIP," *National Review*, 18 (March 8, 1966), p. 200.
2. According to Patrick M. Boarman, Röpke's bibliography at the time of his death numbered over 900 items! "A Fighter for Freedom: Wilhelm Röpke's legacy," *Modern Age*, 10 (Fall, 1966), p. 359.
3. William F. Campbell has recently suggested that "conservative political economy" is better suited to describe the liberalism of Röpke, while Röpke himself seemed to prefer the phrase the "third way" or "economic humanism." See Campbell, William F., "Liberalism vs Conservatism? The Legacy of L. Einaudi and W. Röpke," a paper presented to the Mont Pelerin Society meetings, St. Vincent, Italy, August 31-September 6, 1986. Throughout this essay, the term "liberal" will refer to one who stands for personal freedom, and should not to be confused with its modern American usage.
4. The extent and precise nature of this regulation does not concern us in this study. For a brief survey of what Röpke terms "compatible intervention," see his *The Social Crisis of Our Time,* (Chicago, IL: University of Chicago Press, 1950), pp. 184-191.
5. Röpke, Wilhelm, *A Humane Economy: The Social Framework of the Free Market,* (Chicago, IL: Henry Regnery Company, 1960), p. 123.
6. *Ibid.*, p. 126. See Graham Walker's excellent discussion of this point in a section on the ethics of Röpke in his *The Ethics of F.A. Hayek,* (Lanham, MD: University Press of America, Inc., 1986), pp. 71-75.
7. Röpke, *A Humane Economy*, p. 91.
8. Röpke, Wilhelm, "The Economic Necessity of Freedom, *Modern Age*, 3 (Summer, 1959), p. 233.
9. *Ibid.*
10. Röpke, *A Humane Economy*, p. 121.
11. *Ibid.*, pp. 121-122.
12. *Ibid.*, p. 116.
13. *Ibid.*, pp. 116-117.
14. *Ibid.*, p. 125.
15. *Ibid.*
16. Röpke, *The Social Crises of Our Time*, p. 128. Röpke goes on, "One would have to shut one's eyes to the world and history in order not to see

that individuals, classes and nations have always enjoyed an easy conscience and untroubled prosperity while indulging in cheating, in selling the other fellow short, in exploitation, yes, even spoliation.... One cannot expect that in our day a dispassionate calculation of profit and loss will prevent people from indulging in such conduct." *Ibid.*, pp. 128-129.
17. Röpke, Wilhelm, "Ethics and Economic Life," in *Standard Texts of the Social Market Economy: Two Centuries of Discussion*, Horst Friedrich Wunsche ed., (New York: Gustav Fischer, 1982), p. 374. Röpke continues, "And thus even the prosaic world of business affairs draws on the ethical resources with which it stands or falls and which hold greater importance than the whole gamut of economic laws and principles. It is not the market nor competition nor the interplay between supply and demand which create these reserves. In fact, they consume them and must draw reserves from areas beyond the market." *Ibid.*
18. Röpke, Wilhelm, *International Economic Disintegration,* (New York: The Macmillan Company, 1942), p. 69.
19. *Ibid.*
20. Röpke, *A Humane Economy*, p. 125.
21. Röpke, "The Economic Necessity of Freedom," p. 234.
22. Röpke, Wilhelm, *Civitas Humana: A Humane Order of Society,* (London: William Hodge and Company, 1948), p. 133. Röpke adds, "we can, without exaggeration, describe the decline of the family as one of the gravest symptoms of the disease of our time." *The Social Crisis of Our Time*, p. 16.
23. Röpke, "The Economic Necessity of Freedom," p. 234. Hence, "man must voluntarily accept the community's prior rights as against certain short-term satisfactions of his own, and he must feel that in serving the community he ennobles his own life...." *Ibid.*
24. Röpke, *The Social Crises of Our Time*, p. 52.
25. As Röpke writes, "Mass man is individualistic because of the loosening of the social fabric and the disintegration of com- munity. One of the least well understood aspects of the process of enmassment is that it detaches the individual from his natural social fabric and leaves him to his own resources. Conversely, when individualism became the cult of the isolated individual as such and of the mere millionfold voter, in contrast to true community and social articulation...it also became one of the most corrosive of spiritual acids, dissolving the organic structure of society and thereby contributing to the formation of mass society and mass democracy." *A Humane Economy*, pp. 70-71.
26. See especially *Ibid.*, pp. 36-89.
27. *Ibid.*, p. 40

28. *Ibid.*, p. 32.
29. *Ibid.*, p. 50.
30. *Ibid.*, p. 71.
31. *Ibid.*, p. 78.
32. *Ibid.*, p. 89.
33. *Ibid.*, p. 35. It is beyond the scope of this essay to examine Röpke's vision of social order in any detail. He summarizes it this way: "In such a society, wealth would be widely dispersed; people's lives would have solid foundations; genuine communities, from the family upward, would form a background of moral support for the individual; there would be counterweights to competition and the mechanical operation of prices; people would have roots and would not be adrift in life without anchor; there would be a broad belt of an independent middle class, a healthy balance between town and country, industry and agriculture." In a few places, Röpke makes what seem to us romantic, if not utopian, speculations, especially with regard to his vision of small peasant communities. See, for example, *The Social Crisis of Our Time*, pp. 201-213.
34. Röpke, *A Humane Economy*, p. 35.
35. See Röpke, *The Social Crisis of Our Time*, p. 224.
36. Cited in "Freedom was his Slogan," *The German Tribune*, 204 (February 26, 1966), p. 4.
37. Röpke, *A Humane Economy*, p. 104. He adds, "Economically ignorant moralism is as objectionable as morally callous economism." *Ibid.*
38. *Ibid.*, p. 149.
39. See *Ibid.*, pp. 13-14. Furthermore, Röpke sees an immutable link between genuine liberalism and Christianity. He writes, "the patrimony of Christian social philosophy...merges with all that is essential and enduring in liberalism." Röpke, "Liberalism and Christianity," *Modern Age*, 1 (Fall 1957), p. 134.
40. Röpke, *A Humane Economy*, p. 93. In a recent article, Norman P. Barry identifies Röpke's neo-liberal approach as "end-state" liberalism. It supposes "that a particular pattern or form of economic or social organization is desirable on ethical or metaphysical grounds...." On the other hand, "procedural rules" liberalism (which he identifies with the classical model) "locates the essence of liberalism in the process of free exchange between individuals whatever the outcome of that process." Barry, Norman P., "Political and Economic Thought of German Neo-liberals," in *German Neo-Liberals and the Social Market Economy*, Alan Peacock and Hans Willgerodt eds., (New York: St. Martin's Press, 1989), pp. 111-112. Barry's distinction is helpful in drawing attention to

an important difference between Röpke and many libertarian thinkers. For the latter, the spontaneous processes of the market are self-justifying, whereas for Röpke, they may produce undesirable externalities (such as mass society).

41. Röpke, Wilhelm, "The Place of Economics Among the Sciences," in *On Freedom and Free Enterprise*, Mary Sennholz ed., (Princeton, NJ: D. Van Nostrand Company, Inc., 1956), p. 127.

INDEX

A

Abortion, 392
Abraham, 400-401
Accountant, 453-454, 458-459, 461, 465
Acid rain, 269-270
Adam, Adolph, 114
Adam and Eve, 253, 313, 316
Addison, John T., 515
Advertising, 331
AEI. *See* American Enterprise Institute
American Enterprise Institute (AEI), 65
Affirmative Action, 350
After Communism, 28
Age of Inflation, 161, 200, 530
Aggression, 48-50
Agricultural marketing orders, 52
Agriculture, 455, 477
AIDS, 393
Airline industry, 203
Alexandrin, Glenn, 117
Alienation, 265
Allen, Ernest M., 504
Alliances, 404
Alvarez, Leo Paul de, 29
American Civil Liberties Union, 52
American Hospital Association, 489, 497
American Medical Association, 485-487, 489, 491-492, 497, 504
American Revolution, 55
Anarchism, 14, 22-23, 49
Anderson, Beverly Kline, 159
Anderson, Robert G., 33, 159, 166
Anderson, Odin W., 504
Anthem, 149
Aquinas, Saint Thomas, 77-78, 87, 259, 277, 283, 287
Aristophanes, 107
Aristotle, 14, 75-78, 87, 107, 109, 252, 267, 343, 394
Army, 395, 397-399, 405
Articles of Confederation, 153
Asia, 121
Aschauer, David Alan, 452
Ashenfelter, Orley, 514
Asimov, Isaac, 117
Assets, 453
Auburn University, 69
Audubon Society, 353
Augustine, Saint, 259, 267
Austrian School of Economics, 63, 69-70, 75, 96, 127, 136-137, 155-161, 164-165, 186, 189-190, 198, 242-243, 246-247, 290, 298-299, 301-302, 312, 391, 457
Austrian Economists, 78, 80-81, 83, 85-86, 88, 128, 156, 159, 163, 165, 186-187, 192, 198, 201, 246, 291, 318-319, 355, 367, 391, 419
Austrian Institute for Business Cycle Research, 158
Authority, 414
Ayau, Manuel, 167

B

Babylon, 106
Babylonia, 280
Baghdad, 109
Bailout, 41
Balanced Budget, 232, 292, 434, 437
Balanced Budget and Emergency Deficit Control Act of 1985, 229
Balanced Budget and Emergency Deficit Control Reaffirmation Act of 1987, 229
Bank Insurance Fund (BIF), 425
Bank runs, 418, 421-424
Banking, 111, 161, 197, 304, 394, 402, 417, 420, 424-425, 517, 522, 526
Banking Act of 1933, 418
Bankruptcy, 350, 378, 431, 441, 462
Barro, Robert J., 430, 444, 451-452
Barter, 131
Bartlett's Quotations, 337
Baruch, Bernard, 363
Basic Money Reserves, 519
Bastiat, Frédéric, 148, 310, 336, 398
Bean, C. R., 514
Beethoven, Ludwig van, 114
Bell, Jeff, 298
Benavides, Rosario, 452
Benefits, 483, 500
Benjamin, David, 372
Benson, Bruce L., 61
Bentham, Jeremy, 193, 346
Berger, Peter L., 478, 482
Berlin, Isaiah, 142, 153
Berlin Wall, 281
Berman, Howard J., 489, 504
Berner, Richard B.,
Bernstam, Mikhail S., 273-274, 286
Bernstein, Carl, 53
Bernstein, Edward, 303
Bernstein, Peter, 429, 436-437, 451
Beveridge, Albert J., 221
Bible, 14, 251-252, 257-258, 312, 316-317, 321-323, 394, 400-404, 407, 411, 470
Bidinotto, Robert James, 47
BIF. *See* Bank Insurance Fund
Bill of Rights, 140-141, 144, 195
Biology, 408
Black, Eugene C., 103
Black market, 463, 476
Block, Walter, 150, 154, 530
Blue Cross, 487-490, 492, 495-496, 498
Blue Shield, 489-490, 492, 495-496
Boarman, Patrick M., 542
Boettinger, H. M., 159
Boettke, Peter J., 63, 74
Böhm-Bawerk, Eugen von, 16, 28, 76, 80, 83-88, 93, 103, 156, 158, 161, 211
Bonaparte, Napoleon, 6, 114
Bookkeeping, 460
Boom-bust cycle, 190, 369, 378, 449, 524
Borders, 406
Bounded-rationality, 207
Bowring, John, 115-116
Bracey, Herbert S., 159
Brandeis, Louis D., 145, 153
Brandt, Willy, 342-345
Breakthrough, 267
Bribery, 265, 343

Brock, David, 372
Bronson v. Rodes, 217, 221
Brookings Institute, 65
Brown, C., 515
Brown, John, 57
Brown, James N., 514
Brunner, Emil, 253, 255-256, 258, 262, 267, 268
Bruno, Leoni, 408
Buchanan, James, 232, 239
Budget deficit, 224, 226-227, 230, 435
Budget Enforcement Act of 1990, 229, 231
Bureaucracy, 91, 327, 398-399, 415, 457-459, 463, 502
Bureaucracy, 199, 466
Bureaucrats, 37-38, 42, 194, 283, 425, 448, 479
Burger, Warren, 142
Burke, Edmund, 539
Burton, John, 474
Bush, George, 224, 226, 230, 341, 436
Business, 6-8, 11, 64, 172, 322, 351, 378, 381-382, 384, 456, 503, 523
Business cycle, 319, 370, 429, 508, 524
Byron, Lord, 107, 116-117

C

Cachanosky, Juan C., 75
Califano, Joseph, 498-499
Calvin, John, 255, 470, 481
Calvinism, 260
Cambridge theory, 129
Campbell, William F., 542
Campbell University, 327, 335
Cantillon, Richard, 128
Capital, 7, 12, 102, 110, 120, 124-125, 171, 173-174, 180-181, 205, 335, 356, 382, 398, 425, 430-431, 436-437, 446-447, 449, 455, 490, 501, 513, 521
Capital and Interest, 85, 87, 158, 161, 211
Capital consumption, 463
Capital formation, 297, 383, 429, 436, 443
Capital markets, 172, 296-297
Capitalism, 19-20, 48, 60, 119, 122, 155, 164, 169-171, 175-179, 182-183, 192-193, 196, 201, 311, 320, 339-340, 342-345, 349, 351, 355, 357, 365, 373, 387, 394, 454-455, 531
Capitalism: A Treatise on Economics, 373
Capitalism: The Cure for Racism, 389
Cargo Cults, 122
Carson, Clarence B., 91, 481
Carter, Jimmy, 439
Cash balances, 129-130, 132-134, 137
Castorina, Camille, 105, 117-118
Castro, Fidel, 53, 341-342
Cato Institute, 65, 483
Catron, John, 219
Causation, 247
Central America, 160
Central bank, 197, 424, 525
Central Intelligence Agency (CIA), 49
Central planning, 6, 14, 34, 187, 207, 209-210, 218, 281, 320, 475, 477
Cernushi, Henri, 526
Chafuen, Alejandro A., 88
Chaos, 123

Charitable Institutions, 42, 65
Charity, 43, 323, 395, 485, 489
Charlemagne, 108, 117
Cheney, Richard, 292
Chicago School of Economics, 21, 304, 391
Child labor, 181,
Childs, Roy A., 61, 154
China, 20, 70-71, 92, 108, 203, 281, 287, 441, 477
Christ, 15, 251-252, 258, 313, 393, 396, 400, 402, 411
Christian Economics, 164, 312
Christian reconstructionists, 13-14
Christians, 410-413, 415
Chrysostom, Saint John, 259
Church, 15-16, 258-259, 412
CIO. *See* Committee for Industrial Organization
Citizens for a Sound Economy, 235
City of God, 267
Civil government, 402, 470-471
Civil law, 469
Civil liberties, 52
Civil War, 140
Clark, Gordon H., 408
Class struggle, 92
Classical economists, 76-81, 84, 311
Classical liberalism, 107, 157, 535-536
Classical School of Economics, 310
Club of Rome, 271, 285, 365
Coase, Ronald, 287
Cobden, Richard, 107, 114-116
Code of Hammurabi, 407
Cole, Barbara, 467
Collective bargaining, 146, 494, 509
Collectivism, 8, 53, 162, 170, 179, 206, 357
Collectivist economic planning, 28
Collectivist ownership, 459
Colonialism, 405
Columbus, Christopher, 109, 413
Commager, Henry Steele, 215, 221
Committee for Industrial Organization (CIO), 494
Common law, 469
Common Sense, 336
Communalism, 472-475, 477
Communicating ideas, 58
Communism, 17, 19-20, 91-92, 124, 170, 327, 341-342, 345, 394
Communist Manifesto, The, 115
Community rating, 496
Comparative Advantage, 319
Competition, 39-40, 42, 49, 72, 83, 121, 177, 182, 334, 463, 523, 525, 528, 536, 540
Comprehensive Medical Care, 486
Compulsions, 327
Computers, 368
Congress, 214-215, 219, 223, 230, 232-236, 251, 303, 345, 349-353, 358-360, 434-436, 501-502
Conscription, 148
Conservatism, 291
Constantine the Great, 412
Constitution, 66, 139-140, 144, 153, 177-179, 195, 214-217, 223-224, 232, 234, 237, 346, 349, 360, 409
Constructivism, 209
Consumer, 35, 83, 157, 295, 335, 340, 356, 454, 456

Consumer sovereignty, 335, 337
Consumption, 129-130, 133-134, 272, 305, 323, 346, 436
Contract, 314, 348, 402, 517, 530, 537-538
Contract practice, 491
Convergence, 120, 122
Corn Laws, 114
Corporate ownership, 38
Corporate financing, 448
Corporate personality in ancient Israel, 267
Cost Accounting Standards Board, 462
Cost of production, 79, 81-83, 305, 454, 456, 461
Cost-plus reimbursement, 490
Council of Economic Advisors, 304
Court, 49, 465
Creation, 15, 252, 253
Credit expansion, 297, 305, 370, 524-525, 527-528
Cuba, 340-341
Currency Acts, 216
Currency debasement, 347
Currency principle, 524
Currency School, 524, 527-528, 532

D

Dark Ages, 108, 180
Darman, Richard, 230
Darwin, Charles, 408
Das Capital, 95
Dashkova, Princess, 112, 117
David, King, 106, 400, 405
Davis, John F., 159
Death and Taxes, 45, 161
Debt, 191, 402, 436-437, 439-441, 446, 448
Debts and Deficits, 74, 155, 161, 200, 239, 393, 408, 451
Decalogue, 106, 196, 470
Declaration of Independence, 178
Deficit, 191, 232, 293, 296, 357-358, 429-430, 434-437, 439-444, 446, 448-449
Deficit spending, 320, 349, 429, 431
DeMeza, David, 473, 481
Democracy, 208, 327-328, 330-331, 335-336, 339, 341-343, 346-347, 352, 356-357, 398
Democratic, 359
Democratic government, 458
Democrats, 224, 290
Demosthenes, 383
Demsetz, Harold, 287
Deng Xiaoping, 71
Dent, Ulysses S., 156, 166
Department of Health, Education and Welfare, 497
Deposit insurance, 417-422, 424-427
Depreciation, 7, 93
Depression, 370, 378
Deregulation, 121, 204, 417, 517
Descola, Jean, 117
Diagnostic Related Groups (DRG), 502
Dialectical materialism, 94
Dickinson College, 69
Diplomacy, 404
Disarmament, 49
Discrimination, 350, 373, 375, 379
Distribution, 473, 477
Diversity, 252-253, 256

Division of labor, 33, 110, 136, 173, 175, 177, 387, 456
Doctors, 483, 487
Dolan, Edwin G., 119
Dominion, 413
DRG. *See* Diagnostic Related Groups
Dr. Schmolder, 6
Draft, 395, 397-398

E

Eastern Europe, 19, 64
Ebeling, Richard M., 127, 138, 530
Ebert, Randall W., 514
Echard, Jo Kwong, 281, 285-288
Eckhardt, Meister, 259-260, 267
Econometric, 367, 371
Econometric models, 367-368
Econometrician, 367
Economic calculation, 17, 35, 86, 208, 296, 320-321, 408, 455, 459, 465
Economic Calculation in a Socialist Commonwealth, 28
Economic democracy, 330, 334
Economic development, 36, 176
Economic education, 63-64
Economic growth, 41, 273-274, 442
Economic ownership, 34, 37, 39, 43-44
Economic Policy: Thoughts for Today and Tomorrow, 167
Economic Review, 427
Economics, 19, 28
Economics, 7, 12-13, 18, 21-24, 68, 73, 106-107, 113, 123, 127, 157, 162-164, 171, 177, 186, 189-190, 193, 195-196, 198, 241-242, 248, 269, 295-296, 309-311, 324, 391-392, 454
Economics in One Lesson, 165
Economist, 71, 74
Eden, 254-255
Education, 375, 386, 395
Educators, 66, 68
Edward
Efficient bargain model, 507-508
Egalitarianism, 251, 261-265, 478
Egypt, 105, 316, 404, 406
Ehrlich, Paul, 271, 284, 287
Eighth Commandment, 196, 393-394, 398, 470
Eisner, Robert, 437, 451
Elections, 339-340, 344, 358
Ellsaesser, Hugh W., 284
Ellsberg, Daniel, 53
Eminent Domain, 398
Employee medical programs, 486
Employment, 128, 319-320, 376-377, 379-380, 507-508
Endangered species, 278
Endicott, Kenneth M., 504
Energy, 272
Engels, Friedrich, 94, 103
Enlightenment, 111, 195, 227, 323
Enmassment, 539
Entitlement, 398, 465, 471
Entrepreneur, 23, 26, 40, 72, 79, 85, 157, 163, 178, 181, 208, 245, 247, 274-275, 277, 280, 295, 321, 334-335, 345, 364, 368, 371, 454, 456, 459, 536

Entrepreneurship, 14, 110, 204-205, 314, 370
Environmentalism, 269-271, 273, 281, 283
Environmentalists, 272-273, 275-278, 350, 352
Envy, 16, 26, 262, 264, 345
Epicureans, 252
Epicurus, 147, 152
Epistemology, 13, 15, 27, 86, 185, 193, 318
Equality, 251, 254, 258-260, 263-264, 373
Equality of opportunity, 373-375, 380-381, 387
Equation of exchange, 300-301
Equilibrium, 82-83, 248
Erhard, Ludwig, 6, 542
Esau, 257
Espionage, 405
Ethics, 8-9, 15, 75, 194-196, 272, 392-394, 470, 535, 537-538, 541
Ethiopia, 478
Eucken, Walter, 535
Eudaemonism, 15
Eugenics, 375, 387
Europe, 64, 69, 71-73, 91, 108-109, 121-122, 124, 158, 160, 174, 176, 203, 209, 274, 281, 327, 358, 413, 441
Evans, M. Stanton, 159, 166
Evans, Rowland, 306
Evolution, 408
Exchange, 35, 76-77, 151
Exchange value, 130-133, 217, 223, 520-521, 523
Executive branch, 214
Exit-Voice Model, 507, 509-511
Experience rating, 496
Externalities, 278
Extinction of species, 270

F

Factors of production, 85, 345, 449, 454
Fallacy of composition, 438
Farmers Union Hospital Association, 491
FASB. *See* Financial Accounting Standards Board
Fascism, 19, 41-42, 44, 141, 171, 394
FBI. *See* Federal Bureau of Investigation
FCC. *See* Federal Communications Commission
Federal budget, 223, 358
Federal Bureau of Investigation (FBI), 49
Federal Communications Commission (FCC), 51-52
Federal debt, 289, 429, 431, 433, 438, 442
Federal deficits, 431, 433
Federal Reserve, 56, 191, 225, 299, 304, 322, 357, 369, 418, 424, 439
Federal Reserve Note, 402
Federal Savings and Loan Insurance Corporation (FSLIC), 425
Federalism, 214, 217
Feldman, Jacob J., 504
Feminists, 169-170
Fertig, Lawrence, 17
Feudalism, 174
Fiat money standard, 214, 220, 297, 304, 349
Fichte, Johann, 414
Fiction, 409
Fiduciary media, 519-520, 522-523, 525-526
Fifth Amendment, 142

Financial Accounting Standards Board (FASB), 461
Financial Industry, 417, 425-426, 446
First Amendment, 139, 141-144, 153
Fisher, Irving, 129-131, 300
Fletcher v. Peck, 217, 221
Flexible exchange rates, 303
Flint, Robert, 109, 117
Foley, Thomas, 139, 236, 240
Food, Drug and Cosmetic Act, 503
Food and Drug Administration, 503
Force, 48, 353-354, 377, 379, 458
Fordham University, 22
Forecasting, 363-366
Forecasts and Strategies, 429
Foreign affairs, 394
Foreign policy, 403, 406
Foundation for Economic Education, 6, 8, 29, 33, 164, 166
Foundations of Morality The, 325
Founding Fathers, 5, 55, 68, 112, 195, 224, 260, 409
Fourteenth Amendment, 140, 143-144, 153
Fractional reserve banking system, 304, 401, 424, 517-522, 528, 530
Frankel, Charles, 267
Franklin, Benjamin, 112
Fraternal organizations, 486
Free banking, 69, 162, 305, 517, 522, 523-528, 531
Free good, 37
Free market, 16, 18, 20, 48, 52, 67, 69-71, 86, 107, 162, 164, 172, 177, 187, 192, 203, 205, 269, 273, 276, 283, 290-291, 304, 311, 321, 333, 391, 425, 455, 463, 471, 478, 484, 540
Free speech, 5, 52, 139, 142, 145
Free trade, 14, 48, 56, 71, 110, 120, 125, 349, 406
Freedom, 47, 49-51, 53-55, 67, 73, 105, 107, 111-112, 121, 139, 141-142, 146-147, 169-170, 172, 175, 177, 180, 183, 190, 192-196, 227, 241-242, 248, 251, 263, 266, 295, 305, 320, 343, 345, 373, 385-386, 391, 393-394, 409, 412-415, 465, 469, 471, 480
Freedom and the Law, 408
Freedom of choice, 34, 503, 541
Freedom of contract, 34, 120, 125, 217, 342, 345-346, 354-355
Freedom of opportunity, 375, 379, 386-388
Freedom philosophy, 50
Freedom of press, 5, 139-140, 142
Freedom of religion, 139
The Freeman, 286, 467
Freeman, A., 509, 515
Freeman, R., 515
French Revolution, 55, 414
Friedman, David, 61
Friedman, Milton, 21, 24-25, 70, 134, 138, 302, 304-305, 307, 418, 427, 429-430, 434-436, 439, 451-452
Fringe benefits, 510, 512
Front-end health insurance, 488, 495
Fruin, Richard, 159

FSLIC. *See* Federal Savings and Loan Insurance Corporation
Fugger, Jacob, 111
Futures Markets, 276, 363

G

Gaia, 413
Galbraith, John Kenneth, 192, 295
Garner, John, 225-226, 239
Garrison, Roger W., 438-439, 441, 448, 451-452
Garbarino, Joseph W., 504
Garvin, Glenn, 61
"Geld" in Grundsätze der Volkswirtschaftslehre, 138
Geller, Simon, 51-52, 60
Genealogy, 147
George Mason University, 69
Germany, 6, 19, 111, 176, 439, 440-441, 448, 524, 535
Gerry, Elbridge, 153
Gideon v. Wainwright, 153
Gilder, George, 292-295, 306
Glass-Steagall Act, 418-419
Global warming, 269-270, 273
GNP. *See* Gross National Product
God, 7-9, 15-16, 105, 124, 140, 164, 195-196, 252-262, 264-266, 282, 311, 313-317, 320-321, 323-324, 393, 395-399, 403, 405-406, 410, 412-414, 471
Goethe, 461
Gold, 298, 302-305, 400, 450, 518-520, 523-524
Gold clauses, 216
Gold coins, 216
Gold Commission, 298, 302-303
Gold exchange standard, 450
Gold Is Money, 161
Gold standard, 110, 292, 297, 299, 303-305, 349, 517, 528
Golden Rule, 196
Good Samaritan, 393
Goodman, John C., 504-505
GOP. See Grand Old Party
Gorbachev, Mikhail, 19, 91, 341-345
Gordon, George, 107, 116-117
Gould, J. R., 473, 481
Government, 6, 11, 41, 49-50, 52, 65, 70, 95, 108, 110-111, 124-125, 139-140, 162, 170, 195, 206, 208-209, 213, 215, 217-218, 220, 223-224, 227, 234, 237-238, 272, 275-276, 295-296, 304-305, 319, 335, 342, 344, 347, 349, 352-354, 356-357, 359, 373-375, 377, 394-396, 398, 400, 405-406, 409, 411, 422-423, 441, 457-459, 463-464, 483-485, 494, 496, 498, 500-501, 503, 526-528, 531, 538
The Government Against the Economy, 373
Government control, 170-171, 385-386, 417, 425, 484, 518
Government health legislation, 493, 495-497
Government intervention, 56, 101, 157, 161, 165, 171-172, 176, 178-179, 182, 186, 190-191, 194, 201-202, 217, 228, 270, 273, 282, 340, 352, 355, 431, 453, 462, 465, 483, 495, 497, 503, 532
Government ownership, 36-37, 41, 272

Government power, 237
Government regulations, 423, 453, 503
Government services, 458
Graber, David M., 282
Grace Commission, 450
Gramm-Rudman, 229-231, 305
Grand Old Party (GOP), 289
Grant, Ulysses S., 484
Great Depression, 18, 299, 321, 418, 425, 487
Greaves, Bettina Bien, 27, 155, 159, 167
Greaves, Percy L., Jr., 159, 163-164, 325, 531
Greece, 75, 107, 116
Greeks, 252
Greer, Germaine, 170, 184
Gregory, Paul R., 430
Gresham's Law, 22, 107, 319-320, 421
Grice-Hutchinson, Marjorie, 79, 87-88
Grievances, 509
Grinder, Walter, 211
Gross National Product (GNP), 71, 121, 185-186, 226-227, 293, 298, 300-301, 356-357, 365-367, 371, 439, 441-442
Group plans, 496
Grove City College, 12, 21, 33, 69, 91, 160, 185, 213, 469, 535
Guarnieri, Robert, 169
Guevara, Che, 53
Gunther, Jeffrey W., 427
Gwartney, James, 481
Gwen v. Breedlove, 218-219, 221

H

Haberler, Gottfried, 18, 24, 157
Hagel, John III, 211
Hall, Robert E., 514
Hamilton, Alexander, 139, 223-224
Harman, Nicholas, 474, 481
Harper, F. A., 14-15, 27, 146, 154
Harvard University, 24, 194, 284
Hausman, Daniel M., 451
Hawthorne effect, 510
Hayek, Friedrich A., 14, 18, 24, 27-28, 64, 70, 74, 115, 117, 138, 157-158, 202, 205, 209, 211-212, 246-247, 249, 290, 307, 370, 425, 427, 466
Hazlett, Thomas, 293, 306
Hazlitt, Henry, 148, 159, 164-165, 199, 262, 267, 309, 322, 325-326, 368, 372
Health care, 483-484, 486-488, 498, 500
Health insurance, 485, 487-489, 492, 503
Health Maintenance Organizations (HMO), 501
Hebrew, 470
Hebrew Republic, 394, 397, 405, 407
Hedonic calculation, 408
Hedonism, 15
Heilbroner, Robert, 18-19, 28, 69, 74, 192, 199, 429-430, 436-437, 451
Hendrickson, Mark W., 185
Hepburn v. Griswold, 217
Herdin, Garret, 287
Heritage Foundation, 65
Herodotus, 342
Hertz, Ronald, 159

Herzlinger, Regina E., 504
Hill-Burton Act, 497, 499
Hillsdale College, 69, 127, 327
Hinish v. Meier & Frank Co., 153
Hirsch, Barry T., 515
Hirschman, A., 509
Hiss, Alger, 53
History of Economic Analysis, 87, 138
Hitler, Adolf, 11, 157-158
HMO. See Health Maintenance Organizations
Ho Chi Minh, 53
Hobbes, Thomas, 111
Hodes, I., 159
Holman, Wayne J., Jr., 159
Holy Cross College, 69
Holzer, Henry Mark and Erika, 52, 221
Homeless persons, 203
Honest Money, The Biblical Blueprint for Money and Banking, 400, 408
Honesty, 5, 7, 54, 57, 63, 158, 265, 401, 538
Hong Kong, 70
Hoover, Herbert, 224-226
Hopper, Grace, 27
Hospital plans, 502
Hospitals, 485-490, 493, 497-498
House Banking Committee, 303
House of Representatives, 333, 358
How Can Europe Survive?, 161
Human action, 302, 309-310, 312, 314, 318, 320, 326, 367-368, 376, 525
Human Action: A Treatise on Economics, 15-16, 27, 74, 87-89, 106, 117, 138, 156-157, 162, 204, 212, 241-242, 244-246, 248, 306, 318, 337, 347, 362, 527, 531-533
Human condition, 173
Human nature, 277
Human rights, 139
Humanism, 193, 311-312, 317
Hume, David, 110, 392, 408
Huncke, George D., 211
Husock, Howard, 211
Hutt, W. H., 337

I

IBM. *See* International Business Machines
Ideas, 5, 64-66, 69-70, 72-73, 155-156, 165, 170, 290
Idolatry, 403
Ignorance, 430
Ikeda, Sanford, 201
Image of God, 254-255
Implicit Contract, 508
Incarnation, 15
Incentive, 425, 473
Income, 280, 373-374, 511
Income effect, 302
Income tax, 232, 393, 453, 463
Indemnity coverage, 488
Individual rights, 345
Individualism, 28, 53, 58, 60, 136, 147, 150, 179, 539
Industrial Revolution, 173-175, 178, 180-181, 365
Industrialization, 272-273
Inequality, 252-254, 257, 260, 348
Infanticide, 392
Inflation, 6-7, 108, 164-165, 188, 190-191, 197, 203, 297-298, 300-301, 305, 319, 322-323, 336, 344, 349, 356, 358, 365, 368-369, 378, 429, 431,

433, 437, 439, 441, 444, 448-449, 500, 524, 526
Inheritance, 381, 385, 470
Institute for Christian Economics, 11
Institute for Law and Policy Analysis, 339
Institutes of the Christian Religion, 255
Institutionalists, 16
Insurance, 483-484, 486-487, 490, 495
Intercollegiate Society of Individualists, 22
Intercollegiate Studies Institute, 22
Interest, 92, 134, 296, 314, 385, 418-420, 422, 430-431, 433-434, 438-439, 441-442, 447-449, 523
Internal Revenue Service (IRS), 353, 461, 464, 493
International Business Machines (IBM), 329
Interventionism, 24, 34, 38-39, 70, 162, 169-170, 192, 194, 202, 205-209, 345, 349, 351, 355, 400, 527-528
Investors, 364
Iona College, 20
Iron Curtain, 17, 274, 342
IRS. *See* Internal Revenue Service
Isaiah's Job, 23
Israel, 106, 257, 267, 395-398, 401, 403-406
Italy, 19, 107

J

Jacob, 257
Jacobs, Michael, 452
Japan, 121, 439-440, 448
Jefferson, Thomas, 57, 152-153, 224, 260, 335
Jehovah's Witnesses, 141
Jesus Christ, 410, 415
Jevons, William S., 80-83, 88, 293, 311
Job satisfaction, 510
Job security, 512
Johnson, Lyndon B., 351, 357, 485, 499
Johnson, H. Thomas, 461, 466
Journal of Christian Reconstruction, 27
Joyce, Lucia, 150-151
Joyce, James, 150-151
Joyce, Stephen, 150
Judeo-Christian, 197, 263, 282, 312-313, 323, 394
Judeo-Christian Foundation, 13, 195-196
Julliard v. Greenman, 221
Jurisdiction, 216
Just price, 75
Justice, 54, 59, 251, 263, 375, 387, 400, 458

K

Kane, Edward J., 422, 427
Kant's *Weltanschauung*, 27
Kantianism, 13-14
Kaplan, Robert S., 461, 466
Kauder, Emile, 77, 87
Kaufmann, Felix, 157
Keckeissen, Joseph, 159
Kemp, Jack, 291, 298
Kennedy, John F., 335
Kennedy, Robert, 53
Kenya, 474, 476
Kenyatta, Jomo, 476
Kershner, Howard, 325

Ketler, Bruce W., 213
Keynes, John Maynard, 18, 66, 68, 74, 134, 138, 165, 185, 192, 391, 431, 451
Keynesian, 24-25, 69, 129, 133, 135, 167, 187-188, 191, 197, 291, 429, 436-437, 442-443
Keynesian economics, 302, 391
Keynesianism, 16, 17, 21, 190, 290, 295
Khaldun, Ibn, 109, 111
Kibbe, Matthew W., 223
Kikuyu tribe, 475
King, Martin Luther, Jr., 53
Kirzner, Israel M., 13-14, 21, 23-24, 27-28, 159, 163, 198, 204-205, 211, 241, 249, 317, 325
Klaus, Vaclav, 70
Knight, Virginia Curtin, 482
Knowledge problem, 202, 205, 212
Koether, George, 159, 167
Kohl, Helmut, 342
Köln, University of, 20, 160
Kostiuk, Peter F., 515
Krauss, Melvyn, 268
Kroner, Richard, 27
Krug, Edward C., 284
Kuhn, Thomas S., 325
Kuznets, Simon, 366

L

Labor, 58, 77, 80-81, 93-94, 96-101, 110, 137, 322, 377, 398-399, 471, 473, 507, 513, 521
Labor demand, 508, 514
Labor law, 156, 359
Labor legislation, 182
Labor markets, 172, 174, 371
Labor theory of value, 79, 92-93, 95-96, 294
Labor unions, 95, 507
Lachmann, Ludwig, 13-14, 27
Lafayette, Marquis de, 112
Laffer, Arthur, 292-293, 298-299
Laffer Curve, 292
LaFollette, Karen, 462, 466
Laissez-faire, 47, 51, 58, 60, 164, 177, 182, 206, 339-340
Lamb, David, 482
Lane, Rose Wilder, 117
Lange, Oskar, 18, 28, 167
Laslett, Peter, 408
LeFevre, Robert, 61, 164
Legal ownership, 34-35, 39-40
Legal tender, 213, 218-219, 402
Legislators, 181, 228, 361
Lehrman, Lewis, 291, 302-303
Leisure, 366
Lenin, Vladimir I., 91, 459-460, 466
Lennon, John, 53
Leonidas, 107-108
Leontief, Wassily W., 514
Lesseps, Ferdinand de, 116
Liberal, 24, 179, 540
Liberalism, 68, 155, 158
Liberalism, 349, 466
Libertarian Party, 48-49
Libertarianism, 166, 179, 304, 535
Liberty, 47-53, 55, 57-58, 66, 139, 142, 146, 152-153, 196, 266, 290, 415
Liberty, 49, 105
Liberty bell, 106
Licensing, 379, 393, 410
Lillien, David M., 514
Lindbeck, Assar, 265

Ling Su Fan v. United States, 221
Liturgy, 410
Lobbyists, 65, 276
Locke, John, 110, 195, 392, 408, 471
Lofchie, Michael F., 475, 477, 482
Lopez, Serjio, 341
Losses, 295, 314, 321, 454
Love, Robert D., 5
Lovejoy, David, 267
Loyola University (New Orleans, LA), 69
Lundy, Burrows T., 335

M

Machlup, Fritz, 18, 24, 157, 246
MacKenzie, Charles S., 251
Macroeconomic, 137, 367
Macroeconomics, 127-128, 186, 188, 190-191, 301
Madison, James, 223-224
Mafia, 340, 343, 353-354
Maine, Henry Sumner, 343, 346-348, 357, 362
Malkiel, Burton G., 430, 451
Malthus, Thomas, 270-271, 365
Maltsev, Dr. Yuri, 192
Mammon, 402-403
Management, 42-43, 456-459
Manchester, William, 150, 154
Manchester School of Economics, 115
Mandated benefit laws, 502
Mandela, Nelson, 53
Manufacturing, 82, 98-99, 369
Mao Tse Tung, 53
Marburg, Germany, 11
Marburg University, 160
Marcet, Jane Haldimand, 113-114
Marcos, Luisa Zorraquin de, 269
Marginal cost, 83
Marginal utility, 80-83, 85-86, 129, 133, 158, 293-294
Marginality, 129
Mariam, Mengistu Haile, 478
Market economy, 33-34, 38-40, 44, 119-120, 123, 125, 153-169, 173, 182, 192-193, 535-536
Market failure, 423
Market process, 244, 248
Market Theory and the Price System, 28, 247
Marrakesh, 109
Marshal, Alfred, 80-81, 83, 88, 129, 138
Marshall, Chief Justice John, 214-218, 220
Mason, George, 153
Martineau, Harriet, 113-114
Marx, Karl, 18, 73, 78, 91-92, 94-99, 101-103, 112, 124, 170, 179, 193, 196, 536
Marxism: Philosophy and Economics, 103
Marxists, 53, 56, 92
Mass production, 174
Mathematical economists, 83
Mayer, Hans, 158
McAndrew, Brian, 371-372
McConnell and Brue, 441, 451-452
McCormick, Anne O'Hare, 225, 239
McCulloch v. Maryland, 214-216, 221
McCullough, J. R., 113
McCurdy, Thomas E., 514

Mcans of production, 36, 341, 399, 453, 476
Meat Inspection Act, 484
Media, 65
Medicaid, 351, 498-500
Medical cooperative, 491
Medical industry, 484
Medical insurance, 486
Medicare, 231, 351, 497-499, 501-502
Medium of exchange, 77, 131, 213, 518-520
Medoff, James, 515
Mellon, Andrew, 225
Mencken, H. L., 150-151, 336
Meng, Ronald, 515
Menger, Carl, 16, 76, 78, 80, 84-88, 129, 131, 138, 156, 158, 189, 197, 199, 293, 311-312, 318
Methodological individualism, 127
Methodology, 188, 299, 316, 324
Mexico, 121
Microeconomic, 199
Middle Ages, 111, 175, 347
Militarism, 398
Mill, John Stuart, 80, 82, 88, 310
Miller, James C. III, 235, 240, 310
Miller, Robert H., 289
Millett, Kate, 169, 184
Milton, John, 141
Minimum wage, 96-97, 102, 180, 202, 315, 319, 321-322, 371, 378, 393
Minsky, Hyman, 442, 452
Mints, Lloyd, 304
Mises, Margit von, 17, 27
Mises, Ludwig von, 7, 12-18, 24, 27-28, 69-70, 72-74, 77-78, 85-88, 106, 117, 127-129, 131-133, 135, 138, 155-167, 169, 189, 191-199, 201-202, 208-209, 212, 241-242, 244-247, 249, 290, 296, 306-307, 312, 318, 320, 326, 330, 337, 343, 345-348, 362, 370, 392, 408, 425, 457-458, 466, 517-528, 530-533, 542
Mises Made Easier: A Glossary for Ludwig von Mises's "Human Action," 164
Misesian/Misesian Austrians, 22, 133, 136-137, 192, 196, 204, 207, 242-245, 248, 355, 517, 529
Mitchel v. United States, 221
Mitterand, Francois, 22, 121
Mixed economy, 122, 201-202, 206, 208-210, 453
Monarchy, 396-399, 404-405
Monetarism, 69, 161, 304
Monetarist, 129, 133, 135, 185, 187-188, 191, 297, 300, 429
Monetary policy, 186, 217, 297, 299, 443
Monetary theory, 14, 127, 129, 517
Money, 5-6, 8, 86, 92, 108, 127-128, 130-131, 133, 135-137, 157, 160, 164, 197, 213, 215, 218, 294, 304, 314-315, 319, 323, 329, 331, 333-334, 384, 394-395, 401-402, 417, 454, 517-518, 520, 523, 527, 540
Money, 65, 74
Money, Credit and Commerce, 129, 138
Money, demand for, 128-129, 131-133, 135, 137, 299, 520, 523, 528

Money and Freedom, 161, 200, 403, 408, 517, 530
Money monopoly, 220
Money supply, 7, 298-300, 438-439, 449
Monopoly, 111, 162, 507, 513
Monopoly rights, 275
Montaigne, Fen, 466
Moral foundations, 538
Moral hazard, 420
Moral principles, 8, 55
Moral standards, 63
Morality, 14-16, 161, 309-310, 323, 347
Moral, 9, 16, 54, 56-58, 60-63, 73, 75, 161, 185, 193, 195-196, 198, 228, 311-312, 315, 320-321, 324, 394, 412, 415, 471-472, 480, 535-536, 539-541
Morals and Liberty, 154
Morgenstern, Oskar, 157
Moscow, 53, 119
Moscow State University, 119
Moses, 26, 105-106, 400, 404-405
Mozambique, 478
Mozart, 114
Mueller, Dennis C., 211
Murata, Toshio, 159, 167
Musgrave, Gerald L., 505
My Years with Ludwig von Mises, 27
Mydral, Gunnar, 25, 265
Myers, Norman, 285

N

National Academy of Sciences, 484
National Board of Health, 484
National debt, 349
National health plan, 485, 493, 497-498
National Heart Institute, 496
National Institutes of Health, 353, 493, 496-497
National Labor Relations Board (NLRB), 494
National Recovery Act, 141
National Science Foundation, 496
Natural law, 15, 96, 107, 113, 311, 391-393, 408, 541
Naturalistic fallacy, 392
Nature, 283, 408
The Nature and Destiny of Man
Nature and Significance of Economic Science, 246
Nazis, 56
Neo-fascism, 35-36, 42
Neoliberal, 535
Neutrality of money, 136
New Classical School, 69, 430, 444
New Deal, 164, 260, 497
New Harmony, 473
New Testament, 396
New York University, 13, 17, 22, 63, 69, 155, 159-160, 162-163, 196, 241, 517
Niebuhr, Reinhold, 254, 267-268
Nigeria, 474-475
1984, 149
Ninth Commandment, 394
Niskanen, William, 367
NLRB. *See* National Labor Relations Board
Nobility, 175
Nock, Albert Jay, 23, 146, 152,154
Nomenklatura, 91, 340
Non-ownership, 469, 472, 478-479

Nonaggressors, 50
Nordhaus, William D., 28
Normative economics, 309
North, Gary, 11, 312-313, 315, 325, 400, 408
North Korea, 20
Nortz v. United States, 221
Norwich, John Julius, 117
Notes and Recollections, 166
Novak, Michael, 282, 314, 325
Novak, Robert, 306
Nuclear power, 350
Nuclear weapons, 49
Nyerere, Julius, 477

O

Observations on the Russian Reform Movement, 28
Ogden v. Saunders, 217-218, 221
Old Testament, 105, 394
Olson, Mancur, 71-72, 74
Omnibus Budget Reconciliation Act of 1990, 224, 230
On the Economic Theory of Socialism, 28
On the Manipulation of Money and Credit, 531, 533
Oneida, 473
Opportunity, 375-377, 379-382, 386-388
Opportunity cost, 134, 137
Ortega, Daniel, 53
Orwell, George, 149
Ownership, 33, 36-38, 41-42, 190, 280, 341, 469, 471-472, 479
Ozone layer, 269-270

P

Paganism, 409, 413-414
Paine, Thomas, 336
Paper money, 216-217, 220, 305, 401
Pareto, Vilfredo, 80, 82-83, 88
Parsons, Representative Claude, 225
Patton, Judd, 309, 325
Paul, Saint, 40, 253, 257-258, 402
Paul, Ron, 302-303
Pavesich v. New England Life Ins. Co., 153
Peace, 329, 337, 457
Pearl Harbor, 164
Pencavel, John H., 514
Pension Benefit Guaranty Corporation, 427
Pension Insurance, 427
Pepperdine University, 22, 373
Perestroika, 73
Permoli v. Municipality No. 1 of the City of New Orleans, 153
Pertinax, Publius Helvius, 108
Peru, 478-479
Pescosolido, Carl Jr., 52, 60
Peterson, William H., 159, 167, 327
Petro, Sylvester, 156, 166, 339
Pew, Howard J., 12, 20-22, 25
Phillips Curve, 188
Phoenicia, 106
Physiocrats, 107, 111-112
Pigou, Arthur C., 129-132, 138
Pilgrims, 5
Planned chaos, 457
Planned economy, 123, 172
Planned Parenthood, 280
Plano University, 164

Plato, 107, 109, 112, 252, 374, 394, 406, 412
Pointer v. State of Texas, 153
Politburo, 91
Political action, 171
Political activists, 67
Political freedom, 176
Politicians, 8, 64, 66, 68, 157, 234, 290, 327, 340, 343-344, 358, 361, 509
Politics, 16, 67, 71, 162, 393
Politics, 406
Politics of Unemployment, 161, 200
Pollution, 269
Polo, Marco, 108
Polovchak, Walter, 52, 60
Ponzi, 442
Popular Government, 346, 362
Population, 270
Population growth, 280
Positive economics, 309-310, 319
Positivism, 310
Postrel, Virginia, 288
Poverty, 181, 270, 357, 459, 471, 478
Powell, Lewis, 143, 153
Praxeological/Praxeology, 73, 86, 189, 194, 196, 243-244
Predestination, 259
Prepaid health plan, 491
Price, 33, 80-86, 95-96, 128, 131, 133, 135-137, 190, 271, 277, 294-295, 299, 311, 333, 365, 418, 454, 457-458, 477, 536, 540
Price and wage controls, 493
Price control, 11, 21, 79, 121-122, 319, 347, 391, 502
Price level, 127, 133, 135
Price system, 35, 209, 276, 455
Prices and Production, 138
Principle, 7-9, 11, 16, 51-53, 55-58, 120, 142, 146, 161, 165, 177, 189-190, 272, 291, 309-310, 312, 314, 316, 380, 387, 407, 541
Principles of Economics, 156, 158
Prisoners' dilemma, 228
Privacy, 144, 147, 150-152
Private enterprise, 437, 453-454, 456, 459, 463
Private ownership, 17, 36-37, 41-44, 86, 102, 320, 394, 453, 455, 463, 471, 473, 475, 478
Private property, 33, 35-36, 40, 44, 52, 63, 70, 120, 125, 142, 144, 151, 162, 165, 171, 181-182, 190, 193, 196, 206, 261-262, 264, 277, 311, 321, 329, 342, 345-348, 354-355, 398, 457, 459, 465, 469, 471-472, 474-475, 479-480
Private property rights, 72, 415, 469
Privatization, 121, 193, 476
Production, 64, 72, 77, 82-83, 85, 93, 97-98, 100-102, 129-130, 173-174, 178, 188, 193, 274, 355, 457, 462-463, 473, 521
Productivity, 6, 97, 99, 101-102, 171, 173-174, 176, 181, 194, 274, 282, 295, 328, 376, 391, 455
Professional Standards Review Organization (PSRO), 501
Profit, 14, 34, 37, 41, 72, 79, 84, 110, 157, 205, 207, 274-275, 295, 314, 321, 334, 342, 357, 384-385, 414, 424, 430, 454-455, 457-458, 463, 465, 510, 512-513, 536, 541

Profit and loss, 454, 456-460
Property, 48, 470
Property rights, 151, 278-279, 453, 479
Protectionism, 202, 349
Providence, 255, 259
Pruneyard Shopping Center V. Robins, 143-144, 147
PSRO. *See* Professional Standard Review Organization
Public education, 351-352, 373, 385-386
Public health, 484, 493
Public interest, 328, 335, 361
Public opinion, 272
Public works projects, 443
Public-Choice Economics, 67
Purchasing power, 130, 132-133, 136, 305, 523, 528
Pushkin, Tatyana, 123

Q

Qualitative, 367
Quantitative, 367
Quantity of money, 128, 298, 319
Quantity theory of labor, 91-97, 102
Quasi-public ownership, 41

R

Railroads, 485
Rand, Ayn, 22, 114, 149, 403, 484
Randolph, Edmund, 153
The Ransdell Act, 493
Rationality, 243-244, 247
Read, Leonard, 6-7
Reagan, President Ronald, 25, 66-67, 70-71, 289-291, 298-300, 304-305, 439, 464
Reason, 15, 244, 252
Recession, 191, 224, 322, 356-357, 365, 367, 369, 430, 433, 442-444, 450
Reconstruction, 140
Redistribution, 14, 186, 354, 357, 399, 477
Reductionism, 94
Reed, Lawrence W., 363
Regan, Donald, 302
Regression theorem, 129
Regulation, 161, 172, 401, 419, 423, 427
Rehnquist, Justice William H., 144
Reisman, George, 13, 22, 159, 167, 373, 389
Religion, 410
Religious freedom, 5
Renaissance, 176, 178
Rent, 92, 470
Rent control, 202-203
Rent-seeking activity, 204, 211, 274, 276
Republic, 395-397, 399
Republic, 107, 195, 215, 252, 406
Republicans, 224, 289
Reserve fund, 208
Reserve requirements, 163, 527
Resources, 33, 35-38, 44, 114, 120, 129-130, 132, 137, 176, 205, 270-272, 274-277, 280, 282, 289, 295, 304, 324, 339, 356, 454, 471, 473-474, 501, 522
Responsibility, 415, 480
Restitution, 470
Retribution, 256, 401
Revelation, 391

Revenue Act of 1932, 225
Revolution, 341, 459
Ricardian equivalence theorem, 449
Ricardo, David, 80, 82, 88, 113, 177, 310, 449
Right to know, 151
Right to life and property, 145, 248
Right to privacy, 144-146, 148, 150, 153
Rights, 27, 48, 57, 139-140, 143-144, 149, 165, 328, 342, 354, 392, 469
The Rise and Decline of Nations, 71
Rivlin, Alice, 302
Robbins, John W., 391
Robbins, Lionel, 18, 24, 242, 246
Roberson v. Rochester Folding Box Co., 153
Roberts, Paul Craig, 293, 296-297, 302, 307, 430, 451, 462, 466
Robertson, Dennis H., 134, 138
Robinson, H. Wheeler, 267
Roche, George, 327
Rogers, Will, 333
Roman Empire, 347
Romantic Manifesto The, 114
Rome, 108, 406, 409-410, 412
Roosevelt, Franklin Delano, 141, 226, 260, 493
Roosevelt, Theodore, 484
Röpke, Wilhelm, 18, 24, 116, 118, 535-545
Rose, Tom, 325
Rosenburg, Julius and Ethel, 53
Rosenstein-Roden, 246
Rothbard, Murray N., 13-14, 24, 27, 61, 87, 159, 162-163, 167, 299, 302-303, 307, 318, 325-326, 370, 438, 451, 466, 517-518, 524, 527, 530, 532
Rousseau, Jean Jacques, 394
Ruffin, Roy J., 430, 451
Rule of Law, 33, 355
Rushdoony, Rousas John, 29, 256, 267, 325, 409
Russell, Lewis, 284
Russia, 19, 112, 283
Rüstow, Alexander, 535
Rutledge, John, 367

S

Sade, Marquis de, 392
Safety, 511
Salsman, Richard M., 427
Samuelson, Robert J., 367-368, 372
Samuelson, Paul, 19, 28, 192, 438
Saracens, 108-109
Sartori, Giovanni, 262, 268
Savings, 151, 165, 181, 294, 322, 335, 357, 418, 429, 437-438, 443-444, 446, 450
The Savings and Loan Bailout: Valiant Rescue or Hysterical Reaction?, 45
Savings and Loan crisis, 417
Savings and Loan industry, 41-42, 425
Say, Jean Baptiste, 113, 290, 310
Say's Law, 319-320
Scalia, Justice Antonin, 349
Scarcity of Resources, 78, 270
Scheutz, Alfred, 157
School of Salamanca, 78, 87
Schrof, Joannie M., 467
Schumpeter, Joseph A., 87, 133, 138

Schwartz, Anna, 302-303
Schwartz, Jeffrey, 504
Science, 243
Scientific laws, 242
Scientism, 318
Scully, Gerald W., 481
SEC. *See* Securities and Exchange Commission
Securities and Exchange Commission (SEC), 461
Selected works, 103
Self interest, 329, 335, 537-540
Selfishness, 244-245
Selgin, George A., 427, 532-533
Senate, 358, 360
Senior, Nassau, 310
Sennett, Richard, 414-415
Sennholz, Hans F., 5-9, 11-14, 20-21, 23-25, 27, 44-45, 60-61, 74, 76, 87, 91, 155, 159-161, 167, 169, 196-197, 200-201, 211-212, 221, 225, 229, 234, 239, 241, 272, 276, 283, 286, 288, 290-291, 302-303, 306-307, 321, 324-326, 355, 391, 393-394, 403, 408, 417, 431, 433, 450-451, 454, 466-467, 469, 517, 529, 530
Sennholz, Mary Homan, 8, 159, 167
Separation of powers, 349
Serfdom, 148, 175
Sheppard-Towner Act, 484
Sherman Antitrust Act, 492
Short, Eugenie D., 427
Short, Gary G., 417
Shortages, 295, 320, 328, 391, 463
Shulman, David G., 452
Sierra Club, 353
Silkwood, Karen, 53
Simon, Herbert A., 212
Simon, Paul, 233
Simon, Henry, 304
Simon, Julian, 280, 285, 287
Sin, 257, 259, 315-316, 396
Sixteenth Amendment, 232, 394
Skousen, Mark, 27, 429, 452
Slavery, 120, 173, 175, 350, 392
Smith, Adam, 77, 79, 88, 96, 110, 112, 123, 177, 195, 199, 202, 211, 241, 310-312, 328, 334-335, 337, 450, 520, 531
Smith, Charles W., Jr., 221
Smith, Hedrick, 91, 103
Smith, Vera, 532
Smoot-Hawley Tariff Act, 225, 321
Sobran, Joseph, 223, 239
Social Security, 161, 231, 350, 393, 436-437, 493, 502
Social Security Trust Fund, 436, 450
Socialism, 15, 17-20, 34-36, 102, 112, 122-123, 158, 164, 169-170, 179-180, 182-183, 191-193, 201, 205, 207, 209, 293, 315, 320-321, 341, 344-346, 408, 453-454, 459, 462, 472, 476-477, 536-537
Socialism: An Economic and Sociological Analysis, 16, 28, 191, 199, 362
Socialist, 16, 92, 101, 121, 141, 162, 171, 178-179, 182, 192, 344-345, 352, 358
Socialized medicine, 351
Society for Individual Liberty, 49
Sohm, Rudolph, 481
Solomon, King, 106, 404-405
Solvency, 526
Solzhenitsyn, Aleksander, 185

Sophists, 252
Soto, Hernando de, 478-479, 482
South Africa, 474
South America, 160
Sovereignty, 139, 216, 220, 260
Soviet Union, 19-20, 52, 63, 72, 91-92, 119, 192, 209, 274, 327, 339-340, 342, 409, 412, 425, 454-455, 459, 462
Sowell, Thomas, 103
Spadaro, Louis, 13, 22, 198
Spangler, Mark, 453
Spann, Othmar, 160
Sparks, John A., 469, 482
Special interests, 67-68, 71-72, 332-333, 353, 360, 465, 484
Speculation, 370-371
Spending, 170, 227, 231-232, 234-235, 237, 297, 344, 358, 431, 434, 436, 443, 458, 490
St. Johns College, 22
St. Lawrence College, 69
Stagflation, 69
Stalin, Joseph, 185
Standard of living, 36-38, 44, 122, 173-174, 177, 319, 323, 431, 437, 442
State University of California (Hayward), 69
State University of New York (Oswego), 69
State University of New York (Purchase), 201
Statism, 35, 201, 295, 411, 415
Statistical indicators, 368-369
Statist, 34-35, 38, 41-42, 53
Stein, Herbert, 291
Stein, Gertrude, 335
Stewardship, 315, 319-321, 323-324
Stigler, George J., 88
Stock market, 39, 363, 369, 429, 436, 444, 450
Stockman, David, 289-292, 298, 306-307
Stoic, 252, 255
Strauss, Johann Jr., 115
The Structure of Production, 430
Subjective value theory, 77, 79, 86, 132, 156, 158, 189, 311
Subjectivism, 246
Subsidies, 161, 276, 343, 356
Subsistence, 173
Substitution effect, 302
Subterranean economy, 366
Suez Canal, 116
Suffrage, 260, 343, 346, 348, 356
Sugar, 332-333
Sumeria, 105
Supply and demand, 79, 128, 318, 371, 540
Supply of money, 133, 188
Supply-side economics, 69, 185-187, 191, 289-291, 295-298, 300, 302-303, 430
Supreme Court, 140, 143-144, 213-220, 494
Surplus, 328
Sustainability, 272, 282
Svejnar, Jan, 514

T

Taft-Hartley Labor Relations Act, 494
Taney, Chief Justice Roger, 217-218, 220
Tannehill, Morris and Linda, 61
Tanzania, 477-478
Tariff, 161, 319, 321

Tax, 7, 14, 39-41, 161, 170, 188, 190, 193, 195, 208, 214, 223-226, 228, 230-233, 235-236, 272, 275-276, 289, 292-293, 296, 301-302, 305, 327, 343-344, 349, 351, 353, 356-360, 366, 395, 399, 423, 429, 431, 435-438, 441, 444, 447, 449-450, 453, 458, 461, 463-465, 477, 493-496, 500
The Tax Reform Act of 1986, 464
Taylor, Zachary, 149
Taylor, Fred M., 28
Technology, 63, 83, 179-180
Ten Commandments, 106, 195, 315, 320, 324
Tenth Commandment, 393
Term limitation, 333
Term limits, 235
Thatcher, Margaret, 66-67, 70-71, 121, 348
Thayer, Joseph H., 325
Theft, 401, 470
Theism, 541
Theology 15
Theory of Money and Credit, 13, 518-519, 522-523, 527, 530-533
Thermopolyae, 107
Third-Party Payments, 495, 500
Thompson, Thomas Perronet, 115, 118
Thompson, Dorothy Lampen, 117
Three Economic Commandments, 13, 27, 197, 200, 394, 408
Thurow, Lester, 302
Tiananmen Square/Tiananmen Massacre, 71
Tiawan, 70
Time preference, 319
Tobin, James, 307
"Too big to fail," 421
Torture, 410
Totalitarianism, 34, 392, 394, 409, 412
Toward Liberty, 166
Trade, 121, 329
Trade balance, 438
Trade cycle, 14, 128
Trade deficit, 368, 429, 431, 439, 449
Trade zones, 122
Transfer state, 187, 197
Transportation, 351-352
Treaties, 403
Trend projection, 364
Trinity, 15, 251, 256, 263-264
The Trinity Review, 408
Tropical forests, 269
Ture, Norm, 293, 297
Turgot, Anne Robert Jacques, 112
Two Concepts of Liberty, 153
Tyrmand, Leopold, 27

U

U.S. Bonneville Power Adminstration, 237
Uncertainty, 364, 370
Understanding the Dollar Crisis, 164
Unemployment, 135, 137, 172, 188, 190-191, 226, 322, 356, 369, 371, 377-378, 391, 429-430
Unemployment insurance, 161
Unemployment rate, 369
Union laws, 145
Unions, 92, 97, 333, 349, 351, 377, 393, 485, 494, 507-514, 538

United Kingdom, 67
United Nations, 280
United States v. Marigold, 218-219
University of Chicago, 24
University of Nevada (Las Vegas), 69, 162
Urbanization, 272
Utilitarian theory, 96, 193, 196
Utilitarianism, 13, 15, 165, 194, 391-392, 408
Utility, 76, 81, 83

V

Value, 5-6, 47, 51, 54-55, 58-60, 75-78, 80-82, 85, 93-94, 96, 130-132, 175, 189, 213, 223, 280, 294, 311, 314, 365, 374, 384, 391-392, 455, 458, 519, 539
Value in exchange, 75, 79-80, 83
Value in use, 75, 79
Value of money, 217
Value paradox, 79
Vedder, Richard, 239
Velocity, 188, 298-301
Velocity of money, 131
Verdi, Giuseppi, 106-107, 115
Veterans' Administration, 484, 496
Vinson, Frederick Moore, 414
Virgil, 158
Vögelin, Erich, 157
Volition, 132, 243
Volker, Paul, 296
Voluntary exchange, 44

W

Wage, 79-80, 95-96, 135, 137, 190, 280-281, 314, 364, 378, 430, 463, 498, 500, 507-508, 512-514
Wage controls, 11, 21
Wage Labour and Capital, 103
Wage level, 127
Wagner, Senator Robert, 493
Waldron, Jeremy, 472, 481
Walker, Graham, 542
Wallace v. Jaffree, 153
Walras, Leon, 80, 82-83, 88, 311
Walsh, Vivian C., 249
Walter, David, 61
Wanniski, Jude, 292-294, 298, 306
War, 38, 156, 406
Warren, Samuel D., 144-145, 153
Washington, George, 60, 108, 112
Wasley, Terree P., 483
Wealth, 14, 37-40, 42-44, 93, 182, 188, 190, 195, 205, 224, 243, 245, 251, 282, 323, 335, 343-344, 346-349, 353, 357, 359, 373-374, 381-382, 391, 438, 443, 463, 511
The Wealth of Nations, 337, 531
Weaver, Henry Grady, 117
Weber, Max, 193
Wechslen, Dana, 199
Weeks, Lewis B., 489, 504
Welch, Galbraith, 117
"Welfare capitalism," 486
Welfare programs, 14, 227, 353, 486, 497
Welfare state, 26, 56, 71, 164, 290, 344, 356, 358, 398, 465

Welfarism, 67, 463
Wertfreiheit, 163, 193-194, 391
Wessels, Walter J., 507-509, 512, 514-515
White, Byron, 143
White, Lawrence H., 325, 517, 530, 532
White, Richard A., 535
Whitten, Jamie, 236
Wieser, Friedrich von, 80
Wilson, Edward O., 284
Wilson, Francis G., 29
Wilson, President Woodrow, 484
Winter, Ernst, 20
Women, 169
Wolf, Richard, 65, 74
Wolfe, Gregory, 291, 306
Wolley v. Maynard, 153
Wollstonecraft, Mary, 113
Woodford, Michael, 452
Woodward, Robert, 53
Woodworth, John, 484
Working conditions, 181, 510
World Bank, 280
World War II, 11, 122, 134, 160, 227, 246, 348, 414, 433, 439, 441, 444, 493, 496, 535
Wright, David McCord, 93, 103
Wyman, Walter, 484

Y

Yago, Glenn, 452
Yale, 24
Yeager, Leland B., 531
Yeh Shih, 108
Yellowstone National Park, 278
Yeltsin, Boris, 341, 344
Yuan Hsieh, 108

Z

Zimbabwe, 279, 331, 474